DICTIONARY OF
INFORMATION
TECHNOLOGY

THIRD EDITION

Titles in the series

Workbooks

DICTIONARY OF
INFORMATION
TECHNOLOGY

THIRD EDITION

S.M.H. Collin

PETER COLLIN PUBLISHING

Third edition published 2002
Second edition published 1996
First published in Great Britain 1987

Published by Peter Collin Publishing Ltd
32-34 Great Peter Street, London, SW1P 2DB
© Copyright S.M.H. Collin, 1987, 1996, 2002

British Library Cataloguing-in-Publication Data

A catalogue record for this book is available from the British Library

ISBN 1-901659-55-0

Text computer typeset by PCP
Printed and bound in Italy by Legoprint
Cover artwork by Gary Weston

Preface

This dictionary provides the user with a comprehensive vocabulary used in information technology. It covers computers, programming, networks, communications, database design, the Internet, electronic mail, world wide web, electronics, music, graphics, multimedia, desktop publishing, and many other computer applications. In addition, the dictionary covers communications subjects including film, video, TV and radio.

The 13,000 entries are each explained in simple English, using a limited vocabulary of about 500 words, over and above those words which appear in the dictionary as entries. Many examples are given to show how the words and phrases can be used in context. Words which pose particular problems of grammar have short grammatical notes attached.

General comments about particular items of interest, complex ideas or hardware or software applications are given in separate boxes. Quotations from a wide range of magazines and journals are given to show how the words are used in real text. The supplement at the back of the book provides useful extra information that would be useful for computing and communications studies.

In this edition of the dictionary we have included a number of product names and company names. The trademarked names that are included are those that we have judged to be de-facto, important to users or important in the development of computer technology.

Aa

A = AMPERE

Å *see* ANGSTROM

A: *(used in some operating systems such as DOS and Windows)* denotes the first disk drive on the system; *to see what is stored on your floppy disk, use the DOS command DIR A:*; *see also* C:, FLOPPY DISK, HARD DISK

> COMMENT: a PC usually has two or three disk drives within its casing: a floppy disk drive (called 'A:'), a hard disk ('C:') and, sometimes, a second floppy disk ('B:') and a CD-ROM drive ('D:'). When talking about the different disk drives, you say 'Drive A' for the floppy drive, but normally write 'A:'

A & I = ABSTRACTING AND INDEXING *verb* making summaries and indexes for articles and books

A Programming Language (APL) high-level programming language used in scientific and mathematical work

'A' roll *noun (film)* one of two videotapes or film rolls; the other half is the 'B' roll used in an A/B roll

A to D *or* **A/D** = ANALOG TO DIGITAL; **A to D converter** *or* **A/D converter** = ANALOG TO DIGITAL CONVERTER

A wind *noun (film)* videotape wound onto a reel so that it winds in a clockwise direction; the oxide layer being on the inside

A/UX version of the Unix operating system for the Apple Macintosh range of computers; *see also* UNIX

A1, A2, A3, A4, A5 *noun* ISO recommended international standard sizes of paper *or* sizes of screen; *you must photocopy the spreadsheet on A3 paper; we must order some more A4 headed notepaper; a standard 300 d.p.i. black and white A4 monitor*

AB roll *noun* two video or music segments that are synchronized so that one fades as the second starts; *(film)* **AB roll working** = using two rolls of film to compile a film sequences; one roll using spacing or blanking (the A roll) and one on which the images appear (the B roll)

abandon *verb* to clear a document or file or work from the computer's memory without saving it to disk or tape; *once you have abandoned your spreadsheet, you cannot retrieve it again*

abbreviation *noun* short form of a word *or* command *or* instruction; *use the abbreviation TV for 'television'*; **abbreviated addressing** *or* **abb. add.** = (in a network) user name that has fewer characters than the full name, making it easier to remember or type in; *my full network address is over 60 characters long, so you will find it easier to use my abbreviated address*; *see also* ALIAS; **abbreviated installation** = (during installation) to install new hardware *or* software without restoring the previous backup settings of the operating system

ABC *(film)* = (i) AMERICAN BROADCASTING COMPANY; (ii) AUSTRALIAN BROADCASTING COMMISSION

ABD = APPLE DESKTOP BUS

abend = ABNORMAL END unexpected stoppage of a program being run, due to a fault *or* power failure; **abend code** = special number (generated by the operating system) that identifies the type of error that has caused the problem

aberration *noun* **(a)** distortion of a light beam *or* image due to defects in the optical system **(b)** distortion of a television picture caused by a corrupt signal *or* incorrect adjustment; *see also* SPHERICAL ABERRATION

ablation *noun* method of writing data to an optical storage device; *see also* WORM

COMMENT: a laser burns a hole or pit (that represents digital bits of data) into the thin metal surface of the storage device

abnormal *adjective* not normal; **abnormal end** *or* **abend** *or* **abnormal termination** = unexpected stoppage of a program being run, caused by a fault *or* power failure

abnormally *adverb* not as normal *or* not as usual; *the signal is abnormally weak; the noise level on the line is abnormally high*

abort *verb* to end a process (when a malfunction occurs), by switching the computer off manually *or* by an internal feature; *the program was aborted by pressing the red button; abort the program before it erases any more files;* **aborted connection** = connection to a network or online service that has not been shut down correctly; **abort sequence** = unique sequence of bits that indicates that the transmission will be abnormally terminated

About... *(in the SAA CUA front-end)* menu selection that tells you who developed the program and displays copyright information; *see also* SAA

above-the-line costs *plural noun* variable costs involved in making TV films (such as scriptwriters, actors, sets, etc.) as opposed to below-the-line costs (film crew, technicians, etc.); *compare with* BELOW-THE-LINE

ABS = ABSOLUTE FUNCTION programming instruction that returns the magnitude of a number without the number's sign; *the command ABS(-13) will return the answer 13*

absolute address *or* **actual address** *noun* **(a)** computer storage address that directly, without any modification, accesses a location *or* device; *compare with* INDEXED ADDRESS **(b)** computer storage address that can only access one location; **absolute addressing** = locating a word of data in memory by the use of its absolute address; **absolute assembler** = type of assembly language program designed to produce code which

uses only absolute addresses and values; **absolute cell reference** = spreadsheet reference that always refers to the same cell, even when copied to another location; **absolute code** = binary code which directly operates the central processing unit, using only absolute addresses and values (this is the final form of a program after a compiler *or* assembler pass); *see also* OBJECT CODE; **absolute coordinates** = coordinates that describe the distance of a point from the intersection of axes; *compare with* RELATIVE COORDINATES; **absolute device** = input device such as a tablet or mouse that returns the coordinates of a pointer within specified axes; **absolute error** = value *or* magnitude of an error, ignoring its sign; *(in assembly language)* **absolute expression** = value of an expression that is not affected by program relocation; **absolute function** = programming function that returns the magnitude of a number without the number's sign; **absolute instruction** *or* **code** = (i) instruction which completely describes the operation to be performed (no other data is required); (ii) graphics command that uses absolute coordinates; **absolute loader** = program that loads a section of code into main memory; **absolute positioning** = position of an object in relation to an origin; *(in some operating system)* **absolute priority** = priority of a process that cannot be changed by the operating system; **absolute program** = computer program written in absolute code; *(in CD DA)* **absolute time** = length of time that an audio disc has been playing; **absolute value** = size *or* value of a number, regardless of its sign; *the absolute value of -62.34 is 62.34*

absorb *verb* to take in (light *or* liquid *or* a signal)

absorptance *noun* percentage of light that is absorbed by a material instead of reflecting it (NOTE: the opposite is **reflectance**)

absorption *noun* power loss of a signal when travelling through a medium, due to its absorptance; **absorption filter** = filter that blocks certain colours of light

abstract 1 *noun* short version of a book *or* article; *in our library, abstracts are gathered together in separate volumes allowing an easy and rapid search for a* particular subject; *it's quicker to search through the abstracts than the full text* **2** *verb* **(a)** to remove something from something **(b)** to make a summary of an article

abstract data type *noun* a general data type that can store any kind of information; *the stack is a structure of abstract data types, it can store any type of data from an integer to an address*

abstracting and indexing *verb* making summaries and indexes for articles and books

AC 1 = ALTERNATING CURRENT electric current whose value varies with time in a regular, sinusoidal way **2** = ASSISTANT CAMERAMAN person who carries out camera operations under the instruction of the director of photography (these could be aperture changes, zooming, focusing, etc; in certain situations, he may also operate the camera)

COMMENT: the mains electricity supply uses alternating current to minimize transmission power loss, with a frequency of 50Hz in UK, 60Hz in the USA

Academy *(film) (abbreviation for)* The Academy of Motion Picture Arts and Sciences; **Academy awards** = yearly presentation of the Oscar award by the Academy to artists and technicians for excellence in their area of the film world

ACAP = APPLICATION CONFIGURATION ACCESS PROTOCOL email system developed to work with the IMAP4 email protocol to provide useful secondary features such as managing an address book; originally termed IMSP (Interactive Mail Support Protocol)

ACC *noun* = ACCUMULATOR most important internal CPU storage register, containing the data word that is to be processed

accelerated motion *noun (film)* special effect in which the camera is run at a slower frame rate than the standard 24 frames per second which gives the effect of faster-than-average motion

acceleration *see* MOUSE ACCELERATION

acceleration time *noun* time taken for a disk drive *or* CD-ROM player to spin a disk to the correct speed, from rest

accelerator *see* ACCELERATOR KEY

accelerator board *or* **card** *noun* circuit board that carries a faster or more advanced version of the same processor that runs your computer; *adding an accelerator card to your computer makes it run faster*

accelerator key *noun* combination of keys that, when pressed together, carry out a function that would otherwise have to be selected from a menu using a mouse; *instead of selecting the File menu then the Save option, use the accelerator keys Alt and S to do the same thing and save the file*; *see also* HOT KEY

accent *noun* small sign placed on *or* above a printed *or* written character to show that it is pronounced in a different way; **acute accent** = accent (é) above a character, which slopes upwards to the right; **circumflex accent** = accent (ê) above a character, shaped like an upside down 'v'; **grave accent** = accent (è) above a character, which slopes upwards to the left; *see also* CEDILLA, TILDE, UMLAUT

accented *adjective* (letter) with an accent on it

accept *verb* **(a)** to agree to do something; *he accepted the quoted price for printing; she has accepted our terms; he did not accept the job which he was offered*; **to accept a book for publication** = to agree to publish a book **(b)** to take something which is being offered; *the laser printer will accept a card as small as a business card; the multi-disk reader will accept 3.5 inch disks as well as old 5.25 inch formats* **(c)** to establish a session or connection with another device

acceptable *adjective* which can be accepted; *the error rate was very low, and is acceptable*

acceptable use policy *see* AUP

acceptance *noun* action of accepting something; **acceptance angle** = angle of total field of view of a lens *or* fibre optic; *a light beam at an angle greater than the acceptance angle of the lens will not be transmitted*; **acceptance sampling** = testing a small random part of a batch to see if the whole batch is up to standard; **acceptance**

test *or* **testing** = method of checking that a piece of equipment will perform as required *or* will reach required standards

access 1 *noun* being allowed to use a computer and read *or* alter files held in it (this is usually controlled by a security device such as a password); **to have access to something** = to be able to get *or* examine *or* reach something; *to have access to a file of data; he has access to large amounts of capital*; **to bar access to a system** = to prevent a person from using a system; **access arm** = mechanical device in a disk drive used to position the read/write head over the disk; **access authority** = permission to carry out a particular operation on data; **access barred** = to prevent a user accessing particular data; **access category** = one of several possible predefined access levels; the category defines which files or data a user can access, and which he cannot; *(in token-ring network)* **access channel control** = protocols that manage the data transfer between a station and a medium access control (MAC); **access charge** = cost due when logging onto a system *or* viewing special pages on a bulletin board; **access code** = series of characters *or* symbols that must be entered to identify the user; *see also* PASSWORD; **access control** = security device (such as a password) that only allows selected users into a computer system; *(in token-r+ing network)* **access control byte** = byte following start marker in the token that indicates if the station can access the network; *(in CD-i)* **access control list (ACL)** = security system in which a list that contains user names and passwords is used by an operating system to determine if a particular user is allowed to access or use a resource or feature of the computer or network; **access controller** = electronic device that transfers image data to the video controller; **access counter** = *see* COUNTER; **access head** = part of a disk drive moves to the correct part of the disk's surface and reads information stored on the disk; **access hole** = opening in both sides of a floppy disk's casing allowing the read-write head to be positioned over the disk's surface; **access line** = permanent communications line between a terminal and a DSE *or* two computers; *see also* LEASED LINE; *compare with* DIALUP;

access level = various predefined access categories; the lowest access level might allow the user to only view data, the highest access level allows a user to do anything; **access log** = file that stores a record of every visitor to a website; *our access log shows us which pages on the website are viewed most often; we use an analyzer program to produce reports from our website access log; the access log is vital to check response to email marketing*; **access mechanism** = mechanical device that moves an access arm over the surface of a disk; **access method** = means used for the internal transfer of data between memory and display *or* peripheral devices (differences in the methods used cause compatibility problems); **access method routines** = software routines that move data between main storage and an output device; **access name** = unique name that identifies an object in a database; **access path** = description of the location of a stored file within a directory structure of a disk; **access path journalling** = recording changes to an access path in case of malfunction; **access period** = period of time during which a user can access data; **access permission** = description of all the access rights for a particular user; **access point** = test point on a circuit board *or* software, allowing an engineer to check signals data; **access privilege** = status granted to a user that allows them to see or read or alter files; **access provider** = *see* SERVICE PROVIDER; **access rights** = permission for a particular user to access a particular file or data object; **access time** = (i) total time which a storage device takes between the moment the data is requested and the data being returned; (ii) length of time required to find a file or program, either in main memory or a secondary memory source; CD-ROM drives have a normal access time of 400msec for a single speed and 300msec for a double-speed drive, whilst a hard disk has an access time of around 15msec; *see also* DOUBLE SPEED; *(in token-ring networks)* **access unit** = wiring concentrator; **direct memory access (DMA)** = direct, rapid link between a peripheral and a computer's main memory which avoids the use of accessing routines for each item of data required; **public access terminal** = terminal which can be used by anyone **2** *verb* to call up (data) which is stored in a computer; to obtain data from a storage device; *she accessed the employee's file stored on the computer*

COMMENT: a good access control system should allow valid users to operate the computer easily with the minimum of checks, while barring entry to hackers *or* unauthorized users

access time *noun* **(a)** total length of time which a storage device takes between the moment the data is requested and the data being returned; *the access time of this dynamic RAM chip is around 100nS - we have faster versions if your system clock is running faster* **(b)** length of time required to find a file *or* program, either in main memory *or* a secondary memory source

COMMENT: if you upgrade your computer by adding more memory, you must make sure the RAM has the correct access time for the speed of the processor otherwise data errors will occur

accessible *adjective* which can be reached *or* accessed; *details of customers are easily accessible from the main computer files*

accessions *plural noun* new books which are added to a library; **accession number** = (i) serial number used in a library indexing system; (ii) number in a record that shows in which order each record was entered

accessor *noun* person who accesses data

accessory *noun* extra, add-on device (such as a mouse or printer) which is attached to or used with a computer; *the printer comes with several accessories, such as a soundproof hood; this popular computer has a large range of accessories*; *see also* PERIPHERAL

accidental *adjective* which happens by accident; *always keep backup copies in case of accidental damage to the master file*

accordion fold *or* **fanfold** *noun* method of folding continuous paper, one sheet in one direction, the next sheet in the opposite direction, allowing the paper to be fed into a printer continuously with no action on the part of the user

account 1 *noun (in a network or online system)* record of a user's name, password and rights to access a network or online system; *if you are a new user, you will have to ask the supervisor to create an account for you*; **account name** = unique name of a user on a network or online system; *John Smith's account name is JSMITH* **2** *verb* to keep track of how much time and resources each user of a network or online system uses

accounting package *or* **accounts package** *noun* software that automates a business's accounting functions; *we now type in each transaction into the new accounting package rather than write it into a ledger*

COMMENT: accounting packages typically mimic traditional practice, using disk files to simulate paper ledgers. The main advantage is that a computer system will run a proper double-entry system while allowing details of each transaction to be entered only once. Provided it is used properly, an accounting package can produce summary accounts at any time and speeds up tasks such as making VAT returns. Many accounting packages are sold as a set of separate modules which integrate together so that the user can choose only the functions they require

accumulate *verb* to gather several things together over a period of time; *we have gradually accumulated a databank of names and addresses*

accumulator *or* **ACC** *or*

accumulator register *noun* most important internal CPU storage register, containing the data word that is to be processed; *store the two bytes of data in registers A and B and execute the add instruction - the answer will be in the accumulator*; **accumulator address** = address accessed by an instruction held in the accumulator

accuracy *noun* total number of bits used to define a number in a computer, the more bits allocated the more accurate the definition; **accuracy control character** = code that indicates whether data is accurate or whether the data should be disregarded by a particular device

accurate *adjective* correct; without any errors; *the printed bar code has to be accurate to within a thousandth of a micron*

accurately *adverb* correctly *or* with no errors; *the OCR had difficulty in reading the accents accurately; the error was caused because the data had not been accurately keyed*

ACD *noun* = AUTOMATIC CALL DISTRIBUTION specialised telephone system that can handle lots of incoming calls and direct them to a particular operator according to programmed instructions in a database

ACE *noun (film)* a 1000 watt spotlight

ACES *(film)* = AUTOMATIC CAMERA EFFECTS SYSTEM computer-operated camera movement system developed by Disney Studios which is designed to film repeatable camera moves on separate exposures

acetate *noun* sheet of transparent plastic used for making overlays; *the graphs were plotted on acetate, for use on an overhead projector*; **acetate base** = plastic material used as the standard base for motion picture film; *see also* SAFEBASE; *(film)* **acetate tape** = audio-tape consisting of acetate backing with magnetically sensitive oxide coating

acetone *noun (film)* clear, flammable liquid which is used to clean film print surfaces and splices and other editing and filming apparatus

achieve *verb* to succeed in doing something; *the hardware designers are trying to achieve compatibility between all the components of the system*

achromatic *adjective* (an optical device) that has been corrected for chromatic aberration

achromatic colour *noun* (grey) colour within the range between black and white displayed by a graphics adapter

ACIA = ASYNCHRONOUS COMMUNICATIONS INTERFACE ADAPTER

ACK = ACKNOWLEDGE signal that is sent from a receiver to indicate that a transmitted message has been received and that it is ready for the next one

acknowledge 1 *noun* signal that is sent from a receiver to indicate that a transmitted message has been received and that it is ready for the next one **2** *verb* (i) to tell a sender that a message *or* letter has been received; (ii) to send a signal from a receiver to show that a transmitted message has been received; **acknowledge character** = special code sent by a receiver to indicate to the transmitter that the message has been correctly received

acknowledged mail *noun* function (in an email program) that signals to the sender when an electronic mail message has been read by the recipient

acknowledgements *noun* text printed at the beginning of a book, where the author *or* publisher thanks people who have helped

ACL = *see* ACCESS CONTROL LIST

Acorn Computers *noun* computer company that developed the BBC micro and the Archimedes personal computers

acoustic *adjective* referring to sound; **acoustic delay line** = device that will delay an audio signal for special effects; **acoustic hood** = soundproof hood placed over a printer to reduce the noise; **acoustic panel** = sound-proofed panel placed behind a device to reduce noise

acoustic coupler *noun* device that connects to a telephone handset, converting binary computer data into sound signals to allow data to be transmitted down a telephone line

COMMENT: the acoustic coupler also converts back from sound signals to digital signals when receiving messages; it is basically the same as a modem but uses a handset on which a loudspeaker is placed to send the signals rather than direct connection to the phone line. It is portable, and clips over both ends of a normal telephone handset; it can be used even in a public phone booth

acoustical feedback *noun* distortion in an audio signal, due to a part of an amplified signal being picked up by the microphone and amplified again until the amplifier is overloaded

acoustics *noun* study and science of sound waves

acquisition *noun* accepting or capturing or collecting information

ACR 1 = AUDIO CASSETTE RECORDER; **ACR interface** = interface which allows a cassette recorder to be linked to a computer **2** = AUTOMATIC CASSETTE RECORDER a type of videotape recorder

Acrobat *see* ADOBE ACROBAT

acronym *noun* abbreviation, formed from various letters, which makes up a word which can be pronounced; for example, GUI is an acronym of graphical user interface and is pronounced 'gooey'; *the acronym FORTRAN means Formula Translator; the acronym RAM means Random Access Memory*

actintic light *noun* light which is able to cause chemical change in a material, such as film

action *noun* **(a)** thing which has been done; **to take action** = to do something; **action message** = prompt given for a required user input **(b)** *(in an SAA CUA front-end)* user event, such as pressing a special key, that moves the cursor to the action or menu bar at the top of the screen; **action bar** = top line of the screen that displays the menu names; **action bar pull-down** = standard that defines what happens when a user moves the cursor to a particular menu name on the action bar: the full menu is displayed below the menu name; **action code** = single letter associated with a particular menu option to speed up selection; when the letter action code is pressed, the menu option is selected; for example, in Windows, the convention is F for the file menu, E for the edit menu, and H for the help menu; **action cycle** = complete set of actions involved in one operation (including reading data, processing, storing results, etc.); **action list** = list of choices; **action message** message displayed to inform the user that an action or input is required; **action-object** = object to which a user specifies an action should be applied **(c)** movement; **action field** = area to be photographed by a camera; **action frame** = camera field of view where the filmed action is taking place; **action shot** = still photograph showing action taking place (such as a person running) **(d)** *(film)* the

command to begin a performance, said by a director to an actor

activate *verb* to start a process *or* to make a device start working; *pressing CR activates the printer*

activated *adjective (in an authoring tool or programming language)* button or field in a screen layout that has a script attached to it; the script is executed when the user clicks on the button (NOTE: if the button or field is not activated, it is normally displayed greyed out and does not respond if a user selects it)

active *adjective (in a multitasking operating system)* **active application** = application currently being used by a user; **active area** = (i) *(in a spreadsheet program)* the area that contains data bounded by the top left hand corner and the bottom right hand cell; (ii) *(in a graphical window)* an area that will start or select a function if the user moves the pointer into it with a mouse; **active cell** = spreadsheet cell which is currently selected with a cursor or pointer; **active code page** = code page currently in use by the system; **active database** = database file currently being accessed by a database management program; **active device** = electronic component that provides gain; (in a network) **active document** = standard Windows application that is accessed from within a web browser and controlled by special commands in the web page; **active file** = file which is being worked on; **active gateway** = gateway that exchanges routing information, unlike a passive gateway; **active high** = electronic signal that is logical one when it is high *or* at five volts; **active hub** = network device that selectively directs packets of data according to their address *or* content; *see also* HUB; **active line** = line in a communications link *or* port that is being used to transfer data or carry control signals; **active link** = link currently being used to transfer information; **active low** = electronic signal that is valid when it is low *or* logical zero *or* at zero volts; **active matrix liquid crystal display** way of making liquid crystal displays (for laptop computer screens) in which each pixel is controlled by its own transistor giving a clearer and brighter screen image, but that consumes more power; **active menu** menu selection currently displayed below a menu bar; **active node** = node on a network connected to *or* available to connect to another node; **active printer** = printer that is currently connected to the computer's printer port; *(in a multitasking system)* **active program** = program that is currently in control of the processor; **active record** = record that is being updated or accessed; **active region** area on a screen that will start an action or has been defined as a hotspot; **active state** = electronic state that causes an action to occur; **Active Server Page (ASP)** = technique used to create web pages in real time as the user views the page; the system works with the web server software to run scripts (often written in Visual Basic) and database components to provide information that is then displayed within the web page, for example, a web page that displays a list of products could either be created as a complete HTML file or could be created as an ASP template that extracts data about each product from a database each time a user views the page; **active storage** = main storage, fast access RAM whose locations can be directly and immediately addressed by the CPU; **active window** = (i) area of display screen in which you are currently working; (ii) *(in a GUI or SAA CUA front-end)* the window that is currently the focus of cursor movements and screen displays; *see also* SAA, WINDOW; **ActiveVRML** = *see* VRML; **ActiveX** = programming language and program definition used to create small applications designed to enhance the functionality of a web page; for example, to add multimedia effects to a web page that are not supported by the basic HTML commands, an ActiveX program, called an applet, could be used; *see also* APPLET, JAVA, VBSCRIPT

activity *noun* **(a)** being active *or* busy; **activity level** = maximum number of jobs that can run in a multitasking system; **activity light** = small light or LED on the front of a disk drive or computer that indicates when the disk drive is reading or writing data to disk; **activity loading** = method of organizing disk contents so that the most often accessed files *or* programs can be loaded quickly; **activity ratio** = number of files currently in use compared to the total stored; **activity trail** = record of activities carried out **(b) activities** = jobs *or*

tasks which are being performed on a computer

actual address *or* **absolute address** *noun* computer storage address that directly, without any modification, accesses a location *or* device

actual data transfer rate average number of data bits transferred in a period of time

actuator *noun* mechanical device that can be controlled by an external signal (such as the read/write head in a disk drive)

ACU = AUTOMATIC CALLING UNIT

acuity *noun* **(a)** ability of the eye to define between shades and shapes of an object **(b)** ability of the ear to detect frequency *or* volume changes

acutance *noun* ability of a lens to produce clear edges

acute *adjective* **(a)** very sharp *or* clear **(b) acute accent** = accent above a character, which slopes upwards to the right

AD *(film)* = ASSISTANT DIRECTOR, ASSOCIATE DIRECTOR person who carries out the director's instructions, oversees the work and whereabouts of the actors, technicians and rest of crew and works in close contact with the production unit

ADA *noun* high-level programming language that is used mainly in military, industrial and scientific fields of computing

adapt *verb* to change to fit; *can this computer be adapted to take 31/2-inch disks*

adaptation *noun* ability of a device to adjust its sensitivity range according to various situations; *the adaptation of the eye to respond to different levels of brightness*

adapter *or* **adaptor** *noun* device that allows two *or* more incompatible devices to be connected together; *the cable adapter allows attachment of the scanner to the SCSI interface; the cable to connect the scanner to the adapter is included in the package*; **adapter card** = interface card (that plugs into an expansion slot in a computer) that allows incompatible devices to communicate; for example, a display adapter allows a computer to display text and images on a monitor; **adapter plug** = plug which allows devices with different plugs (two-pin, three-pin, etc.) to be fitted into the same socket; **graphics adapter** = electronic device (normally on an expansion card) in a computer that converts software commands into electrical signals that display graphics on a connected monitor; *the new graphics adapter is capable of displaying higher resolution graphics*; *see also* CGA, EGA, VGA; **network adapter** = add-in board that connects a computer to a network; the board converts the computer's data into electrical signals that are then transmitted along the network cable

adaptive (something) that can change according to the requirements or demand; **adaptive channel allocation** = providing communications channels according to demand rather than a fixed allocation; **adaptive differential pulse-code modulation (ADPCM)** = CCITT standard that defines a method of converting a voice or analog signal into a compressed digital signal; **adaptive interframe transform coding** = class of compression algorithms commonly used with video signals to reduce the data transmission rate; **adaptive packet assembly** = method used by the MNP error correcting protocol to adjust the size of data packets according to the quality of the telephone line (the better the line, the bigger the packet size); **adaptive routing** = ability of a system to change its communications routes according to situations such as line failure; **adaptive systems** = ability of a system to alter its responses and processes according to situations; **adaptive compression** = data compression system that continuously monitors the data it is compressing and adjusts its own algorithm to provide the most efficient compression

adaptor *see* ADAPTER

ADB = APPLE DESKTOP BUS *noun* serial bus built into Apple Macintosh computers that allows low-speed devices, such as the keyboard and mouse, to communicate with the processor; *see also* USB

ADC = ANALOG TO DIGITAL CONVERTER *noun* electronic device that converts an analog input signal to a digital output form, that can be used by a computer

add *verb* **(a)** to put figures together to make a total; *in the spreadsheet each column should be added to make a subtotal* **(b)** to put things together to form a larger

group; *the software house has added a new management package to its range of products; adding or deleting material from the text is easy using the edit program*

added entry *noun* secondary file entry in a library catalogue

addend *noun* number added to the augend in an addition sum

adder *noun* device *or* routine that provides the sum of two *or* more digital inputs; **full adder** *or* **three input adder** = binary addition circuit which can produce the sum of two inputs, and can also accept a carry input, producing a carry output if necessary; **half adder** *or* **two input adder** binary addition circuit which can produce the sum of two inputs and a carry output if necessary, but will not accept a carry input

add-in *noun* & *adjective* (something) which is added; *the first method is to use a page description language, the second is to use an add-in processor card; can you explain the add-in card method? processing is much faster with add-in cards*

additional dialogue replacement *see* ADR

additional *adjective* which is added *or* which is extra; *can we add three additional workstations to the network*

additive colour mixing *verb* to mix different coloured lights to produce the colour which is wanted

add-on *noun* & *adjective* piece of software *or* hardware that is added to a computer system to improve its performance; *the add-on hard disk will boost the computer's storage capabilities; the new add-on board allows colour graphics to be displayed* (NOTE: the opposite is **built-in**)

address 1 *noun* **(a)** details of number, street and town where an office is or a person lives; *my business address and phone number are printed on the card*; **cable address** = short address for sending cables; **home address** = address of a house or flat where someone lives; *please send the documents to my home address*; **address list** = list of addresses; *we keep an address list of two thousand businesses in Europe* **(b)** number allowing a central processing unit to reference a physical location in a storage medium in a computer system; *each separate memory word has its own unique address; this is the address at which the data starts*; **address base** = part of an address that defines the origin to which the logical address is added; **address bus** = physical connection that carries the address data in parallel form from the central processing unit to external devices; *see also* BIT, DATA BUS; *(in programming)* **address code** = part of a computer instruction that contains the location of the operand; **address field** *or* **operand field** = part of a computer instruction that contains the operand address data; *(in a virtual memory system)* **address mapping** = virtual address that is translated to a real address; *see also* VIRTUAL MEMORY; **address modification** = changing the address field, so that it can refer to a different location; **address register** = register in a computer that is able to store all the bits of an address which can then be processed as a single unit; *see also* MAR; **address space** = total number of possible locations that can be directly addressed by the program or CPU; **address track** = track on a magnetic disk containing the addresses of files, etc., stored on other tracks; **address word** = computer word, usually made up of two data words that contain address data **(c)** unique number that identifies a device on a network; **address book** = (i) *(in a network)* list of node addresses; (ii) *(in electronic mail)* list of the network addresses of other users to which electronic mail can be sent; *(in networks)* **address code** = part of a packet that contains the address of the destination node; **address mask** = pattern of bits used to filter out parts of an address from an address; normally used to read the network and subnet parts of an address within an Internet or IP address; **address resolution protocol (ARP)** = protocol used within the TCP/IP standard to link one IP address to a low-level physical address; *see also* TCP/IP; **address translation** = an address produced by calculating an expression; **destination address** = address of the node to which data is being transferred *or* sent; **network address** = unique number that identifies each device on a network **2** *verb* **(a)** to write the details of an address on an envelope, etc.; *to address a letter or a parcel; please address your reply to the*

manager; a letter addressed to the managing director; an incorrectly addressed package **(b)** to put the location data onto an address bus to identify which word in memory *or* storage device is to be accessed; *a larger address word increases the amount of memory a computer can address*

The world's largest open data network, the Internet, links more than 10,000 local networks and 3 million workstations in 50 countries. It has grown so fast that its address space is 'bust' and is being redesigned to allow further expansion

Computing

---

addressability *noun* the control available over pixels on screen

addressable *adjective* which can be addressed; *all the 256Mb of RAM is addressable*; **addressable cursor** = cursor which can be programmed to be placed in a certain position; **addressable point** = any point *or* pixel in a graphics system that can be directly addressed

addressee *noun* person to whom a letter *or* package *or* communication is addressed

addressing *noun* **(a)** process of accessing a location in memory; **addressing method** = manner in which a section of memory is located; **direct addressing** = method of addressing where the storage location address given in the instruction is the location to be used; **immediate addressing** = accessing data immediately because it is held in the address field itself; **indexed addressing** = way of addressing where the storage location is addressed with a start address and an offset word, which is added in to give the destination address; **indirect addressing** = way of addressing data, where the first instruction refers to an address which contains a second address **(b)** process of printing a postal address or label on an envelope or parcel; **addressing machine** = machine which puts addresses on envelopes automatically

adjacent *adjective* which is near *or* next to something; *the address is stored adjacent to the customer name field*; **adjacent domains** = two network domains linked by two adjacent nodes; **adjacent nodes** = two nodes in a network connected by a path that does not connect any other node

adjunct register *noun* 32-bit register in which the top 16 bits are used for control information and only the bottom 16 bits are available for use by a program

adjust *verb* to change something to fit new conditions *or* so that it works better; *you can adjust the brightness and contrast by turning a knob*

adjustment *noun* slight change made to something so that it works better; *the brightness needs adjustment; I think the joystick needs adjustment as it sometimes gets stuck*

AdLib *noun* (older) type of sound card for the PC with basic sound playback and MIDI functions; *see also* SOUND CARD

administrator *noun* **(a)** individual who is responsible for looking after a network; responsibilities include installing, configuring and maintaining the network **(b)** control *or* supervisor *or* executive software *or* person; **data administrator** = control section of a database management system

Adobe *noun* software company that developed products including Acrobat, ATM, and PostScript

Adobe Acrobat software (developed by Adobe Systems) that converts documents and formatted pages into a file format (called PDF) that can be viewed or printed in an identical form on almost any computer platform or using a web browser on the Internet; *we layout this dictionary using DTP software then send convert this to a PDF file using Acrobat before sending this file to the printer*

Adobe Type Manager *or* **ATM**
software technology for describing scalable fonts - most commonly used with Apple System and Microsoft Windows operating systems to provide fonts that can be scaled to almost any point size, and printed on almost any printer; *see also* OUTLINE FONT; *compare with* BITMAPPED FONT

ADP = AUTOMATIC DATA PROCESSING

ADPCM = ADAPTIVE DIFFERENTIAL PULSE-CODE MODULATION *noun* CCITT standard that defines a method of converting a voice or analog signal into a compressed digital signal; *see also* LEVEL A, LEVEL B, LEVEL C

ADR *(film)* = ADDITIONAL DIALOGUE REPLACEMENT *noun* adding words or phrases to a section of film in post production; a continuous loop of film is shown to the artists in which the same scene is shown repeatedly to help them synchronize their speech with their filmed lip movements

ADSL = ASYMMETRIC DIGITAL SUBSCRIBER LINE high-speed transmission standard that uses the same copper telephone wires as a normal telephone service, but is much faster than a standard modem or a digital system such as ISDN. As well as the speed, ADSL provides a user with an 'always on' connection to the Internet - there is no need to dial an access number; *compare with* DIAL-UP, ISDN

advance *verb* to move forward; to make something move forward; *the paper is advanced by turning this knob; advance the cursor two spaces along the line*

advanced *adjective* more complicated *or* more difficult to learn; **advanced peer-to-peer networking (APPN)** = extension to SNA that routes information around a network and dynamically adjusts the route if part of the network is damaged; **advanced program to program communications (APPC)** = set of protocols that allows peer-to-peer communication between workstations connected to an SNA network; also known as LU 6.2 protocols; **advanced run-length limited (ARLL)** = method of storing data onto a hard disk that is faster and more efficient than RLL; **advanced version** = program with more complex features for use by an experienced user; **Advanced Interactive Executive** = *see* AIX; **Advanced Research Projects Agency Network (ARPANET)** = original network of interconnected computers, linked by leased lines, that formed the first prototype for the current Internet; developed by the US Department of Defense (Defense Advanced Research Projects Agency)

adventure game *noun* game played on a computer, where the user pretends to be a hero in an imaginary land and has to get through various dangerous situations, fight monsters, etc.

advisory lock *noun (in a multitasking system)* lock placed on a region of a file by one process to prevent any other process accessing the same data

advisory system *noun* expert system that provides advice to a user

aerial 1 *noun* device for receiving *or* sending radio transmissions by converting electromagnetic impulses into electrical signals and vice-versa; **aerial cable** = wire stretched between poles which acts as an aerial; **aerial perspective** = view of a three-dimensional landscape as if the viewer is above the scene **2** *adjective* in the air; **aerial image** = a view from high above a scene

affect *verb* to touch *or* to influence *or* to change something; *changes in voltage will affect the way the computer functions*

affiliate *verb* to connect *or* join with

affiliated *adjective* connected with *or* owned by another company; *one of our affiliated companies*

affirmative *adjective* meaning 'yes'; **the answer was in the affirmative** = the answer was yes; **affirmative acknowledgement** = acknowledge signal from the receiver that it has accepted the message and is ready for the next one

AFIPS = AMERICAN FEDERATION OF INFORMATION PROCESSING SOCIETIES

AFNOR= ASSOCIATION FRANCE DE NORMALISATION

AFP = APPLETALK FILING PROTOCOL *noun* protocol used to communicate between workstations and servers in a network of Apple Macintosh computers

after-image *noun* copy of a block of data that has been modified

afterglow *see* PERSISTENCE

AGC = AUTOMATIC GAIN CONTROL electronic device that provides a constant amplitude output signal from a varying input signal by changing its gain

agenda *noun* list of tasks *or* appointments *or* activities that have to be carried out on a particular day; *the conference agenda or the agenda of the conference; after two hours we were still discussing the first item on the agenda; the secretary put finance at the top of the agenda; the chairman wants two*

items removed from or taken off the agenda; **agenda item** = topic on an agenda to be discussed; **electronic agenda** = software that allows a user to record appointments for each day

agent *noun* series of commands or actions that are carried out automatically on a particular file or data; the commands can be executed at a particular time or in response to a signal

aggregate *noun & adjective* collection of data objects; **aggregate bandwidth** = total bandwidth of a channel carrying a multiplexed data stream; **aggregate function** = mathematical database function performed on a selected field in every record in a selected database; **aggregate line speed** = maximum speed at which data can be transmitted through a particular channel; **aggregate operator** = command in a database management program that starts an aggregate function

AI = ARTIFICIAL INTELLIGENCE *noun* the design and development of computer programs that imitate human intelligence, providing basic reasoning and other human characteristics

aid 1 *noun* help; *the computer is a great aid to rapid processing of large amounts of information* **2** *verb* to help; *industrial design is aided by computers; see also* COMPUTER-AIDED

aiming symbol *or* **field** *noun* symbol displayed on screen which defines the area in which a light-pen can be detected

air circuit breaker *noun* mechanical device that has an electrical *or* manual switched circuit isolator

air gap *noun* narrow gap between a recording *or* playback head and the magnetic medium

airbrush *noun (in graphics software)* a painting tool that creates a diffuse pattern of dots, like an mechanical airbrush; *we used the airbrush tool to create the cloud effects in this image*

AIX = ADVANCED INTERACTIVE EXECUTIVE version of UNIX produced by IBM to run on its range of PCs, minicomputers and mainframes

alarm *noun* ringing or other sound which warns of a danger; *all staff must leave the* *building if the alarm sounds; an alarm rings when the printer has run out of paper*

albumen plate *noun* photographic plate, with a light-sensitive coating

ALC = AUTOMATIC LEVEL CONTROL; *see* AGC

alert *noun* warning message sent from software to warn a person or application that an error or problem has occurred; **alert box** = dialog box displayed with a sound that warns a user of the implications of the user's actions; *the alert box warned me that I was about to delete all my files*; **alert condition** = status of a particular object *or* device that triggers an alarm; **network alert** = message sent from the network operating system to the user warning that the network hardware is not working properly

algebra *noun* use of letters in certain mathematical operations to represent unknown numbers *or* a range of possible numbers; **Boolean algebra** = rules set down to define, simplify and manipulate logical functions, based on statements that are true or false

algebraic language *noun* context free language

ALGOL = ALGORITHMIC LANGUAGE high level programming language using algorithmic methods for mathematical and technical applications

algorithm *noun* rules used to define *or* perform a specific task *or* to solve a specific problem

COMMENT: programmers write instructions to implement particular algorithms in their programs. The choice of algorithm affects performance, memory requirements, etc. For example, some methods of sorting are very quick while others are slower but do not need as much memory or disk space to operate

algorithmic *adjective* expressed using algorithms; **algorithmic language** = computer language designed to process and express algorithms, such as ALGOL

image processing algorithms are step by step procedures for performing image processing operations

Byte

the steps are: acquiring a digitized image, developing an algorithm to process it, processing the image, modifying the algorithm until you are satisfied with the result

Byte

the complex algorithms needed for geometrical calculations make heavy demands on the processor

PC Business World

alias *noun* **(a)** alternative name for something; often used to provide a new keystroke to access a menu item; *some electronic mail programs allow you to define an alternative name (the alias) for your email address so that any message sent to 'boss@pcp.co.uk' would go to 'simon@pcp.co.uk'; (on a network)* **alias name** = another name that is used instead of the user name **(b)** undesirable value within a digital sample - often because a very high input signal has exceeded the limits of the converter and is wrongly represented as a very low value; *the operating system uses the alias COM1 to represent the serial port address 3FCh*

aliasing *noun* jagged edges that appear along diagonal or curved lines displayed on a computer screen caused by the size of each pixel; **anti-aliasing** = (i) *(in graphics)* method of reducing the effects of jagged edges in graphics by using shades of grey to blend in along edges; (ii) *(in sound)* to add sound signals between the sound samples to create a smoother sound wave

alien *adjective* different *or* not fitting the usual system; **alien disk** = disk formatted on another system *or* containing data in a format which cannot be read; **alien disk reader** = add-on device which allows a computer to read from disks from other computers *or* systems; *when you have an alien disk select the multi-disk option to allow to turn the disk drive into an alien disk reader*

align *verb* **(a)** (i) to make sure that the characters to be printed are spaced and levelled correctly, either vertically or horizontally; (ii) to arrange numbers into a column with all figures lines up against the right hand side (right-aligned) or the left-hand side (left-aligned); *(in a word-processor)* **align text** = to add spaces between words in a line to make sure that the line of text fills the whole line; *see also* JUSTIFY **(b)** to tune two *or* more radio circuits together **(c)** to ensure that a read/write head is correctly positioned over the recording medium

aligner *noun* device used to make sure that the paper is straight on a typewriter

aligning edge *noun* edge of a optical character recognition system used to position a document

alignment *noun* correct spacing and levelling of printed characters; **in alignment** = correctly aligned; **out of alignment** = not aligned correctly; **alignment pin** = peg that fits in a hole to ensure that two devices are correctly aligned

all points addressable (APA) mode *noun* graphics mode in which each pixel can be individually addressed and its colour and attributes defined

allocate *verb* to divide (a sum of money *or* a period of time *or* a piece of work *or* a frequency band) in various ways and share it out between users; *this frequency band has been allocated to the police*

allocation *noun* dividing memory *or* disk space *or* printer use *or* program *or* operating system time *or* device in various ways; *allocation of time or capital to a project*; **allocation unit** = one or more sectors on a hard disk that are used to store a file or part of a file; **band allocation** = range of frequencies allocated to various users *or* for various purposes; *the new band allocation means we will have more channels*; **memory allocation** = process in which an operating system provides an application with the memory it requires in order to run

```
The fix is meant to correct
seven problems. They include
problems with swapper files
and DOS memory allocation
                    Computing
```

allophone *noun* smallest unit of sound from which speech can be formed

ALPHA *noun* processor chip developed by Digital Equipment Corporation; the ALPHA chip is a 64-bit RISC processor

alpha *or* **alpha test** *noun* first working attempt of a computer product; *the new*

software is still in an alpha product stage; *see also* BETA TEST

alpha beta technique *noun* technique used in Artificial Intelligence for solving game and strategy problems by tree structures

alpha channel *noun* **(a)** video channel (often used to hold mattes) **(b)** *(in 32-bit graphics systems)* the top eight bits of a pixel word that define the properties of a pixel; the lower 24 bits define the pixel's colour; *see also* MATTE

alpha wrap *noun* method used for feeding tape into a helical scan video recorder to make sure the alignment is correct

alphabet *noun* the 26 letters used to make words

alphabetic character set *noun* characters (capitals and small letters) that make up the alphabet

alphabetical order *noun* arrangement of records (such as files, index cards) in the order of the letters of the alphabet (A,B,C,D, etc.)

alphabetically *adverb* in alphabetical order; *the files are arranged alphabetically under the customer's name*

alphabetize *verb* to put into alphabetical order; *enter the bibliographical information and alphabetize it*

alphageometric *adjective* (set of codes) that instruct a teletext terminal to display various graphics modes

alphameric *US* = ALPHANUMERIC

alphamosaic *adjective* (character set) used in teletext to provide alphanumeric and graphics characters

alphanumeric *adjective* roman letters and arabic numerals (and other signs such as punctuation marks); **alphanumeric characters** *or* **alphanumerics** = roman letters and arabic numerals (and other signs such as punctuation marks); **alphanumeric data** = data shown by the letters of the alphabet and the arabic numerals; **alphanumeric display** = display device able to show characters as well as numbers; **alphanumeric keyboard** = keyboard containing character keys as well as numerical keys

```
geometrical data takes up more
storage      space      than
alphanumeric data
```
PC Business World

alpha-particle *noun* emitted alpha radiation particle; **alpha-particle sensitivity** = problem experienced by certain (MOS) memory devices exposed to alpha radiation, causing loss of stored charge (data)

alphaphotographic *adjective* which represents pictures using predefined characters, for teletext services

alphasort *verb* to sort data into alphabetical order

Alt key *noun* special key on a PC's keyboard used to activate special functions in an application; *press Alt and P at the same time to print your document*

COMMENT: the Alt key has become the standard method of activating a menu bar in any software running on a PC; for example, Alt-F normally displays the File menu of a program, Alt-X normally exits the program

Alt = ALTERNATIVE collection of Usenet newsgroups on the Internet that cover a wide selection of recreation, discussion and controversial topics

alter *verb* to change; *to alter the terms of a contract; the program specifications have just been altered*

alterable *adjective* which can be altered; *see* EAPROM, EAROM

alteration *noun* change which has been made; *he made some alterations to the terms of a contract; the agreement was signed without any alterations; the new version of the software has many alterations and improvements*

alternate 1 *verb* to change from one to another over and over again **2** *adjective* which change from one to another; **alternate character set** = second set of special characters that can be accessed from a keyboard; *we can print Greek characters by selecting the alternate character set*; **alternate key** = key in a database file that is not the primary key; **alternate mode** = application for multi-user use, where two operators can access and share a single set

of files; **alternate route** = backup method for communications systems

alternately *adverb* switching from one to the other

alternating current *or* **AC** *noun* electric current whose value varies with time in a regular, sinusoidal way (changing direction of flow each half cycle)

alternative 1 *noun* **(a)** something which can be done instead of something else; *what is the alternative to rekeying all the data?*; **we have no alternative** = there is nothing else we can do **(b)** *see* ALT **2** *adjective* other *or* which can take the place of something; **to find someone alternative employment** = to find someone another job

alternator *noun* device which produces an alternating current

ALU = ARITHMETIC LOGIC UNIT section of the CPU that performs all arithmetic and logical functions; *see also* CPU

always on communications link that is permanently active; *compare with* DIAL-UP

COMMENT: Normally used to describe the feature of high-speed broadband communications devices (such as cable modems and ADSL) that link your computer to the Internet - your computer appears to be permanently connected to the Internet and you do not need to dial up a special number

AM = AMPLITUDE MODULATION

A-MAC *noun* low bandwidth variation of MAC

ambient *adjective* normal background (conditions); **ambient noise** = normal background noise that is present all the time; normally given a reference pressure level of 0.00002 pascal in SI units; **ambient noise level** = normal background noise level; *the ambient noise level in the office is greater than in the library*; **ambient temperature** = normal average temperature of the air around a device

ambiguous *adjective* which has two possible meanings; **ambiguous filename** = filename which is not unique to a single file, making it difficult to locate the file

ambisonics *noun* recording more than one audio signal to give the effect of being surrounded by sound

America Online (AOL) large US-based on-line service provider that offers UK and US connections for users to its own collection of databases together with user areas and access to the Internet; electronic mail to or from users of America Online are identified by the suffix 'aol.com'; *see also* SERVICE PROVIDER

American National Standards Institute (ANSI) *noun* organization which specifies computer and software standards including those of high-level programming languages

American Standard Code for Information Interchange (ASCII) *noun* code which represents alphanumeric characters using a standard set of binary codes

American Standards Association (ASA) *noun* organisation that sets standards for the light sensitivity of photographic film emulsion - for example, 100 ASA. The film is numbered in accordance to it's sensitivity to light; the higher the number, the higher the film's sensitivity

Amiga (old) range of personal computers developed by Commodore

> COMMENT: Amiga computers were based on the Motorola 68000 range of CPUs and are not normally IBM PC compatible without add-on hardware or software

AMM = ANALOG MULTIMETER multimeter that uses a graduated scale and a moving needle as a readout for voltage, current and impedance levels; *compare with* DMM

amount 1 *noun* quantity of money *or* data *or* paper, etc.; *what is the largest amount of data which can be processed in one hour?* **2** *verb* **to amount to** = to make a total of; *their debts amount to over $1m; the total keyboarded characters amount to ten million*

amp *or* **ampere (a)** *noun* base SI unit of electrical current; defined as the current flowing through an impedance of one ohm

which has one volt across it (NOTE: used with figures: **a 13-amp plug)**

ampersand *noun* printing sign (&) which means 'and'

amplification *noun* the ratio of the output signal strength compared to the input signal strength

amplifier *noun* electronic circuit that magnifies the power of a signal; **audio amplifier** = domestic amplifier that handles frequencies in the human hearing range; **low noise amplifier** = high-quality amplifier placed very close to a receiving aerial to amplify the received signals before they are corrupted by noise; **amplifier class** = way of classifying the design of amplifiers meant for different jobs; **amplified telephone** = system to allow hands-off telephone conversations

amplify *verb* to magnify a signal power *or* amplitude; *the received signal needs to be amplified before it can be processed*

amplitude *noun* strength or size of a signal; **amplitude distortion** = distortion of a signal due to uneven (non-linear) amplification (high levels amplified less than low); **amplitude modulation (AM)** = method of carrying data by varying the size of a carrier signal (of fixed frequency) according to the data; *compare with* FREQUENCY MODULATION; **amplitude quantization** = conversion of an analog signal to a numerical representation

analog *or* **analogue** *adjective* representation and measurement of numerical data by continuously variable physical quantities, such as: size of electrical voltages, volume of gas *or* gear ratio; *compare with* DIGITAL; **analog channel** = communications line that carries analog signals such as speech; **analog computer** = computer which processes data in analog form (that is, data which is represented by a continuously varying signal - as opposed to digital data); **analog data** = data that is represented as a continuously variable signal; speech is a form of analog data; **analog display** = display or monitor that can display an infinite range of colours or shades of grey (unlike digital displays that can only display a finite range of colours); VGA monitors are a form of analog display; **analog input card** = all circuitry on one PCB required for amplifying and converting analog input signals to a digital form; **analog line** = communications line that carries analog signals, such as a telephone line; **analog loopback** = test mode on a modem used to test the serial port of the local computer or terminal; **analog loopback with selftest** = test mode on a modem used to test the serial port of the modem; **analog monitor** = display screen that uses a continuously variable input signal to control the colours display so it can display a near infinite range of colours; the video monitor accepts analog signals from the computer (digital to analog conversion is performed in the video display board). The monitor may accept only a narrow range of display resolutions; for example, a monitor might only be able to display VGA or VGA and Super VGA, or it may accept a wide range of signals including TV; *see also* MULTIFREQUENCY MONITOR, RGB MONITOR; **analog multimeter** = multimeter that uses a graduated scale and a moving needle as a readout for voltage, current and impedance levels; *compare with* DMM; **analog output card** = all circuitry on one PCB required to convert digital output data from a computer to an analog form; **analog recording** = storing signals in their natural form without conversion to digital form; **analog signal** = continuously varying signal; *when someone speaks, the sound wave is an analog signal - it varies smoothly as the person talks;* **analog to digital (A to D** *or* **A/D)** = change a signal from an analog form to a digitally coded form; **analog to digital converter (ADC** *or* **A to D converter)** = device used to convert an analog input signal to a digital output form, which can be understood by a computer or other digital circuit such as a digital signal processor; *compare with* DIGITAL TO ANALOG CONVERTER; **analog transmission** = data transmission in which the data is sent as a series of changes in a continuously varying signal; *the audio signal was first passed through an A to D converter before being stored on disk; compare with* DIGITAL TO ANALOG CONVERTER

analyse *or* **analyze** *verb* to examine in detail; *to analyse a computer printout; to analyse the market potential for a new computer*

analysis *noun* detailed examination and report; *market analysis; sales analysis; to carry out an analysis of the market potential; to write an analysis of the sales position;* **cost analysis** = examination in advance of the costs of a new product; **systems analysis** = analysing a process *or* system to see if it could be more efficiently carried out by computer (NOTE: plural is **analyses**)

analyst *noun* person who carries out an analysis of a problem; **systems analyst** = person who specializes in systems analysis

analytical engine *noun* mechanical calculating machine developed by Charles Babbage in 1833 that is generally considered the first general-purpose digital computer

analyzer *noun* electronic test equipment that displays various features of a signal; **frequency analyzer** = test equipment that displays the amplitudes of the various frequency components of a signal

anamorphic image *noun* image which has been distorted in one direction

anamorphic lens *noun (film)* motion picture camera lens which allows a wide picture to be compressed on to standard film. When in a projector, it lets the image expand to fill a wide screen

ANAPROP = ANOMALOUS PROPAGATION *noun* distortion of transmitted television signals due to atmospheric conditions

anastigmatic *noun* lens *or* optical device that has been corrected for astigmatism

ancestral file *noun* system of backing up files (son to father to grandfather file), where the son is the current working file

anchor cell *noun* cell in a spreadsheet program that defines the start of a range of cells

anchor *noun (film)* the main presenter of a television programme who sets the style and tone of the show

ancillary equipment *noun* equipment which is used to make a task easier, but which is not absolutely necessary

AND function *noun* logical function whose output is true if both its inputs are true; **AND gate** = gate that performs a logical AND function on electrical signals

> COMMENT: if both inputs are 1, results of the AND will be 1; if one of the input digits is 0, then AND will produce a 0

anechoic *adjective* (room) that produces no echoes, used for testing audio equipment; **anechoic chamber** perfectly quiet room in which sound or radio waves do not reflect off the walls

angle *noun* measure of the change in direction, usually as the distance turned from a reference line; **wide-angle lens** = lens which has a large acceptance angle

angled line line with three or more points (such as a zig-zag)

angstrom (Å) *noun* unit of measurement equal to one thousand millionth of a metre

ANI = AUTOMATIC NUMBER IDENTIFICATION telephone system which displays the telephone number of the caller

animate *verb* to make a series of drawings which, when filmed, will create moving images

animated GIF = way of saving several small graphic images within one file so that they can be repeatedly displayed in sequence giving an impression of animation; often used to create animated buttons or other effects on a web page; *see also* GIF, TRANSPARENT GIF

animated graphics images that move on the screen

animatic *noun (film)* a succession of drawings describing the story of a film, advertisement, animation or multimedia production before filming begins; *see also* STORY BOARD

animation *noun* (i) drawing images on film, especially using a computer to create moving graphical images, such as cartoons; (ii) filming puppets or still drawings in sequence in order to give the appearance of movement; (iii) (with a computer) creating the illusion of movement by displaying a series of slightly different images on screen; the images are displayed very rapidly to give the effect of smooth movement; **animation software** = software that allows a user to create and manipulate a series of images so that when played back they give the effect of movement

ANN *(film)* = ANNOUNCER a voice over or a person on camera who gives information during a broadcast or who introduces and closes a radio or TV programme

annotation *noun* comment *or* note in a program which explains how the program is to be used; **annotation symbol** = symbol used when making flowcharts, to allow comments to be added

announce *verb (a website)* to publicise a new or updated website by informing the main search engines

announcer *see* ANN

annunciator *noun & adjective* signal that can be heard *or* seen that is used to attract attention

anode *noun* positive electrical terminal of a device

anomalistic period *noun* time taken for a satellite to travel between consecutive maximum points in its orbit

anomalous propagation *noun* distortion of transmitted television signals due to atmospheric conditions

anonymous FTP feature of an Internet site that allows any user to login to the computer with the user name 'anonymous' and to transfer files using the FTP protocol; *see also* FTP

ANSI US = AMERICAN NATIONAL STANDARDS INSTITUTE organization which specifies computer and software standards, including those of high-level programming languages; **ANSI C** = standard version of the C programming language; *(in a PC)* **ANSI driver** = small resident software program that interprets ANSI screen control codes and controls the screen appropriately; **ANSI escape sequence** = sequence of ANSI screen control characters that controls the colours and attributes of text on screen; the sequence must begin with the ASCII character Esc (ASCII 27) and the character '[' (ASCII 91); **ANSI screen control** = standard codes developed by ANSI that control how colours and simple graphics are displayed on a computer screen

ANSI.SYS a device driver that is supplied with DOS and allows programs to use a series of special character sequences to change the colour and position of characters displayed on screen; also provides extra controls for the keyboard and is normally used within batch files to enhance the look of a program

COMMENT: before experimenting with ANSI.SYS, it must be loaded when the PC is started by adding a line such as 'DEVICE= \DOS\ANSI.SYS' to the CONFIG.SYS file on the disk used to start the PC. It will be apparent if a program needs ANSI.SYS but does not have it loaded, since the special character sequences will appear on the screen rather than being carried out, leaving the screen display unreadable. These sequences show up as a left arrow, left square bracket and then a combination of letters and numbers

answer 1 *noun* reply *or* letter *or* conversation coming after someone has written or spoken; *I am writing in answer to your letter of October 6th; my letter got no answer or there was no answer to my letter; I tried to phone his office but there was no answer* **2** *verb* **(a)** to speak *or* write after someone has spoken or written to you; **to answer a letter** = to write a letter in reply to a letter which you have received; **to answer the telephone** = to lift the telephone when it rings and listen to what the caller is saying **(b)** to reply to a signal and set up a communications link; *the first modem originates the call and the second answers it*; **answer back** = signal sent by the receiving end of a communications system to identify itself *or* to transmit a message; **answer mode** = modem that is waiting to receive a telephone call and establish a connection; *see also* MODEM; **answer modem** = mode of a modem that emits an answertone used to establish a connection with an originate modem; **answer time** = time taken for a receiving device to respond to a signal; **answertone** = tone an answering modem emits before the carrier is exchanged **(c)** **answer print** = *(film)* the initial composite or graded print (copy) from an edited negative colour film which includes sound, music, titles

answering *noun* **answering machine** = machine which answers the telephone automatically when someone is not in the office; **answering service** = office which answers the telephone and takes messages for someone *or* for a company

answerphone *noun* cassette recorder attached to a telephone, which plays a prerecorded message and records messages from people dialling the number

antenna *noun* aerial *or* device for receiving *or* sending radio transmissions by converting electromagnetic impulses into electrical signals and vice-versa; **antenna array** = series of small transmitting *or* receiving elements connected in parallel, that make up a complex antenna; **antenna gain** = transmitted signal power increase due to using a certain type of antenna

anthropomorphic software *noun (in artificial intelligence)* software that appears to react to what a user says

anti- *prefix* meaning against; **anti-aliasing** = (i) method of reducing the effects of jagged edges in graphics by using shades of grey to blend in along edges and make angled lines appear smooth; (ii) filter used to correct sampling errors (aliases) due to a very high or low input signal; **anti-static mat** = special rubberised mat which dissipates static electricity charge through an electrical earth connection; an operator touches the mat before handling sensitive electronic components that could be damaged by static electricity; **anti-tinkle suppression** = *(in a modem)* switch which prevents other telephones on a line ringing when a modem dials out; **anti-virus program** = software program that looks for virus software on a computer and destroys it before it can damage data or files; *see also* VIRUS

AOL = AMERICA ONLINE

APA = ALL POINTS ADDRESSABLE

APD = AVALANCHE PHOTODIODE

aperture *noun* **(a)** lens diaphragm that allows the amount of light that reaches the film to be regulated according to the user's wishes **(b)** opening in a device that allows a certain amount of light or a signal to pass through it; **aperture card** = method of storing microfilmed information with a card surround, that can contain punched information; *(film)* **aperture correction** = a method of improving image detail by boosting the high frequencies in the video circuits of TV image generating equipment; **aperture illumination** = pattern generated from an aperture antenna; **aperture mask** = metal sheet with holes in colour monitors, used to keep the red, green and blue beams separate

API = APPLICATION PROGRAMMING INTERFACE set of standard program functions and commands that allow any programmer to interface a program with another application; *if I follow the published API for this system, my program will work properly*

APL = A PROGRAMMING LANGUAGE high-level programming language used in scientific and mathematical work

APM = ADVANCED POWER MANAGEMENT specification for computer equipment that allows an operating system, such as Windows, to control the power management features of the equipment; this standard has been replaced by the ACPI standard in newer versions of Windows and Windows NT; *see also* ACPI

apochromatic lens *noun* optical lens that has been corrected for chromatic aberration

apogee *noun* point in a satellite's orbit where it is at its maximum distance from the earth

apostrophe *noun* printing sign ('), which generally indicates that a letter is missing *or* used in ('s), to indicate possession (NOTE: so **computer's** can mean 'belonging to a computer' *or* 'the computer is': **the computer's casing is blue; the computer's broken and has to be repaired.** Note that this is different from **it's =** 'it is' as opposed to **its =** 'belonging to it': **it's easy to program; you cannot edit a disk when its write protect tag is closed**)

APPC = ADVANCED PROGRAM TO PROGRAM COMMUNICATIONS set of protocols that allows peer-to-peer communication between workstations connected to an SNA network; also known as LU 6.2 protocols

append *verb* (i) to add data to an existing file *or* record; (ii) to add a file or data to the end of an existing file; *if you enter the DOS command COPY A+B, the file B will be appended to the end of file A*

appendix *noun* section at the back of a book, containing additional information; *for further details see the appendices; a complete list is printed in the appendix* (NOTE: plural is **appendices**)

Apple Computer Corporation

company (formed in 1975) which has developed a range of personal computers including the Apple II, Apple Lisa and, more recently, the Apple Macintosh; **Apple Desktop Bus** = serial bus built into Apple Macintosh computers that allows low-speed devices, such as the keyboard and mouse, to communicate with the processor; **Apple file exchange** = software program that runs on an Apple Macintosh computer allowing it to read disks from a PC; **Apple filing protocol (AFP)** = method of storing files on a network server so that they can be accessed from an Apple Macintosh computer; **Apple Key** = special key on the keyboard of an Apple Macintosh that, when pressed with another key, provides a short-cut to a menu selection; **Apple Mac** *or* **Apple Macintosh computer** = range of personal computer developed by Apple Inc. that has a graphical user interface and uses the 68000 family of processors; **AppleScript** = *(on an Apple Macintosh)* script language built into the System operation system that allows a user to automate simple tasks; **Appleshare** = software that allows Apple Macintosh computers to share files and printers using a file server; **AppleTalk** = (older) proprietary communications protocol developed by Apple Computer that carries data over network hardware between two or more Apple Macintosh computers and peripherals; similar to the seven-layer OSI protocol model; AppleTalk can link up to 32 devices, uses a CSMA/CA design and transmits data at 230Kbps, now mostly replaced by USB; **AppleTalk Filing Protocol (AFP)** = protocol used to communicate between workstations and servers in a network of Apple Macintosh computers

Apple Computer has fleshed out details of a migration path to the PowerPC RISC architecture for its 7 million Apple Macintosh users. Developments in the pipeline include PowerPC versions of the AppleTalk Remote Access networking protocol

Computing

applet *noun* **(a)** utility application program **(b)** *(in Microsoft Windows)* application started from the Control Panel; *there are applets to help format your disk and configure your keyboard*

appliance *noun* machine, especially one used in the home; *all electrical appliances should be properly earthed*

appliance computer *noun* ready to run computer system that can be bought in a shop, taken home and used immediately for a particular purpose

applicant *noun* person who applies for something; *applicant for a job or job applicant; there were thousands of applicants for shares in the new company*

application *noun* **(a)** asking for something, usually in writing; *application for a job or job application*; **application form** = form to be filled in when applying; *to fill in an application (form) for a job or a job application (form)* **letter of application** = letter in which someone applies for a job **(b)** task which a computer performs *or* problem which a computer solves (as opposed to an operating system which is the way in which a computer works); **application developer** = programmer who designs the look of an application and defines its functions; **application file** = binary file stored on disk that contains the machine code instructions of a program; **application generator** = special software that allows a programmer to define the main functions and look of an application; the generator then automatically creates the instructions to carry out the defined application; **application icon** = small image *or* graphical symbol that represents an application program in a graphical user interface stock control, tax, etc.); **application layer** = top layer in an ISO/OSI network, which requests a transmission (from a users program); **application orientated language** = programming language that provides functions that allow the user to solve certain application problems; **application package** *or* **program** = set of computer programs and manuals that cover all aspects of a particular task (such as payroll, stock control, tax, etc.); **application programming interface (API)** = set of standard program functions and commands that allow any programmer to

interface a program with another application; *if I follow the published API for this system, my program will work properly*; **application service element** = part of a program in the application layer of an OSI environment that interacts with the layers beneath it; **application service provider (ASP)** = specialist company that installs, configures and manages software on its own server and then allows any business to use the software via the Internet (or a private network); the user does not realise that the software is located on a distant server, and the business does not need to buy nor support the software, instead it normally just rents the software; *see also* OUTSOURCING; **application software** *or* **program** = programs which are used by a user to make the computer do what is required, designed to allow a particular task to be performed; *the multi-window editor is used to create and edit applications programs*; **application specific integrated circuits (ASIC)** = specially designed ICs for one particular function *or* to special specifications; **application terminal** = terminal (such as at a sales desk) which is specially configured to carry out certain tasks; **application window** = application program running in a window displayed in a graphical user interface such as Microsoft's Windows; *see also* GUI

```
How do users interact with a
computer    system?    Via    a
terminal    or    PC.    So    what
application layer OSI protocol
do we need first? The Virtual
Terminal. And what do we get?
File    Transfer    Access    and
Maintenance
```
Computing

```
they have announced a fourth
generation        application
development tool which allows
users of PCs and PC networks to
exchange data with mainframe
databases
```
Minicomputer News

apply *verb* **(a)** to ask for something, usually in writing; *to apply for a job; to apply in writing; to apply in person* **(b)** to affect *or* to touch; *this law applies only to sales outside the EU*

APPN = ADVANCED PEER-TO-PEER NETWORKING extension to SNA that routes information around a network and dynamically adjusts the route if part of the network is damaged

appoint *verb* to choose someone for a job; *to appoint James Smith (to the post of) manager; we have appointed a new computer services manager* (NOTE: you appoint a person **to** a job)

appointee *noun* person who is appointed to a job

appointment *noun* **(a)** arrangement to meet; *to make or to fix an appointment for two o'clock; to make an appointment with someone for two o'clock; he was late for his appointment; she had to cancel her appointment;* **appointments book** = desk diary in which appointments are noted **(b)** being appointed to a job; **on his appointment as manager** = when he was made manager; **letter of appointment** = letter in which someone is appointed to a job **(c)** job; **staff appointment** = job on the staff; **computer appointments vacant** = list (in a newspaper) of jobs which are available in the computer industry

approval *noun* **(a)** agreement that something can be used; *a BABT approval is needed for modems;* **certificate of approval** = document showing that an item has been approved officially **(b)** **on approval** = sale where the buyer only pays for goods if they are satisfactory; *to buy a photocopier on approval* (NOTE: no plural)

approve *verb* **(a) to approve of** = to think something is good; *the chairman approves of the new company letter heading; the sales staff do not approve of interference from the accounts division* **(b)** to agree to something; *to approve the terms of a contract; the software has to be approved by the board; an approved modem should carry a label with a green circle and the words 'Approved by ....'*

approximate *adjective* not exact, but almost correct; *we have made an approximate calculation of the time needed for keyboarding*

approximately *adverb* almost correctly; *processing time is approximately 10% lower than during the previous quarter*

approximating *adjective* which is nearly correct; *the figures for running costs are only approximate*

approximation *noun* rough calculation; *approximation of keyboarding time; the final figure is only an approximation;* **approximation error** = error caused by rounding off a real number

Arabic *adjective* **Arabic numbers** *or* **figures** = figures such as 1, 2, 3, 4, etc. (as opposed to the Roman numerals I, II, III. IV, etc.); *the page numbers are written in Arabic figures*

arbitrator *noun* software that is responsible for allocating resources to devices, often used to manage the way Plug and Play adapters use other resources in a computer

arcade game coin-operated console that runs a dedicated games software, with input device (normally a joystick), processor, graphics adapter and sound card built in

archetype *noun* document *or* book that illustrates the styles of a particular time and subject

Archie *noun* program available on the Internet that searches all anonymous FTP sites for a particular file and lists the location of any matching files

COMMENT: Archie can be used via the web or, for users who do not have a full Internet connection, by sending an email message that contains the file names you want to search for to the Archie server; it searches the Internet and sends back an email message with the results

Archimedes *noun* personal computer developed by Acorn Computers; the Archimedes is based around a RISC central processor and is not compatible with either the IBM PC or Apple Macintosh

architecture *noun* layout and interconnection of a computer's internal hardware and the logical relationships between CPU, memory and I/O devices; **onion skin architecture** = design of a computer system in layers, according to function *or* priority; *the onion skin architecture of this computer is made up of a kernel at the centre, an operating system, a low-level language and then the user's programs*

Software giant Microsoft is also interested in using Xerox' Glyph technology as part of its Microsoft At Work architecture that seeks to unite office computers with fax machines and copiers

Computing

archival quality *noun* length of time that a copy can be stored before it becomes illegible

on-line archiving is also used to keep down the interruption needed for archiving to seconds

Computer News

archive 1 *noun* storage of data over a long period; **archive attribute** *or* **bit** *or* **flag** = special attribute attached to a file in some operating systems that indicates if the file has been backed-up or archived since the file was last changed; *see also* ATTRIBUTE; **archive file** = file containing data which is out of date, but which is kept for future reference **2** *verb* to put data in storage; **archived** = (data) stored over a long period of time on backing storage (such as magnetic tape rather than a hard disk); **archived copy** = copy kept in storage

archive site *noun* one computer on the Internet that provides a vast collection of public-domain files and programs (copied from other computers around the Internet) that a user can download; an archive site is a single, convenient site for any user

ARCNET *or* **ARCnet** = ATTACHED RESOURCE COMPUTER NETWORK network hardware and cable standard; developed by Datapoint Corporation, it is a token bus network that transmits data at between 2.5 and 4Mbps

ARCNET uses a single token that moves from one workstation to the next carrying data; ARCNET transmits data at 2.5Mbits per second and uses a star-wired cable topology

area *noun* **(a)** measurement of the space taken up by something (calculated by multiplying the length by the width); *the area of this office is 3,400 square feet; we are looking for a shop with a sales area of about 100 square metres*; **type area** = space on a page which is taken up by printed

characters; **area composition** = organizing and setting up pages before photocomposition; *(in graphics)* **area fill** = instruction to fill an area of the screen *or* an enclosed pattern with a colour *or* pattern; **area graph** = line graph in which the area below the line is filled with a pattern or colour **(b)** section of memory *or* code that is reserved for a certain purpose; **area search** = search for specific data within a certain section of memory *or* files **(c)** part of a country *or* town; *his sales area is the centre of the town; he finds it difficult to cover all his area in a week*; **area code** = part of a telephone number that allows the exchange to identify the part of the country required; *the area code for London is 020 7*; **area exchange** = central point in a part of a country where telephone calls are directed to their correct destination inside the area *or* to another exchange

area manager *noun* manager who deals with a certain part of the country

arg *see* ARGUMENT

argue *verb* to discuss something about which you do not agree; *they argued over or about the design of the cover; we spent hours arguing with the managing director about the layout of the new factory* (NOTE: you argue **with** someone **about** *or* **over** something)

argument *noun* **(a)** discussing something without agreeing; *they got into an argument with the customs officials over the documents; he was sacked after an argument with the managing director* **(b)** **argument** *or* **arg** = variable acted upon by an operator *or* function; for example, if you enter the words 'MULTIPLY A, B', the processor will recognise the operator, MULTIPLY, and use it with the two arguments, A and B; *see also* OPERAND; **argument separator** = punctuation mark or symbol that separates several arguments on one line; *the command 'MULTIPLY A, B' uses a comma as the argument separator*

arithmetic *noun* concerned with mathematical functions such as addition, subtraction, division and multiplication; **arithmetic capability** = ability of a device to perform mathematical functions; **arithmetic functions** = calculations carried out on numbers, such as addition, subtraction, multiplication, division;

arithmetic logic unit (ALU) *or* **arithmetic unit** = hardware section of a CPU that performs all the mathematical and logical functions; **arithmetic operators** = symbol which indicates an arithmetic function (such as + for addition, x for multiplication); **arithmetic register** = memory location which stores operands; **arithmetic shift** = word *or* data moved one bit to the left *or* right inside a register, losing the bit shifted off the end; *compare with* LOGICAL SHIFT

ARP = ADDRESS RESOLUTION PROTOCOL *noun* protocol used within the TCP/IP standard to link one IP address to a low-level physical address; *see also* TCP/IP

ARPANET = ADVANCED RESEARCH PROJECTS AGENCY NETWORK original network of interconnected computers, linked by leased lines, that formed the first prototype for the current Internet; developed by the US Department of Defense (Defense Advanced Research Projects Agency); *see also* INTERNET, TCP/IP

ARQ = AUTOMATIC REPEAT REQUEST *noun* error correction system, used in some modems, which asks for data to be re-transmitted if it contains errors

array *noun* ordered structure containing individually accessible elements referenced by numbers, used to store tables *or* sets of related data; **array bounds** = limits to the number of elements which can be given in an array; **array element** = one individual piece of data within an array; **array processor** = computer that can act upon several arrays of data simultaneously, for very fast mathematical applications

arrow keys *noun* set of four keys on a keyboard that move the cursor or pointer around the screen; the four keys control movement up, down, left and right

arrow pointer *noun* arrow-shaped cursor that is displayed to indicate the position on the screen

arsenide *see* GALLIUM ARSENIDE

art file *noun (film)* digital picture store which has extra graphic and painting facilities

article *noun* **(a)** section of a newspaper *or* magazine; *he wrote an article about the user group for the local newspaper* **(b)**

section of an agreement; *see article 8 of the contract* **(c)** message or comment added to a Usenet newsgroup

artifacts *plural noun* very small errors in a digital version of an analog signal

artificial intelligence (AI) *noun* the design and device of computer programs that imitate human intelligence, providing basic reasoning and other human characteristics

artwork *noun* graphical work *or* images which are to be printed; *the artwork has been sent for filming* (NOTE: no plural)

ASA *(film)* = AMERICAN STANDARDS ASSOCIATION

ascend *verb* to increase; **ascending order** = to arrange data with the smallest value or date first in the list

ascender *noun* part of a character that rises above the main line of printed characters (as the 'tail' of a 'b', 'd', etc.)

ASCII = AMERICAN STANDARD CODE FOR INFORMATION INTERCHANGE code which represents alphanumeric characters in binary code; **ASCII character** = character which is in the ASCII list of codes; **ASCII file** = stored file containing only ASCII coded character data; *use a word processor or other program that generates a standard ASCII file*; **ASCII keyboard** = keyboard which gives all the ASCII characters; **ASCII text** = letter and number characters with an ASCII code between 0 and 127; *(in programming)* **ASCIIZ string** = a sequence of ASCII characters followed by the ASCII code zero that indicates the end of the sequence (NOTE: when speaking say 'as-key')

ASIC = APPLICATION SPECIFIC INTEGRATED CIRCUITS

ASP (i) = ACTIVE SERVER PAGE; (ii) = APPLICATION SERVICE PROVIDER

aspect *noun* way in which something appears; **aspect card** = card containing information on documents in an information retrieval system; **aspect ratio** = ratio of the width to the height of a TV *or* cinema screen *or* of pixel shapes; **aspect system** = method of storing and indexing documents in a retrieval system

COMMENT: the aspect ratio of television is normally four units of width to every three units of height. This is written as 4:3 aspect ratio; a standard 35mm photographic negative frame measures 24 x 36 mm, which means it has an aspect ratio of 3:2

ASR = AUTOMATIC SEND/RECEIVE device *or* terminal that can transmit *or* receive information; *compare with* KSR

COMMENT: an ASR terminal can input information via a keyboard or via a tape cassette or paper tape. It can receive information and store it in internal memory or on tape

assemble *verb* **(a)** to put a product together from various parts; *the parts for the disk drive are made in Japan and assembled in France* **(b)** to translate assembly code into machine code

assemble edit *verb (film)* adding new images, sounds, control tracks or timecodes to previous material on a videotape when in the process of editing

assembler *noun* assembly program *or* program which converts a program written in assembly language into machine code; **absolute assembler** = type of assembly language program designed to produce code which uses only absolute addresses; **cross-assembler** = assembler that produces machine-code code for one computer while running on another

assembly *noun* **(a)** putting an item together from various parts; *there are no assembly instructions to show you how to put the computer together*; **assembly plant** = factory where units are put together from parts made in other factories **(b)** converting a program into machine code; **assembly code** = mnemonics which are used to represent machine code instructions in an assembler program; **assembly language** *or* **assembler language** = programming language used to code information which will then be converted to machine code; **assembly listing** = display of an assembly program ordered according to memory location; **assembly program** = number of assembly code instructions which perform a task; **assembly time** = (i) time taken by an assembler program to translate a program; (ii) period during which an assembler is converting a program from assembly language into machine code

COMMENT: assembly language programs are difficult to write and modify. Each instruction does a simple thing (such as move an item of data from memory into the processor) so many thousands are required to create a program that performs a useful job. In contrast, a language like C, Pascal or Basic is 'high-level'; particular instructions do more complete tasks, such as printing information or writing it to a file. However, assembly language is the most efficient way to program because it allows the programmer to specify exactly what needs to be done and how, resulting in the smallest and fastest programs. Few applications today are written in assembly language, but it is still widely used for system-level software such as device drivers and for parts of large programs that need to run quickly

assertion *noun* program statement of a fact *or* rule

assets *plural noun* separate data elements (such as video, audio, image) that are used in a multimedia application

assign *verb* **(a)** to give a computer *or* someone a job of work; *he was assigned the job of checking the sales figures; two PCs have been assigned to outputting the labels* **(b)** (i) to set a variable equal to a string of characters *or* numbers; (ii) to keep part of a computer system for use while a program is running; **assigned frequency** = frequency reserved for one user *or* application; **assigned numbers** = document that contains a list of unique numbers that are each assigned to an Internet or network manufacturer's device, protocol or other resource; manufacturers apply for a unique number from the IANA organisation

assignment *noun* **(a)** transfer of a property *or* of a right; *assignment of a copyright* **(b)** particular job of work; *he was appointed managing director with the assignment to improve the company's profits; the oil team is on an assignment in the North Sea* **(c)** setting a variable equal to a string of characters; *(in the Pascal programming language);* **assignment compatible** = check to see if a value is allowed according to its type; *(in the C and Fortran programming languages)*

assignment conversion = operation to change the type of a value

assignor *noun* person who assigns something to someone

assist *verb* to help; *can you assist the stock controller in counting the stock? he assists me with my income tax returns* (NOTE: you assist someone **in** doing something or **with** something)

assistance *noun* help; **financial assistance** = help in the form of money (NOTE: no plural)

assistant *noun* person who helps *or* an ordinary employee; **personal assistant** = secretary who also helps the boss in various ways; **shop assistant** = person who serves the customers in a shop; **assistant cameraman** = person who carries out camera operations under the instruction of the director of photography; **assistant** *or* **associate director** = person who carries out the director's instructions, oversees the work and whereabouts of the actors, technicians and rest of crew and works in close contact with the production unit; **assistant manager** = person who helps a manager

associate 1 *adjective* linked; **associate company** = company which is partly owned by another **2** *noun* person who works in the same business as someone; *she is a business associate of mine*

associate producer *noun* *(film)* personal assistant to the producer who is likely to have a particular understanding of the subject of the film or programme being made

associated document *or* **file** *noun* document or file that is linked to its originating application; when you select the file, the operating system automatically starts the originating application

associational editing *noun* way of editing a film *or* video so as to present together scenes which are similar to others

associative processor *noun* processor that uses associative storage; **associative storage** *or* **content-addressable storage** = method of data retrieval that uses part of the data rather than an address to locate the data

AST *(film)* = AUTOMATIC SCAN TRACKING system which permits broadcast quality videotape pictures to be broadcast at different speeds or frame rates

astable multivibrator *noun* electronic current that repeatedly switches an output between two voltage levels

asterisk *noun* graphical symbol used as a wildcard in many operating systems (including DOS) to mean any series of characters in a search; *to view all the files beginning with the letter 'L', use the DOS command DIR L*.**; **asterisk fill** = to fill unused decimal places with the asterisk symbol; *we have used asterisk fill to produce the answer of '***122.33'*

astigmatism *noun* *(film)* a camera lens defect which causes focal problems such as out-of-focus or blurred images

asymmetric *adjective* two sides or parts of something that are not equal or balanced

asymmetric compression *noun* compression system that requires a lot of processing time and power to compress an image (or video sequence) but is very quick to decompress; this type of compression is normally used when creating video sequences for distribution

asymmetric system *noun* *(in video compression)* a system that requires more equipment to compress the data than to decompress it

asymmetric transmission *noun* method of data transmission used in high-speed modems

COMMENT: asymmetric transmission splits a communications channel into two, one that can support fast data transmission at 9,600bps or higher and a slower channel that can support transmission of around 300bps. The slower channel is used to carry control and error-correcting data, the high-speed channel used to transfer the bulk of the data

asymmetric video compression *noun* using a powerful computer to compress video, allowing it to be played back on a less powerful computer

async *(informal)* = ASYNCHRONOUS

asynchronous *adjective* serial data *or* equipment which does not depend on being synchronized with another piece of equipment; **asynchronous access** =

communications using handshaking to synchronize data transmission

asynchronous cache *noun* type of cache memory that provides the slowest performance and uses a type of SDRAM that is cheap but slow; *see also* CACHE, SDRAM; **asynchronous communications interface adapter (ACIA)** = circuit that allows a computer to transmit and receive serial data using asynchronous access; **asynchronous data transfer** = transfer of data between two devices that takes place without any regular or predictable timing signal; **asynchronous mode** = linking a terminal linked to another piece of equipment in a way where the two need not be synchronized; **asynchronous port** = connection to a computer allowing asynchronous data access; *since asynchronous ports are used no special hardware is required*; *(in a program)* **asynchronous procedure call (APC)** = function that runs separately from the main program and will execute when a particular set of conditions exist; **asynchronous sound** = *(film)* sound which is not synchronized to each particular frame but is related to the general action; **asynchronous transfer mode (ATM)** = (i) method of transferring data very rapidly (at up to 155Mbps) across an ISDN link or network; (ii) CCITT and ANSI standard defining cell relay transmission; **asynchronous transmission** = data transmission that uses handshaking signals rather than clock signals to synchronize data pulses

each channel handles two forms of communication: asynchronous communication is mainly for transferring data between computers and peripheral devices, while character communication is for data transfer between computer

Electronics & Power

AT *noun* standard of PC originally developed by IBM that uses a 16-bit 80286 processor; **AT-bus** = expansion bus standard developed by IBM that uses an edge connector to carry 16-bits of data and address information; **AT command set** = standard set of commands to control a modem, developed by Hayes Corporation; **AT-keyboard** = standard keyboard layout for IBM AT personal computers; the keyboard has 102 keys with a row of 12 function keys along the top; *compare with* XT-KEYBOARD; **AT mode** = mode of a modem that is ready to accept commands using the Hayes AT command set

COMMENT: AT originally meant IBM's Advanced Technology personal computer, but is now used to describe any IBM PC compatible that uses a 16-bit processor

Atari ST *noun* (old) range of personal computers developed by Atari Corporation; Atari ST computers use the 68000 range of processor and are not compatible with IBM PCs

ATD = ATTENTION, DIAL; standard command for compatible modems used to dial a telephone number; defined by Hayes

ATM (i) = ADOBE TYPE MANAGER; (ii) = ASYNCHRONOUS TRANSFER MODE; (iii) = AUTOMATED TELLER MACHINE

atmosphere *noun* gas which surrounds the earth

atmospheric *adjective* referring to the atmosphere; **atmospheric absorption** = energy loss of a radio signal due to atmospheric conditions causing dispersion of the signal; **atmospheric conditions** = state of the atmosphere (including clouds, pressures, etc.)

atmospheric interference *noun* electrical disturbances in the earth's atmosphere which causes hissing and crackling sounds on radio or TV channels

atom *noun* smallest particle of an element that has the same properties as the element

atomic *adjective* (a) referring to atoms; **atomic clock** = very accurate clock which uses changes in energy of atoms as a reference (b) an operation that returns data to its original state if it is stopped during processing

attach *verb* (a) to fasten *or* to link; *I am attaching a copy of my previous letter; please find attached a copy of my letter of June 24th; the machine is attached to the floor so it cannot be moved* (b) to connect a node *or* login to a server on a network; *I issued the command to attach to the local server*

attached processor *noun* separate microprocessor in a system that performs certain functions under the control of a central processor

attached resource computer network (ARCNET) *see* ARCNET

attachment *noun* (a) device which is attached to a machine for a special purpose; *there is a special single sheet feed attachment* (b) named file which is transferred together with an electronic mail message; *there is an attachment with my last mail message - it contains the sales report*

attack *noun* start of a sound; **attack envelope** = shape of the initial section of a signal

attend *verb* to be present at; *the chairman has asked all managers to attend the meeting*

attend to *verb* to give careful thought to (something) and deal with it; *the managing director will attend to your complaint himself; we have brought in experts to attend to the problem of installing the new computer*

attended operation *noun* process which has an operator standing by in case of problems

attention *noun* giving careful thought, especially to processing a particular section of a program; *for the attention of the Managing Director; your orders will have our best attention; this routine requires the attention of the processor every minute*; **attention, dial** = *see* ATD; **attention interruption** = interrupt signal that requests the attention of the processor; **attention key** = key on a terminal that sends a interrupt signal to the processor

attention code *noun* the characters AT used within the Hayes AT command set to tell a modem that a command follows

attenuate *verb* to reduce the strength *or* size of peaks (of a signal)

attenuation *noun* reduction or loss of signal strength; the difference between transmitted and received power measured in decibels; *if the cable is too long, the signal attenuation will start to cause data errors* (NOTE: opposite of **gain**)

attribute *noun* (a) *(in printers, display)* a single bit that defines whether the font has a

particular characteristic, for example, whether it is displayed in normal, bold or underlined; **screen attributes** = variables defining the shape, size and colour of text *or* graphics displayed; *pressing Ctrl and B keys at the same time will set the bold attribute for this paragraph of text* (b) *(in a file)* control bits of data stored with each file which control particular functions or aspects of the file; **archive attribute** = special attribute attached to a file in some operating systems that indicates if the file has been archived since it was last changed; **read-only attribute** = special attribute attached to a file which, when switched on, only allows the contents of the file to be viewed, the contents cannot be changed; **system attribute** = special attribute attached to a file used by the operating system; the file is hidden from normal users

audible *adjective* which can be heard; *the printer makes an audible signal when it runs out of paper*

audience *noun* people who watch a TV programme *or* listen to a radio programme; **audience rating** = rating of a programme by calculating the number of people who have watched it

audio *adjective & noun* referring to sound *or* to things which can be heard; the human ear can hear a range of frequencies between around 20Hz-20KHz; **audio active** = system used in a learning laboratory, where the student can hear and respond to questions; **audio board** = *see* SOUND CARD; **audio cassette** = reel of magnetic recording tape in a small protective casing inserted into a cassette recorder (for recording music *or* voice *or* data); **audio cassette recorder (ACR)** = machine to transfer audio signals onto magnetic tape; **audio compressor** = circuit that limits the maximum level of a signal by attenuating any peaks; **audio conferencing** = *see* TELECONFERENCING; **audio file** = digital sound sample stored on disk; often stored in WAV file format on a PC; **audio frequency** = frequency within the audio range that a human can hear; **audio range** = frequency range between 50-20000Hz; **audio response unit** = speech synthesizer that allows a computer to speak responses to requests; **audio slide** = photographic slide that has magnetic tape along an edge allowing sound to be recorded

audio/video interleaved (AVI)

Windows multimedia video format developed by Microsoft; the system interleaves standard waveform audio and digital video frames (stored as bitmaps) to provide reduced speed animation at 15 frames per second at a resolution of 160x120 pixels in eight colours; audio is recorded at 11,025Hz, 8-bit samples

audiotape *noun (film)* tape treated with magnetizable metallic oxide in order to allow sound to be recorded

audiotex *noun* interactive voice response over the telephone in which a computer asks the caller questions and the caller responds by pressing numbers on his telephone

audiovisual (AV) *adjective* which uses sound and images; **audiovisual aids** = equipment used in teaching, which includes both sound and pictures; **audio visual connection** = *see* AVC; *(film)* **audiovisual scripts** = scripts that indicate and separate live and mechanical sources

audit 1 *noun* (a) examination of the books and accounts of a company; **external audit** *or* **independent audit** = audit carried out by an independent auditor; **internal audit** = audit carried out by a department inside the company (b) noting tasks carried out by a computer; **audit trail** = recording details of use of a system by noting transactions carried out (used for checking on illegal use *or* on a malfunction) **2** *verb* to examine the state of a system and check that it is still secure or working properly; *to audit the accounts; the books have not yet been audited*

augend *noun (in an addition)* the number to which another number, the addend, is added to produce the sum

augment *verb* to increase; **augmented addressing** = producing a usable address word from two shorter words

augmenter *noun* value added to another

AUI connector *noun* D-connector used to connect thick Ethernet cable to a network adapter

aural *adjective* by ear

authentic *adjective* which is true

authenticate *verb* to say that something is true *or* genuine

authentication *noun* making sure that something is authentic; **authentication of messages** = using special codes to accurately identify the sender of messages, so that the messages can be recognized as being genuine; *see also* RSA CIPHER SYSTEM, PUBLIC KEY CIPHER SYSTEM

authenticator *noun* trust-worthy company that provides authentication for digital signatures on the Internet; this process is used by secure web sites (shopping or payment sites) to prove to a visitor that the web site has been created by the authorised publisher; *see also* AUTHENTICATION, RSA, SECURE PAYMENTS, SSL

author 1 *noun* person who wrote a book *or* program **2** *verb* to create a multimedia presentation or application by combining text, video, sound and images using a programming language or special multimedia authoring system; **authoring** = creating a multimedia application by combining sound, video and images, usually using a script or authoring language

author level *noun* mode of an authoring software package that is used by the author to design the application; the user uses the finished application at user level

authoring language
noun programming language used to write CAL and training programs, multimedia applications or control a cast of multimedia objects and define how they react to a user's input

authoring system *or* software
noun set of tools normally used to develop multimedia applications; an authoring system provides special commands to control CD-ROM players, play sound files and video clips and display a user-friendly front-end

---

The authoring system is a software product that integrates text and fractally compressed images, using any word-processor line editor, to create an electronic book with hypertext links between different pages

Computing

---

authority *noun* power to do something; *he has no authority to act for the company;*

authority file *or* **list** = list of special terms used by people compiling a database and also by the users of the database

authorization *noun* **(a)** permission *or* power to do something; *do you have authorization for this purchase? he has no authorization to act for the company* **(b)** giving a user permission to access a system; **authorization code** = code used to restrict access to a computer system to authorized users only (NOTE: no plural)

authorize *verb* **(a)** to give permission for something to be done; *to authorize the purchase of a new computer system* **(b)** to give someone the authority to do something; *to authorize someone to act for the company*

authorized *adjective* permitted; **authorized user** = person who is allowed to access a system

auto *adjective & prefix* automatic *or* which works without the user needing to act; **auto advance** = paper in a printer that is automatically moved forward to the next line at the end of a line; **auto-answer** = (modem) that will automatically answer a telephone when called; *(film)* **auto assembly** = process in which a computer carries out a previously entered edit decision list concerning the editing together of videotape programme sections; **auto-baud scanning** = *see* SCANNING; **auto boot** = computer system that will initiate a boot-up procedure when it is switched on; **auto-dial** = to dial a number automatically using stored data; **auto-login** *or* **auto-logon** = phone number, password and user's number transmitted when requested by a remote system to automate logon; *see also* LOGIN, LOGON; **auto-redial** = (modem *or* telephone) that dials a telephone number again if engaged, until it replies; **auto repeat** = facility where a character is automatically repeated if the key is kept pressed down; **auto restart** = computer that can initialize and reload its operating system if there is a fault *or* power failure *or* at switch on; **auto save** = feature of some application programs, such as word-processor or database software, that automatically saves the file being used every few minutes in case of a power failure or system crash; **auto start** = facility to load a program automatically when the computer

is switched on; **auto stop** = feature of a tape player which stops when it has reached the end of a tape; **auto trace** = feature of some graphics programs that will transform a bit-mapped image into a vector image by automatically locating the edges of the shapes in the image and drawing lines around them; **auto verify** = verification procedure carried out automatically, as soon as the data has been saved

```
expansion accessories include
auto-dial and auto-answer
              Electronic & Wireless World
```

autocue *noun (film)* method that enables a person to read out a rolling text which is projected on to an angled mirror in front of the camera lens; *autocue enables a TV presenter to read a script without looking down; an autocue operator controls the speed*

AUTOEXEC.BAT *(in an IBM PC running the MS-DOS operating system)* batch file that contains commands that are executed when the computer is first switched on or reset; *see also* CONFIG.SYS, BATCH FILE

COMMENT: AUTOEXEC.BAT is a plain text file listing DOS commands (or commands to start programs) one per line

autoflow *noun (in DTP or wordprocessor)* text that automatically flows around a graphic image or from one page to the next

autofocus *noun (film)* an infrared sensors in cameras or camcorders that activate the focusing operation

automate *verb* to install machines to do work previously done by people; **automated office** = office where many of the tasks are done by machines; **automated teller machine (ATM)** = automatic telling machine *or* machine linked to a main computer that allows cash to be taken out of a bank account when a special card is inserted and special instructions given

automatic *adjective* which works by itself, without being worked by an operator; **automatic backup** = feature of some application programs, such as word-processor or database software, that automatically saves the file being used every few minutes in case of a power failure or system crash; **automatic call distribution (ACD)** = specialised telephone system that can handle lots of incoming calls and direct them to a particular operator according to programmed instructions in a database; **automatic calling unit (ACU)** = device which allows a computer to call telephone numbers automatically; **automatic camera effects system (ACES)** = computer-operated camera movement system developed by Disney studios which is designed to film repeatable camera moves on separate exposures; **automatic carriage return** = system where the cursor automatically returns to the beginning of a new line when it reaches the end of the previous one; **automatic cassette recorder** = a type of videotape recorder; **automatic data capture** = system where data is automatically recorded in a computer system, as it is input; **automatic data processing (ADP)** = data processing done by a computer; **automatic decimal adjustment** = process of lining up all the decimal points in a column of figures; **automatic font downloading** = process in which special font information is sent to a printer by the application; **automatic gain** electronic circuit which automatically increases the volume when someone is speaking quietly and drops it when someone is speaking loudly; **automatic gain control (AGC)** = electronic device that provides a constant amplitude output signal from a varying input signal, by changing its gain; **automatic hyphenation** = feature of a software program that looks up in an electronic dictionary how to correctly split and hyphenate words; *(film)* **automatic image stabiliser** = device that balances the movement of a camera lens and so smooths out the camera moves by using a floating lens; **automatic letter writing** = writing of form letters; **automatic mailing list** = *see* LISTSERV; **automatic message accounting** = system of logging telephone calls automatically so that details of them can be given to the user; **automatic mode** *or* **frequency switching** = monitor that can adjust its internal circuits to the different frequencies used by different video standards; **automatic number identification** = telephone system which displays the telephone number of the caller;

automatic recalculation = spreadsheet mode in which the answers to new formula are calculated every time any value or cell changes; **automatic repeat** = facility where a character is automatically repeated if the key is kept pressed down; **automatic repeat request (ARQ)** = error correction system used in some modems that asks for data to be re-transmitted if it contains errors; **automatic scan tracking (AST)** = *see* AST; **automatic send/receive** = device *or* terminal that can transmit *or* receive information; **automatic speed matching** = ability of a modem to adjust its data rate to the speed of the remote modem; **automatic telephone exchange** = telephone exchange operated by a computer rather than a human operator; **automatic telling machine** *or US* **automatic teller machine** = machine which allows money to be taken out of a bank account when a special card is inserted and special instructions given; **automatic vending machine** = machine which provides drinks, cigarettes, etc., when money is put in; **automatic volume control** = *see* AVC

automatically *adverb* (machine) working without a person giving instructions; *the statements are sent out automatically; addresses are typed in automatically; a demand note is sent automatically when payment is late*

automation *noun* use of machines to do work with very little supervision by people (NOTE: no plural)

autopositive *noun* photographic process that produces a positive image without a negative stage

auto-reliable mode *noun* modem mode in which the modem will try and establish a reliable connection with another modem using error correction

autosizing *noun* ability of a monitor to maintain the same rectangular image size when changing from one resolution to another

AUX = AUXILIARY abbreviation for a serial communications port under the DOS operating system; *see also* COM1, SERIAL PORT

auxiliary *adjective* which helps; *the computer room has an auxiliary power supply in case there is a mains failure*; **auxiliary audio device** = audio device whose output is mixed with other waveforms, for example the output from a CD-audio; **auxiliary equipment** = backup *or* secondary equipment in case of a breakdown; **auxiliary storage** *or* **store** = any data storage medium (such a magnetic tape *or* floppy disk) that is not the main high speed computer storage (RAM); *disk drives and magnetic tape are auxiliary storage on this machine*

AV *or* **A/V** = AUDIOVISUAL

availability *noun* being easily obtained; **offer subject to availability** = the offer is valid only if the goods are available (NOTE: no plural)

available *adjective* which can be obtained *or* bought; *available in all branches; item no longer available; items available to order only*; **available capital** = capital which is ready to be used; **available light** = light which is present at a place where photographs are being taken, without needing additional artificial light; **available point** = *see* PIXEL; **available time** = time during which a system may be used

avalanche *noun* one action starting a number of other actions; **avalanche photodiode (APD)** = photodiode able to detect very low light levels (since one photon received produces several electrons)

avatar *noun* (i) the graphical image that is used to represent a real person in a cyberspace or three-dimensional system, for example the image of a person in a three-dimensional adventure game; (ii) the name for the superuser account on a UNIX system; *also known as* ROOT

AVC **1** = AUDIO VISUAL CONNECTION multimedia software developed by IBM that works with its Audio Capture and Video Capture boards **2** = AUTOMATIC VOLUME CONTROL electronic circuit that maintains constant sound level despite undesired differences in strength of incoming signal

average 1 *noun* number calculated by adding together several figures and dividing by the number of figures added; *the average for the last three months or the last three months' average; sales average or average of sales*; **weighted average** = average

which is calculated taking several factors into account, giving some more value than others; **on an average** = in general; *on an average, $15 worth of goods are stolen every day* **2** *adjective* middle (figure); *average cost per unit; average price; average sales per representative; the average figures for the last three months; the average increase in prices*; **average access time** = the average time taken between a request being sent and data being returned from a memory device; **average delay** = average time that a user must wait when accessing a communication network; *see also* MEAN **3** *verb* to produce as an average figure; *price increases have averaged 10% per year; days lost through sickness have averaged twenty-two over the last four years*

average out *verb* to come to a figure as an average; *it averages out at 120 dpi*

AVI = AUDIO/VIDEO INTERLEAVED Windows multimedia video format developed by Microsoft

COMMENT: the system interleaves standard waveform audio and digital video frames (stored as bitmaps) to provide reduced speed animation at 15 frames per second at a resolution of 160x120 pixels in eight colours; audio is recorded at 11,025Hz, 8-bit samples

axis *noun* **(a)** line around which something turns **(b)** reference line which is the basis for coordinates on a graph; **horizontal axis** = reference line used for horizontal coordinates on a graph; **vertical axis** = reference line used for vertical coordinates on a graph (NOTE: plural is **axes**)

azerty keyboard *noun* method of arranging the keys on a keyboard where the first line begins AZERTY (used mainly in Europe); *compare with* QWERTY

azimuth *noun* the angle of an aerial *or* tape head to a reference (such as the earth's surface *or* tape plane); **azimuth alignment** = correct horizontal angle of a tape head to the magnetic tape; *to minimize distortion and loss of signal, the playback head should have the same azimuth alignment as the record head*

Bb

b *abbreviation* one bit; **bps (bits per second)** = number of bits transmitted or received per second; *compare with* B

B 1 = BLUE one of the three primary colours used as a base for the colour spectrum of television (the others being red and green) **2** = BYTE one byte; **KB (kilobyte)** = meaning equal to 1024 bytes

B: *(in personal computers)* indicates the second disk drive, normally a floppy disk drive; *copy the files from the hard drive, C:, to the floppy drive, B:;* see also A:

B and C *(film)* = BLACKED AND CODED (videotape) ready for editing; the tape includes the timecode, control track and colour black signals

B and W *or* **B/W** *(film)* = BLACK AND WHITE

B/W *or* **B and W** *(film)* = BLACK AND WHITE

Babbage *noun* Charles Babbage (1792-1871) English inventor of the first automatic calculator and inventor of the forerunner of today's digital computers

babble *noun* crosstalk *or* noise from other sources which interferes with a signal

BABT = BRITISH APPROVAL BOARD FOR TELECOMMUNICATIONS independent organisation that tests and certifies telecommunications equipment; **BABT approval** = official approval for a device to be connected to the public telephone system; *if you design a new modem, you must have BABT approval before you can sell it*

baby *noun* *(film)* spotlight with a 1000 watt bulb

baby legs *or* **tripod** *noun* *(film)* small tripod which is used when shooting low angle shots

back 1 *noun* opposite side to the front; *write your address on the back of the envelope; the conditions of sale are printed on the back of the estimate*; = **back door** = unauthorised route into a computer system that by-passes the main security or password protection scheme; = **back end** = specialised processor (or server) that is designed to carry out one task very efficiently - it is used to provide support to the main server on a network; *see also* FRONT END, SERVER; **back panel** = panel at the rear of a computer which normally holds the connectors to peripherals such as keyboard, printer, video display unit, and mouse; *(in a tree structure)* **back pointer** = a pointer that holds the position of the parent node relative to the current node; used in programming to search backwards through a file **2** *adjective* referring to the past; **back orders** = orders received in the past, but not supplied because the item was out of stock **3** *adverb* as things were before; *the store sent back the cheque because the date was wrong; the company went back on its agreement to supply at £1.50 a unit* **4** *verb* *to back someone* = to help someone with money; *the bank is backing him to the tune of £10,000; he is looking for someone to back his project*

back focus *noun* *(film)* distance between the electronic camera transducer (that converts light into electronic signals) and the rear part of a zoom lens; this gap is adjusted when the lens is set to its widest point to produce a sharp image

back number *noun* old copy of a journal *or* periodical

back pack *noun* *(film)* lightweight television recording equipment which the cameraman carries on his back when filming

back projection *noun* background projection *or* film projected onto the back of a screen, in front of which further action is filmed

COMMENT: often used in animation where the static scene is displayed with back projection, then the foreground characters are displayed and the composite scene photographed

back tab *verb (in SAA CUA front-end)* to move the cursor back to the previous field

back up *verb* (a) to make a copy of important data onto a backing storage media in case the original is corrupted or damaged; *the company accounts were backed up on disk as a protection against fire damage; the program enables users to back up hard disk files* (b) to support *or* to help; *he brought along a file of documents to back up his claim; the finance director said the managing director had refused to back him up in his argument with the tax office*

the system backs up at the rate of 2.5Gb per minute
Microcomputer News

backbone *noun* high-speed, high-capacity connection path that links smaller sub-networks; *we have linked the networks in each office using a high-speed backbone*; **backbone ring** = high-speed ring network that connects a number of smaller ring networks

backdate *verb* to put an earlier date on a cheque *or* a document; *backdate your cheque to April 1st; the pay increase is backdated to January 1st*

backdrop *noun* static background image in front of which are displayed actors or scenes

back-end network *noun* a connection between a mainframe computer and a high-speed mass storage device or file server rather than the network between the user terminals and the mainframe

back-end server *noun* computer connected to a network that carries out tasks requested by client workstations

backer *noun* person who backs someone; *he has an Australian backer; one of the company's backers has withdrawn*

The V3500 has on-board Ethernet and SCSI interfaces, up to 32Mb local DRAM, two programmable timers, a battery-backed real-time clock with 32Kb RAM and four serial ports
Computing

background *noun* (a) past work *or* experience; *his background is in the computer industry; the company is looking for someone with a background of success in the electronics industry; she has a publishing background; what is his background or do you know anything about his background?* (b) part of a picture which is behind the main object of interest; *see also* WALLPAPER; **background colour** = colour of a computer screen display (characters and graphics are displayed in a different foreground colour); **background image** = image displayed as a backdrop behind a program or windows of a GUI; the background image does not move and does not interfere with any programs; *the other machines around this device will produce a lot of background noise*; **background plane** = *see* BACKDROP; **background projection** *or* **back projection** = film projected onto the back of a screen, in front of which further action is filmed (c) system in a computer where low-priority work can be done in the intervals when very important work is not being done; **background communication** = data communication activity (such as downloading a file) carried out as a low-priority task in the background; **background job** = low priority task; **background operation** = low priority process that works as and when resources become available from high-priority foreground tasks; **background printing** = printing from a computer while it is processing another task; *see also* PRINT QUEUE, PRINT SPOOLING; **background processing** = (i) low priority job which is executed when there are no higher priority activities for the computer to attend to; (ii) process which does not use the on-line capabilities of a system (NOTE: opposite is **foreground**); **background program** = computer program with a very low priority; *(in a spreadsheet program)* **background recalculation** = facility that allows a user to enter new numbers or equations while the program recalculates the solutions in the background; **background task** = process executed at any time by the computer system, not normally noticed by the user **(d) background reflectance** = light reflected from a sheet of paper that is being scanned or read by an optical character reader; **(e) background noise** = noise which is present along with the required signal; *see also* AMBIENT NOISE

backing *noun* **(a)** financial help; *he has the backing of an Australian bank; the company will succeed only if it has enough backing; who is providing the backing for the project or where does the backing for the project come from?* **(b) backing store** *or* **backing memory** = permanent storage medium onto which data can be recorded before being processed by the computer *or* after for later retrieval; *by adding another disk drive, I will increase the backing store capabilities*

backlash *(film) noun* fault when slack film, caused by a fault in mechanics, is broken or damaged; common when using take-up or rewind wheels

back-level *noun* earlier release of a product which may not support a current function

backlight 1 *noun* light behind a liquid crystal display (LCD) unit that improves the contrast of characters on the screen and allows it to be read in dim light **2** *verb* to place a light behind the subject which increases the feeling of depth and helps to separate the subject from the background

backlit display *noun* a liquid crystal display (LCD) unit that has a backlight fitted to improve the contrast of the display

backlog *noun* work *or* tasks that have yet to be processed; work (such as orders *or* letters) which has piled up, waiting to be done; *the packing department is trying to deal with a backlog of orders; the programmers can't deal with the backlog of programming work* (NOTE: no plural)

backout *verb* to restore a file to its original condition before any changes were made

backplane *noun* part of the body of a computer which holds the circuit boards,

buses and expansion connectors; *see* MOTHERBOARD

backscatter *noun* reflected *or* scattered radio wave travelling in the opposite direction to the original signal

backslash *noun* ASCII character 92, the sign \ which is used in MS-DOS to represent the root directory of a disk, such as C:\, or to separate subdirectories in a path, such as C:\APPS\DATA

backspace *noun* movement of a cursor *or* printhead back by one character; **backspace character** = code that causes a backspace action in a display device; **backspace key** = key which moves the cursor back one space

backstage *noun* *(film)* area behind a theatrical stage or film set which is not seen by the audience or camera

backtime *noun* *(film)* method of timing the length of rewinding from a specific end point in material to establish a specific start point in order to permit the end point to occur at a precise time

backup *adjective & noun* **(a)** helping; *we offer a free backup service to customers; after a series of sales tours by representatives, the sales director sends backup letters to all the contacts* **(b)** **backup** *or* **backup file** *or* **backup copy** = copy of a file *or* set of data kept for security against original; **backup agent** = software utility that will carry out an automatic backup of files or folders at a regular time and date each week; **backup domain controller** = server in a network that keeps a copy of database of user accounts to validate login requests in case of a fault with the main server; *(in a Token-Ring network)* **backup path** = alternative path for a signal around a network avoiding a malfunctioning device; **backup plan** = set of rules that take effect when normal operation has gone wrong; *the normal UPS has gone wrong, so we will have to use our backup plan to try and restore power;* **backup procedure** = method of making backup copies of files; **backup server** = second computer on a network that contains duplicate files and up-to-date data in case of a problem with the main server; **backup utility** = software that simplifies the process of backing up data; backup utilities often allow a user to backup files automatically at a particular time; **backup version** = copy of a file made during a backup

Backus-Naur-Form (BNF) system of writing and expressing the syntax of a programming language

backward or **backwards** *adjective & adverb* towards the back *or* in the opposite direction; **backward chaining** = method used in artificial intelligence systems to calculate a goal from a set of results; **backward channel** = channel from the receiver to transmitter allowing control and handshaking signals to be transmitted; *(in a broadband network)* **backward LAN channel** = channel from receiver to sender used to carry control signals; **backward recovery** = data retrieval from a system that has crashed; **backwards compatible** = hardware device (normally a processor) that can still run all the same functions as earlier versions; *Windows Me is backwards compatible with Windows 3.x since it can run the same programs; Microsoft Word 2000 is backwards compatible with Word 6*; **backwards learning** = intelligent routing system that switches data to the correct path according to its destination; *(in a word-processor or database)* **backwards search** = search for data that begins at the position of the cursor or end of the file and searches to the beginning of the file; **backwards supervision** = data transmission controlled by the receiver

COMMENT: backward recovery is carried out by passing the semi-processed data from the crashed computer through a routine that reverses the effects of the main program to return the original data

BACS = BANKERS AUTOMATED CLEARANCE SYSTEM

bacterium *see* VIRUS

bad break *noun* wrong hyphenation of a word at the end of a line of text

COMMENT: this is a problem sometimes caused by the automatic hyphenation feature of word-processing software

bad copy *noun* illegible *or* badly edited manuscript which the typesetter will not accept

bad sector *noun* sector which has been wrongly formatted *or* which contains an error *or* fault and is unable to be correctly written to or read from; *you will probably receive error messages when you copy files that are stored on bad sectors on a disk*

badge reader *noun* machine that reads data from an identification badge; *a badge reader makes sure that only authorized personnel can gain access to a computer room*

baffle *noun* **(a)** sound absorber and deflector which is a moveable unit used in recording studios and film and television sets **(b)** a loudspeaker which is built into the unit

BAFTA *(film)* = BRITISH ACADEMY OF FILM AND TELEVISION ARTS

BAK file extension *noun* standard three-letter file extension used in MS-DOS systems to signify a backup or copy of another file

balance 1 *noun* **(a)** placing of text and graphics on a page in an attractive way; *(in a word-processor or DTP system)* **column balance** = method of making sure that the ends of two columns of text are level **(b)** positioning of musical instruments so that they may be recorded to their best advantage **(c)** amplitude control of left and right audio signals in a stereo system; **balance stripe** = thin magnetic stripe on a cine film on the opposite side to the sound track, so that the whole film will lie flat when played back **2** *verb* **(a)** to calculate the amount needed to make the two sides of an account equal; *I have finished balancing the accounts for March*; **the February accounts do not balance** = the two sides are not equal **(b)** *(film)* the adjustment of the blue, green and red TV camera signals in order to create a neutral chart of tones ranging from black to white. This is done to enable the production of a true colour picture on television **(c)** *(film)* lighting equal to that in other takes shot on the same set **(d)** to plan something so that two parts are equal; **balanced circuit** = electronic circuit that presents a correct load to a communications line (the correct load is usually equal to the impedance of a line element); *you must use a balanced circuit at the end of the line to prevent signal reflections*; **balanced line** =

communications line that is terminated at each end with a balanced circuit, preventing signal reflections; **balanced routing =** method of using all possible routes through a network equally

ball printer *noun* impact printer that uses a small metal ball on the surface of which are formed the characters; *see also* GOLF-BALL

balun *noun* transformer that matches two circuits which have different impedances; *we have used a balun to connect the coaxial cable to the twisted-pair circuit*

band *noun* range of frequencies between two limits; *telephone voice band is 300-3400 Hz*

banding *noun* **elastic banding =** method of defining the limits of an image on the computer screen by stretching a boundary round it

bandlimited *adjective* (signal) whose frequency range has been limited to one band

bandpass filter *noun* circuit that allows a certain band of frequencies to pass while stopping any that are higher *or* lower; *compare with* HIGH PASS FILTER

bandwidth *noun* **(a)** range of frequencies **(b)** measure of the amount of data that can be transmitted along a cable *or* channel *or* other medium; *telephone bandwidth is 3100 Hz; this fibre-optic cable has a greater bandwidth than the old copper cable and so it can carry data at higher speeds* **(c)** measure of the range of frequencies that a monitor or CRT will accept and display; high resolution monitors display more pixels per area so need high speed data input and so a higher bandwidth

bank *noun* collection of similar devices; **bank switching =** selection of a particular memory bank; **memory bank =** collection of electronic memory devices connected together to form one large area of memory; *an add-on card has a 128MB memory bank made up of 16 chips*; *see also* DATABANK

bankers automated clearance system (BACS) *noun* system to transfer money between banks using computers linked via a secure network

banner *noun (in printing)* heading *or* title extending to the width of a page; **banner**

headlines = large headlines on a newspaper running across the width of the page; **banner page =** a page that is printed out first with the time, date, name of the document and the name of the person who has printed it

banner advertisement *noun* image that carries an advertising slogan, logo or message and is displayed on a web page; *see also* CTR, IMPRESSION

COMMENT: a short, wide strip is the unofficial standard format for advertisements that appear on almost every commercial website on the net; some banner advertisements are images, others include animation to attract the viewer's attention. If you click on a banner ad, you will usually jump to the advertiser's own site; websites normally charge advertisers according either to the number of times the banner ad is displayed (called the number of impressions) or the number of times that a user clicks on the ad (called the click-through rate)

bar 1 *noun* **(a)** thick line *or* block of colour **(b)** *see* TOOLBAR **2** *verb* to stop someone from doing something; *journalists were barred from entering the house*; **to bar entry to a file =** to stop someone accessing a file

bar chart *or* **bar graph** *noun* graph on which values are represented as vertical *or* horizontal bars

bar code *or* *US* **bar graphics** *noun* data represented as a series of printed stripes of varying widths; **bar-code reader** *or* **optical scanner =** optical device that reads data from a bar code

COMMENT: bar codes are found on most goods and their packages; the width and position of the stripes is sensed by a light pen *or* optical wand and provides information about the goods, such as price, stock quantities, etc.

bare board *noun* circuit board with no components on it; usually refers to a memory expansion board that does not yet have any memory chips mounted on it

barndoor *noun (film)* hinged metal shutters at the front of a studio spotlight used to shield or direct the light

barney *noun (film)* a piece of heavy cloth which is put over a film camera when recording sound in order to help prevent the noise of the camera being heard

barrel *noun* image distortion in which the image appears swollen in the middle and narrower at the top and the bottom

barrel distortion *noun* optical lens distortion causing sides of objects to appear curved

barrel printer *noun* type of printer where characters are located around a rotating barrel

barrier box *noun* device that electrically isolates equipment from a telephone line to prevent damage

baryta paper *noun* coated matt paper used to produce final high quality proofs before printing

base 1 *noun* **(a)** lowest *or* first position; **base year** = first year of an index, against which later years' changes are measured; **bank base rate** = basic rate of interest which a bank charges on money lent to its customers **(b)** place where a company has its main office or factory *or* place where a businessman has his office; *the company has its base in London and branches in all European countries; he has an office in Madrid which he uses as a base while he is travelling in Southern Europe* **(c)** initial *or* original position; **base address** = initial address in a program used as a reference for others; **base addressing** = relative addressing; **base address register** = register (in a CPU) used to store the base address; **base font** = default font and point size used by a word-processing program or DTP package when no particular style or font has been selected; **base line** = (i) lines (that are only displayed during the design stage or author level of an application) which define the size and layout of a page in an application; (ii) horizontal line along which characters are printed or displayed; the descenders of a character drop below the line horizontal line along which characters are printed or displayed; the descenders of a character drop below the baseline; *(in an IBM-compatible PC)* **base memory** *or* **conventional memory** *or* **base RAM** = first 640Kb of random access memory fitted to the PC; *compare with* HIGH MEMORY, EXPANDED MEMORY SYSTEM; **base**

station = fixed radio transmitter/receiver that relays radio signals to and from data terminals or radios **(d)** referring to a number system; **base 2** = binary number system (using the two digits 0 and 1); **base 8** = octal number system (using the eight digits 0 - 7); **base 10** = decimal number system (using the ten digits 0 - 9); **base 16** = hexadecimal number system (using the ten digits 0 - 9 and six letters A - F) **2** *verb* **(a)** to start to calculate from a position; *we based our calculations on the basic keyboarding rate*; **based on** = calculating from; *based on last year's figures; the price is based on estimates of keyboarding costs* **(b)** to set up a company *or* a person in a place; *the European manager is based in our London office; a London-based sales executive*

base film *noun (film)* transparent material which bears the light sensitive emulsion of a film or the magnetic oxide of magnetic recording tape

base hardware *noun* minimum hardware requirements that a particular software package needs in order to run; *graphics programs often demand more sophisticated base hardware with more memory or a faster processor*

base level synthesizer *noun (on a sound card)* synthesizer that supports three melodic instruments and can play six notes simultaneously; *compare with* EXTENDED LEVEL SYNTHESIZER

baseband *or* **base band** *noun* **(a)** frequency range of a signal before it is processed *or* transmitted **(b)** digital signals transmitted without modulation **(c)** information modulated with a single carrier frequency; **baseband local area network** = transmission method in which the whole bandwidth of the cable is used and the data signal is not modulated; Ethernet is a baseband network; *base band local area networks can support a maximum cable length of around 300m*; **base band modem** = communications circuit that transmits an unmodulated signal over a short range; **baseband signalling** = transmitting data as varying voltage levels across a link

BASIC = BEGINNER'S ALL-PURPOSE SYMBOLIC INSTRUCTION CODE high-level programming language for developing programs in a conversational way, providing an easy introduction to computer programming; *see also* VISUAL BASIC

basic *adjective* normal *or* from which everything starts; *basic rates of pay; she has a basic qualification in maths; the basic discount is 20%*; **basic controller** = part of a communications controller that carries out arithmetic and logic functions; **basic direct access method (BDAM)** = method of directly updating or retrieving a particular block of data stored on a direct access device; = **basic encoding rules (BER)** = standard method of encoding data that is stored in the ASN language; often used in libraries and other Internet data sites; **basic exchange format** = standard method of storing data on a disk so that it may be accessed by another type of computer; **basic mode link control** = standardized control of transmission links using special codes; **basic rate access;** *see* BRA; **basic sequential access method (BSAM)** = method of storing or retrieving blocks of data in a continuous sequence; **basic weight** = weight of printing paper per 500 sheets

basic input/output system = BIOS

basically *adverb* seen from the point from which everything starts; *the acoustic coupler is basically the same as a modem*

basis *noun* point *or* number from which calculations are made; *we calculated keyboarding costs on the basis of 5,500 keystrokes per hour*

bass *noun & adjective* low sound *or* sound with a low frequency; **bass control** = knob used to vary the strength of the bass frequencies in an audio signal; **bass driver** *or* **speaker** = large loudspeaker able to produce low frequency sounds; **bass response** = characteristics of a circuit *or* device to bass signals; **bass signal** = audio signals in the frequency range below 100Hz

BAT file extension *noun* standard three-letter file extension used in MS-DOS systems to signify a batch file; a text file containing system commands

batch 1 *noun* **(a)** group of items which are made at one time; *this batch of shoes has the serial number 25-02* **(b)** (i) group of documents which are processed at the same time; (ii) group of tasks *or* amount of data to be processed as a single unit; *today's batch of orders; the director signed a batch of*

cheques; we deal with the orders in batches of fifty; **batch file** *or* **BAT** = stored file containing a sequence of system commands, used instead of typing them in; *this batch file is used to save time and effort when carrying out a routine task; to see if there are any batch files on the hard disk, use the 'DIR *.BAT' command from the MS-DOS prompt or the File Manager/Explorer in Windows and look for the BAT file extension*; **(processing data in) batch mode** = (processing the data) in related groups in one machine run; **batch region** = memory area where the operating system executes batch programs **2** *verb* **(a)** to put data *or* tasks together in groups; **batched communication** = high-speed transmission of large blocks of data without requiring an acknowledgement from the receiver for each data item **(b)** to put items together in groups; *to batch orders or cheques*

batch number *noun* number attached to a batch; *when making a complaint always quote the batch number on the packet*

batch processing *noun* system of data processing where information is collected into batches before being processed by the computer in one machine run

COMMENT: batch processing is the opposite to interactive processing (where the user gives instructions and receives an immediate response)

battery *noun* chemical device that produces electrical current; **battery backup** = use of a battery to provide power to volatile storage devices (RAM chips) to retain data after a computer has been switched off; **battery-backed** = (volatile storage device) that has a battery backup; **battery meter** = small utility (in a laptop computer) that tells you how much life or working time is left in the batteries; **battery voltage level** = size of voltage being provided by a battery

baud *or* **baud rate** *noun* measure of number of signals transmitted per second; *the baud rate of the binary signal was 56,000 bits per second; a modem with auto-baud scanner can automatically sense at which baud rate it should operate*; **baud rate generator** = device that produces various timing signals to synchronize data at different baud rates;

split baud rate = modem which receives data at one baud rate but transmits data at another; *the viewdata modem uses a 1200/75 split baud rate*; *see also* (AUTO-BAUD) SCANNING

> COMMENT: baud rate is often considered the same as bits per second, but in fact it depends on the protocol used, the compression and the error checking (300 baud is roughly equivalent to 30 characters per second at standard error checking)

Baudot code *noun* five-bit character transmission code, used mainly in teletypewriters

bay *or* **drive bay** *noun* space within a computer's case into which you can fit and secure a floppy disk drive or CD-ROM drive or hard disk drive; *to fit the drive into the bay you must open the case and connect the drive to the correct controller card*

bazooka *noun (film)* adjustable pole used as a camera support in restricted locations where a tripod is too big

BBC   *(film)*   =   BRITISH BROADCASTING CORPORATION

BCC 1 = BLOCK CHARACTER CHECK error detection method for blocks of transmitted data **2** *(film)* = BROADCASTING COMPLAINTS COMMISSION

BCD = BINARY CODED DECIMAL representation of single decimal digits as a pattern of four binary digits; *the BCD representation of decimal 8 is 1000*

BCNF = BOYCE-CODD NORMAL FORM; *see* NORMAL FORM

BCPL *noun* high level programming language

BCS   =   BRITISH   COMPUTER SOCIETY

BCU *(film)* = BIG CLOSE UP a camera shot that is so close it only reveals part of the subject in the picture frame

beacon *verb* signal transmitted repeatedly by a device that is malfunctioning on a network

beacon frame *noun* special frame within the FDDI protocol that is sent after a network break has occurred; *see also* FDDI

bead *noun* small section of a program that is used for a single task

beam *noun* narrow radiated stream of waves *or* particles; *a beam of laser light is used in this printer to produce high-resolution graphics*; **beam deflection** = change in beam direction; *a magnetic field is used for beam deflection in a CRT*; **beam diversity** = using a single frequency communications band for two different sets of data; **beam splitter** = device to redirect a part of a beam; **beam width** = maximum size of a transmission beam which should not be exceeded if a constant received power is to maintained

beard *noun* blank section between bottom of a character and the type face limit

bearding *noun (film)* fault that occurs when the electronic limits of a television system have been exceeded and is visible with marks between the horizontally adjacent light and dark areas of a television picture

Beaulieu *noun (film)* lightweight motion picture camera that is popular with people making documentaries or news programmes

BEC = BUS EXTENSION CARD

BEEB *slang term for* BRITISH BROADCASTING CORPORATION (BBC)

beep 1 *noun* audible warning noise; *the printer will make a beep when it runs out of paper* **2** *verb* to make a beep; *the computer beeped when the wrong key was hit*; *see also* BLEEP

begin *verb* to start; *the company began to lose its market share; he began to keyboard the changes to the customer address file* (NOTE: you begin something *or* begin **to do** something *or* begin **with** something. Note also: **beginning - began - has begun**)

Beginner's All-Purpose Symbolic Instruction Code

(BASIC) *noun* high-level programming language for developing programs in a conversational way, providing an easy introduction to computer programming; *see also* VISUAL BASIC

beginning *noun* first part; **beginning of file (bof)** = character *or* symbol that shows the start of a valid section of data; **beginning of information mark (bim)** = symbol indicating the start of a data stream stored on a disk drive *or* tape; **beginning of tape (bot) marker** = section of material that marks the start of the recording area of a reel of magnetic tape

behind-the-lens filter *noun* *(film)* gelatin filter which is able to cut out chosen colours when placed behind the camera lens and in front of the film

BEL *noun* bell character (equivalent to ASCII code 7)

bel *noun* unit used when expressing ratio of signal power in logarithmic form (P bels = Log (A/B) where A and B are signal power)

bell character *noun* control code which causes a machine to produce an audible signal (equivalent to ASCII code 7, EBCDIC 2F)

Bell-compatible modem *noun* modem that operates according to standards set down by AT&T

bells and whistles *plural noun* every possible feature that has been included in an application or peripheral; *this word-processor has all the bells and whistles you would expect - including page preview*

below-the-line *adjective* **below-the-line expenditure** = exceptional payments which are separated from a company's normal accounts; **below-the-line costs** = costs of crew and technicians used in making a TV programme (as opposed to scriptwriters, actors, etc., who are above-the-line costs)

benchmark *noun* **(a)** point in an index which is important, and can be used to compare with other figures **(b)** program used to test the performance of software *or* hardware *or* a system; *the magazine gave the new program's benchmark test results*

benchmarking *noun* testing a system *or* program with a benchmark

COMMENT: the same task *or* program is given to different systems and their results and speeds of working are compared

bending *noun* *(film)* distortion in videotape playback which is a result of defects in the tape or in the video machine itself

BER = BASIC ENCODING RULES standard method of encoding data that is

stored in the ASN language; often used in libraries and other Internet data sites

Berkeley UNIX (BSD) *noun* version of UNIX operating system developed by the University of California, Berkeley

Bernoulli drive *or* **box** *noun* high capacity storage system using exchangeable 20MB cartridges

I use a pair of Bernoulli boxes for back up and simply do a disk-to-disk copy

PC Business World

bespoke software *noun* software that has been written especially for a customer's particular requirements

best boy *noun* second in command on the electrical team on a film set

best fit *noun* **(a)** (something) which is the nearest match to a requirement **(b)** function that selects the smallest free space in main memory for a requested virtual page

Beta *noun* first home VCR format developed by Sony; the system used 1/2-inch tape cassettes; the Beta standard is no longer produced and the prevalent home video standard is currently VHS

beta site *noun* company or person that tests new software (before it is released) in a real environment to make sure it works correctly

beta software *noun* software that has not finished all its testing before release and so may still contain bugs

beta test *noun* second stage of tests performed on new software just before it is due to be released; *see also* ALPHA TEST; *the application has passed the alpha tests and is just entering the beta test phase*

beta version *noun* version of a software application that is almost ready to be released; *we'll try out the beta test software on as many different PCs as possible to try and find all the bugs*

The client was so eager to get his hands on the product that the managing director bypassed internal testing and decided to let it go straight out to beta test

Computing

Betacam *noun* standard developed for video player and cameras

Betacam SP *noun (film)* = BETACAM SUPERIOR PERFORMANCE a more accurate and sharper version of the Betacam system

Betamax *noun* Sony's VHS home video cassette recorder

bezel *noun* front cover of a computer's casing or disk drive unit

Bézier curve *noun* geometric curve; the overall shape is defined by two midpoints, called control handles

> COMMENT: Bézier curves are a feature of many high-end design software packages; they allow a designer to create smooth curves by defining a number of points. The PostScript page description language uses Bézier curves to define the shapes of characters during printing

BFI = BRITISH FILM INSTITUTE

BGP = BORDER GATEWAY PROTOCOL a protocol allows routers to share routing information to allow each router to calculate the most efficient path for information; this protocol is most often used between routers installed at Internet Service Providers (ISPs)

bias *noun* **(a)** electrical reference level **(b)** high frequency signal added to recorded information to minimize noise and distortion (the high frequency is removed on playback) **(c)** deviation of statistical results from a reference level

biased *adjective* which has a bias; **biased data** = data *or* records which point to a certain conclusion

bibliographic *or* **bibliographical** *adjective* referring to books *or* to bibliographies; **bibliographical information** = information about a book (name of author, number of pages, ISBN, etc.) which is used for library cataloguing

bibliography *noun* **(a)** list of documents and books which are relevant to a certain subject; *he printed a bibliography at the end of each chapter* **(b)** catalogue of books

bid *noun* attempt by a computer to gain control of a network in order to transmit data

bi-directional *adjective* (operation *or* process) that can occur in forward *or* reverse directions; *bi-directional file transfer*; **bi-directional bus** = data *or* control lines

that can carry signals travelling in two directions; **bi-directional printer** = printer which is able to print characters from left to right and from right to left as the head is moving forward *or* backward across the paper; *compare with* OMNIDIRECTIONAL

bifurcation *noun* system where there are only two possible results

Big Blue *noun (informal)* = IBM

big close up *see* BCU

billion number equal to one thousand million *or* one million million (NOTE: in the US it means one thousand million, but in GB it usually means one million million. With figures it is usually written **bn: $5bn** (say 'five billion dollars'))

BIM = BEGINNING OF INFORMATION MARK *noun* symbol indicating the start of a data stream stored on a disk drive *or* tape

bin *noun* tray used to hold a supply of paper ready to be fed into a printer

binary *adjective & noun* base 2 *or* number notation system which uses only the digits 0 and 1; **binary arithmetic** = rules and functions governing arithmetic operations in base 2; *computers do all their calculations using binary arithmetic, since the two values are easy to represent electrically*; **binary chop** = *see* BINARY SEARCH; **binary coded decimal (BCD)** = representation of single decimal digits as a pattern of four binary digits; **binary digit** *or* **bit** = smallest unit in (base 2) binary notation, either a 0 or a 1; **binary field** = field (in a database record) that contains binary numbers; often refers to a field that is capable of holding any information, including data, text, graphics images, voice and video; **binary file** = file that contains data rather than alphanumeric characters; a binary file can include any character code and cannot always be displayed or edited; *the program instructions are stored in the binary file; your letter is a text file, not a binary file*; **binary fraction** = representation of a decimal fraction binary form; *the binary fraction 0.011 is equal to one quarter plus one eighth (i.e. three eighths)* **binary large object** *or* **blob** *or* **BLOb** = field in a database record that can contain a large quantity of binary data - normally a bitmap image; **binary notation** = base 2 numerical system using only the digits 0 and 1; **binary number** = quantity represented in base 2; **binary scale** = power of two associated with each bit position in a word; *in a four bit word, the binary scale is 1,2,4,8*; **binary search** *or* **chop** = fast search method for use on ordered lists of data; the search key is compared with the data in the middle of the list and one half is discarded, this is repeated until only one data item remains; **binary split** = method of iteration in which the existing number is compared to a new value calculated as the mid-point between the high and low limits; **binary tree** = tree structure for data, where each item of data can have only two branches; *see also* DIGITAL

---

with this type of compression
you can only retrieve words by
scanning   the   list
sequentially, rather than by
faster means such as a binary
search

Practical Computing

---

binaural *adjective* method of recording two audio channels

COMMENT: separate sound tracks for the left and right ears are recorded to provide enhanced depth of sound

BIND = BERKELEY INTERNET NAME DOMAIN specialist software application that provides the functions of a Domain Name Server (DNS) for server computers running BSD UNIX

bind *verb* to put a stiff cover on the printed pages of a book and to glue or attach sheets of paper along their spine to form a book; *the book is bound in laminated paper; a paperbound book; the sheets have been sent to the bindery for binding* (NOTE: binding - bound)

binder *noun* **(a)** company which specializes in binding books **(b)** program that converts object code into a form that can be executed **(c)** *(film)* substance used to join the metallic oxide particles together and to the base film

Bindery *noun* special database used in a Novell NetWare network operating system to store user account, access and security details; *compare with* REGISTRY

bindery *noun* factory where books are bound

binding *noun* **(a)** action of putting a cover on a book **(b)** cover of a book; *the book has a soft plastic binding*; **binding offset** = extra wide margin on the inside of a printed page (left margin on a right hand page, right margin on a left hand page) to prevent text being hidden during binding

BinHex a method of encoding binary data into ASCII characters; software programs and data files are stored as binary data (using all eight bits of information within one byte of storage space), wheras ASCII characters can be stored in just the first seven of the eight bits of storage space within one byte; *see also* UUENCODE

COMMENT: older email and communication systems only supported the transfer of 7-bit text (ASCII characters); to transfer a data file, the 8-bit data had to be encoded before it could be transferred; now, almost all email software and links between computers support full eight bit transfer so data does not have to be encoded

BIOS = BASIC INPUT/OUTPUT SYSTEM software system-control routines that interface between high-level program instructions and the system peripherals to control the input and output to various standard devices. This often includes controlling the screen, keyboard and disk drives

biosensor *noun* device that allows electrical impulses from an organism to be recorded; *the nerve activity can be measured by attaching a biosensor to your arm*

bipack *noun* *(film)* **(a)** two sections of film that are run in contact through a motion picture camera in order to be printed as one **(b)** the camera which is used for this method of filming

biphase *noun* *(film)* electronic signal that gives information about film speed and direction

bipolar *adjective* with two levels; **bipolar coding** = transmission method which uses alternate positive and negative voltage levels to represent a binary one, with binary zero represented by zero level; **bipolar transistor** = transistor constructed of three layers of alternating types of doped semiconductor (p-n-p or n-p-n)

COMMENT: each layer has a terminal labelled emitter, base and collector, usually the base signal controls the current flow between the emitter and collector

birdseye *noun (film)* reflector type of spotlight

bis used to describe an extension of the V-standards that cover the features of modems providing error detection and correction; *see also* CCITT, V SERIES

B-ISDN = BROADBAND INTEGRATED SERVICES DIGITAL NETWORK; *see* ISDN

bistable *adjective* (device *or* circuit) that has two possible states, on and off

bit *noun* (a) binary digit *or* smallest unit in binary number notation, which can have the value 0 or 1 (b) smallest unit of data that a system can handle; *(in computer graphics)* **bit blit** *or* **bitblt** = to move a block of bits from one memory location to another; if the computer has a memory-mapped display a bitblt effectively moves an image on screen; **bit block** = group of bits treated as one unit; **bit block transfer** = to move a block of bits from one memory location to another; **bit bucket** = area of memory into which data can be discarded; **bit density** = number of bits that can be recorded per unit of storage medium; **bit depth** = number of bits used to represent the number of colours that can be displayed on a screen or printer at one time = bit depth Total number of colours = 4-bit 16 = 8-bit 256 = 16-bit 65,536 = 24-bit 16,777,216; *(normally referring to fibre optics)* **bit error rate (BER)** = ratio of the number of bits received compared to the number of errors in a transmission; **bit flipping** = to invert the state of bits from 0 to 1 and 1 to 0; **bitFTP** = type of server that allows a user to retrieve a file using only an email link; the user sends an email to the bitFTP server, the email contains a series of FTP commands that ask it to fetch the file from a remote server, when it has done this, the bitFTP server sends an email back to the user as an email attachment or encoded mail message; **bit image** = collection of bits that represent the pixels that make up an image on screen or on a printer; **bit interleaving** = form of time domain multiplexing used in some synchronous transmission protocols

such as HDLC and X.25; **bit parallel** = transmission of a collection of bits simultaneously over a number of lines; the parallel printer port uses bit parallel transmission to transfer eight bits at a time to a printer; **bits per inch (bpi)** = number of bits that can be recorded per inch of recording medium; **bits per second (bps)** = measure of the number of binary digits transmitted every second; this is a common way of describing the speed of a modem or serial link between two computers or a computer and a printer; *the transmission rate is 60,000 bits per second (bps) through a parallel connection*; **bit position** = place of a bit of data in a computer word; **bit rate** = measure of the number of bits transmitted per second; **bit slice design** = construction of a large word size CPU by joining a number of smaller word size blocks; *the bit slice design uses four four-bit word processors to construct a sixteen-bit processor*; **most significant bit (MSB)** = bit in a computer word that represents the greatest power of two (in an eight-bit word the MSB is in bit position eight and represents a decimal number of two to the power eight, or 128); **bit stream** = binary data sequence that does not consist of character codes *or* groups; **bit stuffing** = addition of extra bits to a group of data to make up a certain length required for transmission; *see also* BYTE

bit map *or* **bitmp** *noun* (a) image whose individual pixels can be controlled by changing the value of its stored bit (one is on, zero is off; in colour displays, more than one bit is used to provide control for the three colours - Red, Green, Blue); *in Windows, every icon picture is stored as a small bitmap image* (b) binary representation in which each bit or set of bits corresponds to some object (image, font, etc.) or condition (c) file format for storing images in which data in the file represents the value of each pixel; *compare with* VECTOR; **bit-mapped font** = font whose characters are made up of patterns of pixels; *bit-mapped fonts are quick and easy for a computer or printer to use*; *compare with* VECTOR FONT; **bit-mapped graphics** = image whose individual pixels can be controlled by changing the value of its stored bit (one is on, zero is off; in colour displays, more than one bit is used to provide control for the three colours: red, green, blue); **bits per pixel (BPP)** = number of bits assigned to store the colour of each pixel; one bit provides black or white, four bits gives 16 colour combinations, eight bits gives 256 colour combinations; *(in computer graphics)* **bit plane** = one layer of a multiple-layer image; each layer defines one colour of each pixel; **bit significant** = using the bits within a byte to describe something; *testing bit six of a byte containing an ASCII character is bit significant and determines if the ASCII character is upper or lower case*; **bit wise** = action or operation carried out on each bit in a byte, one bit at a time

> it became possible to store more than one bit per pixel
> *Practical Computing*

> the expansion cards fit into the PC's expansion slot and convert bit-mapped screen images to video signals
> *Publish*

> it is easy to turn any page into a bit-mapped graphic
> *PC Business World*

BitNet *noun* wide area network used to connect (mostly) academic sites and computers and allows transfer of electronic mail and listserver application; BitNet is similar to the Internet and is connected to allow the transfer of electronic mail to and from academic users to other users on the Internet

biz type of newsgroup that contains business discussions and opportunities; *compare with* ALT

> COMMENT: Only the biz series of newsgroups are supposed to discuss commercial aspects, the rest of the newsgroups are for technical or academic discussion. For example, 'biz.opportunities' contains messages from users that are offering ways of making money.

black 1 *adjective* **(a)** with no colour; **black and white** = (i) use of shades of grey to represent colours on a monitor or display; (ii) an image in which each pixel is either black or white with no shades of grey; **black box** = device that performs a function without the user knowing how; **black crush** = conversion of a television picture to one with no tones, only black or white; **black leader (black opaque leader)** = strip of black film leader without pinholes which is used to block the light of the printer when adapting the original film for A and B roll printing; **black level** = level of a TV signal that produces no luminescence on screen; **black level clamp** = circuit which makes the black level of a television picture remain at a fixed brightness; **black matrix** = CRT monitor tube in which the colour phosphor dots are surrounded by black for increased contrast **(b) in the black** = not owing any money; *the company has moved into the black; my bank account is still in the black* **2** *verb* to forbid buying *or* selling certain goods *or* dealing with certain suppliers; *three firms were blacked by the government*

black list *noun* list of goods *or* people *or* companies which have been blacked

black writer *noun* printer where toner sticks to the points hit by the laser beam when the image drum is scanned; *compare with* WHITE WRITER

> COMMENT: a black writer produces sharp edges and graphics, but large areas of black are muddy

blacklist *verb* to put goods *or* people *or* a company on a black list; *his firm was blacklisted by the government*

blackout *or* **black-out** *noun* loss of electrical power

blank 1 *adjective* empty *or* with nothing written on it; **blank cell** = empty cell in a spreadsheet; **blank character** = character code that prints a space; **blank tape** *or* **blank disk** = magnetic tape *or* disk that does not have data stored on it; **blank string** = (i) empty string; (ii) string containing spaces **2** *noun* space on a form which has to be completed; *fill in the blanks and return the form to your local office*

blanket *noun* thick woollen cover for a bed; **blanket agreement** = agreement which covers many items; **blanket cylinder** = rubber coated cylinder in a offset lithographic printing machine that transfers ink from the image plate to the paper

blanking *noun* preventing a television signal from reaching the scanning beam on its return trace; **blanking interval** = time taken for the scanning beam in a TV to return from the end of a picture at the bottom right of the screen to top left; **blanking pulse** = electrical signal used to start the blanking of a TV signal

blast-through alphanumerics *noun* characters that can be displayed on a videotext terminal when it is in graphics mode

bleed 1 *noun* **(a)** line of printing that runs off the edge of the paper **(b)** badly adjusted colour monitor in which colours of adjoining pixels blend **2** *verb* to lose distinction between separate areas of an image on film - often caused by the development process; **the photo is bled off** = the photograph is printed so that the image runs off the edge of the page (NOTE: bleeding - bled)

bleep 1 *noun* audible warning noise; *the printer will make a bleep when it runs out of paper* **2** *verb* to make a bleep; *see also* BEEP

bleeper *noun* device which bleeps (often used to mean radio pager); *the doctor's bleeper began to ring, and he went to the telephone; he is in the factory somewhere - we'll try to find him on his bleeper*

blessed folder *noun (in an Apple Macintosh system)* the System Folder that contains files loaded automatically when the Macintosh is switched on

blimp *noun (film)* a soundproofed film camera case which prevents camera noise being detected by the microphone

blind copy receipt *noun (in electronic mail)* method of sending a message to several users, whose identities are not known to the other recipients; *compare with* CARBON COPY

blind dialling *noun* ability of a modem to dial out even if the line appears dead, used on certain private lines; **blind keyboard** = keyboard whose output is not displayed but is stored directly on magnetic tape *or* disk

blink *verb* way a cursor flashes on and off to show you where you are positioned on the screen or in a document

blinking *noun* flashing effect caused by varying the intensity of a displayed character

blip *noun* small mark on a tape or film counted to determine the position

blister pack *noun* type of packing where the item for sale is covered with a thin plastic sheet sealed to a card backing

blit *or* **bitblt** *verb (in computer graphics)* to move a block of bits from one memory location to another; if the computer has a memory-mapped display a bitblt effectively moves an image on screen

blitter *noun* electronic component designed to process or move a bit-mapped image from one area of memory to another; *the new blitter chip speeds up the graphics display*; **blitting** = transferring a bitmap image from a storage device to an output window

blob *or* **BLOb** = BINARY LARGE OBJECT field in a database record that can contain a large quantity of binary data - normally a bitmap image

block 1 *noun* **(a)** series of items grouped together; *he bought a block of 6,000 shares*; **block booking** = booking of several seats *or* rooms at the same time; *the company has a block booking for twenty seats on the plane or for ten rooms at the hotel* **(b)** piece of metal from which a halftone *or* line drawing is printed **(c)** number of stored records treated as a single unit; **block character check (BCC)** = error detection method for blocks of transmitted data; **block copy** = to duplicate a block of data to another section of memory; *(in a word-processor)* **block delete** = to delete a selected area of text; **block device** = device that manipulates many bytes of data at once; *the disk drive is a block device that can transfer 256bytes of data at a time*; **block diagram** = illustration of the way the main components in a system are connected, but without detail; *the first step to designing a new computer is to draw out a block diagram of its main components*; **block error rate** = number of blocks of data that contain errors compared with the total number transmitted; **block length** = number of bytes of data in a block; *(in a word-processor)* **block move** = to move selected text from one area of a document to another; (in memory) to move the contents of an area of memory to another area of memory; **block operation** = process carried out on a block of data; **block parity** = parity error check on a block of data; *(in a word-processor)* **block protection** = to prevent a selected block of text being split by an automatic page break; **block transfer** = moving large numbers of records around in memory; **building block** = self-contained unit that can be joined to others to form a system; **interblock gap (IBG)** = space between two blocks of stored data **(d)** wide printed bar; **block cursor** = cursor the shape of a solid rectangle that fills a character position; **block diagram** = graphical representation of a system *or* program operation **(e) block capitals** *or* **block letters** = capital letters (such as A,B,C); *write your name and address in block letters* **2** *verb* **(a)** to stop something taking place; *he used his casting vote to block the motion* **(b)** to **block in** = to sketch roughly the main items of a design

blocking factor *noun* number of records in a block

blond *noun (film)* film business name for a 20,000 watt variable-beam floodlight

blooding *noun (film)* **(a)** application of a particular opaque ink, paint or tape **(b)** using a triangular opaque patch when dealing with a photographic sound-track to cover up noise caused by a join

bloom *noun* bright spot on the screen of a faulty television

blooming *noun* distortion of a picture on television due to a too high brightness control setting

bloop *verb* to pass a magnet over a tape to erase signals which are not needed

blow *or* **burn in** *verb* to program a PROM device with data

blow-up *noun (film)* the enlargement of a picture from a 16mm to a 35mm film

blue packing shot *noun (film)* foreground action shot in front of a blue background in order to enable the director to mix the scene with another using a travelling matte or chromakey processes; the final picture appears with the blue background replaced

blueprint *noun* copy of an original set of specifications *or* design in graphical form

Bluetooth *noun* a short-range radio communications system that is designed to provide a simple way for devices to communicate; the technology was developed by a group of computer and telecoms companies that included Ericsson, IBM, Intel, Nokia and Toshiba; *a palm-top computer can transfer information to a mobile phone using a Bluetooth link*

blur 1 *noun* image where the edges *or* colours are not clear **2** *verb* to make the edges *or* colours of an image fuzzy; *we can't use this blurred photograph on the book jacket*

BMP *noun (in graphics)* three-letter extension to a filename that indicates that the file contains a bit-mapped graphics image; *this paint package lets you import BMP files*; **BMP file** = filename extension used to represent the Microsoft Windows standard for storing bitmap images

bn = BILLION

BNC connector *noun* cylindrical metal connector with a copper core that is at the end of coaxial cable and is used to connect cables together; it attaches by pushing and twisting the outer cylinder onto two locking pins

BNC T-piece connector *noun* T-shaped metal connector used to connect an adapter card to the ends of two sections of RG-58 'thin' coaxial cable used in many Ethernet network installations

BNF = BACKUS-NAUR-FORM

board *noun* **(a) board of directors** = group of directors elected by the shareholders to run a company; **board meeting** = meeting of the directors of a company; **she was asked to join the board** = she was asked to become a director; **(b)** people who run a group *or* a society; **editorial board** = group of editors **(c)** flat insulation material on which electronic components are mounted and connected; **printed circuit board (PCB)** = flat insulating material that has conducting tracks of metal printed *or* etched onto its surface, which complete a circuit when components are mounted on it

```
both models can be expanded to
the  current  maximum  of  the
terminals  by  adding  further
serial interface boards
```
Micro Decision

body *noun* **(a)** main section of text in a document **(b)** main part of a program; **body size** = length of a section of text from top to bottom in points; **body type** = default font and point size that is used for the main section of text in a document; *compare with* HEADER, FOOTER

bof *or* **BOF** = BEGINNING OF FILE

boilerplate *noun* final document that has been put together using standard sections of text held in a word processor

boilerplating *noun* putting together a final document out of various standard sections of text

bold *adjective & noun* **bold face** = thicker and darker form of a typeface; *the headwords are printed in Helvetica bold; the bold is too dark for the headlines*

bomb 1 *noun* routine in a program designed to crash the system or destroy data at a particular time **2** *verb (of software) (informal)* to fail; *the program bombed, and we lost all the data; the system can bomb if you set up several desk accessories or memory-resident programs at the same time*

bond paper *noun* heavy grade writing paper

book 1 *noun* **(a)** set of sheets of paper attached together; *they can print books up to 96 pages; the book is available in paperback and hard cover* **(b)** cheque book = book of new cheques; phone book *or* telephone book = book which lists names of people *or* companies with their addresses and telephone numbers **(c)** another name for a multimedia application **2** *verb* to order *or* to reserve something; *to book a room in a hotel or a table at a restaurant or a ticket on a plane; I booked a table for 7.45*

book mark *noun* **(a)** special character or code inserted at a particular point in a document that allows the user to move straight back to that point at a later date **(b)** web page address that is stored in a list to allow the user to move straight back to this page at a later date

book palette *noun* set of colours that are used in a particular multimedia application; two different applications could use different palettes and each must load its own palette otherwise the colours will appear corrupted

booklet *noun* small book with a paper cover

bookseller *noun* person who sells books

bookshop *noun* shop which sells books

bookstall *noun* small open bookshop (as in a railway station)

bookstore *noun* US bookshop

bookwork *noun* **(a)** keeping of financial records **(b)** printing and binding of books (NOTE: no plural)

Boolean algebra *or* **logic** *noun* rules set down to define, simplify and manipulate logical functions based on statements which are true or false; **Boolean search** = search that uses the AND and OR functions; **monadic Boolean operation** = logical operation on only one word, such as NOT; **Boolean variable** *or* **data type** = a variable in a program that can only be either 1 or 0 (or true or false); *see* AND FUNCTION, NOT FUNCTION, OR FUNCTION

boom 1 *noun* **(a)** microphone connected to an adjustable pole that can be extended over the performer's heads and steered noiselessly around the set; long metal arm used to position a video camera **(b)** an upright pole on which lights are mounted **(c)** time when sales *or* production *or* business activity are increasing; **boom industry** = industry which is expanding rapidly; **the boom years** = years when there is a boom **2** *verb* to expand *or* to do well in business; *sales are booming; a booming industry or company; technology is a booming sector of the economy*

boost 1 *noun* help received; *the prize was a real boost; the new model gave a boost to the sales figures* **2** *verb* to make something increase; *the extra hard disk will boost our storage capacity by 25Gb*

boot *verb* to automatically execute a set of instructions to reach a required state

boot block *or* **record** *noun* first track (track 0) on a boot disk of an IBM-compatible floppy disk

boot disk *noun* special disk which contains a bootstrap program and the operating system software; *after you switch on the computer, insert the boot disk*

boot partition *noun* on a hard disk with more than one partition, the partition that contains the bootstrap and operating system

boot sector *noun* part of a disk that contains instructions that are read by the computer when it is first switched on or reset; the instructions tell the computer how to load the operating system from the disk

boot up *or* **booting** *noun* automatic execution of a set of instructions usually held in ROM when a computer is switched on; the boot instructions normally check the hardware and load the operating system software from disk

bootable *adjective* storage device that holds the commands to boot up a computer and load the operating system; *the main hard disk on your PC is a bootable device and your computer will normally boot up from this disk unless you insert a floppy disk into drive A:*

booth *noun* small place for one person to stand *or* sit; **telephone booth** = soundproof cabin with a public telephone in it; **ticket booth** = place outdoors where a person sells tickets

bootleg *noun* illegal copy of recorded material

BOOTP (= BOOTSTRAP PROTOCOL) an Internet protocol that is used by a diskless workstation to find out its IP address, then load its operating system from a central server; this protocol allows a workstation to start up and load all its software over the network; a normal workstation would load its operating system software stored on an internal floppy or hard disk drive

bootstrap *noun* set of instructions that are executed by the computer before a program is loaded, usually to load the operating system once the computer is switched on; *compare with* LOADER

```
the digital signal processor
includes  special  on-chip
bootstrap  hardware  to  allow
easy loading of user programs
into the program RAM
```
Electronics & Wireless World

border *noun* (a) area around printed *or* displayed text (b) thin boundary line around a button or field or a graphic image; **border style** = type of graphic line used as a border around an object, button or field; *use a single-line as the border style for the form*

borrow *verb* to take something (such as money *or* a library book) from someone for a time, returning it at the end of the period; *he borrowed $1,000 from the bank; she borrowed a book on computer construction*

borrower *noun* person who borrows; *borrowers from the library are allowed to keep books for two weeks*

borrowing *noun* (a) action of borrowing money; **borrowing power** = amount of money which a company can borrow (b) **borrowings** = money *or* books borrowed

bottom 1 *noun* lowest part *or* point; **bottom price** = lowest price; **bottom line** = last line on a balance sheet indicating profit *or* loss; *the boss is interested only in the bottom line* = he is only interested in the final profit; **bottom space** = blank lines at the bottom of a page of printed text **2** *verb* **to bottom (out)** = to reach the lowest point

bottom up method *noun* combining low-level instructions to form a high-level instruction (which can then be further combined)

bounce *noun* (film) (a) vertical film image distortion when being projected (b) an electronic mail message that could not be correctly delivered and is returned to the sender

boundary *noun* edge *or* limit of an area; **boundary punctuation** = punctuation which marks the beginning *or* end of a file

bounding box *noun* rectangle that determines the size, position and shape of a graphic image or video clip

COMMENT: in graphics software there is normally a tool that allows you to select an area of an image to operate on: this area is shown as a dashed or flashing bounding box that can be adjusted or moved using the mouse

bounds *noun* limits *or* area in which one can operate; **array bounds** = limits to the number of elements which can be given in an array

box *noun* (a) cardboard *or* wood *or* plastic container; *the goods were sent in thin cardboard boxes; the keyboard is packed in plastic foam before being put into the box*; **box file** = file (for papers) made like a box (b) **box number** = reference number used in a post office or an advertisement to avoid giving an address; *please reply to Box No. 209; our address is: P.O. Box 74209, Edinburgh* (c) **cash box** = metal box for keeping cash; **letter box** *or* **mail box** = place where incoming mail is put; **call box** = outdoor telephone booth (d) square of ruled lines round a text *or* illustration; *the comments and quotations are printed in boxes*

box in *verb* to surround a section of text with ruled lines

boxed *adjective* put in a box *or* sold in a box; **boxed set** = set of items sold together in a box

Boyce-Codd normal form (BCNF) *see* NORMAL FORM

bozo bit *noun (in an Apple Macintosh system)* attribute bit that prevents a file being copied or moved

BPI *or* **bpi** = BITS PER INCH

BPP = BITS PER PIXEL

Bps = BYTES PER SECOND

BPS *or* **bps** = BITS PER SECOND rate at which information is sent equal to the number of bits transmitted or received per second; **bps rate adjust** = ability of a modem to automatically adjust the speed of its serial port to match the communications speed

BRA = BASIC RATE ACCESS basic ISDN service that provides two data channels capable of carrying data at a rate of 64Kbps together with a signalling channel used to carry control signals at 16Kbps; *see also* ISDN

braces *noun* curly bracket characters ({ }) used in some programming languages to enclose a routine

bracket 1 *noun* printing sign to show that a piece of text is separated from the rest; *the items in brackets need not be included; the brackets in the phonetics show sounds which are not always pronounced; the four words underlined should be put in brackets*; **curly brackets** *or* **braces** = curly bracket characters ({ }) used in some programming languages to enclose a routine; **round brackets** *or* **square brackets** = different types of bracket (( ), [ ]) **2** *verb* **to bracket together** = to print brackets round several items to show that they are treated in the same way and separated from the rest of the text

bracketed *adjective* (characters) joined together with small lines between serif and main part

bracketing *noun* photographing the same scene with different exposures to make sure there is one good picture

Braille *noun* system of writing using raised dots on the paper to indicate letters, which allows a blind person to read by passing his fingers over the page; *she was reading a Braille book; the book has been published in Braille*; **Braille marks** = raised patterns on equipment *or* in books to permit identification by touch

branch 1 *noun* **(a)** local office of a bank *or* large business; local shop of a large chain of shops; *the bank or the store has branches in most towns in the south of the country; the computer shop has closed its branches in South America; we have decided to open a branch office in Chicago; the manager of our branch in Lagos or of our Lagos branch*; **branch manager** = manager of a branch **(b)** possible path *or* jump from one instruction to another; **branch table** = table that defines where to jump to in a program depending on the result of a test; **program branch** = one or more paths that can be followed after a conditional statement **(c)** line linking one or more devices to the main network; *the faulty station is on this branch* **2** *verb* **(a) to branch out** = to start a new (but usually related) type of business **(b)** to jump from one section of a program to another

COMMENT: in BASIC, the instruction GOTO makes the system jump to the line indicated; this is an unconditional branch. The instruction IF...THEN is a conditional branch, because the jump will only take place if the condition is met

branching *noun (in a program or script)* decision with two or more possible results that lead to two different points in the program

brand *noun* make of product, which can be recognized by a name *or* by a design; *the number one brand of magnetic tape; the company is developing a new brand of screen cleaner*; **brand image** = idea of a product which is associated with the brand name; **brand name** = name of a brand; **own brand** = name of a store which is used on products which are specially packed for that store

brand new *adjective* quite new *or* very new

branded *adjective* **branded goods** = goods sold under brand names

breach *noun* failure to carry out the terms of an agreement; **breach of contract** = failing to do something which is in a contract; **breach of warranty** = supplying goods which do not meet the standards of the warranty applied to them; **the company is in breach of contract** = it has failed to carry out the duties of the contract

breadboard *noun* device that allows prototype electronic circuits to be constructed easily without permanent connections or soldering

break 1 *noun* **(a)** action *or* key pressed to stop a program execution; **break key** = special key on an IBM-compatible keyboard that halts execution of a program when pressed with the Control key; *I stopped the problem by pressing Ctrl-Break* **(b)** short space of time, when you can rest; *she typed for two hours without a break*; **coffee break** *or* **tea break** = rest time during work when the workers can drink coffee or tea **2** *verb* **(a)** to fail to carry out the duties of a contract; *the company has broken the contract or the agreement* **(b)** to cancel (a contract); *the company is hoping to be able to break the contract* **(c)** to decipher a difficult code; *he finally broke the cipher system* (NOTE: **breaking - broke - has broken**)

break down *verb* **(a)** to stop working because of mechanical failure; *the telex machine has broken down; what do you do when your photocopier breaks down?* **(b)** to show all the items in a total list of costs; *can you break down this invoice into spare parts and labour?*

break even *verb* to balance costs and receipts, but not make a profit; *last year the company only just broke even; we broke even in our first two months of operations*

break up *verb* **(a)** to split something large into small sections; *the company was broken up and separate divisions sold off* **(b)** to come to an end; *the meeting broke up at 12.30*

breakdown *noun* **(a)** stopping work because of mechanical failure; *we cannot communicate with our New York office because of the breakdown of the telex lines* **(b)** showing details item by item; *give me a breakdown of costs*

breaker *noun* **circuit breaker** = device which protects equipment by cutting off the electrical supply

breakeven point *noun* point at which sales cover costs, but do not show a profit

breakout box *noun* device that displays the status of lines within an interface, cable or connector; *the serial interface doesn't seem to be working - use the breakout box to see which signals are present*

breakpoint *noun* **(a)** symbol inserted into a program which stops its execution at that point to allow registers, variables and memory locations to be examined (used when debugging a program) **(b)** halt command inserted into a program to stop execution temporarily, allowing the programmer to examine data and registers while debugging a program

breakup *noun* loss *or* distortion of a television picture *or* radio signal

breathing *noun* *(film)* fault in which the image on screen continually comes in and out of focus; caused by buckling of the film during exposure or during high intensity projection

breezeway *noun* signal used to separate the colour information from the horizontal synchronizing pulse in a television signal

bridge 1 *verb* to use bridgeware to help transfer programs, data files, etc., to another system **2** *noun* **bridge** *or* **bridging product** **(a)** device that connects two networks together; bridges function at the data link layer of the OSI network model; *see also* ROUTER, BROUTER **(b)** matching communications equipment that makes sure that power losses are kept to a minimum **(c)** hardware *or* software that allows parts of an old system to be used on a new system; *a bridging product is available for companies with both generations of machines*

Lotus Development and IMRS are jointly developing a bridge linking their respective spreadsheet and client server reporting tools.

Computing

COMMENT: A bridge connects two similar networks, a gateway connects two different networks. To connect two Ethernet networks, use a bridge

bridgeware *noun* software used to make the transfer from one system to another easier

briefcase utility *noun (in Windows)* a utility that allows you to keep files stored on a laptop and a desktop PC up to date

> COMMENT: if you travel away from the office and work on some documents or files on a laptop, when you return to the office you can connect the laptop to your main desktop PC and the briefcase utility will update the files on each computer

brightness *noun* luminance of an object which can be seen; *a control knob allows you to adjust brightness and contrast; the brightness of the monitor can hurt the eyes*

brightness range *noun (film)* the difference in the highest and lowest reflected light in an image shot, measured by a light meter

there is a brightness control
on the front panel
Micro Decision

brilliance *noun* the luminance of an object as seen in a picture

brilliant *adjective* very bright and shining (light *or* colour); *the background colour is a brilliant red; he used brilliant white for the highlights*

bring up *verb* to start a computer system

British Approval Board for Telecommunications *see* BABT

British Standards Institute (BSI) UK organization that monitors design and safety standards in the UK

broad *noun (film)* wide-angled floodlight

broadband *or* **wideband** *noun (in local area networks or communications)* transmission method that combines several channels of data onto a carrier signal and can carry the data over long distances; *compare with* BASEBAND; DIAL UP, MODEM; *see also* ADSL, ISDN

broadband communication device *noun* communication device that allows a computer connect to a network (normally the Internet) at a very high speed

> COMMENT: The three most popular broadband communication standards are ISDN, cable modems and ADSL

(part of the wider DSL standard). Each country has different prevalent standards and pricing models. For example, ISDN provides a digital link that can transfer data at the rate of 64Kbps; it dials an access number and provides a link when required. ADSL, in contrast, provides a direct connection that appears to be 'always on' using a network adapter to link the computer to the Internet provider. ADSL normally supports a transfer speed of up to 2Mbps.

broadcast **1** *noun* **(a)** *(radio communications)* data transmission to many receivers **(b)** *(in a network)* message or data sent to a group of users; **broadcast homes** = homes with at least one TV *or* radio receiver; **broadcast message** = message sent to everyone on a network; *five minutes before we shut down the LAN, we send a broadcast message to all users*; **broadcast network** = network for sending data to a number of receivers; **broadcast satellite technique** = method of providing greatest channel bandwidth for a geostationary satellite; **broadcast quality** = video image *or* signal that is the same as that used by professional television stations; *we can use your multimedia presentation as the advert on TV if it's of broadcast quality* **2** *verb* to distribute information over a wide area *or* audience; *he broadcast the latest news over the radio*; **broadcasting station** = radio station that transmits received signals to other stations

broadsheet *noun* uncut sheet of paper *or* paper which has printing on one side only

broadside *noun US* publicity leaflet

brochure *noun* publicity booklet; *we sent off for a brochure about holidays in Greece or about maintenance services*

bromide *or* **bromide print** *noun* **(a)** positive photographic print from a negative *or* the finished product from a phototypesetting machine; *in 24 hours we had bromides ready to film* **(b)** lithographic plate used for proofing

brouter *noun* device that combines the functions of a router and bridge to connect networks together; *the brouter provides dynamic routing and can bridge two local area networks*; *see also* BRIDGE, ROUTER

browse *verb* **(a)** to view data in a database or online system **(b)** to search through and access database material without permission; **browsing** = to move through a multimedia title or through a list of files or through sites on the Internet in no particular order; you control which page you move to next and what you view; *see also* SURFING

browse mode *noun* mode of operation in multimedia software that allows a user to move between pages in no fixed order

browser *noun* software utility or front-end that allows a user to easily access and search through text or a database; *a browser can decode the HTML tags that are used to format pages on the Internet and can display images and text*; *see also* MOSAIC, NETSCAPE, WWW

brush *noun* tool in paint package software that draws pixels on screen; *the paint package lets you vary the width of the brush (in pixels) and the colour it produces*; **brush style** = width and shape of the brush tool in a paint package; *to fill in a big area, I select a wide, square brush style*

brute *noun* *(film)* large 10,000 watt spotlight, generally an arc lamp

brute force method *noun* problem-solving method which depends on computer power rather than elegant programming techniques

BS = BACKSPACE

BSAM = BASIC SEQUENTIAL ACCESS METHOD

BSC *(film)* = BRITISH SOCIETY OF CINEMATOGRAPHY

BSD = BERKLEY SOFTWARE DISTRIBUTION

BSI = BRITISH STANDARDS INSTITUTE

BTL filter *(film)* *see* BEHIND-THE-LENS FILTER

btree = BINARY TREE

bubble jet printer *see* INK-JET PRINTER

bubble memory *noun* method of storing binary data using the magnetic properties of certain materials, allowing very large amounts of data to be stored in primary memory

bubble pack *noun* = BLISTER PACK

bubble sort *noun* sorting method which repeatedly exchanges various pairs of data items until they are in order

bucket *noun* storage area containing data for an application

buckle switch *noun* *(film)* automatic circuit breaker in a film camera which is activated by a film jam and shuts off the motor to prevent the film tearing or buckling

buckling *noun* distortion and bending of a film due to heat *or* dryness

buffer 1 *noun* temporary storage area for data waiting to be processed; **buffer size** = total number of characters that can be held in a buffer; **I/O buffer** = temporary storage area for data waiting to be input *or* output **2** *verb* to use a temporary storage area to hold data until the processor *or* device is ready to deal with it; **buffered memory** = device that allows instructions *or* data to be entered before it has completed its present ones; **double buffering** = two buffers working together so that one can be read while the other is accepting data

COMMENT: buffers allow two parts of a computer system to work at different speeds (i.e. a high-speed central processing unit and a slower line printer)

the speed is enhanced by the
1Mb RAM printer buffer
included
Which PC?

the software allocates a
portion of cache as a print
buffer to restore program
control faster after sending
data to the printer
Which PC?

bug 1 *noun* *(informal)* **(a)** error in a computer program which makes it run incorrectly; *see also* DEBUG **(b)** hidden microphone which records conversations secretly **2** *verb* to hide a microphone to allow conversations to be recorded secretly; *the conference room was bugged*

buggy *noun* small computer-controlled vehicle

build *noun* particular version of a program; *this is the latest build of the new software*

building block *noun* self-contained unit that can be joined to others to form a system

buildup *noun (film)* blank tape inserted into a videotape or film sequence in order to leave spaces for scenes that have not yet been filmed

built into *adjective* feature that is already a physical part of a system; *there are communications ports built into all modems* (NOTE: opposite is **add-on**)

built-in *adjective* (special feature) that is already included in a system; *the built-in adapter card makes it fully IBM compatible; the computer has a built-in hard disk*; **built-in function** = special function already implemented in a program; **built-in message** = message generated by a system or authoring language in response to an action (such as a mouse click)

bulk *noun* large quantity of goods; **in bulk** = in large quantities; **bulk buying** *or* **bulk purchase** = buying large quantities of goods at a lower price; **bulk erase** = to erase a complete magnetic disk *or* tape in one action; **bulk storage medium** = medium that is able to store large amounts of data in a convenient size and form; *magnetic tape is a reliable bulk storage medium*; **bulk update terminal** = device used by an information provider to prepare videotext pages off-line, then transmit them rapidly to the main computer

bulk eraser *noun (film)* removal of recorded material on a magnetic tape or film by the repositioning of all iron dioxide molecules

bullet *noun* symbol (often a filled circle or square) in front of a line of text, used to draw attention to a particular line in a list

> For a bullet chart use four to six bullet points and no more than six to eight words each
> *Computing*

bulletin board system (BBS) *noun* computer that you can call up and connect to via a modem and a telephone line

> The Council of European Professional Informatics Societies has instituted an experimental Bulletin Board System based at the University of Wageningen
> *Computing*

bullets *noun* (a) solid area of typeset tone indicating the required image intensity (b)

method of indicating an important section of text by the use of large dots on the page

bundle 1 *noun* (a) number of optic fibres gathered together (b) package containing a computer together with software or accessories offered at a special price; *the bundle now includes a PC with spreadsheet and database applications for just £999* **2** *verb* to market at a special price a package that contains a computer together with a range of software or accessories

bundled software *noun* programs included in the price of a computer hardware package

bureau *noun* (a) office which specializes in keyboarding data *or* processing batches of data for other small companies; *the company offers a number of bureau services, such as printing and data collection; our data manipulation is handled by a bureau*; **employment bureau** = office which finds jobs for people; **information bureau** = office which gives information; **visitors' bureau** = office which deals with visitors' questions; **word-processing bureau** = office which specializes in word-processing; *we farm out the office typing to a local bureau* (b) company that specializes in typesetting from disks or outputting DTP or graphics files to bromide or film; **output bureau** = office that converts data from a DTP program or a drawing stored on disk into typeset artwork; (NOTE: the plural is **bureaux**)

> IMC has a colour output bureau that puts images onto the uncommon CD-ROM XA format.
> *Computing*

burn *verb* to destroy by fire; *the managing director burnt the documents before the police arrived* (NOTE: **burning - burnt**)

burn in *verb* (a) to increase the exposure for a part of a photographic image (b) to mark a television screen after displaying a high brightness image for too long (c) to write data into a PROM chip

burner *noun* device which burns in programs onto PROM chips

burn-out *noun* excess heat *or* incorrect use that causes an electronic circuit *or* device to fail

burst 1 *noun* short isolated sequence of transmitted signals; **burst mode** = data transmission using intermittent bursts of data; *see also* COLOUR 2 *verb* to cut continuous printing paper into separate sheets

burster *noun* machine which cuts continuous stationery into separate sheets

bus *noun* (a) communication link consisting of a set of leads *or* wires which connects different parts of a computer hardware system, and over which data is transmitted and received by various circuits in the system; **address bus** = bus carrying address data between a CPU and a memory device; **bi-directional bus** = data and control lines that can carry signals travelling in two directions; **bus board** = PCB containing conducting paths for all the computer signals; **bus clock** = speed at which data is transferred along the main bus in a computer; this is not always the same speed as the processor speed; *see also* WAIT STATE; **bus extender** *or* **bus extension card (BEC)** = (i) device that extends an 8-bit bus to accommodate 16-bit add-in cards; (ii) special board (used by repair engineers) that moves an add-in board up to a position that is easier to work on; **bus master** = device that controls the bus whilst transmitting (bus master status can move between sending stations); normally this is the central processor, but in high-performance computers, secondary processors in a network card or graphics adapter can take over control of the bus from the CPU; **bus master adapter** = adapter card that fits in a EISA or MCA expansion slot in a PC; the adapter can take control of the main bus and transfer data to the computer's main memory independently of the main processor; *the bus master network adapter provides much faster data throughput than the old adapter*; **bus mouse** = mouse that plugs into the main data bus of a computer (using an interface card) rather than using a serial port; **bus network** = network of computers where the machines are connected to a central bus unit which transmits the messages it receives; **bus topology** = network topology in which all devices are connected to a single cable which has terminators at each end; *Ethernet is a network that uses the bus topology; token ring uses a ring topology*; **bus unit** = (within a microprocessor) the place where instructions flow between the main memory and the processor; control bus = bus carrying control signals between a CPU and other circuits; **data bus** = bus carrying data between a CPU and memory and peripheral devices; **dual bus system** = way for linking different parts of a system which keeps the memory bus separate from the input/output bus; **expansion bus** = data and address lines leading to a connector and allowing expansion cards to control and access the data in main memory; **input/output bus (I/O bus)** = links allowing data and control transfer between a CPU and external peripherals; **memory bus** = bus carrying address data between a CPU and memory devices (b) central source of information which supplies several devices; *see also* EISA, LOCAL BUS, MCA

business *noun* (a) work in buying *or* selling; *business is expanding; business is slow; he does a good business in repairing computers; what's your line of business?*; **business call** = visit to talk to someone on business; **business centre** = part of a town where the main banks, shops and offices are located; **business college** *or* **business school** = place where business studies are taught; **business efficiency exhibition** = exhibition which shows products (computers, word-processors) which help a business to be efficient; **business system** *or* **business package** = set of programs adapted for business use (such as payroll, invoicing, customers file, etc.) (b) commercial company; *he owns a small computer repair business; she runs a business from her home; he set up in business as an computer consultant*; **business address** = details of number, street and town where a company is located; **business card** = card showing a businessman's name and the name and address of the company he works for; **business equipment** = machines used in an office (c) things discussed at a meeting; *the main business of the meeting was finished by 3 p.m.*; **any other business** = item at the end of an agenda, where any matter can be raised (NOTE: no plural for (a) and (c); (b) has the plural **businesses**)

busy *adjective* (a) occupied in doing something *or* in working; *he is busy preparing the accounts; the manager is busy at the moment, but he will be free in about fifteen minutes; the busiest time of year for stores is the week before*

Christmas **(b)** electrical signal indicating that a device is not ready to receive data; *when the busy line goes low, the printer will accept more data*; **the line is busy** = the telephone line is being used **(c)** distracting *or* detailed (background to a film shot)

butt splice *noun (film)* a join in film or tape which has been taped together with the edges touching in order to prevent overlapping

button *noun* **(a)** *(on a mouse or joystick)* switch that carries out an action; *use the mouse to move the cursor to the icon and start the application by pressing the mouse button* **(b)** a square shape displayed on screen (or an area of the screen) that will carry out a particular action if selected by the user with a pointer or keyboard; *there are two buttons at the bottom of the status window, select the left button to cancel the operation or the right to continue; to see the range of applications in Windows click on the Start button displayed in the bottom left-hand corner of the screen;* **button-strip** *or* **button bar** = a line of tiny buttons along the top of the screen, just below the menu bar, on which each button has a tiny picture (called an icon) that tells you what will happen when you click the button; *see also* CHECK BOX, HOTSPOT, PUSHBUTTON, RADIO BUTTON

buzz 1 *noun* sound like a loud hum, caused by interference in a receiver **2** *verb* to make a loud hum

buzz track *noun (film)* sound track of a test film which is used to position correctly the visual film in an optical sound reproduction system

buzzer *noun* electrical device which makes a loud hum

buzzword *noun (informal)* word which is popular among a certain group of people

BVA *(film)* = BRITISH VIDEOGRAM ASSOCIATION

bypass *noun* alternative route around a component *or* device, so that it is not used; *there is an automatic bypass around any faulty equipment*

byte *noun* group of bits *or* binary digits (usually eight) which a computer operates on as a single unit; *one byte can hold numbers between zero and 255*; **bytecode** = form of Java instructions that can be executed in a Java Virtual Machine; when a programmer develops a program written in Java, the Java compiler converts the instructions in a bytecode form that can then be run on any computer that supports the Virtual Machine software; *see also* JAVA, VIRTUAL MACHINE; **byte- orientated protocol** = communications protocol which transmits data as characters rather than as a bit-stream; **bytes-per-inch** = measure of data storage capacity of magnetic tape; **byte serial transmission** = transmission of bytes of data sequentially, the individual bits of which can be sent in a serial *or* parallel way

Cc

C 1 hexadecimal number equivalent to decimal 12 **2** high-level programming language developed mainly for writing structured systems programs; **C++ =** high-level programming language based on its predecessor, C, but providing object-oriented programming functions

> COMMENT: the C language was originally developed for the UNIX operating system. Visual C is a Microsoft product that includes a code-generator to create C code for Windows-based applications

> these days a lot of commercial software is written in C
>
> *PC Business World*

C: the letter that is used in some operating systems, including DOS and Windows to denote the hard disk drive on the system. When talking about the different disk drives, you say 'Drive C' for the hard disk, but normally write 'C:'; *see also* FLOPPY DISK, HARD DISK

C band *noun* microwave communications frequency range of 3.9 - 6.2GHz

cable 1 *noun* **(a)** flexible conducting electrical *or* optical link; **cable connector =** connector at either end of a cable; **cable matcher =** impedance matching device that allows non-standard cable to be used with a particular device; **cable modem =** device that links a computer to the Internet via an existing cable television line; this system provides very high speed access to the Internet (up to 2Mbps) sharing the coaxial cable that is used to distribute cable television signals; *see also* ADSL; BROADBAND; **cable plant =** all the cables, connectors and patch panels within a building or office; **cable television** *or* **cable TV =** communications system to which a subscriber must pay a fee in order to receive programmes delivered through broadcasting signals by means of a coaxial cable; **cable tester =** test equipment used to find breaks *or* faults *or* cracks in cabling; **cable TV relay station =** receiving station which retransmits received television signals to a terminal point (where they are then distributed by cable to viewers' homes); *see also* CATV **(b)** telegram *or* message sent by telegraph; *he sent a cable to his office asking for more money*; **cable address =** specially short address for sending cables **2** *verb* to send a message *or* money by telegraph; *he cabled his office to ask them to send more money; the office cabled him $1,000 to cover his expenses*

cablegram *noun* telegram *or* message sent by telegraph

cabling *noun* cable (as a material); *using high-quality cabling will allow the user to achieve very high data transfer rates; cabling costs up to $10 a foot* (NOTE: no plural); **cabling diagram =** drawing showing where the cable runs throughout an office, including connection points

> It has won a £500,000 contract to supply a structured voice and data cabling system to the bank and its stockbroking subsidiary
>
> *Computing*

cache 1 *noun* **cache controller =** logic circuits that determine when to store data in the high-speed cache memory, when to access data in the cache and when to access data stored in the slower storage device; **cache memory =** section of high-speed memory which stores data that the computer can access quickly; *file access time is much quicker if the most frequently used data is stored in cache memory* **2** *verb* to file *or* store in a cache; *this program can cache any size font;*; *this CPU caches instructions so improves performance by 15 percent*

the first range of 5.25 inch Winchester disk drives to feature inbuilt cache
Minicomputer News

a serious user might also want a tape streamer and cache memory
PC Business World

The Alpha AXP PC runs at 150MHz and comes equipped with 256Kb of Cache RAM, 16Mb of RAM (upgradeable to 128Mb) and Microsoft Windows NT
Computing

CAD = COMPUTER AIDED DESIGN *or* COMPUTER ASSISTED DESIGN software that allows a designer to accurately draw objects on screen; **CAD/CAM** = CAD/COMPUTER AIDED MANUFACTURE interaction between computers used for designing and those for manufacturing a product

CAD   software   is memory-intensive
PC Business World

John Smith of CAD supplier CAD/CAM Limited has moved into sales with responsibilities for the North of England. He was previously a technical support specialist
Computing

caddy *see* CD CADDY

CAI = COMPUTER AIDED INSTRUCTION *or* COMPUTER ASSISTED INSTRUCTION use of a computer to assist pupils in learning a subject

CAL = COMPUTER AIDED LEARNING *or* COMPUTER ASSISTED LEARNING use of a computer to assist pupils in learning a subject

calculate *verb* (a) to find the answer to a problem using numbers; *the DP manager calculated the rate for keyboarding*; **calculated field** = field within a database record that contains the results of calculations performed on other fields (b) to

estimate; *I calculate that we have six months' stock left*

calculating machine *noun* machine which calculates

calculation *noun* answer to a problem in mathematics; **rough calculation** = approximate answer; *I made some rough calculations on the back of an envelope; according to my calculations, we have six months' stock left*

Calculator a software utility that is supplied with Windows and works just like a normal calculator

calculator *noun* electronic machine which works out the answers to numerical problems; *my pocket calculator needs a new battery; he worked out the discount on his calculator*

Calendar simple calendar and diary that was supplied with Windows 3.1. This has been replaced by the more sophisticated Schedule+ in Windows 3.11 and by Outlook in current versions of Windows; **calendar program** = software diary utility that allows a user to enter and keep track of appointments; **multi-user** *or* **network calendar program** = software diary utility that allows many users to enter appointments and schedule meetings with other users

calibrate *verb* to adjust a monitor or joystick so that it is responding correctly and accurately to the signals or movements

call 1 *noun* conversation on the telephone; **local call** = call to a number on the same exchange; **trunk call** *or* **long-distance call** = call to a number in a different zone *or* area; **person-to-person call** = call where you ask the operator to connect you with a named person; **transferred charge call** *or* US **collect call** = call where the person receiving the call agrees to pay for it; **to make a call** = to dial and speak to someone on the telephone; **to take a call** = to answer the telephone; **to log calls** = to note all details of telephone calls made **2** *verb* **(a)** to transfer control to a separate program *or* routine from a main program; *after an input is received, the first function is called up; the subroutine call should be at this point*; **call instruction** = programming instruction that directs control to a routine (control is passed back once the routine has finished; before the call, the program counter contents are saved to show the return instruction where to return to in the main program) to try to contact another user by telephone; *I'll call you at your office tomorrow*; **call accepted signal** = signal sent by device meaning willing to accept caller's data; **call back modem** = modem that, on answering a call, immediately hangs up and calls the user back to establish a connection (used to provide better security than a normal dial-up modem); **call control signal** = signal necessary to establish and end a call; **call diverter** = device that on receiving a call, contacts another point and re-routes the call; **call duration** = length of time spent between starting and ending a call; **called party** = person *or* station to which a call is made; **call forwarding** = automatic redirection of calls to another user *or* station; *we are having all calls forwarded from the office to home*; **calling** = signal to request attention, sent from a terminal *or* device to the main computer; *(in a fax server)* **call scheduling** = arranging calls so that long-distance calls are made at off-peak times

call box *noun* outdoor telephone booth

call discrimination *noun* feature of a modem that allows it to check if an incoming telephone call is from a fax machine, another computer with a modem or from a person

call handler *see* HANDLER

call in *verb* to telephone to make contact; *we ask the representatives to call in every Friday to report the weeks' sales*

call up *verb* to ask for information from a backing store to be displayed; *all the customers addresses were called up; call up the previous file*

callback *noun* security system that's used to reduce the risk of any unauthorised user accessing a dial-in network; the system works in a simple but effective way: the user's computer dials the server, the user enters their name and password, if correct, the server then hangs up and dials a preset telephone number to access the user's computer

caller *noun* person who telephones

callier effect *noun* scattering of light as it passes through one *or* more lenses

calligraphy *noun* art of handwriting

calloc *noun* *(in C programming)* instruction to allocate memory to a program

CAM = COMPUTER AIDED MANUFACTURE *or* COMPUTER ASSISTED MANUFACTURING use of a computer to control machinery *or* assist in a manufacturing process

Cambridge ring *noun* local area networking standard used for connecting several devices and computers together in a ring with simple cable links

camcorder *noun* *(film)* compact, portable video camera with built-in video cassette recorder and microphone; records onto VHS, S-VHS or Hi-8 format cassettes

cameo *noun* **(a)** reverse characters, that is, white on a black background **(b)** front-lit subject filmed in front of a dark background

camera *noun* **(a)** photographic device that transfers a scene onto a piece of film, usually via a lens; *(film)* **camera original** = original film in the camera which was used to photograph a scene; **camera-ready copy (crc)** = final text *or* graphics ready to be photographed before printing **(b)** device that transforms a scene into electronic signals that can be displayed on a television; **camera chain** = pieces of equipment necessary to operate a television camera; *(film)* **camera exposure sheets** = in animation photography, the frame by frame instruction sheet for the camera operator; *(film)* **camera operator** *or* **cameraman** = main camera technician who is in charge of the lighting and photography of a shot; **camera script** = script on which information of shots, lighting and sound are listed; **camera speed** = speed with which film moves through camera; rate is measured by frames per second, in feet, or metres per minute

campus environment *noun* large area or location that has lots of users connected by several networks, such as a university or hospital

cancel *verb* to stop a process *or* instruction before it has been fully executed; *we cancelled the order yesterday*; **cancel character** = control code used to indicate that data transmitted was incorrect; **cancel page** = extra printed page inserted into a book to take the place of a page with errors on it

cancellation *noun* action of stopping a process which has been instructed

candela *noun* SI unit of measurement of light intensity

canonical schema *noun* model of a database that is independent of hardware *or* software available

cans *plural noun (film)* headphones

capability *noun* being able to do something; *resolution capabilities; electronic mail capabilities*

capable *adjective* able to do something; *that is the highest speed that this printer is capable of; the software is capable of far more complex functions* (NOTE: a device is capable **of** something)

capacitance *noun* ability of a component to store electrical charge

capacitor *noun* electronic component that can store charge; **capacitor microphone** = microphone that uses variations in capacitance due to sound pressure to generate an electrical signal; **ceramic capacitors** = general purpose, non-polar small capacitors made from ceramic materials; **electrolytic capacitors** = polar, high-capacitance devices made in a variety of materials; **non-electrolytic capacitors** = non-polar, low-capacitance devices made from a variety of materials; **variable capacitor** = device whose capacitance can be varied over a small range, used for tuning purposes; **memory backup capacitor** = very high-capacitance, small device that can provide power for volatile RAM chips for up to two weeks (used instead of a battery)

capacity *noun* (a) amount which can be produced *or* amount of work which can be done; *industrial or manufacturing or production capacity*; **to work at full capacity** = to do as much work as possible; **to use up spare** *or* **excess capacity** = to make use of time *or* space which is not fully used (b) amount of storage space available in a system *or* on a disk; **storage capacity** = space available for storage; *total storage capacity is now 3Mb*

capitalization *noun* function of a word-processor to convert a line or block of text into capitals

capitals *or informal* **caps** *noun* large form of letters (A,B,C,D, etc.) as opposed to lower case (a,b,c,d, etc.); *the word BASIC is always written in caps*; **caps lock** = key on a keyboard *or* typewriter that allows all characters to be entered as capitals

capstan *noun* device in a tape player which ensures that the tape moves at a constant speed

caption *noun* descriptive text that appears at the very top of a window or on a button or below an image; *the captions are printed in italics*

> COMMENT: in Windows, double-click on the My Computer icon and a small window will pop up with the caption 'My Computer' in white characters on a blue background. If you click anywhere outside this window, the blue background to the caption turns grey to show that the window is no longer active

caption generator *noun* computer or electronic device that allows a user to add titles or captions to a video sequence

capture 1 *noun* **data capture** = action of taking data into a computer system (either by keyboarding *or* by scanning, etc.) **2** *verb* (a) to take data into a computer system (b) to store the image currently displayed on screen in a file; useful when creating manuals about a software product; *the software allows captured images to be edited; this scanner can capture an images at a resolution of 1200 dots per inch (dpi)* (c) *(in a token ring network)* to remove a token from the network in order to transmit data across the network; *see also* TOKEN RING NETWORK; **capture (a printer port)** = way of redirecting data intended for a computer's printer port over a network to a shared printer; **capture (a screen)** = to store the image that is currently displayed on the screen as a graphics file; *in Windows, you can save the current screen as a graphics image by pressing the PrintScreen key on the keyboard; this graphics image can then be pasted into a document or paint program*

In July this year it signed a two-year outsourcing and disaster-recovery deal with Unisys for the operation and management of its Birmingham-based data-capture facility

Computing

carbon *noun* (a) carbon paper; *you forgot to put a carbon in the typewriter* (b) carbon copy, a copy made with carbon paper; *give me the original, and file the carbon copy*; *see also* NCR PAPER

carbon microphone *noun* microphone that uses changes of resistance in carbon granules due to sound pressure to produce a signal

carbon paper *noun* thin paper with a coating of ink on one side, used to make copies in a typewriter *or* printer

carbon ribbon *noun* thin plastic ribbon, coated with black ink, used in printers; *compare with* FIBRE RIBBON

carbon set *noun* forms with carbon paper attached

carbon tissue *noun* light sensitive material used to transfer an image to the printing plate of a photogravure process

carbonless *adjective* which makes a copy without using carbon paper; *our representatives use carbonless order pads*; **carbonless paper** = paper that transfers writing without carbon paper

card *noun* (a) stiff paper; *we have printed the instructions on thick white card* (NOTE: no plural) (b) small piece of stiff paper *or* plastic; **cash card** = plastic card containing the owner's details on a magnetic stripe, used to obtain money from a cash dispenser; **charge card** = plastic card which allows you to buy goods and pay for them later; **credit card** = plastic card which allows you to borrow money *or* to buy goods without paying for them immediately; **filing card** = card with information written on it, used to classify information in correct order; **index card** = card used to make a card index; **punched card** = card with holes punched in it that represent data; **smart card** = plastic card with a memory and microprocessor embedded in it, so that it can be used for direct money transfer *or* for identification of the user (c) a punched card; **card code** = representation of characters on a punched card; **card column** = line of punched information about one character, parallel to the shorter side of the card; **card feed** = device which draws punched cards into a reader automatically; **card image** = section of memory that contains an exact representation of the information on a card; **card punch (CP)** = machine that punches the holes in punched cards; **card reader** *or* **punched card reader** = device that transforms data on a punched card to a form that can be recognized by the computer; **card row** = punch positions parallel to the longer edge of a card (d) sheet of insulating material on which electronic components can be mounted; **card cage** *or* **card frame** = frame containing a motherboard into which printed circuit boards can be plugged to provide a flexible system; **expansion card** *or* **expansion board** = printed circuit board that is connected to a system (expansion connector) to increase its functions *or* performance; **hard card** = board containing a hard disk drive and the required interfacing electronics, which can be slotted into a system (expansion connector) (e) single page within a HyperCard program; each card can have text, images, sound, video and buttons on it

card index *noun* series of cards with information written on them, kept in special order so that the information can be found easily; **card-index file** = information kept on filing cards

cardboard *noun* thick stiff brown paper; **cardboard box** = box made of cardboard (NOTE: no plural)

CardBus high-speed (up to 33MHz) version of the original PCMCIA PC Card standard that also allows 32-bits of data to be transferred in one operation compared to the 16-bit capability of the original PC Card standard

cardinal *noun* & *adjective* positive integer; *13, 19 and 27 are cardinal numbers, -2.3 and 7.45 are not*

cardioid microphone *noun* (*film*) highly sensitive microphone which is used to pick up sound in a specific area; not used for general noise recording

cardioid response *noun* heart shaped response curve of an antenna *or* microphone when a signal source is moved around it

caret *noun* symbol ' ^ ' that is often used to mean the Control key

caret mark *or* **sign** *noun* proofreading symbol to indicate that something has to be inserted in the text

carpal tunnel syndrome *see* REPETITIVE STRAIN INJURY

carriage *noun* mechanical section of a typewriter *or* printer that correctly feeds *or* spaces *or* moves paper that is being printed; **carriage control** = codes that control the movements of a printer carriage; **carriage return (CR)** = signal *or* key to move to the beginning of the next line of print *or* display

carrier *noun* (a) substance that holds the ink for photocopying *or* printing processes (b) device that holds a section of microfilm (c) continuous high frequency waveform that can be modulated by a signal; **carrier detect (CD)** = signal generated by a modem to inform the local computer that it has detected a carrier from a remote modem; **carrier frequency** = frequency of the carrier signal before it is modulated; **carrier sense multiple access - collision detection (CSMA-CD)** = network communications protocol that avoids two sources transmitting at the same time by waiting for a quiet moment, then attempting to transmit; **carrier signalling** = simple data transmission by switching on and off a carrier signal; **carrier system** method of transmitting several different signals on one channel by using different carrier frequencies; **carrier telegraphy** = method of transmitting telegraph signals via a carrier signal; **carrier wave** = waveform used as a carrier; **double sideband-suppressed carrier (DSBSC)** = modulation technique that uses two modulated signal sidebands, but no carrier signal

carry 1 *noun* digit resulting from an addition result being greater than the number base; **carry bit** *or* **flag** = indicator that a carry has occurred **2** *verb* to move (something) from one place to another; *the fibre optic link carried all the data; the information-carrying abilities of this link are very good*

cartesian coordinates *noun* positional system that uses two axes at right angles to represent a point which is located with two numbers, giving a position on each; *compare with* AXIS, POLAR COORDINATES

cartridge *noun* removable device made of a closed box, containing a disk *or* tape *or* program *or* data (usually stored in ROM); *(film)* **cartridge camera** = camera which uses film cartridges instead of spools or reels; **cartridge drive** = drive which operates a disk *or* tape in a cartridge; **cartridge fonts** = hardware which can be attached to a printer, providing a choice of typefaces, but still limited to the typefaces and styles included in the cartridge; *compare with* RESIDENT FONT; **cartridge ribbon** = printer ribbon in a closed cartridgedisk cartridge = removable hard disk; **ink cartridge** = (for use in bubble-jet or ink-jet printers) plastic module that contains ink; **ROM cartridge** = module which can be plugged into a computer and contains data *or* extra programs stored in a ROM chip; **tape cartridge** = box containing magnetic tape

cartridge paper *noun* good quality white paper for drawing *or* printing

CAS = COMMUNICATING APPLICATIONS SPECIFICATION standard developed by Intel and DCA to allow communication software to control a fax modems

cascading menu *noun* secondary menu that is displayed to the side of the main pull-down menu

cascading windows *plural noun (in a GUI)* multiple windows that are displayed overlapping so that only the title bar at the top of each window is showing; *see also* GUI, WINDOW

case 1 *noun* (a) protective container for a device *or* circuit (b) box containing metal letters used in composing; **upper case** *or* **lower case** = capital letters *or* ordinary letters; *he corrected the word 'coMputer', replacing the upper case M with a lower case*; **case change** = key used to change from upper to lower case on a word-processor; **case sensitive** = command *or* operation that will only work when the characters are entered in a particular case; *if your password is case-sensitive, then 'Fred' will not be the same as 'fred'*; **case sensitive search** = search function that succeeds only if both the search word and the case of the characters in the search word match (c) programming command that jumps to various points in a program depending on the result of a test; **case branch** = branch to a part of a program that is dependant upon the result of a test (d) cardboard cover for a book; *the library edition has a case and jacket; have you* *remembered to order the blocking for the spine of the case?*; **case binding** = stiff cardboard cover **(e)** cardboard *or* wooden box for packing and carrying goods; **a packing case** = large wooden box for carrying items which can be easily broken **2** *verb* **(a)** to bind a book in a stiff cardboard cover; **cased book** = book with a hard cover **(b)** to pack in a case

cash *noun* money in coins *or* notes; **cash card** = plastic card containing the owner's details on a magnetic stripe, used to obtain money from a cash dispenser; **cash desk** = place in a store where you pay for the goods bought; **cash dispenser** = machine which gives out money when a special card is inserted and instructions given; **cash register** *or* **cash till** = machine which shows and adds the prices of items bought, with a drawer for keeping the cash received

casing *noun* solid protective box in which a computer *or* delicate equipment is housed

cassette *noun* hard container used to store and protect magnetic tape on which speech *or* music *or* data can be recorded; *copy the information from the computer onto a cassette*; **audio cassette** = small cassette containing a reel of narrow magnetic tape on which audio signal can be recorded; **cassette recorder** = machine to transfer audio signals onto magnetic tape; **cassette tape** = narrow reel of magnetic tape housed in a solid case for protection; **data cassette** = special high-quality tape for storing data; **video cassette** = large cassette containing a reel of wide magnetic tape on which video data can be recorded

COMMENT: using cassette tape allows data to be stored for future retrieval; it is used instead of a disk system on small computers or as a slow high-capacity back up medium for very large systems

cast *noun* **(a)** *(in a programming language)* instruction that converts data from one type to another **(b)** collection of individual images, graphical objects and text that are used in a multimedia presentation; *to convert the variable from an integer to a character type, use the cast command*; **cast-based animation** = animation in which everything is an object and has its movement, colour, shape, etc. defined and controlled by a script of

commands; **cast member** = a single object within a cast used in a presentation, such as text, an image or an animated object

cast off 1 *noun* amount of space required to print a text in a certain font **2** *verb* to calculate the amount of space needed to print a text in a certain font

caster machine *noun* machine that produces metal type

casting agent *noun* *(film)* person who chooses the performers for a film or television production

CAT = COMPUTER AIDED *or* ASSISTED TESTING *or* TRAINING

catadiatropic lens *noun* *(film)* telephoto lens incorporating mirrors which are used to diminish the lens size

catalogue 1 *noun* list of contents *or* items in order; *they sent us a catalogue of their office equipment; look in the catalogue to find the price of the listing paper*; **disk catalogue** = list of files stored on a magnetic disk **2** *verb* to make a catalogue of items stored, especially of books in a library; *the books are catalogued under the author's name*

cataloguer *noun* person who makes a catalogue

catastrophe *noun* serious fault, error *or* breakdown of equipment, usually leading to serious damage and shutdown of a system

catastrophic error *noun* error that causes a program to crash *or* files to be accidentally erased

cathode *noun* negative electrode in an electrical circuit; *opposite is* ANODE

cathode ray tube (CRT) *noun* device used for displaying characters *or* figures *or* graphical information, similar to a TV set (NOTE: CRT is now often used to mean 'monitor')

COMMENT: cathode ray tubes are used in television sets, oscilloscopes, computer monitors and VDUs; a CRT consists of a vacuum tube, one end of which is flat and coated with phosphor, the other end containing an electron beam source. Characters *or* graphics are visible when a controllable electron beam causes the phosphor to glow

CATV = COMMUNITY ANTENNA TELEVISION cable television system using a single aerial to pick up television signals and then distribute them over a wide area via cable

CAV = CONSTANT ANGULAR VELOCITY

CB = CITIZENS BAND RADIO cheap popular system of radio communications, usually between vehicles

CBL = COMPUTER-BASED LEARNING education or learning using special programs running on a computer

CBMS = COMPUTER-BASED MESSAGE SYSTEM

CBT = COMPUTER-BASED TRAINING use of a computer system to train students

CBX = COMPUTERIZED BRANCH EXCHANGE

CC = COURTESY COPY a copy of an electronic mail sent to a second user (NOTE: you can say 'I've CC'd you a copy of my mail about the project')

CCD = CHARGE-COUPLED DEVICE electronic device that has an array of tiny elements whose electrical charge changes with light; each element represents a pixel and its state can be examined to record the light intensity at that point; used in video cameras

CCIR 601 *noun* recommended standard for defining digital video

CCITT = COMITE CONSULTATIF INTERNATIONAL TELEGRAPHIQUE ET TELEPHONIQUE international committee that defines communications protocols and standards

CCR = CAMERA CASSETTE RECORDER *see* CAMCORDER

CCTV = CLOSED CIRCUIT TELEVISION

CCU = COMMUNICATIONS CONTROL UNIT

CD (a) = COMPACT DISC; **CD-ROM** = COMPACT DISC READ ONLY MEMORY **(b)** = CHDIR *or* CHANGE DIRECTORY system instruction in MS-DOS and UNIX that moves you around a directory structure; *type in CD DOCS to move into the DOCS subdirectory*

cd *see* CANDELA

CD32 unit with a processor and CD-ROM drive developed by Commodore that uses its Amiga computer - aimed at the games market

CD-audio *see* CD DA

CD-bridge *noun* extension to the CD-ROM XA standard that allows extra data to be added so that the disc can be read on a CD-i player

CD caddy *noun* flat plastic container that holds a CD-ROM disc; the container is inserted into the CD-ROM disc drive

> COMMENT: Some CD-ROM drives use a CD caddy to hold the disc, others use a motorised tray on which you place the disc

CD DA = COMPACT DISC DIGITAL AUDIO standard that provides 73 minutes of high quality digital sound on a CD at a sample rate of 44.1KHz (NOTE: also called **Red Book audio**)

CD+Graphics *or* **CD+G** *noun* CD format that adds a text track to an audio disc - used to store song title information

CD-i = COMPACT DISC INTERACTIVE CD-ROM system developed by Philips aimed for home use; **CD-i digital audio** = a CD-i disc can record audio in digital format in one of four ways: mono or stereo and at two different sample rates; **CD-i digital images** = the compression method used to store images and video frames on a CD-i disc; **CD-i disc** = CD-ROM that contains video, text, images and sound and is read with a CD-i player; **CD-i player** = console that contains all the drive, processing and display electronics to read a CD-i disc and display images on a normal television; users interact either through a track-ball, joystick or mouse; **CD-i sector** = unit of storage on a CD-i disc that can store 2352 bytes

> COMMENT: a CD-i disc provides similar features to the CD-ROM XA standard; the system includes a central unit with a drive, processor, display hardware and electronics to connect to a television; CD-i is a mix of hardware and software standards that combine sound, data, video and text onto a CD-ROM and allow a user to interact with the software stored on a CD-ROM; the standard defines encoding, compression and display functions

CD-R = COMPACT DISC-RECORDABLE type of CD and player that allows a user to store (write) data onto the disc; a CD-R disc can be played in any standard CD-ROM drive but needs a special CD-R drive to write data to the disc

CD real time operating system; *see* CDRTOS

CD-ROM *or* **CD** = COMPACT DISC READ ONLY MEMORY small plastic disc that is used as a high capacity ROM storage device that can store 650Mb of data; **CD-ROM drive** = disc drive that allows a computer to read data stored on a CD-ROM; the player spins the disc and uses a laser beam to read etched patterns on the surface of the CD-ROM that represent data bits; **CD-ROM extensions** = software required to allow an operating system (typically DOS) to access a CD-ROM drive attached to a PC; **CD-ROM player** = disc drive that allows a computer to read data stored on a CD-ROM; the player uses a laser beam to read patterns on the surface of the CD-ROM that represent data bits; *see also* CD-i, DVI

> COMMENT: a CD can store any type of binary data from images to text to music. A CD normally refers to a music disc which can be played in a HiFi or in a PC's CD player. In computing, the same type of plastic disc is used to store files and data and is called a CD-ROM. Data is stored in binary form as tiny holes etched on the surface which are then read by a laser; CD-ROM drives normally have an access time of between 150-300 milliseconds, compared to under 15ms for a fast hard disk drive; a single-speed disc spins at 230rpm

CD-ROM mode 1 *noun* standard, original method of storing data in the High Sierra file format

CD-ROM mode 2 *noun* higher capacity storage format that stores data in the space used in mode 1 for error correction; neither mode 1 nor mode 2 can play audio and simultaneously read data - hence the XA extension

CD-ROM Extended Architecture *or* **CD-ROM/XA** *noun* enhanced CD-ROM format developed by Philips, Sony and Microsoft, that allows data to be read from the disc at the same time as audio is played back

> COMMENT: the XA standard defines how audio, images and data are stored on a CD-ROM disc to allow sound and video to be accessed at the same time; CD-ROM XA drives can read a Kodak Photo CD disc. CD-ROM XA discs can be played on a CD-i player; a CD-ROM XA disc can be read in a standard CD-ROM player, but requires a special CD-ROM XA controller card

CDRTOS = CD REAL TIME OPERATING SYSTEM operating system used to run a CD-i hardware platform

CD-RW = COMPACT DISC REWRITABLE CD-ROM disc and drive technology that allows a user to read or write data to the disc; unlike CD-RO, data can be stored on the CD many times

CDS *(film)* = CINEMA DIGITAL SOUND digital sound recorded on a film track

CDTV = COMMODORE DYNAMIC TOTAL VISION CD-ROM standard developed by Commodore that combines audio, graphics and text

> COMMENT: this standard is mainly intended as an interactive system for home use; the player connects to a television and can also play music CDs

CD-V = COMPACT DISC VIDEO format for storing 5 minutes of video data on a 3-inch disc in analog form (this format is no longer used)

CD-WO = COMPACT DISC WRITE ONCE CD-ROM disc and drive technology that allows a user to write data to the disc once only and is useful for storing archived documents or for testing a CD-ROM before it is duplicated

cedilla *noun* accent under a letter c (ç), used in certain languages to change the pronunciation

cel *noun* single frame within an animation sequence

cell *noun* **(a)** single function *or* number in a spreadsheet program; *(in a spreadsheet)* **cell address** = code that identifies the position of a cell by row and column; the rows are normally numbered and the columns use the letters of the alphabet; **cell definition** = formula that is contained in a cell; **cell**

format = way in which the result or data in a cell is displayed; *the cell format is right-aligned and emboldened*; **cell protection** = to prevent the contents of a particular cell or range of cells from being changed; **current** *or* **active cell** = thicker line surrounding the border of the cell being edited **(b)** single memory location, capable of storing a data word, accessed by an individual address; **cell phone** = mobile telephone system that uses a network of stations to cover a large area

cellular *adjective* **cellular radio** = radio telephone linked to a main telephone system, which uses a network of stations, each covering a certain area, to provide a service over a large area (the radio is switched from one station to another as it moves from area to area); **cellular service** = changing from one transceiver station to another as a cellular radio *or* cell phone user moves from area to area **(c)** clear plastic sheet used for animation and for overhead projectors

celluloid *noun (film)* cellulose nitrate which was used as a film base in the past; *see also* ACETATE

centering *noun* action of putting text in the centre of the piece of paper; *centering of headings is easily done, using this function key*

centi- *prefix* meaning one hundred *or* one hundredth; **centimetre** = one hundredth of a metre

central *adjective* in the middle; **central computer** = HOST COMPUTER; **central memory (CM)** = area of memory whose locations can be directly and immediately addressed by the CPU; **central processing unit (CPU)** *or* **central processor** = group of circuits which perform the basic functions of a computer, made up of three parts: the control unit, the arithmetic and logic unit and the input/output unit

central processing unit *see* CPU

centralized *adjective* which is located in a central position; **centralized data processing** = data processing facilities located in a centralized place that can be accessed by other users; **centralized computer network** = network with processing power provided by a central computer

centre *or US* **center 1** *noun* point in the middle of something; **centre holes** = location holes along the centre of punched tape; **centre operator** = person who looks after central computer operations; **centre sprocket feed** = central paper tape sprocket holes that line up with coding hole positions **2** *verb* **(a)** to align the read/write head correctly with a magnetic disk *or* tape **(b)** to place a piece of text in the centre of the paper *or* display screen; *which key do you press to centre the heading?*; **centre text** = an option in word-processing packages that lets you place the line or paragraph of text in the centre of the page

Centronics interface *noun* parallel printer interface devised by Centronics Inc

CEPT standard *noun* videotex character standard defined by the Conference of European Post Telephone and Telegraph

ceramic *adjective* made from baked clay; *see* CAPACITOR

certificate *noun* unique set of numbers that uniquely identifies something or someone

COMMENT: certificates are used as the basis of security on the Internet - for digital signatures and secure websites. The certificate is generated by a certificate authority (a trusted company); the certificate can now be used by an individual to sign digital documents or by a company to implement a secure website (for example, an online shop).

certificate authority *noun* specialist trusted organization that issues digital certificates to individuals or companies for use in security and authentication systems (such as digital signatures or secure websites); the authority will need to see evidence that the person applying for a certificate is who they claim to be; *see also* DIGITAL CERTIFICATE, DIGITAL SIGNATURE, SECURE WEBSITE, SSL

C-format *noun (film)* popular, broadcast-quality videotape format that uses 1-inch magnetic tape to store analog video recordings; often used before conversion to digital format

CGA = COLOUR GRAPHICS ADAPTER (old) video display standard developed by IBM that provided low-resolution text and graphics; now superseded by EGA and VGA; the CGA standard could display images at a resolution of 320x200 pixels

CGI = COMMON GATEWAY INTERFACE standard that defines how a web page can access special programs and scripts on an Internet server to carry out functions that enhance the web page; for example, if a web page provides a search function, the web page starts and controls the program that carries out the search using CGI commands; *see also* PERL

CGM = COMPUTER GRAPHICS METAFILE device-independent file format that provides one method of storing an image as a collection of separate objects

chad *noun* waste material produced from holes punched in tape *or* card; **chadless tape** = punched tape that retains chad by not punching holes through fully

chain 1 *noun* **(a)** series of files *or* data items linked sequentially **(b)** series of instructions to be executed sequentially; **chain delivery mechanism** = mechanical system to move paper from machine to machine; **chain list** = list of data with each piece of information providing an address for the next consecutive item in the list; **chain printer** = printer whose characters are located on a continuous belt **2** *verb* to link files *or* data items in series by storing a pointer to the next item at each entry; *more than 1,000 articles or chapters can be chained together when printing*

chaining *noun* execution of a very large program by running it in small segments

change *verb* to make something different; to use one thing instead of another; **change dump** = printout of locations where data has been changed; **change file** = file containing records that are to be used to update a master file

changeover cue *noun* *(film)* visual warnings, usually circles or dots, towards the end of a reel of film to warn the operator to change from one projector to the other

changer *noun* device which changes one thing for another; **record changer** = device on a turntable which allows records to be changed automatically

channel 1 *noun* **(a)** physical connection between two points that allows data to be transmitted (such as a link between a CPU and a peripheral); **channel bank** = collection of a number of channels, and circuits to switch between them; **channel capacity** = maximum rate of data transmission over a channel; **channel group** = collection of twelve channels, treated as one group in a multiplexing system; **channel isolation** = separation of channels measured as the amount of crosstalk between two channels (low crosstalk is due to good channel isolation); **channel overload** = transmission of data at a rate greater than the channel capacity; **I/O channel** = link between a processor and peripheral allowing data transfer **(b)** way in which information *or* goods are passed from one place to another; **to go through the official channels** = to deal with government officials (especially when making a request); **to open up new channels of communication** = to find new ways of communicating with someone; **distribution channels** *or* **channels of distribution** = ways of sending goods from the manufacturer for sale in shops **(c)** *(communications)* signal path for transporting information between two points **(d)** *(in a graphics application)* term used to refer to an individual plane within an image that can store a matte or special effect or one part of the final picture **(e)** *(in MIDI)* method of identifying individual tracks or instruments in a MIDI setup; there are 16 channel numbers and an instrument can be set to respond to the instructions on one particular channel; each channel also has a patch associated with it that defines the sound that is played; *(in Windows MIDI Mapper utility)* **channel map** = list that shows which MIDI channel is being redirected to another **(f)** *(in animation or video editing software)* method of organising cast members in a presentation; each channel can hold a cast member, background or a special effect according to time - these are played back together to create the final presentation **2** *verb* to send signals *or* data via a particular path

channelling *noun* protective pipe containing cables *or* wires

chapter *noun* **(a)** sequence of frames on a videodisc; **chapter stop** = code at the end of a videodisc chapter that enables rapid location of a particular chapter **(b)** section of a book *or* document; **chapter heading** = special heading at the beginning of each printed chapter; *chapter headings are in 12 point bold*

char *noun (in programming)* a data type which defines a variable as containing data that represents a character using the ASCII code

character *noun* graphical symbol which appears as a printed *or* displayed mark, such as one of the letters of the alphabet, a number or a punctuation mark; **character assembly** = method of designing characters with pixels on a computer screen; **character-based** = screen design that is drawn using ASCII characters rather than graphical windows; **character block** = the pattern of dots that will make up a character on a screen *or* printer; **character byte** = byte of data containing the character code and any error check bits; **character code** = system where each character is represented by a number; *the ASCII code is the most frequently used character coding system*; **character display** = device that displays data in alphanumeric form; **character generator** = ROM that provides the display circuits with a pattern of dots which represent the character (block); **character interleaving** = transmission of one complete character word at a time in a TDM system; **character key** = word processor control used to process text one character at a time; **Character Map** = a utility that is provided with Windows to allow you access to the full range of 256 characters that make up every font rather than the limited range that you can access from the keyboard; *(of a display adapter)* **character mode** = mode that can only display the characters defined in the built-in character set; **character printer** = device that prints characters one at a time; *a typewriter is a character printer*; **character recognition** = system that reads written *or* printed characters into a computer; *see also* OCR; **character rounding** = making a displayed character more pleasant to look at (within the limits of pixel size); **character set** = list of all the characters that can be displayed; **character skew** = angle of a character in comparison to its correct position; **characters per inch (cpi)** = number of printed characters which fit within the space of one inch; **characters per second (cps)** = number of characters

which are transmitted *or* printed per second; **character stuffing** = addition of blank characters to a file to increase its length to a preset size

characteristic 1 *noun* **(a)** value of exponent in a floating point number **(b)** measurements *or* properties of a component **2** *adjective* which is typical *or* special; **characteristic curve** = response curve of an electronic component *or* circuit

```
This explains a multitude of
the  database's  problems  -
three-letter   months   are
treated like character strings
instead of as dates
                      Computing
```

charge 1 *noun* **(a)** (i) a quantity of electricity; (ii) the number of *or* excess of *or* lack of electrons in a material *or* component; **charge-coupled device (CCD)** = electronic device operated by charge; **electric charge** = a number of atoms that are charged (due to an excess *or* deficiency of electrons) **(b)** money which must be paid *or* price of a service; *to make no charge for maintenance while the system is still under guarantee; there is no charge for service or no charge is made for service*; **free of charge** = free *or* with no money to be paid; **inclusive charge** = charge which includes all items **2** *verb* **(a)** to supply a device with an electric charge; **battery charging** = to replenish the charge stored in a re-chargeable battery **(b)** to ask someone to pay for services later; to ask for money to be paid; *to charge £5 for postage; how much does he charge?*; **to charge the packing to the customer** *or* **to charge the customer with the packing** = the customer has to pay for packing; **he charges £6 an hour** = he asks to be paid £6 for an hour's work

charge-coupled device *see* CCD

chargeable *adjective* which can be charged; *costs of returning a system for repair are chargeable to the owner*; **re-chargeable battery** = battery that can be used to supply power, and then have its charge replenished

```
Compaq Computer and Duracell
are developing a new type of
standard-size  re-chargeable
battery for portable computers
```

chart 69 checksum

```
that lasts 40% longer than
those now available
```
Computing

chart *noun* diagram showing information as a series of lines *or* blocks, etc.; **bar chart** = diagram where quantities and values are shown as thick columns of different heights *or* lengths; **chart recorder** = mechanical device that records input values by drawing lines on a moving reel of paper; **flowchart** *or* **flow diagram** = diagram showing the arrangement of various work processes as a series of stages; *see also* FLOWCHART; **organization chart** = diagram showing how a company *or* an office is organized; **pie chart** = diagram where ratios are shown as slices of a circle; **sales chart** = diagram showing how sales vary from month to month

```
You need a flowchart to
understand Taylor's early
life: he was brought up in
London, Paris and Boston,
secondary school in Paris, and
universities in New York and
Harvard
```
Computing

chassis *noun* metal frame that houses the circuit boards together with the wiring and sockets required in a computer system *or* other equipment

chat room *noun* area of a website where visitors can exchange messages with other visitors; if a visitor types in a message, special software displays the name of the visitor and their message to all the other visitors, allowing them to 'talk' and exchange messages, in real time

CHCP *noun* (*in MS-DOS and Windows*) system command that selects which code page to use

CHDIR = CHANGE DIRECTORY; *see* CD

cheapernet (*informal*) *see* THIN-ETHERNET

check 1 *noun* (a) act of making sure that something is correct; **check bit** = one bit of a binary word that is used to provide a parity function; (*in a GUI or front-end*) **check box** = small box displayed with a cross inside it if the option has been selected, or empty if the option is not selected; unlike a radio button, more than one checkbox can be

selected; *select the option by moving the cursor to the check box and pressing the mouse button*; *see also* BUTTON; **check digit** = additional digit inserted into transmitted text to monitor and correct errors; **check key** = series of characters derived from a text used to check for and correct errors; **check mark** = indicator in a checkbox that shows if the checkbox has been selected; often a cross or tick; **check point** = point in a program where data and program status can be recorded *or* displayed; **check sample** = sample to be used to see if goods which have been supplied are acceptable; **check total** = CHECKSUM (b) examination; *the auditors carried out checks on the company accounts; a routine check of the fire equipment* (c) *US* mark on paper to show that something is correct; *make a check in the box marked 'R'* **2** *verb* (a) to examine *or* to make sure that something is in good working order; *to check that a bill is correct; to check and sign for goods*; **he checked the computer printout against the invoices** = he examined the printout and the invoices to see if the figures were the same (b) *US* to mark with a sign to show that something is correct; *check the box marked 'R'* (NOTE: the GB English is **tick**)

check-in *noun* place where passengers give in their tickets for a flight; *the check-in is on the first floor*; **check-in counter** = counter where passengers check in; **check-in time** = time at which passengers should check in

checking *noun* examination; *the maintenance engineer found some defects during his checking of the equipment* (NOTE: no plural)

checkout *noun* (a) (*in a supermarket*) place where you pay for the goods you have bought (b) (*in a hotel*) **checkout time is 12.00** = time by which you have to leave your room

checksum *noun* number calculated from data, that is used to make sure that the data is correct and valid; *on a barcode, the last digit is a checksum to ensure that the scanner has read the barcode data correctly*

checksum *or* **check total** *noun* program which checks that data (retrieved from memory) is correct, summing it and comparing the sum with a stored value; *the data must be corrupted if the checksum is different*

```
Four bits control three
multiplexers within the
function unit. The last bit is
a check bit to read the block's
output
```
Computing

chemical 1 *adjective* referring to the interaction of substances; **chemical reaction** = interaction between two substances *or* elements **2** *noun* product resulting from the interaction of other substances *or* elements

child process *or* **program** *noun* second program run from within another program; for example, in some DOS applications you can return to the DOS prompt, whilst the main program is still running: the DOS prompt is a child process that has been started by running a second copy of the DOS command interpreter

child window *noun* window within a main window; the smaller window cannot be moved outside the boundary of the main window and is closed when the main window is closed

chinese *noun (film)* camera movement which consists of a zoom out travel with a pan left or right

chip *noun* electronic device consisting of a small piece of a crystal of a semiconductor onto which are etched *or* manufactured (by doping) a number of components such as transistors, resistors and capacitors, which together perform a function; **chip architecture** = design and layout of components on a chip; *(film)* **chip camera** = television camera which works with light-sensitive chips instead of pickup tubes; **chip select line** = connection to a chip that will enable it to function when a signal is present; **diagnostic chip** = chip that contains circuits to carry out tests on circuits *or* other chips; **single chip computer** = complete simple computer including CPU, memory and input/output ports on one chip; **sound chip** = device that will generate a sound *or* tune; *they are carrying out research on diagnostic chips to test computers that contain processors*

```
Where the display is provided
by an LCD system, high levels
of performance must be
achieved with the lowest cost,
smallest chip count and lowest
power consumption
```
Computing

CHKDSK *(in MS-DOS)* system command that runs a check on the status of a disk drive and installed RAM

choke *see* INDUCTOR

Chooser *noun* operating system utility supplied with the Apple Macintosh that allows a user to select the type of printer, network and other peripherals that are connected

chop *see* BINARY

chord keying *noun* action of pressing two *or* more keys at the same time to perform a function

COMMENT: as an example, to access a second window, you may need to press control and F2; pressing shift and character delete keys at the same time will delete a line of text

chroma *noun* measure of the hue and saturation of a colour; **chroma control** = circuit in a TV that alters the colour saturation; **chroma detector** = television circuit that checks whether a signal is monochrome *or* colour

chroma key *or* **colour key** *noun (in video)* special effect in which an object is photographed against a (normally blue) background which is then replaced with another image to give the impression that the object appears against the image; *see* TRAVELLING MATTE

chromatic *adjective* referring to colours; **chromatic aberration** = lens defect which is caused by the refraction of white light into colours; **chromatic dispersion** = uneven refraction index across an optic fibre causing signal distortion

chromaticity *noun* quality of light according to its most prominent colour and purity

chrominance signal *noun* part of a colour video signal containing colour hue and saturation information

COMMENT: Chroma key can be used to

give the appearance of flying; a video sequence of a person against a deep ultramarine blue background is recorded, then this blue background colour (the chroma key) is electronically replaced with footage of sky

chronological order *noun* arrangement of records (files, invoices, etc.) according to their dates

chunk *noun* basic part of a RIFF file that consists of an identifier (chunk ID) and data

CIDR = CLASSLESS INTER-DOMAIN ROUTING method of organising IP addresses that is more compact and efficient than the original, older IP system

COMMENT: the original IP system used three classes of IP address (A, B and C) that could each represent hundreds or thousands of individual addresses; the new system adds a slash and a new IP Prefix number that represents a number of individual addresses. For example, the old system used an IP address such as '194.124.0.0' wheras the new scheme would replace this with '194.124.0.0/12'; the IP Prefix number 12 represents 4,096 unique addresses and the lower the number the more addresses are represented

CIF *noun* videophone ISDN standard which displays colour images at a resolution of 352x288 pixels; this standard uses two ISDN B channels

CIM (a) = COMPUTER INPUT FROM MICROFILM coordinated use of microfilm for computer data storage and the method of reading the data (b) = COMPUTER INTEGRATED MANUFACTURING use of computers in every aspect of design and manufacturing

cine- *prefix* meaning moving pictures *or* film; **cine camera** = camera that records motion pictures onto a roll of film; **cine film** = normally refers to 8mm or 16mm photographic film used to record motion pictures with an optional sound track; **cine orientated image** = data *or* graphics on a microfilm where the image is at right angles to the long edge of the roll of film; *(film)* **cine spool** = magnetic tape spool usually made of plastic and not more than 7 inches in width

cinema *noun* **(a) the cinema** = making of films for showing to the public **(b)** building where films are shown to the public

cinema digital sound *see* CDS

Cinemascope *noun* *(film)* the first wide-screen filming system to be extensively used

cinematographer *noun* *(film)* the person responsible for lighting and photography on a film set

cinematography *noun* *(film)* **(a)** motion picture photography **(b)** special effects giving impression of motion

cipher *noun* system of transforming a message into an unreadable form with a secret key (the message can be read normally after it has passed through the cipher a second time); **cipher key** = secret sequence of characters used with a cipher system to provide a unique ciphertext; **cipher system** = formula used to transform text into a secret form; **ciphertext** = data output from a cipher

circuit *noun* connection between electronic components that perform a function; **circuit analyzer** = device that measures voltage *or* current *or* impedance *or* signal in a circuit; **circuit board** = insulating board used to hold components which are then connected together (electrically) to form a circuit; **circuit breaker** = device which protects equipment by cutting off the electrical supply when conditions are abnormal; **circuit diagram** = graphical description of a circuit; **circuit grade** = ability of a communication channel to carry information (the grades are: wideband, voice, subvoice and telegraph); **circuit noise level** = amplitude of noise in a circuit compared to a reference level; **circuit switched network** = communications network in which each link can be linked to another at a switching centre; **circuit switching** = communications circuit established on demand and held until no longer required; **data circuit** = circuit which allows bi-directional data communications; **printed circuit board (PCB)** = flat insulating material that has conducting tracks of metal printed *or* etched onto its surface, which complete a circuit when components are mounted on it

circuitry *noun* collection of circuits; *the circuitry is still too complex* (NOTE: no plural)

> The biggest shock was to open up the PC and find the motherboard smothered in patch wires (usually a sign that a design fault in the printed circuit board was rectified at the last minute)
>
> *Computing*

circular 1 *adjective* **(a)** which goes round in a circle; **circular buffer** = computer-based queue that uses two markers, for top and bottom of the line of stored items (the markers move as items are read from *or* written to the stack); **circular file** = a data file that has no visible beginning *or* end, each item points the way to the next item with the last pointing back to the first; **circular orbit** = orbit of a satellite that is always at a constant distance from the centre of the earth; *(in a spreadsheet)* **circular reference** = error condition that occurs when two equations in two cells reference each other; **circular waveguide** = microwave beam carrying a channel, of circular cross-section, allowing high frequencies to be carried **(b)** sent to many people; **circular letter of credit** = letter of credit sent to all branches of the bank which sent it out **2** *noun* leaflet *or* letter sent to many people; *they sent out a circular offering 10% off demonstration models*

circularize *verb* to send a circular to; *the committee has agreed to circularize the members; they circularized all their customers with a new list of prices*

circulate *verb* **(a)** to go round in a circle, and return to the first point **(b)** to send information to; *they circulated a new list of prices to all their customers*

circulating *adjective* which is moving about freely; **circulating register** = shift register whose output is fed back to its input to form a closed loop

circulation *noun* **(a)** movement; *the company is trying to improve the circulation of information between departments* **(b)** *(of a newspaper)* number of copies sold; *what is the circulation of this computer magazine? a specialized paper with a circulation of over 10,000*

circumflex *noun* printed accent (like a small 'v' printed upside down) placed above a letter, which may change the pronunciation *or* distinguish the letter from others

CIS = CONTACT IMAGE SENSOR scanner in which the detectors (a flat bar of light-sensitive diodes) touch the original, without any lens that might distort the image

CISC = COMPLEX INSTRUCTION SET COMPUTER central processor chip that can carry out a large number of instructions each of which does a complete job; this compares with a RISC processor which has fewer simple instructions that are executed more quickly but is often more complex to program

citizens band (CB) radio *noun* cheap popular system of radio communications, usually between vehicles

cladding *noun* protective material surrounding a (fibre optic) core

claim frame *noun* *(in an FDDI protocol network)* special frame which is used to determine which station will initialise the network

clamp *verb* to find the voltage of a signal

clamper *noun* circuit which limits the level of a signal from a scanning head or other input device to a maximum before this is converted to a digital value; used to cut out noise and spikes

clapper *noun* mechanical part of a dot matrix printer that drives the printing needles onto the ribbon

clapperboard *noun* *(film)* a board on which is written all relevant information to a shot in a motion picture film

clarity *noun* being clear; *the atmospheric conditions affect the clarity of the signal*

class *noun* *(in a programming language)* definition of what a particular software routine will do or what sort of variable it can operate on; **class interval** = range of values that can be contained in a class

Class 1, Class 2 *noun* standards that define how a to control a fax modem using software; the standard uses extensions to the Hayes AT command set used for data modems. Class 2 expects the modem to carry out more work in managing fax communications; Class 1 units can often be upgraded through software. Only modems advertised as 'Class 2.0' follow the true Class 2 standard.

classification *noun* way of putting into classes

classify *verb* to put into classes *or* under various headings; **classified directory** = book which lists businesses grouped under various headings (such as computer shops *or* newsagents)

claw *noun (film)* mechanism in a camera or projector which moves the film through contact with the holes in the edge of the film

clean 1 *adjective* not dirty *or* with no errors *or* with no programs; **clean copy** = copy which is ready for keyboarding, and does not have many changes on it; **clean machine** = computer that contains only the minimum of ROM based code to boot its system from disk, any languages required must also be loaded in; **clean proof** = proof without any corrections; **clean room** = area where hard disks, wafers and chips are manufactured; the air inside has been filtered to ensure no dust or particles are present which could damage a chip **2** *verb* to make something clean; **head cleaning disk** = special disk which will clean dirt from the read/write head

clear 1 *adjective* easily understood; *the program manual is not clear on copying files; the booklet gives clear instructions how to connect the different parts of the system; he made it clear that the system will only work on IBM-compatible hardware* **2** *verb* **(a)** to sell cheaply in order to get rid of stock; *'demonstration models to clear'* **(b)** to wipe out *or* erase *or* set to zero a computer file *or* variable **(c)** to release a communications link when transmissions have finished; *to clear an area of memory; press ESCAPE to clear the screen; to clear the data register*; **clear to send (CTS)** = RS232C signal that a line *or* device is ready for data transmission

clearance *noun* **(a)** authority to access a file **(b) customs clearance** = passing goods through the customs so that they can enter or leave the country

click 1 *noun* **(a)** short duration sound, often used to indicate that a key has been pressed **(b)** pressing a key *or* button on a keyboard *or* selecting a button or menu option on screen by moving the pointer over the object and pressing the mouse button; *you move through text and graphics with a click of the mouse; Windows uses a click on the left-hand mouse button to select an icon and a click on the right-hand button to display a menu of options that apply to the icon*; = **click through** = action of someone clicking on a banner advertisement and jumping to the advertiser's website.; = **click through rate (CTR)** = a method of charging an advertiser for the display of a banner advertisement on a website. Each time a visitor clicks on a displayed ad (that links to the advertiser's main site), the advertiser is charged a fee. A click through rate of just a few percent is common and most advertisers have to pay per thousand impressions of their banner ad, sometimes written CTM (click through, per thousand).; **double-click** = two rapid press-release actions on a mouse button; normally to start a program or select an option; **drag-and-click** = to hold down a mouse button while moving the mouse, so moving the object selected **2** *verb* to press a key *or* a button on a keyboard *or* the mouse; *use the mouse to enlarge a frame by clicking inside its border*

click-and-mortar Internet-based online shop that also has a real physical shop that customers can visit

> COMMENT: the bookshop Barnes & Noble is a click-and-mortar company: it has a chain of real bookshops and an online shop at www.bn.com; compare this with Amazon.com that has an online shop but does not have real physical bookshops

client *noun* **(a)** *(in a network)* a workstation *or* PC *or* terminal connected to a network that can send instructions to a server and display results **(b) client application** = application that can accept linked or embedded objects from a server application; *see* OLE **(c)** *(in a GUI)* **client area** = area inside a window that can be used to display graphics or text

client-server architecture *noun* distribution of processing power in which a central server computer carries out the main tasks in response to instructions from terminals or workstations; the results are sent back across the network to be displayed on the terminal, the client (the terminal or workstation) does not need to be able to directly access the data stored on the server nor does it need to carry out a lot of processing

client-server network *noun* method of organising a network in which one central dedicated computer, the server, looks after tasks such as security, user accounts, printing and file sharing, while clients (the terminals or workstations connected to the server) run standard applications; *compare with* PEER-TO-PEER NETWORK

clip 1 *noun* short piece of (live) film; *there was a clip of the disaster on the news* **2** *verb* **(a)** to attach papers together with a wire; *the corrections are clipped to the computer printout* **(b)** to cut out with scissors; **clipping service** = service which cuts out references to someone in newspapers *or* magazines and sends them to him **(c)** to remove the peaks of a waveform; *the voltage signal was clipped to prevent excess signal level*

clip-art *noun* set of pre-drawn images or drawings that a user can incorporate into a presentation or graphic; *we have used some clip-art to enhance our presentation*

clipboard *noun* **(a)** temporary storage area for data **(b)** *(in Microsoft Windows and Macintosh Finder)* utility that temporarily stores any type of data, such as a word or image; *copy the text to the clipboard, then paste it back into a new document*

Clipper chip *noun* electronic device that provides data encryption for messages transmitted by computers, over the Internet, telephones, and television programmes

> COMMENT: in the original scheme the US Government held the master key to the Clipper chip and so could decrypt and read any encrypted messages - this angered many groups concerned with freedom of speech and the US Government has since re-designed the original scheme and suggested an alternatives

clipping *noun* cutting off the outer edges of an image or the highest and lowest parts of a signal

clock *noun* **(a)** machine which shows the time; *the office clock is fast; the micro has a built-in clock*; **digital clock** = clock which shows the time using numbers (as 12:05)

(b) circuit that generates pulses used to synchronize equipment; *the central processing unit normally carries out one instruction every clock pulse, so the faster the clock the more instructions it carries out*; **clock cycle** = time period between two consecutive clock pulses; **clock doubler** = component that doubles the speed of the main system clock to effectively double the processing speed of the computer; **clock pulse** = regular pulse used for timing *or* synchronizing purposes; **clock rate** *or* **speed** = number of pulses that a clock generates every second; **clocked signals** = signals that are synchronized with a clock pulse; **clock track** = line of marks on a disk *or* tape which provides data about the read head location

clock in *or* **clock on** *verb (of worker)* to record the time of arriving for work by putting a card into a special timing machine

clock out *or* **clock off** *verb (of worker)* to record the time of leaving work by putting a card into a special timing machine; *the new CPU from Intel has an optional clock doubler that will double performance*

clogging *noun (film)* build up of oxide and binder on a playback head or tape recording which results in drop-outs

clone *noun* computer *or* circuit that behaves in the same way as the original it was copied from; *they have copied our new personal computer and brought out a cheaper clone*

> On the desktop, the IBM/Motorola/Apple triumvirate is planning to energise a worldwide clone industry based on the PowerPC chip
>
> *Computing*

close *noun* command (in a programming language) that means the program has finished accessing a particular file *or* device; **close menu option** = (normally under the File menu) menu option that will shut the document that is currently open, but will not exit the application. If you have not saved the document, the application will warn you before it closes the document and give you the chance to save any changes.

close *verb* to shut down access to a file *or* disk drive; **closed bus system** = computer with no expansion bus that makes it very difficult for a user to upgrade; **closed circuit television (CCTV)** = TV system consisting of a camera connected directly to a television monitor; **closed loop** = number of computer instructions that are repeated; **closed subroutine** = number of computer instructions in a program that can be called at any time, with control being returned on completion to the next instruction; **closed user group (CUG)** = to restrict the entry to a database to certain known users, usually by means of a password; **close file** = to execute a computer instruction to shut down access to a stored file

close up *verb* to move pieces of type *or* typeset words closer together; *if we close up the lines, we should save a page*

close-up *noun* photograph taken very close to the subject; **close-up lens** = extra lens that permits the ordinary lens to focus closer to the subject than normal; *(film)* **close-up shot** *or* **close-up** *or* **cs** = camera shot very close to subject

CLS *(in MS-DOS)* system command to clear the screen, leaving the system prompt and cursor at the top, left-hand corner of the screen

cluster *noun* number of terminals *or* stations *or* devices *or* memory locations grouped together in one place, controlled by a cluster controller; **cluster controller** = central computer that controls communications to a cluster of devices *or* memory locations

```
cluster   controllers   are
available   with   8   or   16
channels
```
Microcomputer News

CLUT = COLOUR LOOK-UP TABLE table of values that define the colours in a palette; this allows a program to use colours without having to calculate them each time

CLV *see* CONSTANT LINEAR VELOCITY

CM = CENTRAL MEMORY

C-MAC *noun* new direct-broadcast TV standard using time division multiplexing for signals

CMI = COMPUTER-MANAGED INSTRUCTION

CMIP = COMMON MANAGEMENT INFORMATION PROTOCOL protocol officially adopted by the ISO used to carry network management information across a network

CMIS = COMMON MANAGEMENT INFORMATION SPECIFICATION powerful network management system

CML = COMPUTER-MANAGED LEARNING

CMOS = COMPLEMENTARY METAL OXIDE SEMICONDUCTOR integrated circuit design and construction method (using a pair of complementary p- and n-type transistors); *see also* MOS, NMOS, PMOS

COMMENT: the final package uses very low power but is relatively slow and sensitive to static electricity as compared to TTL integrated circuits; their main use is in portable computers where battery power is being used

```
Similarly,   customers   who   do
not   rush   to   acquire   CMOS
companion processors for their
mainframes   will   be   rewarded
with   lower   prices   when   they
finally do migrate
```
Computergram

CMOT = CMIP/CMIS OVER TCP use of CMIP and CMIS network management protocols to manage gateways in a TCP/IP network

CMYK = CYAN-MAGENTA-YELLOW-BLACK *(in graphics or DTP)* method of describing a colour by the percentage content of its four component colours; *see also* HSV, RGB, YMCK

CNC = COMPUTER NUMERIC CONTROL machine operated automatically by computer; *see also* NUMERICAL CONTROL

co.uk domain name suffix that indicates a business based in the UK; *the Peter Collin Publishing domain name is 'pcp.co.uk'*; *see also* COM, DOMAIN

coat *verb* to cover with a layer of liquid; **coated papers** = papers which have been covered with a layer of clay to make them shiny

coating *noun* material covering something; *paper which has a coating of clay*

co-axial cable *or* **co-ax** *noun* cable made up of a central core, surrounded by an insulating layer then a second shielding conductor

> COMMENT: co-axial cable is used for high frequency, low loss applications such as television transmission, audio connections and network cabling; co-ax cable provides a higher bandwidth than twisted-pair cabling

COBOL = COMMON ORDINARY BUSINESS ORIENTED LANGUAGE programming language mainly used in business applications

code 1 *noun* **(a)** rules used to convert instructions *or* data from one form to another; **code conversion** = rules used to change characters coded in one form, to another; *(in MS-DOS)* **code page** = table that defines the characters that are produced from each key; *in order to enter Swedish characters from an English keyboard, you have to change the system code page* **(b)** sequence of computer instructions; *(in an IBM-compatible PC)* **code segment** = an area of memory assigned to hold the instructions that form a program **(c)** system of signs *or* numbers *or* letters which mean something; **area code** = numbers which indicate an area for telephoning; *what is the code for Edinburgh?*; **bar code** = data represented as a series of printed stripes of varying widths; **bar-code reader** = optical device that reads data from a bar code; **code bit** = smallest signalling element used by the physical layer (of an OSI model network) for transmission; **code group** = special sequence of five code bits that represent an FDDI symbol; **escape codes** = transmitted code sequence which informs the receiver that all following characters represent control actions; **international dialling code** = numbers used for dialling to another country; **machine-readable codes** = sets of signs *or* letters (such as bar codes *or* post codes) which can be read by computers; **post code** *or* *US* **zip code** = letters and numbers used to indicate a town *or* street in an address on an envelope; **stock code** = numbers and letters which refer to an item of stock **(d)** set of rules; **code of practice** = rules drawn up by an association which the members must follow when doing business **2** *verb* **(a)** to convert instructions *or* data into another form **(b)** to write a program in a programming language

CODEC = CODER/DECODER electronic device that converts an audio or video signal into a digital form (and vice versa) using various analogue to digital conversion techniques such as pulse code modulation; *see also* A/D, D/A, PCM

codepage *noun* the definition of the character that is produced by each key on the keyboard; in order to use your computer when typing in a different language you need to change the keyboard layout and the font that is used for the characters - both are defined by the codepage

coder *noun* device which encodes a signal

coding *noun* act of putting a code on something; *the coding of data*; **coding sheet** *or* **coding form** = special printed sheet used by programmers to write instructions for coding a certain type of program

coercivity *noun* magnetic field required to remove any flux saturation effects from a material

coherent *adjective* referring to waveforms which are all in phase; *the laser produces coherent light*; **coherent bundle** = number of optical fibres, grouped together so that they are all the same length and produce coherent signals from either end

coil *noun* number of turns of wire; *an inductor is made from a coil of wire*

coincidence circuit *noun* electronic circuit that produces an output signal when two inputs occur simultaneously *or* two binary words are equal

cold *adjective* **(a)** not hot; *the machines work badly in cold weather; the office was so cold that the staff started complaining; we have to air-condition the computer room to keep the air cold enough to prevent the computers overheating* **(b)** without being prepared; **cold boot** = switching on a computer; **cold call** = sales call where the salesman has no appointment and the customer is not known to the company; **cold standby** = backup system that will allow the equipment to continue running, but with the loss of any volatile data; *compare with* HOT STANDBY, WARM STANDBY; **cold start** = (i) starting a new business *or* opening a new shop where there was none before; (ii) switching on a computer *or* to run a program from its original start point; *compare with* WARM START

collaboration *noun* two or more people working together to produce or use a multimedia application

collate *verb* **(a)** to compare and put items in order **(b)** to put signatures in order for sewing and binding; **collating marks** = marks printed on the spine of a signature so that the binder can see if they have been collated in correct order; **collating sequence** = (i) characters ordered according to their codes; (ii) order in which signatures are stacked for printing

collator *noun* machine which takes sheets *or* printed signatures and puts them in order for stapling *or* binding

collect 1 *verb* **(a)** to make someone pay money which is owed; **to collect a debt** = to go and make someone pay a debt **(b)** to take things away from a place; *we have to collect the stock from the warehouse; can you collect my letters from the typing pool?*; **letters are collected twice a day** = the post office workers take them from the letter box to the post office to be sent **2** *adverb & adjective* US **collect call** = (phone call) where the person receiving the call agrees to pay for it; *to make a collect call; he called his office collect*

collection *noun* **(a)** gathering together **(b)** series of items put together

collector *noun* **(a)** person who makes people pay money which is owed; *collector of taxes or tax collector; debt collector* **(b)** connection to a bipolar transistor

college *noun* place where people can study after they have left school; **business college** = college which teaches general business methods

collision *noun* two signals that interfere with each other over a network, normally causing an error; **collision detection** = the detecting and reporting of the coincidence of two actions *or* events

co-location *noun* computer used solely by one company as an Internet server that is located at a specialist site which provides maintenance and high-speed links to the Internet

COMMENT: many websites are published on disk space rented from an Internet company; if the website is very complex or large, it might need its own server computer. A company could install a server computer in their office, but it is often easier to rent an entire computer that is located at an Internet service provider's office. The service provider provides maintenance and high-speed connections to the Internet, the customer pays a monthly or yearly rental and has sole use of the computer and its disk storage space.

colon *noun* printing sign (:), which shows a break in a string of words

colophon *noun* design *or* symbol *or* company name, used on a printed item to show who are the publisher and the printer

colorisation *noun* *(film)* an electronic process of adding colour to a videotape transfer of a black and white film to be transmitted on television

colour *noun* sensation sensed by the eye, due to its response to various frequencies of light; **colour balance** = the relationship between colour elements on film or television pictures; elements can be adjusted to provide a pleasing over-all picture; *(film)* **colour bars** = video test waveform; **colour bits** = number of data bits assigned to a pixel to describe its colour; one bit provides two colours, two bits give four colours and eight bits allow 256 colour combinations; **colour burst** = part of a TV signal used to provide information about the hue of the colour; **colour cell** = smallest area on a CRT screen that can display colour information; **colour correction** = altering characteristics such as balance in a colour reproduction system in order to improve the quality of the image; **colour cycling** = to change the colours in a palette over a period of time, normally used to create a special effect or animation; **colour decoder** = device which converts colour burst and picture signals so that they can be displayed on a screen; **colour depth** = number of bits used to describe the colour of a pixel; for example, if four bits are used to describe each pixel, it can support 16 different colours and has a depth of 4-bits; **colour display** = display device able to represent characters *or* graphics in colour; **colour encoder** = device that produces a standard TV signal from separate Red, Green and Blue signals; **colour filter** = filter that blocks all colours of light except one; **colour graphics adapter (CGA)** =

popular microcomputer colour display system; **colour key** = image manipulation technique used to superimpose one image on another; often used with two video sources to create special effects - one image is photographed against a blue (matte) background which is then superimposed with another image to produce a combined picture; see also CHROMA KEY, MATTE; **colour look-up table (CLUT)** = table of values that define the colours in a palette, this allows a program to use colours without having to calculate them each time; **colour monitor** = screen that has a demodulator which shows information in colour; **colour palette** = range of colours which can be used (on a printer or display); **colour printer** = printer that can produce hard copy in colour; includes colour ink-jet, colour dot-matrix and thermal-transfer printers; **colour saturation** = purity of a colour signal; **colour separation** = process by which colours are separated into their primary colours; **colour separation overlay** = special effects technique used in video, similar to chromakey; **colour shift** = (unwanted) change in colour; **colour standard** = one of three international standards used to describe how colour TV and video images are displayed and transmitted: NTSC, PAL and SECAM; **colour temperature** = method of standardizing the colour of a body (at a certain temperature); **colour tool** = utility or icon in a graphics or DTP application that allows the user to create custom colours by specifying the CMYK or RGB values and then draw or fill an area with this colour; **colour transparency** = transparent positive film in colour, which can be used to project on a screen or to make film for printing; (film) **colour under** = recording process of a colour TV signal on to videotape which is common in most domestic video cassette recorders (NOTE: The stroke colour is the colour displayed when a line is drawn in a graphics program or a brush tool is used; fill colour is the colour used when filling an area of an image with colour; true colour normally refers to 24-bit colour image)

COMMENT: Full colour printing using a printing press requires four-colour separation to produce four printing plates for the cyan, magenta, yellow and black (CMYK) inks that together create a colour image

column noun **(a)** series of characters, printed one under the other; **to add up a column of figures; put the total at the bottom of the column; 80-column printer** = printer which has a maximum line width of 80 characters; **column report** = viewing data in columns; each column is one field of a record and each row a separate record **(b)** section of printed words in a newspaper or magazine; **column-centimetre** = space in centimetres in a newspaper column, used for calculating charges for advertising; (in a DTP application) **column guide** = vertical line that indicates the position and width of a column; (in word-processing software) **column indicator** = status bar at the bottom of the screen that displays in which column the cursor is positioned

columnar adjective in columns; **columnar graph** = graph on which values are shown as vertical or horizontal bars; **columnar working** = showing information in columns

COM = COMPUTER OUTPUT ON MICROFILM recording the output from a computer directly onto microfilm or microfiche

.com domain name suffix that indicates a business (originally, a company based in the USA, now refers to any commercial website); we registered two domain names for our US and UK offices: petercollin.com and petercollin.co.uk; see also DOMAIN

COM file noun (in operating systems for the PC) three-letter extension to a file name which indicates that the file contains a machine code in binary format and so can be executed by the operating system; to start the program, type the name of the COM file at the MS-DOS prompt

COM1 (in an IBM-compatible PC) name for the first serial port; see also AUX

COMMENT: if you plug an external modem into the first serial port, you are connecting it to COM1. There are normally two serial ports (COM1 and COM2) in a PC, although it can support four. Some PCs have a mouse plugged into the first serial port and the modem plugged into the second port.

Communications software needs to be configured so that it knows to which port a modem is connected

coma *noun* lens aberration

COMAL = COMMON ALGORITHMIC LANGUAGE structured programming language similar to BASIC

combi player *noun* hardware drive that can read two or more different CD-ROM formats

combination *noun* several things which are joined together; series of numbers which open a lock; *he forgot the combination of the safe*

combinational *adjective* which combines a number of separate elements; **combinational circuit** = electronic circuit consisting of a number of connected components; **combinational logic** = logic function made up from a number of separate logic gates

combine *verb* to join together; **combined station** = high-level data link control station that processes commands and responses

combo box *noun* box that displays a number of different input and output objects; for example, a list of options, together with radio buttons and a field in which the user can type their request

comic-strip oriented *adjective* film-image orientation in which the image runs perpendicular to the outer edge of the film

Comité consultatif International télégraphique et téléphonique *see* CCITT

comma *noun* symbol (,) that is often used to separate data *or* variables *or* arguments; **comma-delimited file** = data file in which each data item is separated by a comma; **inverted commas** = printing sign (" ") which marks the beginning and end of a quotation; *all databases can import and export to a comma-delimited file format*

command *noun* (a) word *or* phrase which is recognized by a computer system and starts *or* terminates an action; *interrupt command; the command to execute the program is RUN* (b) electrical pulse *or* signal that will start *or* stop a process; **command control language** = programming language that allows equipment to be easily controlled; **command-driven** = (software) that is controlled by the user typing in command words rather than making a selection from a menu; **command file** = sequence of frequently used commands stored in a file; **command interpreter** = program within an operating system that recognises a set of system commands and controls the processor, screen and storage devices accordingly; *when you type in the command 'DIR', the command interpreter asks the disk drive for a list of files and instructs the monitor to display the list; (on an Apple Macintosh)* **command key** = special key that gives access to various special functions, similar in effect to the Control key on an IBM PC; **command language** = programming language made up of procedures for various tasks, that can be called up by a series of commands; **command line** = (i) program line that contains a command instruction; (ii) command prompt and system command; **command line argument** = additional items entered following a command; *use the command 'DIR' to view the files on disk, add the command line argument 'A:' to view the files on drive A:;* **command line interface** = user interface in which the user controls the operating system (or program) by typing in commands; for example, DOS is a command line interface, Windows is a graphical user interface that can be controlled by using a mouse; *compare with* GUI; **command mode** = operating mode of a modem in which the user (or communications software) can send instructions to a modem; the standard method of switching a modem to command mode is to type or send it the three characters '+++' the modem will reply with an 'OK' message and is then ready to accept configuration or other commands; = *see also* AT COMMAND SET, HAYES COMPATIBLE; **command line operating system** = computer system software which is controlled by a user typing in commands (as in MS-DOS), now being replaced by GUI front-ends, such as Microsoft Windows, which allow a user to control the system through images; **command prompt** = symbol displayed to indicate a command is expected; **command state** = state of a modem in which it is ready to accept commands; **command string** = character string that contains all the information to carry out an MCI command; the string ends with a null character and is split by MCI into the command message and data structure; **command window** = area of a screen where commands are entered to control the low-level operation of a program, normally whilst another window displays the result; **command window history** = list of previous commands entered in the command window; **embedded command** = printer control command, such as indicating that text should be in italics, inserted into test and used by a word-processor when text formatting

```
This gives Unix a friendly
face instead of the
terrifyingly complex
command-line prompts that make
most users reach for their
manuals
```
Computing

COMMAND.COM *(in MS-DOS)* program file that contains the command interpreter for the operating system; this program is always resident in memory and recognises and translates system commands into actions; *MS-DOS will not work because you deleted the COMMAND.COM file by mistake*

comment *noun* helpful notes in a program to guide the user; **comment out** = temporarily disabling a command by enclosing it in a comment field

commentary *noun* spoken information which describes a film

commerce *see* E-COMMERCE, SECURE WEB SITE, SHOPPING CART

commerce server *noun* computer and specialist web software that provides the main functions of an online shop including managing the shopping cart and dealing with the credit card payment processing; *see also* SERVER, SHOPPING CART, SSL, WEBSITE

commercial *noun* advertising film on TV

Commodore Dynamic Total Vision (CDTV) *noun* CD-ROM standard developed by Commodore that combines audio, graphics and text; this standard is mainly intended as an interactive system for home use; the player connects to a television and can also play music CDs

common *adjective* **(a)** which happens very often; *putting the carbon paper in the wrong way round is a common mistake; being caught by the customs is very common these days* **(b)** belonging to several different people *or* to everyone; **common algorithmic language (COMAL)** = structured programming language similar to BASIC; **common carrier** = (i) firm which carries goods *or* passengers, and which anyone can use; (ii) company which can provide information services to the public; **common channel signalling** = one channel used as a communications link to a number of devices *or* circuits; **common intermediate format (CIF)** = videophone ISDN standard which displays colour images at a resolution of 352x288 pixels; this standard uses two ISDN B channels; **common management information protocol (CMIP)** = protocol officially adopted by the ISO used to carry network management information across a network; **common management information specification (CMIS)** = powerful network management system; **common mode noise** = external noise on all power and ground lines; **common ordinary business orientated language (COBOL)** = programming language mainly used in business applications; **common pricing** = illegal fixing of prices by several businesses so that they all charge the same price; **common real-time applications language (CORAL)** = programming language used in a real-time system

comms *(informal)* = COMMUNICATIONS

communicate *verb* to pass information to someone; *he finds it impossible to communicate with his staff; communicating with head office has been quicker since we installed the telex;* **communicating word processor** = word processor workstation which is able to transmit and receive data

communication *noun* **(a)** passing of information; *communication with the head office has been made easier by the telex;* **to enter into communication with someone** = to start discussing something with someone, usually in writing; *we have* *entered into communication with the relevant government department* **(b)** official message; *we have had a communication from the local tax office* **(c)** communications = process by which data is transmitted and received, by means of telephones, satellites, radio or any medium capable of carrying signals; **communications buffer** = terminal *or* modem that is able to store transmitted data; **communications computer** = computer used to control data transmission in a network; **communications control unit** = electronic device that controls data transmission and routes in a network; **communications interface adapter** = electronic circuit that allows a computer to communicate with a modem; **communications link** = physical path that joins a transmitter to a receiver; **communications link control** = processor that provides various handshaking and error detection functions for a number of links between devices; **communications network** = group of devices such as terminals and printers that are interconnected with a central computer, allowing the rapid and simple transfer of data; **communications network processor** = processor that provides various interfacing and management (buffering *or* code conversion) between a computer and communications link control; **communications package** = software that allows a user to control a modem and use an online service; **communications port** = socket or physical connection allowing a device to communicate; **communications protocol** = parameters that define how the transfer of information will be controlled; *the communications protocol for most dial-up online services is eight-bit words, no stop bit and even parity*; **communications satellite** = satellite used for channelling radio *or* television *or* data signals from one point on the earth to another; **communications scanner** = line monitoring equipment to check for data request signals; **communications server** = computer with a modem or fax card attached that allows users on a network to share the use of the modem; **communications software** = software that allows a user to control a modem and use an online service; *some on-line services, such*

as CompuServe and AOL, come with their own specially-written communications software; **data communications** = transmission and reception of data rather than speech *or* images; **data communications buffer** = buffer on a receiver that allows a slow peripheral to accept data from a fast peripheral, without slowing either down

---

it requires no additional hardware, other than the communications board in the PC
Electronics & Power

---

community *noun* group of people living *or* working in the same place; **the local business community** = the business people living and working in the area

community antenna television

(CATV) *noun* cable television system using a single aerial to pick up television signals and then distribute them over a wide area via cable

compact *adjective* (thing) which does not take up much space; **compact cassette** = audio recording tape contained inside a standard plastic box; **compact code** = minimum number of program instructions required for a task; **compact disc (CD)** = small plastic disc that contains audio signals in digital form etched onto the surface; **compact disc digital audio** = *see* CD DA; **compact disc-interactive** = *see* CD-I; **compact disc player** = machine that reads the digital data from a CD and converts it back to audio signals; **compact disc ROM** *or* **CD-ROM** = small plastic disc that is used as a high capacity ROM device, data is stored in binary form as holes on the surface which are then read by a laser; **compact disc video** = *see* CD-V; **compact disc write once** = *see* CD-WO; **compacting algorithm** = formula for reducing the amount of space required by text; **compact model** = memory model in the Intel 80x86 family of CPUs that allows only 64Kb of space for the code of a program, but 1Mb of space for the program's data

companding = COMPRESSING AND EXPANDING two processes which reduce *or* compact data before transmission *or* storage then restore packed data to its original form

compandor *noun* =
COMPRESSOR/EXPANDER device
used for companding signals

COMPAQ *noun* personal computer
company (founded in 1983) that was the
first manufacturer to produce a clone to the
IBM PC

comparability *noun* being able to be
compared; **pay comparability** = similar
pay system in two different companies
(NOTE: no plural)

comparable *adjective* which can be
compared; *the two sets of figures are not
comparable*; **which is the nearest
company comparable to this one in size?**
= which company is of a similar size and
can be compared with this one?

comparator *noun* electronic circuit
whose output is the difference between two
input signals

compare *verb* **(a)** to look at several things
to see how they differ; *the finance director
compared the figures for the first and
second quarters* **(b)** to check the differences
between two pieces of information

compare with *verb* to put two things
together to see how they differ; *how do the
sales this year compare with last year's?
compared with 2000, last year was a boom
year*

comparison *noun* way of comparing;
*sales are down in comparison with last
year*; **there is no comparison between
speeds of the two processors** = one of the
two is much faster than the other

compatibility *noun (of two hardware or
software devices)* ability to function
together; **compatibility box** = window or
session in an operating system that can
execute programs written for a different, but
related, operating system; *Mac System
software can support a compatibility box to
allow it to run Windows applications*

> COMMENT: by conforming to the
> standards of another manufacturer or
> organization, compatibility of hardware
> or software allows programs or hardware
> to be interchanged with no modifications

check for software
compatibility before choosing
a display or graphics adaptor
PC Business World

The manufacturer claims that
this card does not require
special drivers on the host
machine, as a flash-memory
card does, and therefore has
fewer compatibility problems
Computing

compatible 1 *adjective* (two hardware *or*
software devices) that function correctly
together; *is the hardware IBM-
compatible?* **2** *noun* hardware *or* software
device that functions correctly with other
equipment *or* is a clone; *this computer is
much cheaper than the other compatibles;
buy an IBM PC or a compatible*

low-cost compatibles have
begun to find homes as
terminals on LANS
Minicomputer News

it is a fairly standard
feature on most low-cost PC
compatibles
Which PC?

compilation *noun* translation of an
encoded source program into machine
readable code; **compilation error** = syntax
error found during compilation;
compilation time = length of time it takes
for a computer to compile program; *see also*
DECOMPILATION

compile *verb* to convert a high level
language program into a separate machine
code program that can be executed by itself;
compile and go = computer program not
requiring operator interaction that will load,
compile and execute a high level language
program

compiler (program) *noun* software that
translates a high-level language into
machine code that will run directly on a
processor; **compiler diagnostics** = features
in a compiler that help the programmer to
find any faults; *compare with*
INTERPRETER

This utility divides the
compilation of software into
pieces and performs the
compile in parallel across
available machines on the
network
Computergram

complement 1 *noun* inversion of a
binary digit; *the complement is found by*

changing the 1s to 0s and 0s to 1s; **one's complement** = inversion of a binary digit; **two's complement** = formed by adding one to the one's complement of a number **2** *verb* to invert a binary digit; **complemented** = (binary digit) that has had a complement performed

complementary *adjective* (two things) that complete each other *or* go well together; *(film)* **complementary colours** = colours resulting from subtracting a specific colour from white light, therefore the complementary colour to red is 'minus red,' which is cyan (blue-green); **complementary metal oxide semiconductor (CMOS)** = integrated circuit design and construction method (using a pair of complementary p- and n-type transistors)

complementation *noun* number system used to represent positive and negative numbers

complete 1 *adjective* finished *or* all ready; *the signatures are all complete and ready for binding; the spelling check is complete* **2** *verb* to finish a task; *when you have completed the keyboarding, pass the text through the spelling checker*

completion *noun* time when something is complete; *completion date for dispatch of bound copies is November 15th*

complex instruction set computer *see* CISC

complex 1 *adjective* very complicated *or* difficult to understand; *the complex mathematical formula was difficult to solve; the controller must work hard to operate this complex network* **2** *noun* series of buildings, housing workshops and laboratories, etc.; *the office complex houses all the staff*

complexity *noun* being complicated

complicated *adjective* with many different parts *or* difficult to understand; *this program is very complicated; the computer design is more complicated than necessary*

component *noun* (a) piece of machinery *or* section which will be put into a final product (b) electronic device that produces an electrical signal; *the assembly line stopped because supply of a component was delayed; which component goes on the PCB here? the component burnt out due to*

excessive input signal; **components factory** = factory which makes parts which are used in other factories to make finished products; **Component Object Model (COM)** = set of rules that define the way in which objects within the Windows OLE system interact with other documents, objects and applications

compose *verb* to arrange the required type, in the correct order, prior to printing; **composing room** = room in a typesetters *or* in a newspaper, where the text is composed by compositors

composite circuit *noun* electronic circuit made up of a number of smaller circuits and components

composite display *noun* video display unit that accepts a single composite video signal and can display an infinite number of colours *or* shade of grey

composite print *noun* (film) copy of a film (called the print) that includes both audio and visual effects

composite video signal *noun* single television signal containing synchronizing pulse and video signal in a modulated form

composite video *noun* video signal which combines the colour signals and the monochrome signal into one single signal; *most TV set and video players expect a composite video feed; a composite video display is not as clear or crisp as a display that uses separate red, green and blue signals from a computer or a video source*

composition *noun* creating typeset text, either using metal type *or* by keyboarding on a computer typesetter; **composition size** = printing type size

compositor *noun* person who sets up the required type prior to printing; **electronic compositor** = computer that allows a user to easily arrange text on screen before it is electronically typeset

compound device *noun* Windows MCI multimedia device that requires a data file, such as a sound card that plays back a WAV file controlled by the waveform audio driver

compound document *noun* document that contains information created by several other applications; *see also* OLE

COMMENT: this is a feature of most Microsoft Windows that allows a user to include formatted information from one application in another; for example, if you write a letter using a wordprocessor then embed a WAV file voice message the result is a compound document; the technology to support compound documents was developed with Microsoft Windows 3.1 which included OLE, a feature that allows data from one application to be embedded in a document

compound file *noun* individual files grouped together in one file

compound statement *noun* a number of program instructions in one line of program

compress *verb* to squeeze something to fit into a smaller space; **compressed audio** = audio signals that have been adjusted to fit inside sound level limits; **compressed video** = video signals that have been compressed to reduce the data rate required to transmit the information; *a normal television picture is transmitted at around 50-90Mbits/second, a compressed video signal can be transmitted at around one tenth of the data rate*

compression *noun* varying the gain of a device depending on input level to maintain an output signal within certain limits; *see also* RLE; **compression ratio** = ratio of the size of an original, uncompressed file to the final, compressed file that has been more efficiently encoded; **data compression** = means of reducing the size of blocks of data by removing spaces, empty sections and unused material; **disk compression software** = resident software that compresses data as it is written to disk and de-compresses it as it is read back

compressor *noun* **(a)** electronic circuit which compresses a signal **(b)** (program *or* device) that provides data compression; **audio compressor** = circuit which limits the maximum signal level

comptometer *noun* machine which counts automatically

CompuServe one of the largest online Internet service providers and online information services; the service provides access to the Internet with local telephone access numbers worldwide; users can access the Internet, electronic mail and a range of databases and forums

computable *adjective* which can be calculated

computation *noun* calculation

computational *adjective* referring to computation; **computational error** = mistake made in calculating

compute *verb* to calculate *or* to do calculations

computer *noun* **(a)** machine that receives *or* stores *or* processes data very quickly according to a stored program; **business computer** = powerful small computer which is programmed for special business uses; **mainframe computer** = large scale powerful computer system that can handle high capacity memory and backing storage devices as well as a number of operators simultaneously; **microcomputer** *or* **micro** = complete small-scale, cheap, low-power computer system based around a microprocessor chip and having limited memory capacity; **minicomputer** *or* **mini** = small computer with a greater range of instructions and processing power than a microcomputer, but not able to compete with the speed or data handling capacity of a mainframe computer; **personal computer (PC)** = small computer which can be used in the home; **supercomputer** = very powerful mainframe computer used for high speed mathematical tasks **(b)** **computer animation** = making a series of computer-generated images displayed in sequence to emulate motion; **computer bureau** = office which offers to do work on its computers for companies which do not have their own computers; **computer conferencing** = connecting a number of computers *or* terminals together to allow a group of users to communicate; **computer crime** = theft, fraud or other crimes involving computers; **computer dating** = use of a computer to match single people who may want to get married; **computer department** = department in a company which manages the company's computers; **computer engineer** = person who maintains *or* programs *or* designs computer equipment; **computer error** = mistake made by a computer; **computer file** = section of information on a computer (such as the payroll, list of addresses, customer accounts); **computer graphics** = information represented graphically on a computer display; **computer graphics metafile (CGM)** = device-independent file format that provides one method of storing an image as objects; **computer input from microfilm (CIM)** = use of microfilm for computer data storage, and the method of reading the data; **computer language** = language (formed of figures *or* characters) used to communicate with a computer; **computer listing** = printout of a list of items taken from data stored in a computer; **computer literacy** = understanding the basic principles of computers, related expressions and concepts, and being able to use computers for programming *or* applications; **computer-literate** = (person) able to understand how to use a computer, the expressions and concepts used; *the managing director is simply not computer-literate*; **computer mail** = messages sent between users of a bulletin board *or* network; **computer manager** = person in charge of a computer department; *(in Windows)* **computer name** = identifying name of each computer that is connected to a network; = **computer names** = *(in Windows)* series of words that identify a computer on a network; each computer that is connected to a network is given an identifying name, if you are linked to an office network, you will see an icon on your Desktop called Network Neighborhood. Double-click on this and it will display a list of the other computers on the network, and their computer name; **computer network** = number of computers, terminals and peripherals connected together to allow communications between each; **computer numeric control (CNC)** = control of a machine by computer; **computer office system** = computer and related peripherals used for office tasks (filing, word processing, etc.); **computer operator** = person who operates a computer; **computer output** = data *or* information produced after processing by a computer; **computer output on microfilm (COM)** = information output from a computer, stored directly onto microfilm; **computer program** = series of instructions to a computer, telling it to do a particular piece of work; **computer programmer** = person who writes computer programs; **computer science** = scientific study of computers, the construction of hardware and development

of software; **computer services** = work using a computer, done by a computer bureau; **computer system** = a central processor with storage and associated peripherals that make up a working computer; **computer time** = time when a computer is being used (paid for at an hourly rate); *running all those sales reports costs a lot in computer time*; **computer virus** = program which adds itself to an executable file and copies (or spreads) itself to other executable files each time an infected file is run; a virus can corrupt data, display a message or do nothing

computer- *prefix* referring to a computer; **computer-based learning (CBL)** = learning mainly using a computer; **computer-based message system (CBMS)** = use of a computer system to allow users to send and receive messages from other users (usually in-house); **computer-based training (CBT)** = use of a computer system to train students; **computer-generated** = which has been generated by a computer; *computer-generated graphics*; **computer-integrated manufacturing (CIM)** = coordinated use of computers in every aspect of design and manufacturing; **computer-integrated systems** = coordinated use of computers and other related equipment in a process; *this firm is a very well-known supplier of computer-integrated systems which allow both batch pagination of very long documents with alteration of individual pages*; **computer-managed instruction (CMI)** = using a computer to assist students in learning a subject; **computer-managed learning (CML)** = using a computer to teach students and assess their progress; **computer-readable** = which can be read and understood by a computer; *computer-readable codes*

computer-aided *or* **computer-assisted** *adjective* which uses a computer to make the work easier; **computer-aided** *or* **assisted design (CAD)** = the use of computer and graphics terminal to help designers in their work; **computer-aided** *or* **assisted engineering (CAE)** = use of a computer to help an engineer solve problems *or* calculate design *or* product specifications; **computer-aided** *or* **assisted instruction (CAI)** = use of a computer to assist pupils in learning a subject;

computer-aided *or* **assisted learning (CAL)** = use of a computer to assist pupils to learn a subject; **computer-aided** *or* **assisted manufacture** *or* **manufacturing (CAM)** = use of a computer to control machinery *or* to assist in a manufacturing process; **computer-aided** *or* **assisted testing (CAT)** = use of a computer to test equipment *or* programs to find any faults; **computer-aided** *or* **assisted training (CAT)** = use of a computer to demonstrate to and assist pupils in learning a skill

computer generations *noun* way of defining the advances in the field of computing

COMMENT: the development of computers has been divided into a series of 'generations': **first generation:** computers constructed using valves having limited storage; **second generation:** computers where transistors were used in construction; **third generation:** use of integrated circuits in construction; **fourth generation:** most often used at present, using low cost memory and IC packages; **fifth generation:** future computers using very fast processors, large memory and allowing human input/output

computerization *noun* action of introducing a computer system *or* of changing from a manual to a computer system; *computerization of the financial sector is proceeding very fast*

computerize *verb* to change from a manual system to one using computers; *our stock control has been completely computerized; they operate a computerized invoicing system;* **computerized branch exchange (CBX)** = telephone exchange operated by computer

computing *adjective & noun* referring to computers *or* work done on computers; **computing power** = measure of speed and ability of a computer to perform calculations; **computing speed** = speed at which a computer calculates

CON *noun* (*in IBM-PC compatible systems*) name used to identify the console: the keyboard and monitor

concatenate *noun* to join together two files or variables

concatenation *noun* joining together of two or more sets of data; **concatenation operator** = instruction that joins two pieces of data or variables together

conceal *verb* to hide *or* not display information *or* graphics from a user

concentrate *verb* (**a**) to focus a beam onto a narrow point (**b**) to combine a number of lines *or* circuits *or* data to take up less space; *to concentrate a beam of light on a lens; the concentrated data was transmitted cheaply*

concentrator *noun* (**a**) (*in a Token-Ring network*) device at the centre of a Token-Ring network which provides a logical star topology in which nodes are connected to the concentrator, but connects each arm of the star as a physical ring within the device (**b**) (*in an FDDI network*) node which provides access for one or more stations to the network (**c**) (*in a 10Base-T Ethernet network*) the device at the centre of a star-topology 10Base-T Ethernet network that receives signals from one port and regenerates them before sending them out to the other ports (**d**) (*in general networking*) device where all the cables from nodes are interconnected

conceptual model *noun* description of a database or program in terms of the data it contains and its relationships

concertina fold *noun* accordion fold *or* method of folding continuous paper, one sheet in one direction, the next sheet in the opposite direction, allowing the paper to be fed into a printer continuously with no action on the part of the user

concurrency *noun* data or resources that are accessed by more than one user or application at the same time

concurrent *adjective* almost simultaneous (actions *or* sets); **concurrent operating system** = operating system software that allows several programs *or* activities to be processed at the same time; **concurrent processing** = *see* MULTITASKING; **concurrent programming** = running several programs apparently simultaneously, achieved by executing small sections from each program in turn

concurrently *adverb* running at almost the same time

```
The         system         uses
p a r a l l e l - p r o c e s s i n g
technology  to  allow  support
for    large    numbers    of
concurrent users
```
Computing

condenser lens *noun* optical device, usually made of glass, that concentrates a beam of light onto a certain area

condensor microphone *see* CAPACITOR MICROPHONE

condition 1 *noun* **(a)** term of a contract *or* duties which have to be carried out as part of a contract *or* something which has to be agreed before a contract becomes valid; **conditions of sale** = agreed ways in which a sale takes place (such as discounts *or* credit terms) **(b)** general state; *the staff have complained of the bad working conditions in the factory; a demonstration model sold in good condition; what was the condition of the system when it was returned to the factory?* **2** *verb* to modify data that is to be transmitted so as to meet set parameters

conditional *adjective* **(a)** provided that certain things take place; **to give a conditional acceptance** = to accept, provided that certain things happen *or* certain terms apply; **the offer is conditional on the board's acceptance** = provided the board accepts; **he made a conditional offer** = he offered to buy, provided that certain terms applied **(b)** (process) which is dependent on the result of another; **conditional jump** *or* **branch** = programming instruction that provides a jump to a section of a program if a certain condition is met; **conditional statement** = program instruction that will redirect program control according to the outcome of an event

conduct *verb* to allow an electrical current to flow through a material; *to conduct electricity; copper conducts well*

conduction *noun* ability of a material to conduct; *the conduction of electricity by gold contacts*

conductive *adjective* referring to the ability of a material to conduct

conductor *noun* substance (such as a metal) which conducts electricity; *copper is a good conductor of electricity; see also* SEMICONDUCTOR

conduit *noun* protective pipe *or* channel for wires *or* cables

cone *noun* moving section in most loudspeakers

conference *noun* meeting of people to discuss problems; **to be in conference** = to be in a meeting; **conference phone** = telephone so arranged that several people can speak into it from around a table; **conference room** = room where small meetings can take place; **conference call** = telephone call which connects together three or more telephone lines allowing each person *or* device to communicate with all the others; **press conference** = meeting where newspaper and TV reporters are invited to hear news of a new product *or* a change of management, etc.

conferencing *noun* teleconferencing *or* holding a meeting of people in different places, using the telephones to allow each person to communicate with the others; **computer conferencing** = connecting a number of computers *or* terminals together to allow a group of users to communicate

```
Small    organisations    and
individuals find it convenient
to   use   online   services,
offering email, conferencing
and information services
```
Computing

confidence *noun* **(a)** feeling sure *or* being certain; *the sales teams do not have much confidence in their manager; the board has total confidence in the new system* **(b)** **in confidence** = in secret; *I will show you the report in confidence*

confidence level *noun* likelihood that a number will lie to within a range of values

confident *adjective* certain *or* sure; *I am confident the sales will increase rapidly; are you confident the sales team is capable of handling this product?*

confidential *adjective* secret; *a confidential report on the new product*

CONFIG.SYS *(on a PC, in DOS, and Windows)* configuration text file that contains commands to set parameters and load driver software; this file is read automatically once the PC is switched on and the operating system has loaded; *if you add a new adapter card to your PC you will have to add a new command to the*

CONFIG.SYS file; do not delete an existing CONFIG.SYS file or make inappropriate changes to it as this may prevent software and add-ons from working properly; see also AUTOEXEC.BAT

> COMMENT: CONFIG.SYS is one of two special text files that the user can create to configure the initial environment of the PC and load special device drivers. It is a file stored in the root directory of the disk used to start the PC (usually the hard disk if one is fitted or a floppy in drive A:) and the special commands stored in it are automatically executed when DOS starts up. The other startup file is AUTOEXEC.BAT which contains ordinary DOS commands that are executed after CONFIG.SYS. The CONFIG.SYS file is often altered automatically if you install new programs onto your PC

configuration *noun* way in which the hardware and software of a computer system are planned

configure *verb* to select hardware, software and interconnections to make up a special system; *this terminal has been configured to display graphics*

configured-in *adjective* (device) whose configuration state indicates it is ready and available for use

> COMMENT: when installing a new software application there are two main steps: the first is the installation, which creates a new folder and copies the files onto the hard disk from the floppy disk or CD-ROM. Once the program is installed, it can be configured to work the way you want. For example, to change the way Windows looks, use the Control Panel and select the Start button then the Settings option. This displays a set of icons that let you define the basic look and feel of Windows: from the speed and sensitivity of the mouse to the language used and the type of printer that is connected to your PC. For DOS users, the system is configured with commands stored in two files: AUTOEXEC.BAT and CONFIG.SYS

It had the network configuration and administration capabilities required for implementing an international business plan based on client-server computing

Computing

the machine uses RAM to store system configuration information

PC Business World

several configuration files are provided to assign memory to the program, depending on the available RAM on your system

PC Business World

users can configure four of the eight ports to handle links at speeds of 64K bit/sec

Computer News

if you modify a program with the editor, or with a word-processor specified in the configuration file, it will know that the program has changed and will execute the new one accordingly

PC Business World

confirm *verb* action to indicate that you agree with a particular action; *click on the OK button to confirm that you want to delete all your files*

conform *verb* to work according to set rules; *does the new socket conform to international standards?*

congestion *noun* state that occurs when communication *or* processing demands are greater than the capacity of a system

connect *verb* to link together two points in a circuit *or* communications network; *(in a commercial on-line database or system)* **connect charge** = the cost per minute of time when you are connected to the remote system; **connect state** = state of a modem in which it is transferring data across a communications line; **connect time** = length of time a user is logged onto an interactive system; **direct connect** = (modem) which plugs straight into a standard telephone socket

connection *noun* link *or* something which joins; **connection-oriented** = data transfer that occurs according to a series of fixed, pre-defined steps that will create a known and reliable path between the two devices; for example, TCP/IP is a connection-oriented protocol that uses a known modem or network adapter to contact another known computer and establish a link via TCP/IP commands; **parallel connection** = connector on a computer allowing parallel data to be transferred; *their transmission rate is 60,000 bps through parallel connection*

connectionless data transfer that occurs between two devices that do not have a fixed or permanent link and so can take different routes between the two devices; *see also* CIRCUIT SWITCHING

connectivity *noun* ability of a device to connect with other devices and transfer information

connector *noun* physical device with a number of metal contacts that allow devices to be easily linked together; *the connector at the end of the cable will fit any standard serial port*; *see also* FEMALE CONNECTOR, MALE CONNECTOR; *(in an FDDI network)* **connector plug** = device at the end of a fibre-optic or copper cable that connects to a receptacle; **connector receptacle** = device mounted on a panel that connects to a plug

consecutive *adjective* following one after another; *the computer ran three consecutive files*

consecutively *adverb* one after the other; *the sections of the program run consecutively*

consistency check *noun* check to make sure that objects, data or items conform to their expected formats

console *noun* unit (keyboard and VDU, and usually a printer) which allows an operator to communicate with a computer system; *the console consists of input device such as a keyboard, and an output device such as a printer or CRT*; *see also* CON

constant 1 *noun* item of data, whose value does not change (as opposed to a variable) **2** *adjective* which does not change; *the disk drive motor spins at a constant velocity*; **constant angular velocity (CAV)** = CD-ROM that spins at a constant speed; the size of each data frame on the disc varies so as to maintain a regular data throughput of one frame per second; any frame will be slightly larger than the

one after it and slightly smaller than the one before it; *compare with* CONSTANT LINEAR VELOCITY; **constant linear velocity (CLV)** = disk technology in which the disk spins at different speeds according to the track that is being accessed; by varying the speed of the disk, the physical density of bits in each track remains the same, so the tracks at the outer edge of the disk hold more data than the inner tracks; CLV is normally used with CD-ROM drives; *compare with* CONSTANT ANGULAR VELOCITY; **constant length field** = data field that always contains the same number of characters; **constant ratio code** = character representation code that has a constant number of binary ones per word length

constrain *verb* to set limits that define the maximum movement of an object on screen

construct *verb* to build *or* to make (a device *or* a system)

construction *noun* building *or* making of a system; *construction of the prototype is advancing rapidly; construction techniques have changed over the past few years*

consult *verb* to ask an expert for advice; *he consulted his the maintenance manager about the disk fault*

consultancy *noun* act of giving specialist advice; *a consultancy firm; he offers a consultancy service*

consultant *noun* specialist who gives advice; *engineering consultant; management consultant; computer consultant*

consumable *adjective* **consumable goods** = goods which are bought by members of the public and not by companies

consumables *plural noun* small cheap extra items required in the day-to-day running of a computer system (such as paper and printer ribbons); *put all the printer leads and paper over with the other consumables*

consumer market *noun* potential market for a product that is based on the general public buying advertised products from a shop rather than a specialist or academic market

consumption *noun* buying *or* using goods or services; *a car with low petrol consumption; the office has a heavy consumption of listing paper*; **home consumption** *or* **domestic consumption** = use of something in the home (NOTE: no plural)

contact 1 *noun* **(a)** section of a switch *or* connector that provides an electrical path when it touches another conductor; *the circuit is not working because the contact is dirty*; **contact image sensor (CIS)** = scanner in which the detectors (a flat bar of light-sensitive diodes) touch the original, without any lens that might distort the image; **contact microphone** = microphone which picks up vibrations through physical contact with a person or object; **contact printing** photographic printing process in which the negative touches the light-sensitive paper **(b)** person you know *or* person you can ask for help or advice; *he has many contacts in the city; who is your contact in the German company?* **(c)** act of getting in touch with someone; **I have lost contact with them** = I do not communicate with them any longer; **he put me in contact with a good lawyer** = he told me how to get in touch with a good lawyer (NOTE: no plural for (c)) **2** *verb* **(a)** to get in touch with someone *or* to communicate with someone; *he tried to contact his office by phone; can you contact the managing director at his club?* **(b)** to try to call a user *or* device in a network; *I've been trying to contact the operator, but the line is always busy*

contain *verb* to hold something inside; *each carton contains two computers and their peripherals; a barrel contains 250 litres; we have lost a file containing important documents*

container *noun* **(a)** box *or* bottle *or* can, etc. which can hold goods; *the ink is sold in strong metal containers; the container burst while it was being loaded* **(b)** very large metal case of a standard size for loading and carrying goods on trucks, trains and ships; *container ship; container port; container terminal; to ship goods in containers* **(c)** something that can be set to a value; for example, a variable is a container, as is an object's colour or position or other properties

containerization *noun* putting into containers; carrying goods in containers

containerize *verb* to put goods into containers; to ship goods in containers

content *noun* text, images, sound, video and information within a database or multimedia application; **the content of the letter** = the real meaning of the letter; **to read a manuscript for content** = to read it to see if the ideas in it make sense; **content provider** = company or person who owns the copyright of text or images in an application; **content-rich** = website or multimedia application that contains a lot of useful data or information; *this newspaper website is content-rich*

content-addressable *adjective* **content-addressable file** *or* **location** = method of storing data in which each item may be individually accessed; **content-addressable storage** *or* **associative storage** = method of data retrieval which uses part of the data rather than an address to locate the data

contention *noun* situation that occurs when two or more devices are trying to communicate with the same piece of equipment; **contention bus** = communication control system in which a device must wait for a free moment before transmitting data; **contention delay** = length of time spent waiting for equipment to become free for use

contents *plural noun* **(a)** things contained *or* what is inside something; *the contents of the bottle poured out onto the computer keyboard; the customs officials inspected the contents of the box*; **the contents of the letter** = the words written in the letter **(b)** list of items in a file *or* in a book; **table of contents** *or* **contents list** = list of the main chapters in a book, given usually at the beginning

context *noun* words and phrases among which a word is used; *the example shows how the word is used in context*

context-sensitive *adjective* (information) which relates to the particular context; **context-sensitive help** = help message that gives useful information about the particular function or part of the program you are in rather than general information about the whole program

context-switching *noun* process in which several programs are loaded in memory, but only one at a time can be executed

COMMENT: Unlike a true multi-tasking system which can load several programs into memory and run several programs at once, context-switching only allows one program to be run at a time

contiguous *adjective* items that are next to each other without spacing; **contiguous disk area** = area of disk storage that is made up of one block of adjacent sectors; **contiguous graphics** = graphic cells *or* characters that touch each other; *most display units do not provide contiguous graphics: their characters have a small space on each side to improve legibility*

```
If you later edit the file
again, some of the new data
clusters will not be
contiguous with the original
clusters but spread around the
disk
```
Computing

continual *adjective* which happens again and again; *production was slow because of continual breakdowns; the continual system breakdowns have slowed down the processing*

continually *adverb* again and again; *the photocopier is continually breaking down*

continuation *noun* act of continuing; **continuation page** = page *or* screen of text that follows on from a main page

continue *verb* to go on doing something *or* to do something which you were doing earlier; *the chairman continued speaking in spite of the noise; the meeting started at 10 a.m. and continued until six p.m.; printing will continue all night*

continuity *noun* (a) clear conduction path between two points; **continuity check** = test to see whether a conduction path exists between two points (b) checking that the details of one scene in a film continue into the next scene to be shown, even if the two have been shot at different times; *(film)* **continuity person** = person who makes sure that there are no differences in details such as clothes, props or dialogue between takes in a film or television production;

(film) **continuity still** = photograph, usually a polaroid, taken of a scene to record details of clothes, props, lighting, etc. to enable accurate reproduction of scene for other shots

continuous *adjective* with no end *or* with no breaks; which goes on without stopping; **continuous feed** = device which feeds continuous stationery into a printer; **continuous loop** = endless piece of recording *or* projection tape; **continuous stationery** = paper made as one long sheet, used in computer printers; = **continuous tone** = image that uses all possible values of grey or colours, such as a photograph; = *see also* GREY-SCALE, LINE ART; **continuous wave** = high frequency waveform that can be modulated to carry data; *see also* CARRIER

continuously *adverb* without stopping; *the printer overheated after working continuously for five hours*

contouring *noun* (a) *(in a graphics application)* process that converts a wire-frame drawing into a solid-looking object by adding shadows and texture (b) *(in a graphics application)* function that creates realistic-looking ground or a surface, for example to create the ground in a virtual-reality system

contrast 1 *noun* (a) difference between black and white tones or between colours; *the control allows you to adjust brightness and contrast*; **contrast enhancement filter** = special filter put over a monitor to increase contrast and prevent eye-strain (b) control knob on a display that alters the difference between black and white tones or between colours **2** *verb* to examine the differences between two sets of information; *the old data was contrasted with the latest information*

contrasting *adjective* which show a sharp difference; *a cover design in contrasting colours*

control 1 *verb* to be in charge of something *or* to make sure that something is kept in check; **controlled vocabulary** = set of terms *or* words used in an indexing language (NOTE: **controlling - controlled**) **2** *noun* (a) power *or* being able to direct something; *the company is under the control of three directors; the family lost control of its business; to gain control of a*

business = to buy more than 50% of the shares so that you can direct the business; **to lose control of a business** = to find that you have less than 50% of the shares in a company, and so are not longer able to direct it **(b)** restricting *or* checking something *or* making sure that something is kept in check; **out of control** = not kept in check; **under control** = kept in check; *breaks in production are kept under tight control; the company is trying to bring its costs under control;* **stock control** = making sure that movements of stock are noted **(c)** key on a computer keyboard which sends a control character; **control block** = reserved area of computer memory that contains control data; **control bus** = set of connections to a microcomputer that carry the control signals between CPU, memory and input/output devices; **control cards** = in a punched card system, the first cards which contain the processor control instructions; *(in MIDI)* **control change** = message sent to a synthesizer to instruct it to change a setting, for example to change the volume of a MIDI channel; **control character** = special character that provides a control sequence rather than a alphanumeric character; normally a non-printing character that changes the appearance of text; **control computer** = dedicated computer used to control a process *or* piece of equipment; **control driven** = computer architecture where instructions are executed once a control sequence has been received; *(on IBM-PC compatible systems)* **control key** *or* **Ctrl** = special key (in the lower left corner) that provides a secondary function when pressed with another key; *to halt a program, press Ctrl-C - the control key and letter C - at the same time; to reset your PC, press Ctrl-Alt-Del; (in Microsoft Windows)* **control menu** = menu that allows you to move, resize or close the current window; the menu is accessed by pressing Alt-Space; **control mode** = state of a device in which control signals can be received to select options *or* functions; **control panel** = (i) main computer system control switches and status indicators; (ii) *(in Windows and Macintosh)* utility that displays the user-definable options such as keyboard, country-code and type of mouse; **control program/monitor** *or* **control program for**

microcomputers (CP/M) = popular operating system for microcomputers; **control register** = storage location only used for control data; **control room** = room in a TV studio where the director watches the monitors of the film being shot and switches from one to another; **control signals** = electrical signals transmitted to control the actions of a circuit; **control sequence** = (series of) codes containing a control character and various arguments, used to carry out a process *or* change mode in a device; **control structure** = set of instructions that are run in a particular circumstance; an IF..THEN statement selects a particular control structure depending on the value of a variable; **control token** = special sequence of bits transmitted over a LAN to provide control actions; **control total** = result of summing certain fields in a computer file to provide error detection; **control unit (CU)** = section of central processor that selects and executes instructions **(d) control group** = small group which is used to check a sample group; **control systems** = systems used to check that a computer system is working correctly

controllable *adjective* which can be controlled

controller *noun* **(a)** person who controls (especially a company's money); **stock controller** = person who notes movements of stock **(b)** hardware *or* software device that controls a peripheral (such as a printer) *or* monitors and directs the data transmission over a local area network; **printer's controller** = main device in a printer that translates output from the computer into printing instructions; *see also* DEVICE DRIVER

```
a printer's controller is the
brains of the machine. It
translates the signals coming
from your computer into
printing instructions that
result in a hard copy of your
electronic document
```
Publish

conventional memory *or* **RAM** *noun (in an IBM-PC compatible system)* the random access memory region installed in a PC from 0 up to 640Kb; this area of memory can be directly controlled by MS-DOS and it is where most programs are loaded when they are executed; *compare with* HIGH MEMORY, EXPANDED MEMORY

convergence *noun* a measure of how accurately the three colour beams (red, green, blue) in a colour monitor align and track when drawing an image on the screen; *see also* FOCUS, DOT PITCH

conversational mode *noun* computer system that provides immediate responses to a user's input; *see also* INTERACTIVE MODE

conversion *noun* change from one system to another; **conversion tables** *or* **translation tables** = lookup tables *or* collection of stored results that can be accessed very rapidly by a process without the need to calculate each result when needed; *conversion tables may be created and used in conjunction with the customer's data to convert it to typesetting codes*

convert *verb* to change one thing into another

converter *or* **convertor** *noun* device *or* program that translates data from one form to another; *the convertor allowed the old data to be used on the new system*

convertibility *noun* ability to be changed

convertible *adjective* which can be converted

convey *verb* to carry *or* import information; *the chart conveyed the sales problem graphically*

conveyor *noun* method of carrying paper using a moving belt

cooperative processing *noun* system in which two or more computers in a distributed network can each execute a part of a program or work on a particular set of data

coordinate 1 *noun* **coordinates** = values used to locate a point on a graph *or* map; **coordinate graph** = means of displaying one point on a graph, using two values referring to axes which are usually at right angles to each other; **polar coordinates** = use of a distance and a direction to locate a point; **rectangular coordinates** = two numbers referring to distances along axes at right angles from an origin **2** *verb* to organize complex tasks, so that they fit together efficiently; *she has to coordinate*

the keyboarding of several parts of a file in six different locations

coordination *noun* organizing complex tasks; synchronizing two *or* more processes

copier = COPYING MACHINE, PHOTOCOPIER

copper *noun* red-coloured soft metal, a good conductor of electricity, used in wires and as connecting tracks on PCBs

copperplate printing *noun* printing method that uses a copper plate on which the image is etched

coprocessor *noun* extra, specialized processor, such as a numerical processor that can work with a main CPU to increase execution speed

```
Inmos is hiring designers to
create highly integrated
transputers and co-processors
for diverse computer and
telecoms systems
```
Computing

copy 1 *noun* **(a)** document which looks the same as another; duplicate of an original; **carbon copy** = copy made with carbon paper; **file copy** = copy of a document which is filed in an office for reference **(b)** document; **fair copy** *or* **final copy** = document which is written *or* typed with no changes *or* mistakes; **hard copy** = printout of a text which is on a computer *or* printed copy of something which is on microfilm; **rough copy** = draft of a document which, it is expected, will have changes made to it before it is complete; **top copy** = first *or* top sheet of a document which is typed with carbon copies **(c)** text of material ready to be keyboarded; *Tuesday is the last date for copy for the advertisement*; **copy reader** = person who checks copy before printing **(d)** a book *or* a newspaper; *I kept yesterday's copy of 'The Times'; I read it in the office copy of 'Fortune'; where is my copy of the telephone directory?* **2** *verb* to make a second document which is like the first; to duplicate original data; *he copied the company report at night and took it home*; **COPY** = (operating system command) that copies the contents of one file to another file on a storage device; *make a copy of your data using the COPY command before you edit it*; **copy-and-paste** = to select a file or part of a file and copy it to a new location;

highlight this paragraph and copy-and-paste it at the bottom of the document

copy protect *noun & verb* switch to prevent copies of a disk being made; *the program is not copy protected*

copy protection *noun* preventing copies being made; *a hard disk may crash because of copy protection; the new product will come without copy protection*

copying machine *or* **copier** *noun* machine which makes copies of documents

copyright 1 *noun* legal right (lasting for fifty years after the death of an artist whose work has been published) which a writer or programmer has in his own work, allowing him not to have it copied without the payment of royalties (now extended to 70 years in the EU); **Copyright Act** = (in the UK) Act of Parliament making copyright legal, and controlling the copying of copyright material; **copyright law** = laws concerning the protection of copyright; **work which is out of copyright** = work by a writer, etc., who has been dead for fifty years, and which anyone can publish; **work still in copyright** = work by a living writer, or by a writer who has not been dead for fifty years; **infringement of copyright** *or* **copyright infringement** = act of illegally copying a work which is in copyright; **copyright notice** = note in a book showing who owns the copyright and the date of ownership; **copyright owner** = person who owns the copyright in a work **2** *verb* to state the copyright of a written work by printing a copyright notice and publishing the work **3** *adjective* covered by the laws of copyright; *it is illegal to take copies of a copyright work*

copyrighted *adjective* in copyright

CORAL = COMMON REAL-TIME APPLICATIONS LANGUAGE computer programming language used in a real-time system

cord *noun* wire used to connect a device to a socket; *telephone cord*

cordless telephone *noun* telephone which is not connected to a line by a cord, but which uses a radio link

core *noun* (a) central conducting section of a cable; **core memory** *or* **core store** = non-volatile magnetic storage method used in old computers (b) **core memory** = central memory of a computer; **core program** = computer program stored in core memory

coresident *adjective* (two or more programs) stored in main memory at the same time

corona *noun* electric discharge that is used to charge the toner within a laser printer; **corona wire** = thin wire that charges the powdered toner particles in a laser printer as they pass across it; *if your printouts are smudged, you may have to clean the corona wire*

coroutine *noun* section of a program *or* procedure that can pass data and control to another coroutine then halt itself

corporate video *noun* video produced for internal training or as a publicity tool for a company and not intended to be broadcast

correct 1 *adjective* accurate *or* right; *the published accounts do not give a correct picture of the company's financial position* **2** *verb* to remove mistakes from something; *the accounts department have corrected the invoice; you will have to correct all these typing errors before you send the letter*

correction *noun* making something correct; change which makes something correct; *he made some corrections to the text of the speech*

corrective maintenance *noun* actions to trace, find and repair a fault after it has occurred

correspond *verb* (a) **to correspond with someone** = to write letters to someone (b) **to correspond with something** = to fit *or* to match something

correspondence *noun* (a) letters and messages sent from one person to another; **business correspondence** = letters concerned with a business; **to be in correspondence with someone** = to write letters to someone and receive letters back; **correspondence print quality** = quality of print from a computer printer that is acceptable for business letters (that is daisy-wheel rather than dot-matrix printing) (NOTE: no plural) (b) way in which something fits in with something

correspondent *noun* (a) person who writes letters (b) journalist who writes articles for a newspaper on specialist subjects; *the computer correspondent; the 'Times' business correspondent; he is the Paris correspondent of the 'Telegraph'*

corrupt 1 *adjective* data *or* a program that contains errors **2** *verb* to introduce errors into data *or* a program; *power loss during disk access can corrupt the data*

corruption *noun* **data corruption** = errors introduced into data, due to noise *or* faulty equipment; *acoustic couplers suffer from data corruption more than the direct connect form of modem; data corruption on the disk has made one file unreadable*

coulomb *noun* SI unit of electrical charge

COMMENT: a coulomb is measured as the amount of charge flowing in a conductor when one amp of current is present for one second

count *verb* **(a)** to add figures together to make a total; *he counted up the sales for the six months to December* **(b)** to include; *did you count the sales of software as part of the home sales figures?*

counter *noun* **(a)** device which counts **(b)** register *or* variable whose contents are increased *or* decreased by a set amount every time an action occurs; *the loop will repeat itself until the counter reaches 100; the number of items changed are recorded with the counter;* **decade counter** = electronic device able to count actions *or* events from 0 - 9 before resetting to zero and starting again; **instruction** *or* **program counter** = register in a CPU that contains the location of the next instruction to be processed **(c)** frame or footage indicator in motion picture practice

counter- *prefix* against; turning the opposite way to normal; **counter-rotating ring** = two signal paths transmitted in opposite directions around a ring network; **counterprogramming** = running a popular TV programme at the same time as another station is running a popular series, to try to steal viewers

counting perforator *noun* paper tape punch, used in typesetting, that keeps a record of the characters, their widths, etc., to allow justification operations

country file *noun* file within an operating system that defines the parameters (such as

character set and keyboard layout) for different countries

couple *verb* to join together; *the two systems are coupled together*

coupler *noun* **(a)** mechanical device used to connect three or more conductors; **acoustic coupler** = device that connects to a telephone handset, converting binary computer data into sound signals to allow it to be transmitted down a telephone line **(b)** chemical that forms a dye when it reacts with another substance in a copying machine

Courier *noun* fixed-space *or* monospace typeface that is similar to the type produced by an office typewriter

courseware *plural noun* software, manuals and video that make up a training package or CAL product

courtesy copy *see* CC

coverage *noun* size of the potential audience capable of receiving a broadcast; **press coverage** *or* **media coverage** = reports about something in the newspapers *or* on TV, etc.; *the company had good media coverage for the launch of its new model*

CP = CARD PUNCH

cp UNIX command to make a copy of a file

CP/M = CONTROL PROGRAM/MONITOR popular operating system for microcomputers

CPA = COST PER ACTION cost of displaying a banner advertisement once (called one impression) on a website; *see also* BANNER ADVERTISEMENT

cpi = CHARACTERS PER INCH number of printed characters which fit within a space one inch wide

CPM = CRITICAL PATH METHOD

cps = CHARACTERS PER SECOND number of characters printed *or* processed every second

CPU = CENTRAL PROCESSING UNIT group of circuits which perform the basic functions of a computer made up of three parts, the control unit, the arithmetic and logic unit and the input/output unit; **CPU bound** = performance of a computer which is limited by the number of instructions the CPU can carry out; effectively, the memory and I/O devices can transfer data faster than the CPU can produce it; **CPU cycle** = period of time taken to fetch and execute an instruction (usually a simple ADD instruction) used as a measure of computer speed

COMMENT: the specification of a CPU is defined in several ways: its speed (for example, 666MHz) roughly defines the number of instructions that it can process each second - 666 million in this example. The power of a CPU is also defined in terms of its data handling capabilities: a 32-bit CPU can add, subtract or manipulate numbers that are 32-bits wide. A 16-bit processor can only handle 16-bit numbers, so would take twice as long to deal with a big number. In a file handling program CPU time might be minimal, since data retrieval (from disk) would account for a large part of the program run; in a mathematical program, the CPU time could be much higher in proportion to the total run time. Multimedia programs tend to require fast hard disk and video systems rather than a fast CPU (unless complex graphics are calculated). There are two main families of CPU. The Intel-developed range of CPUs is derived from the 80x86 series and includes the Pentium processor. These are used in IBM-compatible PCs and are backwards compatible with earlier Intel processors. Other manufacturers, such as AMD, are licensed to manufacture these CPUs and they work in exactly the same way. The second main family is dderived from the 680x0 and PowerPC range developed by Motorola. These are used in Apple computers and are not directly compatible with the Intel range

CR = CARRIAGE RETURN, CARD READER

CR/LF = CARRIAGE RETURN/LINE FEED

crab *verb (film)* move a camera or microphone sideways

crane *noun (film)* large camera stand which holds the camera operator and camera; *see also* DOLLY

crash 1 *noun* failure of a component *or* a bug in a program during a run, which halts and prevents further use of the system **2** *verb (of a computer or program)* to come to an sudden stop; *the whole system crashed, and not stock movements were possible;*

the disk has crashed and the data may have been lost

crash-protected *adjective* (disk) which uses a head protection *or* data corruption protection system; *if the disk is crash-protected, you will never lose your data*

COMMENT: it is sometimes possible to recover data from a crashed hard disk before reformatting, if the crash was caused by a bad sector on the disk

crawl *noun* mechanical device that moves television *or* film titles down in front of a camera, to give the impression that they are moving up the screen

crawling title *noun (film)* line of titles moving across the screen

CRC = CAMERA-READY COPY, CYCLIC REDUNDANCY CHECK

create *verb* to make; *a new file was created on disk to store the document; move to the CREATE NEW FILE instruction on the menu*

credit *noun* **(a)** time given to a customer before he has to pay; *they have asked for six months' credit*; **credit card** = plastic card which allows the owner to borrow money and buy goods without paying for them immediately **(b)** money received and placed in an account *or* in the balance sheet **(c)** **credits** = text at the end of a film, giving the names of the actors *or* technical staff

crew *noun* group of technical staff who work together (as on filming a TV programme, recording an outside broadcast, etc.); **camera crew** = group of people who man a TV camera; *the camera crew had to film all day in the snow*

crispener *noun (film)* electronic device used to sharpen the edges of objects in an image

critical error *noun* error that stops processing or crashes the computer

critical fusion frequency *noun* the rate of display of frames of graphics *or* text that makes them appear continuous

critical path analysis *noun* the definition of tasks *or* jobs and the time each requires arranged in order to achieve certain goals (NOTE: also called PERT (Program Evaluation and Review Techniques))

critical path method (CPM) use of analysis and projection of each critical step in a large project to help a management team

> ```
> Surprisingly, critical path
> analysis    and    project
> management, frequently the
> next   career   step   for
> engineers, did not seem to
> warrant a mention
> ```
> *Computing*

crop mark *noun (in DTP software)* printed mark that shows the edge of a page or image and allows it to be cut accurately

crop *verb* to reduce the size or margins of an image *or* to cut out a rectangular section of an image

cropping *noun* removal of areas of artwork *or* of a photograph which are not needed; *the photographs can be edited by cropping, sizing, touching up, etc.*

cross- *prefix* running from one side to another; **cross-assembler** = assembler that produces machine-code code for one computer while running on another; **cross-check** = validation of an answer by using a different method of calculation; **cross-compiler** = cross-assembler *or* compiler that compiles programs for one computer while running on another; **cross fade** = to fade out one signal while bringing in another; **crossfire** = *see* CROSSTALK; **crosshair** = cursor in the shape of a cross, used to indicate the position on screen normally displayed when drawing in a CAD program; *(in DOS and Windows)* **cross-linked files** = error in which two files claim to be using the same cluster on disk; **cross modulation** = two *or* more modulated signals on one channel interfering with each other; **crossover** = change from one system to another; *the crossover to computerized file indexing was difficult*

> COMMENT: Cross-compilers and assemblers are used to compile programs for micros, but are run on larger computers to make the operation faster

cross-reference 1 *noun* reference in a document to another part of the document **2** *verb* to make a reference to another part of the document; *the SI units are cross-referenced to the appendix*

cross-section *noun* view of a material *or* object cut across its centre; *the cross-section of the optical fibre showed the problem*

crosstalk *noun* interference in one channel due to another nearby channel *or* signal (caused by badly isolated signals); *the crosstalk was so bad, the signal was unreadable*

crow's foot *noun (film)* metal stand for a camera tripod

CRT = CATHODE RAY TUBE device used for displaying characters *or* figures *or* graphical information, similar to a TV set

> COMMENT: cathode ray tubes are used in TV sets, oscilloscopes, computer monitors and VDUs; a tube consists of a vacuum tube, one end of which is flat and coated with a phosphor, the other end containing an electron beam source. Characters *or* graphics are visible when a controllable electron beam causes the phosphor to glow

cruncher, crunching *see* NUMBER

crushing *noun* reduced contrast range on a TV image due to a fault

cryogenic memory *noun* storage medium operating at very low temperatures ($4°K$) to use the superconductive properties of a material

cryptanalysis *noun* study and methods of cipher breaking

cryptographic *adjective* referring to cryptography; **cryptographic algorithm** = rules used to encipher and decipher data; **cryptographic key** = number *or* code that is used with a cipher algorithm to personalize the encryption and decryption of data

cryptography *noun* study of encryption and decryption methods and techniques

crystal *noun* small slice of quartz crystal which vibrates at a certain frequency, used as a very accurate clock signal for computer or other high precision timing applications; **crystal microphone** = microphone that uses a piece of piezoelectric crystal which produces a signal when sound waves distort it; **crystal oscillator** = small piece of crystal that resonates at a certain frequency when a voltage is applied across it; this can be used as a high precision clock; **crystal shutter printer** = page printer that uses a powerful light controlled by a liquid crystal display to produce an image on a photo-sensitive drum; *see also* LASER PRINTER; **liquid crystal display (LCD)** = liquid crystals that reflect light when a voltage is applied, used in many watch, calculator and digital displays

CSMA-CD = CARRIER SENSE MULTIPLE ACCESS-COLLISION DETECTION method of controlling access to a network used in Ethernet networks

CTM = CLICK THROUGH PER THOUSAND method of charging an advertiser for the display of a banner advertisement on a website, where the price covers one thousand visitors clicking on the advertisement (and being re-directed to the advertiser's website); *see also* BANNER AD, CPM, CLICK THROUGH

CTR *or* **CTRL** *or* **Ctrl** = CONTROL *(on IBM-PC compatible systems)* special key (in the lower left corner) that provides a secondary function when pressed with another key; **Ctrl-Alt-Del** = pressing these three keys at once will cause a PC to carry out a soft reset

CTS = CLEAR TO SEND RS232C signal that a line *or* device is ready for data transmission

CU = CONTROL UNIT

cue *noun* **(a)** prompt *or* message displayed on a screen to remind the user that input is expected **(b)** *(film)* command or signal for a pre-planned event to commence; **cue dots** = visual marks to signify the end of a section of a programme. In television, they are generally a white square in the top right or left corners; *see* CHANGEOVER CUE; **cue tone** = sound recorded on cue track to indicate prompt or cue; **cue track** = control track used for control purposes on audio tape recorders and cartridge machines

CUG = CLOSED USER GROUP

cumulative index *noun* index made up from several different indexes

cumulative trauma disorder *see* RSI

current 1 *adjective* referring to the present time; **current address** = address being used at this time; **current directory** = directory within the directory tree which is currently being used; **current drive** = disk drive that is currently being used or has been selected **2** *noun* movement of charge carrying

particles in a conductor; **direct current (DC)** = constant value electrical current supply that flows in one direction; **alternating current (AC)** = electrical current whose value varies with time in a regular sinusoidal way (changing direction of flow each half cycle)

cursor *noun* marker on a display device which shows where the next character will appear; **addressable cursor** = cursor whose position on the screen can be defined by a program; **cursor control keys** = keys on a keyboard that allow the cursor to be moved in different directions; **cursor home** = movement of the cursor to the top left hand corner of the screen; **cursor pad** = group of cursor control keys; **cursor resource** = image that is displayed as a cursor; programming languages and authoring tools normally provide an array of different cursor images that a developer can use: for example, an egg-timer cursor when waiting or an arrow when pointing; *see also* CROSSHAIR, I-BEAM, POINTER

> COMMENT: cursors can take several forms, such as a square of bright light, a bright underline or a flashing light take several forms, such as a square of bright light, a bright underline or a flashing light

```
Probably    the    most    exciting
technology    demonstrated    was
ScreenCam,   which  allows  users
to    combine    voice,    cursor
movement     and     on-screen
activities  into  a  movie  which
can be replayed
```
Computing

custom colours *plural noun* range of colours in a palette that are used by an image or application; *see also* SYSTEM PALETTE

custom-built *adjective* made specially for one customer

customer *noun* person who buys *or* uses a computer system *or* any peripherals; **customer engineering** = maintenance and repair of a customer's equipment; **customer service department** = department which deals with customers and their complaints and orders

customize *verb* to modify a system to the customer's requirements; *we used customized computer terminals*

cut 1 *noun* removing a piece from a text; piece removed from a text; *the editors have asked for cuts in the first chapter* **2** *verb* **(a)** to divide something into parts, using scissors *or* knife *or* guillotine; **cut in notes =** printed notes in the outer edge of a paragraph in a page; **cut sheet feeder** mechanism that automatically feeds single sheets of paper into a printer **(b)** *(in video)* to switch from one scene to another in two consecutive frames, with no special transition effect (such as a fade) **(c)** to remove pieces of text to make it shorter; *the author was asked to cut his manuscript to 250 pages* (NOTE: **cuts - cutting - has cut**)

cut-and-paste *noun* selecting section of text or data, copying it to the clipboard, then moving to another point or document and inserting it (often used in word-processors and DTP packages for easy page editing)

cutaway shot *noun (film)* **(a)** action shot that is not part of the main action but is connected to it and occurs at the same time **(b)** camera movement away from the principal interest in a television interview, the interviewee, to the interviewer

cut off *verb* **(a)** to remove part of something; *six metres of paper were cut off the reel* **(b)** to stop something flowing; *the electricity supply was cut off*

cutoff *adjective* point at which (something) stops; **cutoff frequency =** frequency at which the response of a device drops off

cutter *noun (film)* film editor who decides which scenes are to be kept and in which order, and which are to be discarded

cutting *noun* action of cutting; **cutting room =** room in a film studio where the unedited film is cut and joined together; **press cuttings =** pieces cut from newspapers *or* magazines which refer to someone *or* to a company

CWP = COMMUNICATING WORD PROCESSOR

cXML = COMMERCE XML version of the XML web page markup language that offers a standard way of producing an online shop with pages about products for sale; the new features allow designers to include information about the product being displayed and how it can be purchased by the viewer; *see also* DTD, E-COMMERCE, XML

cyan *noun (film)* the complimentary colour to red, which is blue-green

cyan-magenta-yellow-black *see* CMYK, RGB

cybernetics *noun* study of the mechanics of human *or* electronic machine movements, and the way in which electronic devices can be made to work and imitate human actions

cybersquat *verb* act in which someone registers a domain name, normally a trademark or brand name, then tries to sell the name to the rightful owner; although not yet illegal in most countries, court cases almost always find in favour of the company trying to recover its name

cycle *noun* **(a)** period of time when something leaves its original position and then returns to it **(b)** one completed operation in a repeated process; *(film)* **cycle animation =** photographed movement of animated characters through repeated use of a series of cels to give the illusion of repetitive action such as walking; **cycle stealing =** memory access operation by a peripheral that halts a CPU for one *or* more clock cycles; **cycle time =** time between start and stop of an operation, especially between addressing a memory and receiving the data, and then ending the operation

cyclic *adjective* (operation) that is repeated regularly; **cyclic code =** *see* GRAY CODE; **cyclic redundancy check (CRC) =** error checking method for transmitted data; **cyclic shift =** rotation of bits in a word with the previous last bit inserted in the first bit position

cyclorama *noun (film)* large, curved, white backdrop positioned at the back of a stage or set

cylinder *noun* **(a)** round hollow object, like a tube **(b)** group of tracks on a disk that can be accessed without moving the read/write head

cylindrical *adjective* shaped like a cylinder

cypher = CIPHER

Dd

D1 videotape *noun* 19mm videotape format used for professional, digital recordings

DA = DESK ACCESSORY

DAC *or* **D/A converter** *or* **D to A converter** = DIGITAL TO ANALOG CONVERTER circuit that outputs an analog signal that is proportional to the input digital signal, and so converts digital input to an analog form

COMMENT: a D/A converter allows the computer to work outside the computer environment, by driving a machine, imitating speech, etc.

DAD = DIGITAL AUDIO DISK method of recording sound by converting and storing signals in a digital form on magnetic disk

daemon *noun (in a UNIX system)* utility program that performs its job automatically without the knowledge of the user

dagger *noun* printing sign (†) used to mark a special word; **double dagger** = printing sign (‡) used to give a second reference level

dailies *plural noun (film)* the first copy of the footage of a day's filming which is seen by the director and production team on a daily basis

daisy chain *noun* method of connecting equipment with a single cable passing from one machine to the next; this is the method used to connect SCSI devices and Ethernet networks

daisy-chain *verb* to connect equipment using the daisy chain method

you can often daisy-chain cards or plug them into expansion boxes

Byte

daisy-wheel *noun* wheel-shaped printing head, with characters on the end of spokes, used in a serial printer; **daisy-wheel printer** *or* **daisy-wheel typewriter** = serial printer *or* typewriter with characters arranged on interchangeable wheels

DAMA = DEMAND ASSIGNED MULTIPLE ACCESS

damage 1 *noun* harm done to things; **to suffer damage** = to be harmed; **to cause damage** = to harm something; *the breakdown of the electricity supply caused damage estimated at £100,000* (NOTE: no plural) **2** *verb* to harm; *the faulty read/write head appears to have damaged the disks*

damaged *adjective* which has suffered damage *or* which has been harmed; *is it possible to repair the damaged files?*

DAO = DATA ACCESS OBJECTS programming interface provided with many of Microsoft's database applications that allow the developer to access Jet or ODBC compatible data sources; *see also* JET, ODBC

dark current *noun* amount of electrical current that flows in an optoelectrical device when there is no light falling on it

dark trace tube *noun* CRT with a dark image on a bright background

darkroom *noun* special room with no light, where photographic film can be developed

DAS = DUAL ATTACHMENT STATION

DASD = DIRECT ACCESS STORAGE DEVICE

DASH *(film)* = DIGITAL AUDIO STATIONARY HEAD sound tape recording system

dash *noun* short line in printing; **em dash** *or* **em rule** = line as long as an em, used to separate one section of text from another; **en**

dash *or* **en rule** = line as long as an en, used to link two words or parts of words

DAT = DIGITAL AUDIO TAPE compact cassette, smaller than an audio cassette, that provides a system of recording sound as digital information onto magnetic tape with very high-quality reproduction; **DAT drive** = mechanical drive that records data onto a DAT tape and retrieves data from a tape; *we use a DAT drive as the backup device for our network*

COMMENT: also used as a high-capacity tape backup system that can store 1.3Gb of data; sound is recorded at a sample rate of either 32, 44.1 or 48KHz to provide up to two hours of CD-quality sound

data *noun* collection of facts made up of numbers, characters and symbols, stored on a computer in such a way that it can be processed by the computer; *programs act upon data files; data is inputted at one of several workstations; the company stores data on customers in its main computer file; a user needs a password to access data*; **raw data** = (i) pieces of information which have not been input into a computer system; (ii) data in a databank which has to be processed to provide information to the user; **data above voice (DAV)** = data transmission in a frequency range above that of the human voice; **data access management** = regulation of the users who can access stored data; **data acquisition** = converting original image, sound or text into a digital form; **data buffer** = temporary storage location for data transmitted to a device that is not ready to receive it; **data bus** = electrical bus carrying the data between a CPU and memory and peripheral devices; **data bus connector** = D-shape connector normally with two rows of pins used to connect devices that transfer data; **data capture** = act of obtaining data (either by keyboarding or scanning, or often automatically from a recording device *or* peripheral); **data carrier** = any device capable of storing data *or* waveform used as a carrier for data signals; **data carrier detect (DCD)** = RS232C signal from a modem to a computer indicating a carrier is being received; **data cartridge** = cartridge that contains data; **data channel** = communications link able to carry data

signals; **data circuit** = circuit which allows bi-directional data communications; **data collection** = act of receiving data from various sources (either directly from a data capture device *or* from a cartridge) and integrated in a database; **data collection platform** = station that transmits collected data to a central point (usually via satellite); **data communications** = transmission and reception of data rather than speech *or* images; **data communications equipment (DCE)** = equipment (such as a modem) which receives *or* transmits data; **data compacting** = reducing the space taken by data by coding it in a more efficient way; **data compression** = means of reducing size of data by removing spaces, empty sections and unused material from the blocks of data; *scanners use a technique called data compression which manages to reduce, even by a third, the storage demand*; **data concentrator** = data which combines intermittent data from various lines and sends it along a single line in one go; **data connection** = link *or* anything which joins two devices and allows data transmission; **data corruption** = errors introduced into data due to noise *or* faulty equipment; **data delimiter** = special symbol or character that marks the end of a file or data item; **data description language (DDL)** = part of a database system which describes the structure of the system and data; **data dictionary/directory (DD/D)** = software which gives a list of types and forms of data contained in a database; **data division** = part of a (COBOL) program giving full definitions of the data; **data-driven** = (computer architecture) in which instructions are executed once relevant data has been received; **data element** = *see* DATA ITEM; **data encryption standard (DES)** = standard for data cipher system; **data entry** = method of entering data into a system (usually using a keyboard but also direct from disks after data preparation); **data file** = file with data in it (as opposed to a program file); **data format** = rules defining the way in which data is stored *or* transmitted; **data flow** = movement of data through a system; **data flowchart** = diagram used to describe a computer *or* data processing system; **data flow diagram (DFD)** = diagram used to describe the movement of data through a system; **data**

glove electronic glove that fits over a user's hand and contains sensors that transmit the position of the user's hand and fingers to a computer, most often used in a virtual reality system; **data independence** = structure of a database which is such that it may be changed without affecting the user; **data input bus** = *see* DIB; **data integrity** = protection of data against damage *or* errors; **data interchange format (DIF)** = de facto standard method of storing spreadsheet formula and data in a file; **data in voice (DIV)** = digital data transmission in place of a voice channel; **data item** = one unit of data such as the quantity of items in stock, a person's name, age or occupation, the registered number of a company; **data link** = connection between two devices to allow the transmission of data; **data link control** = protocol and rules used to define the way in which data is transmitted *or* received; **data link layer** = one layer in the ISO/OSI network that sends packets of data to the next link and deals with error correction; **data logging** = automatic data collection (such as temperature readings from a weather station); **data management** = maintenance and upkeep of a database; **data medium** = medium which allows data to be stored *or* displayed (such as a VDU *or* magnetic disk *or* screen); **data name** = group of characters used to identify one item of data; **data network** = networking system which transmits data; **data origination** = conversion of data from its original form to one which can be read by a computer; **data pointer** = register containing the location of the next item of data; **data preparation** = conversion of data into a machine-readable form (usually by keyboarding) before data entry; **data processing (DP)** = selecting and operating on data to produce useful information; sorting *or* organizing of data files; **data processing manager** = person who runs a computer department; **data projector** = device that uses three large coloured lights (red, green and blue) to project a colour image output from a computer onto a large screen; compare this with a flat-panel display, a colour LCD screen which is placed on an overhead projector to display an image on a larger screen; **data protection** = means of making sure that data is private and secure; **Data Protection Act** = legislation passed in 1984 in the UK that means any owner of a database that contains personal details must register with a central Government agency; **data retrieval** = process of searching, selecting and reading data from a stored file; **data routing** = defining the path taken by a message in a network; **data security** = protection of data against corruption *or* unauthorized users; **data services** = public services (such as the telephone system) which allow data to be transmitted; **data sharing** = one file *or* set of data that can be accessed by several users; **data signals** = electrical *or* optical pulses *or* waveforms that represent binary data; **data signalling rate** = total amount of data that is transmitted through a system per second; **data sink** = device in a data terminal which receives data; **data source** = device in a data terminal which sends data; **data station** = point that contains a data terminal and a data circuit; **data stream** = data transmitted serially one bit *or* character at a time; **data structure** = number of related items that are treated as one by the computer (in an address book record, the name, address and telephone number form separate entries which would be processed as one by the computer); **data switching exchange** = device used to direct and switch data between lines; **data terminal** = device that is able to display, transmit *or* receive data; *a printer is a data terminal for computer output*; **data terminal equipment (DTE)** = device at which a communications path starts *or* finishes; **data transaction** = one complete operation on data; **data transfer rate** = rate at which data is moved from one point to another; **data translation** = conversion of data from one system to another; **data transmission** = process of sending data from one location to another over a data link; **data type** = sort of data which can be stored in a register (such as string, number, etc.); **data under voice (DUV)** = data transmission in a frequency range *or* channel lower than that of a human voice; **data validation** = process of checking data for errors and relevance in a situation; **data vetting** = process of checking data as it is input for errors and validity; **data word** = piece of data stored as a single word; **data word length** = number of bits that make up a word in a computer

COMMENT: data is different from information in that it is facts stored in machine-readable form. When the facts are processed by the computer into a form which can be understood by people, the data becomes information

data compression is the art of squeezing more and more information into fewer and fewer bytes

Practical Computing

it's new notebook models use the power-saving Intel 486 SL microprocessor which offers 32-bit internal and data bus operation

Computing

databank *noun* **(a)** large amount of data stored in a structured form **(b)** personal records stored in a computer

database *noun* integrated collection of files of data stored in a structured form in a large memory, which can be accessed by one or more users at different terminals; **database administrator (DBA)** = person in charge of running and maintaining a database system; **database engine** = program that provides an interface between a program written to access the functions of a DBMS and the DBMS; **database machine** = hardware and software combination designed for the rapid processing of database information; **database management system (DBMS)** *or* **database manager** = series of programs that allows the user to easily create and modify databases

COMMENT: a database could contain data such as contact names and addresses or customer details. Each separate entry is called a record and each individual part of a record is called a field. For example, in a database of names and addresses, a person's details would be stored on one record, with their first name in one field and surname in another

a database is a file of individual records of information which are stored in some kind of sequential order

Which PC?

this information could include hypertext references to information held within a computer database, or spreadsheet formulae

Computing

datagram *noun* packet of information in a packet switching system that contains its destination address and route

dataline *noun* one line of broadcast TV signal that contains the teletext signals and data (usually transmitted at the start of the image and identified with a special code)

dataplex *noun* multiplexing of data signals

dataset *noun US* modem; **dataset ready** = RS232C signal from a modem to a computer indicating it is ready for use

date 1 *noun* **(a)** number of day, month and year; *I have received your letter of yesterday's date*; **date of receipt** = date when something is received; **date-time** = current time and date stored permanently by one area of a PC's memory by means of a tiny battery inside the PC **(b)** **up to date** = current *or* recent *or* modern; *an up-to-date computer system*; **to bring something up to date** = to add the latest information to something; **to keep something up to date** = to keep adding information to something so that it is always up to date; *we spend a lot of time keeping our files up to date* **(c)** **out of date** = old-fashioned; *their computer system is years out of date*; *they are still using out-of-date equipment* **2** *verb* to put a date on a document; *the cheque was dated March 24th*; *you forgot to date the cheque*

DAV = DATA ABOVE VOICE

day *noun* **(a)** period of 24 hours; *there are thirty days in June*; *the first day of the month is a public holiday*; **day for night** = filming during daylight with filters in order to give the impression that it is night **(b)** period of work from morning to night; **day shift** = shift which works during the daylight hours such as from 8 a.m. to 5.30 p.m.; **to work an eight-hour day** = to spend eight hours at work each day

daylight *noun (film)* colour temperature of sunlight, 5600 degrees Kelvin or higher; **daylight filter** = filter of a camera lens which alters the colour temperature of light as it goes through the lens to allow filming outdoors (in natural light) with film that is meant to be used in artificial light settings; **daylight loading** = cassette or spool which can be loaded into a camera in dim lighting conditions without the film becoming fogged; **daylight saving time** = scheme that defines the changes in time over the course of a year; in the UK this means moving the clocks forward or backward by one hour each season; Windows will automatically detect if the system time and date needs to be adjusted and warn you

db *see* DECIBEL

DB connector = DATA BUS CONNECTOR D-shape connector normally with two rows of pins used to connect devices that transfer data; *the most common DB connectors are DB-9, DB-25 and DB-50 with 9, 25 and 50 connections respectively*

DBA = DATABASE ADMINISTRATOR person in charge of running and maintaining a database system

dBA *(film)* decibels which are measured with A-weighting; usually used to measure noise

dBASE popular database software that includes a built-in programming language

> COMMENT: dBASE has several versions, II, III and IV; the software development is currently carried out by Borland International. There have been several versions of dBASE, and files created in dBASE can normally be imported into other database programs

DBMS = DATABASE MANAGEMENT SYSTEM series of programs that allow to user to create and modify databases

DBS = DIRECT BROADCAST SATELLITE

DC = DIRECT CURRENT

DC signalling *noun* method of communications using pulses of current over a wire circuit, like a telegraph system

DCA = DOCUMENT CONTENT ARCHITECTURE document format defined by IBM that allows documents to be exchanged between computer systems

DCC = DIGITAL COMPACT CASSETTE magnetic tape in a compact cassette box that is used to store computer data or audio signals in a digital format

(DCC is the newer version of the traditional audio cassette, but it can record CD quality sound with its digital storage capability)

DCD = DATA CARRIER DETECT RS232C signal from a modem to a computer indicating a carrier is being received

DCE = DATA COMMUNICATIONS EQUIPMENT; **DCE rates** = number of bits of information that a modem can transmit per second over a telephone line (such as 36,600 bps); this is not the same as the DTE rate which measures how fast a modem can exchange data with another PC and takes into account data compression

DCOM = DISTRIBUTED COMPONENT OBJECT MODEL enhanced version of the COM specification that allows applications to access objects over a network or over the Internet

DD = DATA DICTIONARY, DATA DIRECTORY

DD = DOUBLE DENSITY

DDE (a) = DIRECT DATA ENTRY **(b)** = DYNAMIC DATA EXCHANGE

DDL = DATA DESCRIPTION LANGUAGE part of database system software which describes the structure of the system and data; *many of DDL's advantages come from the fact that it is a second generation language*

DDP = DISTRIBUTED DATA PROCESSING

DDR *(film)* = DIRECT DOMESTIC RECEPTION television transmission by satellite

de facto standard *noun* a design *or* method *or* system which is so widely used that it has become a standard but it has not been officially recognised by any committee

dead *adjective* **(a)** not working; (computer *or* piece of equipment) that does not function; **dead keys** = keys on a keyboard that cause a function rather than a character to occur, such as the shift key; **dead matter** = type that has been used for printing and is no longer required; **the line went dead** = the telephone line suddenly stopped working **(b)** (room *or* space) that has no acoustical reverberation

deaden *verb* to make a sound *or* colour less sharp; *acoustic hoods are used to deaden the noise of printers*

deadline *noun* date by which something has to be done; **to meet a deadline** = to finish something in time; *we've missed our October 1st deadline*

deadlock 1 *noun* **(a)** point where two sides cannot come to an agreement; *the discussions have reached a deadlock*; **to break a deadlock** = to find a way to start discussions again **(b)** situation when two users want to access two resources at the same time, one resource is assigned to each user but neither can use the other **2** *verb* to be unable to agree to continue discussing; **talks have been deadlocked for ten days** = after ten days the talks have not produced any agreement

deadly embrace *noun* = DEADLOCK (b)

deal 1 *noun* business agreement *or* contract; *to arrange a deal or to set up a deal or to do a deal; to sign a deal; the sales director set up a deal with an American software house; the deal will be signed tomorrow; they did a deal with a Japanese disk manufacturer;* **package deal** = agreement where several different items are agreed at the same time; *they agreed a package deal, which involves the development of software, customizing hardware and training of staff;* **to call off a deal** = to stop an agreement **2** *verb* **(a) to deal with an order** = to supply an order; **to deal with** = to organize; *leave it to the DP manager - he'll deal with it;* **(b)** to buy and sell; **to deal with someone** = to do business with someone

dealer *noun* person who buys and sells; *always buy hardware from a recognized dealer*

de-bounce *noun* preventing a single touch on a key giving multiple key contact

DEBUG *noun (in MS-DOS)* software utility that allows a user to view the contents of binary files and assemble small assembly-language programs

debug *verb* to test a program and locate and correct any faults *or* errors; *they spent weeks debugging the system*

debugger *noun* software that helps a programmer find faults *or* errors in a program

the debug monitor makes development and testing very easy

Electronics & Wireless World

Further questions, such as how you debug an application built from multisourced software to be run on multisourced hardware, must be resolved at this stage

Computing

decade *noun* ten items *or* events; **decade counter** = electronic device able to count actions *or* events from 0-9 before resetting to zero and starting again

decay 1 *noun* rate at which an electronic impulse *or* the amplitude of a signal fades away; *with a short decay, it sounds very sharp*; **decay time** = time taken for an impulse to fade **2** *verb* to decrease gradually in amplitude *or* size; *the signal decayed rapidly*

deceleration time *noun* time taken for an access arm to come to a stop after it has moved to the correct location over the surface of a hard disk

decentralized computer network *noun* network where the control is shared between several computers

deci- *prefix* meaning one tenth of a number

decibel *or* **dB** *noun* unit for measuring the power of a sound or the strength of a signal; **decibel meter** = signal power measuring device

decile *noun* one of a series of nine figures below which one tenth *or* several tenths of the total fall

decimal *noun* **correct to three places of decimals** = correct to three figures after the decimal point (e.g. 3.485); **decimal point** = dot which indicates the division between the whole unit and its smaller parts (such as 4.75); **decimal system** = number system using the digits 0 - 9; **decimal tabbing** = adjusting a column of numbers so that the decimal points are vertically aligned; **decimal tab key** = key for entering decimal numbers on a word processor

decimalization *noun* changing to a decimal system

decimalize *verb* to change to a decimal system

decimonic ringing *noun* selecting one telephone by sending a certain ringing frequency

decipher *verb* **(a)** to convert an encoded message into plain text **(b)** to read difficult handwriting

decision *noun* making up one's mind to do something; *to come to a decision or to reach a decision*; **decision making** = act of coming to a decision; **the decision-making processes** = ways in which decisions are reached; **decision support system** = suite of programs that help a manager reach decisions using previous databases; **decision table** = chart which shows the relationships between certain variables and actions available when various conditions are met; **decision tree** = graphical representation of a decision table showing possible paths and actions if certain conditions are met

deck *noun* **(a)** tape deck = drive for magnetic tape **(b)** pile of punched cards

deckle edge *noun* rough edge of paper made by hand

declaration *noun* official statement; **customs declaration** = statement declaring goods brought into a country on which customs duty should be paid

declare *verb* **(a)** to make an official statement; **to declare goods to the customs** = to state that you are importing goods on which duty may be paid; *the customs officials asked him if he had anything to declare* **(b)** to define a computer program variable *or* to set a variable equal to a number; *he declared at the start of the program that X was equal to nine*

decode *verb* to translate encoded data back to its original form

decoder *noun* program *or* device used to convert data into another form; **decode unit** = part of a microprocessor that translates a complex instruction into a simple form that the arithmetic and logic unit (ALU) part of the processor can understand and process; **instruction decoder** = hardware that converts a machine-code code instruction into actions

decoding *noun* converting encoded data back into its original form

decollate *verb* to separate continuous stationery into single sheets; to split

two-part *or* three-part stationery into its separate parts (and remove the carbon paper)

decollator *noun* machine used to separate continuous stationery into single sheets *or* to split 2-part or 3-part stationery into separate parts

decompilation *noun* conversion of a compiled program in object code into a source language; *fast incremental compilation and decompilation*

decompression *noun* expanding a compressed image or data file so that it can be viewed

decrease 1 *noun* fall *or* reduction; *decrease in price; decrease in value; decrease in sales; sales show a 10% decrease on last year* **2** *verb* to fall *or* to become less; *sales are decreasing; the value of the pound has decreased by 5%*

decrement *verb* to subtract a set number from a variable; *the register contents were decremented until they reached zero*

decrypt *verb* to convert encrypted data back into its original form

decryption *noun* converting of encrypted data back into its original form

```
typically a file is encrypted
using a password key and
decrypted using the same key.
A design fault of many systems
means the use of the wrong
password for decryption
results in double and often
irretrievable encryption
                    PC Business World
```

dedicated *verb* (program *or* procedure *or* system) reserved for a particular use; **dedicated channel** = communications line reserved for a special purpose; **dedicated computer** = computer which is only used for a single special purpose; **dedicated line** = telephone line used only for data communications; **dedicated logic** = logical function implemented in hardware for one task; *the person appointed should have a knowledge of micro-based hardware and dedicated logic*; **dedicated word processor** = computer which has been configured specially for word processing

```
the server should reduce
networking costs by using
```

standard networking cable instead of dedicated links

PC Business World

The PBX is changing from a dedicated proprietary hardware product into an open application software development platform

Computing

deduct *verb* to remove something from a total; *to deduct $3 from the price; to deduct a sum for expenses; after deducting costs the margin is only 23%*

deductible *adjective* which can be deducted

deduction *noun* removing of money from a total *or* money removed from a total; *net salary is salary after deduction of tax*

deep field *noun (film)* lens or camera that has very close and very distant objects in focus at the same time; *see* DEEP FOCUS

deep focus *noun (film)* type of cinematography where objects at a great distance and objects very close to the camera are all in focus; *see* DEEP FIELD

default 1 *noun* **(a)** failure to carry out the terms of a contract, especially failure to pay back a debt; **by default** = because no one else will act (NOTE: no plural); **the company is in default** = the company has failed to carry out the terms of the contract **(b)** predefined course of action *or* value that is assumed unless the operator alters it **(c)** value that is used by a program if the user does not make any changes to the settings; *an application may ask the user if he wants to install the application to the default, i.e. the C:\APP directory - the user can accept or change this*; **default drive** = disk drive that is accessed first in a multi-disk system (to try and load the operating system or a program); **default option** = preset value *or* option that is to be used if no other value has been specified; **default palette** *or* **system colours** = range of colours that are available on a particular system; a user or application can often change these to create their own palette range of colours; **default rate** = baud rate (in a modem) that is used if no other is selected; **default response** = value which is used if the user does not enter new data; **default value** = value which is automatically used by the computer if no

other value has been specified **2** *verb* to fail to carry out the terms of a contract, especially to fail to pay back a debt

defaulter *noun* person who defaults

The default values of columns cannot be set in the database schema, so different applications can trash the database

Computing

defect *noun* something which is wrong *or* which stops a machine from working properly; *a computer defect or a defect in the computer*

defect skipping *noun* means of identifying and labelling defective magnetic tracks during manufacture so that the next good track will be used

defective *adjective* **(a)** faulty *or* not working properly; *the machine broke down because of a defective cooling system*; **defective sector** = fault with a hard disk in which data cannot be correctly read from a particular sector; it could be caused by a damaged disk surface or faulty head alignment **(b)** not valid in law; *his title to the property is defective*

defensive computing *noun* method of programming that takes into account any problems *or* errors that might occur

deferred printing *noun* the delaying of printing a document until a later, more convenient time

define *verb* **(a)** to assign a value to a variable **(b)** to assign the characteristics of processes *or* data to something

definition *noun* ability of a screen to display fine detail; *see also* RESOLUTION

deflect *verb* to change the direction of an object *or* beam

deflection *noun* **deflection yokes** = magnetic coils around a television tube used to control the position of the picture beam

defocus *verb* to deliberately focus the lens at a point very close to the camera, leaving the background action out-of-focus; usually used for special effects

DEFRAG *(in MS-DOS and Windows)* defragmentation utility supplied with MS-DOS and Microsoft Windows

defragmentation *noun* reorganisation of files scattered across non-contiguous sectors on a hard disk; **defragmentation utility** = software utility that carries out the process of defragmentation on a hard disk

> COMMENT: when a file is saved to disk, it is not always saved in adjacent sectors; this will increase the retrieval time. Defragmentation moves files back into adjacent sectors so that the read head does not have to move far across the disk, and it increases performance

degauss *verb* to remove unwanted magnetic fields and effects from magnetic tape, disks or read/write heads

degausser *noun* device used to remove magnetic fields from a disk *or* tape *or* recording head

degradation *noun* (a) loss of picture *or* signal quality; *line art can be reproduced on scanners or photocopied without much degradation*; **image degradation** = loss of picture contrast and quality due to signal distortion *or* bad copying of a video signal (b) loss of processing capacity because of a malfunction; **graceful degradation** = allowing some parts of a system to continue to function after a part has broken down

dejagging *see* ANTI-ALIASING, JAGGIES

DEL = DELETE *(in MS-DOS)* command to delete a file; *to delete all files with the extension BAK, use the command DEL *.BAK*; **DEL key** = key on a keyboard that moves the cursor back one character space and deletes any character at that position; *to remove a word from the screen, press the DEL key repeatedly*

delay 1 *noun* time when someone *or* something is later than planned; *there was a delay of thirty seconds before the printer started printing; we are sorry for the delay in supplying your order or in replying to your letter*; **delay distortion** = signal corruption due to echoes; **delay equalizer** = electronic circuit used to compensate for delays caused by a communications line; **delay line** = device that causes a signal to take a certain time in crossing it; **delay vector** = time that a message will take to pass from one packet switching network node to another **2** *verb* to be late; to make someone late; *he was delayed because his taxi had an accident; the company has delayed paying all its staff*; **delayed**

broadcast = filming a TV programme and broadcasting it later than other stations in the network

delete *verb* (a) to cut out words in a document; *they want to delete all references to credit terms from the contract; the lawyers have deleted some sections from the book* (b) to remove text *or* data from a storage device; *the word-processor allows us to delete the whole file by pressing this key*; **delete character** = special code used to indicate data *or* text to be removed; **undelete** = to restore a file *or* text *or* data that was accidentally deleted; *thankfully, we could undelete the files*

deletion *noun* (a) making a cut in a document (b) text removed from a document; *the editors asked the author to make several deletions in the last chapter*; **deletion tracking** = method of allowing deleted files to be undeleted; when a file is deleted, the sectors on disk are monitored for a period of time in case the file was deleted by mistake

> COMMENT: when you delete a file, you are not actually erasing it but you are making its space on disk available for another file

delimited-field file *noun* data file in which each field is separated by a special character (often a tab character or comma) and each record is separated by a carriage return or a second special character; this allows data files to be transferred between database applications; **comma delimited** = file in which each item *or* field of data is separated by a comma

delimiter *noun* (a) character or symbol used to indicate to a language or program the start or end of data or a record or information (b) the boundary between an instruction and its argument

delivery system *noun* hardware and software required to play a particular multimedia title

delta *noun* type of connection used to connect the three wires in a 3-phase electrical supply; **delta-delta** = connection between a delta source and load; **delta modulation** = differential pulse coded modulation that uses only one bit per sample; **delta routing** = means of directing data around a packet switching network; **delta YUV** = digital video encoding technique in which luminance of a pixel is calculated by the RGB input signal (Y0.6G + 0.3R + 0.1B); from the value of Y, U and V are calculated as UR - Y; VB - Y

demagnetize *verb* to remove stray *or* unwanted magnetic fields from a disk *or* tape *or* recording head

demagnetizer *noun* device which demagnetizes something; *he used the demagnetizer to degauss the tape heads*

demand 1 *noun* **(a)** asking for something to be done; **demand assigned multiple access (DAMA)** = means of switching in circuits, usually in a satellite, as and when they are required; **demand multiplexing** = time division multiplexing method which allocates time segments to signals according to demand; **demand processing** = processing data when it appears, rather than waiting; **demand protocol architecture (DPA)** = technique of loading protocol stacks in memory only if they are required for a particular session; **demand staging** = moving files *or* data from a secondary storage device to a fast access device when required by a database program **(b)** need for goods at a certain price; *there was an active demand for oil shares on the stock market*; **to meet a demand** *or* **to fill a demand** = to supply what is needed; *the factory had to increase production to meet the extra demand; the factory had to cut production when demand fell off; the office cleaning company cannot keep up with the demand for its services*; **there is not much demand for this item** = not many people want to buy it; **supply and demand** = amount of a product which is available and the amount which is wanted by customers **2** *verb* to ask for something and expect to get it; *she demanded her money back; the suppliers are demanding immediate payment*

demarcation *noun* showing the difference between two areas; **demarcation strip** = device that electrically isolates equipment from a telephone line (to prevent damage)

demo = DEMONSTRATION

democratic network *noun* synchronized network where each station has equal priority

demodulation *noun* recovery of the original signal from a received modulated carrier wave

demodulator *noun* circuit that recovers a signal from a modulated carrier wave

demonstrate *verb* to show how something works; *he demonstrated the file management program*

demonstration *or* **demo** *noun* act of showing how something works; **demonstration model** = piece of equipment in a shop, used to show customers how the equipment works; **demonstration software** = software that shows what an application is like to use and what it can do, without implementing all the functions; *the company gave away demonstration software that lets you do everything except save your data*

demultiplex *verb* to split one channel into the original signals that were combined at source

demultiplexor *noun* device that separates out the original multiplexed signals from one channel

denary notation *noun* number system in base ten, using the digits 0 to 9

dense index *noun* database index containing an entry for every item

densiometer *noun* photographic device used to measure the density of a photograph

density *noun* **(a)** amount of light that a photographic negative blocks **(b)** darkness of a printed image *or* text; **density dial** = knob that controls the density of a printed image; *when fading occurs, turn the density dial on the printer to full black* **(c)** amount of data that can be packed into a space on a disk *or* tape; **double density** = system to double the storage capacity of a disk drive by doubling the number of bits which can be put on the disk surface; **double density disk (DD)** = disk that can store two bits of data per unit area compared to a standard disk, using a modified write process; **single density disk (SD)** = standard magnetic disk able to store data

COMMENT: scanner software produces various shades of grey by using different densities *or* arrangements of black and white dots and/or different size dots

deny access *verb* to refuse access to a circuit *or* system for reasons of workload *or* security

dependent *adjective* which is variable because of something; *a process which is dependent on the result of another process; the output is dependent on the physical state of the link*

deposit 1 *noun* **(a)** thin layer of a substance which is put on a surface **(b)** printout of the contents of all *or* a selected area of memory **2** *verb* to coat a surface with a thin layer of a substance

deposition *noun* process by which a surface is coated with a thin layer of a substance; *see also* DOPING

depth of field *noun* amount of a scene that will be in focus when photographed with a certain aperture setting; **depth cuing** = reducing the colour and intensity of an object within a three-dimensional image to provide the illusion of distance within an image; **depth of focus** = position of film behind a camera lens that will result in a sharp image

derive *verb* to come from; **derived indexing** = library index entries produced only from material in the book *or* document; **derived sound** = sound signal produced by mixing the left and right hand channels of a stereo signal

DES = DATA ENCRYPTION STANDARD standardized popular method of encrypting data

descender *noun* part of a character that goes below the line (such as the bottom section of a g); *compare with* ASCENDER

de-scramble *verb* to reassemble an original message *or* signal from its scrambled form

de-scrambler *noun* device which produces a clear video signal from an encoded signal that is transmitted to prevent unauthorized viewing

COMMENT: de-scramblers are normally used to receive television channels via a satellite dish - the viewer pays for the de-scrambler and can then watch certain television channels

describe *verb* to say what someone *or* something is like; *the leaflet describes the services the company can offer; the managing director described the company's difficulties with cash flow*

description *noun* words which show what something is like; **data description language (DDL)** = part of a database system which describes the structure of the system and data; **false description of contents** = wrongly stating the contents of a packet to trick customers into buying it; **job description** = official document from the management which says what a job involves; **page description programming language** = programming language that accepts commands to define the size, position and type style for text *or* graphics on a page; **trade description** = description of a product to attract customers

descriptor *noun* identification code used to mean the filename *or* program name *or* pass code to a file

design 1 *noun* planning *or* drawing of a product before it is built *or* manufactured; **industrial design** = design of products made by machines (such as cars and refrigerators); **product design** = design of products; **design department** = department in a large company which designs the company's products *or* its advertising; **design parameters** = specifications for the design of a product; **design studio** = independent firm which specializes in creating designs **2** *verb* to plan *or* to draw something before it is built *or* manufactured; *he designed a new chip factory; she designs typefaces*

designer *noun* person who designs; *she is the designer of the new computer*

desk *noun* **(a)** writing table in an office, usually with drawers for stationery; *desk diary; desk drawer; desk light*; **a three-drawer desk** = desk with three drawers; **desk accessories** = useful devices *or* products used at a person's desk (such as pens, paper, desk light, etc.); **desk pad** = pad of paper kept on a desk for writing notes **(b)** **cash desk** *or* **pay desk** = place in a store where you pay for goods bought

desk accessory (DA) *noun* (*in an Apple Macintosh system*) add-in utility that enhances the system; *we have installed several DAs that help us manage our fonts*

desktop *adjective* **(a)** which sits on top of a desk; which can be done on a desk; **desktop computer** = small microcomputer system that can be placed on a desk; *(in an Apple Macintosh system)* **desktop file** = system file used to store information about all the files on a disk *or* volume (such as version, date, size, author); **desktop media** = combination of presentation graphics, desktop publishing and multimedia; this is a phrase that was originally used by Apple; **desktop PC** = normally refers to an IBM-compatible computer which can be placed on a user's desk: comprises a system unit (with main electronics, disk drive and controllers) and a separate monitor and keyboard.; *compare with* LAPTOP COMPUTER; **desktop presentations** = presentation graphics, text and charts produced and designed on a desktop personal computer; *see also* PRESENTATION SOFTWARE; **desktop publishing (DTP)** = design, layout and printing of documents, books and magazines using special software, a desktop computer and a high-resolution printer; the software normally provides a WYSIWYG preview to show what the printed page will look like; **desktop taskbar** = status bar that is normally displayed along the bottom of the screen in Windows; **desktop video** = software and hardware combination that allow a user to edit video; normally consists of a PC or Macintosh with a digitiser, editing software and control of external VCRs **(b)** *(in a GUI)* workspace that is a graphical representation of a real-life desktop, with icons for telephone, diary, calculator, filing cabinet; **desktop background** = the patter or image that is displayed by Windows as a backdrop (often called the wallpaper) and on top of which icons and program windows appear; **desktop icons** = graphic symbols *or* images that are displayed on the desktop; *the two desktop icons that are always on Windows are My Computer and Recycle Bin*

COMMENT: a desktop makes it easier for a new user to operate a computer, they do not have to type in commands, instead they can point at icons on the desktop using a mouse

desktop publishing or the ability to produce high-quality publications using a minicomputer, essentially boils down to combining words and images on pages

Byte

despotic network *noun* network synchronized and controlled by one single clock

de-spun antenna *noun* satellite aerial that always points to the same place on the earth

destination *noun* place to which something is sent *or* to which something is going; location to which a data is sent; *the ship will take ten weeks to reach its destination*; **final destination** = place reached at the end of a journey after stopping at several place en route; *(in a drag and drop operation)* **destination object** = the object or icon onto which you drop an object; many GUIs have a trashcan icon - a destination object onto which you drag and drop files that you want to delete; **destination page** = the target page within a hyperlink; when a user clicks on the active object in a hyperlink, the software displays the destination page

destructive cursor *noun* cursor that erases the text as it moves over it; **destructive readout** = form of storage medium that loses its data after it has been read

detail 1 *noun* small part of a description; *the catalogue gives all the details of our product range; we are worried by some of the details in the contract*; **in detail** = giving many particulars; *the catalogue lists all the products in detail*; **detail paper** = thin transparent paper used for layouts and tracing **2** *verb* to list in detail; *the catalogue details the shipping arrangements for customers; the terms of the licence are detailed in the contract*

detailed *adjective* in detail; **detailed account** = account which lists every item

detect *verb* to sense something (usually something very slight); *the equipment can detect faint signals from the transducer*

detection *noun* process of detecting something; *the detection of the cause of the fault is proving difficult*

detector *noun* device which can detect; **metal detector** = device which can sense hidden metal objects

determine *verb* to fix *or* to arrange *or* to decide; *to determine prices or quantities; conditions still to be determined*

deuce *noun (film)* 2000 watt Fresnel spotlight

Deutsche Industrienorm *see* DIN

develop *verb* **(a)** to plan and produce; *to develop a new product* **(b)** to apply a chemical process to photographic film and paper to produce an image

developer *noun* **(a)** **a property developer** = person who plans and builds a group of new houses *or* new factories; **software developer** = person *or* company which writes software **(b)** chemical solution used to develop exposed film

developing *noun (film)* method by which an invisible image in an exposed photographic film is made permanently visible

development *noun* **(a)** planning the production of a new product; *research and development* **(b)** **development area** *or* **development zone** = area which has been given special help from a government to encourage businesses and factories to be set up there; **industrial development** = planning and building of new industries in special areas

device *noun* small useful machine *or* piece of equipment; **device address** = location within the memory area that is used by a particular device; the CPU can control the device by placing instructions at this address; **device control** = special code sent in a transmission to a device to instruct it to perform a special function; **device dependent** = software application that will not run correctly without a particular piece of hardware (for example, this could be video editing software that will not run if the PC is not connected to a video player, or a paint-package that needs a 24-bit graphics adapter); **device driver** = program or routine used to interface and manage an I/O device or peripheral; **device element** = data required for an MCI compound device (normally a data file), for example a WAVE file that is played back through a sound card; **device independent** = programming technique that results in a program that is able to run with any peripheral hardware; **device independent bitmap (DIB)** = file format for a Windows graphics image that

consists of a header, colour table (palette) and bitmap data; can be in 1, 4, 8 or 24-bit colour resolution; = **device manager** = software (normally part of the operating system) that lets you change the settings or configure a device such as a printer or monitor; **device name** = abbreviation that denotes a port or I/O device, such as COM for serial port, PRN for printer port, CON for keyboard and monitor; **I/O device** = peripheral which can be used for both inputting and outputting data to a processor (such as a terminal)

> Users in remote locations can share ideas on the Liveboard through the use of a wireless pen-input device and network connections
>
> *Computing*

devise *verb* to plan *or* build a system; *they devised a cheap method of avoiding the problem*

Dewey decimal classification *noun* library cataloguing system using classes and subclasses that are arranged in groups of ten

DFD = DATA FLOW DIAGRAM

DGIS = DIRECT GRAPHICS INTERFACE STANDARD standard graphics interface for video adapters, primarily used with the 340x0 range of graphics chips

DHCP = DYNAMIC HOST CONFIGURATION PROTOCOL TCP/IP protocols that is used to assign an Internet address to nodes (workstations or servers) in a network; a special server running DHCP software manages the process of assigning addresses - a client computer can then ask this server for the address of another node on the network

Dhrystone benchmark *noun* benchmarking system developed to try and measure and compare the performance of computers; *see also* BENCHMARK

DIA/DCA = DOCUMENT INTERCHANGE ARCHITECTURE/ DOCUMENT CONTENT ARCHITECTURE standard method for the transmission and storage of documents, text and video over networks; part of the IBM SNA range of standards

diacritic *noun* accent above *or* below a letter

diagnosis *noun* finding of a fault *or* discovering the cause of a fault

diagnostic aid *noun* hardware *or* software device that helps to find faults; **diagnostic chip** = chip that contains circuits to carry out tests on other circuits *or* chips; **diagnostic message** = message that appears to explain the type, location and probable cause of a software error *or* hardware failure; **diagnostic program** = software that helps find faults in a computer system; **diagnostic routine** = routine in a program which helps to find faults in a computer system; **diagnostic test** = means of locating faults in hardware and software by test circuits *or* programs

diagnostics *noun* features *or* tests that help a user find faults in hardware *or* software; **compiler diagnostics** = features in a compiler that help the programmer find faults

diagonal cut *noun* method of joining two pieces of film *or* magnetic tape together by cutting the ends at an angle so making the join less obvious

diagram *noun* drawing which shows something as a plan *or* a map; *diagram showing sales locations; he drew a diagram to show how the decision-making processes work; the paper gives a diagram of the company's organizational structure*; **flow diagram** = diagram showing the arrangement of work processes in a series

diagrammatic *adjective* **in diagrammatic form** = in the form of a diagram; *the chart showed the sales pattern in diagrammatic form*

diagrammatically *adverb* using a diagram; *the chart shows the sales pattern diagrammatically*

dial 1 *verb* to call a telephone number on a telephone; *to dial a number; to dial the operator; he dialled the code for the USA; you can dial New York direct from London*; **to dial direct** = to contact a phone number without asking the operator to do it for you; **to dial into** = to call a telephone number, which has a modem and computer at the other end; *with the right access it is possible to dial into a customer's computer to extract the files wanted for typesetting* (NOTE: GB English is **dialling - dialled,** but US spelling is **dialing - dialed) 2** *noun* **(a)** circular mechanical device which is turned to select something **(b)** round face on an instrument, with numbers which indicate something (such as the time on a clock); *to tune into the radio station, turn the dial*; **dial conference** = facility on a private exchange that allows one user to call a number of other extensions for a teleconference; **dial modifier** = extra commands sent to a Hayes-compatible modem that instruct the modem to use a particular system when dialing a telephone number; for example, the command 'ATDT123' tells the modem to use tone-dialing to dial the number '123'; *see also* AT COMMAND SET; **dial pulse** = pulse-coded signals transmitted to represent numbers dialled; **dial tone** = sound made by a telephone that indicates that the telephone system is ready for a number to be dialled; **dial-in modem** = auto-answer modem that can be called at any time; **density dial** = knob that controls the density of a printed image; *if the text fades, turn the density dial on the printer to full black*; **dial-up access** = a connection to the Internet that is not permanent but that is established whenever you need access to the Internet; *you will need a modem to use dial-up access to the Internet; in our company we use the Internet a lot so have a leased line rather than dial-up access; most ISPs provide dial-up access to the Internet; the new ADSL standard is not dial-up access, it is always on*; **dial-up connection** = the process of connecting to a computer over a telephone link; **Dial-up Networking (DUN)** = part of the Windows operating system that supports and manages a dial-up link to a remote computer; **dialup** *or* **dial-up service** = online information service that is accessed by dialling into the central computer

dialect *noun* slight variation of a standard language; programming languages from different manufacturers often contain slight differences and enhancements when compared to the standard

Dialer *or* **Phone Dialer** utility provided with Windows that will dial telephone numbers for you, if you have a modem connected to your PC; when the person picks up the telephone, you pick up the handset and talk as normal

dialling *noun* act of calling a telephone number; **dialling code** = special series of numbers which you use to make a call to another town *or* country; **dialling tone** = sound made by a telephone that indicates that the telephone system is ready for a number to be dialled; **international direct dialling (IDD)** = calling telephone numbers in other countries direct (NOTE: no plural)

```
Customers  will  be  able  to
choose  a  wide  variety  of
telephony products, from basic
auto-dial    programs    to
call-centre applications
```
Computing

dialogue *or* **dialog** *noun* speech *or* speaking to another person; communication between devices such as computers; **dialogue box** = on-screen message from a program to the user

diameter *noun* distance across a round object

DIANE = DIRECT INFORMATION ACCESS NETWORK FOR EUROPE services offered over the Euronet network

diaphragm *noun* **(a)** mechanical device in a camera that varies the aperture size **(b)** thin flexible sheet which vibrates in response to sound waves to create an electrical signal (as in a microphone) or in response to electrical signals to create sound waves (as in a speaker)

diapositive *noun* positive transparency

diary *noun* book in which you can write notes *or* appointments for each day of the week; **diary management** = part of an office computer program, which records schedules and appointments

diascope *noun* slide projector *or* device that projects slide images onto a screen

diazo (process) *noun* method for copying documents (using sensitized paper exposed to the original)

DIB 1 = DATA INPUT BUS bus used when transferring data from one section of a computer to another, such as between memory and CPU **2** = DEVICE INDEPENDENT BITMAP file format for a Microsoft Windows graphics image that consists of a header, colour table (palette) and bitmap data; can be in 1, 4, 8 or 24-bit colour resolution

dibit *noun* digit made up of two binary bits

dice *(film)* = DIGITAL INTERNATIONAL CONVERSION

EQUIPMENT early system for broadcast television standards conversion

dichotomizing search *noun* fast search method that is used on ordered list of data

> COMMENT: the dichotomizing search works as follows: the search key is compared with the data in the middle of the list and one half is discarded, this is repeated with the half remaining until only one data item remains

dichroic *noun* chemical coating on the surface of a lens which reflects selectively different colours of light

dichroic filter *noun (film)* transmits certain wavelengths and reflects those which are not transmitted; it is not capable of absorbing a great number of wavelengths

dichroic head *noun (film)* source of colour light which is based on adjustable dichroic filters; generally used with rostrum cameras and enlargers

dictate *verb* to say something to someone who then writes down your words; *to dictate a letter to a secretary; he was dictating orders into his pocket dictating machine*; **dictating machine** = small tape recorder that is used to record notes *or* letters dictated by someone, which a secretary can play back and type out the text

dictation *noun* act of dictating; **to take dictation** = to write down what someone is saying; **dictation speed** = number of words per minute which a secretary can write down in shorthand

dictionary *noun* **(a)** book which lists words and meanings **(b)** data management structure which allows files to be referenced and sorted **(c)** part of a spelling checker program: the list of correctly spelled words against which the program checks a text; *see also* SPELLCHECKER

dielectric *noun* insulating material that allows an electric field to pass, but not an electric current

DIF file = DATA INTERCHANGE FORMAT de facto standard that defines the way a spreadsheet, its formula and data are stored in a file

differ *verb* not to be the same as something else; *the two products differ considerably -*

one has an electric motor, the other runs on oil

difference *noun* way in which two things are not the same; *what is the difference between these two products? differences in price* or *price differences*

different *adjective* not the same; *our product range is quite different in design from the Japanese models; we offer ten models each in six different colours*

differential *adjective* which shows a difference; *(film)* **differential focus** = cinematographic style where the area behind and in front of the action is not as clearly focused as the action itself; *see also* SPLIT-FOCUS SHOT; **differential pulse coded modulation (DPCM)** = method of encoding an analogue signal into a digital form in which the value recorded is equal to the difference between the current sample and the previous sample pulse coded modulation that uses the difference in size of a sample value and the previous one, requiring fewer bits when transmitting

diffraction *noun (film)* bending or spreading of sound waves, radio or light which is caused by contact with objects; **diffraction lens** = lens which is used for special effects

diffuse *verb* to move *or* insert something over an area *or* through a substance; *the smoke from the faulty machine rapidly diffused through the building; the chemical was diffused into the substrate*

diffuser *noun (film)* transparent frosted gel or glass which is attached to lamps in order to soften lighting

diffusion *noun* **(a)** means of transferring doping materials into an integrated circuit substrate **(b)** light dispersion

digipulse telephone *noun* push button telephone dialling method using coded pulses

digit *noun* symbol *or* character which represents an integer that is smaller than the radix of the number base used; *a phone number with eight digits or an eight-digit phone number; the decimal digit 8*; *see also* RADIX

digital *adjective* which represents data *or* physical quantities in numerical form (especially using a binary system in computer related devices); **digital audio**

disk (DAD) = method of recording sound by converting and storing signals in a digital form on magnetic disk, providing very high quality reproduction; *see also* COMPACT DISC; **digital audio stationary head (DASH)** = sound tape recording system; **digital audio tape (DAT)** = compact cassette, smaller than an audio cassette, that provides a system of recording sound as digital information onto magnetic tape with very high-quality reproduction; also used as a high-capacity tape backup system that can store 1.3Gb of data; sound is recorded at a sample rate of either 32, 44.1 or 48KHz to provide up to two hours of CD-quality sound; **digital camera** = (i) camera that uses a bank of CCD units to capture an image and store it digitally on to a miniature disk or in RAM in the camera's body; (ii) video camera that stores images in digital form - the light from the image is converted into thousands of individual pixels which store the intensity of the light at that point as a number, using either a light-sensitive cell or CCD unit; in a colour camera there are three sets of CCD units, each of which detects a particular colour and generates values representing the red, green and blue components of the colour; *see also* PHOTOCD; **digital cash** = method of paying for goods over the Internet; *see also* DIGITAL WALLET; E-COMMERCE; MICROPAYMENTS; **digital cassette** = high quality magnetic tape housed in a standard size cassette with write protect tabs, and a standard format leader; **digital certificate** = *see* CERTIFICATE; **digital channel** = communications path that can only transmit data as digital signals; voice, image or video signals have to be converted from analog to digital form before they can be transmitted over a digital channel; *see also* ANALOG TO DIGITAL CONVERTER; **digital clock** *or* **watch** = clock *or* watch which shows the time as a series of digits (such as 12:22:04); **digital compact cassette (DCC)** = magnetic tape in a compact cassette box that is used to store computer data or audio signals in a digital format; DCC is the newer version of the traditional audio cassette, but it has CD quality sound with the digital storage; **digital computer** = machine which processes data represented in discrete terms, that is, data elements and variables are in binary notation and are made up of several bits, which can be one of only two numbers (0 or 1); *compare with* ANALOG; **digital data** = data represented in (usually binary) numerical form; = **Digital Equipment Corporation** = computer company that produces a range of high-performance workstations, mini computers and developed the new Alpha processor that offers high-performance 64-bit data handling and can run Windows NT and standard Windows applications; **digital international conversion equipment (dice)** = early system for broadcast standards conversion; **digital display** = video display that can only show a fixed number of colours or shades of grey; **digital monitor** = video monitor that can only show a fixed number of colours or shades of grey; the monitor accepts a digital signal from the display adapter in the computer and converts it into an analog signal; examples are MDA, CGA and EGA monitors; *compare with* ANALOG MONITOR; **digital multimeter (DMM)** = multimeter that uses a digital readout (giving better clarity than an AMM); **digital nonlinear editing** = *see* NONLINEAR VIDEO EDITING; **digital optical recording (DOR)** = recording signals in binary form as small holes in the surface of an optical or compact disc which can then be read by laser; *(film)* **digital pitch changer** = system which uses digital technique to change pitch of the original sound; used to reduce onset of threshold howl; **digital plotter** = plotter whose pen position is controllable in discrete steps, so that drawings in the computer can be output graphically; **digital recording** = conversion of sound signals into a digital form and storing them on magnetic disk *or* tape usually in binary form; *see* DIGITAL VIDEO, NONLINEAR VIDEO EDITING, MAGNETIC RECORDING; **digital resolution** = smallest number that can be represented with one digit; the value assigned to the least significant bit of a word or number; **digital signal** = electric signal that has only a number of possible states, as opposed to analog signals which are totally variable; **digital signalling** = control and dialling codes sent down a telephone line in digital form; **digital signal processor (DSP)** = special processor that carries out

mathematical calculations on digital signals which have been converted from original analog signals (such as voice, audio or video); this type of processor is now used in telecommunications, voice processing, multimedia applications and modems; **digital signature** = unique identification code sent by a terminal or device in digital form, often used as a means of confirming the authenticity of a message or instruction; **digital speech** = *see* SPEECH SYNTHESIS; **digital switching** = operating communications connections and switches only by use of digital signals; **digital to analog converter** *or* **D to A converter (DAC)** = circuit that converts a digital signal to an analog one (the analog signal is proportional to an input binary number); **digital subscriber line (DSL)** = system of transmitting data at high speed over standard telephone wire; one of the most popular DSL implementation is the ADSL (asymetric digital subscriber line) scheme that provides a permanent, high-speed connection to the Internet over standard telephone lines; *see also* ADSL, POTS; **digital transmission system** = communications achieved by converting analog signals to a digital form then modulating and transmitting this, the signal is then converted back to analog form at the receiver; **digital versatile disc** = *see* DVD; **digital video** = video recorded in digital form; the output from a video camera is converted to digital form using either a digital camera or a frame grabber - the digital output is then normally compressed before being processed or transmitted or stored on videotape; **digital video effects** = *see* DVE; **Digital Video Interactive (DV-I)** = system that defines how video and audio signals should be compressed onto disk and then decompressed during playback on a computer; *the DV-I technology is currently produced by Intel as a chip-set which can record or playback compressed full-motion video in real time*; **digital wallet** = feature of new web browsers that makes it simpler and more secure to buy goods from online shops; the digital wallet contains a unique personal digital signature and allows the user to pay for your goods in many different ways, including credit card or digital cash

digitally *adverb* (quantity represented) in digital form; *the machine takes digitally recorded data and generates an image*

digitize *verb* to change analog movement *or* signals into a digital form which can be processed by computers, etc.; *if you digitize speech you use an analog-to-digital converter to convert the sound into a series of numbers that can be stored on disk and then played back*; **digitized photograph** = image *or* photograph that has been scanned to produce an analog signal which is then converted to digital form and stored *or* displayed on a computer; **digitizing pad** *or* **tablet** = sensitive surface that translates the position of a pen into numerical form, so that drawings can be entered into a computer

digitizer *noun* analog to digital converter *or* device which converts an analog movement *or* signal to a digital one which can be understood by a computer

The contract covers fibre optic cable and Synchronous Digital Hierarchy transmission equipment to be used to digitize the telecommunications network
Computergram

DIL *see* DUAL IN-LINE PACKAGE

DIM = DOCUMENT IMAGE MANAGEMENT software that allows a user to capture, store and index printed text in a digital form

dimension *noun* measurement of size; *the dimensions of the computer are small enough for it to fit into a case*

dimensioning *noun* definition of the size of something (usually an array *or* matrix); *array dimensioning occurs at this line*

dimmer *noun* *(film)* electronic or electrical device which reduces the brightness of lights

DIN = DEUTSCHE INDUSTRIENORM German industry standards organization; often refers to specification for plugs and sockets

Dingbat *noun* font that contains stars, bullets, symbols, images and drawings in place of characters, designed by Zapf; *to insert a copyright symbol, use the Dingbat font*

diode *noun* electronic component that allows an electrical current to pass in one direction and not the other; **diode transistor logic** = method of constructing logic functions in an integrated circuit using diodes and transistors; **light-emitting diode (LED)** = semiconductor diode that emits light when a current is applied (used in clock and calculator displays, and as an indicator)

Sullivan would not reveal the launch power of the diode, except that it was twice that of existing LEDs because of the higher efficiency of electron injection in the part
Electronic Times

diopter *or* **dioptre** *noun* unit of measurement of the refractive power of a lens; **diopter lens** = optical device that is placed in front of a standard camera lens when close up shots are required

DIP 1 = DOCUMENT IMAGE PROCESSING software that allows a user to capture, store and index printed text in a digital form **2** = DUAL IN-LINE PACKAGE standard layout for integrated circuit packages using two parallel rows of connecting pins along each side; **DIP switch** = number of small switches joined together that are used to configure a device; *use the DIP switches to set the interrupt level for this I/O card*

diplex *noun* simultaneous transmission of two signals over the same line

dipole *noun* **(a)** material *or* molecule *or* object that has two potentials, one end positive and the other negative, due to electron displacement from an applied electric field **(b)** short straight radio aerial that receives a signal from a central connector

DIR = DIRECTORY *(in MS-DOS)* system command that displays a list of files stored on a disk

direct 1 *verb* to manage *or* to organize; *he directs our European operations; she was directing the development unit until last year* **2** *noun* straight *or* with no interference *or* going in a straight way; **direct access** = storage and retrieval of data without the need to read other data first; **direct (access) address** = ABSOLUTE ADDRESS; **direct access storage device (DASD)** =

storage medium whose memory locations can be directly read *or* written to; **direct addressing** = method of addressing where the storage location address given in the instruction is the location to be used; **direct broadcast satellite (DBS)** = TV and radio signal broadcast over a wide area from an earth station via a satellite, received with a dish aerial; **direct cable connection** = a utility supplied free with Windows 95 that allows you to link two computers together using a serial cable plugged into each serial port; *see also* BRIEFCASE UTILITY; **direct changeover** = switching from one computer to another in one go; **direct cinema** = usage of sound recorders and hand-held cameras to film live action with natural sound; *(film)* **direct colour print** = colour print made from the original film; **direct connect** = (modem) which plugs straight into the standard square telephone socket; **direct current (DC)** = constant value electric current that flows in one direction; *(film)* **direct cut** = the joining of two shots in one scene in order to continue the action without interruption; **direct data entry (DDE)** = keying in data directly onto a magnetic disk *or* tape; **direct dialling** = calling a telephone number without passing through an internal exchange; **direct domestic reception (DDR)** = television transmission by satellite; **direct graphics interface standard** = *see* DGIS; **direct image** = image that is composed directly onto the screen rather than being composed off-screen in memory before it is displayed; **direct image film** = photographic film that produces a positive image; **direct impression** = use of a typewriter to compose a piece of text that is to be printed; **direct information access network for Europe (DIANE)** = services offered over the Euronet network; **direct inward dialling** = automatic routing of telephone calls in a private exchange; **direct mail** = selling a product by sending publicity material to possible customers through the post; *these calculators are only sold by direct mail; the company runs a successful direct-mail operation*; **direct-mail advertising** = advertising by sending leaflets to people through the post; **direct memory access (DMA)** = direct rapid link between a peripheral and a computer's main memory which avoids accessing routines

for each item of data required; **direct outward dialling** = automatic access to a telephone network form a private exchange **3** *adverb* straight *or* with no third party involved; *we pay income tax direct to the government*; **to dial direct** = to contact a phone number yourself without asking the operator to do it for you; *you can dial New York direct from London if you want*

direction *noun* **(a)** organizing *or* managing; *he took over the direction of a software distribution group* **(b) directions for use** = instructions showing how to use something (NOTE: no plural for **(a)**)

directional *adjective* which points in a certain direction; **directional antenna** = aerial that transmits *or* receives signals from a single direction; **directional pattern** = chart of the response of an aerial *or* microphone to signals from various directions

directive *noun* programming instruction used to control the language translator

directly *adverb* **(a)** immediately; *he left for the airport directly after receiving the telephone message* **(b)** straight *or* with no third party involved; *we deal directly with the manufacturer, without using a wholesaler*

Director *noun* multimedia authoring software developed by Macromedia that uses a grid to allow a user to control elements over time

director *noun* **(a)** person appointed by the shareholders to help run a company; **managing director** = director who is in charge of the whole company; **board of directors** = all the directors of a company **(b)** person who is in charge of a project, an official institute, etc.; *the director of the government computer research institute; she was appointed director of the organization* **(c)** person who controls the filming of a film *or* TV programme; **director of photography** = *see* CINEMATOGRAPHER; **casting director** = person in charge of choosing the actors for a film *or* TV programme; **lighting director** = person in charge of lighting in a film *or* TV studio; **technical director** = person in charge of the technical equipment (especially the cameras) in a TV studio

directory *noun* **(a)** list of people *or* businesses with information about their addresses and telephone numbers; = **directory website** = website that contains a list of other websites, normally organised into sections and often with a search feature; *Yahoo! (www.yahoo.com) is one of the best-known directories and lists over half a million websites; see also* SEARCH ENGINE; **classified directory** = list of businesses grouped under various headings, such as computer shops *or* newsagents; **commercial directory** *or* **trade directory** = book which lists all the businesses and business people in a town; **street directory** = list of people living in a street; map of a town which lists all the streets in alphabetical order in an index; **telephone directory** = book which lists all people and businesses in alphabetical order with their phone numbers; *to look up a number in the telephone directory; his number is in the London directory* (b) method of organising the files stored on a disk; a directory contains a group of files or further sub-directories; *(in MS-DOS and UNIX)* **change directory (CD)** = system command to move to a directory; **disk directory** = list of names and information about files in a backing storage device; **make directory (MD)** = system command to create a new directory on the disk; **remove directory (RD)** = system command to remove an empty directory from disk; **root directory** = directory at the top of the directory tree structure; **sub-directory** = directory within a directory; *see also* FOLDER, TREE (STRUCTURE) **directory routing** = means of directing messages in a packet switching network by a list of preferred routes at each node

COMMENT: a directory is best imagined as a folder within a draw of a filing cabinet; the folder can contain files or other folders

disable *verb* to prevent a device *or* function from operating; *he disabled the keyboard to prevent anyone changing the data;* **disable interrupt** = command to the CPU to ignore any interrupt signals

disassembler *noun* software that translates a machine code program back into an assembly language form

disc *noun* flat circular plate that can contain data as tiny holes, read by a laser;

'disc' normally refers to optical storage, whereas magnetic media uses the spelling 'disk'; **optical disc** = disk which contains binary data in the form of small holes which are read by a laser beam (also called WORM (write once, read many) when used on computers, and compact discs and videodiscs for sound *or* film); *see also* CD-ROM, COMPACT DISC, DISK

discard *verb* to throw out something which is not needed

disclose *verb* to reveal details of something which were supposed to be secret

disclosure *noun* act of telling details about something

disconnect *verb* to unplug *or* break a connection between two devices; **disconnect signal** = code transmitted over a telephone line to indicate that the connection should be broken

discrete *adjective* (values *or* events *or* energy *or* data) which occurs in small individual units; *the data word is made up of discrete bits;* **discrete component** = a single component; **discrete multi-tone** = *see* DMT

discretionary *adjective* which can be used if wanted *or* not used if not wanted; **discretionary hyphen** *or* **soft hyphen** = hyphen which is inserted to show that a word is broken (as at the end of a line), but which is not present when the word is written normally

discussion group *noun* (i) feature of a website that lets visitors discuss a particular subject; any visitor can write and post a message that is displayed to any other visitors, who can then add their comments in reply to the message; (ii) *see* NEWSGROUP

dish aerial *noun* circular concave directional aerial used to pick up long distance transmissions; *we use a dish aerial to receive signals from the satellite*

disjointed *adjective* (set of information *or* data) that has no common subject

disk *noun* flat circular plate coated with a substance that is capable of being magnetized (data is stored on this by magnetizing selective sections to represent binary digits); disk normally refers to magnetic storage, whereas disc refers to optical storage; **backup disk** = disk which contains a copy of the information from other disks, as a security precaution; **disk cache** = high speed section of memory that is used to temporarily store frequently used data that has been read from the disk; the computer checks the cache to see if the data is there before it accesses the (much slower) disk and by using special controller software, this system can dramatically improve apparent disk performance; **disk cartridge** = protective case containing a removable hard disk; **disk compression** = a method of increasing the apparent capacity of a disk to store data; a special piece of software compresses the data as it is being saved to disk and then decompresses the data when it is read back; **disk controller** = IC or circuits used to translate a request for data by the CPU into control signals for the disk drive (including motor control and access arm movement); **disk compression** = method of increasing the apparent capacity of a disk to store data by using special software to compress the data as it is being saved to disk and then decompresses the data when it is read back from the disk; **disk crash** = fault caused by the read/write head touching the surface of the disk; **disk drive** = device that spins a magnetic disk and controls the position of the read/write head; **disk file** = number of related records *or* data items stored under one name on disk; **disk formatting** = initial setting up of a blank disk with track and sector markers and other control information; **disk map** = display of the organization of data on a disk; **disk mirroring** *or* **duplexing** = data protection system in which all or part of a hard disk is duplicated onto another, separate, disk drive; any changes made to the data on the original drive are duplicated on the mirrored drive; **disk operating system (DOS)** = section of the operating system software that controls disk and file management; **MS disk operating system** *or* **Microsoft DOS (MS-DOS)** = popular DOS for microcomputers; **disk pack** = number of disks on a single hub, each with its own read/write head; **disk partition** = *see* PARTITION; **disk storage** = using disks as a backing store; **disk tools** = a set of software programs that help to monitor the performance of a disk, maintain it and ensure that it is storing data efficiently; **fixed disk** = disk which is permanently

fixed in a computer with its own inbuilt read/write head; **floppy disk** = small disk for storing information which can be removed from a computer; **hard disk** = solid disk which will store a large amount of computer information in a sealed case, and cannot usually be removed from the computer; **Winchester disk** = hard disk with a large storage capacity sealed in a computer

COMMENT: the disk surface is divided into tracks which can be accessed individually; magnetic tapes cannot be accessed in this way

diskette *noun* light, flexible disk that can store data in a magnetic form, used in most personal computers

diskless *adjective* which does not use disks for data storage; *diskless system; they want to create a diskless workstation*

dispenser *noun* device which gives out something; **cash dispenser** = device which gives money when a card is inserted and special instructions keyed in

dispersion *noun* separation of a beam of light into its different wavelengths

displacement *noun* offset used in an indexed address

display 1 *noun* device on which information *or* images can be presented; **display adapter** = device which allows information in a computer to be displayed on a CRT (the adapter interfaces with both the computer and CRT); **composite display** = video display unit that accepts a single composite video signal and can display an infinite number of colours *or* shade of grey; **digital display** = video display unit that can only show a fixed number of colours *or* shades of grey; **display attribute** = variable which defines the shape *or* size *or* colour of text *or* graphics displayed; **display character** = graphical symbol which appears as a printed *or* displayed item, such as one of the letters of the alphabet *or* a number; **display character generator** = ROM that provides the display circuits with a pattern of dots which represent the character; **display colour** = colour of characters in a videotext display system; **display cycle** = operations required to display an image on screen; **display device** = *see* VIDEO DISPLAY; **display element** =

(i) *(in graphics)* a basic graphic component, such as a background, foreground, text or graphics image; (ii) *(in computer graphics)* any component of an image; **display format** = number of characters that can be displayed on a screen, given as row and column lengths; **display highlights** = emphasis of certain words *or* paragraphs by changing character display colour; **display line** = horizontal printing positions for characters in a line of text; **display mode** = way of referring to the character set to be used, usually graphics *or* alphanumerics; **Display PostScript** = an extension of PostScript that allows PostScript commands to be interpreted and displayed on screen so that a user can see exactly what will appear on the printer; **display screen** = the physical part of a Visual Display Unit, terminal *or* monitor, which allows the user to see characters *or* graphics (usually a Cathode Ray Tube, but sometimes LCD *or* LED displays are used); **display size** = character size greater than 14 points, used in composition and headlines rather than normal text; **display space** = memory *or* amount of screen available to show graphics *or* text; **display unit** = computer terminal *or* piece of equipment that is capable of showing data *or* information, usually by means of CRT; **gas discharge** *or* **plasma display** = flat lightweight display screen that is made up of two flat pieces of glass covered with a grid of conductors, separated by a thin layer of gas which luminesces when a point of the grid is selected by two electrical signals; *see also* VISUAL DISPLAY UNIT **2** *verb* to show information; *the customer's details were displayed on the screen; by keying HELP, the screen will display the options available to the user*

Barco Chromatics is to supply colour display monitors to the IBM/Siemens Plessey consortium, which is installing the New En Route Centre for air-traffic control

Computing

---

dissolve *noun* transition effect between two scenes or audio segments in which one fades out as the second fades in

distant *adjective* which is located some way away; *the distant printers are connected with cables*

distinguish *verb* to tell the difference between two things; *the OCR has difficulty in distinguishing certain characters*

distort *verb* to introduce unwanted differences between a signal input and output from a device

distortion *noun* unwanted differences in audio *or* light signals before and after they have passed through a piece of equipment *or* lens; **distortion optics** = optical devices that are attached to a camera or optical printer to create special effects; **image distortion** = fault in an optical lens causing the image to be distorted

distribute *verb* **(a)** to break up (and sometimes melt down) old used metal type **(b)** to send out data *or* information to users in a network *or* system; **distributed adaptive routing** = directing messages in a packet network switching system by an exchange of information between nodes; **distributed database system** = data system where the data is kept on different disks in different places; **distributed data processing** = operations to derive information from data which is kept in different places; **distributed file system** = system that uses files stored in more than one location *or* backing store but are processed at a central point; **distributed (data) processing (DDP)** = system of processing in a large organization with many small computers at different workstations instead of one central computer; **distributed system** = computer system which uses more than one processor in different locations, all connected to a central computer

distribution *noun* act of sending information out, especially via a network; **distribution network** = *see* LAN, WAN; **distribution point** = point from which cable television *or* telephone signals are split up from a main line and sent to individual users' homes

distributor *noun* company which sells goods for another company which manufactures them; *he is the UK distributor for a Japanese software house*

CORBA sets out a standard for how objects in applications,

```
repositories    or    class
libraries should make requests
and receive responses across a
distributed computing network
```
Computing

dither *verb* **(a)** to create a curve or line that looks smoother by adding shaded pixels beside the pixels that make up the image **(b)** to create the appearance of a new colour by a pattern of coloured pixels that appear, to the eye, to combine and form a new, composite colour (for example, a pattern of black and white dots will appear like grey); **dithered colour** = colour that is made up of a pattern of different coloured pixels

dittogram *noun* printing error caused by repeating the same letter twice

DIV = DATA IN VOICE digital satellite data transmission in place of a voice channel

divergence *noun* failure of light *or* particle beams to meet at a certain point

diversity *noun* coming from more than one source; being aimed at more than one use; **beam diversity** = using a single frequency communications band for two different sets of data

diverter *noun* circuit *or* device that redirects a message *or* signal from one path or route to another; **call diverter** = device which, on receiving a telephone call, contacts another point and re-routes the call

divide *verb* **(a) to divide a number by four** = to find out how many fours can be contained in the other number; *twenty-one divided by three gives seven* **(b)** to cut *or* to split into parts; *in the hyphenation program, long words are automatically divided at the end of lines*

divider *noun* **frequency divider** = circuit which divides the frequency of a signal by a certain amount to change the pitch

division *noun* act of dividing

DLL = DYNAMIC LINK LIBRARY; *(in Microsoft Windows)* library of utility programs that can be called from a main program; *the word-processor calls a spell-check program that is stored as a DLL*; **DLL file** = file containing a library of routines that can be used by another program when required during the program's execution

DMA = DIRECT MEMORY ACCESS direct rapid link between a peripheral and a computer's main memory, which avoids accessing routines for each item of data read; **DMA controller** = interface IC that controls high-speed data transfer between a high-speed peripheral and main memory, usually the controller will also halt *or* cycle steal from the CPU; **DMA cycle stealing** = CPU allowing the DMA controller to send data over the bus during clock cycles when it performs internal *or* NOP instructions

```
A  32-bit  DMA  controller,
16-bit video I/O ports and I/O
filters complete the chip.
```
Computing

DMM = DIGITAL MULTIMETER

DMT = DISCRETE MULTI-TONE technology that uses digital signal processors to transmit video, sound, image and data over cable at high speed

DNS = DOMAIN NAME SERVICE

DOC *(film)* = DROP-OUT COMPENSATOR provides a signal which reinstates lost information on a videotape when it has been temporarily misplaced

dock *verb* to connect a laptop computer to a special device that provides extra connections and the same resources as a desktop computer; *he carries his laptop with him and docks it when he is at his office*; **docking station** *or* **docking unit** = device unit that connects to a laptop computer to provide expansion ports, connectors and the same resources as a desktop computer

docket *noun US* record of an official proceeding

document 1 *noun* piece of paper with writing on it; **document assembly** = *see* DOCUMENT MERGE; **document delivery service** = sending of a document which has been selected from an index *or* database; **document image management (DIM) or processing (DIP)** = software that allows a user to capture, store and index printed text in a digital form; **document image processing (DIP)** = process of scanning paper documents, performing OCR on the contents and storing this on disk so that it can be searched for; **document interchange architecture/document content**

architecture = *see* DIA/DCA; **document mark** = mark on a roll of microfilm, to provide a facility for counting frames; **document merge** = creating a new file by combining two or more sections *or* complete documents; **document processing** = processing of documents (such as invoices) by a computer; **document reader** = device which converts written *or* typed information to a form that a computer can understand and process; **document recovery** = program which allows a document which has been accidentally deleted to be recovered; **document retrieval system** = information storage and retrieval system that contains complete documents rather than just quotes *or* references **2** *verb* to write a description of a process

documentation *noun* **(a)** all documents referring to something; *please send all documentation concerning the product* **(b)** information, notes and diagrams that describe the function, use and operation of a piece of hardware *or* software (NOTE: no plural)

Dolby system *noun (film)* system for reducing background noise for recordings

dollar sign *noun* printed *or* written character ($) used in some languages to identify a variable as a string type

dolly *noun (film)* moveable stand on which the camera is mounted in order to be able to follow the action; *see also* TRACKING; **dolly pusher** = grip who moves the dolly during filming; **dolly shot** = shot filmed while the camera is moving away from the action

DOM = DOCUMENT OBJECT MODEL scheme that describes how the different parts of a web page (the text, images, and hyperlinks) are represented; each item is an object and has a set of attributes that defines how it is displayed and managed by a web browser; dynamic HTML (DHTML) uses DOM to modify how a web page is displayed to different users; *see also* CSS; DHTML; XML

domain *noun* **(a)** area of responsibility; **public domain** = land *or* property *or* information which belongs to and is available to the public; **program which is in the public domain** = program which is not copyrighted **(b)** area *or* group of nodes in a network **(c)** *(on the Internet)* part of the way of naming users on the Internet in which the domain name is the name of the service provider or company the user works for; in an electronic mail address, the domain name follows the '@' symbol and is a unique name that identifies the location of an Internet server or computer on the Internet. *our domain name is 'petercollin.com'*; **domain name registration** = to apply for the right to use a domain name; *see also* DNS, IP ADDRESS; **domain name server (DNS)** = computer on the Internet that stores part or all of the domain name system database; **domain name system (DNS)** = distributed database used on the Internet to convert a name to its IP address; for example, the domain name 'pcp.co.uk' is simple to remember and a DNS computer would convert this to its correct IP address such as 158.137.234.112; *see also* DISTRIBUTED DATABASE, IP **(d) domain controller** = a server in a network that is responsible for user security and verifying passwords within a group of other servers

COMMENT: to view a web page a user types in the web page address into a web browser; the browser sends this address to the nearest computer that is part of the domain name service database, asking for the IP address of the domain name entered. The DNS database returns the Internet address that identifies the location of the server that stores the web page. Domain names are followed by a suffix that describes the type of organisation and the country in which it is located. Common suffix letters are: .com - commercial site or business (originally based in the USA); .edu - education organisation; .gov - government organisation; .mil - military organisation; .net - network or service provider company; .org - miscellaneous organisations. Country identifiers are two-letters long and are at the very end of the domain name: .ar - Argentina; .be - Belgium; .ca - Canada; .ch - Switzerland; .de - Germany; .fr - France; jp - Japan; .uk - United Kingdom. New suffix types include .info - for websites providing information and .biz - for an e-commerce site.

domestic *adjective* referring to the home market *or* the market of the country where the business is based; **domestic consumption** = consumption on the home market; **domestic market** = market in the country where a company is based; *they produce goods for the domestic market*; **domestic production** = production of goods for domestic consumption; **domestic satellite** = satellite used for television *or* radio transmission, rather than research *or* military applications

dongle *noun* coded circuit *or* chip that has to be present in a system before a piece of copyright software will run

dopant *noun* chemical substance that is diffused *or* implanted onto the substrate of a chip during manufacture, to provide it with n- or p-type properties

dope *verb* to introduce a dopant into a substance

dope sheet *noun (film)* list consisting of the descriptions of takes on a roll of film which is generally used when filming unscripted shots or documentaries

doped *adjective* (chip) which has had a dopant added

doping *noun* adding of dopant to a chip

DOR = DIGITAL OPTICAL RECORDING

DOS = DISK OPERATING SYSTEM section of the operating system software that controls the disk and file access; **MS-DOS** = operating system developed by Microsoft for the IBM PC; **DR-DOS** = operating system developed by Digital Research for the IBM PC

dot *noun* small round spot; *see also* BIT MAP; **dot addressable** = display adapter that allows software to control each pixel (or dot) on the display; **dot command** = method of writing instructions with a full stop followed by the command, used mainly for embedded commands in word-processor systems; **dot matrix** = method of forming characters by use of dots inside a rectangular matrix; **dot-matrix printer** = printer in which the characters are made up by a series of closely spaced dots, it produces a page line by line; a dot-matrix printer can be used either for printing using a ribbon *or* for thermal *or* electrostatic printing; **dots per inch** *or* **d.p.i.** *or* **dpi** = standard method used to describe the resolution capabilities of a page printer *or*

scanner; the greater the number of dots, the smaller each must be and therefore the more capable the printer is of producing sharper and clearer text and graphics; *some laser printers offer high resolution printing at 1200 dpi*; **dot pitch** = the vertical distance between the centre of two similar-coloured phosphor dots on a colour screen; the smaller the distance between the dots, the sharper the image displayed; typically the dot pitch is between .20 to .40mm; *(in dBASE programming language)* **dot prompt** = command prompt displayed as a single dot on screen; **dot signal** = telegraphy code, made up of marks and spaces

---

the characters are formed from an array of dots like in a dot-matrix printer, except that much higher resolution is used

Practical Computing

Star predicts that 500,000 customers will buy a dot matrix printer in the UK in the next 12 months

Computing

---

dotted-decimal-notation method of writing a domain name, email address or other IP network address using numbers and a decimal point (the full stop) to separate the numeric parts of the address; *the doman name 'petercollin.com' is the domain name is written in dotted-decimal- notation as '133.223.33.22'*

double *adjective* twice; twice as large; twice the size; **double buffering** = use of two buffers, allowing one to be read while the other is being written to; **double-click** = to click twice, rapidly, on a mouse button to start an action; *move the pointer to the icon then start the program with a double-click*; **double dagger** = typeset character (‡) used as a second reference mark; **double density** = system to double the storage capacity of a disk drive by doubling the number of bits which can be put on the disk surface; **double-density disk** = disk that can store two bits of data per unit area, compared to a standard disk; **double document** = error in photographing documents for microfilm, where the same image appears consecutively; **double exposure** = two images exposed on the same piece of photographic film, usually used for special effects; *(film)* **double frame** = in motion picture photography, when the image area is double the standard size; **double frame animation** = when each diagram or drawing in an animation sequence is photographed twice; *(in CD-i)* **double frequency scanning** method of doubling the vertical resolution of a monitor by scanning at twice the normal rate; **double-headed** = film projection equipment which can accept separate sound and picture films and run them at the same time; **double-perforation stock** = perforations on both edges of film stock; **double precision arithmetic** = use of two data words to store a number, providing greater precision; **double sideband** = modulation technique whose frequency spectrum contains two modulated signals above and below the unmodulated carrier frequency; **double-sided disk** = disk which can store information on both sides; **double-sided disk drive** = disk drive which can access data on double-sided disks; **double-sided** *or* **double-edged sound track** = film which has two separate magnetic strips on each edge onto which sound can be recorded; **double-sided printed circuit board (PCB)** = circuit board with conducting tracks on both sides; **double sideband suppressed carrier (DSBSC)** = modulation technique that uses two modulated signal sidebands, but no carrier signal; **double speed** = high speed at which a CD-ROM disc is spun by a drive, normally 460rpm; **double strike** = printing a character twice in order to make it appear bolder; **double system** = cinematographic system where sound and picture are recorded on different films, or on a film and a tape

down *adverb (of computers or programs)* not working; *the computer system went down twice during the afternoon* (NOTE: opposite is **up**); **down stroke** = wide heavy section of a character written with an ink pen

download *verb* **(a)** to load a program *or* section of data from a remote computer via a telephone line **(b)** to send printer font data stored on a disk to a printer (where it will be stored in temporary memory *or* RAM) **(c)** to transfer a file from a remote computer or online system onto your local computer; *he*

downloaded the latest driver files from the website

downloadable *adjective* which can be downloaded; **downloadable fonts** = fonts *or* typefaces stored on a disk, which can be downloaded *or* sent to a printer and stored in temporary memory *or* RAM

```
The cards will also download
the latest version of the
network drivers from the
server
```
Computing

downsize *verb* to move a company from a computer system based around a central mainframe computer to a networked environment (usually using PCs as workstations) in which the workstations are intelligent; *downsizing is more cost effective and gives more processing power to the end-user*

downtime *noun* period during which the computer *or* system is not usable

downward *adjective* towards a lower position; **downward compatibility** = ability of a complex computer system to work with a simple computer; *the mainframe is downward compatible with the micro*

dowser *noun (film)* shutter used to block the beam of light in a film printer or projector

dp = DATA PROCESSING operating on data to produce useful information *or* to sort and organize data files

DPA = DEMAND PROTOCOL ARCHITECTURE technique of loading protocol stacks in memory only if they are required for a particular session; *see also* PROTOCOL, STACK

d.p.i. *or* **dpi** = DOTS PER INCH standard method used to describe the resolution capabilities of a page printer *or* scanner; *a 600 d.p.i. black and white A4 monitor; a 600 dpi image scanner*

DPM = DATA PROCESSING MANAGER

draft 1 *noun* rough copy of a document before errors have been corrected; **draft printing** = low quality, high speed printing **2** *verb* to make a rough copy *or* drawing; *he drafted out the details of the program on a piece of paper*; **draft quality** = printed output that is formatted and readable, but is not of finished quality and might be printed at a low-resolution or not include all the illustrations, but which is faster to print

drag *verb* to move (a mouse) while holding the button down, so moving an image or icon on screen; **drag and drop** = feature of some GUIs (including X, Windows and Macintosh System) in which a user can drag a section of text *or* icon *or* object onto another program icon which starts this program and inserts the data; *drag and drop the document icon onto the word-processor icon and the system will start the program and load the document*; **drag image** = the cursor, icon or outline image that is displayed when you drag an object across the screen

> press the mouse button and drag the mouse: this produces a dotted rectangle on the screen
> *Desktop Publishing*

> you can easily enlarge the frame by dragging from any of the eight black rectangles round the border, showing that it is selected
> *Desktop Publishing*

drain 1 *noun* electrical current provided by a battery *or* power supply; connection to a FET **2** *verb* to remove *or* decrease power *or* energy from a device such as a battery

DRAM = DYNAMIC RANDOM ACCESS MEMORY

> cheap bulk memory systems are always built from DRAMs
> *Electronics & Power*

draw direct *noun* process of drawing an object directly to the screen rather than to an off-screen memory buffer

drawing program software that allows the user to draw and design on screen; *see also* PAINT PROGRAM

drawing tools *plural noun* range of functions in a paint program that allows the user to draw; normally displayed as icons in a toolbar, the drawing tools might include a circle-draw, line-draw and freehand drawing tools

D-region *noun* section of the ionosphere 50-90km above the earth's surface; *the*

D-region is the main cause of attenuation in transmitted radio signals

drift *noun* changes in the characteristics of a circuit with time *or* changing temperature

drill-down *verb (in a database or spreadsheet)* to work backwards and look at the individual items and formulae that produced the final result

drive 1 *noun* mechanical device in a computer which operates a tape or disk, spinning the disk to the correct speed and moving the read/write head to the correct location under software control; **drive letter** *or* **designator** = letter that denotes the disk drive currently being used; A and B are normally floppy disks, C is normally the hard disk in a personal computer; **disk drive** = device which spins a magnetic disk and controls the position of the read/write head; **tape drive** = mechanism that carries magnetic tape over the drive heads **2** *verb* to make a tape *or* disk work; *the disk is driven by a motor*

drive letters *noun (in Windows and DOS)* a system of letters to identify the different drives that are fitted to the PC

> COMMENT: a PC can have up to 26 drives fitted - one for each letter of the alphabet. Each drive is normally given a drive letter and the standard configuration is that A: is a floppy disk drive, B: is a second floppy disk drive, C: is the hard disk drive and D: is a CD-ROM drive. If the PC is connected to an office network, it might have other drive letters that map to a disk drive on someone else's PC. If the hard disk drive is very big, it might have been partitioned into manageable sections when the PC was bought. For example, if you have a hard disk drive with a 10Gb capacity, you might find it more useful to split it up into two sections each 5Gb in size. In this case, the first would be referred to as drive C: and the second as drive D:. If you added a CD-ROM drive to this PC, it would now be called drive E:

driver *or* **device driver** *or* **device handler** *noun* computer program *or* routine used to interface and manage an input/output device *or* other peripheral; **printer driver** = dedicated software that controls and formats users' commands ready for a printer

DRO = DESTRUCTIVE READOUT form of storage medium that loses its data after it has been read

drop *noun* fall to a lower position; **drop cable** = section of cable that links an adapter fitted in a workstation to the main network cable (sometimes to a transceiver or T-connector in the main network cable); **drop cap** = first letter in a sentence, printed in a larger typeface than the rest of the sentence; **drop-down list box** = list of options for an entry that appears when you move the cursor to the entry field; **drop-down menu** = list of options that appears below a menu title when it is selected; **drop line** = cable television line, running from a feeder cable to a user's home

drop in *noun* small piece of dirt that is on a disk *or* tape surface, which does not allow data to be recorded on that section

drop out *noun* **(a)** failure of a small piece of tape *or* disk to be correctly magnetized for the accurate storage of data **(b)** short signal loss in a magnetic recording system caused by faults in the magnetic medium or failure in head-to-tape contact; **drop-out compensator (DOC)** = provides a signal which reinstates lost information on a videotape when it has been temporarily misplaced

drum *noun* **(a)** helical scan video tape head assembly **(b)** rotatable cylinder around which film passes in order to ensure steady movement in a photographic sound reproducer **(c)** early type of magnetic computer storage; **drum plotter** = computer output device that consists of a movable pen and a piece of paper around a drum that can be rotated, creating patterns and text when both are moved in various ways; **magnetic drum** = cylindrical magnetic storage device

dry circuit *noun* voice signal transmitting circuit that contains no DC signals *or* levels; **dry joint** = faulty *or* badly made electrical connection; **dry run** = running a program with test data to check everything works

DSE = DATA SWITCHING EXCHANGE

DSL *see* DIGITAL SUBSCRIBER LINE

DSP = DIGITAL SIGNAL PROCESSOR special processor that carries out mathematical calculations on digital signals which have been converted from original analog signals (such as voice, audio or video); this type of processor is now used in telecommunications, voice processing, multimedia applications and modems

DSTP = DATA SPACE TRANSFER PROTOCOL scheme used to store and retrieve web-based data using the XML page markup system

DTC *(film)* = DUAL TIME CODE videotape recording system which provides two sets of time code information used when editing; *see also* TIME CODE

DTE = DATA TERMINAL EQUIPMENT device at which a communications path starts *or* finishes; = **DTE rates** = measure of how fast a device (normally refers to a modem) can exchange data with another PC taking into account data compression and coding systems; the DTE rate is normally much higher than the DCE rate

DTMF = DUAL TONE, MULTI-FREQUENCY communication signalling system using two different frequencies to transmit binary data

DTP = DESKTOP PUBLISHING the design, layout and printing of documents using special software, a desktop computer and a printer; the software normally provides a WYSIWYG preview to show what the printed page will look like

DTV *see* DESKTOP VIDEO

D-type connector *noun* connector that is shaped like an elongated letter D, which prevents the connector being plugged in upside down; *the serial port on a PC uses a 9-pin D-type connector*

D-type flip-flop *noun* flip-flop device with one input and two outputs

dual *adjective* two *or* a pair; *(in an FDDI system)* **dual attachment station (DAS)** = station that allows two connections to the FDDI ring; **dual channel** = two separate audio recording paths, as found in stereo equipment; **dual column** = two separate parallel lists of information; **dual in-line package (DIP)** = standard layout for IC packages using two parallel rows of connecting pins; **dual processor** = computer system with two processors for faster program execution; **dual time code** = *see* DTC; **dual tone, multifrequency (DTMF)** = communication signalling system using two different frequencies to transmit binary data

dub *verb* to add sound to a film after the film has been shot (usually to add a sound version in another language); **dubbed sound** = sound effects added after the film has been shot

dubbing *noun* (a) putting together two or more sound records into one combined recording (b) moving a sound recording from one intermediary to another; for example from photographic film to magnetic tape (c) making a copy; for example, making a showreel from a group of videotapes (d) *(in cinematographic production)* the method of recording new dialogue which is used instead of the original version

duct *noun* pipe containing cables, providing a tidy and protective surrounding to a group of cables

dumb terminal *noun* peripheral that can only transmit and receive data from a computer, but is not capable of processing data; *compare with* INTELLIGENT TERMINAL

dummy *noun* imitation product to test the reaction of potential customers to its design; **dummy pack** = empty pack for display; **dummy variable** = variable set up to satisfy the syntax of a language, but which is replaced when the program is executed

dump 1 *noun* (a) data which has been copied from one device to another for storage (b) transferring of data to a disk for storage (c) *US* printout of all *or* selected data in memory **2** *verb* (a) to move data from one device *or* storage area to another; *the account results were dumped to the backup disk* (b) **to dump goods on a market** = to get rid of large quantities of excess goods cheaply in another market

duotone *noun* *(film)* two-colour reproduction of an image or photograph using only black and either sepia or yellow

duplex *noun* (a) photographic paper that is light sensitive on both sides (b) simultaneous transmission of two signals on one line; **duplex circuit** = electronic circuit used to transmit data in two directions simultaneously; **duplex operation** = transmission of data in two directions simultaneously; *see also* HALF-DUPLEX,

FULL DUPLEX, SIMPLEX; **duplexing** = technique to increase the fault tolerance of a network or disk drive or other critical device; two identical systems are installed so that if one fails, the second can be used without interruption to the service; *data is written to both duplexed disk drives so that if one goes wrong, the second device is switched in under software control with no effect to the user; compare with* DISK MIRRORING

duplicate 1 *noun* copy; *he sent me the duplicate of the contract*; **duplicate receipt** *or* **duplicate of a receipt** = copy of a receipt; **in duplicate** = with a copy; **receipt in duplicate** = two copies of a receipt; *to print an invoice in duplicate* **2** *verb* to copy; **to duplicate a letter** = to make a copy of a letter

duplicating *noun* copying; **duplicating machine** = machine which makes copies of documents; **duplicating paper** = special paper to be used in a duplicating machine

duplication *noun* copying of documents; **duplication of work** = work which is done twice without being necessary

duplicator *noun* machine which produces multiple copies from a master; **duplicator paper** = absorbent paper used in a duplicator

durable *adjective* which will not be destroyed easily; *durable cartridge*; **durable goods** = goods which will be used for a long time (such as washing machines *or* refrigerators)

duration *noun* length of time for which something lasts; **pulse duration modulation (PDU)** = pulse modulation where the pulse width depends on the input signal

dustcover *noun* protective cover for a machine

duty-rated *adjective* maximum number of operations which a device can perform in a set time to a certain specification

```
the laser printer can provide
letter-quality print on
ordinary cut-sheet paper and
is duty-rated at up to 3,000
pages per month
```
Minicomputer News

DUV = DATA UNDER VOICE data transmission in a frequency range *or* channel lower than that of a human voice

DVD-RAM type of rewritable DVD disc that allows a user to store data on the disc; this standard was developed by the DVD Consortium and competes with the DVD-RW standard; provides storage capacity of 2.6GB per side

DVD-ROM flat plastic disc (a type of compact disc) that can store up to 17GB of data

> COMMENT: In a DVD-ROM, the data is stored in a layer of the disc, which is then coated with a transparent plastic layer to protect the data; the disc is read using a device that shines a laser beam onto the spinning disc; DVD disc players are backward-compatible with older CD formats; DVD-ROMs can be used to store computer data, software programs, images or video

DVD+RW type of rewritable DVD disc that allows a user to store data on the disc; DVD discs offer much greater storage capacity than a standard compact disc in a similar-sized disc; this standard was developed by Hewlett-Packard, Philips and Sony and has a capacity of 3GB per side

DVD-video standard that defines how full-length films can be compressed and stored on a DVD disc and played back on a dedicated player attached to a television set or viewed on a computer fitted with a DVD drive

DVE = DIGITAL VIDEO EFFECTS special effects carried out by a PC on a video sequence; for example, a fade between two sequences or a dissolve

DV-I = DIGITAL VIDEO INTERACTIVE system that defines how video and audio signals should be compressed onto disk and then decompressed during playback on a computer; *the DV-I technology is currently produced as a chip-set by Intel which can record or play back compressed full-motion video in real time*

DVORAK keyboard *noun* keyboard layout that is more efficient to use than a normal QWERTY keyboard layout

dye-polymer recording *noun (in optical disks)* recording method which creates minute changes in a thin layer of dye imbedded in the plastic optical disk; dye-polymer recording has one big advantage - that the data stored on the optical disk using this method can be erased

dye-sublimation printer *noun* high-quality colour printer that produces images by squirting tiny drops of coloured ink onto paper; *the new dye-sublimation printer can produce colour images at a resolution of 600dpi*

dynamic *adjective* referring to data which can change with time; **dynamic allocation** = system where resources allocated during a program run, rather than being determined in advance; **dynamically redefinable character set** = computer *or* videotext character sets that can be changed when required; *(in Windows)* **dynamic data exchange (DDE)** = a method for two programs to exchange data in which both programs must be running and one asks the operating system (Windows) to create a link to the second program; **dynamic data structure** = structure of a data management system which can be changed *or* adapted; **dynamic memory** = DYNAMIC RAM; **dynamic microphone** = microphone using a coil that moves and induces a voltage according to sound pressure; **dynamic multiplexing** = time division multiplexing method which allocates time segments to signals according to demand; **dynamic RAM** *or* **DRAM** = random access memory that requires its contents to be updated regularly; **dynamic range** = range of softest to loudest sounds that a device *or* instrument can produce; **dynamic routing** = process of selecting the shortest or most reliable path for data through exchanges at the time of the connection; **dynamic stop** = stop in a process where the system tells the user that some action must be taken before the processing will continue; **dynamic storage allocation** = to allocate memory to a program when it needs it rather than reserving a block before it has run; **dynamic update** = a display (such as a graph) updated in real time as new data arrives

dynamic data exchange (DDE) *noun (in Microsoft Windows)* method in which two active programs can exchange data; one program asks the operating system to create a link between the two programs

dynamic link library (DLL)   *(in Microsoft Windows)* library of utility programs that can be called from a main program when needed and when the program is running; this saves loading into memory functions that are only occasionally used; *the word-processor calls a spell-check program that is stored as a DLL*

DYUV = DELTA YUV digital video encoding technique in which luminance of a pixel is calculated by the RGB input signal $(Y0.6G + 0.3R + 0.1B)$; from the value of Y, U and V are calculated as UR - Y; VB - Y

Ee

EAN = EUROPEAN ARTICLE NUMBER numbering system for bar codes (European version of UPC)

EAPROM = ELECTRICALLY ALTERABLE PROGRAMMABLE READ-ONLY MEMORY version of EAROM which can be programmed

early token release *noun (in a Token-Ring or FDDI network)* system that allows two tokens to be present on a ring network, used when there is a lot of network traffic; *see also* FDDI; TOKEN-RING

EAROM = ELECTRICALLY ALTERABLE READ-ONLY MEMORY read-only memory device whose contents can be changed by an electric signal

earth 1 *noun* **(a)** the planet on which we live; **earth coverage** = area of the earth's surface able to pick up a satellite's transmissions; **earth station** = dish antenna and circuitry used to communicate with a satellite **(b)** connection in a circuit representing zero potential; **earth wire** = connecting wire between an electrical device and the earth, representing zero potential **2** *verb* to connect an electrical device to the earth; *all appliances must be earthed* (NOTE: US English is **ground**)

EAX = ELECTRONIC AUTOMATIC EXCHANGE

EBCDIC = EXTENDED BINARY CODED DECIMAL INTERCHANGE CODE

ebook *see* ELECTRONIC BOOK

EBR = ELECTRON BEAM RECORDING **(a)** recording the output from a computer directly onto microfilm using an electron beam **(b)** *(film)* transfer system of high quality videotape to film

echo 1 *noun* return of a signal back to the source from which it was transmitted; **echo chamber** = acoustic *or* electronic device used to increase the echo of a sound; **echo check** = on-screen checking of accurate data transmission, where each character received at the terminal is returned and checked; **echo suppressor** = device used on long-distance speech lines to prevent echoing effects **2** *verb* to return a received signal along the same transmission path

ECL = EMITTER-COUPLED LOGIC high-speed logic circuit design using the emitters of the transistors as output connections to other stages

ECMA = EUROPEAN COMPUTER MANUFACTURERS ASSOCIATION; **ECMA symbols** = standard set of symbols used to draw flowcharts

e-commerce = ELECTRONIC COMMERCE general term that refers to the process of buying and selling products on the Internet

EDAC = ERROR DETECTION AND CORRECTION

edge *noun* side of a flat object *or* signal *or* clock pulse; **edge card** = printed circuit board that has a series of contact strips along one edge allowing it to be inserted into an edge connector; **edge connector** = long connector with a slot containing metal contacts to allow it to make electrical contact with an edge card; **edge detection** = algorithm and routines used in graphics software to define the edges of an object, often used to convert a bitmap to a vector image or for special effects or to sharpen an image; **edge notched card** = card which has punched holes along an edge to represent data; *(film)* **edge numbers** = manufacturers of film stock print identification numbers on the edge of the film at regular intervals in order to indicate footage; assists the editing process; *see also* FOOTAGE NUMBERS,

KEY NUMBER, NEGATIVE NUMBERS; **edge track** = magnetic audio strip on the side of film stock that is not perforated; **edge-triggered** = process or circuit which is clocked or synchronized by the changing level (edge) of a clock signal rather than the level itself; **edge wave** = when one or both of the edges of film stock are stretched longer than the centre which results in film distortion

> Connections to the target board are made via IC test clips or the edge connector
> *Electronics Today*

EDI = ELECTRONIC DATA INTERCHANGE system of sending orders, paying invoices or transferring company information over a network *or* telephone line using an electronic mail system; often used to send instructions to pay money direct from one company to another, or from one bank to a company

edit *verb* to change, correct and modify text *or* programs *or* films; *(film)* **edit code** = to record data describing the frames, seconds, minutes and hours of a programme that can then be used when editing; **edit decision list (EDL)** = off-line video editing method in which the operator defines the points where he would like the video to be edited; this list of actions is then used in an on-line edit suite to carry out the edits automatically; *see also* NONLINEAR VIDEO EDITING; **edit key** key which starts a function that makes an editor easier to use; **edit window** = area of the screen in which the user can display and edit text or graphics; **editing block** = device for joining magnetic tape; *(film)* **editing machine** = (i) device for viewing and synchronizing film to be edited; (ii) video tape editing machine; **editing plan** = detailed plan of how a film *or* TV programme is to be edited before being shown; **editing run** = processing to check that new data meets certain requirements before actually analysing the data and its implications; **editing symbol** = character on microfilm to aid positioning, cutting and editing of the frames; **editing terms** = command words and instruction sequences used when editing

edition *noun* all the copies of a book *or* newspaper printed at one time; *the second edition has had some changes to the text;* *did you see the late edition of the evening paper?*

editor *noun* **(a)** person who edits a film *or* book **(b)** **text editor** = piece of software used to enter and correct text *or* modify programs under development **(c)** person in charge of a newspaper *or* a section of a newspaper; *the editor of 'The Times'; the paper's computer editor*

editorial 1 *adjective* referring to an editor *or* to editing; **editorial processing centre** = number of small publishers that share a single computer to provide cheaper computing power **2** *noun* main article in a newspaper, written by the editor

> The Smartbook authoring system is a software product that integrates text and fractally compressed images, using any word-processor line editor
> *Computing*

EDL *(film)* = EDIT DECISION LIST off-line video editing method in which the operator defines the points where he would like the video to be edited; this list of actions is then used in an on-line edit suite to carry out the edits automatically; *see also* NONLINEAR VIDEO EDITING

EDLIN *(in MS-DOS)* system utility that allows a user to make changes to a file on a line-by-line basis

EDO memory EXTENDED DATA OUTPUT MEMORY type of electronic memory component that can provide better performance by temporarily storing the last piece of data that was saved to memory in a cache ready to be read back from memory; this means that the processor can read more data from the memory component within one clock cycle, so increasing the amount of data that can be transferred

EDP = ELECTRONIC DATA PROCESSING data processing using computers and electronic devices; **EDP capability** = word processor that is able to carry out certain data processing functions (NOTE: **EDP** is more common in US English)

EDS = EXCHANGEABLE DISK STORAGE disk drive using removable disk pack (as opposed to a fixed disk)

EDTV = EXTENDED-DEFINITION TELEVISION enhancement to the NTSC standard for television transmission that offers higher definition and a wide aspect ratio; EDTV normally has an aspect ratio of 4:3; if greater than this, the system is called EDTV-wide

educational *adjective* referring to education; which is used to teach; **educational TV** = television programme that is in some way educational

edutainment *noun* software that is a cross between entertainment (or games software) and educational products

EEMS = ENHANCED EXPANDED MEMORY SYSTEM *(in an IBM PC)* development of EMS; standard method of expanding the main memory fitted into a PC; *see also* EMS

EEPROM = ELECTRICALLY ERASABLE PROGRAMMABLE READ-ONLY MEMORY storage chip which can be programmed and erased using electrical signals

conventional EEPROM requires
two transistors to store each
bit of data

Electronics & Power

EEROM = ELECTRICALLY ERASABLE READ-ONLY MEMORY

effective aperture *noun* **(a)** received signal power at the output of an aerial **(b)** amount of light allowed through a lens' aperture after taking into account camera faults and lens defects; *see also* DIFFUSION

COMMENT: the effective aperture is measured as the ratio of focal length of the lens to the diameter of the diaphragm

effective *adjective* which can be used to produce a certain result; **effective address** = address resulting from the modification of an address; **effective bandwidth** = usable frequency range of a system; **effective search speed** = rate of finding a particular section of information from a storage device

effects track *noun (film)* sound track which only contains the audio effects

efficiency *noun* working well; *he is doubtful about the efficiency of the new networking system*

efficient *adjective* which works well; *the program is highly efficient at sorting files*

efficiently *adverb* in an efficient way; *the word-processing package has produced a series of labelled letters very efficiently*

EFT = ELECTRONIC FUNDS TRANSFER system where computers are used to transmit money to and from banks

EFTPOS = ELECTRONIC FUNDS TRANSFER POINT OF SALE

Alphameric has extended its
range specifically for the
hospitality market and has
developed an eftpos package
which allows most credit and
debit cards to be processed

Computing

EGA = ENHANCED GRAPHICS ADAPTER *(in an IBM PC)* popular standard for medium-resolution colour graphics display at a maximum resolution of 640x350 pixels; an EGA graphics adapter requires a digital RGB monitor to display the images; *see also* CGA, VGA

EHF = EXTREMELY HIGH FREQUENCY radio frequencies from 30 - 300GHz

EI *(film)* = EXPOSURE INDEX the sensitivity of a photographic emulsion; *see also* ASA

EIA = ELECTRONIC INDUSTRIES ASSOCIATION

eight millimeter film *noun* eight mm wide film which was superseded by Super 8 film

eight-inch disk *noun* high-capacity floppy disk which is eight inches in diameter; **eight-inch drive** = disk drive for a eight-inch disk

eighty-column screen *noun* screen that can display eighty characters horizontally

eighty-track disk *noun* disk formatted to contain eighty tracks

EIS = EXECUTIVE INFORMATION SYSTEM easy-to-use software providing information to a manager or executive about his company; *the EIS software is very easy to use; with this EIS software, we can see how every part of the company performs*

EISA = ELECTRONICS INDUSTRY STANDARDS ASSOCIATION group of PC manufacturers who formed an association to promote a 32-bit expansion bus standard as a rival to the MCA bus standard from IBM

COMMENT: the EISA expansion bus standard is backwards compatible with the older ISA standard of expansion cards, but also features 32-bit data path and allows bus mastering

either-or operation *noun* logical function that produces a true output if any input is true

elapsed time *noun* time taken by the user to carry out a task on a computer

elastic banding *noun* method of defining the limits of an image on a computer screen by stretching a boundary around it

elastic buffer *noun* buffer size that changes according to demand

electret *noun* piece of dielectric that keeps an electronic charge after a voltage has been applied at manufacture; **electret microphone** = microphone using a section of dielectric as a transducer that provide an electric signal with varying sound pressure

electret microphone *noun* *(film)* reliable, cheap, small and low noise microphone

electric *adjective* worked by electricity; **electric current** = mass movement of electric charge in a conductor; **electric charge** = a number of atoms that are charged (due to excess *or* deficiency of electrons); **electric typewriter** = typewriter whose keys are switches which control motors and solenoids to perform all the functions

electrical *adjective* referring to electricity; *the engineers are trying to repair an electrical fault*

electrically *adverb* referring to electricity; *an electrically-powered motor*; **electrically alterable read-only memory (EAROM)** = read-only memory chip whose contents can be programmed by applying a certain voltage to a write pin, and can be erased by light *or* a reverse voltage; **electrically erasable read-only memory (EEROM)** = *see* EEPROM

electrician *noun* *(film)* person on a set who is responsible for the lighting equipment

electricity *noun* electric current used to provide light *or* heat *or* power; *the electricity was cut off, and the computers crashed; electricity prices are an important factor in the production costs*

electro printing *noun* *(film)* transferring sound from an original magnetic track directly to the final copy of the film; this avoids the use of an optical sound track

electrode *noun* part of an electric circuit *or* device that collects, controls or emits electrons

electroluminescence *noun* light emitted from a phosphor dot when it is struck by an electron *or* charged particle

electroluminescent *adjective* capable of emitting light due to electroluminescence; *the TV screen coating is electroluminescent;* **electroluminescent display** = flat, lightweight display screen made up of two pieces of glass covered with a grid of conductors, separated by a thin layer of gas which luminesces when a point of the grid is selected by two electric signals

electroluminescing *adjective* (object) which is emitting light due to electroluminescence

electromagnet *noun* device that consists of a core and a coil of wire that produces a magnetic field when current is passed through the coil

electromagnetic *adjective* generating a magnetic field *or* magnetic effect when supplied with electrical power; **electromagnetic interference** = corruption of data due to nearby electrically generated magnetic fields; **electromagnetic spectrum** = frequency range of electromagnetic radiation (from light to radio wave)

electromagnetic radiation *noun* energy wave consisting of electric and/or magnetic fields

COMMENT: electromagnetic radiation requires no medium to support it, travels approximately at the speed of light and can support frequency ranges from light to radio waves

electromagnetically *adverb* working due to electromagnetic effects

electromechanical switching *noun* connection of two paths by an electrically operated switch *or* relay

electromotive flow *noun (film)* force of a circuit or system which makes the current flow; the unit is the volt

electromotive force (EMF) *noun* difference in electrical potential across a source of electric current

electron *noun* elementary particle with an elementary negative charge; **electron beam** = narrow, focused stream of electrons moving at high speed in the same direction (often in a vacuum); *the electron beam draws the image on the inside of a CRT screen*; **electron beam recording (EBR)** = recording the output from a computer directly onto microfilm using an electron beam; **electron flow** = movement of electrons from one point to another, causing an electrical current; **electron gun** = electronic component that emits a large number of electrons (usually by heating a filament of metal)

> COMMENT: an electron has a mass of 9.109×10^{-31}, and charge of 1.602×10^{-19}

electronic *adjective* referring to something which is controlled by *or* controls the flow of electrons; **electronic automatic exchange** = telephone routing system that uses electronic circuits to switch signals; *(film)* **electronic beam recording** = process of making a film print from a videotape recording; achieved by stop printing from three grey-scaled black and white negatives based on a digital grey scale; **electronic book** = (i) *see* EBOOK; (ii) general term that describes a multimedia title; **electronic blackboard** = means of transmitting handwritten text and diagrams over a telephone line; **electronic clapper** = camera device that flashes a couple of lengths of film and sound simultaneously to a tape recorder so that the visual and audio can be synchronized for workprints; **electronic commerce** = *see* E-COMMERCE; **electronic composition** = text manipulation by computer before typesetting; **electronic data interchange (EDI)** = system of sending orders, paying invoices or transferring company information over a network *or* telephone line using an electronic mail system; often used to send instructions to pay money direct from one company to another, or from one bank to a company; **electronic data processing**

(EDP) = data processing using computers and electronic devices; **electronic data processing compatibility** = word processor that is able to carry out certain data processing functions; **electronic digital computer** = digital computer constructed with electronic components; a basic digital computer includes a CPU, main memory, backing storage and input/output devices; **electronic editing** = the electronic selecting and assembling of audio and visual material; there are no mechanical splices, lifts or reprints; **electronic engineer** = person who specializes in work on electronic devices; **electronic field production** = recording on location using lightweight television cameras for a full broadcast standard programme, usually drama; **electronic filing** = system of storage of documents which can be easily retrieved; **electronic funds transfer (EFT)** = using a computer to transfer money to and from banks; **electronic funds transfer point of sale (EFTPOS)** = terminal at a POS that is linked to a central computer which automatically transfers money from the customer's account to the shop's; **electronic keyboard** = keyboard that generates characters electronically in response to a switch being pressed rather than mechanical means; **electronic lock** = security device, usually in the form of a password (used to protect a file *or* piece of equipment from unauthorized use); **electronic mail** *or* **email** = sending and receiving messages over a telephone network, usually using a bulletin board; **electronic mailbox** = system for holding messages sent by electronic mail until the person to whom they were sent is ready to accept them; *when I log onto the network, I always check my electronic mailbox for new messages*; **electronic money** = smart cards *or* phonecards, etc., which take the place of money; **electronic news gathering (ENG)** = method of reporting news items for TV news programmes, where the reporter has a cameraman with a portable video camera which can transmit live pictures direct to the studio; **electronic office** = office where all the work is done using computers, which store information, communicate with different workstations, etc.; **electronic pen** *or* **stylus** *or* **wand** = light pen or wand; stylus used to draw on a graphics tablet; **electronic**

pin registration (EPR) = ensures consistent frame-frame steadiness in telecine transfer; **electronic point of sale (EPOS)** = system that uses a computer terminal at a point-of-sale site for electronic funds transfer *or* stock control as well as product identification, etc.; **electronic publishing** = use of desktop publishing packages and laser printers to produce printed matter *or* using computers to write and display information, such as viewdata; **electronic pulse** = short voltage pulse; **electronic shopping** = system of shopping from the home, using computerized catalogues displayed on television or on a computer; software lets you view the goods and pay by credit card, all by means of a home computer terminal and a modem or interactive television; **electronic signature** = special code which identifies the sender of a coded message; **electronic smog** = excessive stray electromagnetic fields and static electricity generated by large numbers of electronic equipment - this can damage equipment *or* a person's health; **electronic switching system** = telephone routing using a computer system to control the line switching circuits; **electronic traffic** = data transmitted in the form of electronic pulses; **electronic typewriter** = typewriter using an electronic keyboard linked, via a buffer, to an electrically driven printing mechanism, also with the facility to send *or* receive character data from a computer; **electronic viewfinder** = miniature cathode ray tube in a television *or* video camera that allows the camera operator to see the images being recorded

Electronic Industry Standards Association *see* EISA

electronically *adverb* referring to operations using electronic methods; *the text is electronically transmitted to an outside typesetter*

electronics *noun* science of applying the study of electrons and their properties to manufactured products, such as components, computers, calculators, *or* telephones; *the electronics industry; an electronics specialist* (NOTE: takes a singular verb)

electro-optic effect *noun* changes in the refractive index of a material due to a nearby electric field

electrophotography *noun* forming an image using electrical and optical effects; **electrophotographic** = printed using a laser printer technique in which a laser beam creates an image on a charged drum that attracts particles of fine black toner and the drum transfers the image to the paper, which is then heated to melt the toner onto the paper

electrosensitive *adjective* **electrosensitive paper** = metal-coated printing paper, which can display characters using localized heating with a special dot-matrix print head; **electrosensitive printing** = printing using electrosensitive paper

electrostatic *adjective* referring to devices using the properties of static; **electrostatic printer** = type of printer which forms an image on the paper by charging certain regions to provide character shapes etc, and using ink with an opposite charge which sticks to the paper where required; **electrostatic speaker** = loudspeaker containing two large charged plates, one flexible which moves when a signal is applied, creating sound signals; **electrostatic storage** = data stored in the form of small electric charged regions on a dielectric material

electrostatically *adverb* using properties of static charge

elegant programming *noun* writing a well-structured program using the minimum number of instructions so that the program is easy to understand and runs efficiently

element *noun* **(a)** small part of an object which is made up of many similar parts **(b)** one number *or* cell of a matrix *or* array **(c)** coil of resistive wire to which an electric current is applied to generate heat **(d)** substance in which all the atoms have the same number of electrons and charge

elementary *adjective* made of many similar small sections *or* objects; **elementary cable section** = model of the characteristics of a short length of transmission cable that can be applied to the whole length of cable

elevator *noun* small, square indicator displayed within a scroll bar that indicates where you are within a long document or image; the user can scroll through the image or text by dragging the elevator up or down the scroll bar

ELF = EXTREMELY LOW FREQUENCY communications frequencies of less than 100Hz

eliminate *verb* to remove something completely; *using a computer should eliminate all possibility of error in the address system; the spelling checker does not eliminate all spelling mistakes*

elimination *noun* removing of something completely; **elimination factor** = during a search, the section of data that is not used

elite *noun* typewriter typeface

ellipse *noun* oval shaped; like an elongated circle

ellipsoidal spotlight *noun (film)* spotlight with a sharp beam produced by a spherical lens

elliptical cutting *or* **editing** *noun (film)* film editing process which eliminates much of the action

elliptical orbit *noun* path of a satellite around the earth that is in the shape of an ellipse

ELT = ELECTRONIC TYPEWRITER

em *noun* space taken by an 'm' in a given typeface (equal to 12 point *or* pica); **em quad** = space printed of a size equal to an em; **em dash** *or* **em rule** = dash as long as an 'm', showing that words are separated; **ems per hour** = rate of production of characters from a machine *or* operator; *see also* EN

E-mail *or* **email** = ELECTRONIC MAIL system of sending messages to and receiving messages from other users on a network or over the Internet; **email-enabled application** = software application (such as a wordprocessor or spreadsheet) that includes a direct link to an email application to allow a user to send the current document as an email attachment; *Microsoft email-enabled applications such as Word include a Send option under the File menu that allows a user to email the document directly*

embedded code *noun* sections *or* routines written in machine code, inserted into a high-level program to speed up *or* perform a special function; **embedded command** = printing command (such as indicating that text should be in italic) which is keyboarded into the text, and which appears on the screen but does not appear in the final printed document; **embedded computer** = dedicated computer controlling a machine; *(in Windows)* **embedded object** = feature of OLE that allows a file or object - such as an image - that is included within another document or file; unlike linking, in which a link to the file or object is included; *see* OLE

embedding *noun (in Windows)* dragging an object and dropping it into a document or file so that it is embedded within the document

emboldening *noun* making a word print in bold type

embrace *see* DEADLY EMBRACE

EMF = ELECTROMOTIVE FORCE

EMI = ELECTROMAGNETIC INTERFERENCE corruption of data due to nearby electrically generated magnetic fields

emission *noun* sending out (of a signal *or* radiation, etc.); *the emission of the electron beam; the receiver picked up the radio emission*

emit *verb* to send out

emitter *noun* connection to a bipolar transistor; **emitter-coupled logic (ECL)** = high-speed logic circuit design using the emitters of the transistors as output connections to other stages

EMM = EXPANDED MEMORY MANAGER software driver which manages the extra expanded memory fitted in an IBM PC and makes it available for programs to use

EMMY *noun (film)* annual prize given by the National Academy of Television, Arts and Sciences for the most outstanding artistic work in each area of film and television

emphasis *noun* **(a)** filter that helps cut down the background noise and so boost a signal **(b)** special effects function in a paint program that will increase the value of a range of colours so that they appear brighter

empty *adjective* with nothing inside; **empty set** = reserved area for related data items, containing no data; **empty slot** = (i) packet of data in a packet-switching LAN that is carrying no information; (ii) unused expansion edge connector on a motherboard; **empty string** = variable containing no characters

EMS *or* **LIM EMS** = EXPANDED MEMORY SYSTEM *or* LOTUS-INTEL-MICROSOFT EXPANDED MEMORY SYSTEM *(in an IBM PC)* standard that defines extra memory added above the 640Kb limit of conventional memory; this memory can only be used by specially-written programs; *see also* LIM EMS

emulate *verb* to copy *or* behave like something else; *some laser printers are able to emulate the more popular office printers; a special piece of software running on an Apple Macintosh can emulate Microsoft Windows and allow you to run PC programs on a Mac*

emulation *noun* behaviour by one computer *or* printer which is exactly the same as another, which allows the same programs to be run and the same data to be processed; **emulation facility** = feature of hardware *or* software to emulate another system

emulator *noun* software *or* hardware that allows a machine to behave like another

```
full communications error
checking built into the
software ensures reliable file
transfers and a terminal
emulation facility enables a
user's terminal to be used as
if it were a terminal to the
remote computer
```
Byte

```
some application programs do
not have the right drivers for
a laser printer, so look out
for laser printers which are
able to emulate the more
popular office printers
```
Publish

```
The London Borough of Hackney
has standardised on terminal
emulator software from
Omniplex to allow its
networked desktop users to
select Unix or DOS
applications from a single
menu
```
Computing

emulsion *noun* light-sensitive coating on photographic film *or* paper; **emulsion laser storage** = digital storage technique using a laser to expose light-sensitive material

en *noun* unit of measure equal to half the width of an em; **en dash** *or* **en rule** = line as long as an en, showing that two words or parts of words are joined together; **en quad** = space that is half the width of an em quad space; *see also* EM

enable *verb* **(a)** to allow something to happen; *a spooling program enables editing work to be carried out which printing is going on* **(b)** to use an electronic signal to start a process *or* access a function (on a chip *or* circuit)

enabled *adjective* menu option, button or hotspot that will carry out a function if selected by a user; when a menu option is not enabled it appears grey and cannot be selected

encapsulated *adjective* (something) contained within something else; **encapsulated PostScript (EPS)** = PostScript commands that describe an image *or* page contained within a file that can be placed within a graphics *or* DTP program; **encapsulated PostScript file (EPSF)** = file that contains encapsulated PostScript instructions together with a preview bitmap image

```
COMMENT: an encapsulated
PostScript file often contains a preview
bitmap image of the page in TIFF or
PICT format that can be easily displayed
by a graphics application
```

encapsulation *noun (in a network)* system of sending a frame of data in one format within a frame of another format

encipher *verb* to convert plaintext into a secure coded form by means of a cipher system

enclose *verb* to surround with something; to put something inside something else; **enclosed object** = graphic object that is closed on all sides and so can be filled with a colour or pattern

enclosure *noun* protective casing for equipment

encode *verb* to apply the rules of a code to a program *or* data

encoder *noun* device that can translate data from one format to another; **colour encoder** = device that produces a standard TV signal from separate Red, Green and Blue signals

encoding *noun* translation of a message according to a coding system

encrypt *verb* to convert plaintext to a secure coded form, using a cipher system; *the encrypted text can be sent along ordinary telephone lines*

encryption *noun* conversion of plaintext to a secure coded form by means of a cipher system; for example, the scrambling of a television programme to secure that it can only be reproduced at stations which possess a matching decoder; **data encryption standard (DES)** = standard for data cipher systems; *see also* RSA; SSL

end 1 *noun* **(a)** final point *or* last part; *at the end of the data transmission*; **end product** = manufactured product, made at the end of a production process; *after six months' trial production, the end product is still not acceptable*; **in the end** = at last *or* after a lot of problems; *in the end the company had to pull out of the US market; in the end the company had to call in a consultant engineer*; **to come to an end** = to finish; *our distribution agreement comes to an end next month* **(b)** statement *or* character to indicate the last word of a source file; **end about carry** = carry generated by the MSB of a mathematical function and added to the LSB of the result; **end of address (EOA)** = transmitted code which indicates that address data has been sent; *(film)* **end board** = a reversed clapperboard which is used at the end of a scene; **end of block (EOB)** = code which shows that the last byte of a block of data has been sent through a communications link; **end of data (EOD)** = code which shows that the end of a stored data file has been reached; **end of document** = *see* END OF FILE; **end of file (EOF)** = marker after the last record in a file; **end of job (EOJ)** = code used in batch processing to show that a job has been finished; *(on an IBM PC keyboard)* **end key** = key that moves the cursor to the end of the current line; **end of message (EOM)** = code used to separate the last character of one message from the first of another message; **end office** = *see* CENTRAL OFFICE; **end**

of page indicator = indicator on a typewriter to show that a page is nearly finished; **end of record (EOR)** = code used to show the end of a record; **end of tape** = code used to indicate the end of a magnetic tape; **end of text (EOT)** = code sent after last character of text **2** *verb* to finish *or* to stop something; *ending the card-based index saved a lot of time*

end user *noun* person who will use the device *or* program *or* product; *the company is creating a computer with a specific end user in mind*

ending *noun* **(a)** action of coming to an end *or* of stopping something **(b)** end part of something; **line endings** = last words on each line of text, which may be hyphenated

endless *adjective* with no end; **endless loop** = continuous piece of recording tape *or* number of computer instructions that are continuously repeated

energy *noun* **(a)** force *or* strength; ability of a body *or* object to do work **(b)** power from electricity *or* petrol, etc.; *we try to save energy by switching off the lights when the rooms are empty; if you reduce the room temperature to eighteen degrees, you will save energy* (NOTE: no plural for (b))

energy-saving *adjective* which saves energy; *the company is introducing energy-saving measures*

Energy Star power management system that allows an electronic device to save electricity when it is switched on but has not been used for a while

ENG = ELECTRONIC NEWS GATHERING

engine *noun* library of software routines optimised to perform a particular task, such as database search or graphics display

COMMENT: in a multimedia application, the front-end is often produced using a high-level programming language that is easy to use, but slow, and the database or display routines are written in a separate engine in low-level code for speed

enhance *verb* to make better *or* clearer; **enhanced dot matrix** = clearer character *or* graphics printout (using smaller dots and more dots per inch); *(in an IBM PC)* **enhanced expanded memory system (EEMS)** = a development of EMS, standard method of expanding the main memory fitted into a PC; *(in an IBM PC)* **enhanced graphics adapter (EGA)** = popular standard for medium-resolution colour graphics display at a maximum resolution of 640x350 pixels; an EGA graphics adapter requires a digital RGB monitor to display the images; *see also* CGA, VGA; **enhanced graphics adapter screen** = digital high-resolution colour monitor that can display EGA system signals and graphics; *(in an IBM PC)* **enhanced keyboard** = keyboard with 101 or 102 keys and a row of 12 function keys arranged along the top of the keyboard, with a separate numeric keypad on the right; *(in an IBM PC with an Intel 80386 CPU)* **enhanced mode** = operation of software which uses the CPU's protected mode to allow several MS-DOS programs to run in a multitasking environment; **enhanced small device interface (ESDI)** = interface standard between a CPU and peripherals such as disk drives (NOTE: this standard is no longer commonly used and has been replaced by the SCSI standard); *see also* IDE, SCSI

enhancement *noun* add-on facility which improves output *or* performance

enlarge *verb* to make (a photograph) larger

enlargement *noun* making larger; a larger version of a photograph; *an enlargement of the photograph was used to provide better detail*; **enlargement printing** = optical printing that enlarges a small frame area, for example 16mm to 35mm; *see* BLOW-UP

enquiry *noun* request for data *or* information from a device *or* database; accessing data in a computer memory without changing the data

ensure *verb* to make sure; *pushing the write-protect tab will ensure that the data on the disk cannot be erased*

enter *verb* (a) to go in; *they all stood up when the chairman entered the room; the company has spent millions trying to enter the home computer market* (b) to write information in a book; to type in information on a terminal *or* keyboard; *to enter a name on a list; the data has been entered on data capture forms*; **enter key** = key pressed to indicate the end of an input *or*

line of text; *see also* CARRIAGE RETURN

entering *noun* act of typing in data *or* writing items in a record (NOTE: no plural)

enterprise network *noun* network which connects all the workstations *or* terminals *or* computers in a company; it can be within one building or linking several buildings in different countries

entity *noun* subject to which the data stored in a file *or* database refers

entry *noun* (a) single record *or* data about one action *or* object in a database *or* library (b) place where you can enter; **entry point** = address from which a program *or* subroutine is to be executed

enumerated type *noun* data storage *or* classification using numbers to represent chosen convenient labels; = **enumeration** = method of identifying resources or objects using a unique number

envelope *noun* (a) flat paper cover for sending letters; **air mail envelope** = very light envelope for air mail letters; **envelope feeder** = special add-on to a printer used to print on an envelope instead of a sheet of paper; **envelope printer** = special printer used to print the address on an envelope; **window envelope** = envelope with a hole covered with film so that the address on the letter inside can be seen; **sealed** *or* **unsealed envelope** = envelope where the flap has been stuck down to close it *or* (b) variation of amplitude of a signal *or* sound with time; **attack envelope** = shape of the initial section of a signal; **envelope delay** = *see* DELAY DISTORTION; **envelope detection** = technique of signal recovery from a modulated waveform (c) transmitted packet of data containing error-detection and control information (d) *(in electronic mail)* name for the data which contains the mail message together with any attachment and the destination address information

environment *noun* (a) condition in a computer system of all the registers and memory locations; **environment space** = the amount of memory free to be used by a program; **environment variable** = variable set by the system *or* by a user at the system command line which can be used by any program (b) surroundings *or* physical conditions (c) the imaginary space in which a user works when using a computer; this can be changed to suit the user's needs - by defining its characteristics such as colour or wallpaper and by setting up a printer, keyboard and fonts

EOA = END OF ADDRESS

EOB = END OF BLOCK

EOD = END OF DATA

EOF = END OF FILE

EOJ = END OF JOB

EOM = END OF MESSAGE

EOR = END OF RECORD

EOT = END OF TEXT code *or* character indicating that a transmission has been completed

epidiascope *noun* optical projector which mixes the function of a diascope (a transparency projector) with that of an episcope

episcope *noun* projector that can display opaque material, such as photographs, and documents onto a screen

epitaxial layer *noun* very thin layer of material *or* doped semiconductor deposited onto a substrate base

epitaxy *noun* method of depositing very thin layers of materials onto a base, for use in chip manufacture

epos *or* **EPOS** = ELECTRONIC POINT OF SALE

EPP *(film)* = ELECTRONIC POST-PRODUCTION; *see* POST PRODUCTION

EPR *(film)* = ELECTRONIC PIN REGISTRATION ensures consistent frame-frame steadiness in telecine transfer

EPROM *noun* = ERASABLE PROGRAMMABLE READ-ONLY MEMORY

---
the densest EPROMs commercially available today are at the 1Mbit level
Electronics & Power

EPS = ENCAPSULATED POSTSCRIPT

EPSF = ENCAPSULATED POSTSCRIPT (FILE)

equal 1 *adjective* exactly the same; *male and female workers have equal pay* **2** *verb* to be the same as; *production this month has equalled our best month ever* (NOTE:

equalling - equalled but US: **equaling - equaled)**

equalization *noun* process of making a signal equal (to preset values)

equalize *verb* to make equal (to preset values); electronic adjustment of the frequency and intensity qualities in an audio or visual source; *the received signal was equalized to an optimum shape*

equalizer *noun* device which changes the amplitude of various parts of a signal according to preset values; **frequency equalizer** = device that changes the amplitude of various frequency components of a signal according to preset values

equally *adverb* in the same way; *costs will be shared equally between the two parties; they were both equally responsible for the successful launch of the new system*

equate *verb* to make the same as; *the variable was equated to the input data*

equator *noun* imaginary line running round the middle of the earth

equatorial orbit *noun* satellite flight path that follows the earth's equator

equip *verb* to provide with machinery; *to equip a factory with new machinery; the office is fully equipped with word-processors*

equipment *noun* machinery and furniture required to make a factory *or* office work; *office equipment or business equipment; computer equipment supplier; office equipment catalogue* (NOTE: no plural)

equivalence *noun* **(a)** being equivalent **(b)** logical operation that is true if all the inputs are the same; **equivalence function** = AND function *or* logical function whose output is true if both inputs are the same; **equivalence gate** = gate which performs an equivalence function

---
COMMENT: output is 1 if both inputs are 1 or if both are 0; if the two inputs are different, the output is 0

---

equivalent *adjective* **to be equivalent to** = to have the same value as *or* to be the same as; *the total characters keyboarded so far is equivalent to one day's printing time*

erasable *adjective* which can be erased; **erasable programmable read-only memory (EPROM)** = read-only memory chip that can be programmed by sending data to the chip and, at the same time, applying a voltage to the write pin; usually erasable by exposing to ultra-violet light; **erasable storage** *or* **erasable memory** = (i) storage medium that can be re-used; (ii) temporary storage

erase *verb* **(a)** to set all the digits in a storage area to zero **(b)** to remove any signal from a magnetic medium **(c)** tool in a graphics program that sets an area of an image to the same colour as the background; **erase head** = small magnet that clears a magnetic tape *or* disk of recorded signals; *see also* DELETE

eraser *(in a graphics program)* **eraser tool** = function that allows areas of an image to be erased, or set to the background colour; **eraser UV** = system to erase EPROM ready for re-programming

ERCC = ERROR CHECKING AND CORRECTING memory which checks and corrects errors

E-region *or* **Heaviside-Kennelly layer** *noun* section of the ionosphere that is 90-150 km above the earth's surface

ergonomics *noun* study of people at work, and their working conditions, concerned with improving safety and making machines easy to use

ergonomist *noun* scientist who studies people at work and tries to improve their working conditions

EROM = ERASABLE READ-ONLY MEMORY; *same as* EAROM

erratum *noun* correction on a separate slip of paper to an error *or* omission from a document (NOTE: plural is **errata**)

error *noun* mistake due to an operator; mistake caused by a hardware *or* software fault; mistake in a program that prevents a program *or* system running correctly; *he made an error in calculating the total; the secretary must have made a typing error;* **compilation error** = error occurring during program compilation time; **diagnostic error message** = explanatory line of text displayed when an error has been found; **error box** = dialog box displayed with a message alerting the user that an error has occurred; **error burst** = group of several consecutive errors in a transmission; **error code** = code which indicates that a particular type of error has occurred; **error**

condition = state that is entered if an attempt is made to operate on data containing errors; **error correction** = hardware *or* software that can detect and correct an error in a transmission; **error detection** = using special hardware *or* software to detect errors in a data; **error detection and correction (EDAC)** = forward error correction system for data communications; **error logging** = record of errors met; *features of the program include error logging*; **error message** = report displayed to the user saying that an error has occurred; **error rate** = (i) number of mistakes per thousand entries *or* per page; (ii) number of corrupt bits of data in relation to the total transmission length; *the error rate is less than 1%*; **errors** = (in a software program) problems caused by mistakes that have not been corrected by the software developer who created the program; *see also* = BUG, PATCH; **error trapping** = detecting and correcting errors before they cause any problems; **execution error** = error occurring during program execution, due to bad inputs *or* faulty program; **in error** *or* **by error** = by mistake; *the letter was sent to the London office in error*; **margin of error** = number of mistakes which are acceptable in a document *or* in a calculation; **rejection error** = error by the scanner which is unable to read a character and leaves a blank; **scanning error** = error introduced while scanning an image; *a wrinkled or torn page may be the cause of scanning errors*; **substitution error** = error made by a scanner which mistakes one character *or* letter for another; **syntax error** = error resulting from incorrect use of programming language syntax

Microcom has launched a new version of its MNP proprietary error correction protocol, MNP10, which automatically slows down the transmission rate when it detects line interference and speeds up again when conditions improve
Computing

ESC *abbreviation for* escape key on a computer

escape codes *noun* transmitted code sequence which informs the receiver that all following characters represent control actions; **escape key** = key on a keyboard which allows the user to enter escape codes to control the computer's basic modes *or* actions; *in Windows, pressing the Esc key is the same as selecting the Cancel button*; **escape sequence** = method of switching a Hayes-compatible modem into command mode by sending the three characters '+++' allowing a user to enter new commands whilst still online; *see also* AT COMMAND SET

escapement *noun* preset vertical movement of a sheet of paper in a typewriter

ESDI = ENHANCED SMALL DEVICE INTERFACE interface standard between a CPU and peripherals such as disk drives (NOTE: this standard is no longer commonly used and has been replaced by the SCSI standard)

ESS = ELECTRONIC SWITCHING SYSTEM

establish *verb* **(a)** to discover and prove something **(b)** to define the use *or* value of something; *they established which component was faulty*

establishing shot *noun* (*film*) atmospheric long shot that establishes the main location of the film or programme and is generally used in the opening scene

etch *verb* to use an acid to remove selected layers of metal from a metal printing plate *or* printed circuit board; **etch type** = type for printing produced from an etched plate

Ethernet (*refers to IEEE 802.3 standard*) standard defining the protocol and signalling method of a local area network; **thick-Ethernet** = network implemented using thick coaxial cable and transceivers to connect branch cables; can stretch long distances; **thin-Ethernet** = network implemented using thin coaxial cable and BNC connectors; it is limited to distances of around 1000m, now generally replaced with unshielded-twisted-pair (UTP) Ethernet networks; **UTP-Ethernet** = network using the Ethernet protocols implemented using unshielded twisted-pair wiring; *compare with* ARCNET, TOKEN RING, UTP

COMMENT: Ethernet has several implementations: 10Base5 (an older, but popular system) is a bus-based topology running over coaxial cable; the more popular and convenient 10BaseT

uses thinner unshielded-twisted-pair cable in a ring-based topology; Ethernet normally has a data transmission rate of 10Mbps or 100Mbps

EtherTalk (*in Apple Macintosh systems*) variation of the standard Ethernet network developed to connect Macintoshes together as an alternative to the slower AppleTalk

ETV = EDUCATIONAL TV

Euronet *noun* telephone connected network, covering the EC countries, that provides access to each country's scientific and economic information

European Article Number *see* EAN

evaluate *verb* to calculate a value *or* a quantity

evaluation *noun* action of calculating a value *or* a quantity

evaluation copy *noun* demonstration version of a software product that lets you try the main functions of a software product before buying it

evaluative abstract *noun* library abstract that contains details of the value and usefulness of the document

even *noun* quantity *or* number that is a multiple of two; *the first three even numbers are 2, 4, 6*; **even parity** = error checking method that only transmits an even number of binary ones in each word; *compare with* ODD PARITY; **even working** = section of printed material in 16, 32 or 64 page format

event *noun* an action or activity

event-driven *noun* computer program *or* process where each step in the execution relies on external actions; *Windows is an event-driven program in that it waits for events and then responds to them - it won't do something until you tell it to do so*

event handler *noun* routine that responds to an event or message within an object-oriented programming environment; *if a user clicks the mouse button this generates a message which can be acted upon by the event handler*

```
Forthcoming          language
extensions    will   include
object-oriented     features,
including  classes  with  full
```

inheritance, as well as
event-driven programming
Computing

e-wallet *noun* feature of new web browsers that allows a user to securely store their credit card and other payment details ready to use when shopping at an e-commerce site; the user's payment information is sent automatically rather than requiring the user to type in the details

except *preposition & conjunction* not including; *all the text has been keyboarded, except the last ten pages; sales are rising in all markets except the Far East*

exception *noun* thing which is different from all others; **exception dictionary** = store of words and their special word-break requirements, for word-processing and photocomposition; **exception handling** *or* **error handling** = routines and procedures that diagnose and correct errors *or* minimise the effects of errors, so that a system will run when an error is detected; **exception report** = report which only gives items which do not fit in the general rule *or* pattern

exceptional *adjective* not usual *or* different; **exceptional items** = items in a balance sheet which do not appear there each year

excess *noun* too much of something; *there was an excess of resistors, but not enough capacitors*

excessive *adjective* too much *or* too large; *the number of faulty components was excessive*

Exchange (older) program developed by Microsoft that was supplied with Windows 95 to manage fax and electronic mail messages; now replaced by Microsoft Outlook

exchange 1 *noun* **(a)** giving of one thing for another; **part exchange** = giving an old product as part of the payment for a new one **(b)** telephone equipment required to connect incoming and outgoing calls; **exchange line** = *see* LOCAL LOOP **2** *verb* **(a) to exchange one article for another** = to give one thing in place of something else **(b)** to swap data between two locations

exchangeable *adjective* which can be exchanged; **exchangeable disk storage (EDS)** = disk drive using a removable disk pack (as opposed to a fixed disk)

exciter light *noun (film)* high-intensity lamp which is used to record and reproduce optical sound tracks on film

exclamation mark *noun* printed *or* written sign (!), which shows surprise

exclude *verb* to keep out *or* not to include; *the interest charges have been excluded from the document; the password is supposed to exclude hackers from the database*

excluding *preposition* not including; *all salesmen, excluding those living in London, can stay at hotels during the sales conference*

exclusion *noun* **(a)** act of not including; **exclusion clause** = section of an insurance policy *or* warranty which says which items are not covered **(b)** restriction of access to a telephone line *or* system

exclusive *adjective* which excludes; **exclusive agreement** = agreement where a person is made sole agent for a product in a market

exclusive NOR (EXNOR) logical function whose output is true if both inputs are the same; **exclusive NOR gate** = electronic implementation of the EXNOR function

exclusive OR (EXOR) logical function whose output is true if A or B is true, and false if both inputs are the same; **exclusive OR gate** = electronic implementation of the EXOR function

EXE file *noun (in an operating system)* three-letter extension to a filename which indicates that the file contains binary data of a program; the file can be executed directly by the operating system

COMMENT: by typing 'DIR' in DOS you can see the names of all the files stored in the current directory on your hard disk. To the right of the file name is the three-letter filename extension that describes the type of file: DOC means document, WAV means Wave or sound file, EXE means executable - a program file that can be run. To run a file with an EXE extension, just type in its name and press return

executable file *noun* file that contains a program rather than data

executable form *noun* program translated or compiled into a machine code form that a processor can execute

execute *verb* to run *or* carry out a computer program *or* process; **execute cycle** = events required to fetch, decode and carry out an instruction stored in memory; **execute phase** = section of the execute cycle when the instruction is carried out; **execute time** = EXECUTION TIME

execution *noun* carrying out of a computer program *or* process; **execution address** = location in memory at which the first instruction in a program is stored; **execution error** = error detected while a program is being run; **execution phase** = section of the execute cycle when the instruction is carried out; **execution time** = time taken to run *or* carry out a program *or* series of instructions

executive 1 *adjective* (person) who puts decisions into action; **executive producer** = person who organizes and arranges for the finance for a film *or* TV programme but does not play an active part in making the film; **executive program** *or* **supervisor program** = master program in a computer system that controls the execution of other programs; **executive control program** = OPERATING SYSTEM **2** *noun* person in a business who takes decisions (such a manager *or* director); **executive terminal** = terminal which is specially adapted for use by company executives

executive information system (EIS) *noun* easy-to-use software providing information to a manager or executive about his company; *the EIS software is very easy to use; with this EIS software, we can see how every part of the company performs*

exhaustive search *noun* search through every record in a database

EXIT *noun (in MS-DOS)* system command to stop and leave a child process and return to the parent process; *to quit and close a DOS session within MS Windows, type EXIT*

exit *verb* to stop program execution *or* to leave a program and return control to the operating system *or* interpreter; **exit point** = point in a subroutine where control is returned to the main program; *you have to exit to another editing system to add headlines*

EXNOR = EXCLUSIVE NOR; **EXNOR gate** = electronic implementation of the EXNOR function; *see also* NOR

EXOR = EXCLUSIVE OR; **EXOR gate** = electronic implementation of the EXOR function; *see also* OR

expand *verb* to make larger; *if you want to hold so much data, you will have to expand the disk capacity*

expandable *adjective* which can be expanded; **expandable system** = computer system that is designed to be able to grow (in power *or* memory) by hardware *or* software additions

expanded memory system (EMS) *noun (in an IBM PC)* standard that defines extra memory added above the 640Kb limit of conventional memory; this memory can only be used by specially-written programs; *see also* LIM EMS; **expanded memory board** = expansion card used to add extra memory to an IBM PC; the memory follows the EMS standard; **expanded memory manager (EMM)** = utility which manages the extra expanded memory fitted in an IBM PC and makes it available for programs to use

expander *noun* **video expander** = device that stores one frame of a video image as it is slowly received over a voice grade communications link, with a video compressor used at the transmitting end

expansion *noun* increase in computing power *or* storage size; **expansion box** = device that plugs into an expansion bus and provides several more free expansion slots; **expansion bus** = data and address lines leading to a connector and allowing expansion cards to control and access the data in main memory; **expansion card** *or* **expansion board** = printed circuit board that is connected to a system to increase its functions *or* performance; *a graphics expansion card provides an interface between a computer and a monitor*; **expansion slot** = connector inside a computer into which an expansion card can be plugged; *insert the board in the expansion slot*

expert *noun* person who knows a lot about something; *he is a computer expert; she is an expert in programming languages*; **expert system** = software that applies the knowledge, advice and rules defined by experts in a particular field to a user's data to help solve a problem; *some expert systems carry details of every type of medical symptom and link these to the cause so that if you, the patient, type in that you have a runny nose and a fever, the software will work out that this means you have a cold and not that you have sprained your back!*

expiration *noun* coming to an end; **expiration date** = (i) last date at which photographic film *or* paper can be used with good results; (ii) date when a computer file is no longer protected from deletion by the operating system

expire *verb* to come to an end *or* to be no longer valid

explicit reference *noun (within a program or script)* a way of identifying a particular object, such as a field or button, by a unique name

Explorer utility software developed by Microsoft and supplied with Windows; allows a user to manage all the files stored on a disk

exponent *noun* number indicating the power to which a base number is to be raised

exponentiation *noun* raising a base number to a certain power

export *verb* to save data in a different file format from the default; *to use this data with dBASE, you will have to export it as a DBF file; if you use Microsoft Word you would normally save the file as a DOC format file, if you want to use the Viewer authoring tool, you would need to export the document as an RTF format file*

expose *verb* to allow light to reach photographic film *or* paper to form an image

exposure *noun* letting light fall on a photographic film to form an image; **exposure end point** = quantity of light required to produce a certain image density; **exposure index** = the sensitivity of a photographic emulsion; **exposure latitude** = the extent to which film can be over-exposed or under-exposed and still provide a clear picture; **exposure meter** = device for measuring the light intensity on or reflected by a scene which is to be filmed

express *verb* to state *or* to describe; *express the formula in its simplest form;*

the computer structure was expressed graphically

expression *noun* (a) mathematical formula *or* relationship (b) definition of a value *or* variable in a program; *compare with* CONTAINER

extend *verb* to make longer; **extended addressing** = *see* ABSOLUTE ADDRESSING; **extended binary coded decimal interchange code (EBCDIC)** = 8-bit character coding system; **extended character set** = symbols or foreign characters within a character set with an ASCII value between 128 and 255; **extended-definition television (EDTV)** = enhancement to the NTSC standard for television transmission that offers higher definition and a wider aspect ratio; EDTV normally has an aspect ratio of 4:3, if the broadcaster wants to provide a greater aspect ratio than this, the standard is called EDTV-wide; **extended graphics array (XGA)** = high resolution graphics standard developed by IBM; capable of displaying resolutions of up to 1024x768 pixels; **extended industry standard architecture (EISA)** = group of PC manufacturers who formed an association to promote a 32-bit expansion bus standard as a rival to the MCA bus standard from IBM; **extended level synthesizer** = synthesizer on a sound card that supports nine melodic instruments and can play 16 notes simultaneously; waveform synthesizers are extended level synthesizers; *compare with* BASE LEVEL SYNTHESIZER; *(in an IBM PC)* **extended memory** = most popular standard method of adding extra memory above 1Mb which can be used directly by many operating systems or programs; **extended memory manager** = software utility that configures extra memory fitted in a PC to conform to the extended memory standard; **extended memory specification (XMS)** = rules that define how a program should access extended memory fitted in a PC; **extending serial file** = file that can be added to *or* that has no maximum size

extensible *adjective* software that can be extended by the user or by third-party software; **extensible language** = computer programming language that allows the user to add his own data types and commands

extension *noun* making longer; thing which makes something longer; **extension cable** = cable that allows a device located at some distance to be connected; **extension tube** = device that moves photographic lens away from the camera to allow close-up shots; **filename extension** = additional information after a filename, indicating the type *or* use of the file

COMMENT: in MS-DOS there is a three-character filename extension that normally indicates the type of file; for example, a TIFF file has a .TIF extension, a sound file either a .WAV or .SND or .MDI extension and an application program either a .EXE or .COM extension

extent *noun* number of pages in a printed document, such as a book; *by adding the appendix, we will increase the page extent to 256*

external *adjective* outside a program *or* device; **external clock** = clock *or* synchronizing signal supplied from outside a device; **external data file** = file containing data for a program that is stored separately from it; **external disk drive** = device not built into the computer, but which is added to increase its storage capabilities; **external label** = identifying piece of paper stuck to the outside of a device *or* disk; **external memory** = memory which is located outside the main computer system confines but which can be accessed by the CPU; **external modem** = modem which is self-contained with its own power supply unit that connects to a serial port of a computer; **external schema** = user's view of the structure of data *or* a program; **external sort** = method of sorting which uses a file stored in secondary memory, such as a disk, as its data source and uses the disk as temporary memory during sorting; **external storage** *or* **external store** = storage device which is located outside the main computer system but which can be accessed by the CPU

extra 1 *adjective* added *or* which is more than usual **2** *noun* **(a)** item which is additional to the package; *the mouse and cabling are sold as extras* **(b)** mark at the end of a telegraphic transmission, induced by noise; **extra-terrestrial noise** = random noise coming from the air, space and planets

extract 1 *noun* information selected from a database; printed document which is part of a longer document **2** *verb* to remove required data *or* information from a database; *we can extract the files required for typesetting*

extranet *noun* internal company network (an intranet) that has a connection to the public Internet and allows users to gain access via the Internet; often used to provide access for employees who are working away from the office; *our Intranet was for internal use only, but the new extranet lets us access our data via the public Internet; the extranet has very sophisticated security against hackers*

extrapolation *noun* process of predicting future quantities *or* trends by the analysis of current and past data

extremely *adverb* to a very high degree; **extremely high frequency (EHF)** = radio frequencies from 30-300GHz; **extremely low frequency (ELF)** = communication frequencies of less than 100Hz

eye-lighting *noun* *(film)* illuminating a close shot in order to produce a small highlight reflection on the actor's eyeball which causes the eye to sparkle

eyepiece *noun* camera viewfinder; **eyepiece lens** = lens in the viewfinder of a camera through which the cameraman looks

eye-strain *noun* pain in the eyes, caused by looking at bright lights *or* at a VDU for too long

Ff

F = FARAD

face *see* TYPEFACE

facet *noun* one surface *or* plane

faceted code *noun* code which indicates various details of an item, by assigning each one a value

facility *noun* **(a)** being able to do something easily; *we offer facilities for processing a customer's own disks* **(b)** **facilities** = equipment *or* buildings which make it easy to do something; *storage facilities; harbour facilities; transport facilities; there are no facilities for passengers; there are no facilities for unloading or there are no unloading facilities* **(c)** communications path between two or more locations, with no ancillary line equipment **(d)** *US* single large building; *we have opened our new data processing facility*

facsimile *noun* exact copy of an original; **facsimile character generator** = means of displaying characters on a computer screen by copying preprogrammed images from memory; **facsimile copy** = exact copy of a document; **facsimile transmission (FAX)** = method of sending and receiving images in digital form over a telephone *or* radio link

COMMENT: a PC can send and receive faxes - just like an office fax machine - if it has a special modem and software that support this function. Windows and Macintosh System include software to manage fax data to send and receive faxes. When the computer receives a fax, it is stored as a graphic image file, which can then be viewed on screen or printed out.

FACT *(film)* = FEDERATION AGAINST COPYRIGHT THEFT organization that prevents illegal copying of film and TV material; *see also* FAST

factor *noun* **(a)** thing which is important *or* which has an influence on something else; **deciding factor** = most important factor which influences someone's decision **(b)** any number in a multiplication that is the operand; **by a factor of ten** = ten times

factorize *verb* to break down a number into two whole numbers which when multiplied will give the original number; *when factorized, 15 gives the factors 1, 15 or 3, 5*

factory *noun* building where products are manufactured; *computer factory; they have opened a new components factory*; **factory price** *or* **price ex factory** = price not including transport from the maker's factory; **factory unit** = single factory building on an industrial estate

fade *verb (of radio or electrical signal)* to become less strong;; *(of colour or photograph)* to become less dark; **fade-down** = slow reduction of the brightness of a lamp or the strength of an audio signal; **fade-in** = gradual forming of a picture, generally from black, or the increase of an audio signal; **fade-out** = gradual disappearance of a picture, generally to black, or the decrease of an audio signal; **to fade out** = to reduce the strength of an audio signal or image; **fade-up** = gradual increase of lamp brightness or of an audio signal

fader *noun (film)* instrument which brightens or darkens the picture, or decreases or increases the audio levels; **fader shutter** *or* **fading shutter** = shutter with two blades in a film camera; an adjustable opening can be used to vary the exposure for fade or dissolve effects

fading *noun* **(a)** variation in strength of radio and television broadcast signals **(b)** *(of photograph or colour)* becoming less dark; *when fading occurs turn the density dial on the printer to full black*

fail *verb* not to do something which should be done; not to work properly; *the company failed to carry out routine maintenance of its equipment; the prototype disk drive failed its first test; a computer has failed if you turn on the power supply and nothing happens;* **fail safe system** = system that has a predetermined state it will go to if a main program *or* device fails, so avoiding a total catastrophe that a complete system shutdown would produce; **fail soft system** = system that will still be partly operational even after a part of the system has failed; *see also* GRACEFUL DEGRADATION

failure *noun* breaking down *or* stopping; not doing something which should be done; **power failure** = stopping of the electric power supply; **failure to pay a bill** = not having paid the bill

```
if one processor system fails,
the  other  takes  recovery
action on the database, before
taking on the workload of the
failed system
```
Computer News

```
The DTI is publishing a new
code of best practice which
covers  hardware  reliability
and fail-safe software systems
```
Computing

fall back routines *noun* routines that are called *or* procedures which are executed by a user when a machine *or* system has failed

fall-off *noun (film)* gradual decrease in brightness from the centre of a screen to the edges

false *adjective* wrong; not true *or* not correct; **false code** = code that contains values not within specified limits; **false drop** = unwanted files retrieved from a database through the use of incorrect search codes

FAM = FAST ACCESS MEMORY

family *noun* **(a)** range of different designs of a particular typeface **(b)** range of machines from one manufacturer that are compatible with other products in the same line from the same manufacturer

fan 1 *noun* (i) mechanism that circulates air for cooling; (ii) a spread of data items *or*

devices; *if the fan fails, the system will rapidly overheat* **2** *verb* (i) to cool a device by blowing air over it; (ii) to spread out a series of items *or* devices; **fan antenna** = antenna whose elements are arranged in a semicircle; **fan-in** = maximum number of inputs that a circuit *or* chip can deal with; **fan-out** = maximum number of outputs that a circuit *or* chip can drive without exceeding its power dissipation limit; **fanning strip** = cable supporting insulated strip

```
Intel  is  investigating  other
options  to  solve  the  Pentium
system  overheating  problems,
including  selling  the  chip
with its own miniature fan
```
Computing

fanfold paper = ACCORDION FOLD

FAQ = FREQUENTLY ASKED QUESTIONS file that contains the answers to questions users most often ask about a particular topic

farad (F) *noun* SI unit of capacitance, defined as coulombs over volts

fascia plate *noun* front panel on a device; *the fascia plate on the disk drive of this model is smaller than those on other models*

FAST = FEDERATION AGAINST COPYRIGHT THEFT organization that prevents illegal copying of software

fast *adjective* **(a)** which moves quickly; which works quickly; (storage *or* peripheral device) that performs its functions very rapidly; **fast access memory (FAM)** = storage locations that can be read from *or* written to very rapidly; **fast peripheral** = peripheral that communicates with the computer at very high speeds, limited only by the speed of the electronic circuits, as opposed to a slow peripheral such as a card reader, where mechanical movement determines speed **(b)** (photographic lens) with a very wide aperture; highly light-sensitive photographic film; **fast film** = film which is very sensitive to light; **fast lens** = lens which can hold a vast amount of light

FAT = FILE ALLOCATION TABLE *(in DOS, and some other operating systems)* data file stored on disk that contains the names of each file stored on the disk, together with its starting sector position, date and size

fatal error *noun* fault in a program *or* device that causes the system to crash

FatBits *noun* MacPaint option which allows a user to edit an image one pixel at a time

father file *noun* backup of the previous version of a file; *see also* GRANDFATHER FILE, SON FILE

fault *noun* situation where something has gone wrong with software *or* hardware, causing it to malfunction; *the technical staff are trying to correct a programming fault; we think there is a basic fault in the product design*; *see also* BUG, ERROR; **fault detection** = (automatic) process which logically *or* mathematically determines that a fault exists in a circuit; **fault diagnosis** = process by which the cause of a fault is located; **fault trace** = program that checks and records the occurrences of faults in a system

fault-tolerant *adjective* (system *or* device) that is able to continue functioning even when a fault occurs; *they market a highly successful range of fault-tolerant minis; see also* DUPLEX, MIRROR

```
before          fault-tolerant
systems, users had to rely on
cold standby
```
Computer News

```
fault  tolerance  is  usually
associated  with  a  system's
reliability
```
Computer News

faulty *adjective* which does not work properly; *there must be a faulty piece of equipment in the system; they traced the fault to a faulty cable*; **faulty sector** = sector of a magnetic disk that cannot be written to *or* read from correctly

fax *or* **FAX** *noun & verb* (*informal*) = FACSIMILE COPY, FACSIMILE TRANSMISSION; *we will send a fax of the design plan; I've faxed the documents to our New York office; the fax machine is next to the telephone switchboard*; **fax card** *or* **board** *or* **adapter** = adapter card which plugs into an expansion slot and allows a computer to send or receive fax data; **fax group** = method of defining the basic features of a fax machine or modem:

groups 1 and 2 are old and rarely used now, group 3 is the most common standard used today, groups 3bis and 4 provide higher speed and better resolution of transmission; **fax server** = computer connected to a network and fitted with a fax modem so that all users on the network can send and receive faxes

FCB = FILE CONTROL BLOCK area of memory (used by the operating system) that contains information about the files in use *or* those stored on a disk drive

FCC (*film*) (a) US = FEDERAL COMMUNICATIONS COMMISSION (b) = FRAME COUNT CUEING in the printing of film, this is a control cue device based on the electronic counting of the amount of frames moving through the machine

fd *or* **FD** (a) = FULL DUPLEX data transmission down a channel in two directions simultaneously (b) = FLOPPY DISK

fdc = FLOPPY DISK CONTROLLER

FDDI = FIBRE DISTRIBUTED DATA INTERFACE ANSI standard for high-speed networks which use fibre optic cable in a dual ring topology; data is transmitted at 100Mbps; **FDDI II** = extension to FDDI standard to allow transmission of analog data in digital form

FDISK (*in MS-DOS*) system utility that configures the partitions on a hard disk

FDM = FREQUENCY DIVISION MULTIPLEXING assigning a number of different signals to different frequencies (or bands) to allow many signals to be sent along one channel; *using FDM we can transmit 100 telephone calls along one main cable*

fdx *or* **FDX** = FULL DUPLEX

feasibility *noun* ability to be done; *he has been asked to report on the feasibility of a project*; **feasibility report** = report saying if something can be done; **feasibility study** = examination and report into the usefulness and cost of a new product that is being considered for purchase; **to carry out a feasibility study on a project** = to carry out an examination of costs and profits to see if the project should be started (NOTE: no plural)

feature film *noun* commercial, full-length film production to be shown in a cinema; usually ninety minutes in length

feature *noun* special function *or* ability *or* design of hardware *or* software; *the key features of this system are: 20Gb of formatted storage with an access time of 10ms*

FED *see* FIELD EMISSION DISPLAY

Federation Against Copyright Theft *see* FACT

FEDS = FIXED AND EXCHANGEABLE DISK STORAGE

feed 1 *noun* device which puts paper *or* tape into and through a machine, such as a printer *or* photocopier; **continuous feed** = device which feeds in continuous computer stationery into a printer; **front feed** *or* **sheet feed attachment** = device which can be attached to a line printer to allow individual sheets of paper to be fed in automatically; **feed holes** = punched sprocket holes along the edge of continuous paper; **feed horn** = microwave channelling device used to direct transmitted signals; **feed reel** = reel of tape *or* film which is being fed into a machine; **sheet feed** = device which puts in one sheet at a time into a printer; **paper feed** = slot into which the paper is introduced **2** *verb* to put paper into a machine *or* information into a computer; *this paper should be manually fed into the printer; data is fed into the computer* (NOTE: feeding - fed)

feedback *noun* **(a)** part of an output signal that is fed back to the input and amplified; **feedback loop** = path from output to input by which feedback occurs; **negative feedback** = subtraction of part of the output from a device from its input signal; **positive feedback** = addition of part of the output from a device to its input; *if a microphone is too close to a speaker the result is positive feedback or a howl; see also* ACOUSTICAL FEEDBACK **(b)** information from one source which can be used to modify something *or* provide a constructive criticism of something; *we are getting customer feedback on the new system; they asked the sales teams for feedback on the reception of the new model; have you any feedback from the sales force about the customers' reaction to the new model?* (NOTE: no plural)

COMMENT: negative or positive feedback can be accidental (when it may cause severe overloading of the circuit) or designed into the circuit to make it more stable

feeder *noun* **(a)** channel that carries signals from one point to another; **feeder cable** = (i) main transmission line that carries signals from a central point for distribution; (ii) cable from an antenna to a circuit **(b)** mechanism that automatically inserts the paper into a printer

feevee *noun (US informal)* form of cable TV where the viewer pays an extra fee for extra channels

feint *noun* very light lines on writing paper

female *adjective* **female connector** = connector with connecting sockets into which the pins *or* plugs of a male connector can be inserted; **female socket** = hole into which a pin *or* plug can be inserted to make a connection

femto- (f) *prefix* equal to ten exponent minus fifteen (10^{-15}); **femto second** = thousandth of a picosecond

FEP = FRONT-END PROCESSOR processor placed between an input source and the central computer, whose function is to preprocess received data to relieve the workload of the main computer

ferric oxide *noun* substance used as tape *or* disk coating that can be magnetized to store data *or* signals

ferrite *noun* low loss radio frequency material, usually used as a coil former

ferromagnetic *adjective* (material) that has a high magnetic permeability

FET = FIELD EFFECT TRANSISTOR

fetch *noun* command that retrieves the next instruction from memory; **fetch-execute cycle** = events required to retrieve, decode and carry out an instruction stored in memory; **fetch phase** = section of the fetch-execute cycle that retrieves and decodes the instructions from memory

FF = FLIP-FLOP, FORM FEED

fibre distributed data interface (FDDI) *noun* ANSI standard for high-speed networks that uses fibre optic cable in a dual ring topology; data is transmitted at 100Mbps

fibre optics *noun* light transmission through thin strands of glass *or* plastic, which allows data to be transmitted; **fibre optic cable** *or* **connection** = fine strands of glass *or* plastic protected by a surrounding material, used for transmission of light signals; *fibre optic connections enabling nodes up to one kilometre apart to be used*

```
Honeywell has won a contract
worth £380,000 to cable Abbey
National's          Milton
Keynes-based   administration
offices. The installation will
be based on copper wire and
fibre optics and will be
carried out by Honeywell's PDS
Group
```
Computing

fibre ribbon *noun* fabric-based ribbon used in printers and typewriters

fiche *see* MICROFICHE

fidelity *noun* ability of an audio system to reproduce sound correctly; **high fidelity system (hi fi)** = high-quality equipment for playing records *or* compact discs *or* tapes *or* for listening to the radio (tape recorder, turntable, amplifier and speakers); *see also* HI FI

field emission display (FED) *noun* method of producing thin, flat displays for laptop computers in which a miniature colour CRT is located at each pixel point; this method uses less energy and provides a sharper image than active matrix LCD colour screen; **field strength** = amplitude of the magnetic *or* electric field at one point in that field **(b)** sections containing individual data items in a record; *the employee record does have a field for age*; **field separator** = code used to indicate the end of one field and the start of the next **(c)** method of building up a picture on a television screen; **field blanking** = interval when television signal field synchronizing pulses are transmitted; **field frequency** = number of field scans per second; **field fly back** = return of electron beam to top left hand corner of a screen; **field sweep** = vertical electron beam movement over a television screen; **field sync pulse** = pulse in a TV signal that makes sure that the receiver's field sweep is in sync **(d)** section of an image that is available after the light has passed through the camera and lens **(e)** in

the field = outside an office *or* factory; **field engineer** = engineer who does not work at one single company, but travels between customers carrying out maintenance on their computers; **field sales manager** = manager in charge of a group of salesmen working in a particular area of the country; **field tested** = product tested outside a company *or* research laboratory, in a real situation; **field work** = examining the situation among several potential customers

field *noun* **(a)** area of force and energy distribution, caused by magnetic *or* electric energy sources; **field effect transistor (FET)** = electronic device that can act as a variable current flow control, an external signal varies the resistance of the device and current flow by changing the width of a conducting channel

fielding *noun* arrangement of field allocations inside a record and file

FIF = FRACTAL IMAGE FORMAT file format used to store graphics images which have been highly-compressed using fractals

FIFO = FIRST IN FIRST OUT **(a)** accounting policy where the stock is valued at the price of the oldest purchases **(b)** temporary queue where the first item stored is the first read; *compare with* LIFO

fifth generation computers *noun* next stage of computer system design using fast VLSI circuits and powerful programming languages to allow human interaction

figure *noun* **(a)** printed line illustration in a book; *see figure 10 for a chart of ASCII codes* **(b)** printed number; **figures case** = characters in a telegraphic transmission that are mainly numbers *or* signs; **figures shift** = (i) transmitted code that indicates to the receiver that all following characters should be read as upper case; (ii) mechanical switch which allows a typewriter to print special characters and symbols located on the same keys as the numbers; **in round figures** = not totally accurate, but correct to the nearest 10 *or* 100; *they have a workforce of 2,500 in round figures*

file 1 *noun* **(a)** cardboard holder for documents, which can fit in the drawer of a filing cabinet; *put these letters in the customer file; look in the file marked 'Scottish sales'*; **box file** = cardboard box for holding documents **(b)** documents kept for reference; **file copy** = copy of a document which is kept for reference in an office; **card-index file** = information kept on filing cards; **to keep someone's name on file** = to keep someone's name on a list for reference; **to place something on file** = to keep a record of something (c) section of data on a computer (such as payroll, address list, customer accounts), in the form of individual records which may contain data, characters, digits *or* graphics; **distributed file system** = system that uses files stored in more than one location *or* backing store, but which are processed at a central point; *(in a PC operating system)* **file allocation table (FAT)** = data file stored on disk containing the names of each file stored on the disk, together with its starting sector position, date and size; **file attributes** = control bits of data stored with each file which control particular functions *or* aspects of the file such as read-only, archived or system file; **file cleanup** = tidying and removing unnecessary data from a file; **file control block** = *see* FCB; **file conversion** = change of format *or* structure of a file system, usually when using a new program *or* file handling routine; **file defragmentation** = *see* DEFRAGMENTATION; **file element** = complete file contained within a RIFF compound file; *see also* RIFF; **file format** = standard way in which information is stored within a file; *a graphics image can be stored in many different ways according to the file format used*; *see also* TIFF, EPS, CGM; **file fragmentation** = file that is stored in non contiguous sectors on a disk; **file gap** = section of blank tape *or* disk that indicates the end of a file; **file handle** = number by which an open file is identified within a program; *the new data is written to the file identified by file handle 1*; **file handling routine** = short computer program that manages the reading/writing and organization of stored files; **file header** = information about the file stored at the beginning of the file; *the file header in the database file shows the total number of records and lists the index fields*; **file layout** = set of rules defining internal file structure; **file locking** = software mechanism that prevents data in a file being updated by two different users at the same time; only one user can change the particular information at any one time; **file**

maintenance = process of updating a file by changing, adding *or* deleting entries; **file management** = routines used to create and maintain a file; **File Manager** = a program supplied with Windows 3.x that lets the user manage all the files stored on a disk; **file organization** = *see* FILE LAYOUT; **file processing** = applying a set of rules *or* search limits to a file, in order to update *or* find information; **file properties** = (in Windows) attributes that are assigned to a particular file, including its name, date that it was created and owner; *to view the file's properties, highlight the file with a single click from within Windows Explorer and click on the right-hand mouse button, choose the Properties menu option to view the properties of the file;* **file protection** = (i) software *or* physical device used to prevent any accidental deletion *or* modification of a file *or* its records; (ii) *see* FILE SECURITY; **file protect tab** = plastic tab on a disk which prevents accidental erasure of a file; **file-recovery utility** = software that allows files that have been accidentally deleted *or* damaged to be read again; *a lost file cannot be found without a file-recovery utility*; **file security** = hardware *or* software organization of a computer system to protect users files from unauthorized access; **file server** = small microcomputer and large backing store device that is used for the management and storage of a user's files in a network; **file sharing** = one file that can be used by two or more users *or* programs in a network (often using file locking); **file size** = the number of bytes a file occupies on disk; **file storage** = physical means of preserving data in a file, such as a disk drive *or* tape machine; **file store** = files that are available in main memory at any time; **file transfer** = moving a file from one area of memory to another *or* to another storage device; **file transfer access and management (FTAM)** = standard method of transferring files between different computer systems; **file transfer protocol (FTP)** = TCP/IP standard for transferring files between computers; it is a file sharing protocol that operates at layers 5, 6 and 7 of an OSI model network; **file transfer utility** = software utility that links two computers together (normally via a physical serial cable) and allows files to be transferred between the computers; **file type**

= method of classifying what a file contains; (in an MS-DOS system this is often by the filename extension); *files with the extension EXE are file types that contain program code*; **output file** = set of records that have been completely processed according to various parameters **2** *verb* to **file documents** = to put documents in order so that they can be found easily; *the correspondence is filed under 'complaints'; he filed the new papers in chronological order*

filename *noun* unique identification code allocated to a program; *in MS-DOS, a filename can be up to eight characters long together with a three-character filename extension; in Windows, long filenames that are not limited to eight characters can be entered*; **filename extension** = additional information after a filename, indicating the type *or* use of the file; *the filename extension SYS indicates that this is a system file*

> it allows users to back up or restore read-only security files and hidden system files independently
>
> *Minicomputer News*

> the lost file, while inaccessible without a file-recovery utility, remains on disk until new information writes over it
>
> *Publish*

> The first problem was solved by configuring a Windows swap file, which I hadn't done before because my 4Mb 486 had never been overloaded
>
> *Computing*

> when the filename is entered at the prompt, the operating system looks in the file and executes any instructions stored there
>
> *PC User*

filing *noun* (a) documents which have to be put in order (b) putting documents in order; *there is a lot of filing to do at the end of the week; the manager looked through the week's filing to see what letters had been sent*; **filing basket** *or* **filing tray** = container kept on a desk for documents

which have to be filed; **filing cabinet** = metal box with several drawers for keeping files; **filing card** = card with information written on it, used to classify information into the correct order (NOTE: no plural)

filing system *noun* (a) way of putting documents in order for reference (b) software which organizes files

fill *verb* (a) to make something full; *we have filled our order book with orders for Africa; the production department has filled the warehouse with products we cannot sell* (b) to put characters into gaps in a field so that there are no spaces left; **fill character** = character added to a string of characters to make up a required length; **filled cable** = cable which uses a substance to fill any gaps between outer and conductors, so preventing water getting in (c) to draw an enclosed area in one colour *or* shading

fill light *or* **filler** *or* **fill-in light** *noun* *(film)* additional studio lamp used to provide extra light in shadows

fill up *verb* (a) to make something completely full; *the disk was quickly filled up* (b) to finish writing on a form; *he filled up the form and sent it to the bank*

film 1 *noun* (a) transparent strip of plastic, coated with a light-sensitive compound and used to produce photographs with the aid of a camera; **film advance** = (i) lever on a camera used to wind on a roll of film to the next frame; (ii) the distance a phototypesetting machine has to move prior to the next line to be set; **film assembly** = correct arrangement of photographs *or* negatives prior to the production of a printing plate; **film base** = thin transparent roll of plastic used as a supporting material for photographic film; **film chain** = all the necessary equipment needed when showing film *or* slides on television, such as a projector, TV camera and synchronizer; **film cutter** *or* **film editor** = *see* EDITOR; **film gate** = the alliance of the aperture and pressure plates in a camera or a projector to guide the film through, and to also ensure the correct focal distance between the film and the lens; **film gauge** = diameter of different types of cinematographic film; **film optical scanning device for input into computers (FOSDIC)** = storage device for computer data using microfilm; **film**

pickup = transmission of a motion picture film by television by electronically scanning each frame; **film recorder** = device that produces a 35mm slide from a computer image; a film recorder can produce slides at very high resolution, normally around 3,000 lines, by re-generating the image on an internal screen; **film running speed** = speed in frames per second or meters per minute at which film passes through a camera or a projector; **film speed** = light sensitivity of photographic film, as determined by ASA or DIN; **film strip** = set of related images on a reel of film, usually for educational purposes; **photographic film** = light-sensitive film used in a camera to record images **(b)** projection at high speed of a series of still images that creates the impression of movement **2** *verb* to expose a photographic film to light by means of a camera, and so to produce images

filming *noun* shooting of a cinema film *or* TV film; *filming will start next week if the weather is fine*

filmsetting *noun* photocomposition

filter 1 *noun* **(a)** electronic circuit that allows certain frequencies to pass while stopping others; **bandpass filter** = circuit that allows a certain band of frequencies to pass while stopping any that are higher or lower; **high pass filter** = circuit that allows frequencies above a certain limit to pass, but blocks those below that limit; **low pass filter** = circuit that blocks signals above a certain frequency **(b)** option in a software application that allows it to import or export a particular file type; *most graphics packages have import filters that will decode TIFF, BMP and PCX file formats* **(c)** optical coloured glass, which stops certain frequencies of light; **absorption filter** = filter that blocks certain colours; **character enhancement filter** = filter placed over a monitor to increase contrast, and also to prevent eye-strain; **filter factor** = indicator of the amount of light that an optical filter absorbs when light passes through it; *(film)* **filter heat** = translucent material which transmits light visible to the eye but absorbs or reflects infra-red radiation **2** *verb* to remove unwanted elements from a signal *or* file

final *adjective* last *or* coming at the end of a period; *to keyboard the final data files; to make the final changes to a document*

final cut *noun (film)* **(a)** original negative when it has been altered to conform with the workprint **(b)** the final version of the edited film on which the sound track can now be placed

find 1 *verb* to get something back which has been lost (NOTE: **finding - found**) **2** *noun* command to locate a piece of information; **Find** = (in Windows) utility software that searches for a file on a disk drive; **find and replace** = feature on a word-processor that allows certain words *or* sections of text to be located and replaced with others

final trial composite *noun (film)* film containing audio and visual effects; this is the final and approved version of all former trial composites

Finder *noun (in an Apple Macintosh system)* graphical user interface that is used to operate the Macintosh; allows a user to view files, organise files into folders and start and control applications using a mouse

fine *adjective* **(a)** very thin *or* very small; *the engraving has some very fine lines* **(b)** excellent *or* of very high quality

fine tune *verb* to adjust by small amounts the features *or* parameters of hardware *or* software to improve performance

finger *verb (in a program)* to question the status of a remote computer on a network or on the Internet and display the user name and status

finish 1 *noun* **(a)** final appearance; *the product has an attractive finish* **(b)** end of a process *or* function **2** *verb* **(a)** to do something *or* to make something completely; *the order was finished in time; she finished all the keyboarding before lunch* **(b)** to come to an end; *the contract is due to finish next month*

finished *adjective* which has been completed; **finished document** = document which is typed, and is ready to be printed; **finished goods** = manufactured goods which are ready to be sold

firewall *noun* device connected between a local area network and the Internet that is used to protect an internal network from unauthorised access via the Internet; *a firewall computer normally has two* *network adapters that connect the two networks and special software that checks the identity of each user before allowing access*

firmware *noun* computer program *or* data that is permanently stored in a hardware memory chip, such as a ROM *or* EPROM; *compare with* HARDWARE, SOFTWARE

first cameraman *noun (film)* person who is the main operator of a camera

first fit *noun* routine or algorithm that selects the first, largest section of free memory in which to store a (virtual) page

first generation computer *noun* original computer made with valve based electronic technology, started around 1951

first generation image *noun* master copy of an original image, text *or* document

first grip *noun (film)* on a film set, the principal stagehand who is responsible for the other stagehands; *see* GRIP

first in first out (FIFO) *noun* temporary queue where the first item stored is the first read; *see also* FIFO

first party release *noun* ending of a telephone connection as soon as either party puts his phone down *or* disconnects his modem

fisheye lens *noun* extremely wide angle photographic lens that has a field of view of 180 degrees and produces a distorted circular image

fishpole *noun (film)* hand-held pole (about two metres long) which holds a microphone

fit *verb* to plot or calculate a curve that most closely approximates a number of points *or* data

fix 1 *noun* chemical stage in processing a film that sets permanently the developed image on a film *or* paper **2** *verb* **(a)** to make something permanent *or* to attach something permanently; *the computer is fixed to the workstation*; **fixed and exchangeable disk storage (FEDS)** = magnetic disk storage system that contains some removable disks, such as floppy disks and some fixed *or* hard disk drives; **fixed data** = data written to a file *or* screen for information *or* identification purposes and which cannot be altered by the user; **fixed disk storage** = hard disk *or* magnetic disk which cannot be removed from the disk drive; **fixed field** =

area in a stored record that can only contain a certain amount of data; **fixed-field file** = data file in which each field consists of a pre-defined and fixed number of characters; spaces are used to pad out each field to the correct length; *compare with* DELIMITED-FIELD FILE; **fixed-frequency monitor** = monitor that can only accept one frequency and type of video signal, such as VGA-only monitor; *compare with* MULTI-SCAN MONITOR; **fixed head disk (drive)** = use of a separate read/write head over each disk track making access time very short; **fixed-length record** = record whose size is preset; **fixed-length word** = preset number of bits that make up a computer word; **fixed-point notation** = number representation that retains the position of the digits and decimal points in the computer, so limiting the maximum manageable numbers; **fixed-point arithmetic** = arithmetic rules and methods using fixed-point numbers; **fixed routing** = communications direction routing that does not consider traffic *or* efficient paths **(b)** to mend; *the technicians are trying to fix the switchboard; can you fix the photocopier?*

fixing *or* **fixation** *noun* chemical stage in processing a film that sets permanently the developed image on a film *or* paper

flag 1 *noun* **(a)** (i) way of showing the end of field *or* of indicating something special in a database; (ii) method of reporting the status of a register after a mathematical *or* logical operation; *if the result is zero, the zero flag is set*; **carry flag** = indicator that a carry has occurred after a subtraction *or* addition; **flag bit** = single bit of a word used as a flag for certain operations; **flag code** = *see* ESCAPE CODES; **flag sequence** = sequence of codes sent on a packet switching network as identification of the start and finish of a frame of data; **overflow bit** *or* **flag** = single bit in a word that is set to one (1) if a mathematical overflow has occurred **(b)** square or rectangular opaque sheet which is used to stop light from the camera lens hitting places where it is not needed on the set **2** *verb* to attract the attention of a program while it is running to provide a result *or* to report an action *or* to indicate something special

flagging *noun* **(a)** putting an indicator against an item so that it can be found later;

see also BOOK MARK **(b)** distortion in a television picture which is created by timing mistakes in a video tape recorder's playback signal

flame *verb* to send rude electronic mail messages with whose opinion you disagree

flare *noun* **(a)** an error in which dispersion of light in a lens undesirably brightens the dark areas of an image **(b)** areas of film that have been exposed to light on account of the camera not being fully light proof

flared *adjective* image with unwanted bright spots *or* lines due to internal lens *or* camera reflections

flash 1 *verb* to switch a light on and off; to increase and lower the brightness of a cursor to provide an indicator **2** *noun* overexposure in the film frame or an unwanted refection causing a bright spot on the film; **flash A/D** = parallel high speed A/D converter; **flash card** = card containing indexing information photographed with a document; *(film)* **flash frame** = (i) in a film negative, a heavily exposed frame which produces a clear area in the matching positive print; (ii) one frame added to a sequence in order to provide a diverse image for a split second; **flash memory** = non-volatile memory similar to an EEPROM device but that operates with blocks of data rather than single bytes; most often used as an alternative to a disk drive

flashing *noun* signal sent over a telephone line to get the attention of an operator *or* user

flat *adjective* **(a)** lacking contrast (in an image *or* photograph) **(b)** smooth (surface); *compare with* SEGMENTED ADDRESS SPACE; **flat file** = two-dimensional file of data items; **flat file database** = database program that does not allow relational data; it can only access data stored in one file at a time; **flat pack** = integrated circuit package whose leads extend horizontally, allowing the device to be mounted directly onto a PCB without the need for holes; **flat screen** = monitor tube that has a very flat display area with nearly square corners, rather than the usual tube with a curved display with rounded edges; a flat screen distorts an image less than a conventional CRT **(c)** fixed *or* not changing; **flat rate** = set pricing rate that covers all the use of a facility

flat address space *noun* area of memory in which each location has a unique address (the Macintosh operating system uses a flat address space, MS-DOS does not)

flatbed *noun* printing *or* scanning machine that holds the paper *or* image on a flat surface while processing; *scanners are either flatbed models or platen type, paper-fed models; paper cannot be rolled through flatbed scanners*; **flatbed plotter** = movable pen that draws diagrams under the control of a computer onto a flat piece of paper; **flatbed press** = mechanical printing machine where the inked printing plate lies flat on the bed of the machine; **flatbed scanner** = device with a flat sheet of glass on which an image or photograph is placed; the scan head moves below the glass and converts the image into data which can be manipulated by computer; *see also* SCANNER; **flatbed transmitter** = device that keeps a document flat while it is being scanned before being transmitted by facsimile means

flex *noun* wire *or* cable used to connect an appliance to the mains electricity supply (NOTE: no plural: **a piece of flex**)

flexibility *noun* ability of hardware *or* software to adapt to various conditions *or* tasks

flexible *adjective* which can be altered *or* changed; **flexible disk** = FLOPPY DISK; **flexible machining system (FMS)** = computer numeric control (CNC) *or* control of a machine by a computer; **flexible manufacturing system (FMS)** = use of CNC machines, robots and other automated devices in manufacturing; **flexible working hours** = system where workers can start *or* stop working at different hours of the morning or evening, provided that they work a certain number of hours per week

flicker 1 *noun* **(a)** random variation of brightness in a television picture **(b)** effect that occurs when a frame from a videodisc is frozen and two different pictures are displayed alternately at high speed due to the incorrect field matching **(c)** very short interruption in a film which is caused by a fault in the film projector or by a slow film projector **(d)** computer graphic image whose brightness alternates due to a low image refresh rate **2** *verb* to move very slightly; *the image flickers where the printer is switched on*

flicker-free *adjective* (display) that does not flicker

flier *noun* small advertising leaflet designed to encourage customers to ask for more information about a product *or* service

flip-flop (FF) *noun* electronic circuit *or* chip whose output can be one of two states, which can be used to store one bit of digital data; **D-flip-flop** = flip-flop device with one input and two outputs; **JK-flip-flop** = flip-flop device with two inputs (J and K) and two outputs whose states are always complementary and dependent on the inputs

flippy *noun* disk that is double-sided but used in a single-sided drive, so it has to be turned over to read the other side

float *noun* *(film)* **(a)** *(in film projection)* slow shake of the image up and down due to faulty synchronization **(b)** overlapping images in multiple exposure rostrum camera work **(c)** part of a studio set which can easily be moved into or out of position

floating *adjective* not fixed; character which is separate from the character it should be attached to; **floating accent** = method of printing an accent in text where the accent is separate from the letter above which it is printed (on a typewriter, an accented letter may need three keystrokes, one for the accent, then backspace, then key the letter); **floating point** = numerical notation in which a fractional number is represented with a point after the first digit and a power, so that any number can be stored in a standard form; *56.47 in floating-point arithmetic would be 0.5647 and a power of 2*; **floating point unit** *or* **processor (FPU)** = specialized CPU that can process floating point numbers very rapidly; *the floating point processor speeds up the processing of the graphics software; this model includes a built-in floating point processor*; **floating voltage** = voltage in a network *or* device that has no related ground *or* reference plane; **floating window** = window that can be moved anywhere on screen; often used to describe a toolbar that can be moved around

flood *or* **floodlight** *noun* *(film)* lamp which gives a wide range of light

flood track *noun* *(film)* sound track on a photographic film which is not used for sound and reveals the standard maximum width of a picture area

flooding *noun* rapid, reliable but not very efficient means of routing packet-switched data, in which each node sends the data received to each of its neighbours

floppy disk *or* **floppy** *or* **FD** *noun* secondary storage device, in the form of a flat, circular flexible disk onto which data can be stored in a magnetic form (a floppy disk cannot store as much data as a hard disk, but is easily removed, and is protected by a flexible paper *or* plastic sleeve); **floppy disk controller (FDC)** = combination of hardware and software devices that control and manage the read/write operations of a disk drive from a computer; **floppy disk unit** = disk drive for floppy disks and ancillary electronics as a separate assembly; **floppy tape** *or* **tape streamer** = continuous loop of tape, used for backing storage; *see also* MICROFLOPPY

COMMENT: floppies are available in various sizes: the commonest is 3.5 inch; older disks were made in 5.25 inch and 8 inch formats. The size refers to the diameter of the disk inside the sleeve.

flow 1 *noun* regular movement; *automatic text flow across pages; the device controls the copy flow; current flow is regulated by a resistor* **2** *verb* to move smoothly; *work is flowing normally again after the breakdown of the printer*

flow control *noun* management of the flow of data into queues and buffers, to prevent spillage *or* lost data

flow text *verb* to insert text into a page format in a DTP system; the text fills all the space around pictures, and between set margins

flowchart 1 *noun* chart which shows the arrangement of the steps in a process *or* program; **flowchart symbol** = special symbols used to represent devices, decisions and operations in a flowchart; **flowchart template** = plastic sheet with template symbols cut out, to allow symbols to be drawn quickly and clearly **2** *verb* to describe a process, its control and routes graphically

fluctuate *verb* to move up and down; *the electric current fluctuates between 1 Amp and 1.3 Amp*

fluctuating *adjective* moving up and down; *fluctuating signal strength*

fluctuation *noun* up and down movement; *current fluctuations can affect the functioning of the computer system*

fluid head *noun (film)* camera head for a tripod which possesses smooth pan and tilt facilities

flush 1 *verb* to clear *or* erase all the contents of a queue, buffer, file or section of memory; **flush buffers** = to erase any data remaining in a buffer, ready for a new job or after a job has been aborted **2** *adjective* level *or* in line with; *the covers are trimmed flush with the pages*; **flush left** *or* **flush right** = *see* JUSTIFY LEFT, JUSTIFY RIGHT

fluting *noun (film)* twisting and bending of film edges created by humidity or by winding the film too tightly around a spool

flutter *noun* fluctuations of tape speed due to mechanical *or* circuit problems, causing signal distortion; *wow and flutter and common faults on cheap tape recorders*

flux *noun* **(a)** measure of magnetic field strength; **flux density** = intensity of a magnetic flux **(b)** amount of reflected light from an object

fly *verb* to move (through the air)

flyback *or* **line flyback** *noun* electron beam return from the end of a scan to the beginning of the next

FM synthesizer *noun* synthesizer that generates sounds by combining base signals of different frequencies; *compare with* WAVEFORM SYNTHESIZER

FM = FREQUENCY MODULATION

FMS (a) = FLEXIBLE MACHINING SYSTEM **(b)** = FLEXIBLE MANUFACTURING SYSTEM

FNP = FRONT-END PROCESSOR

f-number *noun* measurement of the amount of light that an optical lens can collect, measured as the ratio of focal length to maximum aperture

COMMENT: the measurement calculated is very important for focusing, lighting and film development laboratory notes

FO = FIBRE OPTICS

focal length *noun* distance between the centre of an optical lens and the focusing plane, when the lens is focused at infinity

focal plane *noun (film)* plane through the main focus of a camera lens which is at right angles to its optical axis

focus 1 *noun* **(a)** image *or* beam that is clear and well defined; **the picture is out of focus** *or* **is not in focus** = the picture is not clear **(b)** object that is currently accepting user input or is being controlled by a program and accepting commands from the program (for example, a button or check-box on screen); **focus window** = window in a GUI that is currently active and accepting user input or is being controlled by a program and accepting commands from the program (in Microsoft Windows, the focus window is indicated by a different colour title bar) **2** *verb* to adjust the focal length of a lens *or* beam deflection system so that the image *or* beam is clear and well defined; *the camera is focused on the foreground; they adjusted the lens position so that the beam focused correctly*

fog *noun* effect on photographic material which has been accidentally exposed to unwanted light, causing a loss of picture contrast

fog filter *noun (film)* filter placed in front of the camera lens that diffuses the light to produce a softer image; also used to create the impression of fog

fog level *noun (film)* minimum density of the unexposed part of film which has been processed

-fold *suffix* times; **four-fold** = four times

fold *verb* to bend a flat thing, so that part of it is on top of the rest; *she folded the letter so that the address was clearly visible*; **accordion fold** *or* **fanfold** = method of folding continuous stationery, one sheet in one direction, the next sheet in the opposite direction, allowing the paper to stored conveniently and fed into a printer continuously

folder *noun* **(a)** *(in Windows and Apple Macintosh)* location for a group of files stored together under a name, similar to a directory under MS-DOS; to open a folder and see the files it contains, double click on the folder's icon; *see also* DIRECTORY **(b)** cardboard envelope for carrying papers; *put all the documents in a folder for the chairman*

folding machine *noun* machine which automatically folds sheets of paper

folio 1 *noun* page with a number, especially two facing pages in an account book which have the same number **2** *verb* to put a number on a page

follow focus *verb (film)* to keep an object in focus even if it is moving away from the camera

follow spot *noun (film)* very strong spotlight which follows a performer

font *or* **fount** *noun* set of characters all of the same style, size and typeface; **downloadable fonts** = fonts *or* typefaces which are stored on a disk and can be downloaded to a printer and stored in temporary memory; **font card** = ROM device that fits into a socket on a printer and adds another resident font; **font change** = function on a computer to change the style of characters used on a display screen; *(in an Apple Macintosh system)* **Font/DA Mover** = system utility that allows a user to add fonts and DA files to the system environment; **font disk** = (i) transparent disk that contains the master images of a particular font, used in a phototypesetting machine; (ii) magnetic disk that contains the data to drive a character generator to make up the various fonts on a computer display; *(in Windows)* **Fonts Folder** = a special folder which stores all fonts that are currently installed on your PC and that can be displayed or printed; *to add a new font or to view the existing fonts, open the Fonts Folder by clicking on Start/Settings/Fonts;* **resident fonts** = fonts that can be used by any software application; the font data is stored in a printer's memory and does not have to be downloaded

```
laser printers store fonts in
several ways:  as  resident,
cartridge  and  downloadable
fonts
```
Desktop Publishing Today

```
Word Assistant is designed to
help  word-processing  users
produce     better-looking
documents.  It  has  style
templates and forms providing
25  TrueType  fonts,  100
clip-art images and two font
utility programs
```
Computing

foobar term used by programmers to refer to whatever is being discussed; for example,

if a programmer is explaining how a graphic program works, he might refer to an example graphic file that stores the image as 'foobar.gif'; many programmers refer to example variables or example user details as foobar; you will often see this term used in books and lessons about software and systems

foolscap *noun* large size of writing paper, longer than A4; *the letter was on six sheets of foolscap*; **a foolscap envelope** = large envelope which takes foolscap paper (NOTE: no plural)

foot *noun* **(a)** bottom part; *he signed his name at the foot of the letter* **(b)** measurement of length (= 30cm); *the table is six feet long; my office is ten feet by twelve* **(c)** *(film)* measurement of length of film which represents a certain number of frames, for example: one foot contains 72 frames for Super 8, 40 for 16mm and 16 for 35mm (NOTE: the plural is **feet** for **(a)** and **(c)**; there is no plural for **(b)**. In measurements, **foot** is usually written **ft** or ' after figures: **10ft; 10'**)

foot candle *noun* amount of light illumination in one square foot when the incident flux is one lumen

footage *noun (film)* measurement of film length in metres or feet; **footage numbers;** *see* EDGE NUMBERS

footer *or* **footing** *noun* text at the bottom of all the pages in a printed document (such as the page number)

footnote *noun* note at the bottom of a page, which refers to the text above it, usually using a superior number as a reference

footprint *noun* **(a)** area covered by a transmitting device such as a satellite *or* antenna **(b)** area that a computer takes up on a desk

```
Acer  has  overhauled  its
desktop  PC  range  with  the
launch  of  16  new  models
ranging from small-footprint,
single-processing systems to
large multiprocessing boxes
```
Computing

for your information (FYI) document that contains general background information related to the Internet or the TCP/IP protocols; specific technical information is normally contained in RFC documents; *see also* FAQ, RFC

forbid *verb* to say that something must not be done; *the contract forbids sale of the goods to the USA*; **forbidden combination** = bit combination in a computer word that is not allowed according to the rules defined by the programmer *or* system designer (NOTE: **forbidding - forbade - forbidden**)

force 1 *noun* **(a)** strength; **to be in force** = to be operating *or* working; *the rules have been in force since 1946*; **to come into force** = to start to operate *or* work; *the new regulations will come into force on January 1st* **(b)** group of people; **sales force** = group of salesmen **2** *verb* to make someone do something; *competition has forced the company to lower its prices*; *(film)* **forced development** = film processing which uses increased temperature or time to make up for the under-exposure of the original film; **forced page break** = embedded character which makes a new page start

foreground *noun* **(a)** front part of an illustration (as opposed to the background); **foreground colour** = colour of characters and text displayed on a videotext screen **(b)** area in a shot which is closest to the camera **(c)** very important work done by a computer; **foreground processing memory** = region of a multi-tasking operating system in which high priority jobs *or* programs are executed; **foreground program** = high priority program in a multi-tasking system, whose results are usually visible to the user **(d)** image displayed in front of another image in a video clip (for example, Windows Movie Player displays an object in a high score channel in front of an object in a low score channel); *compare with* BACKGROUND

This brighter - but still anti-glare - type of screen is especially useful for people using colourful graphic applications, where both the background and foreground are visually important
Computing

forelengthen *noun* to create an illusion of depth by using a wide angle lens on a camera

foreshorten *verb* to create an illusion that all objects are very close together by using a long (telephoto) lens on a camera

forest *noun* number of interconnected data structure trees

fork *noun (in an Apple Macintosh)* special folder that contains system files and information about a file or application

form 1 *noun* **(a)** preprinted document with blank spaces where information can be entered **(b)** graphical display that looks like an existing printed form and is used to enter data into a database; *it's been easy to train the operators to use the new software since its display looks like the existing printed forms* **(c)** complete plate *or* block of type, ready for printing **(d)** page of computer stationery; **form factor** = size and shape of a device, normally used to refer to a computer's motherboard or other printed circuit board; *a PC motherboard tends to be the size of the motherboard in the first IBM desktop PC computer (full form factor) or smaller;* **form feed** = command to a printer to move to the next sheet of paper; **form handling equipment** = peripherals (such as a decollator) which deal with output from a printer; **form letter** = standard letter into which personal details of each addressee are inserted, such as name, address and job; **form mode** = display method on a data entry terminal, the form is displayed on the screen and the operator enters relevant details; **form overlay** = heading *or* other matter held in store and printed out at the same time as the text; **form stop** = sensor on a printer which indicates when the paper has run out; **form type** = four-character code that identifies the type of data chunk within a RIFF file (for example, WAVE means waveform data) **2** *verb* to create a shape; to construct; *the system is formed of five separate modules*

format 1 *noun* **(a)** size and shape of a book; *the printer can deal with all formats up to quarto* **(b)** specific method of arranging text *or* data; way of arranging data on disk; **low-level format** = process that defines the physical pattern and arrangement of tracks and sectors on a disk **(c)** precise syntax of instructions and arguments **(d)** way of arranging a TV programme; **magazine format** = type of information programme which contains several different items linked together **2** *verb* **(a)** to arrange text as it will appear in printed form on paper; *style sheets are used to format documents*; **formatted dump** = text *or* data printed in a certain format **(b)** **disk formatting** = setting up a blank disk by writing control and track location information on it; *disk formatting has to be done before you can use a new floppy disk*; **to format a disk** = (i) to set up a blank disk so that it is ready for data, by writing control and track information on it; (ii) to define the areas of a disk reserved for data and control

formatter *noun* hardware *or* software that arranges text *or* data according to certain rules; **print formatter** = software that converts embedded codes and print commands to printer control signals

```
there   are   three   models,
offering 53, 80 and 160 Gb of
formatted capacity
```
Minicomputer News

```
As  an  increasing  amount  of
information within businesses
is generated in word-processed
format, text retrieval tools
are    becoming    a    highly
attractive pragmatic solution
```
Computing

formula *noun* set of mathematical rules applied to solve a problem; **formula portability** = feature in a spreadsheet program to find a value in a single cell from data in others, with the possibility of using the same formula in other cells; **formula translator** = FORTRAN (NOTE: plural is **formulae**)

FORTH computer programming language mainly used in control applications

```
the main attraction of FORTH
over other computer languages
is that it is not simply a
language,  rather  it  is  a
programming tool in which it
is possible to write other
application         specific
languages
```
Electronics & Power

FORTRAN = FORMULA TRANSLATOR programming language developed in the first place for scientific use

forty-track disk *noun* floppy disk formatted to contain forty tracks of data

forward 1 *adjective* moving in advance *or* in front; **forward channel** = communications line containing data transmitted from the user to another party; **forward clearing** = switching telephone systems back to their clear state, starting from the point where the call was made and travelling forward towards the destination; **forward error correction** = method of detecting and correcting certain error conditions with the use of redundant codes; *(in a linked list)* **forward pointer** = pointer that contains the address of the next item in the list; **forward reference** = reference to something which has not yet been established; **forward scatter** = scattered sections of wave travelling in the same direction as the incident **2** *verb* to pass a call on to another point

FOSDIC = FILM OPTICAL SCANNING DEVICE FOR INPUT INTO COMPUTERS storage device for computer data using microfilm

fount = FONT

fourcc = FOUR-CHARACTER CODE method of identifying the type of data within a RIFF file

Fourier series *noun* mathematical representation of waveforms by a combination of fundamental and harmonic components of a frequency

fourth generation computers *noun* computer technology using LSI circuits, developed around 1970 and still in current use; **fourth generation languages** = languages that are user-friendly and have been designed with the non-expert in mind

four-track recorder *noun* tape recorder that is able to record and play back four independent audio tracks at once

FP *(film)* = FRONT PROJECTION

FPS = FRAMES PER SECOND **(a)** speed of single frames of a motion picture through a projector *or* camera every second **(b)** number of television picture frames transmitted per second **(c)** number of individual images (or frames) that can be displayed each second to give the impression of movement

FPU = FLOATING POINT UNIT

FQDN = FULLY QUALIFIED DOMAIN NAME complete domain name, for example 'pcp.co.uk' is a fully qualified domain name that can be used to identify a server; 'pcp' is just the hostname

fractal *noun* geometric shape that repeats itself within itself and always appears the same, however much you magnify the image

fractal compression *noun* technique used to compress images; uses complex alogrithms to analyse an image and discover if there are any repeated patterns within the image; the process can offer up to 200:1 size reduction and is used in JPEG and MPEG file formats

fractal image format (FIF) *noun* file format used to store graphics images which have been highly compressed using fractals

fraction *noun* part of a whole unit, expressed as one figure above another (such as 1/4, 1/2, etc.)

fractional *adjective* made of fractions; referring to fractions; *the root is the fractional power of a number*; **fractional services** = allocation of parts of a bandwidth to different signals or customers; *the commercial carrier will sell you fractional services that provide 64Kbps data transmission*

fragment *noun* one small part of a larger piece of information that has had to be split up into several smaller units before being transmitted; the receiver re-assembles these small parts in the correct order to re-create the larger piece of information

fragmentation *noun* **(a)** *(in main memory)* memory allocation to a number of files, which has resulted in many small, free sections *or* fragments that are too small to be of any use, but waste a lot of space **(b)** *(on a disk drive)* files stored scattered across non-contiguous sectors on a hard disk; **defragmentation utility** = software utility that carries out the process of defragmentation on a hard disk

COMMENT: when a file is saved to disk, it is not always saved in adjacent sectors; this will increase the retrieval time. Defragmentation moves files back into adjacent sectors so that the read head does not have to move far across the disk, thus increasing performance

frame *noun* **(a)** packet of transmitted data including control and route information; **frame relay** = communications protocol (similar to X.25 and fast packet switching)

that operates at OSI level 2 and routes data packets directly to the destination **(b)** one complete image displayed on a television screen (in the US this is made up of 525 lines, in the UK it is 625 lines); **frame** = (in a web page) way of dividing a web page into separate sections that can each display different separate files containing HTML commands; *we used frames in this website design to provide a navigation panel on the left of the window; see also* HTML; **frame** = (in communications) standard unit of information (also called a packet) that contains the destination address (header) and the sender's address followed by the information and a trailer that contains error detection information; *see also* PACKET **frame-based animation** = series of screens displayed in quick succession, each one slightly different, that gives the impression of movement; *compare with* CAST-BASED ANIMATION; **frame buffer** = section of memory used to store an image before it is displayed on screen; **frame count cueing** = *see* FCC; **frame counter** = in cinematographic equipment, it is a counter which notes the number of film frames moving through it; **frame flyback** = electron beam return from the bottom right to the top left corner of the screen to start building up a new field; **frame frequency** = number of television frames transmitted per second; *in the UK the frame frequency is 25 fps*; **frame grabber** = high speed digital sampling circuit that stores a television picture frame in memory so that it can then be processed by a computer; **frame hook** = function executed by the Windows Movie Player for each frame of the video; **frame index** = variable used by the Movie Player that identifies the current frame of the video; **frame rate** = speed at which frames in a video sequence are displayed; measured in frames (one still image) displayed per second; PAL is 25fps, NTSC is 30fps and film is 24fps; **frame store** = video system which can store a complete frame of video information in digital form; it is used for special effects and for television standards conversion; *the frame store can be used to display weather satellite pictures*; **video frame** = one complete image on a video film; *with the image processor you can freeze a video frame; the image processor allows you to store a video frame in a* *built-in 8-bit frame store* **(c)** one individual shot in a film or the area it occupies in the camera lens **(d)** one screen of data **(e)** *(in DTP)* a movable, resizable box that holds text or an image; **frame window** = controls (including the minimise and maximise buttons, scroll bar and window title) and border that surround a window area

frames per second (fps) *noun* **(a)** speed of single frames of a motion picture through a projector *or* camera every second **(b)** number of television picture frames transmitted per second **(c)** number of individual images (or frames) that can be displayed each second to give the impression of movement

> COMMENT: TV displays 25 frames per second which is fast enough to appear as continuous movement to the eye

framework *noun* basic structure of a database *or* process *or* program; *the program framework was designed first*

framing *noun* **(a)** positioning of a camera's field of view for a required image **(b)** synchronization of time division multiplexed frames of data; **framing bit** = sync bit *or* transmitted bit used to synchronize devices; **framing code** = method of synchronizing a receiver with a broadcast teletext stream of data

fraud *noun* making money by tricking people *or* by making them believe something which is not true; **computer fraud** = theft of data *or* dishonest use *or* other crimes involving computers

> the offences led to the arrest of nine teenagers who were all charged with computer fraud
> *Computer News*

free 1 *adjective* available for use *or* not currently being used; (spare bytes) available on disk *or* in memory; **free form database** = database that can store any type of data and does not have a fixed record structure; **free indexing** = library entries having references to documents which the indexer considers useful, even if they do not appear in the text; **free line** = telephone line that is not connected and so is available for use; **free running mode** = interactive computer mode that allows more than one user to have simultaneous use of a program; **free space loss** = measure of the loss of transmitted

signals from a satellite antenna to an earth station; **free space media** = empty space between a transmitter and a receiving aerial which is used for transmission; **free wheeling** = transmission protocol where the computer transmitting receives no status signals from the receiver **2** *verb* to erase *or* remove *or* backup programs *or* files to provide space in memory

freedom *noun* being free to do something without restriction; **freedom of information** = being able to examine computer records (both referring to government activities and to records kept about individuals); **freedom of the press** = being able to write and publish in a newspaper what you wish without being afraid of prosecution, provided that you do not break the law; **freedom of speech** = being able to say what you want without being afraid of prosecution, provided that you do not break the law

freely *adverb* with no restrictions; **free WAIS** = (non-commercial) version of the WAIS search index server that can be used without charge; *see also* WAIS

freeware *noun* software that is in the public domain and can be used by anyone without having to pay

freeze *verb* see HANG, CRASH; **to freeze (frame)** = to stop and display a single frame from a film *or* TV *or* videodisc *or* video tape machine; *the image processor will freeze a single TV frame*

F-region *noun* section of the ionosphere that is 150-400Km from the earth's surface

frequency *noun* number of cycles *or* periods of a regular waveform that are repeated per second; one cycle per second is called a Hertz (Hz); **frequency changer** = electronic circuit that shifts the frequency of a signal up *or* down; **frequency divider** = electronic circuit that reduces the frequency of a signal by a multiple of two; **frequency division multiplexing (FDM)** = transmission of several independent signals along a single channel, achieved by shifting each signal up in frequency by a different amount; *using FDM we can transmit 100 telephone calls along one main cable*; **frequency domain** = effects of a certain circuit on the frequency range of a signal; **frequency modulation (FM)** = varying the frequency of one signal according to the level of a second signal; sound synthesizers use FM synthesis to create a sound like an instrument, radio transmission uses frequency modulation in which a very high frequency carrier signal is modified in level by the sound to be transmitted; *see also* WAVEFORM; **frequency range** = range of allowable frequencies, between two limits; **frequency response** = electronic circuit parameter given as the ratio of output to input signal amplitudes at various frequencies; **frequency shift keying (FSK)** = transmission system using the translation of two state binary data into two different frequencies, one for on, one for off; **frequency variation** = change of frequency of a signal from normal; *(in a CRT)* **line frequency** = the number of times that the picture beam scans a horizontal row of pixels in a monitor

frequent *adjective* which comes *or* goes *or* takes place often; *we send frequent telexes to New York; how frequent are the planes to Birmingham?*

frequently *adverb* often; *the photocopier is frequently out of use; we telex our New York office very frequently - at least four times a day*; **frequently asked questions**; *see* FAQ

fresnel lens *noun (film)* condenser or convex lens which is used to focus the beam of a spotlight

friction feed *noun* printer mechanism where the paper is advanced by holding it between two rollers (as opposed to tractor feed)

friendly front-end *noun* design of the display of a program that is easy to use and understand

front *noun* part of something which faces away from the back; *the disks are inserted in slots in the front of the terminal*; *(film)* **front axial projection** = special effects shot where the background of the shot is created by projecting an image along the line of the camera lens on to a highly directional beaded reflecting screen; *see also* REFLEX PROJECTION; **front panel** = main computer system control switches and status indicators; **front porch** = section of television signal between the line blanking pulse and the line sync pulse; **front projection** = projection of background images onto a screen located behind a person

front-end *adjective* **(a)** display presented by a program that is seen by an end user; *the program is very easy to use thanks to the uncomplicated front-end* **(b)** located at the start *or* most important point of a circuit *or* network; **front-end processor (FEP)** = processor placed between an input source and the central computer whose function is to preprocess received data to relieve the workload of the main computer; **front-end system** = typesetting system, where text is keyboarded on a terminal directly connected to the typesetting computer

FSK = FREQUENCY SHIFT KEYING

FTP = FILE TRANSFER PROTOCOL TCP/IP standard for transferring files between computers; it is a file sharing protocol that operates at layers 5, 6 and 7 of an OSI model network; **ftp mail** = *see* BITFTP

full *adjective* **(a)** with as much inside as possible; *the disk is full, so the material will have to be stored on another disk* **(b)** complete *or* including everything; **full adder** = binary addition circuit that can produce the sum of two inputs and can also accept a carry input, producing a carry output if necessary; *(film)* **full aperture** = camera lens iris opened to its full circumference; **full duplex** = data transmission down a channel in two directions simultaneously; *see also* DUPLEX, HALF DUPLEX, SIMPLEX; **full-frame time code** = standard method of counting video frames rather than using a time check signal for synchronization with music and effects; **full motion video** = transmission of video or television data that is displayed in real time and shows smooth, continuous movement rather than single frame or jerky movements; it needs a computer fitted with a digitising card that is fast enough to capture and display moving video images; *compare with* FREEZE (FRAME); **full motion video adapter** = computer fitted with a digitising card that is fast enough to capture and display moving video images (at a rate of 25 or 30 frames per second); **full path** = description of the position of a directory (in relation to the root directory) in which a file is stored; **full-screen** = (program display) that uses all the available screen; it is not displayed within a window; **full shot** *or* **full figure shot** = when the whole of the subject being filmed or when the performer's entire body is shown in the camera shot; **full-size display** = large screen VDU which can display a whole page of text; **full-text search** = to carry out a search for something through all the text in a file or database rather than limiting the search to an area or block

fully *adverb* completely; **fully connected network** = situation where each node in a network is connected with every other; **fully formed characters** = characters produced by a printer in a single action; **fully populated board** = circuit board which has all components in place, including any optional or extra components; *a daisy wheel printer produces fully formed characters*

> transmitter and receiver can be operated independently, making full duplex communication possible
> *Electronics & Power*

function 1 *noun* **(a)** mathematical formula, where a result is dependent upon several other numbers **(b)** sequence of computer program instructions in a main program that perform a certain task; **function call** = program instruction that moves execution to a predefined function *or* named sequence of instructions; **function code** = printing codes that control an action rather than representing a character **(c)** special feature available on a computer *or* word-processor; *the word-processor had a spelling-checker function but no built-in text-editing function*; **function library** = collection of functions that can be used by a program; **function overloading** = programming system in which several different functions can have the same name, but are differentiated because they operate on different data types **2** *verb* to operate *or* perform correctly; *the new system has not functioned properly since it was installed*

function key *noun* key *or* switch that has been assigned a particular task *or* sequence of instructions; *tags can be allocated to function keys; hitting F5 will put you into insert mode*

> COMMENT: function keys often form a separate group of keys on the keyboard, and have specific functions attached to them. On a PC's keyboard there are 12 function keys located in a row above the

> main characters and labelled F1, F2, etc.

> they made it clear that the PC was to take its place as part of a much larger computing function that comprised LANS, wide area networks, small systems, distributed systems and mainframes
> *Minicomputer News*

function key *or* programmable

functional *adjective* which refers to the way something works; **functional diagram** = drawing of the internal workings and processes of a machine *or* piece of software; **functional specification** = specification which defines the results which a program is expected to produce; **functional unit** = hardware *or* software that works as it should

fundamental frequency *noun* most prominent frequency in a complex signal

> COMMENT: almost all signals contain parts of other frequencies (harmonics) at lower amplitudes to the fundamental, which often causes distortion

fuse 1 *noun* electrical protection device consisting of a small piece of metal, which will melt when too much power passes through it; **to blow a fuse** = to melt a fuse by passing too much current through it **2** *verb* to draw too much current, causing a fuse to melt; *when the air-conditioning was switched on, it fused the whole system*

fusible link *noun* small link in a PLA that can be blown to program the device permanently

fusion *noun* combining two hardware devices *or* programs *or* chemical substances to create a single form

fuzzy *noun* not clear; *top quality paper will eliminate fuzzy characters*; **fuzzy logic** *or* **fuzzy theory** = type of logic applied to computer programming, which tries to replicate the reasoning methods of the human brain

FYI = FOR YOUR INFORMATION document that contains general background information related to the Internet or the TCP/IP protocols; specific technical information is normally contained in RFC documents; *see also* FAQ, RFC

Gg

G/V *(film)* = GENERAL VIEW establishing a film or video shot

G = GIGA *prefix* meaning one thousand million; in computing G refers to 2^{30} equal to 1,073,741,824; **GHz** = gigahertz

GaAs = GALLIUM ARSENIDE

gaffer *noun (film)* principal lighting electrician on a film or television set

gaffer tape *noun (film)* sticky tape which is used on set or location

gain 1 *noun* **(a)** increase *or* becoming larger **(b)** amount by which a signal amplitude is changed as it passes through a circuit, usually given as a ratio of output to input amplitude; **gain control** = variable control that sets the amount of gain a circuit *or* amplifier will provide **2** *verb* to obtain *or* to get; **to gain access to a file** = to be able to access a file; *the user cannot gain access to the confidential information in the file without a password*

galactic noise *noun* random electrical noise which originates from planets and stars in space

galley proof *or* **slip** *noun* rough initial proof of a column *or* section of text, printed on a long piece of paper

gallium arsenide (GaAs) *noun* semiconductor compound, a new material for chip construction, that allows for faster operation than silicon chips

game *noun* something which is played for enjoyment *or* relaxation; **computer game** = game played on a computer; **game cartridge** = ROM device that contains the program code for a computer game, and which is plugged into a game console; **game console** = dedicated computer, joystick and display adapter that is designed to be only used to play games; **game paddle** = device held in the hand to move a cursor *or* graphics in a computer game; **game port** = connection that allows a joystick to be plugged into a computer; **gaming gear** = accessories (for a computer) that are designed to increase the enjoyment of playing a computer game; for example, a joystick for action games or a steering wheel and foot pedals for a driving game

gamma *noun* **(a)** unit of magnetic intensity **(b)** measurement of the degree of contrast in a television picture; for television cameras and receivers, the measurement is found from the input and output voltage and the light input or output **(c)** measure of the contrast of a film emulsion

ganged *adjective* mechanically linked devices that are operated by a single action; **ganged switch** = series of switches that operate on different parts of a circuit, but which are all switched by a single action

gap *noun* **(a)** space between recorded data; **interblock gap (IBG)** = blank magnetic tape between the end of one block of data and the start of the next in backing store **(b)** space between a read head and the magnetic medium; **air gap** = narrow gap between a recording *or* playback head and the magnetic medium; **gap loss** = signal attenuation due to incorrect alignment of the read/write head with the storage medium **(c)** method of radio communications using a carrier signal that is switched on and off, as in a telegraphic system

garbage *noun* **(a)** radio interference from adjacent channels **(b)** data *or* information that is no longer required due to being out of date *or* containing errors; **garbage collection** = reorganization and removal of unwanted *or* out of date files and records; clearing a section of memory of a program *or* its data that is not in use; **garbage in**

garbage out (GIGO) = expression meaning that the accuracy and quality of information that is output depends on the quality of the input

> COMMENT: GIGO is sometimes taken to mean 'garbage in gospel out': i.e. that whatever wrong information is put into a computer, people will always believe that the output results are true

gas discharge display *or* **gas plasma display** *noun* flat, lightweight display screen that is made of two flat pieces of glass covered with a grid of conductors, separated by a thin layer of a gas which luminesces when one point of the grid is selected by two electric signals; *see also* LCD

> COMMENT: mainly used in modern portable computer displays, but the definition is not as good as in cathode ray tube displays

gate *noun* **(a)** logical electronic switch whose output depends on the states of the inputs and the type of logical function implemented; **AND gate** = gate that performs a logical AND function; **EXNOR gate** = electronic implementation of the EXNOR function; **EXOR** = electronic implementation of the EXOR function; **gate array** = number of interconnected logic gates built into an integrated circuit to perform a complex function; **NAND gate** = electronic circuit that provides a NAND function; **NOR gate** = electronic circuit which performs a NOR function; **NOT gate** = single input gate whose output is equal to the inverse of the input; **OR gate** = electronic circuit that provides the OR function **(b)** connection pin of a FET device **(c)** mechanical film *or* slide frame aligner in a camera *or* projector **(d)** *(of a camera or projector)* the aperture in which the frame is exposed or projected; **gated**= GATE DAEMON (pronounced 'gate-dee') software that redirects network traffic (normally Internet traffic) according to a set of rules; it can also be used to limit access to a site or to route information to another site; *see also* ROUTED

gateway *noun* **(a)** (i) device that links two dissimilar networks; (ii) software protocol translation device that allows users working in one network to access another; *we use a*

gateway to link the LAN to WAN **(b)** *(in electronic mail)* software that allows mail messages to be sent via a different route *or* to another network; *to send messages by fax instead of across the network, you'll need to install a fax gateway*; **gateway interface** = *see* CGI; **fax gateway** = computer or software that allows users to send an email or information as a fax transmission to a remote fax machine

gauge 1 *noun* **(a)** device which measures thickness *or* width **(b)** film or tape diameter, usually described in millimetres **2** *verb* to measure the thickness *or* width of something

gauss *noun* unit of magnetic induction

gauze *noun* *(film)* material which is transparent or translucent and is used for special effects

Gb = gigabyte

gel *noun* *(film)* translucent sheet of coloured plastic used to alter the colour characteristics of the source of light

gelatin filter *or* **gel filter** *noun* *(film)* sheet of coloured gelatin which is used with a camera to alter the colour of the source light

gender changer *noun* *(informal)* device for changing a female connector to a male and vice versa

general *adjective* **(a)** ordinary *or* not special; **general office** = main administrative office **(b)** dealing with everything; **general purpose computer** = computer whose processing power may be applied to many different sorts of applications, depending on its hardware *or* software instructions; **general purpose interface bus (GPIB)** = standard for an interface bus between a computer and laboratory equipment; **general purpose program** = program *or* device able to perform many different jobs *or* applications; **general register** = data register in a computer processing unit that can store items of data for many different mathematical *or* logical operations; **general view** = establishing a film or video shot

general MIDI standards for a synthesizer that set out the first 128 different instrument sounds in a synthesizer and the patch number that refers to it; for example, patch 40 is always a violin

generate *verb* to use software *or* a device to produce codes *or* a program automatically; *to generate an image from digitally recorded data*; **computer-generated** = produced using a computer; *they analyzed the computer-generated image*

generation *noun* **(a)** producing software *or* programs using a computer; *the computer is used in the generation of graphic images* **(b)** state *or* age of the technology used in the design of a system; **(c)** distance between a file and the original version, used when making backups; *the father file is a first generation backup*; **(d)** generation loss = degradation of signal quality with each successive recording of a video or audio signal

COMMENT: computer technology is normally divided into different generations; each refers to a different development: **first generation =** earliest type of technology; **first generation computers =** original computers made with valve-based electronic technology, started around 1951; **first generation image =** master copy of an original image, text *or* document; **second generation computers =** computers which used transistors instead of valves; **third generation computers =** computers which used integrated circuits instead of transistors; **fourth generation computers =** computer technology using LSI circuits, developed around 1970 and still in current use; **fourth generation languages =** languages that are user-friendly and have been designed with the non-expert in mind; **fifth generation computers =** next stage of computer system design using fast VLSI circuits and powerful programming languages to allow human interaction

generator *noun* device which generates electricity; *the factory has its own independent generator, in case of mains power failure*

generator lock *or* **genlock** *noun* device that synchronizes two video signals from different sources so that they can be successfully combined or mixed; often used to synchronise the output of a computer's display adapter with an external video source when using the computer to create overlays or titles

generic *adjective* (something) that is compatible with a whole family of hardware or software devices from one manufacturer

genuine *adjective* real *or* correct; *authentication allows the system to recognize that a sender's message is genuine*

geometric distortion *noun* linear distortion of a television picture, which can be caused by fluctuations in the speed of a video tape

geostationary satellite *noun* satellite which moves at the same velocity as the earth, so remains above the same area of the earth's surface, and appears stationary when viewed from the earth

geotarget *verb* to analyse the actions of a visitor to a website to determine their location and so display custom advertisements or content relevant to them; *we use geotargetting to provide local weather reports; if you check the weather website for a forecast for London, geotargetting will display banner ads for London hotels*

germanium *noun* semiconductor material, used as a substrate in some transistors instead of silicon

get *noun* instruction to obtain a record from a file *or* database

ghost *noun* **(a)** effect on a television image where a weaker copy of the picture is displayed to one side of the main image, caused by signal reflections **(b)** sometimes used to mean 'greyed' menu items that are displayed in grey and are not currently available; **ghost cursor** = second cursor which can be used in some programs

ghosting *noun* *(film)* hazy double images appearing in a picture

COMMENT: in film projection, ghosting can be a result of an out-of-phase shutter and in television, it can result from undesirable reflections in a cable system or from physical objects in a radiated signal. Can also be used on purpose to give the illusion of the presence of a phantom on film through double exposure or double printing

GHz = GIGAHERTZ

GIF = GRAPHICS INTERFACE FORMAT graphics file format of a file containing a bit-mapped image; originally used on the CompuServe on-line system, now a standard for encoding colour bit-mapped images normally in either 16 or 256 colours with options for compression; **GIF file** = graphics file format of a file containing a bit-mapped image

giga- or **G** *prefix* meaning one thousand million; in computing G refers to 2^{30} equal to 1,073,741,824; **gigabyte** = 10^9 bytes; **gigahertz (GHz)** = frequency of 10^9 Hertz

gigaflop *noun* one thousand million floating-point operations per second

GIGO = GARBAGE IN GARBAGE OUT expression meaning that the accuracy and quality of information that is output depends on the quality of the input

COMMENT: GIGO is sometimes taken to mean 'garbage in gospel out': i.e. that whatever wrong information is put into a computer, people will always believe that the output results are true

GINO = GRAPHICAL INPUT OUTPUT graphical control routine written in FORTRAN

GKS = GRAPHICS KERNEL SYSTEM standard for software command and functions describing graphical input/output to provide the same functions, etc., on any type of hardware

glare *noun* very bright light reflections, especially on a VDU screen; *the glare from the screen makes my eyes hurt*; **glare filter** = coated glass or plastic sheet placed in front of a screen to cut out bright light reflections (NOTE: no plural)

glitch *noun (informal)* anything which causes the sudden unexpected failure of a computer *or* equipment

The programmer was upgrading a verification system at Visa's UK data centre when his work triggered a software glitch causing hundreds of valid cards to be rejected for several hours
Computing

global *adjective* covering everything; **global backup** = (i) backup of all data stored on all nodes *or* workstations connected to a network; (ii) backup of all files on a hard disk *or* file server; **global exchange** = replace function which replaces one piece of text (such as a word) with another throughout a whole text; *(in Microsoft Windows)* **global memory** = memory available to all Windows applications; **global search and replace** = word-processor search and replace function covering a complete file *or* document; **global variable** = variable *or* number that can be accessed by any routine *or* structure in a program; *compare with* LOCAL VARIABLE

In an attempt to bring order to an electronic Tower of Babel, pharmaceutical giant Rhone-Poulenc has assembled an X.400-based global messaging network and a patchwork directory system that will be used until a single email system is deployed worldwide
Computing

glossy 1 *adjective* shiny (paper); *the illustrations are printed on glossy art paper* **2** *noun (informal)* **the glossies** = expensive magazines

GND = GROUND

go ahead *noun* signal to indicate that a receiver *or* device is ready to accept information

go to black *verb* to fade gradually from an image to a dark or empty screen

goal *noun* (a) aim *or* what you are trying to do (b) final state reached when a task has been finished *or* has produced satisfactory results

gobo *noun (film)* moveable opaque shield which is used to hide light between a lamp and a camera lens

gofer *or* **gopher** *noun (informal)* person who does all types of work in an office *or* studio, etc.

gold contacts *plural noun* electrical contacts (usually for low-level signals) that are coated with gold to reduce the electrical resistance

golf-ball *noun* metal ball with characters on its surface, which print on paper; **golf-ball typewriter** = typewriter that uses a golf-ball printhead

COMMENT: a golf-ball contains all the characters of a single typeface; to change the face, the ball is taken out and replaced by another. The main defect of a golf-ball typewriter when used as a printer, is that it is slower than a dot-matrix printer

gooseneck *noun* adjustable microphone stand

GOSIP = GOVERNMENT OPEN SYSTEMS INTERCONNECT PROFILE standards defined by the government of a country to ensure that computers and communications systems can interact

gospel *see note at* GARBAGE

GOSUB programming command which executes a routine then returns to the following instruction

GOTO programming command which instructs a jump

Gouraud shading *noun* mathematical equation that is used to create the effect of shade in a three-dimensional computer image; the equation is applied to each side of each object and produces a gradual change in colour to give the impression of light and shade.

Government Open Systems Interconnect Profile *see* GOSIP

GPF = GENERAL PROTECTION FAULT serious error that occurs in Windows and causes an application to malfunction or stop (crash); new versions of Windows minimise the effects of this type of error; *the GPF was caused by using an incompatible device driver*

GPIB = GENERAL PURPOSE INTERFACE BUS standard for an interface bus between a computer and laboratory equipment

GPRS = GENERAL PACKET RADIO SERVICE standard for wireless radio and mobile telephone communications

COMMENT: GPRS replaces GSM (Global System for Mobile Communications); GPRS supports high-speed data transfer rates of up to 150Kbps compared to the GSM limit of 9.6Kbps; mobile telephones that use the GPRS system will make mobile access to the Internet and email much faster.

grab *verb* to take something and hold it

grabber *or* **frame grabber** *noun* high speed digital sampling circuit that stores a TV picture in memory so that it can then be processed by a computer

```
sometimes a program can grab
all the available memory, even
if it is not going to use it
```
Byte

```
the    frame    grabber    is
distinguished by its ability
to acquire a TV image in a
single frame interval
```
Electronics & Wireless World

graceful degradation *noun* allowing some parts of a system to continue to function after a part has broken down

grade *noun* level *or* rank; *a top-grade computer expert*; **grade of service** = quality of telephone service at a given time, defined by the likelihood of a successful connection via a telephone network at its busiest time

grading *noun* (*in cinematographic work*) choosing the colour and density printing values needed for each scene on a negative; (*in the editing of videotapes*) matching colour balance between shots

graduated *adjective* which has a scale *or* measurements marked on it

graduated filter *noun* (*film*) coloured filter which has a colour on edge and gradually fades into a clear filter on the other side of the filter

grain *noun* molecular make-up of film emulsion (fine grain film has very small particles that provide a very sharp, clear image)

graininess *noun* collection of visible silver particles which create a granular effect on a film's picture; the more visible the particles are, the grainier the picture

gram *or* **gramme** *noun* unit of measurement of weight, one thousandth of a kilogram; *the book is printed on 70 gram paper*

grammage *noun* weight of paper, calculated as grams per square metre (NOTE: usually shown as **gsm** : **80 gsm paper**)

grammar *noun* rules for the correct use of language; **grammar checker** = software utility used to check a document or letter to make sure it is grammatically correct

grammatical error *noun* incorrect use of a computer programming language syntax

grandfather file *noun* third most recent version of a backed up file, after father and son files

granularity *noun* size of memory segments in a virtual memory system, such as Microsoft Windows

graph *noun* diagram showing the relationship between two *or* more variables as a line *or* series of points; **graph paper** = paper with many little squares, used for drawing graphs; **graph plotter** = printing device with a pen which takes data from a computer and plots it in graphic form

graphic *adjective* (representation of information) in the form of pictures *or* plots instead of by text; **graphic display** = computer screen able to present graphical information; **graphic display resolution** = number of pixels that a computer is able to display on the screen; **graphic language** = computer programming language with inbuilt commands that are useful when displaying graphics; *this graphic language can plot lines, circles and graphs with a single command*; **graphic object** = small graphic image imported from another drawing application and placed on a page; in most DTP, paint or drawing packages, the object can be moved, sized and positioned independently from the other elements on the page

graphical *adjective* referring to something represented by graphics; **graphical input output** = *see* GINO; **graphical user interface (GUI)** = interface between an operating system *or* program and the user; it uses graphics *or* icons to represent functions or files and allow the software to be controlled more easily; system commands do not have to be typed in; *compare with* COMMAND LINE INTERFACE

COMMENT: GUIs normally use a combination of windows, icons and a mouse to control the operating system. In many GUIs, such as Microsoft Windows, Apple Macintosh System and X, you can control all the functions of the operating system just using the mouse. Icons represent programs and files; instead of entering the file name, you select it by moving a pointer with a mouse

graphically *adverb* using pictures; *the sales figures are graphically represented as a pie chart*

graphics *noun* pictures *or* lines which can be drawn on paper *or* on a screen to represent information; **graphics output** such as bar charts, pie charts, line drawings, etc.; **graphics accelerator** = video display board with its own graphics coprocessor and high-speed RAM that can carry out graphical drawing operations (such as fill) at high speed; often used to speed up GUIs such as Windows or for graphics-intensive applications such as multimedia or DTP; **graphics adapter** = electronic device (normally on an expansion card) in a computer that provides converts software commands into electrical signals that display graphics on a connected monitor; *the new graphics adapter is capable of displaying higher resolution graphics*; **graphics art terminal** = typesetting terminal that is used with a phototypesetter; **graphics character** = preprogrammed shape that can be displayed on a non-graphical screen instead of a character, used extensively in videotext systems to display simple pictures; **graphics coprocessor** = *see* GRAPHICS PROCESSOR; **graphics file** = (binary) file which contains data describing an image; *there are many standards for graphics files including TIFF, IMG and EPS*; **graphics file format** = method in which data describing an image is stored; *see also* GIF, PCX, PICT, TIFF; **graphics interface format** = *see* GIFF; **graphics kernel system (GKS)** = standard for software command and functions describing graphical input/output to provide the same functions, etc., on any type of hardware; **graphics library** = number of routines stored in a library file that can be added to any user program to simplify the task of writing graphics programs; **graphics mode** = videotext terminal whose displayed characters are taken from a range of graphics characters instead of text; **graphics overlay card** = expansion card for a PC or Macintosh that combines generated text or images with an external video source; **graphics pad** *or* **tablet** = flat device that allows a user to input graphical information into a computer by drawing on its surface; **graphics primitive** = basic shape (such as an arc, line or filled square) that is used to create other shapes or objects; **graphics printer** = printer capable of printing bit-mapped images; **graphics processor** *or* **graphics coprocessor** = secondary processor used to speed up the display of graphics: it calculates the position of pixels that form a line *or* shape and display graphic lines *or* shapes; *this graphics adapter has a graphics coprocessor fitted and is much faster*; **graphics software** = prewritten routines which perform standard graphics commands such as line drawing, plotting, etc., that can be called from within a program to simplify program writing; **graphics terminal** = special terminal with a high-resolution graphic display and graphics pad or other input device; **graphics VDU** = special VDU which can display graphics; **graphics: vector and raster** = there are two methods generally used to store an image: vector graphics (also known as object-oriented graphics) stores the image as a series of points, lines, arcs and other geometric shapes; raster graphics (or bitmap graphics) represents the image as a grid of pixels or dots; paint packages generally let you work on bitmap graphics, a drawing package or CAD software uses vector graphics

one interesting feature of this model is graphics amplification, which permits graphic or text enlargement of up to 800 per cent

Byte

the custom graphics chips can display an image that has 640 columns by 400 rows of 4-bit pixel

Byte

several tools exist for manipulating image and graphical data: some were designed for graphics manipulation

Byte

gravure *see* PHOTOGRAVURE

Gray code *noun* coding system in which the binary representation of (decimal)

numbers changes by only one bit at a time from one number to the next

COMMENT: used in communications systems to provide error detection facilities

gray scale *see* GREY SCALE

greeked *adjective (in a DTP program)* font with a point size too small to display accurately, shown as a line rather than individual characters; thumbnail displays of a page or image use greeked text to give a representation of the final layout

Green Book formal specification for CD-i standard published by Philips; *see also* CD-i, RED BOOK AUDIO, WHITE BOOK, YELLOW BOOK

gremlin *noun (informal)* unexplained fault in a system; **line gremlin** = unexplained fault when data is lost during transmission

grey scale *noun* **(a)** shades of grey that are used to measure the correct exposure when filming **(b)** shades which are produced from displaying what should be colour information on a monochrome monitor; *see also* HALFTONE

COMMENT: a line drawing has no grey scale information, only black or white. A scanner will scan a photograph with grey levels representing the tones. Like colour information, a grey scale needs multiple bits of data for each pixel - 256 grey scales per pixel requires one byte (8 bits)

grid *noun* system of numbered squares used to help when drawing; matrix of lines at right angles allowing points to be easily plotted *or* located; **grid gauge** = positioning tool for microfiche image display; *(in a graphics program)* **grid snap** = feature that limits the position of the cursor to a point on the grid, so ensuring that drawings are aligned; *if you want to draw accurate lines, you'll find it easier with grid snap turned on*

grip 1 *noun* person on film set who is responsible for pushing a camera or moving equipment **2** *verb* to hold something tightly; *in friction feed, the paper is gripped by the rollers*

ground *noun* **(a)** electrical circuit connection to earth *or* to a point with a zero voltage level; **ground absorption** = loss of transmitted power in radio waves that are near the ground (NOTE: **ground** is more common in US English; the GB English is **earth**) (b) the earth's surface; **ground station =** equipment and antenna on the earth used to communicate with an orbiting satellite

ground glass *noun (film)* translucent sheet of glass (which has been etched on one side) on which an image is seen in a film camera's viewfinder

group 1 *noun* **(a)** collection of objects that can be moved or resized as a single object; (in a GUI) collection of icons of files *or* programs displayed together in a window; *all the icons in this group are to do with painting;* **group icon** = (in a GUI) icon that represents a window which contains a collection of icons of files *or* programs **(b)** set of computer records that contain related information **(c)** six-character word used in telegraphic communications **(d)** single communications channel made up from a number of others that have been multiplexed together **(e)** *(in a network)* collection of users conveniently identified by one name; *the group ACCOUNTS contains all the users who work in the accounts department* **2** *verb* to bring several things together

Group 3 *see* FAX GROUP

groupware *noun (on a network)* software specially written to be used by a group of people connected to a network and help them carry out a particular task; it provides useful functions such as a diary or electronic mail that can be accessed by all users

GSM = GLOBAL SYSTEM FOR MOBILE COMMUNICATIONS popular system used for wireless cellular telephone communications throughout Europe, Asia and parts of North America; *see also* GPRS, MOBILE PHONE, PCS

COMMENT:The GSM system allows eight calls to share the same radio frequency and transmits voice signals as digital data. The main drawback of GSM is that it does not offer very fast data transfer rates which has become more important as users want to access the Internet and read email via a mobile telephone connection. GSM provides data transfer at up to 9.6Kbps, is being replaced by the GPRS system that can

support high-speed data transfer at up to 150Kbps

gsm *or* **g/m²** = GRAMS PER SQUARE METRE (per sheet) way of showing the weight of paper used in printing; *the book is printed on 70 gsm coated paper*

guarantee *noun* legal document promising that a machine will work properly *or* that an item is of good quality; *the system is still under guarantee and will be repaired free of charge*

guard band *noun* **(a)** frequency gap between two communication bands to prevent data corruption due to interference between each other **(b)** section of magnetic tape between two channels recorded on the same tape

guarding *noun* joining a single sheet to a book *or* magazine

GUI = GRAPHICAL USER INTERFACE (NOTE: pronounced 'gooey')

guide bars *noun* special lines in a bar code that show the start and finish of the code; *the standard guide bars are two thin lines that are a little longer than the coding lines*

guide path *noun (film)* in audio and video recorders, the posts and mechanical guides that ensure that the tape follows the correct path

guide track *noun (film)* a sound track of low quality which is recorded with the picture only as a guide for post synchronization

guillotine *noun* office machine for cutting paper

gulp *noun* a group of words; *see also* BYTE, NIBBLE

gun *or* **electron gun** *noun* source of an electron beam located inside a cathode ray tube; *black and white TVs have a single beam gun, while colour TVs contain three, one for each primary colour*

gun microphone *noun (film)* a highly directional microphone, also called a rifle microphone, often mounted on a rifle stock that allows it to be easily aimed at the source of the sound

gutter *noun (in a DTP system)* space between two adjacent columns of text *or* blank space or inner margin between two facing pages

Hh

hack *verb* **(a)** to experiment and explore computer software and hardware **(b)** to break into a computer system for criminal purposes

hacker *noun* person who hacks

> software manufacturers try more and more sophisticated methods to protect their programs and the hackers use equally clever methods to break into them
>
> *Electronics & Wireless World*

> the hackers used their own software to break into the credit card centre
>
> *Computer News*

> any computer linked to the system will be alerted if a hacker uses its code number
>
> *Practical Computing*

> The two were also charged with offences under the Computer Misuse Act and found guilty of the very actions upon which every hacker is intent
>
> *Computing*

hair in the gate *noun (film)* hair-shaped particles visible on the edge of film images after the development process

hairline rule *noun (in a DTP system)* very thin line

halation *noun* photographic effect seen as a dark region with a very bright surround, caused by pointing the camera into the light

half *noun* one of two equal parts; *half the data was lost in transmission; the second half of the program contains some errors*; **half adder** = binary adder that can produce the sum of two inputs, producing a carry output if necessary, but cannot accept a carry input; **half card** = expansion card that is half full length; **half duplex** = data transmission in one direction at a time over a bidirectional channel; **half-duplex modem** = modem which works in one mode at a time (either transmitting *or* receiving); *some modems can operate in half-duplex mode if required; see also* DUPLEX; *(film)* **half frame** = frame with smaller dimensions than the standard 35mm frame; **half space** = paper movement in a printer by a half the amount of a normal character; **half title** = first page of a book, with the title, but not the publisher's colophon *or* details of the author; *(film)* **half track** = sound recording that has taken up less than half of the availble surface of the tapes; **half wave rectifier** = circuit that allows current to pass in one direction only; **half word** = sequence of bits occupying half a standard computer word, but that can be accessed as a single unit

halftone *or* **half-tone 1** *adjective* **(a)** continuous shading of a printed area **(b)** grey shade half way between white and black; **halftone process** *or* **half-toning** = making halftones from photographs **2** *noun* photograph *or* image that originally had continuous tones, displayed *or* printed by a computer using groups of dots to represent the tones; *the book is illustrated with twenty halftones*

> COMMENT: small dots represent lighter tones and larger dots the darker tones - halftones are produced before printing since printers (laser and offset) can only print dots or line drawings

halide *noun* silver compound that is used to provide a light-sensitive coating on photographic film and paper

hall effect *noun* description of the effect of a magnetic field on electron flow; **hall effect switch** = solid state electronic switch operated by a magnetic field

halo *noun* photographic effect seen as a dark region with a very bright line around it, caused by pointing the camera into the light

halt 1 *noun* computer instruction to stop a CPU carrying out any further instructions until restarted, or until the program is restarted, usually by external means (such as a reset button) **2** *verb* to stop; *hitting CTRL S will halt the program*

ham *noun* **radio ham** = private radio operator who works especially with a short-wave transceiver

hamming code *noun* coding system that uses check bits and check sums to detect and correct errors in transmitted data, mainly used in teletext systems

hand *noun* part of the body at the end of each arm; **hands on** = working system where the operator controls the operations by keying instructions on the keyboard; *the sales representatives have received hands-on experience of the new computer; the computer firm gives a two day hands-on training course*; **hands off** = working system where (i) the operator does not control the operation which is automatic; (ii) the operator does not need to touch the device in use; **hand camera** = small film camera which can be operated by hand without the use of a dolly or tripod; **hand portable set** *or* **handy talkies** *or* **HTs** = small low-range portable transceiver; **hand receiver** = device containing all necessary electronics to allow reception of broadcast radio signals; **hand viewer** = hand-held magnifying lens with a mount to allow photographic slides to be viewed

hand-held *adjective* which can be held in the hand; **hand-held camera** = cine-camera held by the operator and not supported; **hand-held programmable** = very small computer which can be held in the hand, useful for basic information input, when a terminal is not available; **hand-held scanner** = device that is held in your hand and contains a row of photo-electric cells which, when moved over an image, convert it into data which can be displayed as an image on a computer

all acquisition, data reduction, processing, and memory circuitry is contained in the single hand-held unit

Byte

A year ago the hand-held computer business resembled that of PCs a decade ago, with a large number of incompatible models, often software incompatible and using proprietary displays, operating systems and storage media

Computing

hand off *noun* passing control of a communications channel from one transmitter to another

handle *noun* **(a)** *(in programming)* number used to identify an active file within the program that is accessing the file **(b)** *(in a GUI)* small square displayed that can be dragged to change the shape of a window or graphical object; *to stretch the box in the DTP program, select it once to display the handles then drag one handle to change its shape*

handler *or* **driver** *noun* special software routine that controls a device or function; *the disk drive handler code is supplied in the library*; *see also* DEVICE DRIVER; **error handler** = software routine that controls and reports on an error when it occurs

handset *noun* telephone receiver, with both microphone and loudspeaker; *see also* ACOUSTIC COUPLER

handshake *or* **handshaking** *noun* standardized signals between two devices to make sure that the system is working correctly, equipment is compatible and data transfer is correct (signals would include ready to receive, ready to transmit, data OK); **full handshaking** = RS232C signals transmitted between two communicating devices indicating ready to transmit, ready to receive, received, transmitted, etc.

if a line is free, the device waits another 400ms before reserving the line with a quick handshake process

Practical Computing

handwriting *noun* words written by hand; *the keyboarders are having difficulty in reading the author's handwriting*; **handwriting recognition** = software that is capable of recognising handwritten text and converting it into ASCII characters; *the new PDA has excellent handwriting recognition*

handwritten *adjective* written by hand, using a pen or pencil, not typed; *the author sent in two hundred pages of handwritten manuscript*

handy talkies *see* HT

hang *verb* *(slang)* (a computer) to stop responding to instructions because of temporary fault

hang up *verb* to cut off a communications line; *after she had finished talking on the telephone, she hung up*

hangover *noun* **(a)** effect on a TV screen where the previous image can still be seen when the next image appears **(b)** sudden tone change on a document that is transmitted over a fax machine as a gradual change, due to equipment faults

hangup *noun* sudden stop of a working program

hard *adjective* **(a)** solid, as opposed to soft; (parts of a computer system) that cannot be programmed *or* altered; **hard card** = board containing a hard disk drive and the required interfacing electronics, which can be slotted into a system; **hard copy** = printed document *or* copy of information contained in a computer *or* system, in a form that is readable (as opposed to soft copy); **hard disk** = rigid magnetic disk that is able to store many times more data than a floppy drive, and usually cannot be removed from the disk drive; **hard disk drive** = unit used to store and retrieve data from a hard disk, on the commands of a computer; hard disk drives are normally compact (3.5-inch diameter) and offer low access times (around 10ms) and high capacity (normal is 10Gb); **hard disk model** = model of computer with a hard disk; *(film)* **hard edge** = clearly defined edge to a picture area, as in a matte or wipe; **hard error** = error which is permanent in a system; **hard return** = code in a word-processing document that (normally) indicates the end of a paragraph **(b)** high contrast (photographic paper *or* film)

hard reset *noun* switch or signal that controls the CPU and resets the processor and any attached devices to their initial condition, equivalent to switching the computer off then back on again

hardbound *adjective* (book) with a hard cased cover, as opposed to a paperback

hardcover *noun & adjective* version of a book with a cased binding (as opposed to paperback); *we printed 4,000 copies of the hardcover edition, and 10,000 of the paperback*

hard-sectoring *noun* method of permanently formatting a disk, where each track is split into sectors, sometimes preformatted by a series of punched holes around the central hub, where a hole marks the start of sector

hardware *noun* **(a)** physical units, components, integrated circuits, disks and mechanisms that make up a computer *or* its peripherals; **hardware compatibility** = architecture of two different computers that allows one to run the programs of the other without changing any device drivers or memory locations, or the ability of one to use the add-on boards of the other; **hardware configuration** = way in which the hardware of a computer system is connected together and configured; **hardware dependent** = something which will only work with a particular model *or* brand of hardware; *the communications software is hardware dependent and will only work with Hayes-compatible modems*; **hardware failure** = fault with a hardware device *or* hardware that has stopped working properly; **hardware interrupt** = interrupt signal generated by a piece of hardware rather than by software; **hardware platform** = standard of a particular computer (such as IBM PC, Apple Macintosh); **hardware reliability** = ability of a piece of hardware to function normally over a period of time; **hardware reset** = switch that generates an electrical signal to reset the CPU and all devices, equivalent to turning a computer off and back on again; **hardware security** = making a system secure by means of hardware (such as keys, cards, etc.) (NOTE: no plural); *compare with* SOFTWARE **(b)** equipment used on set or location

COMMENT: computer hardware can include the computer itself, the disks and disk drive, printer, VDU, etc.

Sequent's Platform division will focus on hardware and software manufacture, procurement and marketing, with the Enterprise division concentrating on services and client-server implementation

Computing

hardwired connection *noun* **(a)** permanent phone line connection, rather than using a plug and socket **(b)** logical function *or* program, which is built into the hardware, using electronic devices, such as gates, rather than in software

harmonic *noun* frequency of an order of magnitude greater *or* smaller than a fundamental; **harmonic distortion** = unwanted harmonics produced by a non-linear circuit from an input signal; **harmonic telephone ringer** = telephone that will only detect a certain range of ringing frequencies, this allows many telephones on a single line to be rung individually

hash 1 *verb* to produce a unique number derived from the entry itself, for each entry in a database **2** *noun* **(a)** *see* HASHMARK **(b) hash code** = coding system derived from the ASCII codes, where the code numbers for the first three letters are added up giving a new number used as hash code; **hash-code system** = coding system using hash codes; **hashing function** = algorithm used to produce a hash code for an entry and ensure that it is different from every other entry; **hash index** = list of entries according to their hashed numbers; **hash total** = total of a number of hashed entries used for error detection

hashmark *or* **hash mark** *noun* printed sign (#) used as a hard copy marker *or* as an indicator (NOTE: in US usage (#) means number; # 32 = number 32 (apartment number in an address, paragraph number in a text, etc.)

Hayes Corporation modem manufacturer who developed standard control language for modems; **Hayes AT command set** = set of commands to control a modem prefixed with the letters AT; *to dial the number 1234, use the Hayes AT command ATD1234*; **Hayes compatible** = modem that is compatible with the Hayes AT command set

hazard *noun* fault in hardware due to incorrect signal timing; **hazard-free implementation** = logical function design that has taken into account any hazards that could occur, and solved them

haze filter *or* **haze-cutting filter** *noun* *(film)* lens filter which cuts out ultraviolet light and reduces haziness

HCI = HOST CONTROLLER INTERFACE

HD = HALF DUPLEX data transmission in one direction only, over a bidirectional channel

HDLC = HIGH-LEVEL DATA LINK CONTROL

HDTV = HIGH DEFINITION TELEVISION proposed new television format made up of 1125 lines and requiring a wide screen and high bandwidth equipment to view it on, so limited at present to satellite and cable television installations

HDX = HALF DUPLEX

head 1 *noun* **(a) (read/write) head** = transducer that can read *or* write data from the surface of a magnetic storage medium, such as a floppy disk; **cleaning disk** = special disk which is used to clean the drive heads; **disk head** = head which reads *or* writes on a floppy disk; **head alignment** = (i) correct position of a tape *or* disk head in relation to the magnetic surface, to give the best performance and correct track location; (ii) location of the read head in the same position as the write head was (in relation to the magnetic medium); **head crash** = component failure in a disk drive, where the head is allowed to hit the surface of the spinning disk, causing disk surface damage and data corruption; **head demagnetizer** = device used to remove any stray magnetic effects that might have built up on the surface of the tape head; **head positioning** = moving the read/write head to the correct track on a disk; **head wheel** = wheel that keeps video tape in contact with the head; **tape head** = head which reads *or* writes signals on a magnetic tape **(b)** data that indicates the start address of a list of items stored in memory **(c)** top edge of a book *or* of a page; **head of form** = first line on a form *or* sheet of paper that can be printed on **(d)** start of a reel of photographic film *or* recording tape; *(film)* **head out** = film or tape which is wound on a reel ready to be used; **head wheel** = *see* DRUM **(e)** top part of a device, network or body; **head end** = interconnection equipment between an antenna and a cable television network; *(film)* **head shot** = when the performers in a shot move straight towards the camera **(f)** adjustable mounting for a camera on its tripod **2** *verb* to be the first item of data in a list; *the queue was headed by my file*

header *noun* **(a)** in a local area network, a packet of data that is sent before a transmission to provide information on destination and routing **(b)** information at the beginning of a list of data relating to the rest of the data; **header block** = block of data at the beginning of a file containing data about file characteristics; **header card** = punched card containing information about the rest of the cards in the set **(c)** words at the top of a page of a document (such as title, author's name, page number, etc.); *see also* FOOTER

heading *noun* **(a)** title *or* name of a document or file **(b)** header *or* words at the top of each page of a document (such as the title, the page numbers, etc.) **(c)** title for a page within a multimedia book

headlife *noun* length of time that a video *or* tape head can work before being serviced *or* replaced

headline = HEADING

headset *or* **headphones** *noun* small speakers with padding, worn over a person's ears (used for private listening, instead of loudspeakers)

headword *noun* main entry word in a printed dictionary

heap *noun* temporary data storage area that allows random access; *compare with* STACK

heat-absorbing filter *or* **heat filter** *noun* filter that is able to reflect or absorb infrared radiation; used in projectors to reduce the amount of heat on a film

heat sink *noun* metal device used to conduct heat away from an electronic component to prevent damage

Heaviside-Kennelly layer *see* E-REGION

helical scan *noun* method of accessing data stored on video tape which is stored at an angle to the tape edge

helios noise *noun* noise originating from the sun that is picked up by an earth- based antenna when it points in the direction of the sun

help *noun* **(a)** thing which makes it easy to do something; *he finds his word- processor a great help in the office; they need some help with their programming* **(b)** function in a program *or* system that provides the user useful information about the program in use; **help key** = (i) (on an Apple Macintosh) special key that displays help information; (ii) (on an IBM PC) F1 function key used to display help information; **help screen** = display of information about a program or function; **context sensitive help** = help message that gives useful information about the particular function or part of the program you are in, rather than general information about the whole program; *hit the HELP key if you want information about what to do next*; **helper application** = program that works with a web browser to add a new function; if you want to view Adobe Acrobat pages in your web browser you will need to get the Adobe helper application; *see also* BROWSER, PLUG-IN

COMMENT: Most software applications for PCs have standardized the use of the F1 function key to display help text explaining how something can be done.

Hercules graphics adapter (HGA) *noun* standard for high-resolution mono graphics adapter developed by Hercules Corporation that can display text or graphics at a resolution of 720x348 pixels

Hertz *noun* SI unit of frequency, defined as the number of cycles per second of time; *see also* GHZ, KHZ, MHZ

COMMENT: Hertz rate is the frequency at which mains electricity is supplied to the consumer. The Hertz rate in the USA and Canada is 60; in Europe it is 50

heterodyne *noun* circuit producing two outputs equal to the sum and difference in frequency of two inputs; method used in television and radio reception

heterogeneous network *noun* computer network joining computers of many different types and makes; **heterogeneous multiplexing** = communications multiplexing system that can deal with channels with different transmission rates and protocols

heuristic *noun* which learns from past experiences; *a heuristic program learns from its previous actions and decisions*

Hewlett Packard manufacturer of computers, test equipment, and printers; **Hewlett Packard Graphics Language (HPGL)** = standard set of commands used to describe graphics; **Hewlett Packard Interface Bus (HPIB)** = standard method of interfacing peripheral devices *or* test equipment and computers; **Hewlett Packard LaserJet** *or* **HP LaserJet** = laser printer manufactured by Hewlett Packard that uses its PCL language to describe a page; **Hewlett Packard Printer Control Language (HP-PCL)** = standard set of commands developed by Hewlett Packard to allow a software application to control a laser printer's functions

hex *or* **hexadecimal notation** number system using base 16 and digits 0-9 and A-F; **hex dump** = display of a section of memory in hexadecimal form; **hex pad** = keypad with keys for each hexadecimal digit

HF = HIGH FREQUENCY radio communications range of frequencies from 3 - 30 MHz

HFS = HIERARCHICAL FILING SYSTEM *(in an Apple Macintosh system)* method used to store and organise files on disk or CD-ROM; *see also* HIGH SIERRA SPECIFICATION

HGA = HERCULES GRAPHICS ADAPTER

HI arc *(film)* = HIGH INTENSITY ARC carbon arc lamp which produces a very bright beam of light

hi fi *or* **hifi** = HIGH FIDELITY accurate reproduction of audio signals by equipment such as a record player and amplifier; **a hi fi system** *or* **a hi fi** = equipment for playing records *or* compact discs *or* tapes *or* listening

to the radio (including tape recorder, turntable, amplifier and speakers)

Hi-8 video cassette tape format that uses 8mm wide tape; mostly used in camcorders

hidden *adjective* which cannot be seen; **hidden defect in a program** = defect which was not seen when the program was tested; **hidden files** = important system files which are not displayed in a directory listing and cannot normally be read by a user; *it allows users to backup or restore hidden system files independently*; **hidden lines** = lines which make up a three-dimensional object, but are obscured when displayed as a two-dimensional image; **hidden line algorithm** = mathematical formula that removes hidden lines from a two-dimensional computer image of a 3-D object; **hidden line removal** = erasure of lines which should not be visible when looking at a two-dimensional image of a three-dimensional object

hierarchical classification *noun* library classification system where the list of subjects is divided down into more and more selective subsets; **hierarchical communications system** = network in which each branch has a number of separate minor branches dividing from it; **hierarchical computer network** = method of allocating control and processing functions in a network to the computers which are most suited to the task; **hierarchical database** = database in which records can be related to each other in a defined structure; **hierarchical directory** = directory listing of files on a disk, showing the main directory and its files, branches and any sub-directories; *(in an Apple Macintosh system)* **hierarchical filing system (HFS)** = method used to store and organise files on a disk or CD-ROM; **hierarchical routing** = method of moving information across a network by organising the structure of the network into separate levels: each level is responsible for directing traffic within its area; for example, the Internet has a three-level hierarchical routing system (backbone, mid-level, server) in which the backbone can direct traffic from one mid-level to another, the mid-levels can direct traffic from one server site to another and each server site can direct traffic internally; **hierarchical vector**

quantization (HVQ) = video compression standard which allows colour video images to be transmitted in a bandwidth of 112Kbps

high *adjective* large *or* very great; *(film)* **high angle shot** = shot made by positioning the camera above the action and pointing it down; **high band** = videotape recording system which produces broadcast quality pictures; for example, the 1-inch format and 3/4-inch BVU; **high definition television** *or* **HDTV** = broadcast television standard that can display very clear images with much better definition than existing television sets; there are several standards: the Japanese standard, MUSE, uses 1125 lines/screen, the European standard, HD-MAC, uses 1250 lines/screen; **high density storage** = very large number of bits stored per area of storage medium; *a hard disk is a high density storage medium compared to paper tape*; **high-end** = expensive or high-performance device; **high fidelity** *or* **hifi** *or* **hi fi** = accurate reproduction of audio signals by equipment such as a record player and amplifier; **high frequency** = radio communications range of frequencies between 3-30 MHz; **high intensity arc** = *see* HI ARC; **high-level data link control (HLDLC)** = ISO defined communications interface protocol which allows several computers to be linked; **high-level data link control station** = equipment and programs which correctly receive and transmit standard HLDLC data frames; **high-level (programming) language (HLL)** = computer programming language that is easy to learn and allows the user to write programs using words and commands that are easy to understand and look like English words, the program is then translated into machine code, with one HLL command often representing a number of machine code instructions; *programmers should have a knowledge of high-level languages (particularly PASCAL)* compare with LOW-LEVEL LANGUAGE; *(in an IBM PC)* **high memory** = memory area between 640Kb and 1Mb; *(in an IBM PC)* **high memory area (HMA)** = first 64Kb of extended memory above 1Mb that can be used by programs; **high pass filter** = circuit that allows frequencies above a certain limit to pass, while blocking those below that frequency limit; **high reduction** = reduction of text *or* graphics for use in micrographics,

usually reduced by 30 to 60 times; **high specification** *or* **high spec** = giving a high degree of accuracy *or* having a large number of features; *high spec cabling needs to be very carefully handled*; **high usage trunk** = main communications line that carries a large number of calls

highlight 1 *noun* **highlights** = characters *or* symbols treated to make them stand out from the rest of the text, often by using bold type **2** *verb* **(a)** to make part of the text stand out from the rest; *the headings are highlighted in bold* **(b)** to select an object or text by dragging the pointer across it; when text is highlighted it normally appears inverted (white on a black background); **highlight bar** = bar that a user can move up and down a list of options to choose an option

high-resolution *or* **hi-res** *noun* ability to display *or* detect a very large number of pixels per unit area; *high-resolution graphics; this high-resolution monitor can display 640 x 320 pixels; the new hi-res optical scanner can detect 1200 dots per inch*

COMMENT: currently, high-resolution graphics displays can show images at a resolution of at least 1024x1024 pixels, high-resolution printers can print at 1200 dots per inch and a high-resolution scanner can scan at a resolution of 1200 or 2400 dots per inch

```
the computer is uniquely
suited to image processing
because of its high-
resolution graphics
```

Byte

High Sierra specification *noun* early CD-ROM standard that then became the ISO 9660 standard (it was named after an area near Lake Tahoe, USA)

high-speed *adjective* which operates faster than normal data transmission *or* processing; **high-speed camera** = camera that operates at a higher speed than normal and is used to obtain slow-motion effects when the film is run at ordinary speed; **high-speed duplicator** = machine that copies video *or* audio tapes by running them at a faster speed than normal; **high-speed film** = (i) extremely light-sensitive film; (ii) film used in a high-speed camera; (iii) film with extra perforations to enable it to be used in a high-speed camera; **high-speed photography** = *see* SLOW MOTION; **high-speed skip** = rapid movement in a printer to miss the perforations in continuous stationery

high-tech *or* **high technology** *adjective* technologically advanced

highway *or* **bus** *noun* communications link consisting of a set of leads *or* wires which connect different parts of a computer hardware system and over which data is transmitted and received by various circuits inside the system

hill climbing *noun* method of achieving a goal in an expert system

hi-res = HIGH-RESOLUTION *hi-res graphics; this hi-res monitor can display 640 x 320 pixels; the new hi-res optical scanner can detect 1200 dots per inch*

hiss *noun* high-frequency noise mixed with a signal

histogram *noun* graph on which values are represented as vertical *or* horizontal bars

history *noun* a feature of some applications that keeps a log of the actions that the user has carried out, the places within a hypertext document that they have visited or the sites on the Internet that they have explored; *you can return to any point you had previously visited by looking at the history list*

hit 1 *noun* successful match *or* search of a database; **cache hit** = data retrieved from cache memory rather than from the storage device; indicates that time was saved and the cache was useful; **hit on the line** = short period of noise on a communications line, causing data corruption **2** *verb* to press a key; *to save the text, hit ESCAPE S*

the cause of the data disaster is usually due to your finger hitting the wrong key
PC Business World

HLDLC = HIGH-LEVEL DATA LINK CONTROL

HLL = HIGH-LEVEL (PROGRAMMING) LANGUAGE

HMA = HIGH MEMORY AREA *(in an IBM PC)* first 64Kb of extended memory above 1Mb that can be used by programs

HMI = HUMAN MACHINE INTERFACE study of ergonomics and the way in which a user interacts with hardware or software; software that has been designed to be easy to use

HMS time format *noun* system used by MCI to express time in hours, minutes and seconds - normally used only for videodisc devices; *see* MCI

HOF = HEAD OF FORM

hold 1 *noun* synchronization timing pulse for a television time base signal **2** *verb* to retain *or* keep a value *or* communications line *or* section of memory; **hold current** = amount of electrical current that has to be supplied to a device in its operating state, but not operating; **hold frame** = *see* FREEZE (FRAME) **holding line** = boundary line indicating the limits of an area of artwork *or* tone; **holding loop** = section of program that loops until it is broken by some action, most often used when waiting for a response from the keyboard *or* a device; **holding time** = time spent by a communications circuit on call

holdup *noun* **(a)** time period over which power will be supplied by a UPS **(b)** pause in a program *or* device due to a malfunction

COMMENT: the hold feature keeps the picture steady and central on the screen; some televisions have horizontal and vertical hold controls to allow the picture to be moved and set up according to various conditions

hole *noun* method of describing the absence of an electron from an atomic structure

COMMENT: a hole may move, but in the opposite direction to the flow of electrons in a material; it is also considered to have a positive charge as compared to a electron. This concept is mostly used in semiconductor physics, where the bulk movement of holes and electrons in an electronic device are studied

Hollerith code *noun* a coding system that uses punched holes in a card to represent characters and symbols, the system uses two sets of twelve rows to provide possible positions for each code

hologram *noun* imagined three-dimensional image produced by the interference pattern when a part of a coherent light source, such as a laser, is reflected from an object and mixed with the main beam

holograph *noun* handwritten manuscript, as written by the author using a pen *or* pencil, but not typed

holographic image *noun* hologram of a three-dimensional object; **holographic storage** = storage of data as a holographic image which is then read by a bank of photocells and a laser, a new storage medium with massive storage potential

holography *noun* science and study of holograms and their manufacture

home *noun* (a) place where a person lives; *his business card gives his home address as well as his business address*; **home address** = address of a house *or* flat where someone lives; **home banking** = method of examining and carrying out bank transactions via a terminal and modem in the user's home; **home computer** = microcomputer designed for home use, whose applications might include teaching, games, personal finance and word-processing (b) starting point for printing on a screen, usually taken as the top left hand corner; *(on an IBM PC keyboard)* **home key** = key that moves the cursor to the beginning of a line of text

home page *noun (on the Internet)* first page that is displayed when you visit a website; *if you visit the Peter Collin Publishing website at 'www.petercollin.com' the home page is the first page that is displayed*

homing *noun* location of the source of a transmitted signal *or* data item

homogeneous computer network *noun* network made up of similar machines, that are compatible *or* from the same manufacturer; **homogeneous multiplexing** = switching multiplexor system where all the channels contain data using the same protocol and transmission rate

hood *noun* cover which protects something; **acoustic hood** = soundproof cover put over a line printer to cut down its noise

hook *noun* point in a program at which a programmer can insert test code or debugging code

hooking *noun* distortion of a video picture caused by tape head timing errors

hop *noun* (i) *(radio or TV transmissions)* direct transmission path, using the reflections from only the ionosphere, not the earth, to propagate the signal from one point on the earth to another; (ii) *(in networks)* link between two devices or computers; *the connection between the two offices has two sections of cable and a bridge so takes two hops;* **hop count** = number of individal connections that data has to cross to travel from one computer to another over a network

hopper *noun* device which holds punched cards and feeds them into the reader

horizontal *adjective* lying flat *or* going from side to side, not up and down; **horizontal blanking** = prevention of a picture signal reaching a television beam during the time it contains no picture information on its return trace; **horizontal blanking period** = time taken for the picture beam in a monitor to return to the start of the next line from the end of the previous line; **horizontal scan frequency** = the number of lines on a video display that are refreshed each second; *a display with a resolution of 200 lines refreshed 60 times per second requires a horizontal scan frequency of 12KHz*; *compare with* VERTICAL SCAN FREQUENCY; *(in a GUI)* **horizontal scrollbar** = bar along the bottom of a window that indicates that the page is wider than the window; a user can move horizontally across the page by dragging the indicator bar on the scrollbar; **horizontal scrolling** = to move across a page, horizontally; **horizontal synchronization pulse** = pulse in a television broadcast signal that synchronizes the receiver sweep circuitry; **horizontal wraparound** = movement of a cursor on a computer display from the end of one line to the beginning of the next

horn *noun* directional radio device with a wider open end leading to a narrow section, used for the reception and transmission of radio waves; **feed horn** = microwave channelling device used to direct transmitted signals

host *noun & adjective* **host adapter** = adapter which connects to a host computer; *the cable to connect the scanner to the host* *adapter is included*; **host address or host number** = *see* INTERNET ADDRESS

host computer   *noun*   **(a)** main controlling computer in a multi-user *or* distributed system **(b)** computer used to write and debug software for another computer, often using a cross compiler **(c)** computer in a network that provides special services *or* programming languages to all users; **hosting service** = company (normally called an ISP) that provides storage space on its web server to store the pages that form a website; the company also maintains the server and its connections to the Internet; *see also* ISP

> you select fonts manually or
> through commands sent from the
> host computer along with the
> text
>
> *Byte*

hot *adjective* **(a)** connected to electricity; **hot chassis** = metal framework *or* case around a computer that is connected to a voltage supply rather than being earthed; **hot fix** = to detect and repair a fault (normally a corrupt sector on a hard disk) without affecting normal operations; **hot frame** = very bright film frame caused by overexposure; **hot plugging** *or* **hot swapping** = feature of a computer that lets you plug in or remove a device while the computer is running; the computer's operating system software automatically detects the change and alters its configuration; to support hot plugging the computer needs a special connection and operating system software that can manage this feature; currently USB, IEEE and PC-Card ports support hot plugging; *hot plugging lets you plug a PC-Card modem into a PC-Card slot and the computer will automatically detect this change and configure the PC to use the modem;* **hot standby** = piece of hardware that is kept operational at all times and is used as backup in case of system failure **(b)** active or something that will start a process; **hot key** = special key or key combination which starts a process or activates a program; *a useful hot key shortcut is Alt-F4 which will quit any Windows program*; **hot link** = command within a hypertext program that links a hotspot or hotword on one page with a second destination page which is

displayed if the user selects the hotspot; **hot zone** = text area to the left of the right margin in a word-processed document (if a word does not fit in completely, a hyphen is automatically inserted) **(c)** high temperature; **hot metal composition** = old method of producing typeset pages from individual metal letters which were cast from hot liquid metal, now mainly replaced by phototypesetting; **hot type** = characters cast from hot liquid metal

hotspot *noun* **(a)** special area on an image or display that does something when the cursor is moved onto it; *the image of the trumpet is a hotspot and will play a sound when you move the pointer over it* **(b)** region of high brightness on a film *or* display screen

hotword *noun* word within displayed text that does something when the cursor is moved onto it or it is selected; often displayed in a different colour and used to define complex words or link one text to another

house 1 *noun* company (especially a publishing company); *one of the biggest software houses in the US*; **house corrections** = printing *or* composition errors, caused by and corrected by the printers of a document; **house style** = (i) style of spelling and layout, used by a publishing company in all its books; (ii) method *or* design of products of a company, used to identify them from the products of competitors **2** *verb* to put a device in a case; *the magnetic tape is housed in a solid plastic case*

housekeeping *noun* tasks that have to be regularly carried out to maintain a computer system (checking backups, deleting unwanted files, etc.); *see also* IN-HOUSE

houselights *plural noun (film)* studio lighting, or lights illuminating where the audience is seated

housing *noun* solid case; *the computer housing was damaged when it fell on the floor*

howler *noun* **(a)** buzzer that indicates to a telephone exchange operator that a user's telephone handset is not on the receiver **(b)** very bad and obvious mistake; *what a howler, no wonder your program won't work*

HP = HEWLETT PACKARD

HPFS = HIGH PERFORMANCE FILING SYSTEM *(in OS/2 operating system)* method of storing file information that is faster and more flexible than MS-DOS FAT

HPGL = HEWLETT PACKARD GRAPHICS LANGUAGE

HPIB = HEWLETT PACKARD INTERFACE BUS

HP-PCL = HEWLETT PACKARD PRINTER CONTROL LANGUAGE

HRG = HIGH RESOLUTION GRAPHICS

HSV = HUE, SATURATION AND VALUE

HTs = HANDY TALKIES small portable transceivers

HTML = HYPERTEXT MARKUP LANGUAGE series of special codes inserted into a text file to define the typeface and style of the text and the layout and images used in a page; also allows hypertext links to be inserted to link to other parts of the document or to other documents; *see also* INTERNET, SGML, WML, WWW, XML

COMMENT: HTML is most commonly used to create the pages in a website that are displayed in a web browser; many software programs can create HTML documents, including wordprocessors, and specialist page-layout software

HTTP = HYPERTEXT TRANSFER PROTOCOL protocol (that is part of the TCP/IP set of protocols) used to request information (such as a web page) from a web server; *when you type in the address of a web page in your web browser, it requests this web page from the remote web server using the HTTP protocol; web page addresses should be written starting 'http://';* see also FTP, TCP/IP

hub *noun* **(a)** *(in a floppy disk)* central part of a disk, usually with a hole and ring which the disk drive grips to spin the disk **(b)** *(in a star-topology network)* central ring *or* wiring cabinet where all circuits meet (and form an electrical path for signals) **(c)** continuous audible sound of low frequency

hue *noun* description of a colour according to its frequency of light

hue, saturation and value (HSV) *noun* method of defining a colour through its three properties: hue (the wavelength); saturation (the purity of the hue); and value (the brightness); *see also* RGB, CMYK

Huffman code *noun* data compression code, where frequent characters occupy less bit space than less frequent ones

huge model *noun* *(in programming)* memory model of an Intel processor that allows data and program code to exceed 64Kb (but the total of both must be less than 1Mb)

hum *noun* low frequency electrical noise *or* interference on a signal; *(film)* **hum bars** = slow-moving horizontal bars on a television picture which are created by the input of an undesirable mains hum into the video signal

human-computer *or* **human-machine interface (HMI)** *noun* facilities provided to improve the interaction between a user and a computer system

hung *see* CRASH

hunting *noun* **(a)** process of searching out (i) a free line *or* channel on a telephone exchange; (ii) a data record in a file **(b)** *(in video tape reproduction)* low-frequency instability of sound or picture created by cyclic variations in tape or film transport speed

hybrid circuit *noun* connection of a number of different electronic components such as integrated circuits, transistors, resistors and capacitors in a small package, which since the components are not contained in their own protective packages, requires far less space than the individual discrete components; **hybrid computer** = combination of analog and digital circuits in a computer system to achieve a particular goal

hyper-cardoid microphone *noun* *(film)* microphone with a directional sensitivity pattern similar to a figure-of-eight

hyperlink *noun* series of commands attached to a button or word in one page that link it to another page in a multimedia book, so that if a user clicks on the button or word, the hyperlink will move the user to another position in the book or display another page

hypermedia *noun* hypertext document that is also capable of displaying images and sound

HyperTalk *noun* programming language used to define the elements in a HyperCard database, document or card

HyperTerminal communications program that is included with Windows that allows you to call a remote computer via a modem and transfer files; it is not used to access the Internet but can be used to access a bulletin board or other on-line service

hypertext *adjective* system of organising information where certain words or objects in a document link to and display another document when the word is selected; *in this web page, click once on the word 'weather' and you will see a new page with a weather forecast for the city;* **hypertext markup language** = *see* HTML; **hypertext transfer protocol** = *see* HTTP; **hypertext transfer protocol daemon** = *see* HTTPd

hyphen *noun* printing sign (-) to show that a word has been split; **soft hyphen** = hyphen which is inserted when a word is split at the end of a line in word-processed text, but is not present when the word is written normally

hyphenated *adjective* written with a hyphen; *the word 'high-level' is usually hyphenated*

hyphenation *noun* splitting of a word (as at the end of a line, when the word is too long to fit); **hyphenation and justification** *or* **H & J** = justifying lines to a set width, splitting the long words correctly at the end of each line; *an American hyphenation and justification program will not work with British English spellings*

```
the hyphenation program is
useful    for    giving    a
professional  appearance  to
documents  and for getting  as
many  words  onto  the  page  as
possible
```
Micro Decision

hypo *abbreviation* photographic fixing solution

Hz = HERTZ

Ii

IAM = INTERMEDIATE ACCESS MEMORY

IANA = INTERNET ASSIGNED NUMBERS AUTHORITY

IAR = INSTRUCTION ADDRESS REGISTER

IAS = IMMEDIATE ACCESS STORE

I-beam *noun* cursor shaped like the letter 'I' used (in a GUI) to edit text *or* indicate text operations

IBG = INTERBLOCK GAP

IBM = INTERNATIONAL BUSINESS MACHINES largest computer company in the world; developed the first PC based on the Intel processor; **IBM AT** = personal computer based on the Intel 80286 16-bit processor and featured an ISA expansion bus; **IBM AT keyboard** = keyboard layout that features 12 function keys in a row along the top of the keyboard, with a separate numeric keypad; **IBM- compatible** = generic term for a personal computer that is hardware and software compatible with the IBM PC regardless of which Intel processor it uses; it normally features an ISA, EISA or MCA expansion bus; **IBM PC** = personal computer based on the Intel 8088 8-bit processor; **IBM PC keyboard** = keyboard layout that features 10 function keys arranged to the left of the main keys, with no separate numeric keypad; **IBM PS/2** *or* **IBM Personal System/2** = range of personal computers based on the Intel 8086, 80286 and 80386 processors that feature an MCA expansion bus; **IBM XT** = personal computer based on the IBM PC but with an internal hard disk drive and featuring an ISA expansion bus

IC = INTEGRATED CIRCUIT device consisting of a small piece of a crystal of a semiconductor onto which are etched or manufactured (by doping) a number of components such as transistors, resistors and capacitors, which together perform a function (NOTE: plural is **ICs**)

ICE = INSERTION COMMUNICATION EQUIPMENT communication system (developed by the BBC) which transmits data in the field blanking period

ICMP = INTERNET CONTROL MESSAGE PROTOCOL extension to the Internet Protocol (IP) that provides error detection and control information; *the Internet command 'ping' uses ICMP to test if a named node is working correctly and displays any errors; see also* IP, PING

icon *or* **ikon** *noun* graphic symbol *or* picture displayed on screen, used in an interactive computer system to provide an easy way of identifying a function; *the icon for a word-processor icon might be a small picture of a typewriter*; **icon resource** = file that contains the bitmap image of an icon, used by a programmer when writing an application

the system has on-screen icons and pop-up menus and is easy to control using the mouse
Electronics & Power

an icon-based system allows easy use of a computer without the need to memorize the complicated command structure of the native operating system
Micro Decision

Despite (or because of?) the swap file, loading was slow and the hourglass icon of the mouse pointer frequently returned to the arrow symbol well before loading was complete
Computing

iconoscope *noun* early camera picture tube which was replaced by the image orthicon tube; it is an electron tube that turns visual images into electric impulses for television signals; **iconoscope camera** = television camera which holds an iconoscope tube

ID = IDENTIFICATION; **ID card** = card which identifies a person, and is carried about to prove their identity; **ID code** = password *or* word that identifies a user so that he can access a system

IDA = INTEGRATED DIGITAL ACCESS

IDD = INTERNATIONAL DIRECT DIALLING

IDE = INTEGRATED DRIVE ELECTRONICS *or* INTELLIGENT DEVICE ELECTRONICS popular standard for hard disk drive unit that includes the control electronics on the drive; *IDE drives are the standard fitted to most PCs*

ideal *adjective* perfect *or* very good for something; *she is the ideal designer for children's books*; **ideal format** = standard large format for photographic negatives, used mainly in professional equipment

identical *adjective* exactly the same; *the two systems use identical software*

identification *noun* procedure used by a host computer to establish the identity and nature of the calling computer *or* user (this could be for security and access restriction purposes *or* to provide transmission protocol information); **identification character** = single code character used to establish the identity and location of a remote computer *or* terminal with the host computer

identifier *noun* set of characters used to distinguish between different blocks of data *or* files

identify *verb* to note who someone is *or* what something is; *the user has to identify himself by using a password before accessing the system; the maintenance engineers have identified the cause of the system failure*

identity *noun* who someone is; **identity number** = unique number, used usually with a password to identify a user when logging into a system; *don't forget to log in your identity number*; **identity operation** = logical function whose output is true only if all the operands are of the same value; **identity palette** = 256-colour palette in which the first and last 10 colours are the system colours; used to speed up the process of loading bitmap files

idiot tape *noun* tape containing unformatted text, which cannot be typeset until formatting data, such as justification, line width, and page size, has been added by a computer

idle *adjective* (machine *or* telephone line *or* device) which is not being used, but is ready and waiting to be used; **idle character** = symbol *or* code that means 'do nothing' *or* a code that is transmitted when there is no data available for transmission at that time; **idle time** = period of time when a device is switched on but not doing anything

IDP = INTEGRATED DATA PROCESSING

IEC connector *noun* standard for a three-pin connector used on sockets that carry mains electricity to the computer; *all PCs use a male IEC connector and a mains lead with a female IEC connector*

IEE *UK* = INSTITUTION OF ELECTRICAL ENGINEERS

IEEE *US* = INSTITUTE OF ELECTRICAL AND ELECTRONIC ENGINEERS; **IEEE bus** = interface that conforms to IEEE standards; **IEEE-488** = interfacing standard as laid down by the IEEE, where only data and handshaking signals are used, mainly used in laboratories to connect computers and measuring equipment; **IEEE-802.2** = standard defining data links used with 802.3, 802.4 and 802.5; **IEEE-802.3** = standard defining Ethernet network system (CSMA/CD access using a bus-topology); **IEEE-802.4** = standard defining Token Bus; **IEEE-802.5** = standard defining IBM Token-Ring network system (access using a token passed around a ring network)

IEN = INTERNET EXPERIMENT NOTE

if = INTERMEDIATE FREQUENCY

IF statement *noun* computer programming statement, meaning do an action IF a condition is true (usually followed by THEN); **IF-THEN-ELSE** = high-level programming language statement, meaning IF something cannot be done, THEN do this, or ELSE do that

IFF (a) = INTERCHANGE FILE FORMAT standard that defines how palette data is stored in an Amiga and some graphics program **(b)** = INTERNATIONAL FILE FORMAT *(in CD-i)* standard for compressed files stored on a CD-i

IGMP = INTERNET GROUP MANAGEMENT PROTOCOL network protocol that helps manage how data is transferred during an IP Multicast operation in which one server computer sends packets of data to several destinations at the same time; the IGMP standard is defined in RFC1112

ignore *verb* not to recognize *or* not to do what someone says; *this command instructs the computer to ignore all punctuation*

IGP = INTERIOR GATEWAY PROTOCOL protocol that distributes information to gateways (now normally called routers) within a particular network

IH = INTERRUPT HANDLER

IIL = INTEGRATED INJECTION LOGIC (NOTE: say 'I squared L')

IKBS = INTELLIGENT KNOWLEDGE-BASED SYSTEM

ikon *or* **icon** *noun* graphic symbol *or* picture displayed on screen, used in an interactive computer system to provide an easy way of identifying a function

ILF = INFRA-LOW FREQUENCY

ILL = INTER-LIBRARY LOAN

illegal *adjective* which is not legal *or* which is against the law *or* against (syntax) rules; **illegal character** = invalid combination of bits in a computer word, according to preset rules; **illegal operation** = instruction *or* process that does not follow the computer system's protocol *or* language syntax

illegally *adverb* against the law *or* against rules; *the company has been illegally copying copyright software*

illegible *adjective* which cannot be read; *if the manuscript is illegible, send it back to the author to have it typed*

illiterate *adjective* (person) who cannot read; **computer illiterate** = (person) who does not understand computer-related

expressions *or* operations; *see also* LITERATE

> three years ago the number of people who were computer illiterate was much higher than today
>
> *Minicomputer News*

illuminance *noun* measurement of the amount of light that strikes a surface, measured in lux

illuminate *verb* to shine a light on something; *the screen is illuminated by a low-power light*

illumination *noun* lighting; **aperture illumination** = pattern generated from an aperture antenna

illustrate *verb* to add pictures to a text; *the book is illustrated in colour; the manual is illustrated with charts and pictures of the networking connections*

illustration *noun* picture (in a book); *the book has twenty-five pages of full-colour illustrations*

IMA (a) = INTERACTIVE MULTIMEDIA ASSOCIATION professional organisation that covers subjects including authoring languages, formats, and intellectual property **(b)** = INTERACTIVE MIDI ASSOCIATION association that distributes information on the MIDI specification

iMac personal computer developed by Apple Computer that has a stylish transparent casing that houses the monitor and main computer system with the mouse and keyboard as the only separate items

image *noun* **(a)** exact duplicate of an area of memory **(b)** copy of an original picture *or* design **(c)** projected picture that is shown when light is shone through a photograph film; **image enhancer** = electronic device that improves the clarity of an image; **image intensifier** = system which allows a camera to shoot in very low light, such as starlight; **image master** = data describing fonts and character shapes in a phototypesetter; **image orthicon tube** = standard television picture tube; **image pickup tube** = system that changes visual images into electrical signals through the use of an electronic scanning operation; **image plane** = region where the photographic film is located in a camera, where a sharp image of a scene is formed when the lens is correctly focused;

image point = point behind the lens where an object being filmed is clearly focused when the lens is set at infinity **(d)** picture displayed on a screen or monitor; **image area** = region of microfilm *or* display screen on which characters *or* designs can be displayed; **image buffer** = area of memory that is used to build up an image before it is transferred to screen; **image carrier** = storage medium containing data that defines the typefaces used in a phototypesetter; **image compression** = compressing the data that forms an image; **image degradation** = picture contrast and quality loss due to signal distortion *or* bad copying of a video signal; **image distortion** = optical lens fault causing an image to be distorted; **image editing** = altering or adjusting an image using a paint package or special image editing program; normally this means cropping, cutting and pasting, changing colours or retouching parts of an image; **image enhancement** = adjusting parts of an image using special image editing program, normally to change the contrast, brightness or sharpness of an image; **imagemap** = graphic image that has areas of the image defined as hotspots that link to other web pages; an image map can either be created with special HTML commands that define the coordinates of the areas and are interpreted by a user's web browser (this is called a client-side image map) and is the usual method of creating an imagemap, the alternative is to use a special program that runs on a web server; **image processing** = analysis of information contained in an image, usually to enhance the image or to create special effects; for example, to adjust the colour balance, sharpen the image, etc.; **image processor** = electronic *or* computer system used for image processing, giving digitized pictures; **image retention** = time taken for a TV image to disappear after it has been displayed, caused by long persistence phosphor; **image scanner** = input device which converts documents *or* drawings *or* photographs into a digitized, machine-readable form; **image sensor** = photoelectric device that produces a signal related to the amount of light falling on it; **image setter** = typesetting device that can process a PostScript page and produce a high-resolution output; *see also* TYPESETTER; **image stability** = ability

of a display screen to provide a flicker-free picture; **image storage space** = region of memory in which a digitized image is stored; **image table** = two bit-mapped tables used to control input and output devices or processes

imaging *noun* technique for creating pictures on a screen (in medicine used to provide pictures of sections of the body, using scanners attached to computers); **imaging system** = equipment and software used to capture, digitize and compress video or still images; **magnetic resonance imaging** = scanning technique, using magnetic fields and radio waves; **X-ray imaging** = showing X-ray pictures of the inside of part of the body on a screen

> The Max FX also acts as a server to a growing number of printers, including a Varityper 5300 with emerald raster image processor and a Canon CLC 500 colour photocopier
>
> *Computing*

IMAP = INTERNET MESSAGE ACCESS PROTOCOL standard that defines how electronic mail messages can be managed and read; *see also* POP3, SMTP

> COMMENT: the IMAP standard (currently at version four) provides an alternative to the POP3 standard. The IMAP standard stores a user's messages on a shared server (for example, at your ISP) and allows a user to connect from any computer and read, send or manage messages. In contrast, the POP3 protocol downloads all messages from a shared server onto the user's computer. This makes it very difficult for a user to access messages from different computer - for example, if you are travelling. Regardless of whether IMAP or POP3 is used to read messages, the SMTP protocol is normally used to send messages

IMAX wide-screen motion picture system using 70 mm film and having a frame size of 70 multiplied by 46 mm

immediate *adjective* which happens at once; **immediate access store (IAS)** = high speed main memory area in a computer system; **immediate addressing** = accessing data immediately because it is held in the address field itself; **immediate mode** = mode where a computer that executes an instruction as soon as it is entered

immunity *see* INTERFERENCE

impact *noun* hitting *or* striking something; **impact paper** = carbonless paper used to provide multiple copies without the use of carbon paper; **impact printer** = printer that prints text and symbols by striking an ink ribbon onto paper with a metal character (such as a daisy-wheel printer, as opposed to a non-impact printer like a laser printer); *see also* DAISY-WHEEL PRINTER, DOT-MATRIX PRINTER

```
Lexmark   is   shipping   the
Wheelwriter   family   of
typewriters  that  can  be
connected to a PC using the
parallel  printer  port, making
it act like a PC impact printer
```
Computing

impairment scale *noun* scale of the loss of quality in sound or picture reproduction in both film and video; *scale 5 is negligible loss and scale 1 is unacceptable*

impedance *noun* measurement of the effect an electrical circuit has on signal current magnitude and phase when a steady voltage is applied; **impedance matching** = means of making the best signal power transfer between two circuits by making sure that their output and input impedances are the same as the transmission line; *impedance matching a transmitter and receiver minimizes power losses to transmitted signals*; **impedance mismatch** = situation where the impedance of the transmission *or* receiving end of a system does not match the other, resulting in loss of signal power (due to increased attenuation effects of the two different impedances); *see also* OHM

implant *verb* to fix deeply into something; to bond one substance into another chemically; *the dopant is implanted into the substrate*

implement *verb* to carry out *or* to put something into action

implementation *noun* version of something that works; *the latest implementation of the software runs much faster*

import *verb* (a) to bring goods into a country for sale (b) to bring something in from outside a system; **imported signal** = broadcast television signal from outside a normal reception area, that is routed into and distributed over a cable network (c) to convert a file stored in one format to the default format used by a program

importation *noun* the act of importing; *compare with* EXPORT

```
text and graphics importation
from other systems is possible
```
Publish

```
At  the  moment,  Acrobat
supports only the sending and
viewing of documents. There
are   legal   implications
associated with allowing users
to edit documents in the style
of the original application,
without having the tool itself
on their desks, and there is no
import  facility  back  into
applications
```
Computing

impression *noun* number of books *or* documents printed all on the same printrun; **impression cylinder** = roller in a printing press that presses the sheets of paper against the inked type

imprint *noun* publisher's *or* printer's name which appears on the title page *or* in the bibliographical details of a book; **imprint position** = on a sheet of paper, place where the next letter *or* symbol is to be printed

impulse *noun* (voltage) pulse which last a very short time

impulsive *adjective* lasting a very short time; **impulsive noise** = interference on a signal caused by short periods of noise

in camera process *noun* film processing which takes place inside the camera

in circuit emulator *noun* electronic circuit that emulates the actions of another circuit *or* device and is connected to a device that is being tested

in phase *adverb* (a) (two electrical signals) that have no phase difference between them, i.e. there is no delay *or* a delay of one complete cycle between them (b) synchronization of film frames and projector shutter timing

inaccuracy *noun* mistake *or* error; *the bibliography is full of inaccuracies*

inaccurate *adjective* not correct *or* wrong; *he entered an inaccurate password*

inactive *adjective* (process or window or program or device) which is not being used or is not currently active; *(in a GUI)* **inactive window** = window still displayed, but not currently being used

in-band signalling *noun* use of a normal voice grade channel for data transmission

InBox software that is part of Windows and is used to manage electronic messages, including mail sent over the network, fax messages and email sent over the Internet

inbuilt *adjective* (feature *or* device) included in a system; *this software has inbuilt error correction*

in-camera matte shot *noun* camera shot where some of the action area is obscured by a black mask positioned in front of the camera so that other action can be recorded on the same film by using a second mask

incandescence *noun* generation of light by heating a wire in an inert gas (as in a light bulb)

incandescent *adjective* shining because of heat produced in an inert gas; *current passing through gas and heating a filament in a light bulb causes it to produce incandescent light*; *(film)* **incandescent lighting** *or* **inkie** *or* **inky** = a light using heated tungsten, gas-filled bulbs or tubes instead of bulbs with carbon arcs

incident *noun* *(film)* light that is reflected from an object

inclined orbit *noun* orbit that is not polar *or* equatorial

inclusive *adjective* which counts something in with other things; *prices are inclusive of VAT*; **inclusive OR** = *see* OR FUNCTION

incoming *adjective* which is coming in from outside; **incoming message** = message received in a computer; *(film)* **incoming shot** = shot that follows the one presently being watched or the next to be put into the editing machine; **incoming traffic** = amount of data *or* messages received

incompatible *adjective* not compatible; *they tried to link the two systems, but found they were incompatible*

incorrect *adjective* not correct *or* with mistakes; *the input data was incorrect, so the output is also incorrect*

incorrectly *adverb* not correctly *or* with mistakes; *the data was incorrectly keyboarded*

increment 1 *noun* **(a)** addition of a set number, usually one, to a register, often for counting purposes **(b)** value of the number added to a register **2** *verb* **(a)** to add something *or* to increase a number **(b)** to move forward to the next location **(c)** to move a document *or* card forward to its next preset location for printing *or* reading

incremental backup *noun* backup procedure that only backs up the files which have changed since the last full *or* incremental backup

incremental plotter *noun* graphical output device that can only move in small steps, so drawing lines and curves as a series of short straight lines

indent 1 *noun* space *or* series of spaces from the left margin, when starting a line of text **2** *verb* to start a line of text with a space in from the left margin; *the first line of the paragraph is indented two ens*

indentation *noun* leaving a space at the beginning of a line of text

independent *adjective* free *or* not controlled by anyone

independently *adverb* freely *or* without being controlled *or* without being connected; *in spooling, the printer is acting independently of the keyboard; the item is indexed independently*

index 1 *noun* **(a)** list of items in a computer memory, usually arranged alphabetically; **index build** = creation of an ordered list from the results of a database *or* file search; **index page** = videotext page that tells the user the locations of other pages *or* areas of interest; **index register** = computer address register that is added to a reference address to provide the location to be accessed **(b)** list of subjects and contents of a book in alphabetical order (usually at the back of a book) **(c)** list of terms classified into groups *or* put in alphabetical order; **index card** = small card used for storing information; **index letter** or **index number** = letter or number which identifies an item in an index **(d)** address to be used that is the result of an offset value added to a start location; see INDEXED ADDRESSING **(e)** guide marks along the edge of a piece of film or strip of microfilm; **index hole** = hole in the edge of a hand-sectored disk **(f)** (on the Internet) **index.html** = name given to the file that is used to store the home page on a website; see HOMEPAGE **2** verb **(a)** to write an index (for a book); **the book was sent out for indexing; the book has been badly indexed (b)** to put marks against items, so that they form an index

indexed address noun address of the location to be accessed is found in an index register; **indexed addressing** = method of addressing where the storage location is addressed with a start address and an offset word, which is added to give the destination address; **indexed sequential access method (ISAM)** = data retrieval method using a list containing the address of each stored record; **indexed sequential storage** = method of storing records in a consecutive order, but in such a way that they can be accessed rapidly

indexer noun person who writes an index

indexing noun **(a)** use of indexed addressing methods in a computer **(b)** process of building and sorting a list of records; **indexing language** = language used in building library or book indexes **(c)** writing an index for a book; **computer indexing** = using a computer to compile an index for a book by selecting relevant words or items in the text

indicate verb to show

indication noun sign or thing which shows

indicator noun something which shows the state of a process, usually a light or buzzer; **indicator flag** = register or single bit that indicates the state of the processor and its registers, such as a carry or overflow; **indicator light** = light used to warn or to indicate the condition of equipment

indirect adjective not direct; **indirect addressing** = way of addressing data, where the first instruction refers to an address which contains a second address; **indirect ray** = transmission path of a radio wave that does not take the shortest route, such as a reflection

individual 1 noun single person; **each individual has his own password to access the system 2** adjective single or belonging to a single person; **the individual workstations are all linked to the mainframe**

induce verb to generate an electrical current in a (coil of) wire by electromagnetic effects; **induced interference** = electrical noise on a signal due to induced signals from nearby electromagnetic sources

inductance noun measurement of the amount of energy a device can store in its magnetic field

induction noun generation of an electrical current due to electromagnetic effects from a nearby source; **induction coil** = transformer consisting of two nearby coils of insulated wire, one inducing a signal in the other; is often used either to isolate a signal supply from a some equipment or as a method of stepping up or down a voltage; see also TRANSFORMER

inductive coordination noun agreement between electrical power suppliers and communications providers on methods of reducing induced interference

inductor noun electrical component consisting of a coil of wire used to introduce inductance effects into a circuit (by storing energy in its magnetic field)

Industry Standard Architecture (ISA) noun standard used for the 16-bit expansion bus in an IBM PC or compatible; compare with EISA; MCA

inequality operator noun symbol used to indicate that two variables or quantities are not equal; **the C programming language uses the symbol '!=' as its inequality operator**

inert adjective (chemical substance or gas) that does not react with other chemicals

COMMENT: inert gas is used to protect a filament from oxidizing

INF file noun configuration file supplied by a hardware manufacturer to allow Windows to correctly install the device or peripheral

infected computer *noun* computer that carries a virus program

inference *noun* **(a)** deduction of results from data according to certain rules; **inference engine** *or* **machine** = set of rules used in an expert system to deduce goals or results from data **(b)** method of deducing a result about confidential information concerning an individual by using various data related to groups of people; **inference control** = determining which information may be released without disclosing personal information about a single individual

inferior figures *noun* smaller numbers *or* characters that are printed slightly below normal characters, used in mathematical and chemical formulae; *see also* SUBSCRIPT, SUPERSCRIPT, SUPERIOR NUMBER (NOTE: used in chemical formula: CO_2)

infinite *adjective* with no end; **infinite loop** = loop which has no exit (except by ending the running of the program)

infinity *noun* **(a)** very large incomprehensible quantity even bigger than the biggest you can think of **(b)** distance of an object from a viewer where beams of light from the object would be seen to be parallel (i.e. very far away) **(c)** distance setting on a camera lens beyond which all images are in focus

infix notation *noun* method of computer programming syntax where operators are embedded inside operands (such as C - D or X + Y); *compare with* PREFIX, POSTFIX NOTATION

informatics *noun* science and study of ways and means of information processing and transmission (NOTE: no plural)

information *noun* **(a)** knowledge presented to a person in a form which can be understood **(b)** data that has been processed *or* arranged to provide facts which have a meaning; **information bearer channel** = communications channel that is able to carry control and message data, usually at a higher rate than a data only channel; **information content** = measurement of the amount of information conveyed by the transmission of a symbol *or* character, often measured in shannons; **information flow control** = regulation of access to certain information; **information line** = line running across the screen which gives the user information about the program running *or* the file being edited, etc.; **information management system** = computer program that allows information to be easily stored, retrieved, searched and updated; **information networks** = number of databases linked together, usually by telephone lines and modems, allowing a large amount of data to be accessed by a wider section of users; **information processing** = organizing, processing and extracting information from data; **information processor** = machine that processes a received signal, according to a program, using stored information and provides an output, this is an example of a computer that is not dealing with mathematical functions; **information provider (IP)** = company *or* user that provides an information source for use in a videotext system (such as the company providing weather information *or* stock market reports); **information rate** = amount of information content per character multiplied by the number of characters transmitted per second; **information retrieval** = locating quantities of data stored in a database and producing information from the data; **information retrieval centre** = information search system, providing specific information from a database for a user; **information storage** = storing data in a form which allows it to be processed at a later date; **information storage and retrieval (ISR)** = techniques involved in storing information and retrieving data from a store; **information system** = computer system which provides information according to a user's requests; **information technology (IT)** = technology involved in acquiring, storing, processing and distributing information by electronic means (including radio, television, telephone, computers); **information theory** = formulae and mathematics concerned with data transmission equipment and signals; **information transfer channel** = connection between a data transmitter and a receiver; *see also* DATA TERMINAL EQUIPMENT

Information Technology is still too young to be an established discipline. However, the national and international IT research programmes are reasonably agreed that it comprises electronics, computing and telecommunications

Electronics and Power

Racal-Datacom has picked up a 1.5 million order for its ISDN digital access multiplexers from financial information provider Telerate, its second from the company this year

Computing

infra- *prefix* meaning below *or* less than; **infra-low frequency (ILF)** = range of audio frequencies between 300Hz-3KHz

infrared 1 *adjective* section of the electromagnetic radiation spectrum extending from visible red to microwaves; **infrared cinematography** = filming that uses film which is sensitive to infrared light; **infrared communications** = line of sight of communications path using a modulated infrared light beam rather than electrical signals down a cable; **infrared controller** = remote control unit used to control a slide projector or camera; **infrared detector** = photoelectric cell that is sensitive to the infrared region of the electromagnetic spectrum; **infrared film** = film that is sensitive to infrared radiation and is used to photograph at night; **infrared photography** = part of the photographic field that uses a special film, sensitive to infrared radiation that can be used for very low level light photography; **infrared sights** = camera and specialized optical equipment that can be used in situations where the light level is low, providing bright, enhanced images **2** *noun* film emulsion which is sensitive to longer light waves than visible red

infrasonic frequency *noun* sound wave frequency that is in the range below that audible by the human ear

infrastructure *noun* basic structure *or* basic services

infringement *noun* breaking the law *or* a rule; **copyright infringement** = illegally making a copy of a book which is in copyright

inherit *verb* *(in object-oriented programming)* one class *or* data type that acquires the characteristics of another

inheritance *noun* *(in object-oriented programming)* the characteristics of one class *or* data type that are passed to another (called its descendant)

inhibit *verb* to stop a process taking place *or* to prevent an integrated circuit *or* gate from operating, by means of an applied signal *or* command

in-house *adverb & adjective* working inside a company; *all the data processing is done in-house; the in-house maintenance staff deal with all our equipment*

INI file *noun* configuration file used in Windows 3.x (and earlier) that contains information to allow Windows to load and run an application; the INI file could contain the working directory, user name, and user settings; *see also* REGISTRY

initial 1 *adjective* first *or* at the beginning; **initial program header** = small machine-code program usually stored in a read-only memory device that directs the CPU to load a larger program *or* operating system from store into main memory (such as a boot up routine that loads the operating system when a computer is switched on); **initial value** = starting point (usually zero) set when initializing variables at the beginning of a program **2** *noun* first letter of a word, especially of a name; *what do the initials IBM stand for?*

initialize *verb* to set values *or* parameters *or* control lines to their initial values, to allow a program *or* process to be re-started

injection laser *noun* solid state laser device used to transmit data as pulses of light down an optic fibre

injection logic *see* INTEGRATED INJECTION LOGIC

ink 1 *noun* **(a)** dark liquid used to mark *or* write with **(b)** colour selected that appears when you paint *or* draw using a drawing program on a computer; **ink effect** = features of Windows Movie Player utility that defines how cast members are drawn; for example, transparent ink effect displays the cast member with the background showing through; **ink-jet printer** = computer printer that produces characters by sending a stream of tiny drops of electrically charged ink onto the paper (the movement of the ink drops is controlled by an electric field, producing a non-impact printer with few moving parts); *colour* *ink-jet technology and thermal transfer technology compete with each other* **2** *verb* **(a)** to apply ink to printing rollers in a printing machine **(b)** to draw lines on paper by pen *or* by the use of a plotter device

inkie *or* **inky** *noun (informal)* = INCANDESCENT LIGHTING

inking *noun* applying ink; **overinking** = applying too much ink

---
ink-jet printers work by squirting a fine stream of ink onto the paper
Personal Computer World

---

inlay *noun* combination of two television *or* video signals to produce a single picture; **inlay card** = identification card inside a tape *or* disk box

inline 1 *noun* connection pins on a chip arranged in one or two rows **2** *adverb* to process unsorted *or* unedited data

inline image *noun* graphical image that is part of a web page

inline plug-in *see* PLUG-IN

inner loop *noun* loop contained inside another loop; *see also* NESTED LOOP

input (i/p *or* **I/P) 1** *verb* to transfer data *or* information from outside a computer to its main memory; *the data was input via a modem* (NOTE: **inputs - inputting - input**) **2** *noun* **(a)** action of inputting information **(b)** data *or* information that is transferred into a computer; **input device** = device such as a keyboard *or* bar code reader, which converts actions *or* information into a form which a computer can understand and transfers the data to the processor; **input lead** = lead which connects an input device to a computer; **input port** = circuit *or* connector that allows a computer to receive data from other external devices; **input statement** = computer programming command that waits for data entry from a port *or* keyboard **(c)** electrical signals which are applied to relevant circuits to perform the operation

input-bound *or* **input-limited** *adjective* (program) which is not running as fast as it could, due to limiting input rate from a slower peripheral

input/output (I/O) *noun* receiving *or* transmitting of data between a computer and its peripherals, and other points outside the system; **input/output buffer** = temporary storage area for data waiting to be input *or* output; **input/output bus** = parallel link allowing transfer of data and control signals between a CPU and memory *or* peripheral device; **input/output channel** = link between a processor and peripheral allowing data transfer; **input/output device** = peripheral (such as a terminal in a workstation) which can be used both for inputting and outputting data to a processor; **input/output instruction** = programming instruction that transfers data from memory to an input/output port; **input/output port** = circuit *or* connector that provides an input/output channel to another device

---
In fact, the non-Qwerty format of the Maltron keyboard did cause a few gasps when it was first shown to the staff, but within a month all the Maltron users had regained normal input speeds
Computing

---

inquiry *noun* **(a)** asking a question **(b)** accessing data held in a computer system; **inquiry/response** = interactive computer mode, in which a user's commands and enquiries are responded to very quickly

insert 1 *verb* **(a)** to put something into something; *first insert the system disk in the left slot* **(b)** to add new text inside a word *or* sentence; **insert key** *or* **Ins key** = key that switches a word-processor or editor program into insert mode rather than overwrite mode; **insert mode** = interactive computer mode used for editing and correcting documents **(c)** *(in video tape editing)* to replace a part of an existing recording with inserted material **2** *noun (in film)* generally a scene shot separately which is added during the editing process

---
COMMENT: insert mode is a standard feature on most word-processing packages where the cursor is placed at the required point in the document and any characters typed will be added, with the existing text moving on as necessary

---

insertion communication equipment *see* ICE

insertion loss *noun* attenuation to a signal caused by adding a device into an existing channel *or* circuit

insertion point *noun* cursor positioned to show where any text typed in will be entered within a document; usually shown by an I-beam cursor

install *verb* to put a machine into an office *or* factory; to set up a new computer system to the user's requirements *or* to configure a new program to the existing system capabilities; *the system is easy to install and simple to use*; **install program** *or* **software** = software utility that transfers program code from the distribution disks onto a computer's hard disk and configures the program

installable device driver *noun* device driver that is loaded into memory and remains resident, replacing a similar function built-into the operating system

installation *noun* **(a)** a computer and equipment used for one type of work and processing **(b)** setting up a new computer system *or* software; *the installation of the equipment took only a few hours*

instance *noun* **(a)** *(in object-oriented programming)* object *or* duplicate object that has been created **(b)** one copy of an application, routine or object; *Microsoft Windows will let you run several copies of the same program at the same time; each is called an instance of the original*

instant jump *noun* *(in a videodisc player)* hardware feature that allows the player to skip a number of frames (up to 200) in the time it takes to refresh the screen

instant messaging (IM) software that allows users to type in and instantly exchange messages with one or more other people connected to a network (normally used on the Internet); each person runs special software that tells them when a friend or colleague has connected to the Internet and is available to receive messages; *unlike email, when you type something in this instant messaging software, it is sent instantly to the other user*

instant replay *noun* feature found in video recording systems that allows the action that has just been recorded to be viewed immediately

instruct *verb* to tell someone *or* a computer what to do

instruction *noun* word used in a programming language that is understood by the computer to represent an action; *the instruction PRINT is used in this BASIC dialect as an operand to display the following data*; **instruction counter** *or* **instruction address register (IAR)** *or* **program counter** = register in a CPU that contains the location of the next instruction to be processed; **instruction cycle** = sequence of events and their timing that is involved when fetching and executing an instruction stored in memory; **instruction cycle time** = amount of time taken for one instruction cycle; **instruction decoder** = program which decodes instructions in machine code; **instruction execution time** = time taken to carry out an instruction; **instruction pointer** = register in a CPU that contains the location of the next instruction to be processed; **instruction processor** = section of the central processing unit that decodes the instruction and performs the necessary arithmetic and logical functions; **instruction register** = register in a central processing unit that stores an instruction during decoding and execution operations; **instruction set** = total number of instructions that a processor can recognize and execute; **instruction time** = amount of time taken for a central processing unit to carry out a complete instruction; **instruction word** = fixed set of characters used to initiate an instruction; *the manufacturers of this CPU have decided that JMP will be the instruction word to call the jump function*; **input/output instruction** = computer programming instruction that allows data to be input *or* output from a processor

COMMENT: in a high level language the instructions are translated by the compiler *or* interpreter to a form that is understood by the computer

A Taos kernel, typically 15Kb in size, resides at each processing node to 'translate', non-native instructions – on the fly when needed. This kernel contains the only code which has to be written in the processor's native instruction set

Computing

instrument *noun* electronic device that can produce a sound in response to a MIDI note or to a keyboard press

instrumentation *noun* equipment for testing, display or recording signals; *we've improved the instrumentation on this model to keep you better informed of the machine's position*

insufficient *adjective* not enough; *there is insufficient time to train the keyboarders properly*

insulate *verb* to prevent energy from a conductor reaching another point by separating the two points with an insulation material

insulation material *noun* substance that is very bad conductor, used to prevent energy reaching a point

insulator *noun* material that does not conduct electricity; *plastic is a good insulator*

integer *noun* a mathematical term used to describe a whole number, such as 12, 135 or 987; *an integer cannot have fractions or decimal points*; **integer BASIC** = faster version of BASIC that uses only integer mathematics and cannot support fractions

integral *adjective* (a feature or hardware device) that is already built into the program or computer; *the Print Manager utility within Windows provides printer control as an integral part of Windows*

integrated *adjective* (system) that contains many peripherals grouped together in order to provide a neat, complete system; **integrated database** = database that is able to provide information for varied requirements without any redundant data; **integrated data processing (IDP)** = organizational method for the entry and retrieval of data to provide maximum efficiency; **integrated device** = device that is part of another machine *or* device; *our competitor's computer doesn't have an integrated disk drive like this model*; **integrated device electronics** *or* **integrated drive electronics (IDE)** = popular standard for hard disk drive unit that combines the drive and control electronics in one device; **integrated digital access (IDA)** = system where subscribers can make two telephone calls and be linked (from their office *or* home) to a database, and send material by fax, all at the same time; **integrated digital**

network = communications network that uses digital signals to transmit data; **integrated injection logic (IIL)** = method of designing and constructing logical circuits on an integrated circuit to provide low power consumption with medium speed gates; **integrated modem** = modem that is an internal part of the system; **integrated office** = office environment in which all operations are carried out using a central computer (to store information, print, etc.); **integrated optical circuit** = optoelectronic circuit that can generate, detect and transmit light for communications over optical fibres; **integrated services digital network (ISDN)** = international digital communications network which can transmit sound, fax and data over the same channel; **integrated software** = software such as an operating system *or* word-processor that is stored in the computer system and has been tailored to the requirements of the system

integrated circuit (IC) *noun* circuit where all the active and passive components are formed on one small piece of semiconductor, by means of etching and chemical processes; *the central processor of a computer is a very complex integrated circuit that can perform mathematical operations on numbers*

> COMMENT: integrated circuits can be classified as follows: Small Scale Integration (SSI): 1 to 10 components per IC; Medium Scale Integration (MSI): 10 to 500 components per IC; Large Scale Integration (LSI): 500 to 10,000 components per IC; Very Large Scale Integration (VLSI): 10,000 to 100,000 components per IC

integration *noun* bringing several operations together

integrity *noun* reliability of data (when being processed *or* stored on disk); **integrity of a file** = the fact that a file that has been stored on disk is not corrupted *or* distorted in any way; **the data in this file has integrity** = the data has not been corrupted

it is intended for use in applications demanding high data integrity, such as archival storage or permanent databases
Minicomputer News

Intel company which developed the first commercially available microprocessor (the 4004); it developed the range of processors that is used in IBM PCs and compatible computers; **Intel 8086** = microprocessor that uses a 16-bit data bus and can address up to 1Mb of RAM; **Intel 8088** = microprocessor that uses a 16-bit data bus internally, but uses an 8-bit data bus externally; used in the first IBM PC computers; **Intel 80286** = microprocessor that uses a 16-bit data bus and can address up to 16Mb of RAM; **Intel 80386** = microprocessor that uses a 32-bit data bus and can address up to 4Gb of RAM; **Intel 80486** = microprocessor that uses a 32-bit data bus and can address up to 64Gb of RAM; **Intel Celeron** = advanced microprocessor that uses a 32-bit data bus; **Intel Pentium** = advanced microprocessor that uses a 32-bit data bus; versions of this processor are used in the current range of purchase; *see also* AMD, MOTOROLA

intelligence *noun* (a) ability to reason (b) ability of a device to carry out processing *or* run a program

intelligent *noun (in machine)* (program *or* device) that is capable of limited reasoning facilities, giving it human-like responses; **intelligent device** = peripheral device that contains a central processing unit allowing it to process data; **intelligent knowledge-based system (IKBS)** *or* **expert system** = software that applies the knowledge, advice and rules defined by an expert in a particular field to a user's data to help solve a problem; **intelligent spacer** = facility on a word-processing system used to prevent words from being hyphenated *or* separated at the wrong point; **intelligent terminal** = computer terminal which contains a CPU and memory, usually with a facility to allow the user to program it independently of the main CPU (NOTE: the opposite is **dumb terminal**); **intelligent tutoring system** = computer-aided learning system that provides responsive and interactive teaching facilities for users; **intelligent wiring hub** = wiring hub that can be controlled from a workstation to direct which circuits to connect to each other

INTELSAT = INTERNATIONAL TELECOMMUNICATIONS SATELLITE ORGANIZATION international group that deals with the design, construction and allocation of space to various communications satellite projects

intensity *noun* measure of the strength of a signal *or* loudness of a noise *or* the brightness of a light source

COMMENT: sound intensity is usually measured in decibels

inter- *prefix* meaning between; **interblock** = between blocks; **inter-library** = between two libraries

interact *verb (of two things)* to act on each other

interaction *noun* action of two things on each other

interactive *adjective* (system *or* piece of software) that allows communication between the user and the computer (in conversational mode); **interactive cable television** = cable television system that allows the viewer to transmit signals such as program choice, teleshopping *or* answers to game questions back to the television transmission centre; **interactive graphics** = display system that is able to react to different inputs from the user; *the space invaders machine has great interactive graphics, the player controls the position of his spaceship on the screen with the joystick*; **interactive media** = communication between a group of people using different transmission means; **interactive processing** = computer mode that allows the user to enter commands *or* programs *or* data and receive immediate responses; *see also* INQUIRY/RESPONSE; **interactive routine** = computer program that can accept data from an operator, process it and provide a real-time reaction to it; **interactive system** = system which provides an immediate response to the user's commands *or* programs *or* data; **interactive terminal** = terminal in an interactive system which sends and receives information; **interactive TV** = channel that allows two-way communication between the viewer and broadcasting station; this feature often allows the user to choose which programme to watch or respond directly to questions displayed on-screen; **interactive video (IV)** = system that uses a computer linked to a videodisc player to provide processing power and real images *or* moving pictures; **interactive videotext** = viewdata service that allows the operator to select pages, display them, ask questions *or* use a service such as teleshopping

COMMENT: interactive video is often used in teaching to ask a student questions, which if answered correctly will provide him with a filmed sequence from the videodisc

Interactive Multimedia Association (IMA) *noun* professional organisation that covers subjects including authoring languages, formats, and intellectual property

soon pupils will be able to go shopping in a French town from the comfort of their classroom - carried to their destination by interactive video, a medium which combines the power of the computer with the audiovisual impact of video

Electronics & Power

Oracle today details its interactive information superhighway aims, endorsed by 17 industry partners. The lynchpin to the announcement will be software based on the Oracle Media Server, a multimedia database designed to run on massively parallel computers

Computing

interblock gap (IBG) *noun* blank magnetic tape between the end of one block of data and the start of the next in backing store

intercarrier noise *noun* interference caused by two different signal carriers getting mixed; *television intercarrier noise is noticed when the picture and the sound signal carriers clash*

interchange 1 *noun* exchange of one thing for another; *the machine allows document interchange between it and other machines without reformatting* **2** *verb* to exchange one thing for another

interchange file format (IFF) *noun* standard that defines how palette data is stored in an Amiga and some graphics programs

interchangeable *adjective* which can be exchanged

intercharacter spacing *noun* word-processor feature that provides variable spacing between words to create a justified line

intercom *noun* short-range voice communications system

COMMENT: used mainly in offices *or* in automatic door systems where room-to-room communication of voice signals is required

interconnect *verb (of several things)* to connect together; *a series of interconnected terminals*

interconnection *noun* **(a)** section of connecting material between two devices **(b)** connection between a telephone set and a telephone network

interface 1 *noun* **(a)** point at which one computer system ends and another begins **(b)** circuit *or* device *or* port that allows two or more incompatible units to be linked together in a standard communication system, allowing data to be transferred between them; **interface card** = add-on board that allows a computer to interface to certain equipment or conform to a certain standard **(c)** section of a program which allows transmission of data to another program; **interface message processor** = computer in a packet switching network that deals with the flow of data, acting as an interface processor; **interface processor** = computer that controls data transfer between a processor and a terminal *or* network; **parallel interface** = computer circuit *or* connector that allows parallel data to be transmitted *or* received; **serial interface** = circuit that converts parallel data in a computer to and from a serial form, allowing serial data to be transmitted to *or* received from other equipment (NOTE: the most common serial interface is RS232C) **2** *verb* **(a)** to modify a device by adding a circuit *or* connector to allow it to conform to a standard communications system **(b)** to connect two or more incompatible devices together with a circuit, to allow them to communicate

The original release of ODBC only included a driver for Microsoft's own SQL Server database. Microsoft has subsequently published the ODBC application program interface enabling third-party vendors to create drivers for other databases and tools

Computing

interfacing *noun* hardware *or* software used to interface two computers *or* programs *or* devices

interfere *verb* **to interfere with something** = to stop something working properly *or* to get in the way

interference *noun* **(a)** unwanted addition of signals *or* noise to a transmitted signal **(b)** effect seen when two signals are added, creating constructive interference when both signals are in phase *or* destructive interference when they are out of phase; **interference fading** = effect in radio reception when destructive interference occurs; **interference immunity** = ability of a system (i) to ignore interference signals; (ii) to function correctly even with interference; **interference pattern** = effect seen when light *or* radio *or* X-ray waves interact and produce destructive and constructive interference, causing patterns; **constructive interference** = increase in peak and trough amplitude when two in phase signals are added; **destructive interference** = cancellation of peaks and troughs when two out of phase signals are added (if the signals are exactly out of phase, they completely cancel out each other)

COMMENT: interference can be due to electrical noise (such as from a relay), natural galactic noise or two signals mixing due to insufficient insulation

interframe coding *noun* system of compressing video images such that only the differences between each frame are recorded

interlace *verb* method of building up an image on a television screen using two passes, each displaying alternate lines; **interlaced video** = video signal made up of

two separate fields; this is the normal display mode for home video

COMMENT: this system uses two picture fields made up of alternate lines to reduce picture flicker effects

interleave *verb* to store data on alternate tracks on a hard disk drive, used to slow down data transfer from a fast disk drive so that it can be used by a slower processor; **interleave factor** = ratio of sectors skipped between access operations on a hard disk

COMMENT: in a hard disk with an interleave of 3, the first sector is read, then three sectors are skipped and the next sector is read. This is used to allow hard disks with slow access time to store more data on the disk

interleaved *adjective* **(a)** (thin sheets of paper) which are stuck between the pages of a book; *blank paper was interleaved with the newly printed text to prevent the ink running* **(b)** sections of two programs executed alternately to give the impression that they are running simultaneously; **interleaved memory** = two separate banks of memory used together in sequence

interleaving *noun* **(a)** processor dealing with slices *or* sections of processes alternately, so that they appear to be executed simultaneously **(b)** addition of blank paper between printed sheets to prevent the ink from making other sheets dirty **(c)** dividing data storage into sections so that each can be accessed separately

inter-library loan (ILL) *noun* lending of books *or* documents from one library to another

interlinear spacing *noun* (*on a phototypesetter*) insertion of spaces between lines of text

interlock 1 *noun* **(a)** security device which is part of the logon prompt and requires a password **(b)** method of synchronizing audio tape with a video *or* filmed sequence (this can be achieved by using a frame counter *or* a timer *or* by running both audio and visual tapes on the same motor); **interlock projector** = film display machine that can also provide synchronized sound **2** *verb* to prevent a device from performing another task until the present one has been completed

intermediate *adjective* **(a)** which is at a stage between two others; **intermediate access memory (IAM)** = memory storage that has an access time between that of main memory and disk based systems; **intermediate code** = code used by a computer *or* assembler during the translation of a high-level code to machine code; **intermediate file** = series of records that contain partially processed data, that will be used at a later date to complete that task; **intermediate materials** = medium *or* format used for recording prior to the transfer to another format; *those slides, photographs, video and film are the intermediate materials to be mastered onto the videodisc*; **intermediate storage** = temporary area of memory for items that are currently being processed **(b)** widespread term for colour master positives and duplicate negatives which are printed on an integral colour masking film stock

intermediate frequency (if) *noun* frequency in a radio receiver to which the incoming received signal is transformed

COMMENT: this is to allow high frequency signals to be converted to a lower intermediate frequency so that they can be processed with standard components, rather than more expensive high-frequency versions

intermittent error *noun* error which apparently occurs randomly in a computer *or* communications system due to a program fault *or* noise

COMMENT: these errors are very difficult to trace and correct due to their apparent random appearance

internal *adjective* which is inside; **internal character code** = representation of characters in a particular operating system; **internal command** = command that is part of the operating system, rather than a separate utility program; *in MS-DOS, the internal command DIR is used frequently*; **internal** *or* **resident font** = font that is stored on a ROM in a printer; **internal hard disk** = hard disk drive mounted inside the main case of a computer; **internal language** = language used in a computer system that is not under the direct control of the operator

COMMENT: many compiled languages are translated to an internal language

internal memory *noun* section of RAM and ROM to which the central processing unit is directly connected without the use of an interface (as in external memory devices such as disk drives)

internal modem *noun* modem on an expansion card that fits into an expansion connector and transfers information to the processor through the bus rather than connecting to a serial port

internal sort *noun* sorting program using only the main memory of a system

internally stored program *noun* computer program code that is stored in a ROM device in a computer system (and does not have to be loaded)

international *adjective* referring to different countries; **international direct dialling (IDD)** = system using an international dialling code that allow a user to telephone any country without going through an operator; **international dialling code** = INTERNATIONAL PREFIX CODE; *(in CD-i)* **international file format (IFF)** = standard for compressed files stored on a CD-i; **International MIDI Association (IMA)** = professional organisation that covers subjects including authoring languages, formats, and intellectual property; **international number** = digits to be dialled after the international prefix code to reach a subscriber in another country; **international prefix code** = code number to be dialled at the start of a number to select another country's exchange system; **international standard book number (ISBN)** = ten-digit identifying number allocated to every new book published; **international standard serial number (ISSN)** = identifying number allocated to every journal *or* magazine published

International Standards Organization (ISO) organization which regulates standards for many types of product; **International Standards Organization Open System Interconnection (ISO/OSI)** = standardized ISO network design which is constructed in layered form, with each layer having a specific task, allowing different systems to communicate if they conform to the standard

International Telecommunications Satellite Organization *see* INTELSAT

inter-negative *noun (film)* duplicate colour negative film which is prepared directly from an original colour negative film exposed in the camera

Internet *noun* international wide area network that provides file and data transfer, together with electronic mail functions for millions of users around the world; *I used the Internet to check the share prices; it's cheaper to buy the book on the Internet; see also* EMAIL, NEWSGROUPS, WEB

internet *noun* wide area network formed of many local area networks; **internet protocol (IP)** = TCP/IP standard that defines how data is transferred across a network; **internet protocol address (IP Address)** = unique, 32-bit number which identifies each computer connected to a TCP/IP network

Internet address *noun* unique number that identifies the precise location of a particular node on the Internet; this address is also called an IP address and is a 32-bit number usually written in dotted decimal format; it used by the TCP/IP protocol and is normally of the form '123.33.22.32'; *see also* DNS, IP

Internet architecture board

(IAB) group of people who monitor and manage the development of the Internet; the group includes the IETF and the IRTF

Internet assigned numbers authority (IANA) group of people who assign unique identifying numbers to the different protocols and network products used on the Internet

Internet-draft (I-D) draft documents produced by the IETF that often lead to RFCs

Internet engineering steering group (IESG) group of people who review Internet standards and manage the IETF

Internet engineering task force

(IETF) large group of network designers, researchers, programmers, vendors and engineers that work together to improve and

develop the Internet (further information is at www.info.isoc.org)

Internet Explorer (IE) *noun* web browser developed by Microsoft that allows a user to view web pages and HTML documents; it supports many features including ActiveX applets; *see also* BROWSER, HTML, NETSCAPE

Internet Information Server (IIS)

Internet web server software developed by Microsoft

Internet merchant account

(IMA) business bank account that allows a company to accept credit card payments via the Internet

Internet message access protocol *see* IMAP

Internet number *see* INTERNET ADDRESS

Internet protocol (IP) protocol used to carry data over the Internet; it is part of the TCP/IP protocol suite; *see also* PROTOCOL, TCP/IP

internet relay chat (IRC) function of the Internet that allows several users to send and receive text messages in real-time as if they were all in a room

Internet research steering group (IRSG) group that manages the Internet research task force; part of the Internet Society

Internet research task force

(IRTF) group that considers the long-term technical objectives and standards for the Internet; part of the Internet Society

Internet service provider (ISP) *noun* company that provides a link to the Internet for individual users and small businesses dialling in via a modem; the ISP provides telephone numbers for dial-up customers using modems and has direct high-speed links to the Internet to send and receive information to other computers on the Internet; *see also* BACKBONE; DIAL-UP; POP

Internet Society organisation that looks after the maintenance and future developments of the Internet; it is not linked to any government nor company so provides an independent view of the future of the Internet; it is made up of committees, such as the Internet Advisory Board and the Internet Engineering Task Force, that are responsible for developing and approving new Internet standards

Internet telephony system that allows someone to make a telephone call using the Internet to transfer the voice signals rather than the normal telephone lines

COMMENT: If you have low-cost dial-up access to the Internet, Internet telephony allows you to make long distance calls for the low-price you pay for your Internet connection. To make a telephone call, you need a computer with a sound card fitted and a microphone and loudspeaker plugged in; special software manages the connection and transfers the voice data over the Internet to the person you are calling. Some systems let you call and speak to anyone else connected to the Internet who is using the same software. More sophisticated software links you to a real telephone exchange and lets you call any normal telephone number and so speak to anyone in the world. This type of system normally charges an extra fee to manage the link to the real telephone exchange, but this is often cheaper than the cost of a normal long-distance telephone call.

InterNIC organisation that was originally responsible for managing the way domain names were registered, assigned and paid for by organisations; this has recently changed and now groups of companies in different countries manage the registration and payment process

interoperability *noun* the ability of two devices or computers to exchange information

interpolation *noun* calculation of intermediate values between two points

inter-positive *noun (film)* positive colour duplicate film made from an original negative

interpret *verb* to translate what is said in one language into another; **interpreted language** = programming language that is executed by an interpreter

interpreter *noun* software that is used to translate (at the time of execution) a user's high-level program into machine code

COMMENT: compare with a compiler, that takes time to translate the high-level language into machine code and then executes it, rather than real-time translation with an interpreter

interrecord gap = INTERBLOCK GAP

interrogation *noun* asking questions; **file interrogation** = questions asked to select various records *or* data items from a file

interrupt 1 *verb* to stop something happening while it is happening **2** *noun* **(a)** stopping of a transmission due to an action at the receiving end of a system **(b)** signal which diverts a central processing unit from one task to another which has higher priority, allowing the CPU to return to the first task later; *this printer port design uses an interrupt line to let the CPU know it is ready to receive data*; **interrupt-driven** = (program) that works in response to an interrupt; **interrupt handler (IH)** = software that accepts interrupt signals and acts on them (such as running a program *or* sending data to a peripheral); **interrupt level** = priority assigned to the interrupt from a peripheral; **interrupt line** = connection to a central processing unit from outside the system that allows external devices to use the CPU's interrupt facility; **interrupt mask** = term in computer programming that selects which interrupt lines are to be activated; **interrupt request (IRQ)** = signal from a device that indicates to the CPU that it requires attention; **priority interrupt table** = list of peripherals and their priorities when they send an interrupt signal (used instead of a hardware priority scheduler); **vectored interrupt** = interrupt which directs the CPU to transfer to a particular location

interstation muting *noun* ability of a radio receiver to prevent the noise found between radio stations from being amplified and heard by the user

interval *noun* short pause between two actions; *there was an interval between pressing the key and the starting of the printout*

intervention *noun* acting to make a change in a system

interword spacing *noun* variable spacing between words in a text, used to justify lines

intrinsic *adjective* pure (substance) which has had no other chemicals (such as dopants) added; *the base material for ICs is an intrinsic semiconductor which is then doped*

introduce *verb* to put something into something; *errors were introduced into the text at keyboarding*

intruder *noun* person who is not authorized to use a computer or connect to a network

intrusion *noun* action by a telephone operator to allow both parties on each end of the telephone line to hear his *or* her message

invalid *adjective* not valid; *he tried to use an invalid password; the message was that the instruction was invalid*

inverse video *noun* television effect created by swapping the background and foreground text display colours

inversion *noun* changing over the numbers in a binary word (one to zero, zero to one); *the inversion of a binary digit takes place in one's complement*

invert *verb* (i) to change one item or colour for another; *the image looks better with the black inverted to white* (ii) to change all binary ones to zeros and zeros to ones

inverted commas *noun* printing sign (" ") which is usually used to indicate a quotation

inverted file *noun* file in which indexes exist for every data item

inverter *noun* **(a)** logical gate that provides inversion facilities **(b)** circuit used to provide alternating current supply from a DC battery source; **inverter AC/DC** = device which changes alternating current to direct current, or direct current to alternating current

invisible *adjective* guide or object visible on a DTP page or graphics layout during the design phase, but is not printed

invitation *noun* action by a processor to contact another device to allow it to send a message; **invitation to send** = special character transmitted to indicate to a device that the host computer is willing to receive messages

invite *verb* to ask someone to do something

involve *verb* to have to do with; to include (something) in a process; *backing up involves copying current working files onto a separate storage disk*

I/O = INPUT/OUTPUT referring to the receiving *or* transmitting of data; **I/O address** = the memory location that is used by an I/O port to transfer data with the CPU; **I/O bound** = processor that is doing very little processing since its time is taken up reading *or* writing data from a I/O port; **I/O buffer** = temporary storage area for data waiting to be input *or* output; **I/O bus** = cable linking peripherals (such as a keyboard *or* printer) to a CPU parallel link, allowing transfer of data and control signals between a CPU and memory *or* peripheral devices; **I/O channel** = link between a processor and peripheral, allowing data transfer; **I/O device** = peripheral (such as a terminal in a workstation) which can be used for both inputting and outputting data to a processor; **I/O instruction** = computer programming instruction that allows data to be input *or* output from a processor; **I/O mapping** = method of assigning a special address to each I/O port that does not use any memory locations; *compare with* MEMORY MAPPED; **I/O port** = circuit *or* connector that provides an input/output channel to another device; *see also* SERIAL PORT, PARALLEL PORT

ion *noun* charged particle

COMMENT: an ion is an atom that has gained *or* lost an extra electron, producing a negative *or* positive ion

ion deposition *noun* printing technology that works in a similar way to a laser printer, but instead of using light, it uses a printhead that deposits ions to create a charged image which attracts the toner; used for very high-speed printers

ionosphere *noun* layer of charged particles surrounding the earth

COMMENT: the ionosphere extends from 50km above the surface of the earth

i/p *or* **I/P** = INPUT

IP (a) = INFORMATION PROVIDER company or user that provides an information source for use in a videotext system or on the Internet (such as a company providing weather information or stock market reports); **ip terminal** = special visual display unit that allows users to create and edit videotext pages before sending to the main videotext page database **(b)** = INTERNET PROTOCOL TCP/IP standard that defines how data is transferred over a network; **IP address** = unique, 32-bit number which identifies computers that want to connect to a TCP/IP network; **IP datagram** = packet of data transferred across a TCP/IP network; **IP multicast** = process of sending out one set of data to several recipients simultaneously

IP spoofing method of gaining unauthorised access to a computer (or network) by immitating the IP address of an authorised computer or device

> COMMENT: Each device on the network has its own unique address (its IP address) and many security systems block or allow access to networks based on the computer's IP address. A hacker needs to find out which IP address is allowed (or trusted), then modifies the header information in the data packets from his computer to include this IP address and so allowing access to the target computer. Newer routers and firewalls use a range of techniques to spot this scheme and block the data.

IPng = INTERNET PROTOCOL NEXT GENERATION new version of IP (Internet Protocol) that allows more computers to connect to the Internet and supports more data traffic; *see also* IP

ips *(film)* **(a)** = INCHES PER SECOND **(b)** = INSTRUCTIONS PER SECOND

IPsec = IP SECURITY security protocol that allows information to be transferred securely over the Internet and is used primarily to run and support secure virtual private networks (VPNs); *see also* = HEADER, PACKET, PUBLIC-KEY ENCRYPTION, VPN

> COMMENT: The system works with packets of data at the IP layer and supports two types of public-key data encryption. The first, called Transport mode encrypts the data within a packet, but does not touch the header information (that contains the destination address, subject and source of a packet); a second mode, Tunnel mode, provides a greater level of

> security by encrypting all of the packet, including the header information.

IR = INFORMATION RETRIEVAL

IRC (i) = INFORMATION RETRIEVAL CENTRE; (ii) = INTERNET RELAY CHAT

iris *noun* small, adjustable hole in a camera between the lens and the film; the size can be changed to regulate the amount of light passing through it to the film

IRQs = INTERRUPT REQUESTS

> COMMENT: an IRQ is a signal sent to the central processing unit (CPU) to temporarily suspend normal processing and transfer control to an interrupt handling routine IRQ Device (in a PC): 0=System timer, 1=Keyboard, 2=Bus mouse or network card, 3=COM2, COM4, 4=COM1, COM3, 5=LPT2, CD-ROM, 6=Floppy disk, 7=LPT1, sound card, 8=Realtime clock, 9=not used, 10=not used, 11=not used, 12=not used, 13=Maths coprocessor, 14=Hard disk, 15=not used

irradiation *noun* light diffused by the silver grains contained in the film emulsion

irretrievable *adjective* which cannot be retrieved; *the files are irretrievable since the computer crashed*

IRSG = INTERNET RESEARCH STEERING GROUP

IS = INDEXED SEQUENTIAL (STORAGE)

ISA = INDUSTRY STANDARD ARCHITECTURE standard used for the 16-bit expansion bus in an IBM PC or compatible; *compare with* EISA, MCA

> COMMENT: this has been replaced as a standard in more powerful PCs by either the MCA or EISA bus which provide a 32-bit data path and bus-mastering; local bus is often used for peripherals that require high-speed data transfer, such as a network or graphics adapter; there are two types: the VL-bus (from VESA) and Intel's PCI bus - both allow direct data transfer between main memory and the peripheral

ISAM = INDEXED SEQUENTIAL ACCESS METHOD

ISAPI = INTERNET SERVER APPLICATION PROGRAM

INTERFACE (on a Windows NT server) set of commands and procedures that allow web server software to access other applications on the same server running Windows NT

ISBN = INTERNATIONAL STANDARD BOOK NUMBER

ISDN = INTEGRATED SERVICES DIGITAL NETWORK standard method of transmitting digital data over a telephone network at high speeds - faster than a normal modem

ISO = INTERNATIONAL STANDARDS ORGANIZATION; **ISO 9660** = standard method of storing files on a CD-ROM, used in many formats including PhotoCD; its predecessor was High Sierra; **ISO/OSI model** = INTERNATIONAL STANDARDS ORGANIZATION/OPEN SYSTEM INTERCONNECTION layered architecture that defines how computers and networks should interact

isolate *verb* (a) to separate something from a system (b) to insulate (something) electrically; **isolated adaptive routing** = method of controlling message transmission path

isolation *noun* being isolated; **isolation transformer** = transformer used to isolate equipment from direct connection with the mains electricity supply, in case of voltage spikes, etc.

isolator *noun* device *or* material which isolates

isometric view *noun* (*in graphics*) a drawing that shows all three dimensions of an object in equal proportion; an isometric view does not show any perspective

isotropic *adjective* with the same properties in all dimensions and directions; **isotropic radiator** = antenna that transmits in all directions

ISP = INTERNET SERVICE PROVIDER

ISR = INFORMATION STORAGE AND RETRIEVAL

ISSN = INTERNATIONAL STANDARD SERIAL NUMBER

IT = INFORMATION TECHNOLOGY

italic *adjective & noun* type of character font in which the characters slope to the right; *the headline is printed in 10 point italic*; **italics** = italic characters; *all the footnotes are printed in italics*

item *noun* single thing among many; *a data item can be a word or a series of figures or a record in a file*

iterate *noun* loop *or* series of instructions in a program which repeat over and over again until the program is completed

iteration *noun* repeated application of a program to solve a problem

ITS = INVITATION TO SEND

IV = INTERACTIVE VIDEO

Jj

jabber *noun* continuous random signal transmitted by a faulty adapter card *or* node on a network

jack *or* **jack plug** *noun* plug which consists of a single pin; normally used with audio equipment (such as a headphone or microphone)

jacket *noun* cover for a book *or* disk; *the book jacket has the author's name on it*

jaggies *plural noun* jagged edges which appear along diagonal or curved lines displayed on a computer screen, caused by the size of each pixel; *see also* ALIASING, ANTI-ALIASING

jam 1 *noun* process *or* mechanism which has stopped working due to a fault; *a jam in the paper feed* **2** *verb* **(a)** *(of a device)* to stop working because something is blocking the functioning; *the recorder's not working because the tape is jammed in the motor; lightweight copier paper will feed without jamming; the switchboard was jammed with incoming calls* **(b)** to prevent a transmission from being correctly received by transmitting a strong noise at the same frequency (often used to prevent unauthorized transmission); *the TV signals are being jammed from that tower*

jam-sync *noun* regeneration of a time-code, especially when video tape editing, to make sure that the numbers are in ascending order throughout the tape

JANET = JOINT ACADEMIC NETWORK wide area network that connects universities and academic establishments

jar *verb* to give a sharp shock to a device; *you can cause trouble by turning off or jarring the PC while the disk read heads are moving*

Java programming language developed by Sun Microsystems; it is used to develop software and is often used to create applets for the Internet that enhance the functions of a web page; **Java Beans** = software system (developed by Sun Microsystems) that provides objects within the Java programming language, that is similar to COM and CORBA and can work with both these standards; **JavaScript** = programming language made up of instructions that can be included within a web page (the commands are included within the HTML file that contains the web page); *see also* ACTIVEX APPLET, VBSCRIPT

COMMENT: JavaScript commands carry out a function to enhance the web page, such as providing the time of day, animation or form processing; Java applet is a self-contained program file that is downloaded separately from the web page and run on the user's computer; a JavaScript program is a series of commands included within a web page HTML file and executed by the web browser. To write JavaScript you need to learn the script commands and then use an editor to add them to your web page file; to create a Java application you need a program compiler and programming skills;

JCL = JOB CONTROL LANGUAGE commands that describe the identification of and resources required by a job that a computer has to process

JDBC = JAVA DATABASE CONNECTIVITY

jelly *noun (film)* colour filter which is put in front of a lighting source; *see* GEL

jet *see* INK-JET PRINTER

jingle *noun* short easily-remembered tune used to advertise a product on television

jitter *noun* rapid small up and down movements of characters *or* pixels on a screen *or* movement of image bits in a facsimile transmission; *looking at this screen jitter is giving me a headache*

JK-flip-flop *noun* flip-flop device with two inputs (J and K) and two complementary outputs that are dependent on the inputs

job *noun* task *or* number of tasks *or* work to be processed as a single unit; *the next job to be processed is to sort all the records*; **job control file** = file which contains instructions in a JCL; **job control language (JCL)** = commands that describe the identification of and resources required by a job that a computer has to process; **job number** = number which is given to a job to be processed; **job orientated language** = computer programming language that provides specialized instructions relating to job control tasks and processing; **job orientated terminal** = computer terminal used for a particular task; **job priority** = importance of a job compared to others; **job queue** *or* **job stream** = number of tasks arranged in an order waiting to be processed in a multitasking *or* batch system; **job scheduling** = arranging the order in which jobs are processed; **job step** = one unit of processing involved in a task

jobbing printer *noun* person who does small printing jobs, such as printing business cards

jog *verb* to advance a video tape by one frame at a time

joggle *verb* to align a stack of punched cards *or* sheets of paper

join 1 *verb* **(a)** to put several things together; *they joined several pieces of paper to make an extra large sheet* **(b)** to combine two or more pieces of information to produce a single unit of information; **join files** = instruction to produce a new file consisting of one file added to the end of another **2** *noun* an edit or splice between two shots

joint academic network *see* JANET

joint photographic expert group *see* JPEG

journal *noun* **(a)** note of all communications to and from a terminal; **journal file** = stored record of every communication between a user and the central computer, used to help retrieve files

after a system crash *or* fault **(b)** list of any changes *or* updates to a file; *the modified records were added to the master file and noted in the journal* **(c)** learned journal = specialized magazine

journalist *noun* person who writes for a newspaper

joystick *noun* device that allows a user either to move a cursor around the screen by moving an upright rod connected to the computer *or* to control the remote action of a robot or device; **joystick port** = circuit and connector used to interface a joystick with a computer; *(film)* **joystick zoom control** = zoom lens control button which starts the motor which zooms the lens in or out; *a joystick port is provided with the home computer*

COMMENT: joysticks are mostly used for computer games and CAD *or* desktop publishing packages. In order to use a joystick, a joystick controller card needs to be fitted inside your PC. The first PCs had joystick ports fitted, but now it is common for the sound card to provide the joystick port

JPEG JOINT PHOTOGRAPHIC EXPERT GROUP ISO/CCITT standard for compressing images; **JPEG++** = an extension to JPEG that allows parts of an image to be compressed in different ways

COMMENT: the compressed image is not as sharp as the original; JPEG can either work through hardware or software routines and works as follows: the image is divided into a matrix of tiny pixels, every other pixel is ignored and the grid is divided into blocks of 8x8 pixels, the algorithm then calculates the average of the blocks and so can delete one block - the decompression is the reverse of this process. MPEG is a similar standard that is used with full-motion colour digital video

JScript scripting language, similar to JavaScript, developed by Microsoft

judder *noun* unwanted movement in a printing *or* facsimile machine that results in a distorted picture

jukebox *noun* CD-ROM player that can hold several discs at the same time and load and play a disc automatically

jumbo chip *noun* integrated circuit made using the whole of a semiconductor wafer; *see also* WAFER SCALE INTEGRATION

jump *verb* **(a)** programming command to end one set of instructions and direct the processor to another section of the program; **conditional jump** = situation where the processor is directed to another section of the program only if a condition is met; **jump on zero** = conditional jump executed if a flag *or* register is zero **(b)** to miss a page *or* a line *or* a space when printing; *the typewriter jumped two lines; the paging system has jumped two folio numbers*

jump cut *verb (in film and video editing)* to eliminate a part of the continuous action within a scene

jump out *verb (film)* to delete frames in film or video tape editing

jumper *noun* temporary wire connection on a circuit board; **jumper-selectable** = circuit *or* device whose options can be selected by positioning various wire connections; *the printer's typeface was jumper-selectable*

junction *noun* **(a)** connection between wires *or* cables; **junction box** = small box where a number of wires can be interconnected **(b)** region between two areas of semiconductor which have different doping levels (such as a p-type and n-type area), resulting in a potential difference between them; **bipolar junction transistor (BJT)** = transistor constructed of 3 layers of alternating types of doped semiconductor (p-n-p *or* n-p-n), each layer having a terminal labelled as emitter, base and

collector; usually the base controls the current flow between emitter and collector

junior (spot) *noun (film)* spotlight which uses a 1,000 to 2,000 watt lamp

junk 1 *noun* information *or* hardware which is useless *or* out-of-date *or* non-functional; **junk mail** = form letters containing special offers *or* advertisements; **space junk** = satellites and hardware that are out of action and no longer used, but are still in orbit in space **2** *verb* to get rid of a file; to make a file *or* piece of hardware redundant; **to junk a file** = to erase *or* delete from storage a file that is no longer used

justification *noun* moving data bits *or* characters to the left *or* right so that the lines have straight margins; **hyphenation and justification** *or* **H & J** = justifying lines to a set width, splitting the long words correctly at the end of each line; *an American hyphenation and justification program will not work with British English spellings*

justify *verb* **(a)** to align text so that it is level on both right and left margins, normally by adding spaces between words; **justify inhibit** = to prevent a word processor justifying a document; **hyphenate and justify** = to break long words correctly where they split at the ends of lines, so as to give a straight right margin; **left justify** = to print with a straight left-hand margin; **right justify** = to print with a straight right-hand margin; *this book would look far neater if you right justified each line* **(b)** to shift the contents of a computer register by a set amount **(c)** to set lines of printed text as wide as possible in a certain page size

Kk

K *prefix* **(a)** = KILO symbol used to represent one thousand **(b)** symbol used to represent 1,024

K56flex communications standard developed by Hayes Corporation and other manufacturers for a range of high-speed modems that can transfer data at 56,000 bits per second; *see also* V SERIES, X2

Kaleida Labs *noun* company formed as a joint venture between Apple and IBM to produce cross-platform multimedia authoring tools, the first of which is called ScriptX; *see also* SCRIPTX

Karnaugh map *noun* graphical representation of states and conditions in a logic circuit; *the prototype was checked for hazards with a Karnaugh map*

Kb *or* **Kbit** = KILOBIT measure of 1,024 bits

KB *or* **Kbyte** = KILOBYTE unit of measure for high capacity storage devices meaning 1,024 bytes; *the new disk drive has a 100KB capacity; the original PC cannot access more than 640K bytes of RAM*

COMMENT: 1,024 is the strict definition in computer *or* electronics applications, being equal to a convenient power of two; these abbreviations can also be taken to equal approximately one thousand, even in computing applications. 1KB is roughly equal to 1,000 output characters in a PC

Kermit *noun* file transfer protocol usually used when downloading data from a mainframe or via a modem

kern *verb* to adjust the space between pairs of letters so that they are printed closer together; *we have kerned 'T' and 'o' so they are closer together*

kernel *noun* basic essential instruction routines required as a basis for any operations in a computer system; **graphics kernel** = number of basic commands required to illuminate in various shades and colours the pixels on a screen; these are then used to provide more complex functions such as line *or* shape plotting

COMMENT: kernel routines are usually hidden from the user; they are used by the operating system for tasks such as loading a program or displaying text on a screen

kerning *noun* slight overlapping of certain printed character areas to prevent large spaces between them, giving a neater appearance

key 1 *noun* **(a)** button on a keyboard that operates a switch; *there are 64 keys on the keyboard*; **key click** = sound produced by a computer to allow the operator to know that the key he pressed has been registered; **key force** = pressure required to close the switch in a key; **key matrix** = design of interconnections between keys on a keyboard; **key number** = numeric code used to identify which key has been pressed; **key overlay** = paper placed over the keys on a keyboard describing their functions for a particular application; **key punch** = machine used for punching data into punched cards by means of a keyboard; **key rollover** = use of a buffer between the keyboard and computer to provide rapid key stroke storage for fast typists who hit several keys in rapid succession; **key strip** = piece of paper above certain keys used to remind the operator of their special function; **key travel** = distance a key has to be pressed before it registers **(b)** *(names of keys)* **alphanumeric key** *or* **character key** = key which produces a character (letter *or* symbol *or* figure); **function key** = key which has a specific task *or* sequence of instructions; *tags can be allocated to function keys*; **shift key** = key which provides a second function for a key (usually by moving the output into upper case); **carriage return key** = key which moves a cursor *or* printhead to the beginning of the next line on screen *or* on a typewriter *or* in printing **(c)** important object *or* group of characters in a computer system, used to represent an instruction *or* set of data; **key plate** = initial printing plate used when printing colour images; **key terminal** = most important terminal in a computer system *or* one with the highest priority **(d)** special combination of numbers *or* characters that are used with a cipher to encrypt *or* decrypt a message; *type this key into the machine, that will decode the last message*; **key management** = the selection, protection and safe transmission of cipher keys **(e)** identification code *or* word used for a stored record *or* data item; *we selected all the records with the word disk in their keys*; **key field** = field which identifies entries in a record **2** *verb* **to key in** = to enter text *or* commands via a keyboard; *they keyed in the latest data*

key frame *noun* **(a)** single picture in an animation that describes the main actions in the sequence **(b)** *(in hypertext document)* a page that gives the user a choice of destination **(c)** *(in full motion video)* a frame that is recorded in full rather than being compressed or differentially recorded

key grip *(film)* = FIRST GRIP

key light *noun* *(film)* main light which projects the most brightness on to the subject being filmed

keyboard 1 *noun* number of keys fixed together in some order, used to enter information into a computer *or* to produce characters on a typewriter; **ASCII keyboard** = keyboard that provides for every ASCII code; **keyboard layout** = way in which various function and character keys are arranged; **keyboard scan** = method for a computer to determine if a key has been pressed by applying a voltage across each key switch (if the key is pressed a signal will be read by the computer); **keyboard send/receive** = *see* KSAM; **keyboard to disk entry** = system where information entered on a keyboard is stored directly on to disk with no processing; **QWERTY keyboard** = standard English language key layout (the first 6 letters on the top left row of keys are QWERTY) **2** *verb* to enter information by using a keyboard; *it was cheaper to have the manuscript keyboarded by another company*

keyboarder *noun* person who enters data via a keyboard

keyboarding *noun* action of entering data using a keyboard; *the cost of keyboarding is calculated in keystrokes per hour*

keyed sequential access method *see* KSAM

keyer *noun* *(film)* an effect from a vision mixer which is created by cutting a hole in the principal picture whose outline is decided by another camera output; in this way, captions or titles may be keyed into a picture; *see* CHROMA KEY

keying *noun* method of overlaying one particular video signal onto another

keypad *noun* group of special keys used for certain applications; *you can use the numeric keypad to enter the figures*; **numeric keypad** = set of nine keys with figures, included in most computer keyboards as a separate group, used for entering large amounts of data in numeric form

keystroke *noun* action of pressing a key; **keystroke count** = counting of each keystroke made, often used to calculate keyboarding costs; **keystroke verification** = check made on each key pressed to make sure it is valid for a particular application

key-to-disk *noun* system where data is keyed in and stored directly on disk without any processing

keyword *noun* **(a)** command word used in a programming language to provide a function **(b)** important *or* informative word in a title *or* document that describes its contents **(c)** word which is relevant *or* important to a text; *the BASIC keyword PRINT will display text on the screen*; *computer is a keyword in IT*; **keyword and context (KWAC)** = library index system using important words from the text and title as index entries; **keyword in context (KWIC)** = library index system that uses keywords from the title *or* text of a book *or* document as an indexed entry, followed by the title *or* text it relates to; **keyword out of context (KWOC)** = library index system that indexes book *or* document titles under any relevant keywords

---

the new keyboard is almost unchanged, and features sixteen programmable function keys

Micro Decision

---

it uses a six button keypad to select the devices and functions

Byte

KHz = KILOHERTZ unit of frequency measurement equal to one thousand Hertz; *see also* HERTZ

COMMENT: the higher the KHz number, the higher pitched the sound. Normal speech has a very limited frequency range - mostly between 300Hz and 2.4KHz - whereas music and other sounds can be heard at far higher and lower frequencies. In the specification of a sound card, KHz can define two separate functions: the first is the range of frequencies that the sound card can output and the second, and more usual use, is the frequency at which the sound card takes samples of a sound when recording it onto a disk. A sound card looks at the level of a sound (from a microphone) thousands of times each second and so builds up a picture of the sound. The more times it takes a sample, the more accurate the recording - and the number of times the sound card takes a sample per second is described in KHz. A good sound card would cope with 22KHz or 44KHz samples - 22,000 or 44,000 samples each second

---

kicker *noun (film)* spotlight which is used to produce a highlight effect in backlighting

kill *verb* to erase a file *or* stop a program during execution; **kill file** = command to erase a stored file completely; **kill job** = command to halt a computer job while it is running

kilo *prefix* **(a)** meaning one thousand; **kilobaud** = 1,000 bits per second; **kilohertz** *or* **KHz** = unit of frequency measurement equal to one thousand Hertz; **kilo instructions per second (KIPS)** = one thousand computer instructions processed every second, used as a measure of computer power; **kilo-ohm** = resistance of one thousand ohms; **kiloVolt-ampere output rating (KVA)** = method of measuring the power rating of a device; **kilowatt** *or* **kW** = power measurement equal to one thousand watts **(b)** meaning 1,024 units (used only in computer and electronics applications); **kilobit** *or* **Kb** = 1,024 bits of data; **kilobyte** *or* **KB** *or* **Kbyte** = unit of measurement for high capacity storage devices meaning 1,024 bytes of data; **kiloword** *or* **KW** = unit of measurement of 1,024 computer words; *see also* WORD

kimball tag *noun* coded card attached to a product in a shop, containing information about the product that is read by a scanner when the product is sold

kinetograph *noun (film)* early cinematographic film strip machine

kiosk *noun* small booth with a screen, means of user input and a computer, used to provide information for the general public

KIPS = KILO INSTRUCTIONS PER SECOND one thousand computer instructions processed every second, used as a measure of computer power

kludge *or* **kluge** *noun (informal)* **(a)** temporary correction made to a badly written *or* constructed piece of software *or* to a keyboarding error **(b)** hardware which should be used for demonstration purposes only

kluged *adjective* temporarily repaired

knob *noun* round button (such as on a receiver *or* TV set), which can be turned to control some process; *turn the on/off knob; the brightness can be regulated by turning a knob at the back of the monitor*

knowledge *noun* what is known; **knowledge-based system** = computer system that applies the stored reactions, instructions and knowledge of experts in a particular field to a problem; *see also* EXPERT SYSTEM; **knowledge engineering** = designing and writing expert computer systems

Kodak PhotoCD *see* PHOTOCD

KSAM = KEYED SEQUENTIAL ACCESS METHOD file structure that allows data to be accessed using key fields or key field content

KSR = KEYBOARD SEND/RECEIVE terminal which has a keyboard and monitor, and is linked to a CPU; *compare with* ASR

KVA = KILOVOLT-AMPERE OUTPUT RATING

KW (a) = KILOWATT **(b)** = KILOWORD

KWAC = KEYWORD AND CONTEXT library indexing system using important words from the text and title as indexed entries

KWIC = KEYWORD IN CONTEXT library indexing system that uses keywords from the title *or* text of a book *or* document as an indexed entry followed by the text it relates to

KWOC = KEYWORD OUT OF CONTEXT library indexing system that indexes books *or* document titles under any relevant keywords

LI

L *(film)* = LAMBERT unit of surface brightness

L2TP = LAYER TWO TUNNELING PROTOCOL network protocol (an extension to the PPP protocol) that allows the data from small Virtual Private Networks (VPN) to be transferred over a network (such as the public Internet) by enclosing the network packets from the VPN within a special packet that can then travel over the Internet (a process called tunneling); *see also* PPP, TUNNELING, VIRTUAL PRIVATE NETWORK

label 1 *noun* **(a)** (i) word *or* other symbol used in a computer program to identify a routine *or* statement; (ii) character(s) used to identify a piece of data *or* a file; *BASIC uses many program labels such as line numbers*; **label field** = an item of data in a record that contains a label; **label record** = record containing identification for a stored file **(b)** piece of paper *or* card attached to something to show its price *or* an address *or* instructions for use; **address label** = label with an address on it; **continuous labels** = removable adhesive labels attached to a backing sheet that can be fed into a printer; **label printer** = special printer used to print addresses onto continuous labels; **price label** = label showing a price **2** *verb* to print an address *or* a price on a label (NOTE: **labelling - labelled** but US **labeling - labeled**)

labelling *noun* (i) putting a label on something; (ii) printing labels; *the word-processor has a special utility allowing simple and rapid labelling* (NOTE: no plural)

COMMENT: there are two ways of labelling a floppy disk - the first is to stick a paper label on the outside and write on it, and the second is to give the disk an electronic label. This is called the volume name. If you want to give a short description to a floppy disk (which will appear at the top of any DIR command or within the MyComputer window), use the LABEL command at the DOS prompt or, in Windows 95, highlight the floppy disk icon, select its properties window and type in the new volume name

laboratory *noun* place where scientists work on research and development of new products; *the new chip is being developed in the university laboratories*

lace *verb* to thread film on to a projector or tape on to a cassette recorder

lag *noun* **(a)** time taken for a signal to pass through a circuit, such that the output is delayed compared to the input; *time lag is noticeable on international phone calls* **(b)** time taken for an image to be no longer visible after it has been displayed on a TV screen (this is caused by long persistence phosphor)

lambert *see* L

laminate *verb* to cover a paper with a thin film of plastic, to give it a glossy look; *the book has a laminated cover*

lamp *noun* an electrical component which provides artificial light by heating a thin wire within a glass bulb filled with an inert gas

LAN *or* **lan** = LOCAL AREA NETWORK network where various terminals and equipment are all within a short distance of one another (at a maximum distance of about 500m, for example in the same building), and can be interconnected by cables; **LAN segment** = part of a network separated from the rest by a bridge; **LAN server** = dedicated computer and backing storage facility used by terminals and operators of a LAN; *see also* PEER-TO-PEER NETWORK; *compare with* WAN

The opportunities to delete and destroy data are far greater on our LAN than in the days when we had a mainframe. PC people are culturally different from mainframe people. You really don't think about security problems when you can physically lock your system up in a closet

Computing

---

since most of the LAN hardware is already present, the installation costs are only $50 per connection

Practical Computing

landing zone *noun* area of a hard disk which does not carry data, the head can come into contact with the disk in this area without damaging the disk or data; *see also* PARK

landline *noun* communications link that uses cable laid in the ground to physically and electrically link two devices

landscape *noun* orientation of a page *or* piece of paper where the longest edge is horizontal; *compare with* PORTRAIT

language *noun* (a) spoken *or* written words which are used to communicate with other people; *he speaks several European languages*; **foreign language** = language which is spoken by people of another country (b) system of words *or* symbols which allows communication with computers (such as one that allows computer instructions to be entered as words which are easy to understand, and then translates them into machine code); **assembly language** *or* **assembler language** = programming language used to code information which will then be converted to machine code; **command language** = programming language made up of procedures for various tasks, that can be called up by a series of commands; **graphic language** = computer programming language with inbuilt commands that are useful when displaying graphics; **high-level language (HLL)** = computer programming language that is easy to learn and allows the user to write programs using words and commands that are easy to understand and look like English words, the program is then translated into machine code, with one HLL instruction often representing more than one machine code instruction; **language assembler** = program used to translate and assemble a source code program into a machine executable binary form; **language interpreter** = any program that takes each consecutive line of source program and translates it into another language; **language support environment** = hardware and software tools supplied to help the programmer write programs in a particular language; **language translation** = using a computer to translate text from one language to another; **language translator** = program that converts code written in one language into equivalent code in another language; **low-level language** = language which is long and complex to program, where each instruction represents a single machine code instruction; **programming language** = software that allows a user to enter a program in a certain language and then to execute it; *assembly language uses mnemonics to represent machine code instructions; machine code is the basic binary patterns that instruct the processor to perform various tasks*

COMMENT: There are three main types of computer languages: machine code, assembler and high-level language. The higher the level the language is, the easier it is to program and understand, but the slower it is to execute. The following are the commonest high-level languages: ADA, ALGOL, APL, BASIC, C, COBOL, COMAL, CORAL, FORTH, FORTRAN, LISP, LOGO, PASCAL, PL/1, POP-2, PROLOG

LAP = LINK ACCESS PROTOCOL CCITT standard protocol used to start and maintain links over an X.25 network; **LAP-B** = CCITT standard setup routine to establish a link between a DCE and DTE (such as a computer and modem); **LAP-M** = LINK ACCESS PROTOCOL FOR MODEMS variation of LAP-B protocol used in V.42 error correcting modems

lap *noun* (a) a person's knees, when he is sitting down; *he placed the computer on his lap and keyboarded some orders while* *sitting in his car* **(b)** overlap of printed colours which prevents any gaps showing

lapel microphone *noun* small microphone that is pinned to the someone's jacket

laptop computer *noun* computer that is light enough to carry (but not so small as to fit in a pocket) and normally has a clam-shell construction with a fold-down lid that houses the screen, a keyboard and a floppy disk and hard disk drive; an internal battery pack provides power for a few hours' use; *compare with* PDA

Michael Business Systems has provided research company BMRB with 240 Toshiba laptop computers in a deal valued at $300,000. The deal includes a three-year maintenance contract

Computing

large model *noun (in an Intel processor)* memory model in which both code and data can exceed 64Kb in size, but combined size should be less than 1Mb

large-scale integration (LSI) *noun* integrated circuit with 500 to 10,000 components

laser *noun* = LIGHT AMPLIFICATION BY STIMULATED EMISSION OF RADIATION electrical device that produces coherent light of a single wavelength in a narrow beam, used to read data from a CD-ROM and to charge points in a laser printer; **laser beam recording** = production of characters on a light-sensitive film by a laser beam controlled directly from a computer; **laser beam communications** = use of a modulated laser beam as a line-of-sight communications medium; **laser disc** = COMPACT DISC plastic disc containing binary data in the form of small etched dots that can be read by a laser, used to record high quality TV images *or* sound in digital form; **laser emulsion storage** = digital storage technique using a laser to expose light-sensitive material; **injection laser** = solid-state laser device used to transmit data as pulses of light down an optic fibre

laser printer *noun* high-resolution computer printer that uses a laser source to print high-quality dot matrix character

patterns on paper; *see also* DOT-MATRIX PRINTER, INK-JET PRINTER

COMMENT: a laser printer creates an image on a charged drum (using a laser). This then attracts particles of fine black toner and the drum transfers the image to the paper which is then heated to melt the toner onto the paper. A laser printer offers high-resolution printing with, typically 600dpi. There are actually very few printers that use a laser; most use a laser diode or an LED light source for the same effect

LaserDisc *noun* optical disc that is either 12, 20 or 30cm in diameter, used to store analog video and digital sound and generally used to refer to videodiscs that use the Philips LaserVision system

LaserJet *or* **Hewlett Packard LaserJet** *or* **HP LaserJet** *noun* laser printer manufactured by Hewlett Packard that uses its PCL language to describe a page (or PostScript in the newer LaserJet 4M series)

LaserVision original interactive videodisc format, developed by Philips, that provides analog video and two analog audio signals on a 30cm diameter disc; two formats are used to store the video images: CAV and CLV; *see* CAV, CLV, VIDEODISC

LaserWriter *noun* laser printer manufactured by Apple that uses the PostScript page description language

last in first out (LIFO) *noun* queue system that reads the last item stored, first; *this computer stack uses a last in first out data retrieval method*; *compare with* FIRST IN FIRST OUT

latch 1 *noun* electronic component that maintains an output condition until it receives an input signal to change; *see also* FLIP-FLOP **2** *verb* to set an output state; *the output latched high until we reset the computer*

other features of the device include a programmable latch bypass which allows any number of latches from 0 to 8 so that this device may be used as latched or combinatorial

Electronics & Power

latency *noun* time delay between the moment when an instruction is given to a computer and the performance of the instruction (as between a request for data and the data being transferred from memory)

latent image *noun* the recorded invisible image in exposed but undeveloped film

lateral reversal *noun* creating the mirror image of a picture by swapping left and right

latitude *noun* *(film)* acceptable range of exposure that is possible in film stock

launch 1 *noun* **(a)** putting a new product on the market; *the launch of the new PC has been put back six months* **(b)** putting a satellite in space; *the launch date for the network will be September* **2** *verb* **(a)** to put a new product on the market; *the new PC was launched at the Personal Computer Show; launching costs for the computer range were calculated at $250,000* **(b)** to put a satellite into space **(c)** to start *or* run a program; *you launch the word-processor by double-clicking on this icon*

launch amplifier *noun* amplifier used to boost the television signals before they are transmitted over a cable network

launch vehicle *noun* spacecraft used to transport a satellite from earth into space

lavacier *noun* microphone which is hung around the neck

lay in *verb* to synchronize a frame of film with the music *or* sound tracks

lay out *verb* to plan and design the positions and sizes of a piece of work to be printed; *the designers have laid out the pages in A4 format*

layer *noun* **(a)** division of sections of space at certain distances from the earth into separate regions used for various radio communications (these are: D-Region from 50 - 90km above earth's surface, E-Region from 90 - 150km above earth's surface, F-Region from 150 - 400km above the earth's surface) **(b)** ISO/OSI standards defining the stages a message has to pass through when being transmitted from one computer to another over a local area network; **application layer** = the program that requests a transmission; **data link layer** = layer that sends packets of data to the next link, and deals with error correction;

network layer = layer that decides on the routes to be used, the costs, etc.; **physical layer** = layer that defines the rules for bit rate, power, medium for transmission, etc.; **presentation layer** = section that agrees on format, codes and request for start/end of a connection; **session layer** = layer that makes the connection/disconnection between a transmitter and receiver; **transport layer** = layer that checks and controls the quality of the connection **(c)** feature of graphics software that provides a stack of separate drawing areas that can be overlaid to produce the final image, or controlled and manipulated independently; often used in complex images: for example, the background might be on layer 1, an image of a house on layer 2 and any special effects on layer 3; the finished picture is made up of the three layers combined and viewed together

layered *adjective* consisting of layers

layout *noun* **(a)** mock-up of a finished piece of printed work showing the positioning and sizes of text and graphics; *the design team is working on the layouts for the new magazine* **(b)** rules governing the data input and output from a computer; **keyboard layout** = arrangement of the keys on a keyboard; different countries have different keyboard layouts - the UK and US have a standard QWERTY layout which refers to the order of the first keys on the top left-hand corner of the keyboard; other countries have different key layouts according to their accents and local requirements; **page** *or* **paper layout** = way of using a sheet of paper with the long edge horizontally (called landscape) or with the long edge vertically (called portrait); *see also* LANDSCAPE, PORTRAIT

LBR = LASER BEAM RECORDING producing characters on a light sensitive film by laser beam directly controlled from a computer

LC circuit *noun* simple inductor-capacitor circuit that acts as a filter *or* oscillator

LCD = LIQUID CRYSTAL DISPLAY liquid crystal that turns black when a voltage is applied, used in many watches, calculators and other small digital displays; **LCD shutter printer** = page printer that uses an LCD panel in front of a bright light to describe images onto the photosensitive drum; the LCD panel stops the light passing through, except at pixels that describe the image

COMMENT: there are several types of LCD display. Passive Matrix, in which the transistors controlling the LCD pixels are outside of the display, provides sharp monochrome but a less defined colour image. There are two types of Passive Matrix: TN (twisted nematic) is used in cheaper screens and provides black on a grey background; STN (supertwisted nematic) is used on most laptops for both mono and colour displays. Active Addressing provides a sharper display than an equivalent Passive Matrix display. Dual Scan Passive Matrix effectively doubles the refresh rate of the screen and improves the sharpness of Passive Matrix colour screens. Active Matrix or thin film transistor LCD (TFT) is used in most high-end colour laptop screens; the controlling transistors are built into each pixel for each colour - this provides the best quality colour and contrast, but is the most expensive

LCD screens can run for long periods on ordinary or rechargeable batteries

Micro Decision

LCP = LINK CONTROL PROCEDURE rules defining the transmission of data over a channel

LDAP LIGHTWEIGHT DIRECTORY ACCESS PROTOCOL standard system that provides directory services over the Internet; derived from the X.500 standard, LDAP is beginning to be included in many Internet applications and provides a way of organising, locating and using resources over the Internet listed within its database

LDS = LOCAL DISTRIBUTION SERVICE TV signal relay station that transmits signals to another point from which they are distributed over cable

lead in page *noun* videotext page that directs the user to other pages of interest

lead *noun* (a) electrical conducting wire (b) thin piece of metal used to give extra space between lines of type before printing

leader *noun* (a) section of magnetic tape *or* photographic film that contains no signal *or* images, used at the beginning of the reel for

identification and to aid the tape machine to pick up the tape (b) row of printed dots

leading *noun* (a) extra space between lines of print, normally measured in points; (b) something that is first or before something else

leading edge *noun* first edge of a punched card that enters the card reader

leading zero *noun* zero digit used to pad out the beginning of a stored number

leaf *noun* (a) page of a book (printed on both sides) (b) final node in a data tree structure

leaflet *noun* small publicity sheet (usually one page folded in half)

leak 1 *noun* (a) loss of secret documents *or* a breach of security; *a leak informed the press of our new designs* (b) gradual loss of charge from a charged component due to faulty insulation **2** *verb* (a) to provide secret information to unauthorized people; *the details of our new software package have been leaked to the press* (b) to lose electric charge gradually; *in this circuit, the capacitor charge leaks out at 10% per second*

leakage *noun* loss of signal strength

signal leakages in both directions can be a major problem in co-axial cable systems

Electronics & Wireless World

learning curve *noun* graphical description of how someone can acquire knowledge (about a product or subject) over time; **steep learning curve** = (a product) that is very difficult to use

lease 1 *noun* written contract for letting *or* renting a piece of equipment for a period against payment of a fee **2** *verb* to let *or* rent equipment for a period; *the company has a policy of only using leased equipment; all the company's computers are leased*; **leased circuit** = electronic circuit *or* communications channel rented for a period; **leased line** = communications channel such as a telephone line, which is rented for the exclusive use of the subscriber

least cost design *noun* best money-saving use of space *or* components; *the budget is only £1000, we need the least cost design for the new circuit*

least recently used algorithm   *see* LRU

least significant digit (LSD)   *noun* digit which occupies the right hand position in a number and so carries least power (equal to the number radix raised to zero = 1); **least significant bit (LSB)** = binary digit occupying the right hand position of a word and carrying the least power of two in the word (usually equal to two raised to zero = 1)

leaving files open *phrase* meaning that a file has not been closed *or* does not contain an end of text marker (this will result in the loss of data since the text will not have been saved)

LED = LIGHT EMITTING DIODE semiconductor diode that emits light when a current is applied; **LED printer** = page printer (similar to a laser printer) that uses an LED light source instead of a laser; *see also* LASER PRINTER

COMMENT: LED displays are used to display small amounts of information, as in pocket calculators, watches, etc.

left justification *noun* **(a)** shifting a binary number to the left hand end of the word containing it **(b)** printing command that makes sure that the left hand margin of the text is even

left-handed mouse *noun* configuration of a mouse so that the function of the two buttons are reversed; if you are left-handed you can swap the functions of the two keys using the setup software supplied with the mouse or by using the Settings function of Windows

legacy older technology or a previous version that is still supported in new developments to allow existing applications and hardware to still be used

legibility *noun* being able to be read; *the keyboarders find the manuscript lacks legibility*

legible *adjective* which can be read easily; *the manuscript is written in pencil and is hardly legible*

length *noun* how long something is; the number of data items in a variable *or* list; **buffer length** = number of data item that can be stored in a buffer while waiting for the processor to attend to them; **file length** = number of characters *or* bytes in a stored file; **length of filename** = number of characters allowed for identification of a file; **line length** = number of characters which can fit into a set line of type

lens *noun* an optical system of transparent glass through which light is refracted on curved surfaces to produce photographic images; **concave lens** = lens that is thinner in the centre than at the edges, bending light out; **convex lens** = lens that is thicker in the centre than the edges, bending light in; **lens aperture** = the opening of a lens system; it may be expressed as a fraction (f)-number, the ratio of focal length to physical opening, or as a measured factor of transmission, T number; **lens coating** = fluoride coating which is used to decrease reflection and to let more light through the lens of the camera; **lens flare** = luminous spot which appears on a film image, caused by the lens having received overbright light from a natural or artificial source; **lens hood** = extension of outer part of lens which prevents unwanted light entering the lens; **lens mount** = device used to fix a lens to a camera; **lens prism** = device which is used for multiple-image photography and is attached to the lens; **lens speed** = the maximum aperture of a lens, relating to the amount of light that can enter the lens; **lens stop** = lens aperture size; **lens spotlight** = a light whose beam is controlled by a single, sliding lens; **lens turret** = a revolving mounting which carries two or more lenses, making it possible to change lenses very quickly

letter *noun* **(a)** piece of writing sent from one person to another *or* from a company to another, to give information, to send an instruction, etc.; **business letter** = letter dealing with business matters; **circular letter** = letter sent to many people; **form letter** *or* **standard letter** = letter sent to several addressees by name without any change to the text **(b)** written *or* printed sign, which goes to make a word (such as A, B, C, etc.); *his name was written in capital letters*

letterhead *noun* name and address of a company printed at the top of the company's notepaper; *business forms and letterheads can now be designed on a PC*

letter-quality (LQ) printing   *noun* feature of some dot-matrix printers to provide characters of the same quality as a typewriter by using dots which are very close together; *see also* NLQ

---

the printer offers reasonable speeds of printing in both draft and letter-quality modes
Which PC?

---

level *noun* **(a)** strength *or* power of an electrical signal; *turn the sound level down, it's far too loud*; **sound pressure level (SPL)** = measurement of the magnitude of the pressure wave conveying sound **(b)** quantity of bits that make up a digital transmitted signal

Level 1 cache *see* L1 CACHE

Level 2 cache *see* L2 CACHE

Level A ADPCM audio quality level with a 20KHz bandwidth, 38.7KHz sample rate and 8-bit samples

Level B ADPCM audio quality level with a 17KHz bandwidth, 38.7KHz sample rate and 4-bit samples

Level C ADPCM audio quality level with an 8.5KHz bandwidth, 18.9KHz sample rate and 4-bit samples

lexical analysis *noun* stage in program translation when the compiling *or* translating software replaces program keywords with machine code instructions

lexicographical order *noun* order of items, where the words are listed in the order of the letters of the alphabet, as in a dictionary

LF (a) = LOW FREQUENCY range of audio frequencies between 5 - 300Hz *or* range of radio frequencies between 30 - 300KHz **(b)** = LINE FEED

librarian *noun* person who works in a library

---

a library of popular shapes and images is supplied
Practical Computing

---

library *noun* **(a)** collection of files *or* documents *or* books *or* records, etc., which can be consulted *or* borrowed by the public, usually kept in a public place; *the editors have checked all the references in the local library; a copy of each new book has to be deposited in the British Library; look up the bibliographical details in the library catalogue* **(b)** collection of programs *or* books belonging to a person; *he has a large*

library of computer games **(c)** **library program** = (i) number of specially written *or* relevant software routines, which a user can insert into his own program, saving time and effort; (ii) group of functions which a computer needs to refer to often, but which are not kept in memory; *the square root function is already in the library program*; **library function** = software routine that a user can insert into his program to provide the function with no effort; **library routine** = prewritten routine that can be inserted into a main program and called up when required

licence *noun* permission given by one manufacturer to another manufacturer to make copies of his products against payment of a fee; *the software is manufactured in this country under licence*

licence agreement *noun* the legal document that accompanies any commercial software product, defining how the software can be used and, importantly, how many people can use it; *unless you buy a network version of a software product, the licence allows one person to use the software*

lifetime *noun* period of time during which a device is useful *or* not outdated; *this new computer has a four-year lifetime*

LIFO = LAST IN FIRST OUT queue system that reads the last item stored, first; *this computer stack uses a LIFO data retrieval method*; *see also* FIFO

lifter *noun* mechanical device that lifts magnetic tape away from the heads when rewinding the tape

ligature *noun* two characters printed together to form a combined character *or* a short line connecting two characters

light 1 *noun* perception of brightness due to electromagnetic effects in the frequency range 400 - 750 nm, which allows a person to see; *the VDU should not be placed under a bright light*; **coherent light** = light beam in which all the waveforms are in phase; **infrared light (IR light)** = electromagnetic radiation just below visible red (often used for communications purposes such as remote control); *(film)* **light box** = a box which is covered by frosted glass against which film or slides can be examined; **light changes** = changes in intensity of the printer light, used to correct overexposed or underexposed film; **light conduit** = fibre optics used to transmit light from one place to another rather than for the transmission of data; **light emitting diode (LED)** = semiconductor diode that emits light when a current is applied (used in calculators and clock displays and as indicators); **light guide** = fine strands of glass or plastic protected by a surrounding material, used for the transmission of light; **light level** = light intensity which is measured in candelas; **light meter** = device which is used to measure light intensity in candelas; **light pen** = computer accessory in the shape of a pen that contains a light-sensitive device that can detect pixels on a video screen (often used with suitable software to draw graphics on a screen or position a cursor); **light pipe** = LIGHT GUIDE; (film) **light source filter** = filter which is used to change the colour or colour temperature of light; **visible light** = range of light colours that can be seen with the human eye; **ultra-violet light (UV light)** = electromagnetic radiation with wavelengths just greater than the visible spectrum, from 200 to 4,000 angstrom (often used to erase data from EPROMs) **2** adjective not dark; **light face** = typeface with thin lines, which appears light on the page

light-sensitive adjective which is sensitive to light; *the photograph is printed on light-sensitive paper*; **light-sensitive device** = device (such as a phototransistor) which is sensitive to light, and produces a change in signal strength or resistance

lighting noun (a) any regulated illumination of an object or person which is being filmed (b) source of this illumination, whether natural or artificial; **lighting rig** = a group of lights and their stands and controls

lightweight adjective which is not heavy; *a lightweight computer which can easily fit into a suitcase; the book is printed on thin, lightweight paper*

LIM EMS = LOTUS, INTEL, MICROSOFT EXPANDED MEMORY SYSTEM; (in an IBM PC) standard that defines extra memory added above the 640Kb limit of conventional memory; this memory can only be used by specially-written programs

limited distance modem noun data transmission device with a very short range that sends pure digital data rather than on a modulated carrier

limiter noun electronic circuit that prevents a signal from going above a certain level; used with audio and video signals to prevent overloading an amplifier

limiting resolution noun maximum number of lines that make up a television picture

limits noun predefined maximum ranges for numbers in a computer

line noun **(a)** physical connection for data transmission (such as a cable between parts of a system or a telephone wire); **line adapter** = electronic circuit that matches the correct signal voltage and impedance for a particular line; **line analyzer** = test equipment that displays the characteristics of a line or the signals carried on the line; **line busy tone** = signal generated to indicate that a connection or telephone line is already in use; **line communications** = signal transmission using a cable link or telegraph wire; **line conditioning** = (techniques) used to keep the quality of data transmissions or signals on a line to a certain standard; **line control** = special codes used to control a communications channel; **line extender** = circuit used to boost a television signal; **line impedance** = impedance of a communications line or cable (equipment should have a matching load to minimize power loss); **line level** = amplitude of a signal transmitted over a cable; **line load** = number of messages transmitted over a line compared to the maximum capacity; **line speed** = rate at which data is sent along a line; **line switching** = communications line and circuit established on demand and held until no longer required; **line transient** = large voltage spike on a line; **telephone line** = cable used to connect a telephone handset with a central exchange **(b)** single long thin mark drawn by a pen or printed on a surface; *the printer has difficulty in reproducing very fine lines*; **line art** = black and white graphics, with no shades of grey; **line drawing** = illustration in which objects are drawn using thin lines, without shading or surface texture; see also WIRE FRAME MODEL; *the book is illustrated with line drawings and halftones* **(c)** one trace by the electron picture beam on a television screen; **line blanking interval** = period of time when the picture beam is not displayed, this is during line flyback; **line drive signal** = signal to start the scanning procedure in a television camera; **line flyback** = electron beam returning from the end of one line to the beginning of the next; **line frequency** = number of picture lines that are scanned per second **(d)** row of characters (printed on a page *or* displayed on a computer screen *or* printer); *each page has 52 lines of text; several lines of manuscript seem to have been missed by the compositor; can we insert an extra line of spacing between the paragraphs?*; **line editor** = piece of software that allows the operator to modify one line of text from a file at a time; **line ending** = character which shows that a line has ended (instructed by pressing the carriage return key); **line feed (LF)** = control on a printer *or* computer terminal that moves the cursor down by one line; **line folding** = move a section of a long line of text onto the next row; **line frequency** = number of picture lines that are scanned per second; **line increment** = minimum distance between two lines of type, which can be as small as one eighteenth of a point; **line length** = number of characters contained in a displayed line (on a computer screen this is normally 80 characters, on a printer often 132 characters); **line noise** = unwanted interference on a telephone or communications line that causes errors in a data transmission; **lines per minute (LPM)** = number of lines printed by a line printer per minute; **line spacing** = distance between two rows of characters; *see also* LEADING; **line style** = appearance of a line displayed on screen or printed **(e)** series of characters received as a single input by a computer; **line input** = command to receive all characters including punctuation entered up to a carriage return code **(f)** one row of commands *or* arguments in a computer program; **line number** = number that refers to a line of program code in a computer program

COMMENT: the programming language will sort out the program into order according to line number

straight lines are drawn by clicking the points on the

screen where you would like the line to start and finish
Personal Computer World

while pixel editing is handy for line art, most desktop scanners have trouble producing the shades of grey or half-tones found in black and white photography
Publish

line of sight *noun* clear transmission path for radio communications in a straight line

COMMENT: line of sight paths are used with a very directional transmission medium such as a laser beam rather than uni-directional one such as radio

line printer *noun* device for printing draft quality information at high speeds, typical output is 200 to 300 lines per minute

COMMENT: line printers print a whole line at a time, running from right to left and left to right, and are usually dot matrix printers with not very high quality print. Compare page printers, which print a whole page at a time

linear *adjective* (circuit output) that varies directly with the input signal so that the output to input characteristics are a straight line (in practice this is never achieved since all components have maximum and minimum output limits at which points the signal becomes distorted); **linear array** = antenna whose elements lie in a straight line; **linear function** = mathematical expression where the input is not raised to a power above one and contains no multiplications other than by a constant; *the expression Y = 10 + 5X - 3W is a linear function; the expression Y = (10 + 5X²) is not a linear function*; **linear integrated circuit** = electronic device whose output varies linearly with its input over a restricted range (device usually used to provide gain to an analog signal); **linear program** = computer program that contains no loops *or* branches; **linear programming** = method of mathematically breaking down a problem so that it can be solved by computer; **linear search** = search method which compares each item in a list with the search key until the correct entry is found (starting with the first item and working sequentially towards the end); **linear video** = (i) continuous playback of a video sequence from videotape; (ii) normal video that is played back in a continuous sequence rather than a single frame at a time as in interactive video; **linear video editing** = video sequence (on videotape) that is edited by inserting or deleting new frames but without changing the order of the frames; *see also* EDL

linearity *noun* the shape of the frequency response curve of a device (such as a microphone or A/D converter); if the curve is straight, the device is very accurate, if it is not, the device is introducing frequency distortion

line-up *verb* to prepare a camera ready to photograph a scene

Lingo scripting language used to control the actions in the Macromedia Director authoring software

link 1 *noun* (a) communications path *or* channel between two components *or* devices; *to transmit faster, you can use the direct link with the mainframe*; **link access protocol** = *see* LAP; **link access protocol for modems** = *see* LAP-M; **link control procedure (LCP)** = rules defining the transmission of data over a channel; **link loss** = attenuation of signals transmitted over a link; **satellite link** = use of a satellite to allow the transmission of data from one point on earth to another (b) software routine that allows data transfer between incompatible programs; **link trials** = testing computer programs so as to see if each module works in conjunction with the others **2** *verb* (a) to combine separate routines from different files and library files to create a program (b) *(in hypertext)* to create an association between two objects in a title, for example to link a button to another page in the title that is displayed when the user selects the button; *the two computers are linked*; **link files** = command to merge together a list of separate files; **linked list** = list of data where each entry carries the address of the next consecutive entry; *(in Windows)* **linked object** = feature of OLE that allows one object or document or image to be referenced and displayed in another document; only a link is inserted and the

originating application must be present; *compare with* EMBEDDED OBJECT; **linked subroutine** = number of computer instructions in a program that can be called at any time, with control being returned on completion to the next instruction in the main program

linkage *noun* act of linking two things; **linkage software** = special software which links; *graphics and text are joined without linkage software*

linking *noun* merging of a number of small programs together to enable them to run as one unit; *(in Microsoft Windows)* **linking information** = linking together different types of data using the OLE function; *see also* OLE; **linking loader** = short software routine that merges sections of programs to allow them to be run as one

Linux *(normally pronounced 'lee-nucks')* popular version of the UNIX operating system originally developed by Linus Torvalds, who then distributed it free of charge over the Internet.

COMMENT: Enthusiasts and other developers have extended and enhanced the Linux software, normally also publishing their software free of charge. Linux has a very enthusiastic and loyal following and is one of the most popular operating systems for developers and people running web-based applications. Unlike many other operating systems, such as Microsoft Windows, the Linux software runs on a range of different types of computer hardware including the PC and Macintosh.

lip sync *noun (film)* voice recorded at the same time that a person is filmed to ensure that the movement of the mouth matches the speech

LIPS = LOGICAL INFERENCES PER SECOND standard for the measurement of processing power of an inference engine

COMMENT: one inference often requires thousands of computer instructions

liquid crystal display (LCD) *noun* liquid crystals that turn black when a voltage is applied, used in many watch, calculator and digital displays; **liquid**

crystal display shutter printer = *see* LCD SHUTTER PRINTER

COMMENT: LCDs do not generate light and so cannot be seen in the dark without an external light source (as opposed to LEDs)

LISP = LIST PROCESSING high-level language used mainly in processing lists of instructions *or* data and in artificial intelligence work

LIST chunk *noun (in a RIFF file)* four-character code LIST that contains a series of subchunks

list 1 *noun* series of ordered items of data; **list box** = display element in GUIs that can show a list of items (such as files in a directory) and allows a user to move a bar up and down the list to choose an item; the list box is normally intelligent enough to add a scroll bar if there are more items that can fit in the box; **list processing** = (i) computation of a series of items of data such as adding *or* deleting *or* sorting *or* updating entries; (ii) LISP *or* a high-level language used mainly in processing lists of instructions *or* data, and in artificial intelligence work **2** *verb* to print *or* display certain items of information; **to list a program** = to display a program line by line in correct order

listing *noun* (a) program lines printed *or* displayed in an ordered way; **a program listing** = a printed copy of the lines of a program; **computer listing** = printout of a list of items, taken from data stored in a computer; **listing paper** = continuous stationery (b) **listings** = series of information items (such as cinema times, etc.) listed in a newspaper

literacy *noun* being able to read; **computer literacy** = understanding the basic principles of computers, related expressions and being able to use computers for programming *or* applications

literal *noun* (a) computer instruction that contains a number rather than its location (b) printing error when one character is replaced by another *or* when two characters are transposed

literate *adjective* (person) who can read; **computer-literate** = able to understand expressions relating to computers and how to use a computer

lith film *noun* high quality and contrast photographic film used in lithographic printing

Lithium-Ion battery rechargeable battery that provides high output power in a compact and lightweight unit; this type of battery is often used in mobile telephones, PDAs and lightweight laptop computers; *Lithium-Ion batteries are light, powerful, and do not suffer from memory effect; see also* MEMORY EFFECT, NICAD, NIMH

lithographic *adjective* referring to lithography; **lithographic film** = LITH FILM

lithography *or (informal)* **litho** *noun* **offset lithography** = printing process used for printing books, where the ink sticks to dry areas on the film and is transferred to rubber rollers from which it is printed on to the paper

live *adjective (in television)* action transmitted as it happens rather than being transmitted from a recording; *(film)* **live recording** = original recording; **live-on-tape** = action which is recorded without any break, is not edited and is filmed to fit into a particular time frame; **Live3D** = *see* VRML

liveware *noun* the operators and users of a computer system (as opposed to the hardware and software)

LLC = LOGICAL LINK CONTROL IEEE 802.2 standard defining the protocol for data-link-level transmissions

LLL = LOW-LEVEL LANGUAGE

lm = LUMEN unit of luminous flux

load 1 *noun* (a) job *or* piece of work to be done; **line load** = number of messages transmitted over a line compared to the maximum capacity of the line; **load sharing** = use of more than one computer in a network to even out the work load on each processor; **work load** = number of tasks that a machine has to complete (b) impedance presented to a line *or* device; **load life** = length of time an impedance can operate with a certain power before it is no longer usable; **matched load** = load that is the same as the impedance of the transmission line *or* device connected to it **2** *verb* (a) to transfer a file *or* program from disk *or* tape to main memory; **load and run** *or* **load and go** = computer program that is loaded into main memory and then starts to execute itself automatically; **load high** = (using MS-DOS on a PC) to transfer a program into high *or* expanded memory **(b)** to insert disk, film, tape or cassette into a machine **(c)** to place an impedance *or* device at the end of a line

load point *noun* start of a recording section in a reel of magnetic tape

loader *noun* **(a)** *(film)* **loader boy** = person on set who is responsible for loading the camera **(b)** program which loads another file *or* program into computer memory; **absolute loader** = program that loads a section of code into main memory; *compare with* BOOTSTRAP

```
this windowing system is
particularly handy when you
want to load or save a file or
change directories
```
Byte

---

loading *noun* action of transferring a file *or* program from disk to memory; *loading can be a long process*

lobe *noun* section of a response curve around an antenna *or* microphone

local *adjective & noun* **(a) local bridge** = bridge that links two local networks; *we use a local bridge to link the two LANs in the office*; **local bus** = direct link *or* bus between a device and the processor; with no logic circuits *or* buffers *or* decoders in between; *the fastest expansion cards fit into this local bus connector*; **local drive** = disk drive that is physically attached to a computer rather than a resource being accessed across a network; **local printer** = printer physically attached to a computer rather than a shared resource available on a network **(b)** (variable *or* argument) that is only used in a certain section of a computer program *or* structure; **local declaration** = assignment of a variable that is only valid in a section of a computer program *or* structure; **local variable** = variable which can only be accessed by certain routines in a certain section of a computer program; *compare with* GLOBAL VARIABLE **(c)** referring to a system with limited access; **local distribution service** = TV signal relay station that transmits signals to another point from which they are distributed over cable; **local loop** = exchange line *or* communications line connecting a user to the main computer; **local mode** = operating state of a computer terminal that does not receive messages; *(of a terminal)* **on local** = not working with a CPU, but being used as a stand-alone terminal

local area network (LAN *or* **lan)** *noun* network where various terminals and equipment are all a short distance from one another (at a maximum distance of about 500m, for example in the same building) and can be interconnected by cables; *compare with* WAN; **local area network server** = dedicated computer and backing storage facility used by terminals and operators of a LAN

LocalTalk *noun* cabling system and connectors used in Apple's AppleTalk network

---

COMMENT: LANs use cables *or* optical fibre links; WANs use modems, radio and other long distance transmission methods

---

locate *verb* **(a)** to place *or* to set; *the computer is located in the main office building* **(b)** to find *have you managed to locate the programming fault?*

location *noun* **(a)** number *or* absolute address which specifies the point in memory where a data word can be found and accessed **(b)** any setting away from the studio, whether outdoors or indoors, where a film or programme is recorded; **location shots** = sections of a film which are shot on location; **on location** = filming in real situations, and not in the studio

lock *verb* **(a)** to prevent access to a system *or* file; **locking a file** = the action of preventing any further writing to a file; often used in multi-user database applications to prevent someone writing changes to a file when another user is reading the data **(b)** to synchronize two devices or signals, such as two video recorders or two clocks; **to lock onto** = to synchronize an internal clock with a received signal

lock up *noun* faulty operating state of computer that cannot be recovered from without switching off the power

---

COMMENT: this can be caused by an infinite program loop *or* a deadly embrace

---

lockout *noun* preventing a user sending messages over a network by continuously transmitting data

log 1 *noun* **(a)** record of computer processing operations; **log file** = (i) file that contains a record of actions; (ii) (on a web server) file that contains details of the visitors to a web site, recorded automatically with the visitor's DNS address, time and the name of the web page that they viewed; *see also* ACCESS LOG; **log on script** = series of batch instructions that are automatically executed when you connect *or* log on to network a server; **log on server** = computer that checks user identification and password data against a user database to authorize connection to a network *or* server; **log sheet** = a single page of a log; **(b)** *(film)* a detailed record of camera and sound-recording operations during filming **2** *verb* to record a series of actions; **automatic log on** = telephone number, password and user number transmitted when requested by a remote system to automate logon; **to log in** *or* **log on** = to enter various identification data, such as a password, usually by means of a terminal, to the central computer before accessing a program *or* data (used as a means of making sure that only authorized users can access the computer system); **to log calls** = to keep a record of telephone calls; **to log off** *or* **log out** = to enter a symbol *or* instruction at the end of a computing session to close all files and break the channel between the user's terminal and the main computer (NOTE: the verbs can be spelled **log on, log-on,** or **logon; log off, log-off** or **logoff**)

logarithm *noun* mathematical operation that gives the power a number must be raised to, to give the required number; *decimal logarithm of 1,000 is 3 (= 10 x 10 x 10)*

logarithmic *adjective* referring to variations in the logarithm of a scale; *bel is a unit in the logarithmic scale*; **logarithmic graph** = graph whose axes have a scale that is the logarithm of the linear measurement

logger *noun* **call logger** = device which logs telephone calls (and notes the number called, the time when the call was made, and the length of the call)

logging *noun* input of data into a system; **call logging** = system of monitoring telephone calls; **error logging** = recording errors met; *features of the program include error logging*; **logging on** *or* **logging off** = process of opening *or* ending operations with a system

> logging on and off from terminals is simple, requiring only a user name and password
>
> *Micro Decision*

> once the server is up and running it is possible for users to log-on
>
> *Micro Decision*

> facilities for protection against hardware failure and software malfunction include log files
>
> *Computer News*

logic *noun* **(a)** science which deals with thought and reasoning **(b)** mathematical treatment of formal logic operations such as AND, OR, etc., and their transformation into various circuits; *see also* BOOLEAN ALGEBRA; **logic map** = graphical representation of states and conditions in a logic circuit; **logic state** = one out of two possible levels in a digital circuit, the levels being 1 and 0 or TRUE and FALSE; **logic state analyzer** = test equipment that displays the logic states of a number of components *or* circuits; **logic symbol** = graphical symbol used to represent a type of logic function **(c)** *(in computing and electronics)* system for deducing results from binary data; **logic bomb** = section of code that performs various unpleasant functions such as fraud *or* system crash when a number of conditions are true (the logic bomb is installed by unpleasant hackers *or* very annoyed programmers); **logic level** = voltage used to represent a particular logic state (this is often five volts for a one and zero volts for a zero); **logic operation** = computer operation *or* procedure in which a decision is made **(d)** components of a computer *or* digital system; **logic card** *or* **logic board** = printed circuit board containing binary logic gates rather than analog components; **logic circuit** = electronic circuit made up of various logical gates such as AND, OR and EXOR; **logic element** = gate *or* combination of logic gates; **logic gate** = electronic circuit that applies a logical operator to an input signal and produces an output; *see also* GATE

---

a reduction in the number of logic gates leads to faster operation and lower silicon costs

Electronics & Power

---

the removal of complex but infrequently used logic makes the core of the processor simpler and faster, so simple operations execute faster

Electronics & Power

---

logical *adjective* that uses logic in its operation; *logical reasoning can be simulated by an artificial intelligence machine*; **logical channel** = electronic circuit between a terminal and a network node in a packet switching system; **logical comparison** = function to see if two logic signals are the same; **logical drive** = letter assigned to a disk drive *or* storage area on a disk drive that can be used as if it were a local drive; *the logical drive F: actually stores data on part of the server's disk drive*; **logical error** = fault in a program design causing incorrect branching *or* operations; **logical expression** = function made up from a series of logical operators such as AND and OR; **logical inferences per second (LIPS)** = standard for the measurement of processing power of an inference engine; **logical link control (LLC)** = IEEE 802.2 standard defining the protocol for data-link-level transmissions; **logical operator** = character *or* word that describes the logical action it will perform (the most common logical operators are AND, NOT, and OR); *(in Windows)* **logical palette** = graphics object that includes the colour palette information it requires; the application asks Windows if it can use these colours (in a process called realizing the palette); **logical record** = unit of information ready for processing that is not necessarily the same as the original data item in storage, which might contain control data, etc.; *(in a token ring or FDDI network)* **logical ring** = the path a token follows through the layers of each node; in FDDI the physical topology does not effect the logical ring; **logical shift** = data

movement to the left *or* right in a word, the bits falling outside the word boundary are discarded, the free positions are filled with zeros; *compare with* ARITHMETIC SHIFT

logic-seeking *adjective* printer that can print the required information with the minimum head movement, detecting end of lines, justification commands, etc.

login = LOGGING IN

login script *noun* a series of instructions that are automatically run when you log into a network; *if you log into your office network in the morning by typing your name and password, the login script might remind you of important information or just display 'good morning'*

LOGO *noun* high-level programming language used mainly for educational purposes, with graphical commands that are easy to use

logo *noun* special printed set of characters *or* symbols used to identify a company *or* product

logoff = LOG OFF, LOGGING OFF

logon = LOG ON, LOGGING ON

logout = LOGOUT

long filename *noun* feature of Windows (introduced with Windows 95) that allows files to have long descriptive names (up to 254 characters long); the old system only allowed file names to be eight-characters long

long focal-length lens *or* **long lens** *see* TELEPHOTO LENS

long haul network *noun* communications network between distant computers that usually uses the public telephone system

long integer *noun* *(in programming languages)* an integer represented by several bytes of data

long persistence phosphor *noun* television screen coating that retains the displayed image for a period of time longer than the refresh rate, reducing flicker effects

long shot *noun* *(film)* photograph of a general view of the setting where the action takes place

longitudinal time code (LTC) *noun* method of recording a time code signal on a linear audio track along a video tape; the disadvantage of this method is that the code is not readable at slow speeds or when the tape has stopped; *compare with* VITC

look ahead *noun* action by some CPUs to fetch instructions and examine them before they are executed (to speed up operations)

look-up table *or* **LUT** *noun* collection of stored results that can be accessed very rapidly by a program without the need to calculate each result whenever needed; *lookup tables are preprogrammed then used in processing so saving calculations for each result required*

---

a lookup table changes a pixel's value based on the values in a table

Byte

---

loop 1 *noun* **(a)** procedure *or* series of instructions in a computer program that are performed again and again until a test shows that a specific condition has been met *or* until the program is completed; **endless loop** *or* **infinite loop** = loop which has no end, except when the program is stopped; **holding loop** = section of program that loops until it is broken by some action, most often used when waiting for a response from the keyboard *or* a device; **loop check** = check that data has been correctly transmitted down a line by returning the data to the transmitter; **nested loop** = loop contained inside another **(b)** long piece of tape with the two ends joined; **loop film** = (i) endless piece of magnetic *or* photographic film that plays continuously; (ii) the parts of slack film above and below the gate in a camera or film projector **(c)** communications channel that is passed via all receivers and is terminated where it started from; **loopback** = diagnostic test that returns the transmitted signal to the sending device after it has passed through a device *or* across a link **(d)** length of wire coiled in the shape of a circle; **loop antenna** = aerial in the shape of a circle; **loop network** = communications network that consists of a ring of cable joining all terminals **2** *verb* to make a piece of wire *or* tape into a circle; **looping program** = computer program that runs continuously

loose gate *noun* (*film*) the gate of a projector which is loosened in order to prevent damage occurring to the film

lose *verb* not to have something any more; *we have lost the signal in the noise; all the current files were lost when the system crashed and we had no backup copies*; (*film*) **lose the loop** = the accidental tightening of the loop in the slack film between the projector picture and the sound head which causes loss of synchronization; **lost call** = telephone call that cannot be established; **lost cluster** = number of sectors on a disk whose identification bits have been corrupted; the operating system has marked this area of disk as being used by a file, but the data they contain can no longer be identified with a particular file; **lost time** = period of a transmitted facsimile signal when the image is being scanned, that contains no image data

loss *noun* the power of a signal that is lost when passing through a circuit

lossless compression *noun* image compression techniques that can reduce the number of bits used for each pixel in an image, without losing any information or sharpness (such as Huffman Encoding)

lossy compression *noun* image compression techniques that can reduce the number of bits used for each pixel in an image, but in doing so loses information; *see also* JPEG

Lotus software company best known for its desktop applications such as the spreadsheet program 1-2-3 and networking products such as cc:Mail and Notes

Lotus, Intel, Microsoft Expanded Memory System *see* LIM EMS

loudness *noun* volume of a signal which you can hear

loudspeaker *noun* electromagnetic device that converts electrical signals into audible noise

low angle shot *noun* (*film*) camera shot taken from below the subject with the camera tilted up towards subject

low band video *noun* (*film*) video tape recording system which is usually used for low-quality home use and does not meet television broadcast standards

low contrast *noun* (*film*) **(a)** muted colours in a film **(b)** film which does not have a great contrast between its black and white tones; **low contrast filter** = a camera lens which mutes colours

low end *noun* hardware *or* software that is not very powerful or sophisticated and is designed for beginners

low frequency (LF) *noun* range of audio frequencies between 5-300Hz *or* range of radio frequencies between 30-300kHz; **low pass filter** = electronic circuit that blocks signals above a certain frequency

low key *noun (film)* **(a)** pictures in which the lower grey scale tones, or shadowy parts, are emphasized **(b)** low lighting of subject

low speed communications *noun* data transmission at less than 2400 bits per second

low-level format *noun* process that defines the physical pattern and arrangement of tracks and sectors on a disk

low-level language (LLL) *noun* programming language similar to assembler and in which each instruction has a single equivalent machine code instruction (the language is particular to one system *or* computer); *see also* HIGH-LEVEL LANGUAGE

low-memory *noun (in a PC)* memory locations from zero up to 640Kb; *compare with* HIGH MEMORY

low-power standby *noun* an energy-saving feature of laptop computers and many monitors connected to a desktop; if the computer is not used for a few minutes, it will shut down some parts of the electronics - normally the hard disk drive and the screen or monitor - and when you start typing or move the mouse, the computer switches these parts back on to normal power levels; *see also* ENERGY STAR

low-priority work *noun* task which is not particularly important

low-resolution graphics *or*
low-res graphics *plural noun* character-sized graphic blocks *or* preset shapes, rather than individual pixels, displayed on a screen; *compare with* HIGH-RESOLUTION

lower case *noun* small characters (such as a, b, c, as opposed to upper case A, B, C)

LPM = LINES PER MINUTE

LPT1 *(in a PC)* name given to the first, main parallel printer port in the system; *the laser printer is connected to LPT1*

LQ = LETTER QUALITY

LRU = LEAST RECENTLY USED ALGORITHM *noun* algorithm which finds the page of memory that was last accessed before any other, and erases it to make room for another page

LS (a) = LONG SHOT **(b)** = LOUDSPEAKER

LSB = LEAST SIGNIFICANT BIT binary digit occupying the right hand position of a word and carrying the least power of two in the word, usually equal to two raised to zero = 1

LSD = LEAST SIGNIFICANT DIGIT digit which occupies the right hand position in a number and so carries least power (equal to the number radix raised to zero = 1)

LSI = LARGE-SCALE INTEGRATION system with between 500 and 10,000 circuits on a single IC

LTC = LONGITUDINAL TIME CODE occasionally referred to as audio time code, recorded in the audio track of video tapes in off-line editing

lumen *noun* SI unit of illumination, defined as the amount of flux emitted from a candela into an angle of one steradion

luminance *noun* amount of light radiated from a source; **luminance signal** = part of television signal providing luminance data

luminous flux *noun* rate of stream of visible light coming from a source, measured in lumens

lurk *verb* to join an online conference, discussion group or chat room and listen to the messages without contributing anything yourself

COMMENT: Most discussion forums do not object to users lurking, since it helps to build the confidence of new users and allows a user to check the content before joining in. However, some chat rooms do not approve of lurking and immediately identify anyone joining to discourage people who do not contribute to the forum.

LUT = LOOK-UP TABLE

an image processing system can have three LUTs that map the image memory to the display device

Byte

lux *noun* SI unit of measurement of one lumen per square metre

LV *see* LASERVISION

LV-ROM 12-inch diameter optical disc developed by Philips that can store both analog video and digital data

Mm

m *prefix* = MILLI one thousandth; **mA** = milliampere

M *prefix* = MEGA **(a)** one million; **Mbps** = MEGABITS PER SECOND number of million bits transmitted every second **(b)** symbol for 1,048,576, used only in computer and electronic related applications; **MByte (MB)** = measurement of mass storage equal to 1048576 bytes; *300Mbyte hard disk*

M and S microphone *(film)* = MIDDLE AND SIDE MICROPHONE combination used for stereo sound recording

M out of N code *noun* coding system providing error detection; each valid character which is N bits long must contain M binary 'one' bits

M signal *noun* signal produced from the sum of left and right signals in a stereophonic system

mA = MILLIAMPERE electrical current measure equal to one thousandth of an ampere

MAC (a) = MULTIPLEXED ANALOG COMPONENTS standard colour television broadcast signal format **(b)** = MESSAGE AUTHENTICATION CODE special code transmitted at the same time as a message as proof of its authenticity

Mac *see* MACINTOSH

MacBinary *noun* file storage and transfer system that allows Macintosh files, together with their icons and long file names, to be stored on other computer systems

machine *noun* **(a)** number of separate moving parts *or* components, acting together to carry out a process; **copying machine** *or* **duplicating machine** = machine which makes copies of documents; **dictating machine** = recording machine which records what someone dictates, so that the text can be typed **(b)** computer *or* system *or* processor made of various components connected together to provide a function *or* perform a task; **machine address** = number *or* absolute address which specifies the point in memory where a data word can be found and accessed; **machine check** = fault caused by equipment failure; **machine code** *or* **machine language** = programming language that consists of commands in binary code that can be directly understood by the central processing unit without the need for translation; **machine code instruction** = instruction that directly controls the CPU and is recognized without the need for translation; **machine cycle** = minimum period of time taken by the CPU for the execution of an instruction; **machine dependent** = not standardized; cannot be used on hardware *or* software from a different manufacturer without modifications; **machine error** = error caused by a hardware malfunction; **machine independent** = computer software that can be run on any computer system; **machine instruction** = an instruction which can be recognized by a machine and is part of its limited set of commands; **machine language** = MACHINE CODE; *(film)* **machine leader** = leader which is used to pull film through the film processor; **machine proof** = proof of sheets of a book, taken from the printing machine; **machine-readable** = (commands *or* data) stored on a medium that can be directly input to the computer; *the disk stores data in machine-readable form*; **machine translation** = computer system that is used to translate text and commands from one language and syntax to another; **source machine** = computer which can compile source code

machinery *noun* machines (NOTE: no plural)

machining *noun* making a product using a machine; printing the sheets of a book

machinist *noun* person who works a machine

Macintosh *noun* range of personal computers designed by Apple Corporation

COMMENT: the Macintosh uses the Motorola family of processors, originally the 68000 and now the PowerPC, and offers similar computing power to a PC. The Macintosh is best known for its graphical user interface which allows a user to control the computer using icons and a mouse; Macintosh computers are not hardware compatible with an IBM PC unless you use special emulation software running on the Macintosh that can run Microsoft Windows-compatible software

macro *noun* program routine *or* block of instructions identified by a single word *or* label; **macro assembler** = assembler program that is able to decode macro instructions; **macro code** *or* **macro instruction** = one word that is used to represent a number of instructions, simplifying program writing; **macro language** = programming language that allows the programmer to define and use macro instructions; **macro programming** = writing a program using macro instructions *or* defining macro instructions; **macro virus** = type of virus that is created using a macro language and attached to a document or email message

COMMENT: A macro virus can hit advanced software applications, such as Microsoft Word (wordprocessor) or Excel (spreadsheet) or Outlook (email software); these applications provide a macro language that allows a user to extend the application and add automate features. However, as macro languages become more advanced and powerful, they also provide an opportunity for someone to create a macro that can delete files or corrupt data when run. The macro virus will run when the document is opened; some viruses are benign, others carry out malicious damage on your files and data. The virus will also try and spread to other compatible documents and applications on your computer, so that any new documents you create are also infected. The latest macro virus attacks have targetted the Microsoft Outlook email software; the virus uses the macro feature of Outlook to re-send itself to all the email addresses stored in the email address book. The last major macro virus created so much extra network email traffic on the Internet that many servers were overloaded. The best way to avoid a macro virus is to regularly run virus detection software that can check and remove viruses attached to documents and new email messages.

```
Microsoft has released a
developer's kit for its Word
6.0      for      Windows
word-processing package. The
900-page kit explains how to
use   the   WordBasic   macro
language  supplied  with  the
software
```

Computing

macro- *prefix* very large *or* applying to the whole system

macrocinematography *noun* filming of very small objects with the use of special camera attachments

macro-focusing telephoto lens *or* **macro-telephoto lens** *noun* special telephoto lens which is able to focus on objects which are placed very close to the camera

macro lens *noun* a magnifying lens which is used for close-up shots

Macromedia Director authoring software for the PC and Macintosh using the Lingo scripting language

macrozoom *noun* zoom lens that can focus on very close objects

mag tape *noun (informal)* = MAGNETIC TAPE

magazine *noun* (a) paper, usually with illustrations which comes out regularly, every month or every week; *a weekly magazine; he edits a computer magazine* (b) number of pages in a multimedia book or videotext system (c) light-tight film container which is used with a camera, printer or film processing machine

magnet *noun* something that produces a magnetic field

magnetic *adjective* which has a magnetic field associated with it; **magnetic bubble memory** = method of storing large amounts of binary data as small magnetized areas in the medium (certain pure materials); **magnetic card** = plastic card with a strip of magnetic recording material on its surface, allowing data to be stored (used in automatic cash dispensers); **magnetic card reader** *or* **magnetic strip reader** = machine that can read data stored on a magnetic card; **magnetic cartridge** *or* **cassette** = small box containing a reel of magnetic tape and a pick up reel; **magnetic cell** = small piece of material whose magnetic field can be altered to represent the two states of binary data; **magnetic core** = early main memory system for storing data in the first types of computer, each bit of data was stored in a magnetic cell; **magnetic disk** = flat circular piece of coated material onto the surface of which signals can be stored magnetically; *see also* FLOPPY DISK, HARD DISK; **magnetic disk unit** = computer peripheral made up of a disk drive and necessary control electronics; **magnetic drum** = computer data storage peripheral that uses a coated cylinder to store data (not often used now); **magnetic encoding** = storage of (binary) data signals on a magnetic medium; **magnetic field** = description of the polarity and strength of magnetic effects at a point; **magnetic film** *or* **mag film** = iron oxide-coated film which is used to record sound and from which sound can be reproduced; **magnetic film recorder** = sound recorder which uses perforated magnetic film instead of tape; **magnetic flux** = measure of magnetic field strength per unit area; **magnetic focusing** = use of magnetic field to focus a beam of electrons (in a television); **magnetic head** = electromagnetic component that converts electrical signals into a magnetic field, allowing them to be stored on a magnetic medium; **magnetic ink** = printing ink that contains a magnetic material, used in character recognition systems; **magnetic ink character recognition (MICR)** = system that identifies characters by sensing the magnetic ink patterns (as used on bank cheques); **magnetic master** = original version of a recorded tape *or* disk; **magnetic material** *or* **medium** = substance that will retain a magnetic flux pattern when a magnetic field is applied; **magnetic media** = magnetic materials used to store signals, such as disk, tape, etc.; **magnetic recording** = transferring an electrical signal onto a moving magnetic tape or disk by means of a magnetic field generated by a write head; **magnetic screen** = metal screen used to prevent stray magnetic fields affecting electronic components; **magnetic storm** = disturbance in the earth's magnetic fields affecting radio and cable communications; **magnetic strip** = layer of magnetic material on the surface of a plastic card, used for recording data; **magnetic stripe** *or* **mag stripe** = iron oxide stripe which is put on one edge of clear photographic film, used for recording a single or mixed soundtrack; **magnetic thin film storage** = high-speed access RAM device using a matrix of magnetic cells and a matrix of read/write heads to access them; **magnetic track** = a magnetically recorded sound track which is imprinted on to a composite film base; **magnetic transfer** = copy signals stored on one type of magnetic medium to another

magnetic tape *noun* audiotape *or* narrow length of thin plastic coated with a magnetic material used to store signals magnetically; *see also* AUDIOTAPE, VIDEOTAPE; **magnetic tape cartridge** *or* **cassette** = small box containing a reel of magnetic tape and a pick up reel; **magnetic tape encoder** = device that directly writes data entered at a keyboard onto magnetic tape; **magnetic tape recorder** = device with a magnetic head, motor and circuitry to allow electrical signals to be recorded onto *or* played back from a magnetic tape; **magnetic tape transport** = (computer) controlled magnetic tape drive mechanism

COMMENT: magnetic tape is available on spools of between 200 and 800 metres. The tape is magnetized by the read/write head. Tape is a storage medium which only allows serial access, that is, all the tape has to be read until the required location is found (as opposed to disk storage, which can be accessed randomly)

magnetize *verb* to convert a material *or* object into a magnet

magneto-optical disc *noun* optical disc that is used in a magneto-optical recording device

magneto-optical recording   *noun*
storage media that uses an optical disc

> COMMENT: the optical disk has a thin
> layer of magnetic film which is heated by
> a laser, the particles are then polarised
> by a weak magnetic field.
> Magneto-optical media is high capacity
> (over 600Mb) and is re-writable

magnification *noun* amount by which
something has been made to appear larger;
the lens gives a magnification of 10 times

magnify *verb* to make something appear
larger; *the photograph has been magnified
200 times*

magnitude *noun* level *or* strength of a
signal *or* variable; **signal magnitude** =
strength of an electrical current and voltage
or power signal

mag-opt *noun (film)* motion picture print
which contains both magnetic and optical
sound tracks

mail 1 *noun* **(a)** system of sending letters
and parcels from one place to another; *to
put a letter in the mail; the cheque was lost
in the mail; the letter was put in the mail
yesterday; mail to some of the islands in
the Pacific can take six weeks*; **by mail** =
using the postal services, not sending
something by hand *or* by messenger **(b)**
letters sent *or* received; *has the mail arrived
yet? to open the mail; your cheque arrived
in yesterday's mail; my secretary opens my
mail as soon as it arrives; the receipt was in
this morning's mail*; **incoming mail** = mail
which arrives; **mail exchange record (MX
record)** = (in an electronic mail system)
information stored in the DNS that tells an
email system how to deliver a mail message
to a particular domain; **outgoing mail** =
mail which is sent out **(c) direct mail** =
selling a product by sending publicity
material to possible buyers through the post;
direct-mail advertising = advertising by
sending leaflets to people by post; **mail shot**
= leaflets sent by mail to possible
customers; *he company runs a successful
direct-mail operation; these calculators are
sold only by direct mail* **(d)** electronic
messages sent to and from users of a
network; **mail-enabled** = application that
has access to an electronic mail system
without leaving the application; *this
word-processor is mail-enabled - you can*

*send messages to other users from within
it;* **mail server** = computer that stores
incoming mail and sends it to the correct
user and stores outgoing mail and transfers
it to the correct destination server on the
Internet; **mail transfer agent (MTA)** =
software program that manages the way
electronic mail messages are transferred
over a network; *see also* EMAIL, MAIL
USER AGENT, MAPI, POP3, SMTP;
mail user agent (MUA) = software used to
create and read electronic mail messages;
this software creates a message in the
correct format and standard and passes this
to the mail transfer agent that is responsible
for transferring the message over the
network; *see also* EMAIL, MAIL
TRANSFER AGENT, MAPI, POP3,
SMTP **2** *verb* to send something by post; *to
mail a letter; we mailed our order last
Wednesday*

mail-merge   *noun*   word-processing
program which allows a standard letter to be
printed out to a series of different names and
addresses

```
Spreadsheet views for data and
graphical forms for data entry
have been added to the Q&A
database, with the traditional
reporting, mail-merge, and
labels improved through
Windows facilities
```
Computing

mail-order *noun* system of buying and
selling from a catalogue, placing orders and
sending goods by mail; **mail-order
business** *or* **mail-order firm** *or* **mail-order
house** = company which sells a product by
mail; **mail-order catalogue** = catalogue
from which a customer can order items to be
sent by mail

mailbox *or* **mail box** *noun* **(a)** one of
several boxes where incoming mail is put in
a large building; box for putting letters, etc.
which you want to post **(b)** electronic
storage space with an address in which a
user's incoming messages are stored

mailing *noun* sending something using the
post; *the mailing of publicity material*;
direct mailing = sending of publicity
material by post to possible buyers; **mailing
list** = list of names and addresses of people
who might be interested in a product *or* list
of names and addresses of members of a

society; *his name is on our mailing list; to build up a mailing list;* **mailing piece** = leaflet suitable for sending by direct mail; **mailing shot** = leaflets sent by mail to possible customers; **to buy a mailing list** = to pay a society, etc. money to buy the list of members so that you can use it to mail publicity material

main *adjective* most important; *main office; main building; one of our main customers*; **main beam** = direction of the central most powerful region of an antenna's transmission pattern; **main body (of a program)** = set of instructions that form the main part of a program and from which other subroutines are called; **main clock** = clock signal that synchronizes all the components in a system; **main distributing frame** = racks of termination circuits for the cables in a telephone network; **main entry** = entry in a catalogue under which is contained the most important information about the document; **main index** = more general index that directs the user gradually to more specific index areas; **main memory** *or* **main storage** = area of fast access time RAM whose locations can be directly and immediately addressed by the CPU; *the 16-bit system includes up to 3Mb of main memory*; **main loop (of a program)** = series of instructions performed repeatedly that carry out the main action of a program; this loop is often used to wait for user input before processing the event

mainframe (computer) *noun* large-scale high power computer system that can handle high capacity memory and backing storage devices as well as a number of operators simultaneously

mainly *adverb* mostly *or* usually; *their sales are mainly in the home market; we are interested mainly in buying colour printing*

mains electricity *noun* normal domestic electricity supply to consumers

COMMENT: in UK this is 240 volts at 50Hz; in the USA, it is 120 volts at 60Hz

maintain *verb* to ensure a system is in good condition and functioning correctly

maintainability *noun* the ability to have repairs carried out quickly and efficiently if a failure occurs

maintenance *noun* **(a)** keeping a machine in good working condition **(b)** tasks carried out in order to keep a system running, such as repairing faults, replacing components, etc.; **maintenance contract** = arrangement with a repair company that provides regular checks and special repair prices in the event of a fault; **maintenance release** = program revision that corrects a minor problem or bug but does not offer any major new features; *the maintenance release of the database program, version 2.01, corrects the problem with the margins*; **preventive maintenance** = regular inspection and cleaning of a system to prevent faults occurring

majordomo *see* LISTSERV

majuscule *noun* capital letter

make up *verb* to arrange type into the correct page formats before printing

make up *or* **makeup** *noun* arrangement and layout of type into correct page formats before printing; *corrections after the page makeup are very expensive*

make-ready time *noun* time taken by a printer to prepare the machines and film for printing

male connector *noun* plug with conducting pins that can be inserted into a female connector

malfunction 1 *noun (of hardware or software)* not working correctly; *the data was lost due to a software malfunction* **2** *verb* not to work properly; *some of the keys on the keyboard have started to malfunction*

malfunctioning *noun* not working properly

maltese cross *noun (film)* a mechanical device which provides the frame-by-frame movement of film through a camera or projector

man 1 *noun* person *or* ordinary worker; *all the men went back to work yesterday* **2** *verb* to provide the workforce for something; *to man a shift; to man an exhibition; the exhibition stand was manned by three members of the sales department*

MAN = METROPOLITAN AREA NETWORK network extending over a limited area (normally a city); *compare with* LAN, WAN

man machine interface (MMI) *noun* hardware and software designed to make it easier for users to communicate effectively with a machine; *see also* HMI

manage *verb* to direct *or* to be in charge of; *to manage a department; to manage a branch office*

manageable *adjective* which can be dealt with easily; *processing problems which are still manageable; the problems are too large to be manageable; data should be split into manageable files*

management *noun* directing *or* running a business; *to study management; good management or efficient management; bad management or inefficient management;* **management information service (MIS)** = department within a company that is responsible for information and data processing; in practice, this department is often responsible for the computer system in a company; **management information system (MIS)** = software that allows managers in a company to access and analyse data; **management training** = training managers by making them study problems and work out ways of solving them; **product management** = directing the making and selling of a product as an independent item (NOTE: no plural)

manager *noun* head of a department in a company; *a department manager; data processing manager; production manager; sales manager*

managerial *adjective* referring to managers; *managerial staff*

Manchester coding *noun* method of encoding data and timing signals that is used in communications; the first half of the bit period indicates the value of the bit (1 or 0) and the second half is used as a timing signal

Mandlebrot set *noun* mathematical equation that is called recursively to generate a set of values; when plotted these form a fractal image; *see also* FRACTAL

manipulate *verb* to move, edit and change text *or* data; *an image processor that captures, displays and manipulates video images*

manipulation *noun* moving *or* editing *or* changing text *or* data; *the high-speed database management program allows the manipulation of very large amounts of data*

man-made *adjective* not natural, produced by man; **man-made noise** = electrical interference caused by machines *or* motors; *compare with* GALACTIC NOISE

mantissa *noun* fractional part of a number; *the mantissa of the number 45.897 is 0.897*

manual 1 *noun* document containing instructions about the operation of a system *or* piece of software; *the manual is included with the system;* **installation manual** = booklet showing how a system should be installed; **user's manual** = booklet showing how a device *or* system should be used **2** *adjective* (work) done by hand; (process) carried out by the operator without the help of a machine; **manual data processing** = sorting and processing information without the help of a computer; **manual entry** *or* **manual input** = act of entering data into a computer, by an operator via a keyboard

manually *adverb* done by hand, not automatically; *the paper has to be manually fed into the printer*

manufacture *verb* to make in a factory; *the company manufactures diskettes and magnetic tape*

manufacturer *noun* company which manufactures a product; *if the system develops a fault it should be returned to the manufacturer for checking; the manufacturer guarantees the system for 12 months*

manuscript *or* **MS** *noun* original draft copy of a book written *or* typed by the author; *this manuscript was all written on computer*

map 1 *noun* **(a)** diagram representing the internal layout of a computer's memory *or* communications regions; **memory map** = diagram indicating the allocation of address ranges to various memory devices, such as RAM, ROM and memory-mapped input/output devices; **memory-mapped (input/output)** = allocation of addresses to a computer's input/output devices to allow them to be accessed as if they are a memory location; *a memory-mapped screen has an address allocated to each pixel allowing direct access to the screen by the CPU* **(b)**

data that is linked to another set of data **(c)** list of data items or objects within an application or multimedia book **2** *verb* **(a)** to retrieve data and display it as a map; **to map out** = to draw *or* set down the basic way in which something should be done; **(b)** (i) to link and represent a network directory path on a remote computer with a local drive letter; *you can map E: to point to a disk drive that is actually located on another computer on the network; map drive G: to the \\files\work path on the network server;* (ii) to link and represent a remote shared printer with a local printer name; *map the shared laser printer so that you can use it on your PC;* **(c)** to transform a two-dimensional image into a three-dimensional form that can then be rotated or manipulated **(d)** to transfer data from one region of memory to another; *the graphic image is mapped in main memory and on the display* **(e)** to relate or link one set of data items with another; *see also* BIT MAP

MAR = MEMORY ADDRESS REGISTER register within the CPU that contains the next location to be accessed

marching display *noun* display device that contains a buffer to show the last few characters entered

margin *noun* **(a)** blank space around a section of printed text; *when typing the contract leave wide margins; the left margin and right margin are the two sections of blank paper on either side of the page;* **to set the margin** = to define the size of a margin **(b)** extra time *or* space; **margin of error** = number of mistakes which are accepted in a document *or* in a calculation; **safety margin** = time *or* space allowed for something to be safe;

margination *noun* giving margins to a printed page

mark 1 *noun* **(a)** sign put on a page to show something; **proof correction marks** = special marks used to show changes to a proof **(b)** transmitted signal that represents a logical one *or* true condition; **mark hold** = continuously transmitted mark signal that indicates there are no messages on the network; **mark space** = two-state transmission code using a mark and a space without a mark as signals **2** *verb* to put a mark on something; **mark block** = to put a

block marker at the beginning and end of a block of text; **marking interval** = time when a mark signal is being carried out; **mark sense** = to write characters with conductive *or* magnetic ink so that they are then machine readable; **mark sense device** *or* **reader** = device that reads data from special cards containing conductive *or* magnetic marks; **mark sensing card** = preprinted card with spaces for mark sense characters

mark up *verb* to prepare copy for the compositor to set, by showing on the copy the typeface to be used, the line width, and other typesetting instructions

marker *noun* **(a) marker pen** = coloured pen used to indicate *or* highlight sections of text **(b)** code inserted in a file *or* text to indicate a special section; **block markers** = two markers inserted at the start and finish of a section of data to indicate a special block which can then be moved *or* deleted *or* copied as a single unit

marquee *noun (in a graphics application)* area selected by a selection tool

married print *noun (film)* motion picture film which has synchronised picture and sound on the film strip ready for projection

MASER = MICROWAVE AMPLIFICATION BY STIMULATED EMISSION OF RADIATION low noise amplifier, formerly used for microwave signals from satellites

mask 1 *noun* **(a)** integrated circuit layout that is used to define the pattern to be etched *or* doped onto a slice of semiconductor; *a mask or stencil is used to transfer the transistor design onto silicon* **(b)** photographic device used to prevent light reaching selected areas of the film **(c)** pattern of binary digits used to select various bits from a binary word (a one in the mask retains that bit in the word); **interrupt mask** = data word in a computer that selects which interrupt lines are to be activated; **mask register** = storage location in a computer that contains the pattern of bits used as a mask **2** *verb* to cover an area of (something) with (something) so that the area is not transformed by subsequent special effects or paint operations; *an image of a man in a field could be masked out and the background blurred to make him stand out more as a sharp image on a* *blurred background*; **masked ROM** = read-only memory device that is programmed during manufacture, by depositing metal onto selected regions dictated by the shape of a mask

maskable *adjective* which can be masked

masking *noun* **(a)** operation used to select various bits in a word **(b)** the adjustment of the colour balance by matrixing the RGB signals; this method is used to match colour film primaries to the television standard

---

the device features a maskable interrupt feature which reduces CPU overheads

Electronics & Power

---

mass media *noun* media which aim to reach a large public (such as television, radio, mass-market newspapers)

mass storage *noun* storage and retrieval of large amounts of data; **mass storage device** = computer backing store device that is able to store large amounts of data; *the hard disk is definitely a mass storage device*; **mass storage system** = data storage system that can hold more than one million million bits of data

mast *noun* **radio mast** = tall structure used to position an aerial above natural obstacles (such as houses, hills, etc.)

master 1 *noun* **(a)** main *or* most important device *or* person in a system; most up-to-date and correct file; *the master computer controls everything else* **(b)** *(film)* special positive print which is made from an original negative for duplication or protection instead of for projection **(c)** *(film)* the finished version of any type of programme from which release or show copies will be made **(d)** *(film)* output gain control on an audio mixer or video chain; **image master** = data describing fonts and character shapes in a phototypesetter; **master antenna television system (MATV)** = single main receiving antenna that provides television signals to a number of nearby receivers; **master clock** = timing signal to which all components in a system are synchronized; **master disk** = (i) disk containing all the files for a task; (ii) disk containing the code for a computer's operating system that must be loaded before the system will operate; (iii) (in CD-ROM or optical disc technology) glass disc onto which a laser etches pits to represent data; the glass disc is then used to press the plastic discs ready for distribution; **master file** = set of all the records of reference data required, can be updated periodically; **master proof** = final proof of a section of text before it is printed **2** *verb* to learn and understand a language *or* process; *we mastered the new word-processor quite quickly*

mastering *noun* process to convert finished data to a master disc

mat *noun* plain coloured border that is displayed around an image that is smaller than the window in which it is displayed

match *verb* **(a)** to search through a database for a similar piece of information **(b)** to set a register *or* electrical impedance equal to another; **impedance matching** = means of making the best signal power transfer between two circuits by making sure that their output and input impedances are the same; **matched load** = impedance of the same value as the cable across which it is connected, so minimizing signal reflections; **matching transformer** = transformer used to connect and match two lines of differing impedance, while isolating them electrically

material *noun* **(a)** substance which can be used to make a finished product; *gold is the ideal material for electrical connections*; **materials control** = system to check that a company has enough materials in stock to do its work; **materials handling** = moving materials from one part of a factory to another in an efficient way; **synthetic materials** = substances made as products of a chemical process **(b)** **display material** = posters, photographs, etc., which can be used to attract attention to goods which are for sale

mathematical *adjective* referring to mathematics; **mathematical model** = representation of a system using mathematical ideas and formulae

mathematics *noun* study of the relationship between numbers, their manipulation and organization to (logically) prove facts and theories; *see also* ALGEBRA

matrix *noun* **(a)** array of numbers *or* data items arranged in rows and columns; **matrix rotation** = swapping the rows with the columns in an array (equal to rotating by 90 degrees) **(b)** array of connections between logic gates providing a number of possible logical functions; **key matrix** = keyboard whose keys are arranged as an array of connections **(c)** pattern of the dots that make up a character in phototypesetting *or* on a computer screen; **character matrix** = pattern of dots that makes up a displayed character; **matrix printer** *or* **dot-matrix printer** = printer in which the characters are made up by a series of dots printed close together, producing a page line by line; a dot-matrix printer can be used either for printing using a ribbon or for thermal *or* electrostatic printing **(d)** *(film)* a filmstrip of images which contains dyed emulsion and is combined with two other filmstrips on a film base to create colour film

matt way in which an object or surface of an object reflects light equally in all directions

matt *or* **matte 1** *noun* **(a)** addition of an image onto a film of a background **(b)** an opaque mask limiting the picture area which is exposed in special effects; the mask can be a cut-out aperture, a high density image on film, or, in video, it may be electronically created in order to blank off the particular signal **(c)** device put before the camera which is used to soften or block light from sections of the action area, or from exposure in the printer **2** *adjective* (print) which is not shiny; *see also* CHROMA KEY

matte bleed *or* **ride** *noun* *(film)* an abnormality in the matte image which causes the matte lines to become visible

matte shot *noun* *(film)* any shot in which some of the action is blocked out so that other action can be added later

matter *noun* **(a)** problem; **it is a matter of concern to the members of the committee** = the members of the committee are worried about it **(b)** main section of text on a page as opposed to titles *or* headlines; **printed matter** = printed books, newspapers, publicity sheets, etc.; **publicity matter** = sheets *or* posters *or* leaflets used for publicity **(c)** question *or* problem to be discussed; *the most important matter on the agenda; we shall consider first the matter of last month's fall in prices* (NOTE: no plural for (b))

matting *noun* *(film)* inserting an image into a background, whether electronically or optically

MATV = MASTER ANTENNA TELEVISION SYSTEM

maximise *verb* *(in MS-Windows)* to expand an application icon back to its original display window; *you maximise a window by clicking once on the up arrow in the top right hand corner*; *compare with* MINIMISE

> COMMENT: you maximise a window by clicking once on the up arrow in the top right hand corner

maximum *adjective & noun* highest value used *or* which is allowed; **maximum capacity** = greatest amount of data that can be stored; **maximum reading** = greatest signal magnitude recorded; **maximum transmission rate** = greatest number of data that can be transmitted every second; **maximum usable frequency** = highest signal frequency which can be used in a circuit without distortion; **maximum users** = greatest number of users that a system can support at any one time

MB or MByte = MEGABYTE equal to 1,048,576 bytes of storage, or equal to 220 bytes; megabytes are used to measure the storage capacity of hard disk drives or main memory (RAM); *see also* KBYTE

> the maximum storage capacity is restricted to 8 Mbytes
> *Micro Decision*

Mb = MEGABIT equal to 1,048,576 bits of storage, or equal to 131,072 bytes

Mbps = MEGABITS PER SECOND number of million bits transmitted every second

MBR = MEMORY BUFFER REGISTER register in a CPU that temporarily buffers all inputs and outputs

MC = MILLICOULOMB

MCA = MICROCHANNEL ARCHITECTURE (old) design of the expansion bus within IBM's PS/2 range of personal computers that replaced the older ISA/AT bus; MCA is a 32-bit bus that supports bus master devices; **MCA chipset** = number of electronic components required to manage the timing and data signals over an MCA expansion bus

MCGA = MULTICOLOUR GRAPHICS ADAPTER colour graphics adapter standard fitted in low-end IBM PS/2 computers

MCI = MEDIA CONTROL INTERFACE device-independent programming interface, developed by IBM and Microsoft, that provides basic control (such as play, stop, rewind) of installed multimedia devices from within a programming language such as C and Visual Basic

COMMENT: MCI is part of Microsoft Windows; the Windows Media Player is a simple front-end that issues MCI commands to any installed multimedia device (such as to play a CD audio disc, video clip or sound file)

MCI device *noun* recognised multimedia device that is installed in a computer with the correct drivers; for example, a sound card could either be installed with an MCI driver or with its own proprietary driver

MCS *(film)* = MEDIUM CLOSE SHOT shot which pictures the subject from waist and above

MCU *(film)* = MEDIUM CLOSE-UP shot showing the head and shoulders of a subject

MD *or* **MKDIR** = MAKE DIRECTORY DOS command used to create a new directory on a disk

MDA = MONOCHROME DISPLAY ADAPTER video adapter standard used in early PC systems that could display text in 25 lines of 80 columns

MDR = MEMORY DATA REGISTER register in a CPU that holds data before it is processed *or* moved to a memory location

mean 1 *noun & adjective* average value of a set of numbers *or* values; **mean grade** = average quality from a series of products; **mean time between failures (MTBF)** = average period of time that a piece of equipment will operate before a failure; **mean time to repair** = average period of time required to repair a faulty piece of equipment **2** *verb* to signify something; *the message DISK FULL means that there is no more room on the disk for further data*

measure 1 *noun* (a) way of calculating size *or* quantity; **square measure** = area in square feet *or* metres, calculated by multiplying width and length (b) **tape measure** = long tape with centimetres or inches marked on it, used to measure how long something is (c) total width of a printed line of text (shown in picas) (d) type of action; **to take measures to prevent something happening** = to act to stop something happening; **safety measures** = actions to make sure that something is safe **2** *verb* (a) to find out the size *or* quantity of something (b) to be of a certain size *or* quantity; *to measure the size of a package; a package which measures 10cm by 25cm or a package measuring 10cm by 25cm*

measurement *noun* (a) **measurements** = size (in inches, centimetres, etc.); *to write down the measurements of a package* (b) way of judging something; *performance measurement or measurement of performance*

mechanical *adjective* referring to machines; **mechanical paper** = paper (such as newsprint) made from rough wood, which has not been processed

mechanical mouse *noun* pointing device that is operated by moving it across a flat surface; as the mouse is moved, a ball inside spins and turns two sensors that feed the horizontal and vertical movement back to the computer; *compare with* OPTICAL MOUSE

mechanism *noun* piece of machinery; *the printer mechanism is very simple; the drive mechanism appears to be faulty*

media *noun* (a) means of communicating information to the public (such as television, radio, newspapers); *the product attracted a lot of interest in the media or a lot of media interest*; **media analysis** *or* **media research** = examining different types of media (such as the readers of newspapers, television viewers) to see which is best for advertising a certain type of product; **media control interface** = *see* MCI; **media coverage** = number of reports about an event *or* product in newspapers, magazines and on TV; *we got good media coverage for the launch of the new model* (NOTE: **media** is followed by a singular or plural verb) (b) any physical material that can be used to store data; *computers can store data on a variety of media, such as disk, punched card or CD-ROM*; **media conversion** = to copy data from one type of storage media to another; *to transfer from magnetic tape to floppy disk, you need a* *media conversion device*; **media error** = fault in the storage media that corrupts data; **media server** = file server on a local area network that is primarily used to store multimedia data (such as sound, images, and video); *see also* MEDIUM

Media Player utility supplied with Windows that allows the user to control installed multimedia hardware and pass data to the device - such as playing an audio CD-ROM, a video clip or a sound file through a sound card

> COMMENT: the Media Player utility is actually a simple front-end that issues MCI commands to a multimedia device

medium 1 *adjective* middle *or* average; *the company is of medium size; a medium-sized computer system*; **medium close shot** = *see* MCS; **medium long shot** = *see* MLS **2** *noun* **(a)** way of doing something *or* means of doing something; method used to communicate with an end-user, for example, film, sound, or text; **advertising medium** = type of advertisement (such as a TV commercial); *the product was advertised through the medium of the trade press* **(b)** any physical material that can be used to store data for a computer application; *data storage mediums such as paper tape, magnetic disk, magnetic tape, paper, card and microfiche are available* (NOTE: plural is mediums or media)

medium frequency *noun* radio frequency range between 300 to 3000KHz (often referred to as medium wave (MW), especially on radio receivers)

medium lens *noun* optical photographic lens that has a focal length near the standard for the film size

medium model *noun* memory model of the Intel 80x86 processor family that allows 64Kb of data and up to 1MB of code; used when writing applications in assembly language, C or C++

medium scale integration (MSI) *noun* integrated circuit with 10 to 500 components

medium speed *noun* data communication speed between 2400 and 9600 bits per second

> COMMENT: medium speed transmission describes the maximum rate of transfer for a normal voice grade channel

medium wave (MW) *see* MEDIUM FREQUENCY

meg *abbreviation* *(informal)* = MEGABYTE; *this computer has a ninety-meg hard disk*

mega- *prefix* meaning one million; **megabit (Mb)** = equal to 1,048,576 bits, or equal to 131,072 bytes; **megabits per second** = *see* MBPS; **megabyte (MB)** = equal to 1,048,576 bytes of storage, or equal to 10^{22} bytes; **MegaCD** = add-on to a console games system with a built-in CD-ROM drive to play interactive titles; developed by Sega, the MegaCD plugs into a Mega-Drive console; **Mega-Drive** = interactive console that can run titles from cartridge or CD; developed by Sega; **megaflops (MFLOPS)** = measure of computing power equal to one million floating point operations per second; **megahertz (MHz)** = measure of frequency equal to one million cycles per second; **megapixel display** = display adapter and monitor that are capable of displaying over one million pixels; this means a resolution of at least 1,024x1,024 pixels; **Megastream** = data link provided by British Telecom that offers data transfer at rates up to 8Mbits/second; **Mega VGA** = 256 colour Super VGA mode with a resolution of 1024x768 that requires one megabyte of video RAM; **megawatt** = one million watts

> The component manufacturers sell flash memory at an average price of $30 a megabyte. By comparison, the hard-disk components sell at $3 a megabyte
>
> *Computing*

melody *noun* series of musical notes that form the basis for a musical tune

member *noun* **(a)** one object on a page of a multimedia book **(b)** individual record or item in a field

membrane keyboard *noun* keyboard that uses a thin plastic or rubber sheet with key shapes moulded into it; when the user presses on a key, it activates a pressure sensor

COMMENT: the keys in a membrane keyboard have less travel than normal mechanical keys, but since they have no moving parts, they are more robust and reliable

memo field *noun* field in a database *or* text window in an application that allows a user to add comments or a memo about the entry

COMMENT: memo fields cannot normally be searched but can store a larger amount of text than a normal text field

memomotion *noun (film)* a photographic method used to show a very slow process at normal projection speeds; *see* TIME-LAPSE

memorize *verb* to remember *or* to retain in the memory

The lower-power design, together with an additional 8Kb of on-board cache memory, will increase the chip's performance to 75 million instructions per second
Computing

memory *noun* storage space in a computer system *or* medium that is capable of retaining data *or* instructions; **bubble memory** = method of storing large amounts of binary data, as small magnetized areas in the medium (certain pure materials); **core memory** *or* **primary memory** = central fast-access memory which stores the programs and data currently in use; **disk memory** = memory held on magnetic disk, not on tape; **external memory** = memory which is located outside the main computer system confines, but which can be accessed by the CPU; **fast access memory (FAM)** = storage locations that can be read from *or* written to very rapidly; **memory access time** = time delay between requesting access to a location and being able to do so; **memory address register (MAR)** = register within the CPU that contains the address of the next location to be accessed; **memory bank** = number of smaller storage devices connected together to form one large area of memory; **memory buffer register (MBR)** = register in a CPU that temporarily buffers all inputs and outputs;

memory chip = electronic component that is able to store binary data; **memory cycle** = period of time from when the CPU reads *or* writes to a location and the action being performed; **memory data register (MDR)** = register in a CPU which holds data before it is processed *or* moved to a memory location; **memory dump** = printout of all the contents of an area of memory; **memory edit** = to change selectively the contents of various memory locations; **memory effect** = (unwanted) feature of nickel-cadmium (NiCad) rechargeable batteries in which the battery's capacity to hold charge is reduced if the battery is recharged before it has been fully discharged; *if a battery is already half-charged when it is recharged, it appears only to have the capacity to carry the new half-charge rather than a full charge; the newer Lithium Ion battery, do not suffer from memory effect; see also* LITHIUM ION BATTERY, NICAD, NIMH; **memory expansion** = the addition of more electronic memory chips to a computer; **memory-intensive software** = software that uses large amounts of RAM or disk storage during run-time, such as programs whose entire code has to be in main memory during execution; **memory management** = software that controls and regulates the flow and position in memory of files and data; **memory management unit (MMU)** = electronic logic circuits that generate the memory refresh signals and manage the mapping of virtual memory addresses to physical memory locations; the MMU is normally integrated into the processor chip; **memory map** = diagram indicating the allocation of address ranges to various devices such as RAM, ROM and memory-mapped input/output devices; **memory-mapped** = with addresses allocated to a computer's input *or* output devices to allow them to be accessed as if they were a memory location; *a memory-mapped screen has an address allocated to each pixel, allowing direct access to the screen by the CPU;* **memory model** = method used in a program to address the code and data that is used within that program; the memory model defines how much memory is available for code and data; processors with a segmented address space (like the Intel 80x86 range) can support multiple memory models; **memory**

page = one section of main store which is divided into pages, and which contains data or programs; **memory protect** = feature on most storage systems to prevent the accidental overwriting of data; **memory-resident** *or* **resident** = (program) that is held permanently in memory; *the system can bomb if you set up too many memory-residentat the same time*; **memory switching system** = system which communicates information, stores it in memory and then transmits it according to instructions; **memory workspace** = amount of extra memory required by a program to store data used during execution; **virtual memory** = system where the workspace is held in both backing store and memory at the same time

menu *noun* list of options *or* programs available to the user; *(in a GUI)* **main menu** = list of primary options available; **menu-bar** = list of options available to a user which are displayed on a horizontal line along the top of the screen or window: each menu option activates a pull-down menu; *almost all Windows programs have a menu-bar that starts with the word 'File', which if you select it displays the options that include Open, Save and Exit*; **menu-driven software** = program where commands *or* options are selected from a menu by the operator; **menu item** = one of the choices in a menu; **menu selection** = choosing commands from a list of options presented to the operator; **menu shortcut** = a combination of two or more keys that activate the same function as selecting the menu option; *Ctrl-S is the standard menu shortcut for saving a document you are working on*; **pop-up menu** = set of options that are displayed in the centre of the screen; **pull-down menu** = menu of options that can be displayed at any time, usually overwriting any other text; *the pull-down menu is viewed by clicking on the menu bar at the top of the screen*

merge *verb* to combine two data files, but still retaining an overall order; *the system automatically merges text and illustrations into the document*; **merge sort** = software application in which the sorted files are merged into a new file; *see also* MAIL-MERGE

mesh *noun* any system with two *or* more possible paths at each interconnection; **mesh network** = method of connecting several machines together, where each pair of devices has two *or* more connections

message *noun* **(a)** information sent from one person to another; *he sent a message to his head office; there are two messages on your answerphone* **(b)** certain defined amount of information **(c)** *(in an object-oriented programming system)* code generated by an action or object and interpreted by another object; *if a user presses the mouse button it generates a 'button_down' message that can then be interpreted by a user-interface or program*; **message authentication code** = *see* MAC **(b)**; **message format** = predetermined rules defining the coding, size and speed of transmitted messages; **message heading** = section of a message that contains routing and destination information; **message numbering** = identification of messages by allocating a number to each one; **message routing** = selection of a suitable path between the source and destination of a message in a network; **message slot** = number of bits that can hold a message which circulates around a ring network; **message switching** = storing, arranging and making up batches of convenient sizes of data to allow for their economical transmission over a network; **message text** = information that concerns the user at the destination without routing *or* network control data **(d)** text displayed to a user to report on a condition or program; **message box** = small window displayed on screen with text that informs the user of a condition, error or report **(e)** *(in MIDI)* data that is sent to control an instrument

metafile *noun* (i) file that contains other files; (ii) file that defines or contains data about other files; *the operating system uses a metafile to hold data that defines where each file is stored on disk*

metal halide lamp *noun* *(film)* a mercury arc light

metal oxide *noun* *(film)* mixture of oxygen and a metal; **complementary metal oxide semiconductor (CMOS)** = integrated circuit design and construction method, using a pair of complementary p- and n-type transistors; **metal oxide semiconductor (MOS)** = production and design method for a certain family of integrated circuits using patterns of metal conductors and oxide deposited onto a semiconductor; **metal oxide semiconductor field effect transistor (MOSFET)** = high-powered and high-speed field effect transistor manufactured using MOS techniques;

metalanguage *noun* language which describes a programming language

meter 1 *noun* **(a)** device which counts *or* records something; *an electricity meter; a meter attached to the photocopier records the number of copies made*; *see also* MULTIMETER **(b)** *(in Windows)* an icon in the bottom right-hand corner of the status bar that indicates how much power is left in a laptop's battery and whether the laptop is running off battery or mains electricity power **2** *verb* to record and count; *the calls from each office are metered by the call logger*

metre kilogram second *see* MKS

metropolitan area network (MAN) *noun* network extending over a limited area (normally a city); *compare with* LAN, WAN

MF = MEDIUM FREQUENCY

MFLOPS = MEGA FLOATING POINT OPERATIONS PER SECOND measure of computing speed calculated as the number of floating point operations that can be processed each second

MFM = MODIFIED FREQUENCY MODULATION method of storing data on magnetic media (such as a magnetic disk) that encodes the data bit according to the state of the previous bit; MFM is more

efficient than FM, but less efficient than RLL encoding

M-format *or* **M-wrap** *noun* *(film)* a tape path which is used in the VHS video cassette recorder

MHz = MEGAHERTZ a measure of the frequency of a timing signal that is equal to one million cycles per second

> COMMENT: the higher the MHz number, the faster the clock that is generating the timing signal. This normally refers to the main clock that sets the timing signal for the processor chip in a PC. The faster the timing signal, the faster the processor will operate and so the faster the software will run

MIC = MICROPHONE device which converts sound to an electrical analogue signal

MICR = MAGNETIC INK CHARACTER RECOGNITION system that identifies characters by sensing magnetic ink patterns (as used on bank cheques)

micro *noun* = MICROCOMPUTER

micro- *prefix* **(a)** meaning one millionth of a unit; **micrometre** = one millionth of a metre; **microsecond** = one millionth of a second **(b)** meaning very small; **microcassette** = small format audio cassette used mainly in pocket dictating equipment; **microcontroller** = small self-contained microcomputer for use in dedicated control applications; **microdevice** = very small device, such as a microprocessor

Microchannel Architecture *see* MCA

microcircuit *noun* complex integrated circuit

microcode *noun* ALU control instructions implemented as hardwired software

Microcom Networking Protocol *see* MNP

microcomputer *or* **micro** *noun* complete small-scale, cheap, low-power computer system based around a microprocessor chip and having limited memory capacity; **microcomputing** = referring to microcomputers and their use; *the microcomputing industry*

COMMENT: micros are particularly used as home computers *or* as small office computers

microelectronics *noun* design and manufacture of electronic circuits with integrated circuits and chips

microfiche *noun* sheet of text and graphics in highly reduced form on a photographic film

microfilm 1 *noun* reel of film containing a sequence of very small images used for document storage; *we hold all our records on microfilm* **2** *verb* to take very small photographs; *the 2000 records have been sent away for microfilming*

microfloppy *noun* small size magnetic floppy disk (usually refers to 3.5 inch disks)

microform *noun* medium used for storing information in microimage form

micrographics *noun* images and graphics stored as microimages

microimage *noun* graphical image too small to be seen with the naked eye

microinstruction *noun* one hardwired instruction (part of a microcode) that controls the actions of the ALU

micron *noun* one millionth of a metre

microphone *noun* device that converts sound waves into an electrical analogue signal; **dynamic microphone** = microphone using a coil that moves and induces a voltage according to sound pressure; **lapel microphone** = small microphone that is pinned to someone's jacket; **moving coil microphone** = microphone hat uses a coil of wire moved by sound waves to generate an electrical signal; *(film)* **microphone boom** = a pole to which a microphone is attached and which can be extended over the area where the action is taking place; **microphone presence** = unwanted noise such as breathing which appears when the performer and microphone are too close together;

microphotography *noun* photographic production of microimages (too small to be seen with the naked eye)

microprocessor *noun* small central processing unit contained on a single integrated circuit chip; **microprocessor unit (MPU)** = unit containing the main elements of a microprocessor

microprogram *noun* series of microinstructions; **microprogram store** = storage device used to hold a microprogram

microprogramming *noun* writing microcode using microinstructions

microreciprocal degree *noun (film)* numerical value which is used to indicate the colour temperature of a light or filter

microsecond *noun* one millionth of a second

Microsoft major developer and publisher of software for the PC and Macintosh; Microsoft developed the MS-DOS operating system for the IBM PC and later Windows together with a wide range of application software; **Microsoft Compact Disc Extensions** = *see* MSCDEX; **Microsoft DOS (MS-DOS)** = operating system for IBM PC range of personal computers that manages data storage onto disks, display output and user input; MS-DOS is a single-user, single-tasking operating system that is controlled by a command-line interface; **Microsoft Exchange** = a program included in Windows 95 that coordinates the electronic mail, fax and network messages sent and received on a PC, now replaced by Outlook; **Microsoft Fax** = a series of programs supplied with Windows 3.1 and 95 that let the user send and receive fax transmissions from their PC; coversheets for fax transmissions can also be created with the Fax software; **Microsoft Network (MSN)** = a vast on-line service to provide information, weather reports, database links to the Internet and electronic mail; **Microsoft Outlook** = application that provides a range of features to manage email, fax messages, contacts, diary appointments, notes and projects; = **Microsoft Outlook Express** = free version of Outlook that has fewer extra features for managing contacts and appointments; **Microsoft Windows 3.1** = multi-tasking graphical user interface designed to be easy to use; Windows uses icons to represent files and devices and can be controlled using a mouse, unlike MS-DOS which requires commands to be typed in; **Microsoft Windows 9x** = multi-tasking graphical user interface that has superseded

Windows 3.1; with versions 95 and 98 each providing full 32-bit software support and pre-emptive multitasking together with built-in networking and Internet support; **Microsoft Windows for Workgroups** = multi-tasking GUI designed to be easy to use, that is compatible and nearly identical to Windows 3.1 but includes built-in networking support; **Microsoft Windows Me** = version of Windows with improvements designed to appeal to home users; **Microsoft Windows NT** = high-performance multitasking version of Windows that is used on servers and high-performance workstations

microwave *noun* radio frequency range from 1 to 3000GHz; **microwave amplification by stimulated emission of radiation** = *see* MASER; **microwave communications link** = use of a microwave beam to transmit data between two points; **microwave relay** = radiocommunications equipment used to receive microwave signals, then boost and retransmit them; **microwave transmission** = communication using modulated microwaves allowing high data rates, used for international telephone and satellite communications

microwriter *noun* portable keyboard and display, used for keyboarding when travelling

middle and side microphone *see* M AND S MICROPHONE

MID-F1 *(in CD-i)* mid-quality sound at Level B; *see* LEVEL B

MIDI = MUSICAL INSTRUMENT DIGITAL INTERFACE serial interface that connects electronic instruments; the MIDI interface carries signals from a controller or computer that instructs the different instruments to play notes; **MIDI connector** = standard 5-pin, round DIN connector used to connect MIDI devices; **MIDI control-change message** = message sent to a synthesizer to control the volume or pitch of a sound or to change the instrument patch used to generate a sound; **MIDI device** = device that can receive or send MIDI data; **MIDI file** = file format used to store a MIDI song, made up of notes and control-change messages (normally has a MIDI file extension); **MIDI interface card** = adapter card that plugs into an expansion connector in a PC and allows it to send and receive

MIDI data; **MIDI Mapper** = utility provided with Microsoft Windows that allows a user to redefine the way MIDI channels are used - for example, it can be used to send any data marked for channel two to channel four and also modify its controls, such as the volume setting; **MIDI mapping** = translating and redirecting MIDI messages between channels according to settings in a MIDI map; **MIDI program-change message** = message sent to a synthesizer to request a patch change for a particular MIDI channel; **MIDI sequence** = data that has time-sequence data embedded and that can be played by a MIDI sequencer; **MIDI sequencer** = (i) software that allows a user to record, edit, add special effects and playback MIDI data through a synthesizer; (ii) hardware device that records or plays back stored MIDI data; **MIDI setup map** = (used with MIDI Mapper) file that contains all the data required to define the settings for MIDI Mapper; **MIDI time code (MTC)** = messages used to synchronize MIDI sequences with an external device, such as an SMPTE time code

COMMENT: the MIDI interface can connect up to 32 different instruments and carries signals from a sequencer or computer that instructs the different instruments - such as a drum machine or synthesizer - to play notes together with instructions called control-change messages, which control the volume, pitch and type of instrument used. A MIDI interface does not carry sounds, rather it carries notes and instructions to change to a different preset sound; many PC sound cards include electronics to generate sounds from MIDI data on-board. There are two kinds of MIDI sound generation: FM synthesis simulates musical notes by modulating the frequency of a base carrier wave, whereas waveform synthesis uses digitized samples of the notes to produce a more realistic sound. MIDI also allows multiple different voices, or notes, to be played back simultaneously (MPC requires an 8-voice synthesizer, but studio-quality instruments can have up to 32 MIDI voices)

mid-user *noun* operator who retrieves relevant information from a database for a customer *or* end user

migration *noun* moving users from one hardware platform to another

milk disk *noun* disk used to transfer data from a small machine onto a larger computer, which provides greater processing power

milking machine *noun* portable machine which can accept data from different machines, then transfer it to another larger computer

Millennium compliance computer or software that has been designed to work correctly after the year 2000; *see* Y2K, YEAR 2000

milli- *prefix* meaning one thousandth; **milliampere** *or* **mA** = electrical current measure equal to one thousandth of an ampere; **millicoulomb** *or* **mC** = one thousandth of a coulomb; **millisecond** *or* **mS** = one thousandth of a second

million instructions per second *see* MIPS

MIMD = MULTIPLE INSTRUCTION STREAM-MULTIPLE DATA STREAM architecture of a parallel processor that uses a number of ALUs and memory devices in parallel to provide high speed processing

mini- *prefix* meaning small; **minidisk** = magnetic disk smaller than the 5.25 inch standard, usually 3.5 inch; **minifloppy** = magnetic disk (usually refers to the 5.25 inch standard); *(slang)* **miniwinny** = small Winchester hard disk

minicam *noun* *(film)* a hand-held, lightweight video camera

minicomputer *or* **mini** *noun* small computer, with a greater range of instructions and processing power than a microcomputer, but not able to compete with the speed *or* data handling capacity of a mainframe computer

minimise *or* **minimize** *verb* **(a)** to make as small as possible; *we minimized costs by cutting down the number of components* **(b)** *(in MS-Windows)* to shrink an application window to an icon; *compare with* MAXIMISE

COMMENT: the application can continue to run in the background; you minimise a window by clicking once on the first icon, that displays a '_', of the three small icons in the top right-hand corner of every window

minimum *noun* the smallest amount of something; **minimum weight routing** = method of optimizing the transmission path of a message through a network

minmax *noun* method used in artificial intelligence to solve problems

minuend *noun* number from which another is subtracted

minus *or* **minus sign** *noun* printed *or* written sign (like a small dash) to indicate subtraction *or* to show a negative value

minuscule *noun* lower case printed character

MIPS = MILLION INSTRUCTIONS PER SECOND measure of processor speed

```
ICL has staked its claim to the
massively parallel market with
the launch of the Goldrush
MegaServer, providing up to
16,000 Unix MIPS of processing
power
```
Computing

mirror 1 *noun* glass with a metal backing, which reflects an image; **mirror image** = image produced that is equivalent to that which would be seen in a mirror; *(film)* **mirror shutter** = a reflex shutter system which enables the cameraman to see the shot as it is being filmed **2** *verb* **(a)** to create an identical copy **(b)** to duplicate all disk operations onto a second disk drive that can be used if the first breaks down; *there's less chance of losing our data now that we have mirrored the server's disk drive* **(c)** to rotate an image by 180 degrees

```
they also offer mirror-disk
protection against disk
failure, providing automatic
backup of a database
```
Computer News

```
disks are also mirrored so
that the system can continue
to run in the event of a disk
crash
```
Computer News

```
mirroring of the database is
handled automatically by
systems software
```
Computer News

MIS = MANAGEMENT INFORMATION SYSTEM

MISD = MULTIPLE INSTRUCTION STREAM-SINGLE DATA STREAM architecture of a parallel computer that has a single ALU and data bus with a number of control units

mismatch *noun* situation occurring when two things are not correctly matched; **impedance mismatch** = situation where the impedance of the transmission *or* receiving end of a system does not match the other, resulting in loss of signal power

mission-critical *adjective* (application or hardware) on which your company depends; **mission-critical application** = software program without which your company cannot function

mix 1 *noun* **(a)** creative blending together of audio or video sources **(b)** a visual effect which is similar to a dissolve **2** *verb* to combine several separate signals into a single signal; **to mix down** = to combine the signals from several sources such as a number of recorded audio tracks *or* instruments into a single signal

mixed highs *noun* fine colour detail that is in monochrome in a TV signal

mixer *noun* electronic circuit used to combine two *or* more separate signals into a single output

mixing *noun* **(a)** combining several audio signals into a single signal; **mixing studio** = room with audio mixers and sound processors used when recording music **(b)** printing a line of text with several different typefaces

MKS = METRE KILOGRAM SECOND widely used measurement system based on the metre, kilogram and second; *see also* SI UNITS

MLS *(film)* = MEDIUM LONG SHOT shot picturing almost the whole of a subject

MMA = MIDI MANUFACTURERS ASSOCIATION

MME = MULTIMEDIA EXTENSIONS

MMI = MAN MACHINE INTERFACE hardware and software designed to make it easier for users to communicate effectively with a machine

MMU = MEMORY MANAGEMENT UNIT electronic logic circuits that generate the memory refresh signals and manage the mapping of virtual memory addresses to physical memory locations; the MMU is normally integrated into the processor chip

mnemonic *noun* shortened form of a word *or* function that is helpful as a reminder (such as INCA for increment register A); **assembler mnemonics** = standard word abbreviations used when writing a program for a particular CPU in assembly language (such as LDA for load register A); **mnemonic keyboard shortcut** = combination of keys (on a keyboard) that provide direct access to a menu option or function

COMMENT: normally a mnemonic keyboard shortcut is a combination of the Alt key on a PC or the Apple key on a Mac at the same time as another key; the convention is that the second key is underlined. For example, the standard shortcut to pull-down the File menu in Windows is Alt-F (the F in File is underlined to show that it is the shortcut key)

MNP = MICROCOM NETWORKING PROTOCOL error detection and correction system developed by Microcom Inc., used in modems and some communications software

mobile *adjective* **(a)** which can move about; **mobile earth terminal** = satellite communications equipment that is mobile; **mobile unit** = complete set of television filming and editing equipment carried in a vehicle (for outside broadcasts) **(b)** *(informal)* meaning a portable telephone or radio base such as a car transceiver; **mobile phone** *or* **cellular phone** = small, portable device that lets someone make and receive telephone calls; *see also* = BLUETOOTH, GPRS, GSM, PCS, SMS, WAP; **mobile radiophone** = radio telephone linked to a main telephone system, which uses a network of stations, each covering a certain area, to provide a service over a large area

COMMENT: older mobile phone standards transmitted the user's voice as an analogue radio signal, current phones convert the voice to digital data and transmit this via a radio signal, new mobile phones provide data transmission, messaging services and access to online services, as well as basic telephone functions: some phones include built-in modems to provide dial-up access to the Internet, many allow text messages to be transmitted to other phone users and some incorporate an electronic diary, organiser and address book; current mobile telephones transmit information using the GSM, PCS or GPRS standard and can provide basic Internet access using WAP and GPRS

mock-up *noun* model of a new product for testing *or* to show to possible customers

modal *adjective* **(a)** referring to modes **(b)** method of displaying a window so that the user cannot do anything outside this window; *dialog boxes are normally modal windows and will not let you do anything outside the window until you choose an option or close the dialog box*

Mode 1 encoding format used on compact discs, that has error-detection and correction codes, and is used in CD-ROM, DV-I and CD-TV; supports a data area of 2048bytes per sector

Mode 2 encoding format with two forms: form 1 is the same as Mode 1, form 2 requires no processing and the data can be sent straight to the output channel; this is used in CD-ROM XA, PhotoCD and CD-i. Mode 2 form 2 has a larger data area than Mode 1, since there is less error correction code

the printer gives print quality in three modes: high speed, data processing and letter-quality

Minicomputer News

The approach being established by the Jedec committee provides for burst mode data transfer clocked at up to 100MHz

Computing

mode *noun* **(a)** way of doing something; method of operating a computer; *when you want to type in text, press this function key which will put the terminal in its alphanumeric mode*; **execute mode** = entering a command in direct mode to start a program run; **input mode** = mode in which a computer is receiving data; **insert mode** = interactive computer mode in which new text is entered within the previous text, which adjusts to accept it; **interactive mode** = mode in which a computer allows the user to enter commands *or* programs *or* data and receive an immediate response; **replace mode** = interactive computer mode in which new text entered replaces any previous text in its place **(b)** number of paths taken by light when travelling down an optical fibre; **mode dispersion** = loss of power in a light signal transmitted down an optic fibre due to dispersion from transmission paths that are not directly along the axis of the fibre; *see* MONOMODE FIBRE, MULTIMODE FIBRE **(c)** number that occurs most frequently in a series of samples

model 1 *noun* **(a)** small copy of something to show what it will look like when finished; *he showed us a model of the new computer centre building* **(b)** style *or* type of product; version of a product; *the new model B has taken the place of model A; this is the latest model; the model on display is last year's; they are selling off the old models at half price*; **demonstration model** = piece of equipment used in demonstrations (and then sold cheaply) **2** *adjective* which is a perfect example to be copied; *a model agreement* **3** *verb* to make a computerized model of a new product *or* of the economic system, etc. (NOTE: **modelling - modelled** but *US* **modeling - modeled**)

modelling *noun* **(a)** creating computer models **(b)** colouring and shading a (normally wire-frame or vecto) graphic object so that it looks solid and real; *(film)* **modelling light** = lighting which creates both highlights and creates shadows on objects or performers in the area of action

modem *or* **MODEM** *noun* = MODULATOR/DEMODULATOR device that allows data to be sent over telephone lines by converting binary signals from a computer into analog sound signals, which can be transmitted over a telephone line; **dial-in modem** = auto-answer modem that can be called at any time; **modem eliminator** = cable *or* device that allows two computers to communicate via their serial ports without using modems; **null modem** = circuit *or* cable that allows two computers to communicate via their serial ports; *this cable is configured as a null modem, which will allow me to connect these two computers together easily*; *see also*

STANDARD; *compare with* ACOUSTIC COUPLER

> COMMENT: the process of converting binary signals to analog is called 'modulation'. When the signal is received, another modem reverses the process (called 'demodulation'). Both modems must be working according to the same standards

AST Research has bundled together a notebook PC with a third-party PCMCIA fax modem technology for a limited-period special offer
Computing

moderated newsgroup *noun* newsgroup in which someone (the moderator) reads all the material that has been submitted before it is published in the newsgroup; most newsgroups are not moderated and anyone can write anything; moderated newsgroups usually have a '-d' after their name

moderator *noun* person responsible for reading messages sent to a mailing list and editing any messages that do not conform to the rules of the list, for example by deleting commercial messages

modification *noun* change made to something; *they are using the stock control system without any modifications; the modifications to the system, allow it to be run as part of a LAN*

modified frequency modulation (MFM) *noun* method of storing data on magnetic media (such as a magnetic disk) that encodes the data bit according to the state of the previous bit; MFM is more efficient than FM, but less efficient than RLL encoding

modified NTSC *noun* (*film*) colour television system which uses NTSC coding but with a colour sub-carrier frequency of 4.43 MHz instead of 3.8 MHz; this is occasionally used in video cassette recorders and monitors

modifier *noun* programming instruction that alters the normal action of a command

modify *verb* to change something *or* to make something fit a different use; *the keyboard was modified for European users; we are running a modified version of the mail-merge system; the software will have to be modified to run on a small PC*

Modula-2 *noun* high-level programming language derived from Pascal that supports modular programming techniques and data abstraction

modular *adjective* (method of constructing hardware *or* software products) by connecting several smaller blocks together to produce a customized product; **modular programming** = programming small individually written sections of computer code that can be made to fit into a structured program and can be called up from a main program

modularity *noun* being made up from modules; *the modularity of the software or hardware allows the system to be changed*

modularization *verb* designing programs from a set of standard modules

modulate *verb* to change a carrier wave so that it can carry data; **modulated signal** = constant frequency and amplitude carrier signal that is used in a modulated form to transmit data; **modulating signal** = signal to be transmitted that is used to modulate a carrier

modulation *noun* process of varying a carrier's amplitude *or* frequency *or* phase according to an applied signal; **amplitude modulation (AM)** = system that varies the amplitude of a constant carrier signal according to an external signal; **frequency modulation (FM)** = system that varies the frequency of a constant amplitude carrier signal according to an external signal

modulator *noun* electronic circuit that varies a carrier signal according to an applied signal; often used to convert the output of a computer to a composite signal (by varying a generated carrier signal) that can be displayed on a standard television set; **modulator/demodulator** = MODEM

module *noun* (a) small section of a large program that can if required function independently as a program in its own right (b) self-contained piece of hardware that can be connected with other modules to form a new system; *a multifunction analog interface module includes analog to digital and digital to analog converters* (c) (*film*) (i) a system for imprinting a signal on a radio frequency carrier; (ii) a system for producing audio effects where one sound is modulated by another

modulo arithmetic *noun* branch of arithmetic that uses the remainder of one number when divided by another

modulus *or* **MOD** *noun* the remainder after the division of one number by another; *7 mod 3 = 1*

moiré *noun* **(a)** picture distortion which is caused by interference beats of similar frequencies **(b)** unwanted optical effect when images are printed by a printing press using the wrong screen angle for the images for this particular printer; *see also* SCREEN ANGLE

momentary switch *noun* switch that only conducts while it is being pressed

monitor 1 *noun* **(a)** visual display unit used to display high quality text *or* graphics, generated by a computer **(b)** loudspeaker used to listen to the sound signals produced during recording *or* mixing; *(film)* **monitor loudspeaker** = high-quality loudspeaker which is used to listen to all sound elements during the recording and mixing of audio **(c)** TV screen in a TV studio control room, which shows the image being filmed by one of the cameras; **monitor viewfinder** = viewfinder where the picture is seen on a small screen **(d)** computer program that allows basic commands to be entered to operate a system (such as load a program, examine the state of devices, etc.); *see also* OPERATING SYSTEM **(e)** system that watches for faults *or* failures in a circuit; **power monitor** = circuit that shuts off the electricity supply if it is faulty *or* likely to damage equipment **2** *verb* **(a)** to check *or* to examine how something is working **(b)** to look after and supervise a process *or* experiment to make sure it is operating correctly; *he is monitoring the progress of the trainee programmers; the machine monitors each signal as it is sent out*; *see also* ANALOG MONITOR, DIGITAL MONITOR, MULTI-SCAN MONITOR

mono = MONOAURAL

mono- *prefix* meaning single *or* one

monoaural *adjective* single audio channel presented to only one ear

monochromatic light *noun (film)* light of a single colour

monochrome *adjective & noun* (image) in one colour, usually shades of grey and black and white; **monochrome display adapter (MDA)** = video adapter standard used in early PC systems that could display text in 25 lines of 80 columns; **monochrome monitor** = computer monitor that displays text and graphics in black, white and shades of grey instead of colours

monolithic *adjective* (integrated circuit) manufactured on a single crystal of semiconductor; **monolithic driver** = driver software that has a range of different functions or applications within one program; *see also* = DRIVER

monomode fibre *noun* optical fibre that only allows light to travel along its axis without any internal reflections, as the result of having a very fine core diameter; *see also* MODE

monophonic *adjective* system where one audio signal is used to feed one *or* more loudspeakers; *compare with* STEREOPHONIC

monoprogramming system *noun* computer batch processing system that executes one program at a time; *compare with* MULTI-PROGRAMMING SYSTEM

monospacing *noun* system of printing where each character occupies the same amount of space, as on a typewriter (as opposed to proportional spacing)

monostable *noun* electronic circuit that produces a output pulse for a predetermined period when it receives an input signal

montage *noun* **(a)** series of quickly changing images, sometimes with general pictures seen simultaneously on the screen **(b)** combining several still or video images

Monte Carlo method *noun* statistical analysis technique

morphing *noun* process of transforming one image into another over a period of time; usually used for special effects; *we morphed an image of a house into a bird in 20 separate frames so that the change appears animated when played back*

Morse code *noun* system of signalling using only two symbols: dots and dashes; **morse key** = switch used to send morse messages by hand

MOS = METAL OXIDE SEMICONDUCTOR production and

design method for a certain family of integrated circuits using patterns of metal conductors and oxide deposited onto a semiconductor; *see also* MOSFET, NMOS; **CMOS = COMPLEMENTARY METAL OXIDE SEMICONDUCTOR** integrated circuit design and construction (using a pair of complementary p- and n-type transistors)

integrated circuits fall into one of two distinct classes, based either on bipolar or metal oxide semiconductor (MOS) transistors

Electronics & Power

Mosaic *noun* (old) web browser software used to view web pages on the Internet; *see also* BROWSER, HTML, MICROSOFT IE, NETSCAPE, WWW

mosaic *noun* **(a)** display character used in videotext systems that is made up of small dots **(b)** light-sensitive surface of a television camera pick-up tube which is scanned by the electron beam

MOSFET = METAL OXIDE SEMICONDUCTOR FIELD EFFECT TRANSISTOR high power and high speed field effect transistor manufactured using MOS techniques

most significant bit *or* **msb** *or* **MSB** *noun* bit in a word that represents the greatest value *or* weighting (usually the bit which is furthest to the left); *the most significant bit in an eight bit binary word represents 128 in decimal notation*

most significant character *or* **most significant digit (MSD)** *noun* digit at the far left of a number, that represents the greatest power of the base

motherboard *noun* main printed circuit board of a system, containing most of the components and connections for expansion boards, etc.

motion blur *noun* blurring of an object that moves too fast to be frozen by the camera

motion control *noun* computer that allows a user to control all the aspects of a camera to allow special effects in video or still images

motion picture *noun* series of still pictures (each slightly different) which give an object the appearance of motion when projected on to a screen; **motion-picture camera** = a box with lens, shutter, viewfinder and film advance system in which motion-picture film is exposed; **motion picture experts group** = *see* MPEG; **motion-picture film** = light-sensitive film which is used in a motion picture camera

motor *noun* electromagnetic machine that converts an electrical supply into (rotary) motion (by means of a magnetic field)

Motorola manufacturer of electronic components, including the 68000 range of processors used in original Apple Macintosh computers; **Motorola 68000** = processor that can manage 32-bit words internally, but transfers data externally via a 16-bit data bus; used in the original Apple Macintosh; **Motorola PowerPC** = RISC-based 32-bit processor used in high-end Macintosh computers and other high-performance workstations; it is still downwards compatible with the 68000 range; *see also* AMD, INTEL

mount 1 *noun* stand on which a camera is put when needed to be raised **2** *verb* **(a)** to fix a device *or* a circuit onto a base; *the chips are mounted in sockets on the PCB* **(b)** operation to insert a disk in a disk drive or inform an operating system that a disk drive is ready to be used

mouse *noun* small hand-held input device moved on a flat surface to control the position of a cursor on the screen; **bus mouse** = mouse that connects to a special expansion card plugged into the computer's expansion bus; **mechanical mouse** = pointing device that is operated by moving it across a flat surface; as the mouse is moved, a ball inside spins and turns two sensors that feed the horizontal and vertical movement back to the computer; **mouse-driven** = (software) which uses a mouse rather than a keyboard for input; **mouse driver** = program which controls the use of a mouse; **mouse pointer** = small arrow displayed on screen that moves around as the mouse is moved; **optical mouse** = pointing device that is operated by moving it across a special flat mat; on the mat is printed a grid of lines, as the mouse is moved, two light sensors count the number of lines that have been passed to produce a measure of the distance and direction of travel; an optical mouse has fewer moving parts than a mechanical mouse and so is more reliable, but requires an accurately printed mat; **serial mouse** = mouse that connects to the serial port of a PC and transfers positional data via the serial port (NOTE: the plural is **mice** or sometimes **mouses**)

```
Other   areas   of   research
include a sound system which
allows   a   sound   to   'move',
mirroring the movement of a
mouse
```
Computing

mouth *noun* open end of an antenna

movable *adjective* which can be moved; **movable head disk** = magnetic disk head assembly that moves across the disk until the required track is reached

move *verb* to change the place of something; **move block** = command which changes the place of a block of text identified by block markers; **moving coil microphone** = microphone which uses a coil of wire moved by sound waves to generate an electrical signal

movement *noun* changing the place of something; **movement file** = file continuing recent changes *or* transactions to records, which is then used to update a master file

movie file *noun* file that contains data used to display a moving image or animation when viewed with special software; *Windows Movie Player can display movie files with an .MMM or .MPG extension; the movie file contains graphic objects (the cast members) together with information that defines how they move around the screen*

movie ID *noun* unique ID number assigned to a movie in Movie Player; each separate instance has a different ID number

Movie Player Windows utility that can playback AVI-format video clips or movie files with the MMM extension

Movie Player instance *noun* one copy of the Movie Player program that is running

moving pictures expert group *see* MPEG

moving shot *noun (film)* shot filmed while the camera is moving; camera movement is created by use of a dolly, crane or car

MP3 = MPEG AUDIO LEVEL 3 method of encoding digital audio data into a compressed format that is approximately one twelfth the size of the original without perceptible loss of quality

> COMMENT: MP3 files (that normally have the file name extension 'MP3') are now one of the most popular ways of storing and distributing music over the Internet. Because MP3 files are compact and easy to copy, they are relatively quick to download and very easy to distribute - which is causing problems for the original artists who are trying to protect their copyright material. Once you have an MP3 file you can listen to it by opening it and playing it with special software on your computer or by transferring it to a dedicated pocket-sized device that stores the file in its memory, has no moving parts and but can play back CD-quality music.

MPC = MULTIMEDIA PC minimum hardware requirements for a multimedia PC specified by the Multimedia PC Marketing Council; this gives the user a guide when buying a PC that is capable of running multimedia applications

MPEG = MOTION PICTURE EXPERTS GROUP full-motion video compression technique that is more efficient than the similar still-image compression scheme, JPEG

> COMMENT: MPEG compares two successive frames and only records the changes between the two; MPEG-1 is used for data rates of 2Mb per second, MPEG-2 for data rates of 2-10Mb per second

MPPP = MULTI-LINK POINT TO POINT PROTOCOL communications protocol used with ISDN to link the two B-channels in a standard ISDN adapter to create a transmission channel that can transfer data at a higher speed

MPU = MICROPROCESSOR UNIT

MS = MANUSCRIPT (NOTE: plural is **MSS**)

ms = MILLISECOND one thousandth of a second

msb *or* **MSB** = MOST SIGNIFICANT BIT

MSCDEX = MICROSOFT COMPACT DISC EXTENSIONS driver software installed on a PC to allow DOS and Windows to access a CD-ROM drive as a normal disk drive letter; normally drive D:

MSD = MOST SIGNIFICANT DIGIT

MS-DOS = MICROSOFT DOS operating system for IBM PC range of personal computers that manages data storage onto disks, display output and user input

> COMMENT: MS-DOS is a single-user, single-tasking operating system that is controlled by a command-line interface

MSF time format *noun* time format that counts frames per second used by MCI, normally used by CD-audio devices (in a CD-A device there are 75 frames per second)

MSI = MEDIUM SCALE INTEGRATION

MS-Windows *see* MICROSOFT WINDOWS

MSX *noun* hardware and software standard for home computers using compatible software

MTBF = MEAN TIME BETWEEN FAILURES average period of time that a piece of equipment will operate between failures

MTC = MIDI TIME CODE messages used to synchronize MIDI sequences with an external device, such as a SMPTE time code

MUA = MAIL USER AGENT software used to create and read electronic mail messages; this software creates a message in the correct format and standard and passes this to the mail transfer agent that is responsible for transferring the message over the network; *see also* EMAIL, MAIL TRANSFER AGENT, MAPI, POP3, SMTP

MUD = MULTI-USER DUNGEON adventure game played by multiple users over the Internet

multi statement line *noun* line from a computer program that contains more than one instruction *or* statement

multi- *prefix* meaning many *or* more than one; *multimegabyte memory card; a multistandard unit*

multi-access system *noun* computer system that allows several users to access one file *or* program at the same time; *see also* MULTI-USER SYSTEM

multi-board computer *noun* computer which has several integrated circuit boards connected with a mother board

multiburst signal *noun* television test signal

multicast *noun* to transmit one message to a group of recipients; *see also* BROADCAST, MAILING LIST, NARROWCAST

> COMMENT: a multicast could be as simple as sending an email message to a list of email addresses or posting a message to a mailing list. It can also refer to more complex transfers such as a teleconference or video-conference in which several users link together by telephone or video link. A broadcast, in comparison, refers to the process of sending a message to anyone who could receive the message rather than a select group of recipients. Narrowcasting is very similar in concept to a multicast, but is normally used to refer to the concept, whereas multicast refers to the technology used

multicasting *noun* broadcasting to a number of receivers *or* nodes, with an address in each message to indicate the node required

multichannel *adjective* with more than one channel

multicolour graphics adapter (MCGA) *noun* colour graphics adapter standard fitted in low-end IBM PS/2 computers

multicolour *adjective* with several colours

multidimensional *adjective* with features in more than one dimension; **multidimensional array** = number of arrays arranged in parallel, providing depth; **multidimensional language** = programming language that can be represented in a number of ways

multi-disk *adjective* referring to several types of disk; **multi-disk option** = system that can have disk drives installed in a number of sizes; **multi-disk reader** = device which car read from various sizes and formats of disk

multidrop circuit *noun* network allowing communications between a number of terminals and a central computer, but not directly between terminals

MultiFinder version of Apple Macintosh Finder that supports multi-tasking

multifrequency *noun* **dual tone, multifrequency (DTMF)** = communication signalling system using two different frequencies to transmit binary data

multifunction *adjective* which has several functions; *a multifunction analog interface module includes analog to digital and digital to analog converters*; **multifunction card** = add-on circuit board that provides many features to upgrade a computer; **multifunction workstation** = workstation where several tasks can be carried out

multifunctional *adjective* which has several functions; *a multifunctional scanner*

multilayer *noun* printed circuit board that has several layers *or* interconnecting conduction tracks; **multilayer colour film** = photographic film with two or more layers, each being sensitive to a different colour

multilevel *noun* signal with a number of possible values (quaternary signals have four levels)

multilink system *noun* system where there is more than one connection between two points

multimedia *adjective* the combination of sound, graphics, animation, video and text within an application; **multimedia developer's kit (MDK)** = product developed by Microsoft that allows developers to produce multimedia applications more easily using the supplied libraries of routines to control video playback, process images and display text; **multimedia extensions (MME)** = part of Microsoft Windows 3.1 that supports multimedia functions, specifically audio recording and playback, animation playback, MIDI, and MCI devices such as for CD-ROM and video players; **multimedia mail** = messages that can contain voice, sound, images or data; **multimedia PC** = computer that can run multimedia application; normally equipped with a sound card, CD-ROM drive and

high-resolution colour monitor; **multimedia ready** = computer that has the necessary extra hardware to allow it to run multimedia applications; this normally means a PC or Macintosh that has a CD-ROM drive, sound card and graphics adapter, or that conforms to the MPC specification

multimeter *noun* testing equipment that provides an indication of the voltage *or* current *or* impedance at a point or of a component; **analog multimeter (AMM)** = testing equipment using a moving needle to indicate voltage, current *or* impedance levels; **digital multimeter (DMM)** = multimeter that uses a digital readout to indicate voltage, current *or* impedance levels

multimode fibre *noun* optical fibre that allows many different paths in addition to the direct straight path for light beams, causing pulse stretching and interference on reception of the signal

multi-part stationery *noun* continuous stationery with two or more sheets together, either with carbons between *or* carbonless

multipass overlap *noun* system of producing higher quality print from a dot matrix printer by repeating the line of characters but shifted slightly,

multi-platform *noun* software that can run on several different hardware platforms

> The Oracle Media Server is a multimedia database designed to run on massively parallel computers, running hundreds of transactions per second and managing multiple data types, such as video, audio and text
> *Computing*

multiple *adjective* having many parts *or* acting in many ways; *(film)* **multiple image** = when a number of images are combined, all from different sources; **multiple instruction stream - multiple data stream (MIMD)** = architecture of a parallel processor that uses a number of ALUs and memories in parallel to provide high speed processing; **multiple instruction stream - single data stream (MISD)** = architecture of a parallel computer that has a single ALU and data bus with a number of control units; **multiple precision** = use of more than one byte of data for number storage to increase possible precision

multiplex *verb* to combine several messages in the same transmission medium; **multiplexed analog components (MAC)** = standard television broadcast signal format

multiplexing *noun* combining several messages in the same transmission medium; **dynamic multiplexing** = multiplexing method which allocates time segments to signals according to demand; **homogeneous multiplexing** = switching multiplexor system where all the channels contain data using the same protocol and transmission rate; **optical multiplexing** = sending several light beams down a single path *or* fibre

multiplexor (MUX) *noun* circuit that combines a number of inputs into a smaller number of outputs; *compare with* DEMULTIPLEXOR; *a 4 to 1 multiplexor combines four inputs into a single output*

```
the displays use BCD input
signals and can be multiplexed
to provide up to six digits
```
Electronics & Power

multiplication *noun* mathematical operation that adds one number to itself a number of times; *the multiplication of 5 x 3 = 15*; **multiplication sign** = printed *or* written sign (x) used to show that numbers are multiplied

multiply *verb* to perform a multiplication of a number (the multiplicand) by another number (the multiplier)

multipoint *adjective* (connection) with several lines, attaching several terminals to a single line to a single computer

multiprocessing system *noun* system where several processing units work together sharing the same memory

multiprocessor *noun* number of processing units acting together *or* separately but sharing the same area of memory

multi-programming system *noun* operating system used to execute more than one program apparently simultaneously (each program being executed a little at a time)

multipurpose Internet mail extensions = MIME

multi-scan monitor *noun* monitor which contains circuitry to lock onto the required scanning frequency of any type of graphics card; *see also* MULTIFREQUENCY

multisession *noun* CD-ROM which has had data stored onto it at different times (each time is called a session); this normally applies to PhotoCD discs: with a multisession PhotoCD disc, you can store extra images onto it until it is full

multisession compatible *adjective* (drive) that can read multisession discs; if you want to access a PhotoCD disc, you normally require a multisession compatible drive

multi-strike printer ribbon *noun* inked ribbon in a printer that can be used more than once

multisync monitor *see* MULTIFREQUENCY

multitasking *or* **multi-tasking** *noun* ability of a computer system to run two or more programs at the same time; *the system is multi-user and multi-tasking*

COMMENT: few small systems are capable of simultaneous multitasking, since each program would require its own processor; this is overcome by allocating to each program an amount of processing time, executing each a little at a time so that they will appear to run simultaneously due to the speed of the processor and the relatively short gaps between programs; Microsoft Windows and Apple System are operating systems which are capable of multitasking several programs at the same time

```
this is a true multi-tasking
system, meaning that several
computer applications can be
running at the same time
```
Which PC?

```
page management programs are
so greedy for memory that it is
not a good idea to ask them to
share RAM space with anything
else, so the question of
multi-tasking does not arise
here
```
Desktop Publishing

```
X is the underlying technology
which allows Unix applications
```

```
to  run  under  a  multi-user,
multitasking GUI.
```
Computing

multi-terminal system *noun* system where several terminals are linked to a single CPU

multithreading *noun* running several different processes in rapid succession within a program (effectively multitasking within a program)

multi-user system *noun* computer system that can support more than one user at a time; *the program runs on a standalone machine or a multi-user system*

multivibrator *noun* electronic circuit that switches continuously between two output states, often used for clock generation; **astable multivibrator** = electronic circuit that repeatedly switches an output betweenvoltage levels

multi-window editor *noun* program used for creating and editing a number of applications programs on screen at the same time

mung up *verb (informal)* to distort data *or* to ruin a file

Murray code *noun* code used for teleprinters that uses only 5 bits

mush *noun* distortion and loss of signal; **mush area** = distortion and loss of signal due to two transmissions interfering

music chip *noun* integrated circuit capable of generating musical sounds and tunes; **music synthesizer** = device able to generate musical notes which are similar to those made by musical instruments

music track *noun (film)* sound track on which is recorded music for a film

musical instrument digital interface (MIDI) *noun* serial interface that connects electronic instruments

COMMENT: the MIDI interface carries signals from a controller or computer that instructs the different instruments to play notes

mute neg *noun (film)* picture negative with no sound track

mute print *noun (film)* positive film print with no sound track

muting *noun* **interstation muting** = ability of a radio receiver to prevent the noise found between radio signals from being amplified and heard by the user

MUX = MULTIPLEXOR circuit that combines a number of inputs into a smaller number of outputs; *compare with* DEMULTIPLEXOR

MW 1 = MEDIUM WAVE **2** *(film)* = MEGAWATT one million watts

MX record = MAIL EXCHANGE RECORD (in an electronic mail system) information stored in the DNS that tells a mail system how to deliver a mail message to a particular domain; *the MX record will ensure that any email message sent to the user 'smith@pcp.co.uk' will be correctly routed to the pcp.co.uk domain*

Nn

n *prefix* meaning nano-

NAB *(film)* = NATIONAL ASSOCIATION OF BROADCASTERS US term used to describe standards specified by this organisation; **NAB cartridge** = NAB approved continuous loop magnetic tape cartridge which is broadcast standard and is made in three tape capacity sizes; **NAB curve** = the standard for audio playback equalization; **NAB spool** = NAB approved magnetic tape spool which has a large central hole and is made in three tape capacity sizes

NAK = NEGATIVE ACKNOWLEDGEMENT

name *noun* **(a)** word used to call a thing *or* a person; **brand name** = name of a particular make of product; **corporate name** = name of a large corporation; *the company buys computer parts from several suppliers, and packages them together to make their own name product* **(b)** ordinary word used to identify an address in machine language; **name table** *or* **symbol table** = list of reserved words *or* commands in a language and the addresses in the computer that refer to them; **name registration** = *see* DOMAIN NAME REGISTRATION; **name resolution** = process of converting a domain name into its numerical IP address; *see also* DNS; **namespace** = group of unique names; for example, in a small office network the namespace might include 20 users, in the Internet the namespace runs into hundreds of millions

NAND function *noun* logical function whose output is false if both inputs are true, and true if any input is false; **NAND gate** = electronic circuit that provides a NAND function (NOTE: the NAND function is equivalent to an AND function with a NOT function at the output)

COMMENT: the output is 0 only if both inputs are 1; if one input is 1 and the other 0, or if both inputs are 0, then the output is 1

nano- *or* **n** *prefix* meaning one thousand millionth *or US* one billionth; **nanometre** *or* **nm** one thousand millionth of a metre; **nanosecond** *or* **ns** = one thousand millionth of a second (NOTE: US billion is the same as UK one thousand million (10 to the power of nine); UK billion is one million million (10 to the power of 10))

```
the cache's internal RAM is
accessed in under 70ns from
address strobe to ready signal
```
Electronics & Power

Napster software that allows users to share MP3-format music files over the Internet

COMMENT: the software, developed by Shawn Fanning, allows anyone to download music files from any another Napster users' computer; once installed, the software searches your hard disk for any MP3 music files, then allows other Napster users online to access these files from your hard disk, via the Internet; the software has now been modified after complaints that it was used to allegedly distribute copyright material

narrative *noun* text or story that describes a video or animation

narrow band *noun* communication method that uses a bandwidth less than that of a voice channel; **narrow band FM (NBFM)** = frequency modulation system using very small bandwidth (with only one pair of sidebands); *compare with* WIDEBAND; **narrowcast** = *see* MULTICAST

narrow-gauge film *noun* *(film)* film diameter that is less than 35mm

NAT = NETWORK ADDRESS TRANSLATION system that allows a local area network to work with two sets of IP addresses for each computer or node in the network: one for internal traffic, the other for external traffic

COMMENT: This system provides basic security against external attacks, for example using IP spoofing. Its main purpose is that it allows the local area network to use as many IP addresses as are required, but only using a minimal number of public IP addresses

National Association of Broadcasters *see* NAB

National Center for Supercomputing Applications (NCSA) organisation that helped define and create the world wide web with its Mosaic web browser

National Television Standards Committee (NTSC) *noun* official body that defines television and video formats *or* standards used mainly in the USA and in Japan; *see also* VIDEO STANDARDS

COMMENT: NTSC standards for television transmission and reception use a 525-line picture refreshed at 30 frames per second; the picture is broadcast using amplitude modulation and the sound using frequency modulation. NTSC is the standard in the USA, Central America and Japan. Most of Europe uses the PAL standard, except France which uses SECAM

native *adjective* **native compiler** = compiler that produces code that will run on the same system on which it is running (a cross-compiler produces code that will run on another hardware platform); **native file format** = (normally proprietary) default file format that is used by an application to store its data on disk; **native format** = first *or* basic format; **native language** = language that can be executed by a processor without the need for any special software (normally this means the processor's native machine code)

natural *adjective* occurring in nature *or* not created artificially; **natural binary coded decimal (NBCD)** = *see* BCD; **natural**

language = language that is used *or* understood by humans; *the expert system can be programmed in a natural language*

```
there are two main types of
natural-language interface:
those based on menus, and
those where the user has to
discover what questions the
computer will respond to by
trial and error
```
Electronics & Power

navigation *noun* moving around a multimedia title using hotspots, buttons and a user interface

NBCD = NATURAL BINARY CODED DECIMAL

NBFM = NARROW BAND FREQUENCY MODULATION

NC *see* NETWORK COMPUTER

NC *see* NUMERICAL CONTROL

n-channel metal oxide Semiconductor *noun* transistor design, with MOS techniques, that uses an n-type region for conduction

NCR paper = NO CARBON REQUIRED special type of paper impregnated with chemicals and used in multipart forms; when NCR paper is printed on by an impact printer, the writing also appears on the sheets below

NCSA = NATIONAL CENTER FOR SUPERCOMPUTING APPLICATIONS organisation that helped define and create the world wide web with its Mosaic web browser

ND *(film)* = NEUTRAL DENSITY FILTER used to lower the level of light without altering the colour

NDIS = NETWORK DRIVER INTERFACE SPECIFICATION standard command interface (defined by Microsoft) between network driver software and network adapter cards

NDR = NON DESTRUCTIVE READOUT display system that continues to display previous characters when new ones are displayed

near instantaneously compounded audio multiplex *see* NICAM

near letter-quality (NLQ) *noun* printing by a dot-matrix printer that provides higher quality type, which is almost as good as a typewriter, by decreasing the spaces between the dots; *switch the printer to NLQ for these circular letters*

needle *noun* tiny metal pin on a dot matrix printer which prints one of the dots

negate *verb* to reverse the sign of a number; *if you negate 23.4 the result is -23.4*

negation *noun* reversing the sign of a number (such as from 5 to -5)

negative 1 *adjective* meaning 'no'; **negative acknowledgement (NAK)** = signal sent by a receiver to indicate that data has been incorrectly *or* incompletely received; **negative feedback** = loop around a circuit in which part of the output signal is subtracted from the input signal; **negative number** = number which represents zero minus the number **2** *noun* normal photographic film where the colours are reversed (black is white and white is black); **contact negative** = film which can be used to produce a print without any reduction *or* enlargement; **negative film** *or* **neg stock** = (i) specially designed film which produces a clear negative image when it is exposed or processed; (ii) film which creates images which have reverse tones; **negative numbers** = the manufacturer's numbers which are imprinted on the film edge;

neg-pos *noun (film)* method where the film in the camera is processed as a negative image from which a separate positive is printed

NEQ = NON-EQUIVALENCE; **NEQ function** = logical function where the output is true if the inputs are not the same, otherwise false; **NEQ gate** = electronic implementation of an NEQ function

nested loop *noun* loop inside another loop in the same program

nested macro call *noun* a macro called from within another macro

nested structure *noun* section of a program in which one control loop or subroutine is used within another

NetBIOS = NETWORK BASIC INPUT OUTPUT SYSTEM commonly used standard set of commands (originally developed by IBM) that allow application programs to carry out basic operations over

a network (operations such as file sharing and transferring data between nodes); *this software uses NetBIOS calls to manage file sharing*

netiquette unofficial rules that define good manners on the Internet

NetScape (i) software company that develops Internet applications, now part of AOL; (ii) popular browser software used to view web pages on the Internet; *see also* WEB BROWSER, MOSAIC, MICROSOFT

network 1 *noun* any system made of a number of points *or* circuits that are interconnected; **computer network** = shared use of a series of interconnected computers, peripherals and terminals; **local area network (LAN)** = network where the various terminals and equipment are all within a short distance of one another (at a maximum distance of 500m, for example in the same building) and can be interconnected by cables; **network adapter** = add-in board that connects a computer to a network; the board converts the computer's data into electrical signals that are then transmitted along the network cable; = **network address** = part of an IP address that defines the main network on which the domain is located: for class A networks this is the first byte of the address, for class B networks it is the first two bytes and for class C networks it is the first three bytes. The rest of the IP address forms the host address; **network address translation** = *see* NAT; **network administrator** = individual who is responsible for looking after a network; responsibilities include installing, configuring and maintaining the network; **network analysis** = study of messages, destinations and routes in a network to provide a better operation; **network architecture** = method in which a network is constructed, such as layers in an OSI system; **Network Basic Input Output System** = *see* NETBIOS; **network computer (NC)** = design of desktop computer that does not have a floppy disk drive and downloads any software and applications required from a central server; network computers are cheaper and simpler in design than current desktop computers, have few moving parts (so are more reliable), and are designed to be easier to manage in a large company; **network control program** = software that regulates the flow of and channels for data transmitted in a network; **network controller** = network user responsible for allocating disk space, answering queries and solving problems from other users of the same network; **network database** = database structure in which data items can be linked together; **network device driver** = software which controls and manages a network adapter card to ensure that it functions correctly with other hardware and software in the computer; **network diagram** = graphical representation describing the interconnections between points; **network directory** = directory that is stored on a disk drive on another computer in the network, but it can be accessed by anyone on the network; not on the local disk drive; **network drive** = disk drive that is part of another computer on a network, but it can be used by anyone on the network; **network driver interface specification** = see NDIS; **network file system (NFS)** = network protocol developed by Sun Microsystems that allows a computer to share its local disk drives with other users on a network and is now used as a standard across most of the Internet; **network interface card (NIC)** = add-in board that connects a computer to a network; the board converts the computer's data into electrical signals that are then transmitted along the network cable; **network layer** = ISO/OSI standard layer that decides on the routes to be used, the costs, etc.; see also LAYER; **network hardware** = NETWORKING HARDWARE; **network management** = organization, planning, running and upkeep of a network; **network operating system (NOS)** = operating system running on a (normally dedicated) server computer that controls access to the network resources, manages network links, printing, and users; **network printer** = printer attached to a server or workstation that can be used by any user connected to the network; **network processor** = signal multiplexor controlled by a microprocessor in a network; **network protocol** = set of handshaking signals that defines how a workstation sends data over a network without clashing with other data transmissions; **network redundancy** = extra links between points allowing continued operation in the event of one failing; **network server** = computer which runs a network operating system and controls the basic network operations; all the workstations in a LAN are connected to the central network server and users log onto a network server; **network software** = NETWORKING SOFTWARE; **network structure** = data structure that allows each node to be connected to any of the others; = **network time protocol (NTP)** = protocol that provides an accurate time signal to computers on the Internet based on an atomic clock; allows local computers to synchronise their clocks; **network timing** = signals that correctly synchronize the transmission of data; **network topology** = arrangement of nodes and links within a network; *a bus network topology; ring network topology;* **neural network** = system running an artificial intelligence program that attempts to simulate the way the brain works, how it learns and remembers; *see also* BUS NETWORK, MESH NETWORK; PROTOCOL, RING NETWORK, STAR NETWORK, TOPOLOGY; **radio** *or* **television network** = series of local radio *or* TV stations linked to a main central station; **wide area network (WAN)** = network where the various terminals are far apart and linked by radio *or* satellite; *see also* BUS NETWORK, MESH NETWORK, PROTOCOL, RING NETWORK, STAR NETWORK, TOPOLOGY **2** *verb* to link points together in a network; *they run a system of networked micros; the workstations have been networked together rather than used as standalone systems;* **networked TV programme** = programme which is broadcast (usually simultaneously) by all the stations in a TV network

networking *noun* **(a)** broadcasting a prime-time TV programme over several local stations at the same time **(b)** (i) working *or* organization of a network; (ii) interconnecting two *or* more computers either in the same room *or* different buildings, in the same *or* different towns, allowing them to exchange information; **networking hardware** *or* **network hardware** = physical links, computers and control equipment that make up a network;

networking software or **network software** = software which is used to establish the link between a user's program and the network; **networking specialist** = company or person who specializes in designing and setting up networks; *this computer firm is a UK networking specialist*

COMMENT: networking allows a machine with floppy disk to use another PC's hard disk when both machines are linked by a cable and use networking software

the traditional way of operating networks involves have a network manager and training network users to familiarize themselves with a special set of new commands

Which PC?

workstations are cheaper the more you buy, because they are usually networked and share resources

PC Business World

neutral *adjective* with no state or bias or voltage; *(film)* **neutral density filter** or **nd filter** = a filter with a grey lens which reduces the light which is transmitted in order to leave colours, definition and contrast unaffected; **neutral transmission** = (transmission) system in which a voltage pulse or zero volts represent the binary digits

new *adjective* recent or not old; *they have installed a new computer system; the new programmer does not seem as efficient as the old one*; **new line character** = character that moves a cursor or printhead to the beginning of the next line; *see also* CARRIAGE RETURN (CR) **new technology** = electronic instruments which have recently been invented

newbie *noun* person who is new to the Internet and is still learning how to use it

news *noun* information about things which have happened; *business news; financial news; financial markets were shocked by the news of the collapse of the computer company*; **news agency** = office which distributes news to newspapers and television companies; **newsgroup** = collection of articles on the Usenet relating to one particular subject; **news release** = sheet giving information about a new event

which is sent to newspapers and TV and radio stations so that they can use it; *the company sent out a news release about the new managing director*

newsletter *noun* **company newsletter** = printed sheet or small newspaper giving news about a company

newsprint *noun* mechanical paper used for printing newspapers (NOTE: no plural)

next instruction register *noun* register in a CPU that contains the location where the next instruction to be executed is stored; *see also* REGISTER

nexus *noun* connection

NFS *see* NETWORK FILE SYSTEM

nibble or **nybble** *noun* half the length of a standard byte (NOTE: a nibble is normally 4 bits, but can vary according to different micros or people)

NIC = NETWORK INTERFACE CARD add-in board that connects a computer to a network; the board converts the computer's data into electrical signals that are then transmitted along the network cable

NICAM *(film)* = NEAR INSTANTANEOUSLY COMPOUNDED AUDIO MULTIPLEX digital system used for coding in the television transmission of stereo sound

night filter *noun (film)* filter which alters the colour of a shot filmed during the day to give the impression that it was filmed at night

n-key rollover *noun* use of a buffer between the keyboard and computer to provide key stroke storage (up to 'n' keys can be stored) for fast typists who hit several keys in rapid succession

NLQ = NEAR LETTER-QUALITY

NMI = NON-MASKABLE INTERRUPT

NMOS = N-CHANNEL METAL OXIDE SEMICONDUCTOR

NNTP = NETWORK NEWS TRANSFER PROTOCOL network standard used to distribute news messages over the Internet, the NNTP is one of the protocols within the TCP/IP protocol suite and provides a way of creating, reading and distributing messages within newsgroups over the Internet; *see also* NEWSGROUP

no carbon required paper *see* NCR PAPER

no op = NO OPERATION programming instruction which does nothing

no parity *noun* data transmission which does not use a parity bit

no-break *adjective* (power supply system) which will not be affected by a power failure; *see also* UPS

nodal point *noun* optical centre of an objective lens through which all rays pass

node *noun* interconnection point in a structure *or* network; *a tree is made of branches that connect together at nodes; this network has fibre optic connection with nodes up to one kilometre apart*

no-drop image *noun* (in a GUI) icon image displayed during a drag and drop operation when the pointer is over an object that cannot be the destination object (the object being dragged cannot be dropped onto it)

noise *noun* random signal present in addition to any wanted signal, caused by static, temperature, power supply, magnetic *or* electric fields and also from stars and the sun; **noise immunity** = ability of a circuit to ignore *or* filter out *or* be protected from noise; **noise margin** = maximum amplitude of noise that will affect a device, such as switch a logic gate; *(film)* **noise reduction** = system which reduces noise to improve quality in sound *or* picture; **noise temperature** = temperature of a component for it to produce the same thermal noise as a source; **galactic noise** = electrical noise which originates from planets and stars in space; **impulsive noise** = interference on a signal caused by short periods of noise; **thermal noise** = background noise signal caused by temperature variations in components

---

the photographs were grainy, out of focus, and distorted by signal noise

Byte

---

nomenclature *noun* predefined system for assigning words and symbols

nomogram *or* **nomograph** *noun* graphical system for solving one value given two others

non- *prefix* meaning not

non return to zero (NRZ) *noun* signalling system in which a positive voltage represents one binary digit and a negative voltage the other

nonaligned *adjective* two devices that are not correctly positioned in relation to each other, for optimum performance; **nonaligned read head** = read head that is not in the same position on a magnetic medium as the write head was

non-breaking space *noun* (in word-processing or DTP software) space character that prevents two words being separated by a line break

noncompatibility *noun* two or more pieces of hardware *or* software that cannot exchange data *or* peripherals

non-composite video signal *noun* video signal which has no synchronising signals but contains picture and blanking information

noncounting keyboard *noun* entry keyboard on a phototypesetter that does not allow page format instructions to be entered

non-dedicated server *noun* computer that runs a network operating system in the background and can also be used to run normal applications at the same time

non-destructive cursor *noun* cursor on a display that does not erase characters already displayed as it passes over them; *the screen quickly became unreadable when using a non-destructive cursor*; **non-destructive readout (NDR)** = display device that retains previous characters when displaying new characters; **non-destructive test** = series of tests carried out on a piece of equipment without destroying it; *I will carry out a number of non-destructive tests on your computer, if it passes, you can start using it again*

nondirectional microphone *noun* (film) microphone which picks up sound equally in every direction

non-equivalence function (NEQ) *noun* logical function where the output is true if the inputs are not the same otherwise false; **non-equivalence gate** = electronic implementation of an NEQ function

nonerasable storage *noun* storage medium that cannot be erased and re-used; *paper tape is a nonerasable storage*

non-impact printer *noun* printer (like an ink-jet printer) where the character form does not hit the paper

non-interlaced *adjective (in a monitor)* system in which the picture electron beam scans each line of the display once during each refresh cycle; the beam in an interlaced display scans every alternate line

100 sets of test results can be stored in non-volatile memory for later hard-copy printout
Computing

nonlinear *adjective* electronic circuit whose output does not change linearly in proportion to its input; **nonlinear video editing** = method of editing a video sequence in which the video is digitized and stored in a computer; the editor can then cut and move frames in any order before outputting the finished sequence

non-maskable interrupt (NMI) *noun* computer interrupt signal that cannot be blocked by software and overrides other commands

nonmodal *adjective (in a GUI)* displaying a window but still allowing a user to access other windows that are on-screen before closing the nonmodal window; *compare with* MODAL

non-printing codes *noun* codes that represent an action of the printer rather than a printed character

non-scrollable *adjective* (part of the screen display) which is always displayed (in a WP, the text can scroll while the menu bar or status line are always visible)

non-synchronous sound *or*
non-sync sound *noun (film)* any sound recorded without a camera operating at the same time

non-volatile *adjective* **non-volatile memory** *or* **non-volatile store** *or* **storage** = storage medium *or* memory that retains data even when the power has been switched off; *bubble memory is a non-volatile storage; using magnetic tape provides non-volatile memory* (NOTE: opposite is **volatile**)

COMMENT: disks (both hard and floppy) and tapes are non-volatile memory stores; RAM chips are volatile

NOR function *noun* logical function whose output is false if either input is true;

NOR gate = electric circuit *or* chip which performs a NOR function

COMMENT: the output is 1 only if both inputs are 0; if the two inputs are different *or* if both are 1, the output is 0

normal *adjective* usual *or* which happens regularly; *the normal procedure is for backup copies to be made at the end of each day's work*; **normal form** = method of structuring information in a database to avoid redundancy and improve storage efficiency

normal lens *noun (film)* motion picture lens with a focal length double the diagonal width of the area where the action is occurring

normalization *noun* process of normalizing data

normalize *verb* **(a)** to convert data into a form which can be read by a particular computer system **(b)** to store and represent numbers in a pre-agreed form, usually to provide maximum precision; *all the new data has been normalized to 10 decimal places*

northlight *see* FILL LIGHT

NOS = NETWORK OPERATING SYSTEM

NOT function *noun* logical inverse function where the output is true if the input is false; **NOT gate** = electronic circuit *or* chip which performs a NOT function

COMMENT: if the input is 1, the output is 0; if the input is 0, the output is 1

notation *noun* method of writing or representing numbers; **decimal notation** = number representation in base 10; *binary, hexadecimal notation*; **prefix notation** =; *normal notation: (x-y) + z, but using prefix notation: - xy + z*

notch *noun (film)* a small emulsion mark made on a filmstrip's edge which is used in the dark room for identification

notched *see* EDGE NOTCHED CARD

notepad *noun* pad of paper for writing notes; **screen notepad** = part of the screen used to store information even when the terminal is switched off

notice board *noun* **(a)** board fixed to a wall where notices can be pinned up **(b)**

type of bulletin board on which messages to all users can be left

notification message *noun* message within authoring software to notify other objects that a particular task has been completed; *if an object is moved, the application will generate a notification message to tell other processes when it has finished moving the object*

notify handler *noun* series of commands that are executed when a particular notification message is received; *the programmer could create a notify handler to carry out a task when it receives a message from a button object that says it has been selected with the mouse pointer*

npn transistor *noun* bipolar transistor design using p-type semiconductor for the base and n-type for the collector and emitter; *see also* TRANSISTOR, BIPOLAR TRANSISTOR

NRZ = NON RETURN TO ZERO

ns *abbreviation* nanosecond

NSFnet wide area network developed by the National Science Foundation (NSF) to replace ArpaNet as the main government-funded network linking together universities and research laboratories; *see also* ARPANET, INTERNET

COMMENT: NSFnet was a crucial stepping-stone in the development history of the Internet; it was closed down in 1995 and replaced by a commercial high-speed network backbone that formed one of the foundations for the current commercial Internet

NTFS *see* WINDOWS NT FILE SYSTEM

NTP *see* NETWORK TIME PROTOCOL

NTSC = NATIONAL TELEVISION STANDARDS COMMITTEE; official body that defines television and video formats *or* standards used mainly in the USA and in Japan; *see also* VIDEO STANDARDS

COMMENT: the NTSC standard is based on 525 horizontal lines and 60 frames per seconds

the system has a composite video output port that conforms to the NTSC video specification
Byte

n-type material *or* **n-type semiconductor** *noun* semiconductor that has been doped with a substance that provides extra electrons in the material giving it an overall negative charge compared to the intrinsic semiconductor; *see also* NPN TRANSISTOR

NuBus *noun* (old) 96-pin expansion bus used within Apple Macintosh II computers

null *noun* nothing; **null character** = character which means nothing (usually code 0); **null list** = list which contains nothing; **null modem** = emulator circuit that allows two pieces of equipment, that normally require modems to communicate, to be connected together over a short distance; *this cable is configured as a null modem, which will allow me to easily connect these two computers together*; **null set** = set that only contains zeros; **null string** = string that contains no characters; **null terminated string** = string of characters that has a null character to indicate the end of the string

you have to connect the two RS-232 ports together using a crossed cable, or null modem
PC Business World

Num Lock key *noun* (on a keyboard) key that switches the function of a numeric keypad from cursor control to numeric entry

number 1 *noun* (a) representation of a quantity; **number cruncher** = dedicated processor used for high-speed calculations; **number crunching** = performing high-speed calculations; *a very powerful processor is needed for graphics applications which require extensive number crunching capabilities*; **number range** = set of allowable values (b) written figure; *each piece of hardware has a production number; please note the reference number of your order*; **box number** = reference number used when asking for mail to be sent to a post office *or* to a newspaper, in reply to advertisements **2** *verb* (a) to put a figure on a document; *the pages of the manuscript are numbered 1 to*

395 **(b)** to assign digits to a list of items in an ordered manner

numeral *noun* character *or* symbol which represents a number; **Arabic numerals** = figures written 1, 2, 3, 4, etc.; **Roman numerals** = figures written I, II, III, IV, etc.

numeric *adjective* **(a)** referring to numbers **(b)** (field, etc.) which contains only numbers; **numeric keypad** = set of nine keys with figures, included in most computer keyboards as a separate group, used for entering large amounts of data in numeric form

numerical *adjective* referring to numbers; **numerical analysis** = study of ways of solving mathematical problems; **numerical control (NC)** *or* **computer numerical control (CNC)** = machine operated automatically by computer *or* circuits controlled by stored data

```
Hewlett-Packard's    100LX
Palmtop PC weighs 11oz and has
a separate numeric keypad
```
Computing

nybble *or* **nibble** *noun (informal)* half the length of a standard byte (NOTE: a nybble is normally 4 bits, but can vary according to different computer architectures)

Oo

O.K. used as a prompt in place of 'ready' in some systems; *(in a GUI)* **OK button** = button with 'OK' label that is used to start or confirm an action

O/P *or* **o/p** = OUTPUT

OA = OFFICE AUTOMATION

object *noun* **(a)** the data that makes up a particular image or sound **(b)** variable used in an expert system within a reasoning operation **(c)** data in a statement which is to be operated on by the operator; *see also* ARGUMENT, OPERAND; **object animation** = *see* CAST-BASED ANIMATION; **object** *or* **object-orientated architecture** = structure where all files, outputs, etc., in a system are represented as objects; **object code** = binary code which directly operates a central processing unit, a program code after it has been translated, compiled or assembled (into machine code); **object file** = file that contains object code for a routine *or* program; **object hierarchy** = order in which messages are passed from one object to another; **object language** = the language of a program after it has been translated; *compare with* SOURCE LANGUAGE; *(in Microsoft Windows 3.x)* **Object Packager** = Microsoft Windows utility that combines a data file with information about the application that created it so that the combined package can be inserted into another application; *see also* OLE; **object program** = computer program in object code form, produced by a compiler *or* assembler

object linking and embedding

(OLE) *noun (in Microsoft Windows)* method of sharing data between applications; an object (such as an image or sound) can be linked to a document or spreadsheet; *compare with* DDE; *see also* EMBEDDING, LINKING, OBJECT PACKAGER

object-oriented *adjective* (system or language) that uses objects which respond to messages from the system (such as a mouse click) or from other objects; **object-oriented graphics** = image which uses vector definitions (lines, curves) to describe the shapes of the image rather than pixels in a bit-map image; *this object-oriented graphics program lets you move shapes around very easily*; **object-oriented language** = programming language that is used for object-oriented programming, such as C++; **object-oriented programming (OOP)** = method of programming, such as C++, in which each element of the program is treated as an object that can interact with other objects within the program; *see also* OBJECT

> It has signed a strategic agreement with NeXT Computer designed to create a volume market in Europe for NeXT's pioneering object based operating system
>
> *Computing*

objective *noun* **(a)** something which someone tries to do **(b)** optical lens nearest the object viewed **(c)** any optical device which has the ability to form images; *(film)* **objective camera** *or* **objective camera angle** = camera angle producing shots which give the cinema audience the illusion that they are actually seeing the action happen while they are sitting in their seats; *objective camera shots exclude establishing shots, long shots, etc.*

obtain *verb* to get *or* to receive; *to obtain data from a storage device; a clear signal is obtained after filtering*

OCCAM computer programming language, used in large multiprocessor *or* multi-user systems

occur *verb* to happen *or* to take place; *data loss can occur because of power supply variations*

OCE = OPEN COLLABORATION ENVIRONMENT set of standards that allow networked Macintosh users to share objects and files

OCP = ORDER CODE PROCESSOR

OCR (a) = OPTICAL CHARACTER READER device which scans printed *or* written characters, recognizes them, and converts them into machine-readable form for processing in a computer **(b)** = OPTICAL CHARACTER RECOGNITION process that allows printed *or* written characters to be recognized optically and converted into machine-readable code that can be input into a computer, using an optical character reader; **OCR font** = character design that can be easily read using an OCR reader

COMMENT: there are two OCR fonts in common use: OCR-A, which is easy for scanners to read, and OCR-B, which is easier for people to read than the OCR-A font

```
This      is      the      first
neural-network-based      OCR
system that can read complex
pages containing any mixture
of    non-decorative    fonts
without manual training
                        Computing
```

octal (notation) *noun* number notation using base 8, with digits 0 to 7; **octal digit** = digit (0 to 7) used in the octal system; **octal scale** = power of eight associated with each digit position in a number

COMMENT: in octal, the digits used are 0 to 7; so decimal 9 is octal 11

octave *noun* series of 8 musical notes, each a semitone higher than the previous one

octet *noun* a group of eight bits treated as one unit; *see also* BYTE

OCX small program that carries out a particular function and is stored in a separate file with an OCX file extension; the program is normally an ActiveX component that provides a particular function for an application (such as a web browser) running under Microsoft Windows; *the spellchecker function is implemented in an OCX file; the web browser automatically downloads the OCX to support this multimedia feature*

ODBC = OPEN DATABASE CONNECTIVITY standard software system that provides a link between a database and an application; developed by Microsoft, any application that supports the standard can access any compatible data source; *the accounts software stores all the records in an ODBC database*

odd *adjective* (number, such as 5 or 7) which cannot be divided by two (NOTE: opposite is **even**); **odd even check** = method of checking that transmitted binary data has not been corrupted; **odd parity** = error checking system in which any series of bits transmitted must have an odd number of binary ones

ODI = OPEN DATALINK INTERFACE standard interface, defined by Novell, between a network driver and network interface card; *compare with* NDIS

OEM = ORIGINAL EQUIPMENT MANUFACTURER company which produces equipment using basic parts made by other manufacturers, and customizes the product for a particular application

off hook *adverb* state of a telephone unit indicating to incoming calls that it is being used (NOTE: opposite is **on hook**)

off microphone *or* **off mike** *adverb* **(a)** dialogue which is spoken away from the microphone in order to give the impression of sound being heard at a distance **(b)** sound that is too far away to be picked up by the microphone

off screen *adverb (in television or film)* action that is taking place off the screen, outside the viewer's field of vision; **off-screen buffer** = area of RAM used to hold an off-screen image before it is displayed on screen; **off-screen image** = image that is first drawn into a memory area and then is transferred to the display memory

off-cut *noun* scrap paper that is left when a sheet is trimmed to size

office *noun* room *or* building where a company works *or* where business is done; **office automation** = use of machines and computers to carry out normal office tasks; **office computer** = small computer (sometimes with a hard disk and several terminals) suitable for office use; **office copier** = copying machine in an office; **office equipment** = desks, typewriters, and other furniture and machines needed in an office; **office of the future** = design of an office that is completely coordinated by a computer; *see also* PAPERLESS OFFICE

off-line *adjective* **(a)** (processor *or* printer *or* terminal) that is not connected to a network *or* central computer (usually temporarily) **(b)** peripheral connected to a network, but not available for use; *before changing the paper in the printer, switch it off-line*; *(film)* **off-line edit** = the editing of video material using inexpensive equipment to create a rough edit before using expensive broadcast standard equipment to make the final edit; **off-line editing** = editing process in which copies of the original sound or video tape are used, cut, edited to create an EDL that is then used in an on-line editing suite to automatically assemble all the sectors of the tape according to the instructions in the EDL; **off-line printing** = printout operation that is not supervised by a computer; **off-line processing** processing by devices not under the control of a central computer; **off-line reader (OLR)** = software that will dial and connect to an on-line service, download any electronic mail and new messages from newsgroups and then disconnect, minimising the telephone charges; **off-line storage** = storage that is not currently available for access, such as a magnetic tape that must first be loaded into the tape machine (NOTE: opposite is **on-line**)

offprint *noun* section of a journal reprinted separately

off-scale *adverb* *(in film printing)* outside the area of the standard light point scale of a printer

offset 1 *noun* **(a)** **offset lithography** = printing process used for printing books, where the ink sticks to dry areas on the film and is transferred to rubber rollers from which it is printed on to the paper; **offset printing** = printing method that transfers the ink image to the paper via a second roller **(b)** **offset word** = value to be added to a base address to provide a final indexed address **(c)** positive or negative time displacement in systems using time code synchronisation **2** *verb* to balance one thing against another, with the result that they cancel each other

ohm *noun* unit of measurement of electrical resistance; *this resistance has a value of 100 ohms*; **kilo-ohm** = one thousand ohms

Ohm's Law *noun* definition of one ohm as: one volt drop across a resistance of one ohm when one amp of current is flowing

OLE = OBJECT LINKING AND EMBEDDING; *(in Microsoft Windows)* method of sharing data between applications; *see also* EMBEDDING, LINKING, OBJECT PACKAGER; **OLE container object** = object that contains a reference to a linked object or a copy of an embedded object; **OLE-2** = extends the functions of OLE to include visual editing to allow an embedded object to be edited without leaving the document in which it is embedded

COMMENT: an object (such as an image or sound file) can be linked to a document. The application that creates the document that holds an embedded object is the client application, whereas the application that creates the object that is embedded is called the server application - an application can be both client and server

omega wrap *noun* system of threading video tape around a video head

COMMENT: the tape passes over most of the circular head and is held in place by two small rollers

omission factor *noun* number of relevant documents that were missed in a search

omnidirectional *adjective* device that can pick up signals from all directions; *omnidirectional aerial*; *(film)* **omnidirectional microphone** = microphone which is able to pick up sound evenly in all directions

OMR (a) = OPTICAL MARK READER device that can recognize marks, lines on a special forms (such as on an order form *or* a reply to a questionnaire) and that inputs them into a computer **(b)** = OPTICAL MARK RECOGNITION process that allows certain marks *or* lines on special forms (such as on an order form *or* a reply to a questionnaire) to be recognized by an optical mark reader, and input in a computer

on chip *noun* circuit constructed on a chip

on hook *adverb* state of a telephone unit indicating that it is not busy and can receive incoming calls

on the fly *adverb* (to examine and modify data) during a program run without stopping the run

on-board *adjective* feature *or* circuit which is contained on a motherboard *or* main PCB; *the electronic page is converted to a printer-readable video image by the on-board raster image processor*

the key intelligence features of these laser printers are emulation modes and on-board memory

Byte

on-chip *adjective* (circuit) constructed on a chip; *the processor uses on-chip bootstrap hardware to allow programs to be loaded rapidly*

one address computer *noun* computer structure whose machine code only uses one address at a time

one for one *noun* programming language, usually assembler, that produces one machine code instruction for each instruction *or* command word in the language

one's complement *noun* binary representation for positive and negative numbers, formed by inverting each bit of the binary number for negative numbers; *the one's complement of 10011 is 01100; compare with* TWO'S COMPLEMENT

one-light print *noun (film)* film print which is made at a single exposure level, without changing from scene to scene

one-pass assembler *noun* assembler program that translates the source code in one action; *this new one-pass assembler is very quick in operation*

one-time pad *noun* coding system that uses a unique cipher key each time it is used

COMMENT: two identical pieces of paper with an encrypted alphabet printed on each one are used, one by the sender, one by the receiver; this is one of the most secure cipher systems

one-to-one position *noun* camera setting where the object and the image in the camera are the same size

onion skin architecture *noun* design of a computer system in layers, according to function *or* priority; *the onion skin architecture of this computer is made up of a kernel at the centre, an operating system, a low-level language and then the user's program*

onion skin language *noun* database manipulation language that can process hierarchical data structures

on-line 1 *adverb* (terminal *or* device) connected to and under the control of a central processor; anything which is 'live', or actively connected to the line or system, etc.; *the terminal is on-line to the mainframe* **2** *adjective* data or information that is available when a terminal is connected to a central computer via a modem; **on-line editing** = process of creating a finished audio or film sequence from original tape using editing instructions in an EDL list; **on-line help** = text screen displayed from within an application that explains how to use the application; **on-line information retrieval** = system that allows an operator of an on-line terminal to access, search and display data held in a main computer; **on-line processing** = processing by devices connected to and under the control of the central computer (the user remains in contact with the central computer while processing); **on-line storage** = data storage equipment that is directly controlled by a computer; **on-line system** = computer system that allows users who are on-line to transmit and receive information; **on-line transaction processing** = interactive processing in which a user enters commands and data on a terminal which is linked to a central computer, with results being displayed on-screen

OnNow power management standard that adds power management and control within a computer or peripheral; OnNow allows the development of a computer that is dormant but will be ready to use almost immediately after it has been switched on; *see also* ENERGYSTAR

on-screen *adjective* (information) that is displayed on a computer screen rather than printed out

on-site *adjective* at the place where something is; *the new model has an on-site upgrade facility*

OOP = OBJECT-ORIENTED PROGRAMMING

op amp = OPERATIONAL AMPLIFIER term for a versatile electronic component that provides amplification, integration, addition, subtraction and many other functions on signals depending on external components added

> COMMENT: an op amp component is usually in the form of an 8 pin IC package with 2 inputs (inverting and non-inverting), output, power supply and other control functions

op code = OPERATION CODE part of the machine code instruction that defines the action to be performed

opacity *noun* measure of how opaque an optical lens is (NOTE: opposite is **transmittance)**

opaque *adjective* will not allow light to pass through it; *the screen is opaque - you cannot see through it*; *(film)* **opaque leader** = part of a filmstrip which is used as a leader: no image is present; **opaque projector** = device that is able to project an image of an opaque object

open 1 *adjective* **(a)** command to prepare a file before reading *or* writing actions can occur; *you cannot access the data unless the file is open* **(b)** not closed; **open access** = system where many workstations are available for anyone to use; **open architecture** = computer with a published expansion interface that has been designed to allow add-on hardware to be plugged in; **Open Collaboration Environment (OCE)** = set of standards that allow networked Macintosh users to share objects and files; **open datalink interface;** *see* ODI; **open file** = file that can be read from or written to; the application opens the file which locates the file on disk and prepares it for an operation; **open loop** = control system whose input is free of feedback; *see also* FEEDBACK; **open reel** = film *or* tape on a reel that is not enclosed in a cartridge *or* cassette; **OpenScript** = object-oriented programming language used in Asymetrix' Toolbook authoring software; **open subroutine** = code for a subroutine which is copied into memory whenever a call instruction is found; **open system** = system which is constructed in such a way that different operating systems can work together; **Open System Interconnection (OSI)** = standardized ISO network which is constructed in layered form, with each layer having a specific task, allowing different systems to communicate if they conform to the standard; *see also* LAYER, INTERNATIONAL STANDARDS ORGANIZATION OPEN SYSTEM INTERCONNECTION **2** *verb* **(a)** to take the cover off *or* to make a door open; *open the disk drive door; open the top of the computer here* **(b)** to prepare a file before editing *or* carrying out other transactions; *open a file; you cannot access the data unless the file has been opened*

> X.400 messaging company Isocor has appointed Steve McDaniel to the position of sales director. Steve previously worked for Retix, where he was European sales manager for the company's OSI products
>
> *Computing*

operand *noun* data (in a computer instruction) which is to be operated on by the operator; *in the instruction ADD 74, the operator ADD will add the operand 74 to the accumulator*; **operand field** = space allocated for an operand in a program instruction; *see also* ARGUMENT, MACHINE-CODE INSTRUCTION

operate *verb* to work *or* to make a machine work; *do you know how to operate the telephone switchboard*; **operating instructions** = commands and instructions used to operate a computer; **operating system (OS)** = basic software that controls the running of the hardware, and the management of data files; the operating system is usually supplied with the computer, for example Unix on a server, Windows XP for a PC or SystemX on a Macintosh; *see also* DISK OPERATING

SYSTEM (DOS); **operating time** = total time required to carry out a task

operation *noun* working (of a machine); **operation code (OP-CODE)** = the part of a machine-code instruction that defines the action to be performed; **operation trial** = series of tests to check programs and data preparation

operational amplifier (op amp) *noun* versatile electronic component that provides amplification, integration, addition, subtraction and many other functions on signals depending on external components added

> COMMENT: usually in the form of an 8 pin IC package with 2 inputs (inverting and non-inverting) output, power supply and other control functions

operational *adjective* which is working *or* which refers to the way a machine works; **operational information** = information about the normal operations of a system

operator *noun* (a) person who makes a machine *or* process work; *the operator was sitting at his console*; **operator's console** = input and output devices used by an operator to control a computer (usually consisting of a keyboard and VDU); **computer operator** = person who operates a computer (b) character *or* symbol *or* word that defines a function *or* operation; *x is the multiplication operator*; **operator overloading** = assigning more than one function to a particular operator (the function often depends on the type of data being operated on and is used in the C++ and Ada programming languages); **operator precedence** = order in which a number of (mathematical) operations will be carried out; **operator procedure** = set of actions that an operator has to carry out to work a machine *or* process

optic *adjective* referring to sight; **optic fibre** = OPTICAL FIBRE

optical *adjective* (i) referring to *or* making use of light; (ii) referring to the eyes; *an optical reader uses a light beam to scan characters or patterns or lines*; **optical axis** = axis in an optical system about which all light properties *or* images are symmetrical; **optical bar reader** *or* **bar code reader** *or* **optical wand** = optical device that reads data from a bar code; **optical character**

reader (OCR) = device which scans printed *or* written characters, recognizes them, and converts them into machine-readable code for processing in a computer; **optical character recognition (OCR)** = process that allows printed *or* written characters to be recognized optically and converted into machine-readable code that can be input into a computer, using an optical character reader; **optical communication system** = communication system using fibre optics; **optical disc** = disc that contains binary data in the form of small holes which are read by a laser beam (NOTE: also called WORM (write one, read many, for computers) or compact disc (CD) and videodisc for sound *or* images); **optical effects** = special visual effects that are created by an optical printer after filming is finished, such as dissolves, wipes, fades, etc.; **optical fibre** = fine strand of glass *or* plastic protected by a surrounding material, that is used for the convenient transmission of light signals; **optical flop** = an image which is reversed in an optical printer; **optical font** *or* **OCR font** = character design that can be easily read using an OCR reader; **optical mark reader (OMR)** = device that can recognize marks *or* lines on a special form (such as on an order form *or* a reply to a questionnaire) and that inputs them into a computer; **optical mark recognition (OMR)** = process that allows certain marks *or* lines on special forms (such as on an order form *or* a reply to a questionnaire) to be recognized by an optical mark reader, and input into a computer; **optical memory** = optical disks; **optical mouse** = pointing device that is operated by moving it across a special flat mat; on the mat is printed a grid of lines and, as the mouse is moved, two light sensors count the number of lines that have been passed to produce a measure of the distance and direction of travel; *compare with* MECHANICAL MOUSE; **optical negative** = a negative which is used in the final picture printing process; **optical printing** = photographic printing method where an image of the original is created on print stock by a copy lens; **optical scanner** = equipment that converts an image into electrical signals which can be stored in and displayed on a computer; **optical sound** = sound that is recorded from a photographic sound track rather than from magnetic film, tapes or records; **optical storage** = data storage using mediums such as microfiche, optical disk, etc.; *(film)* **optical system** = parts of a film camera which create visual images on film; **optical transfer** = transfer of sound to an optical sound recorder from a magnetic tape track in order to produce a positive or negative film sound track; **optical transmission** = use of fibre optic cables, laser beams and other light sources to carry data, in the form of pulses of light; **optical viewfinder** = system in a camera consisting of an objective lens and an eyepiece which enables the camera operator to accurately frame a scene; **optical wand** = OPTICAL BAR READER

optically *adverb* by using an optical device; *the text is scanned optically*

optics *noun* science of light and sight; **fibre optics** = using optical fibres (fine strands of glass *or* plastic protected by a surrounding material) for the transmission of light signals

optimization *noun* making something work as efficiently as possible

optimize *verb* to make something work as efficiently as possible; **optimized code** = program that has had any inefficient code or statements removed to make it run faster or to use less memory

optimizer *noun* program which adapts another program to run more efficiently

optimizing compiler *noun* compiler that analyses the machine code it produces in order to improve the speed or efficiency of the code

optimum *noun & adjective* best possible; *this is the optimum PCB design*

opt-in mailing list *noun* list of email addresses in which each recipient has specifically asked to receive advertising email messages - normally so that they can keep up to date with a topic or industry; *see also* EMAIL, MAILING LIST

option *noun* action *or* member of a list which can be chosen by a user; *there are usually four options along the top of the screen*; *(on an Apple Macintosh)* **Option key** = key on the keyboard that gives access to secondary functions of keys; similar to Ctrl or Alt keys on an IBM PC keyboard, located to the left of the space bar

optional *adjective* which can be chosen; *the system comes with optional 3.5 or 5.25 disk drives*

> with the colour palette option, remarkable colour effects can be achieved on an RGB colour monitor
> *Electronics & Wireless World*

optoelectrical *adjective* which converts light to electrical signals *or* electrical signals into light

optoelectronic *adjective* (microelectronic component) that has optoelectrical properties

optoelectronics *noun* electronic components that can generate *or* detect light, such as phototransistors, light-emitting diodes

optomechanical mouse *see* MECHANICAL MOUSE

OR function *noun* logical function that produces a true output if either input is true; **OR gate** = electronic implementation of the OR function

> COMMENT: the result of the OR function will be 1 if either *or* both inputs is 1; if both inputs are 0, then the result is 0

Orange Book set of standards published by Philips that define the format for a recordable CD-ROM; *see also* GREEN BOOK, RED BOOK, WHITE BOOK, YELLOW BOOK

orbit 1 *noun* path in space that a satellite follows around the earth; *the satellite's orbit is 100km from the earth's surface*; **elliptical orbit** = path of a satellite around the earth that is in the shape of an ellipse; **geostationary orbit** = satellite which moves at the same velocity as the earth, so remains above the same area of the earth's surface, and appears stationary when viewed from earth; **polar orbit** = satellite flight path that goes over the earth's poles **2** *verb* to follow a path in space around the earth; *the weather satellite orbits the earth every four hours*

order *verb* to sort according to a key

order code processor (OCP) *noun* *(in a multiprocessor system)* a processor which decodes and performs the arithmetic and logical operations according to the program code

ordered list *noun* list of data items which has been sorted into an order

organization *noun* **(a)** way of arranging something so that it works efficiently; *the chairman handles the organization of the sales force; the organization of the group is too centralized to be efficient; the organization of the head office into departments*; **organization and methods** = examining how an office works, and suggesting how it can be made more efficient; **organization chart** = list of people working in various departments, showing how a company *or* office is organized **(b)** group of people which is arranged for efficient work; **a government organization** = official body, run by the government; **an employers' organization** = group of employers with similar interests (NOTE: no plural for **(a)**)

organizational *adjective* referring to the way in which something is organized; *the paper gives a diagram of the company's organizational structure*

organize *verb* to arrange something so that it works efficiently; *the company is organized into six profit centres; the group is organized by areas of sales*

orientated *adjective* aimed towards; *the aerial was orientated towards the satellite*

orientation *noun* **(a)** direction *or* position of an object **(b)** *(when printing or in word-processing or DTP software)* direction of a page, either landscape (long edge horizontal) or portrait (long edge vertical)

origin *noun* **(a)** position on a display screen to which all coordinates are referenced, usually the top left hand corner of the screen **(b)** location in memory at which the first instruction of a program is stored

original equipment manufacturer (OEM) *noun* company which produces equipment using basic parts made by other manufacturers, and customizes the product for a particular application; *an OEM supplies the disk drive, another the monitor; he started in business as a manufacturer of PCs for the OEM market*

original 1 *adjective* used *or* made first; *this is the original artwork for the advertisement* **2** *noun* **(a)** first document, from which a copy is made; *did you keep the original of the letter? the original*

document is too faint to photocopy well **(b)** (first) master data disk *or* photographic film *or* sound recording used, from which a copy can be made

originate *verb* to start *or* come from; *the data originated from the new computer*; **originate modem** = modem that (normally) makes a call to another modem that is waiting to answer calls; the originate modem emits a carrier in response to an answertone from the remote modem

origination *noun* work involved in creating something; *the origination of the artwork will take several weeks*

```
IBM UK has appointed Steve
Wainwright as regional sales
manager, northern Europe, for
micro-electronics  products.
He was previously OEM sales
manager, north Europe,  for
Harris Corporation
```
Computing

orphan (line) *noun* first line of a paragraph of text printed alone at the bottom of a column, with the rest of the paragraph at the top of the next column; an orphan makes a page look ugly; *see also* WIDOW

ortho *or* **orthochromatic film** *noun* photographic black and white film that is not sensitive to red light; used to achieve a correct colour tone

OS = OPERATING SYSTEM

OS/2 (old) multitasking operating system for PC computers developed by IBM and Microsoft

COMMENT: OS/2 provides a 32-bit software kernel with both a graphical user interface (called Presentation Manager) and a command line user interface

oscillator *noun* electronic circuit that produces a pulse *or* signal at a particular frequency

oscilloscope *noun* electronic test equipment that displays on a CRT the size and shape of an electrical signal

OSI = OPEN SYSTEM INTERCONNECTION

OTF *(film)* = OPTICAL TRANSFER FUNCTION system of accurately measuring the features of lenses *or* photographic reproduction systems

out of band signalling *noun* transmission of signals outside the frequency limits of a normal voice channel

out of phase *adverb* situation where a waveform is delayed in comparison to another

out of range *adjective* (number *or* quantity) that is outside the limits of a system

outage *noun* time during which a system is not operational; *see also* SUN OUTAGE

outdent *verb* to move part of a line of text into the margin (NOTE: opposite is **indent**)

outlet *noun* connection *or* point in a circuit *or* network where a signal *or* data can be accessed

outline 1 *noun* edge round an image; **outline font** = printer or display font (collection of characters) stored as a set of outlines that mathematically describe the shape of each character (which are then used to draw each character rather than actual patterns of dots); outline fonts can be easily scaled, unlike bit-map fonts; *see also* BIT-MAPPED FONT **2** *verb* to describe the main features of something

outliner *noun* utility program used to help a user order sections and sub-sections of a list of things to do or parts of a project

out-of-sync *adjective* fault when the sound and picture are not synchronised

output (o/p *or* **O/P) 1** *noun* **(a)** information *or* data that is transferred from a CPU *or* the main memory to another device such as a monitor *or* printer *or* secondary storage device (NOTE: opposite is **input**) **(b)** action of transferring the information *or* data from store to a user; **output bound** = processor that cannot function at normal speed because of a slower peripheral; **output device** = device (such as a monitor *or* printer) which allows information to be displayed to the user; **output file** = set of records that have been completely processed according to various parameters; **output port** = circuit and connector that allow a computer to output *or* transmit data to other devices *or* machines; *connect the printer to the printer output port*; **output stream** = communications channel carrying data output to a peripheral; **output port** = circuit and connector that allow a computer to output *or* transmit data to other devices *or*

machines; *printer output port*; **input/output (I/O)** = (i) receiving *or* transmitting of data between a computer and its peripherals and other points outside the system; (ii) all data received *or* transmitted by a computer; *see also* INPUT **2** *verb* to transfer data from a computer to a monitor *or* printer; *finished documents can be output to phototypesetters* (NOTE: **outputting - output)**

---

most CAD users output to a colour plotter

PC Business World

OV = OVERFLOW

overcranking *noun (film)* filming at a faster speed than the final projection speed, resulting in slowing down the action

overdevelop *verb (film)* to develop a filmstrip longer than is necessary; results in a fogging effect and is sometimes done on purpose

overdub *verb* to record a new voice or sound to replace an existing sound on a film or video

overexpose *verb (film)* to expose film for a greater period of time than is necessary by using a too-slow shutter speed or an overly enlarged aperture; produces a dark negative and a light print

overflow *or* **OV** *noun* **(a)** mathematical result that is greater than the limits of the computer's number storage system; **overflow bit** *or* **flag** = single bit in a word that is set to one (1) if a mathematical overflow has occurred **(b)** situation in a network when the number of transmissions is greater than the line capacity and are transferred by another route

overhead *noun* **(a)** extra code that has to be stored to organize the program; *the line numbers in a BASIC program are an overhead*; **overhead bit** = single bit used for error detection in a transmission **(b)** **overhead projector** = projector which projects an image of transparent artwork onto a screen; *(film)* **overhead shot** = camera positioned above the action

overheat *verb* to become too hot; *the system may overheat if the room is not air-conditioned*

overink *verb* to put on too much ink when printing; *two signatures were spoilt by overinking*

overlap 1 *noun* (a) two things where one covers part of the other *or* two sections of data that are placed on top of each other; **multipass overlap** = system of producing higher quality print from a dot matrix printer by repeating the line of characters but shifted slightly, so making the dots less noticeable (b) *(film)* the continuation of the sound track into the following scene for smooth continuity **2** *verb* to cover part of an item with another

overlay *noun* (a) strip of paper that is placed over keys on a keyboard to indicate their function (b) small section of a program that is larger than the main memory capacity of a computer, that is loaded into memory when required, such that main memory only contains the sections it requires to run a program (c) device that converts composite video or television signals into a digital format so that they can be displayed on a computer

overlay function *see* MATTE, CHROMA KEY

overlay network *noun* two communications networks that have some common interconnections

overlay segments *plural noun* short sections of a long program that can be loaded into memory when required, and executed; *compare with* VIRTUAL MEMORY

Many packages also boast useful drawing and overlay facilities which enable the user to annotate specific maps

Computing

overlaying *noun* putting an overlay into action

overload *verb* to demand more than the device is capable of; *the computer is overloaded with that amount of processing; if you turn the volume down, the amplifier won't be overloaded*

overmodulation *noun* situation where an amplitude modulated carrier signal is reduced to zero by excessive input signal

overpunching *noun* altering data on a paper tape by punching additional holes

overscan *noun* (a) faulty or badly adjusted monitor in which the displayed image runs off the edge of the screen (b) display equipment in which the picture beam scans past the screen boundaries to ensure that the image fills the screen

overstrike *verb* to print on top of an existing character to produce a new one

overtones *see* HARMONIC

over-voltage protection *noun* safety device that prevents a power supply voltage exceeding certain specified limits

overwrite *verb* to write data to a location (memory *or* tape *or* disk) and, in doing so, to destroy any data already contained in that location; *the latest data input has overwritten the old information*

oxide *noun* chemical compound of oxygen; **ferric oxide** = iron oxide used as a coating for magnetic disks and tapes; **metal oxide semiconductors (MOS)** = production and design method for a certain family of integrated circuits using patterns of metal conductors and oxide deposited onto a semiconductor; *see also* MOSFET, CMOS

Pp

p = PICO-

P (a) = PASCAL unit of pressure **(b)** = PETA equal to one quadrillion (2^{50})

PA (a) *(film)* = PRODUCTION ASSISTANT **(b)** = PUBLIC ADDRESS SYSTEM

PABX = PRIVATE AUTOMATIC BRANCH EXCHANGE

pack 1 *noun* **pack of items** = items put together in a container for selling; **blister pack** *or* **bubble pack** = type of packing where the item for sale is covered with a stiff plastic cover sealed to a card backing; **display pack** = specially attractive box for showing goods for sale **2** *verb* **(a)** to put things into a container for selling *or* sending; *to pack goods into cartons; the diskettes are packed in plastic wrappers; the computer is packed in expanded polystyrene before being shipped* **(b)** to store a quantity of data in a reduced form, often by representing several characters of data with one stored character; **packed decimal** = way of storing decimal digits in a small space, by using only four bits for each digit (NOTE: opposite is **padding**)

package 1 *noun* **(a)** goods packed and wrapped for sending by mail; *the Post Office does not accept very large packages; the goods are to be sent in airtight packages* **(b)** group of different items joined together in one deal; **package deal** = agreement where several different items are agreed at the same time; *we are offering a package deal which includes the whole office computer system, staff training and hardware maintenance* **(c)** applications **package** = set of computer programs and manuals that cover all aspects of a particular task (such as payroll, stock control, invoicing, etc.); **software package** = computer programs and manuals designed for a special purpose; *the computer is sold with accounting and word-processing packages* **2** *verb* **packaged software** = SOFTWARE PACKAGE; **to package goods** = to wrap and pack goods in an attractive way

packager *noun* person who creates a book for a publisher

packaging *noun* **(a)** the action of putting things into packages **(b)** material used to protect goods which are being packed; attractive material used to wrap goods for display; *airtight packaging; packaging material* **(c)** creating books for publishers (NOTE: no plural)

packet *noun* **(a)** small box *or* bundle of goods for selling; *packet of carbon paper or of envelopes or of filing cards*; **postal packet** = small container of goods sent by post **(b)** group of bits of uniform size which can be transmitted as a group, using a packet switched network; **packet Internet groper** = *see* PING; **packet switched data service** *or* **packet switched network (PSN)** = service which transmits data in packets of a set length; **packet switching** = method of sending messages *or* data in uniform-sized packets; **packet switching service (PSS)** = commercial data transmission service that sends data over its WAN using packet switching; *compare with* STORE-AND-FORWARD

```
The network is based on
Northern Telecom DPN data
switches over which it will
offer X.25 packet switching,
IBM SNA, and frame-relay
transmission
```
Computing

packing *noun* **(a)** action of putting goods into boxes and wrapping them for shipping; *what is the cost of the packing? packing is* *included in the price*; **packing charges** = money charged for putting goods into boxes; **packing list** *or* **packing slip** = list of goods which have been packed, sent with the goods to show they have been checked **(b)** putting large amounts of data into a small area of storage; **packing density** = amount of bits of data which can be stored in a unit area of a disk *or* tape; **packing routine** = program which packs data into a small storage area **(c)** material used to protect goods; *packed in airtight packing*; **non-returnable packing** = packing which is to be thrown away when it has been used and not returned to the sender (NOTE: no plural; opposite is **padding**)

pad 1 *noun* **(a)** pile of sheets of paper attached together on one side; **desk pad** = pad of paper kept on a desk for writing notes; **memo pad** *or* **note pad** = pad of paper for writing memos *or* notes; **phone pad** = pad of paper kept by a telephone for noting messages; *see also* NOTEPAD, SCRATCHPAD **(b)** soft material like a cushion; *the machine is protected by rubber pads*; **inking pad** = cushion with ink in it, used to put ink on a rubber stamp **(c)** **cursor pad** = group of four arrowed cursor control keys, used to move the cursor up and down or to the right or left **2** *verb* to fill out

padding *noun* material added to fill out a string *or* packet until it is the right length (NOTE: opposite is **packing**)

paddle *noun* computer peripheral consisting of a knob *or* device which is turned to move a cursor *or* pointer on the screen; **games paddle** = device held in the hand to move a cursor *or* graphics in a computer game

page *noun* **(a)** sheet of paper **(b)** one side of a printed sheet of paper in a book *or* newspaper *or* magazine *or* catalogue, etc. **(c)** text held on a computer monitor screen (which if printed out will fill a page of paper *or* which fills the screen); **page addressing** = main memory which has been split into blocks, with a unique address allocated to each block of memory, which can then be called up and accessed individually when required; **page break** = (i) point at which a page ends and a new page starts (in continuous text); (ii) marker used when word-processing to show where a new page should start; **page description language**

(PDL) = software that controls a printer's actions to print a page of text to a particular format according to a user's instructions; *see also* PCL, POSTSCRIPT; **page display** = showing on the screen a page of text as it will appear when printed out; **page down key** = (on a keyboard) key that moves the cursor position down by the number of lines on one screen; **page image buffer** = memory in a page printer that holds the image as it is built up before it is printed; **page impression** = action of displaying a web page to a visitor to a website; often used as a simple measure to count how many visitors have seen a website; *see also* ACCESS LOG, BANNER ADVERTISEMENT, IMPRESSION; **page layout** = arrangement of text and pictures within a page of a document; *we do all our page layout using desktop publishing software*; **page length** = length of a page (either in printing *or* in word-processing); **page makeup** = action of pasting images and text into a page ready for printing; **page number** = unique number assigned to each page within a multimedia application, to be used within hyperlinks and when moving between pages; **page orientation** = direction of the long edge of a piece of paper; *see* PORTRAIT, LANDSCAPE; **pages per minute (ppm)** = measurement of the speed of a printer shown as the number of pages of text printed every minute; *this laser printer can output eight pages per minute*; *(in word-processing or DTP software)* **page preview** = graphical representation of how a page will look when printed, with different type styles, margins, and graphics correctly displayed; **page printer** = printer which composes one page of text within memory and then prints it in one pass (normally refers to laser printers); *this dot-matrix printer is not a page printer, it only prints one line at a time*; **page reader** = device which converts written *or* typed information to a form that a computer can understand and process; **page request** = measure of the number of pages viewed in a day, providing an indication of the popularity of a website; *see also* ACCESS LOG, IMPRESSION; **page setup** = options within software that allow a user to set up how the page will look when printed, normally setting the margins, size of paper, and scaling of a page; **page up**

key = key on a keyboard that moves the cursor position up by the number of lines in one screen **(d)** section of main store, which contains data *or* programs; **page frame** = physical address to which a page of virtual (or logical) memory can be mapped; **page-mode RAM** = dynamic RAM designed to access sequential memory locations very quickly; *the video adapter uses page-mode RAM to speed up the display* **(e)** blank area of the screen used as a background for a multimedia book; the design of each page is created by pasting objects, such as windows, buttons, graphic images and text, onto the page **2** *verb* **(a) to page someone** = to try to find someone in a building (using a PA *or* radio pager); *see also* RADIO PAGING **(b)** to make up a text into pages **(c) paging system** = system of dividing computer backing storage into sections to allow long programs to be executed in a small main memory

paged address *noun* (in a *paged-memory scheme*) actual physical memory address that is calculated from a logical address and its page address; **paged-memory scheme** = way of dividing memory into areas (pages) which are then allocated a page number; memory addresses are relative to a page which is then mapped to the real, physical memory (this system is normally used to implement virtual memory); **paged-memory management unit** = electronic logic circuit that manages the translation between logical addresses that refer to a particular page and the real physical address that is being referenced

pager *noun* small device carried by someone, which allows him to be called from a central office, by using a radio signal

pagination *noun* process of dividing text into pages; arrangement of pages in a book

Mannesmann Tally has launched the T9005, a five-page-a-minute page printer designed to handle over 3,000 pages a month
Computing

paint 1 *noun (in a graphics program)* colour and pattern used to fill an area **2** *verb (in a graphics program)* to fill an enclosed graphics shape with a colour; **paint object** = BIT MAP (a)

paint pots *plural noun (film)* video controls which are used to change the colour balance in a camera

paint program *noun* software that allows a user to draw pictures on screen in different colours, with different styles of brush and special effects; *I drew a rough of our new logo with this paint program*

COMMENT: paint programs normally operate on bitmap images; drafting or design software normally works with vector-based images

PAL = PHASE ALTERNATING LINE standard that defines television and video formats, using 625 horizontal scan lines and 50 frames per second; *(film)* **PAL plus** = widescreen adaptation of the PAL system which produces 16:9 aspect ratio pictures

COMMENT: mainly used in Western Europe, Australia, some parts of the Middle East and Africa. France uses SECAM; the USA and Japan use NTSC. PAL provides a clearer image than NTSC

palette *noun* **(a)** range of colours which can be used (in an image, on a web page, on a colour printer or on a computer display) **(b)** *(in Windows)* data structure that defines the colours used in a bitmap image; the palette data defines each colour, the bitmap includes references to the colours in the palette; **palette shift** = image displayed using the wrong palette so that the colours appear distorted

the colour palette option offer sixteen colours from a range of over four thousand
Electronics & Wireless World

palm computer *noun* tiny computer that is about half the size of a paperback book; it does not have a keyboard, but uses a touch-sensitive screen and character recognition to allow the user to enter information and control applications; *I use a palm computer for contact management, calendar and email*; *see also* PDA

palmtop *noun* personal computer that is small enough to be held in one hand and operated with the other; *this palmtop has a tiny keyboard and twenty-line LCD screen*

PAM = PULSE AMPLITUDE MODULATION pulse modulation in which the height of the pulse varies with the input signal

pan *verb* **(a)** *(in computer graphics)* to move a viewing window horizontally across an image that is too wide to display all at once **(b)** *(in film)* the rotation of a camera in a horizontal direction in order to film action, subject or background; sometimes used to mean 'follow the action' **(c)** *(in MIDI or sound)* to adjust the balance of a sound between the two stereo channels

pan and tilt head *noun (film)* the mount on a tripod for a film or television camera which permits camera movement in both horizontal and vertical directions

pan pot *noun (film)* a potentiometer which controls the amount of an audio signal when it is divided between two or more components, such as between two programme channels or two loudspeakers

panachromatic master *or* **pan master** *noun (film)* a black and white positive which is made from a colour negative so that a black and white duplicate negative can be made

panaglide *noun (film)* a harness with stabilised camera mounting which permits steady movement of a hand-held camera

panchromatic film *or* **pan film** *noun* black and white film which is sensitive to all colours

panel *noun* flat section of a casing with control knobs *or* sockets; **back panel** = panel at the rear of a computer which normally holds the connectors to peripherals such as keyboard, printer, video display unit, and mouse; *the socket is on the back panel*

panorama *noun (film)* a wide-angle shot which reveals the whole of the scene through a pan shot

Pantone Matching System (PMS) method of ensuring that the colours seen on a computer screen match the colours printed by a printer

paper *noun* thin material used for making books *or* newspapers *or* stationery items; *the book is printed on 80gsm paper; glossy paper is used for printing half-tones; bad quality paper gives too much show-through*; **paper feed** = slot into which paper is introduced (in a printer); US **paper slew** = PAPER THROW; **paper**

tape = long strip of paper on which data can be recorded, usually in the form of punched holes; **paper tape feed** = method by which paper tape is passed into a machine; **paper tape punch** = device which punches holes in paper tape to carry data; **paper tape reader** = device which accepts punched paper tape and converts the punched information stored on it into signals which a computer can process; **paper throw** = rapid vertical movement of paper in a printer; **paper tray** = container used to hold paper to be fed into a printer; **paper weight** = weight of paper used in printing (usually measured in gsm *or* grams per square metre)

paperback *noun* book which has a paper cover; *we are publishing the book as a hardback and as a paperback*

paperbound *adjective* (book) bound with a paper cover (as opposed to hardbound)

paper-fed *adjective* (device) which is activated when paper is introduced into it; *paper-fed scanner*

paperless *adjective* without using paper; **paperless office** = electronic office *or* office which uses computers and other electronic devices for office tasks and does not use much paper

paper-white monitor *noun* monitor that normally displays black text on a white background, rather than the normal illuminated text on a black background

Indeed, the concept of the paperless office may have been a direct attack on Xerox and its close ties to the paper document. Yet, as we all know, the paperless office has so far been an empty promise

Computing

parabolic (spotlight) *noun (film)* a spotlight which produces a narrow beam of light

parabolic reflector *noun (film)* a concave reflector which is used when focusing light or sound

paragraph *noun* **(a)** *(in a document)* section of text between two carriage return characters; **paragraph marker** = non-printing character that shows where a carriage return is within a document **(b)** *(in a memory map)* 16-byte section of memory which starts at a hexadecimal address that can be evenly divided by 16

parallax *noun (film)* the angle of divergence between the viewfinder objective and the lens of the camera which can cause mistakes in framing; this type of error is solved by using a reflex camera

parallel *adjective* (lines) which run side by side and never join; (computer system) in which two or more processors operate simultaneously on one or more items of data *or* bits of a word transmitted over separate lines at the same time; **parallel action** = a sequence of shots of two or more action scenes which are shown alternately to give the audience the illusion that they are occurring simultaneously; **parallel computer** = computer with one or more logic *or* arithmetic units, allowing parallel processing; **parallel connection** = transmission link that handles parallel data; *their average transmission rate is 60,000 bps through parallel connection*; **parallel data transmission** = transmission of bits of data simultaneously along a number of data lines; **parallel editing** = the intercutting of two or more shots in order to show that the action is occurring simultaneously; **parallel input/output (PIO)** = data input *or* output from a computer in parallel; **parallel input/parallel output (PIPO)** = device that can accept and transmit parallel data; **parallel input/serial output (PISO)** = device that can accept parallel data and transmit serial data; **parallel interface** *or* **port** = circuit *or* connector that allows parallel data to be received *or* transmitted; **parallel operation** = number of processes carried out simultaneously on a number of inputs; **parallel port** = connector on a computer or peripheral that allows several bits of data to be transmitted simultaneously, normally eight bits at a time; *see* PARALLEL INTERFACE; **parallel printer** = printer that is connected to a computer via a parallel interface and accepts character data in parallel form (eight bits at a time sent over eight wires); **parallel processing** = computer operating on several tasks simultaneously; **parallel running** = running an old and a new computer system together to allow the new system to be checked before it becomes the only system used; **parallel transmission** = number of data lines carrying the bits of a data word

simultaneously (NOTE: opposite is **serial transmission**)

parameter *noun* information which defines the limits of something; **parameter-driven software** = software whose main functions can be modified and tailored to a user's needs by a number of variables; **parameter passing** = value in a program passed to a routine or program when it is called; **parameter testing** = using a program to examine the parameters and set up the system *or* program accordingly; **parametric equalizer** = device that can enhance or reduce the levels of particular frequencies within an audio signal; used to remove distortion from a signal and cut out excessive bass or high-pitch noise from an audio signal; **physical parameter** = description of the size, weight, voltage or power of a system

parent directory *noun (in DOS filing system)* the directory above a sub-directory

parent folder *noun (on a disk used for storing data)* one folder that contains other folders; *I have created a new parent folder on the hard drive*

parent object *noun* page that contains the object that is being referenced

parent program *noun* program that starts another program (a child program), whilst it is still running; control passes back to the parent program when the child program has finished

parity *noun* being equal; **even parity** = error checking system in which any series of bits transmitted must have an even number of binary ones; **no parity** = data transmission which does not use a parity bit; **odd parity** = error checking system in which any series of bits transmitted must have an odd number of binary ones; **parity bit** = extra bit added to a data word as a parity checking device; **parity check** = method of checking that transmitted binary data has not been corrupted; **parity track** = one track on magnetic *or* paper tape that carries the parity bit

The difference between them is that RAID level one offers mirroring, whereas level five stripes records in parity across the disks in the system

Computing

park *verb* to move the read/write head of a hard disk drive over a point on the disk where no data is stored; *when parked, the disk head will not damage any data if it touches the disk surface*

parse *verb* to break down high-level language code into its element parts when translating into machine code

parsing *noun* operation to break down high-level language code into its element parts when translating into machine code

part *noun* (a) section of something; **part page display** = display of only a section of a page, and not the whole page (b) **spare part** = small piece of a machine which is needed to replace a piece which is broken *or* missing; *the printer won't work - we need to a spare part* (c) one of a series; **four-part invoices** = invoices with four sheets (a top sheet and three copies); **two part stationery** = stationery (invoices, receipts, etc.) with a top sheet and a copy sheet; *see also* MULTI-PART STATIONERY

particle *noun* very small piece of matter

partition 1 *noun* area of a hard disk that is treated as a logical drive and can be accessed as a separate drive; *I defined two partitions on this hard disk - called drive C: and D:* **2** *verb* to divide a hard disk into two or more logical drives that can be accessed as separate drives

parts per quarter note *see* PPQN

party line *or* **shared line** *noun* one telephone line shared by a number of subscribers

PASCAL high-level structured programming language used both on micros and for teaching programming

Pascal *noun* unit of pressure

passage *noun* a number of notes that form a small section of a musical score

password *noun* word which identifies a user so that he can access a system; *the user has to key in the password before he can access the database*; **password protection** = computer *or* software that requires the user to enter a password before he can gain access

paste *verb* to insert text or graphics that has been copied or cut into a file; *now that I have cut this paragraph from the end of the document, I can paste it in here*; **cut-and-paste** = action of taking a section

of text *or* data from one point and inserting it at another (often used in word-processors and DTP packages for easy page editing)

patch *noun* (a) (temporary) correction made to a program; small correction made to software by the user, on the instructions of the software publisher (b) thin piece of translucent film which is used to repair a tear in the film (c) data that defines a sound in a synthesizer; a patch is also called a program and can be altered by issuing a program-change message

patch cord *noun* cord with a plug at each end, which is used to link sockets in a patchboard; **patch panel** = electrical terminals that can be interconnected using short patch cords, allowing quick and simple re-configuration of a network

patchboard *noun* board with a number of sockets connected to devices, into which plugs can be inserted to connect other devices *or* functions

path *noun* (a) route from one point in a communications network to another (b) *(in the DOS operating system)* list of subdirectories where the operating system should look for a named file; *you cannot run the program from the root directory until its directory is added to the path*; **pathname** = location of a file with a listing of the subdirectories leading to it; *the pathname for the letter file is \FILES\SIMON\DOCS\LETTER.DOC*

pattern *noun* series of regular lines *or* shapes which are repeated again and again; **pattern palette** = range of predefined patterns that can be used to fill an area of an image; **pattern recognition** = algorithms *or* program functions that can identify a shape from a video camera, etc.

patterned *adjective* with patterns

pause control *noun* control which temporarily stops something; *the video tape recorder has a pause control that temporarily stops the tape playback and displays a still frame*

pause key *noun (in a keyboard)* key that temporarily stops a process, often a scrolling screen display, until the key is pressed a second time

PAX = PRIVATE AUTOMATIC EXCHANGE

paycable *noun* *US* form of cable television where the viewer pays an extra fee for extra channels

payTV *noun* form of cable television, where the viewer pays for programs *or* channels watched

PB = PETABYTE one quadrillion bytes

PBX = PRIVATE BRANCH EXCHANGE

PC (a) = PROGRAM COUNTER **(b)** = PERSONAL COMPUTER *(originally referring to a microcomputer specification that used an 8086 CPU)* now normally used to refer to any computer that uses an Intel 80x86 processor and is based on the IBM PC-style architecture; **PC/AT** = (IBM PC compatible) computer that used an Intel 80286 processor and was fitted with 16-bit ISA expansion connectors; **PC/AT keyboard** = keyboard that features twelve function keys arranged in one row along the top of the keyboard; **PC-compatible** = computer that is compatible with the IBM PC; **PC/XT** = (IBM PC compatible) computer that was fitted with a hard disk drive and used a 8086 Intel processor; **PC/XT keyboard** = keyboard that features ten function keys arranged in two columns along the left hand side of the keyboard

in the UK, the company is known not for PCs but for PC printers
Which PC?

PC *or* **PCB** = PRINTED CIRCUIT (BOARD)

PC Card *noun* electronic device, about the same size as a thick credit-card, that can be plugged into a PCMCIA adapter to provide a particular function; *PC Cards are available that provide a modem, network adapter, extra memory or hard disk drive functions*; *see also* PCMCIA

PC spot = *see* PIANO-CONVEX SPOTLIGHT

PC/TV feature of a personal computer that allows it to receive, decode and display standard television images

PC-DOS version of MS-DOS that is sold by IBM

p-channel *noun* section of semiconductor that is p-type; **p-channel MOS** = MOS transistor that conducts via a small region of p-type semiconductor; *see also* MOS, P-TYPE SEMICONDUCTOR

PCI = PERIPHERAL COMPONENT INTERCONNECT hardware specification, produced by Intel, defining a type of fast local bus that allows high-speed data transfer between the processor and a peripheral or expansion cards (normally a video adapter, disk controller or network card)

COMMENT: the PCI bus can work with either an ISA or EISA expansion bus system and runs at 33MHz with either 32 or 64-bit data path between the CPU and the peripheral

PCL = PRINTER CONTROL LANGUAGE standard set of commands, defined by Hewlett Packard, that allow a computer to control a printer

PCM (a) = PULSE CODE MODULATION pulse stream that carries data about a signal in binary form; *see also* PULSE AMPLITUDE MODULATION, PULSE DURATION MODULATION, PULSE POSITION MODULATION **(b)** = PLUG-COMPATIBLE MANUFACTURER company that produces add-on boards that are compatible with another manufacturer's computer

PCMCIA = PERSONAL COMPUTER MEMORY CARD INTERNATIONAL ASSOCIATION specification for add-in expansion cards that are the size of a credit card with a connector at one end; now called PC Card; *the extra memory is stored on this PCMCIA card and I use it on my laptop*; **PCMCIA card** = memory *or* peripheral which complies with the PCMCIA standard; **PCMCIA connector** = 68-pin connector that is inside a PCMCIA slot and on the end of a PCMCIA card; **PCMCIA slot** = expansion slot (normally on a laptop) that can accept a PCMCIA expansion card

P-code *noun* intermediate code produced by a compiler that is ready for an interpreter to process, usually for PASCAL programs

PCU = PERIPHERAL CONTROL UNIT device that converts input and output signals and instructions to a form that a peripheral device will understand

PCX standard file format for storing colour graphics images

PD *see* PUBLIC DOMAIN

PDA = PERSONAL DIGITAL ASSISTANT lightweight palmtop

computer that provides the basic functions of a diary, notepad, address-book and to-do list together with fax or modem communications

COMMENT: current PDA designs do not have a keyboard, but use a touch-sensitive screen with a pen and handwriting-recognition to control the software

PDL (a) = PAGE DESCRIPTION LANGUAGE **(b)** = PROGRAM DESIGN LANGUAGE

PDM = PULSE DURATION MODULATION pulse modulation system where the pulse width varies with the magnitude of the input signal

PDN = PUBLIC DATA NETWORK

peak 1 *noun* highest point; maximum value of a variable *or* signal; *keep the peak power below 60 watts or the amplifier will overheat; the marker on the thermometer shows the peak temperature for today*; **peaks and troughs** = maximum and minimum points of a waveform; **peak output** = highest output; **peak period** = time of the day when most power is being used, etc.; *(film)* **peak white** = largest amplitude of a video signal which matches the brightest white part possible in the picture; **time of peak demand** = time when something is being used most **2** *verb* to reach the highest point; *the power peaked at 1,200 volts; sales peaked in January*

pedestal *noun (film)* **(a)** in a television signal it is an artificial black level which is put in to a circuit in order to increase the black level of the picture a small amount above the blanking level **(b)** a support for the camera with adjustable height

peek *noun* BASIC computer instruction that allows the user to read the contents of a memory location; *you need the instruction PEEK 1452 here to examine the contents of memory location 1452; compare with* POKE

peer *noun* any two similar devices operating on the same network protocol level

peer-to-peer network *noun* local area network (normally using network adapter cards in each computer) that does not use a central dedicated server, instead each computer in the network shares the jobs; *we have linked the four PCs in our small office using a peer-to-peer network*

pegging *verb* sudden swing of an analog meter to its maximum readout due to a large signal; *after he turned up the input level, the signal level meter was pegging on its maximum stop*

pel = PICTURE ELEMENT the smallest area on a screen that can be individually controlled (NOTE: this is not necessarily the same as a pixel, since a pel could be made up of several pixels)

pen *noun* object used to write or draw on something; **light pen** = computer accessory in the shape of a pen that contains a light-sensitive device that can detect pixels on a video screen (often used with special software to draw graphics on screen or control the position of a cursor); **pen computer** = type of computer that uses a pen instead of a keyboard for input; the computer has a touch-sensitive screen and uses handwriting recognition software to interpret the commands written on the screen using the pen; **pen plotter** = plotter that uses removable pens to draw on paper

Pentium *noun* range of processors developed by Intel, used by a large number of PC manufacturers; *the PC has a Pentium 4 running at 1.6GHz*

COMMENT: the processor is backwards compatible with the 80x86 family used in IBM PCs and uses a 32-bit address bus and a 64-bit data bus

per *preposition* **(a)** **as per** = according to; **as per sample** = as shown in the sample; **as per specification** = according to the details given in the specification **(b)** at a rate of; **per hour** *or* **per day** *or* **per week** *or* **per year** = for each hour *or* day *or* week *or* year **(c)** out of; *the rate of imperfect items is about twenty-five per thousand; the error rate has fallen to twelve per hundred*

per cent *adjective & adverb* out of each hundred *or* for each hundred; **10 per cent** = ten in every hundred; *what is the increase per cent? fifty per cent of nothing is still nothing*

perambulator *noun (film)* a moveable platform support for the microphone boom and the boom operator

percentage *noun* amount shown as part of one hundred; **percentage increase** =

increase calculated on the basis of a rate for one hundred; **percentage point** = one per cent

percentile *noun* one of a series of ninety-nine figures below which a certain percentage of the total falls

perfect 1 *adjective* completely correct *or* with no mistakes; *we check each batch to make sure it is perfect; she did a perfect typing test* **2** *verb* to make something which is completely correct; *he perfected the process for making high grade steel*

perfect binding *noun* method of binding paperback books, where the pages are trimmed at the spine, and glued to the cover

perfect bound *adjective* (book, usually a paperback) bound without sewing, where the pages are trimmed at the spine and glued to the cover with strong glue

perfectly *adverb* with no mistakes *or* correctly; *she typed the letter perfectly*

perfector *noun* printing machine that prints on both sides of a sheet of paper

perforated tape *noun* paper tape *or* long strip of tape on which data can be recorded in the form of punched holes

perforations *noun* line of very small holes in a sheet of paper *or* continuous stationery, to help when tearing; holes which are cut into a filmstrip's edge to enable movement

perforator *noun* machine that punches holes in a paper tape

perform *verb* to do well *or* badly

performance *noun* way in which someone *or* something acts; *as a measure of the system's performance* = as a way of judging if the system is working well; *in benchmarking, the performances of several systems or devices are tested against a standard benchmark*

perigee *noun* point during the orbit of a satellite when it closest to the earth

period *noun* (a) length of time; *for a period of time or for a period of months or for a six-year period; sales over a period of three months; sales over the holiday period* (b) **accounting period** = period of time at the end of which the firm's accounts are made up (c) *US* full stop *or* printing sign used at the end of a piece of text (NOTE: GB English is **full stop**)

periodic *or* **periodical 1** *adjective* (a) from time to time; *a periodic review of the company's performance* (b) periodic = (signal *or* event) that occurs regularly; *the clock signal is periodic* **2** *noun* periodical = magazine which comes out regularly

periodically *adverb* from time to time

peripheral 1 *adjective* which is not essential *or* which is attached to something else **2** *noun* (a) item of hardware (such as terminals, printers, monitors, etc.) which is attached to a main computer system (b) any device that allows communication between a system and itself, but is not operated only by the system; *peripherals such as disk drives or printers allow data transfer and are controlled by a system, but contain independent circuits for their operation*; **peripheral component interconnect** = *see* PCI; **peripheral control unit (PCU)** = device that converts the input/output signals and instructions from a computer to a form and protocol which the peripheral will understand; **peripheral interface adapter (PIA)** = circuit that allows a computer to communicate with a peripheral by providing serial and parallel ports and other handshaking signals required to interface the peripheral; **peripheral software driver** = short section of computer program that allows a user to access a peripheral easily; *same as* DEVICE DRIVER

perlux *noun* (film) material used for a projection screen which is highly reflective and also wide-angle

permanent *adjective* which will last for a very long time *or* for ever; **permanent error** = error in a system which cannot be mended; **permanent file** = data file that is stored in a backing storage device such as a disk drive; **permanent memory** = computer memory that retains data even when power is removed; *see also* NON-VOLATILE MEMORY; **permanent swap file** = file on a hard disk, made up of contiguous disk sectors, which stores a swap file for software that implements virtual memory, such as Microsoft's Windows (NOTE: Windows supports either permanent or temporary swap files, but a permanent file is faster)

permanently *adverb* done in a way which will last for a long time; *the production number is permanently* engraved on the back of the computer casing

permeability *noun* measure of the ratio of the magnetic flux in a material to the size of the generating field

permission *noun* authorization given to a particular user to access a certain shared resource or area of disk; *this user cannot access the file on the server because he does not have permission*

permutation *noun* number of different ways in which something can be arranged; *the cipher system is very secure since there are so many possible permutations for the key*

persistence *noun* length of time that a CRT will continue to display an image after the picture beam has stopped tracing it on the screen; *slow scan rate monitors need long persistence phosphor to prevent the image flickering*

person *noun* human being; **person-to-person call** = telephone call placed through an operator, where the caller will only speak to a certain person

personal *adjective* referring to one person; **personal computer (PC)** = low-cost microcomputer intended mainly for home and light business use; **Personal Computer Memory Card International Association** = *see* PCMCIA; **personal digital assistant (PDA)** = lightweight palmtop computer that provides the basic functions of a diary, notepad, address-book and to-do list together with fax or modem communications; current PDA designs do not have a keyboard, but use a touch-sensitive screen with a pen and handwriting-recognition to control the software; **personal identification device (PID)** = device (such as a card) connected *or* inserted into a system to identify *or* provide authorization for a user; **personal identification number (PIN)** = unique sequence of digits that identifies a user to provide authorization to access a system (often used on automatic cash dispensers *or* with a PID or password to enter a system); **personal information manager (PIM)** = software utility that stores and manages a user's everyday data, such as diary, telephone numbers, address book and notes

personalize *verb* to customize *or* to adapt a product specially for a certain person; to write someone's name *or* initials on a product; **personalizing** = *(term used with Microsoft Windows)* features of an operating system that can be customized by the user to change the background wallpaper, fonts and colours displayed

personnel *noun* staff *or* all the people working in an office *or* factory

perspective *noun* *(film)* appearance of depth in an image in which objects that are further away from the viewer appear smaller

PERT = PROGRAM EVALUATION AND REVIEW TECHNIQUE definition of tasks *or* jobs and the time each requires, arranged in order to achieve a goal

peta (P) equal to one quadrillion (2^{50})

petabyte (PB) *noun* one quadrillion bytes

petal printer = DAISY-WHEEL PRINTER

pF = PICOFARAD unit of measurement of capacitance equal to one million millionth of a farad

PFL *(film)* = PRE-FADE LISTEN

PgDn *see* PAGE DOWN KEY

PGP *see* PRETTY GOOD PRIVACY

PgUp *see* PAGE UP KEY

phantom ROM *noun* duplicate area of read-only memory that is accessed by a special code

phase 1 *noun* **(a)** delay between two similar waveforms; **in phase** = two signals that have no time delay between them; **out of phase** = one signal that has a time delay when compared to another; **phase alternating line (PAL)** = method of providing colour information in a television signal, used in standard receivers in certain countries; **phase angle** = measurement of the phase difference between two signals, where a phase angle of 0 degrees represents signals that are in phase; *(film)* **phase control** = control of the phase angle; **phase distortion** = alterations in the colour wanted in the picture; **phase equalizer** = circuit that introduces delays into signal paths to produce a phase angle of zero degrees; **phase modulation** = modulation method in which the phase of a carrier signal varies with the input **(b)** *(film)* the coincidence of reference signal and colour burst **2** *verb* **phased changeover** = new device that is gradually introduced as the old one is used less and less; **to phase in** *or* **to phase out** = to introduce something gradually *or* to reduce something gradually;

COMMENT: when two signals are in phase there is no time delay between them, when one is delayed they are said to be out of phase by a certain phase angle

phase alternation line (PAL)
standard for television transmission and reception using a 625-line picture transmitted at 25 frames per second; PAL provides a clearer image than NTSC and is used in most of Europe, except for France which uses SECAM. The USA and Japan use NTSC

phasing *noun (film)* **(a)** two systems or circuits which are adjusted so that they operate in phase **(b)** television and video tape recorder standard alignment process **(c)** the loss of quality in transmitted sound when two microphones are placed too near each other

PHIGS = **PROGRAMMER'S HIERARCHICAL INTERACTIVE GRAPHICS STANDARDS** standard application interface between software and a graphics adapter that uses a set of standard commands to draw and manipulate 2D and 3D images

phon *noun* measure of sound equal to a one thousand Hertz signal at one decibel; zero is just audible to the human ear

phone 1 *noun* telephone *or* machine used for speaking to someone over a long distance; *we had a new phone system installed last week*; **by phone** = using the telephone; **card phone** = public telephone that accepts a phonecard instead of money; **house phone** *or* **internal phone** = telephone for calling from one office to another; **phone book** = book which lists names of people and companies with their addresses and phone numbers; *look up his address in the phone book*; **phone call** = speaking to someone on the phone; **phonecard** = special plastic card which allows the user to use a card phone for a certain length of time; **phone number** = set of figures for a particular telephone; *he keeps a list of phone numbers in a little black book; the phone number is on the company notepaper; can you give me your phone number?*; **to be on the phone** = to be speaking to someone on the telephone; *she has been on the phone all morning; he spoke to the manager on the phone;* **to answer the phone** *or* **to take a phone call** = to reply to a call on the phone; **to make a phone call** = to speak to someone on the telephone **2** *verb* **to phone about something** = to make a phone call to speak about something; **to phone for something** = to make a phone call to ask for something; *he phoned for a taxi; he phoned about the order for computer stationery;* **to phone someone** = to call someone by telephone; *don't phone me, I'll phone you; his secretary phoned to say he would be late; he phoned the order through to the warehouse*

phone back *verb* to reply by phone; *the chairman is in a meeting, can you phone back in about half an hour? Mr Smith called while you were out and asked if you would phone him back*

phoneme *noun* single item of sound used in speech; used to analyse voice input to recognise words or to produce speech by playing back a sequence of phonemes; *the phoneme 'oo' is present in the words too and zoo*

phonetic *adjective* referring to phonetics; *the pronunciation is indicated in phonetic script*

phonetics *noun* written symbols that are used to represent the correct pronunciation of a word

phono connector *or* **RCA connector** *noun* plug and socket standard used to connect audio and video devices; the male plug has a 1/8-inch metal central core that sticks out from within the centre of an insulated core

phosphor *noun* substance that produces light when excited by some form of energy, usually an electron beam; used for coating the inside of cathode ray tubes; *see* TELEVISION; **long persistence phosphor** = television screen coating that retains the displayed image for a period of time longer than the refresh rate, so reducing flicker effects; **phosphor coating** = thin layer of phosphor on the inside of a CRT screen; *(film)* **phosphor decay** = the amount of time taken for an image to fade away after the electron beam stops writing; **phosphor dots**

= individual dots of red, green and blue phosphor on a colour CRT screen; **phosphor efficiency** = measure of the amount of light produced in ratio to the energy received from an electron beam; **phosphor triad** = group of three individual phosphor dots (representing red, green and blue) that together form a single pixel on a colour screen.

> COMMENT: a thin layer of phosphor is arranged in a pattern of small dots on the inside of a television screen which produces an image when scanned by the picture beam

phosphorescence *noun* ability of a material to produce light when excited by some form of energy

photo 1 *prefix* referring to light **2** *abbreviation of* PHOTOGRAPH

PhotoCD standard that defines a way of storing images from 35mm photographic slides or negatives in digital format on a CD-ROM

> COMMENT: the Photo CD is normally created at the same time as the photographic film is developed - by digitizing each frame at a resolution of 2048x3072 pixels with 24bit colour (together with a lower-resolution preview image file); one Photo CD can hold 100 photographs. To read a Photo CD disc, the CD-ROM drive must conform to the CD-ROM XA standard. If all the images are recorded onto the Photo CD at the same time, then the disc can be read by a single-session drive; if further images are recorded onto the Photo CD at a later date, then the disc can only be read by a multi-session CD-ROM drive; developed by Kodak and Philips

photocell *noun* electronic device that produces *or* varies an electrical signal according to the amount of light shining on it

photocomposition *noun* composition of typeset text direct onto film

photoconductivity *noun* material which varies its resistance according to the amount of light striking it

photoconductor *noun* photocell whose resistance varies with the amount of light shining on it

photocopier *noun* machine which makes a copy of a document by photographing and printing it

photocopy 1 *noun* copy of a document made by photographing and printing it; *make six photocopies of the contract* **2** *verb* to make a copy of a document by photographing and printing it; *she photocopied the contract*

photocopying *noun* making photocopies; *photocopying costs are rising each year*; **photocopying bureau** = office which photocopies documents for companies which do not possess their own photocopiers; **there is a mass of photocopying to be done** = there are many documents waiting to be photocopied (NOTE: no plural)

photodigital memory *noun* computer memory system that uses a LASER to write data onto a piece of film which can then be read many times but not written to again (NOTE: also called WORM (Write Once Read Many times memory))

photodiode *noun* electronic component displaying the electrical properties of a diode but whose resistance varies with the amount of light that shines on it; *see also* AVALANCHE

photoelectric *adjective* (material) that generates an electrical signal when light shines on it; **photoelectric cell** = component which produces *or* varies an electrical signal when a light shines on it; *the photoelectric cell detects the amount of light passing through the liquid*

photoelectricity *noun* production of an electrical signal from a material that has light shining on it

photoemission *noun* material that emits electrons when light strikes it

photoflood *noun* (film) a high wattage luminous light bulb

photograph *noun* image formed by light striking a light-sensitive surface, usually coated paper; *colour photograph; black and white photograph; it's a photograph of the author; he took six photographs of the set; we will be using a colour photograph of the author on the back of the jacket*

photographic *adjective* referring to photography *or* photographs; *the copier* *makes a photographic reproduction of the printed page*

photographic sound *noun* *(film)* method of recording and reproducing on film where the sound track takes the form of variations in the density or width of a photographic image

photographically *adverb* using photography; *the text film can be reproduced photographically*

photography *noun* method of creating images by exposing light-sensitive paper to light, using a camera

photogravure *noun* printing method in which the paper is pressed directly onto the etched printing plate

photolithography *noun* printing using a lithographic printing plate formed photographically

photomechanical transfer (PMT) *noun* system for transferring line drawings and text onto film before printing

photometer *noun* *(film)* device which measures the brightness of light

photometry *noun* study and measurement of light

photon *noun* packet of electromagnetic radiation

photoprint *noun* *(in typesetting)* final proof

photorealistic *adjective* (digital computer image) having almost the same quality and clarity as a photograph; *the software created a photorealistic landscape using complex mathematical algorithms*

photoresistant *adjective* (chemical *or* material) that hardens into an etch resistant material when light is shone on it; *to make the PCB, coat the board with photoresist, place the opaque pattern above, expose, then develop and etch, leaving the conducting tracks*; **positive photoresist** = method of forming photographic images where exposed areas of photoresist are removed, used in making PCBs

photosensitive *adjective (film)* sensitive to light

photosensor *noun* component *or* circuit that can produce a signal related to the amount of light striking it

photostat 1 *noun* type of photocopy **2** *verb* to make a photostat of a document

phototelegraphy *noun* transmission of images over a telephone line; *see also* FACSIMILE TRANSMISSION

phototext *noun* characters and text that have been produced by a phototypesetter

phototransistor *noun* electronic component that can detect light and amplify the generated signal *or* vary a supply according to light intensity

phototypesetter *noun* **(a)** company which specializes in phototypesetting **(b)** device that can produce very high-resolution text on photo-sensitive paper or film

COMMENT: the phototypesetter, rather like a large laser printer, normally uses the PostScript page description language and can print text at a resolution of 2,540 dpi; if the device is capable of outputting text and half-tone images, it is normally called an image setter

phototypesetting *noun* method of typesetting that creates characters using a computer and exposing a sensitive film in front of a mask containing the required character shape

COMMENT: this is the method by which most new publications are typeset, superseding metal type, since it produces a good quality result in a shorter time

photovoltaic *adjective* which produces a voltage across a material due to light shining on it

physical *adjective* solid *or* which can be touched; **physical address** = memory address that corresponds with a hardware memory location in a memory device; **physical database** = organization and structure of a stored database; **physical layer** = the ISO/OSI defined network layer that defines rules for bit rate, power and medium for signal transmission; *see also* LAYER; **physical memory** = memory fitted in a computer; *compare with* VIRTUAL MEMORY; **physical topology** = actual arrangement of the cables in a network

physical record *noun* **(a)** maximum unit of data that can be transmitted in a single operation **(b)** all the information, including control data for one record stored in a computer system

PIA = PERIPHERAL INTERFACE ADAPTER circuit that allows a computer to communicate with a peripheral by providing serial and parallel ports and other handshaking signals required to interface the peripheral

piano-convex spotlight (pc-spot) *noun (film)* spotlight which has a flat lens on one side and a convex on the other and creates a thin beam of light

PIC 1 = PICTURE method of storing vector graphic images, developed by Lotus for its 1-2-3 spreadsheet charts and graphs **2** = PICTURE IMAGE COMPRESSION image compression algorithm used in Intel's DVI video system; *see also* DVI

pica *noun* **(a)** method of measurement used in printing and typesetting (equal to twelve point type) **(b)** width of characters in a typeface, usually 12 characters to the inch

PICK *noun* multiuser, multitasking operating system that runs on mainframe, mini or PC computers

pickup *noun* **(a)** arm and cartridge used to playback music from a record **(b)** inserting of a shot in a film **(c)** graph showing the sensitivity of a microphone according to the direction of the source; the two most common patterns are omni-directional (the microphone will pick up sound from any direction) and uni-directional (the microphone is focused and responds to sound from one direction only)

pickup reel *noun* empty reel used to take the tape as it is played from a full reel

pick-up tube *noun (film)* video camera tube

pico- (p) *prefix* representing one million millionth of a unit; **picofarad (pF)** = measure of capacitance equal to one million millionth of a farad; **picosecond (pS)** = one million millionth of a second

PICS file format used to import a sequence of PICT files on a Macintosh

PICT = PICTURE *(Apple Macintosh)* graphics file format that stores images in the QuickDraw vector format

picture 1 *noun* printed *or* drawn image of an object or scene; *this picture shows the new design*; **picture beam** = moving electron beam in a TV, that produces an image on the screen by illuminating the phosphor coating and by varying its intensity according to the received signal; **picture element** *or* **pixel** = smallest single unit *or* point on a display whose colour *or* brightness can be controlled; *see also* PIXEL; **picture image compression** = *see* PIC; **picture level benchmark** = *see* PLB; **picture object** = an image created with a vector drawing package and stored as vectors rather than as a bitmap; **picture phone** = communications system that allows sound and images of the user to be transmitted and received; **picture processing** = analysis of information contained in an image, usually by computer *or* electronic methods, providing analysis *or* recognition of objects in the image; **picture search** = device that finds a desired frame on video tape or film; **pictures per second** = *see* PPS; **picture transmission** = transmission of images over a telephone line; *see also* FACSIMILE TRANSMISSION; **picture tube** = cathode ray tubes of a television receiver which change electronic signals to fluorescent optical images through varying the intensity of the scanning beam **2** *verb* to visualize an object *or* scene; *try to picture the layout before starting to draw it in*

PID = PERSONAL IDENTIFICATION DEVICE device (such as a card) connected *or* inserted into a system to identify or provide authorization for a user

pie chart *noun* diagram where ratios are shown as slices of a circle

piece accent *noun* floating accent

piece fraction *noun* printed fraction contained in one character space

piezoelectric *adjective (of certain crystals)* being able to change their electrical properties when a force is applied *or* to change their physical dimensions when an electrical signal is applied

PIF *see* PROGRAM INFORMATION FILE

piggyback *verb* to connect two integrated circuits in parallel, on top of each other to save space; *piggyback those two memory chips to boost the memory capacity*; **piggyback entry** = to gain unauthorized access to a computer system by using an authorized user's password *or* terminal

piggybacking *noun* using transmitted messages to carry acknowledgements from a message which has been received earlier

pilot 1 *noun* **(a)** person who flies a plane *or* guides a ship into port **(b)** used as a test, which if successful will then be expanded into a full operation; *the company set up a pilot project to see if the proposed manufacturing system was efficient; the pilot factory has been built to test the new production processes; he is directing a pilot scheme for training unemployed young people*; *(film)* **pilot pin** = small prongs which connect with the film's perforation holes so that the frame is held steady in the gate of the camera or projector; **pilot print** = first film print; **pilot programme** = test TV programme which may be developed into a full series if it is popular **2** *verb* to test; *they are piloting the new system*

PILOT computer programming language that uses a text based format and is mainly used in computer-aided learning

PIM = PERSONAL INFORMATION MANAGER software utility that stores and manages a user's everyday data, such as diary, telephone numbers, address book and notes

pin 1 *noun* **(a)** sharp piece of metal for attaching papers together, etc.; **drawing pin** = pin with a flat head for attaching a sheet of paper to something hard; *she used drawing pins to pin the poster to the door* **(b)** one of several short pieces of wire attached to an integrated circuit package that allows the IC to be connected to a circuit board **(c)** short piece of metal, part of a plug which fits into a hole in a socket; *use a three-pin plug to connect the printer to the mains*; **pin compatible** = an electronic chip that can directly replace another because the arrangement of the pins is the same and they carry the same signals; *it's easy to upgrade the processor because the new one is pin-compatible*; **three-pin mains plug** = plug with three pins (one neutral, one live and one earthed); **two-pin mains plug** = plug with two pins (one neutral, one live) **(d)** part of a mechanism in a camera or a projector which engages in the perforation hole in order to find the frame **2** *verb* to attach with a pin; *she pinned the papers together; pin your cheque to the application form*

PIN = PERSONAL IDENTIFICATION NUMBER unique sequence of digits that identifies the user

COMMENT: the PIN is commonly used in automatic cash machines in banks, along with a card which allows the user to be identified

pin cushion distortion *noun* optical image distortion in which objects are seen with stretched corners due to lens aberration

pin photodiode *noun* electronic photodiode that can detect light made up of layers of P-type, Intrinsic and N-type semiconductor

pin registration *noun* *(film)* finding the exact position of a film frame in the gate of a camera or projector through pins engaging the perforation holes

pinchwheel *noun* small rubber wheel in a tape machine that holds the tape in place and prevents flutter

pinfeed *noun* *see* TRACTOR FEED

PING software that will test all the nodes on a network or Internet to ensure that they are working correctly

pinhole *noun* *(film)* a transparent dot which appears on the developed emulsion of a film and is often caused by too little movement in the developing liquids

pinout *noun* description of the position of all the pins on an integrated circuit together with their function and signal

PIO = PARALLEL INPUT/OUTPUT; *see also* PIPO, PISO

pipe boom *noun* *(film)* microphone support which is made up of two lengths of tube

pipe *noun* *(in DOS and UNIX)* symbol, normally (|), that tells the operating system to send the output of one command to another command, instead of displaying it

pipelining *noun* **(a)** method of scheduling inputs to arrive at the microprocessor when nothing else is happening, so increasing apparent speed **(b)** beginning the processing of a second instruction while still processing the present one to increase speed of execution of a program

PIPO = PARALLEL INPUT/PARALLEL OUTPUT

piracy *noun* copying of patented inventions *or* copyright works (NOTE: no plural)

> COMMENT: the items most frequently pirated are programs on magnetic disks and tapes which are relatively simple to copy, or books which can easily be printed from photocopied originals

pirate 1 *noun* person who copies a patented invention *or* a copyright work and sells it; *the company is trying to take the software pirates to court; a pirate copy of a computer program* **2** *adjective* **pirate copy** = copy of software or other copyright material which has been made illegally; *a pirate copy of a computer program* **3** *verb* to manufacture copies of an original copyrighted work illegally; *a pirated tape or a pirated design; the designs for the new system were pirated in the Far East; he used a cheap pirated disk and found the program had bugs in it*

PISO = PARALLEL INPUT/SERIAL OUTPUT

pitch *noun* **(a)** measurement of the horizontal spacing of typed characters **(b)** actual frequency of a sound; *(film)* **pitch changer** = system which changes the frequency or pitch of an audio signal; sometimes used to decrease the chance of threshold howl; **pitch envelope** = shape that defines how the frequency of a sound will vary with time; **pitch scale factor** = instruction to a waveform audio device to change the pitch of the sound by a factor; a factor of two is equal to an increase in pitch of one octave and requires complex sound hardware to carry this out without changing the sample rate or playback rate **(c)** satellite *or* antenna movement about the horizontal axis **(d)** **sales pitch** = talk by a salesman to persuade someone to buy **(e)** standard distance between the leading edges of the perforation holes on a film which is to be used as film stock

pix *noun* picture *or* pictures

pix lock *noun* synchronization of a video playback circuit by an external signal

pixel *or* **picture element** *noun* smallest single unit *or* point of a display whose colour *or* brightness can be controlled; *see also* CRT, PEL, RESOLUTION

> COMMENT: in high resolution display systems the colour or brightness of a single pixel can be controlled; in low resolution systems a group of pixels are controlled at the same time

```
adding   40  to  each  pixel
brightens  the  image  and  can
improve    the    display's
appearance
```
Byte

pixillation *noun (film)* **(a)** film and video visual effect where action is shown as a sequence of stills **(b)** an effect in video where the picture is reproduced as a number of enlarged pictures

PL 1 = PROGRAMMING LANGUAGE 1 high level programming language mainly used in commercial and scientific work on large computers, containing features of ALGOL, COBOL and FORTRAN

PL/M = PROGRAMMING LANGUAGE FOR MICROPROCESSORS high level programming language derived from PL/1 for use on microprocessors

PLA = PROGRAMMABLE LOGIC ARRAY (electronic device) integrated circuit that can be permanently programmed to perform logic operations on data

> COMMENT: a PLA consists of a large matrix of paths between input and output pins, with a fusible link at each point which can be broken or left to conduct when programming to define a function from input to output

plain old telephone service *see* POTS

plaintext *noun* text *or* information that has not been encrypted *or* coded; *the messages were sent as plaintext by telephone; enter the plaintext message into the cipher machine*

plan 1 *noun* **(a)** organized way of doing something; **contingency plan** = plan which will be put into action if something happens which no one expects to happen **(b)** drawing which shows how something is arranged *or* how something will be built; *the designers showed us the first plans for the new offices*; **floor plan** = drawing of a floor in a building, showing where different departments are; **street plan** *or* **town plan** = map of a town showing streets and buildings

2 *verb* to organize carefully how something should be done (NOTE: **planning - planned**)

PLAN low-level programming language

planar *noun* **(a)** method of producing integrated circuits by diffusing chemicals into a slice of silicon to create the different components **(b)** graphical objects or images arranged on the same plane

planchest *noun* piece of furniture with wide flat drawers, in which large plans *or* artwork can be kept

plane *noun (in a graphics image)* one layer of an image that can be manipulated independently within a graphics program

planet *noun* large body in space (such as the earth), moving in orbit round the sun

planetary camera *noun* microfilm camera in which the film and article being photographed are stationary

planner *noun* **(a)** person who plans; **the government's economic planners** = people who plan the future economy of the country for the government **(b)** software program that allows appointments and important meetings to be recorded and arranged in the most efficient way **(c) desk planner** *or* **wall planner** = book *or* chart which shows days *or* weeks *or* months so that the work of an office can be shown by diagrams

planning *noun* **(a)** organizing how something should be done, especially how a company should be run to make increased profits; *long-term planning or short-term planning* **(b) the planning department** = section of a local government office which deals with requests for planning permission (NOTE: no plural)

plasma display *or* **gas plasma display** *noun* display screen using the electroluminescing properties of certain gases to display text; *compare with* LCD

COMMENT: this is a modern thin display usually used in small portable computers

the disadvantage of using plasma technology is that it really needs mains power to work for any length of time
Micro Decision

the plasma panel came out of the extended use test well
Micro Decision

plastic bubble keyboard *noun* keyboard whose keys are small bubbles in a plastic sheet over a contact which when pressed completes a circuit

COMMENT: these are very solid and cheap keyboards but are not ideal for rapid typing

plate *noun* **(a)** illustration in a book, usually printed separately and on better quality paper than the text **(b)** etched *or* patterned printing surface that carries the ink to the paper **(c)** photographic image using a sheet of glass as the backing material; **plate camera** = camera which takes pictures on glass plates **(d)** photographic print, film or still transparency which is used in the background of special effect scenes such as travelling matte and back projection

COMMENT: photographic plates are now used mainly in high quality, large-format professional cameras while the most popular backing material is still plastic as in a film

platen *noun* **(a)** roller which supports the paper in a printer *or* typewriter; **platen press** = printing press where the paper passes under a flat printing plate **(b)** device that keeps film in a camera in the correct position

platform *noun* standard type of hardware that makes up a particular range of computers; *this software will only work on the IBM PC platform*; **platform independence** = software or a network that can work with or connect to different types of incompatible hardware

platter *noun* one disk within a hard disk drive

COMMENT: the disks are made of metal or glass and coated with a magnetic compound; each platter has a read/write head that moves across its surface to access stored data

play back *verb* to read data *or* a signal from a recording medium; *after you have recorded the music, press this button to* *play back the tape and hear what it sounds like*

playback head *noun* transducer that reads signals recorded on a storage medium and (usually) converts them to an electrical signal; *disk playback head; tape playback head*

playback rate scale factor *noun* **(a)** *(in waveform audio)* sound played back at a different rate, directed by another application, to create a special effect - created by skipping samples rather than changing the sample rate **(b)** *(video displayed on a computer)* point at which video playback is no longer smooth and appears jerky due to missed frames; this is determined by the size of the playback window and the power of the processor

playback *noun* *(film)* recording reproduction; running a multimedia title, viewing a video clip or listening to a recorded sound

player missile graphics *see* SPRITE

PLB = PICTURE LEVEL BENCHMARK benchmark used to measure the performance (not the quality) of a graphics adapter or workstation

plex database *noun* database structure in which data items can be linked together

plex structure *noun* network structure *or* data structure that has each node connected to all the others

plot 1 *noun* graph *or* map **2** *verb* to draw an image (especially a graph) based on information supplied as a series of coordinates; used to print vector images rather than bitmap images; **plotting mode** = ability of some word-processors to produce graphs by printing a number of closely spaced characters rather than individual pixels (this results in a broad low-resolution line)

plotter *noun* computer peripheral that draws straight lines between two coordinates; **digital plotter** = plotter which receives the coordinates to plot to in a digital form; **drum plotter** = computer output device that consists of a movable pen and a piece of paper wrapped round a drum that rotates, creating patterns and text; **incremental plotter** = plotter which receives positional data as increments to its current position rather than separate

coordinates; **pen plotter** = plotter that uses removable pens to draw an image on paper; **plotter driver** = dedicated software that converts simple instructions issued by a user into complex control instructions to direct the plotter; **plotter pen** = writing instrument used in a plotter to mark the paper with ink as it moves over the paper; **x-y plotter** *or* **graph plotter** = plotter which plots to coordinates supplied, by moving the pen in two planes while the paper remains stationary

COMMENT: plotters are used for graph and diagram plotting and can plot curved lines as a number of short straight lines

plug 1 *noun* **(a)** connector with protruding pins that is inserted into a socket to provide an electrical connection; *the printer is supplied with a plug*; **adapter plug** = plug which allows devices with different plugs (two-pin, three-pin, etc.) to be fitted into the same socket; **plug-compatible** = equipment manufactured to operate with another system when connected to it by a connector *or* cable; *this new plug-compatible board works much faster than any of its rivals, we can install it by simply plugging it into the expansion port*; **plug-compatible manufacturer** = *see* PCM **(b)** to give a **plug to a new product** = to publicize a new product **2** *verb* **(a) to plug in** = to make an electrical connection by pushing a plug into a socket; *no wonder the computer does nothing, you have not plugged it in at the mains*; **plug-in unit** = small electronic circuit that can be simply plugged into a system to increase its power (NOTE: opposite is **unplug**) **(b)** to publicize *or* to advertise; *they ran six commercials plugging holidays in Spain*

plugboard *or* **patchboard** *noun* board with a number of sockets connected to devices into which plugs can be inserted to connect various other devices

it allows room for up to 4Mb of RAM via plug-in memory cartridges

Which PC?

adding memory is simply a matter of plugging a card into an expansion bus connector

Byte

plus *or* **plus sign** *noun* printed *or* written sign (+) showing that figures are added *or* showing a positive value

PLV = PRODUCTION LEVEL VIDEO highest-quality video compression algorithm used with DVI full-motion video sequences; the compression ratio is around 120:1 but has to be carried out off-line by a separate device once the video has been recorded; the compressed videodata can be decompressed in real time during playback

PMBX = PRIVATE MANUAL BRANCH EXCHANGE small telephone exchange inside a company where all calls coming in or going out have to be placed through the switchboard

PMOS = P-CHANNEL METAL OXIDE SEMICONDUCTOR metal oxide semiconductor transistor that conducts via a small region of p-type semiconductor

PMR = PRIVATE MOBILE RADIO

PMS *see* PANTONE MATCHING SYSTEM

PMT = PHOTOMECHANICAL TRANSFER

pn-junction *noun* area where regions of p-type and n-type semiconductor meet, resulting in a diode characteristic; **diffused pn-junction** = practical result of doping one section of semiconductor as p-type and an adjacent section as n-type, where the doping concentration drops gradually over a short distance between the two areas; **step pn-junction** = ideal junction between p-type and n-type areas in a semiconductor where the doping changes occur suddenly

pnp transistor *noun* layout of a bipolar transistor whose collector and emitter are of p-type semiconductor and whose base is n-type semiconductor

pocket *noun* **pocket calculator** *or* **pocket diary** = calculator *or* diary which can be carried in the pocket

point 1 *noun* **(a)** place *or* position; **starting point** = place where something starts **(b)** **decimal point** = dot (in a decimal number) which indicates the division between a whole unit and its fractional parts (such as 4.25); **half a percentage point** = 0.5 per cent; **percentage point** = 1 per cent **(c)** measurement system used in typesetting (one point is equal to 0.351 mm); *the text of the book is set in 9 point Times; if we increase the point size to 10, will the page extent increase?* (NOTE: usually written **pt** after figures: **10pt Times Bold**) **(d)** the exposure increment which is used in a film printing machine; a printer point scale of 1 to 50 is normally used **2** *verb* to move an on-screen cursor using a mouse or arrow keys; **to point out** = to show; *the report points out the mistakes made by the company over the last year; he pointed out that the results were better than in previous years*

point of presence (POP) *noun* a telephone access number for a service provider that can be used to connect to the Internet via a modem

point-of-sale (POS) *noun* the place where goods in a shop are paid for; **point-of-sale material** = display material (such as posters, dump bins) to advertise a product where it is being sold; **point-of-sale terminal** *or* **POS terminal** = computer terminal at a point-of-sale, used to provide detailed product information and connected to a central computer to give immediate stock control information; **electronic point-of-sale (EPOS)** = system that uses a computer terminal at a point-of-sale site for electronic funds transfer, as well as for product identification and stock control

point of view shot *noun* *(film)* camera shot which is positioned behind the performer's shoulder so that the audience sees what the performer is seeing

point size *noun* *(typography)* a unit of measurement equal to 1/72-inch; it indicates the height of a character

pointer *noun* **(a)** variable in a computer program that contains the address to a data item *or* instruction; *increment the contents of the pointer to the address of the next instruction*; **pointer file** = file of pointers referring to large amounts of stored data **(b)** graphical symbol used to indicate the position of a cursor on a computer display; *desktop publishing on a PC is greatly helped by the use of a pointer and mouse*

pointing device *noun* input device that controls the position of a cursor on screen as it is moved by the user; *see also* MOUSE

point to point *noun* communications network where every point is connected to every other; **point to point protocol** = *see* PPP

COMMENT: point to point provides rapid reliable transmissions but is very expensive and wasteful in cabling

point-to-point tunneling protocol
see PPTP

poke *noun* computer instruction that modifies an entry in a memory by writing a number to an address in memory; *poke 1423,74 will write the data 74 into location 1423; compare with* PEEK

POL = PROBLEM-ORIENTATED LANGUAGE

polar *adjective* referring to poles; **polar coordinates** = system of defining positions as an angle and distance from the origin; *compare with* CARTESIAN COORDINATES; **polar diagram** = graphical representation of polar coordinates; **polar orbit** = satellite flight path that flies over the earth's poles; **polar signal** = signal that uses positive and negative voltage levels; **unipolar signal** = signal that uses only positive voltage levels

polarity *noun* **(a)** definition of direction of flow of flux *or* current in an object **(b)** negative or positive elements in a black and white television image; **electrical polarity** = definition of whether an electrical signal is positive *or* negative, indicating if a point is a source or collector of electrical current (positive polarity terminals are usually marked red, negative are black); **magnetic polarity** = method of indicating if a point is a source *or* collector of magnetic flux patterns; **polarity test** = check to see which electrical terminal is positive and which negative; **reverse polarity** = situation where positive and negative terminals have been confused, resulting in the equipment not functioning

polarized *adjective* broadcast signal waveforms are all aligned in one plane; **polarized light** = a light that moves through lenses or crystal plates which stops all waves apart from those vibrating in the same plane; decreases reflections and glare; **vertically polarized** = signal whose waveforms travel horizontally while alternating vertically

polarizing filter *noun (film)* **(a)** lens filter which has thousands of tiny lines which allow light of a certain polarity through, reducing glare **(b)** filter which is used to decrease the amount of polarized light passing through the lens by the specific angling of the slits

Polaroid *noun (film)* **(a)** instant-picture photographic camera **(b)** translucent plastic material which is able to polarize visible light

polaroid filter *noun* photographic filter that only allows light in one plane, vertical *or* horizontal, to be transmitted

COMMENT: often used to remove glare by placing in front of a camera lens or as glasses in front of a person's eyes

policy *see* ACCEPTABLE USER POLICY

Polish notation *see* REVERSE POLISH NOTATION

poll *verb (of computer)* to determine the state of a peripheral in a network

polling *noun* system of communication between a controlling computer and a number of networked terminals (the computer checks each terminal in turn to see if it is ready to receive *or* transmit data, and takes the required action); **polling list** = order in which terminals are to be polled by a computer; **polling overhead** = amount of time spent by a computer in calling and checking each terminal in a network

COMMENT: the polling system differs from other communications systems in that the computer asks the terminals to transmit *or* receive, not the other way round

polyester *noun (film)* tape and film base which consists of polythylene glycol terephthalate

polygon *noun* graphics shape with three or more sides

polynomial code *noun* error detection system that uses a set of mathematical rules applied to the message before it is transmitted and again when it is received to reproduce the original message

POP = POINT OF PRESENCE

pop *verb* instruction to a computer to read and remove the last piece of data from a stack; **pop-down menu** *or* **pop-up menu** = menu that can be displayed on the screen at any time by pressing the appropriate key, usually displayed over material already on the screen; **pop-up window** = window that can be displayed on the screen at any time on top of anything that is already on the screen; when the window is removed, the original screen display is restored; *see also* WINDOW, MODAL; **to pop off** *or* **pop on** = to remove *or* add suddenly an image *or* section of image from a frame; *this is the last frame of the film so pop on the titles*

POP 2 high level programming language used for list processing applications

pop filter *noun* electronic circuit used when recording voices to attenuate signals caused by wind *or* breathing; *every time you say a 'p' you overload the tape recorder, so put this pop filter in to stop it*

populate *verb* to fill the sockets on a printed circuit board with components; **fully-populated** = (i) all the options or memory is fitted into a computer; (ii) printed circuit board that has components in all free sockets

porch *see* FRONT PORCH

port 1 *noun* socket *or* physical connection allowing data transfer between a computer's internal communications channel and another external device; *interface port; parallel port; joystick port; serial port; plug the terminal into the input port*; **input port** = circuit *or* connector that allows a computer to receive data from other external devices; **output port** = circuit *or* connector that allows a computer to output *or* **2** *verb* to transfer an application between platforms

```
the 40Mb hard disk model is
provided with eight terminal
ports
```
Micro Decision

port replicator *noun* device that plugs into a laptop computer and has the same connection ports that are on the back of the laptop; the port replicator stays on a desk and is permanently connected to a mouse, power cable, or printer and the laptop can be easily removed when the user needs to travel with the laptop; *see also* DOCKING STATION

portability *noun* extent to which software *or* hardware can be used on several systems

portable 1 *noun* compact self-contained computer that can be carried around and used either with a battery pack *or* mains power supply **2** *adjective* (any hardware *or*

software *or* data files) that can used on a range of different computers; **portable operating system interface** = *see* POSIX; **portable software** *or* **portable programs** = programs that can be run on several different computer systems

portapack *noun (film)* a battery-operated, portable video camera and recorder

portholing *noun (film)* an even shadowing effect which is created by an error in the beam adjustment in a camera pick-up tube

portrait *noun* orientation of a page or piece of paper where the longest edge is vertical

POS = POINT-OF-SALE place in a shop where goods are paid for; *see also* EPOS

position 1 *noun* place where something is; *this is the position of that chip on the PCB* **2** *verb* to place something in a special place; *the VDU should not be positioned in front of a window; position this photograph at the top right-hand corner of the page*; **positioning time** = amount of time required to access data stored in a disk drive *or* tape machine, including all mechanical movements of the read head and arm

positional *adjective* referring to position; in a certain position

positive 1 *adjective* **(a)** meaning 'yes'; **positive interlace** = precise positioning of a TV camera *or* set interlace scans; **positive photoresist** = photographic image forming system where exposed areas of photoresist are removed, often used in making printed circuit boards; **positive response** = communication signal that indicates correct reception of a message; **positive sound track** = a clear sound track; **positive terminal** = connection to a power supply source that is at a higher electrical potential than ground and supplies current to a component **(b)** (image *or* film) which shows objects as they are seen; **positive display** = (screen) where the text and graphics are shown as black on a white background to imitate a printed page; **positive presentation** = screen image which is coloured on a white background; *compare with* NEGATIVE **2** *noun* **(a)** photographic image where the colours and tones match those of the original scene **(b)** polarity of an electrical signal

positive feedback *noun* part of an output signal that is added into the input of a device; *make sure the microphone is not too close to the loudspeaker or positive feedback will occur and you will overload the amplifier*

> COMMENT: positive feedback is often accidental, resulting in a stronger output which provides a bigger positive feedback signal which rapidly overloads the system

POSIX = PORTABLE OPERATING SYSTEM INTERFACE IEEE standard that defines a set of services provided by an operating system; software that works to the POSIX standard can be easily ported between hardware platforms

POST = POWER-ON SELF-TEST series of checks that are carried out by a computer when it is first switched on and before it loads the operating system (such as Windows)

post *verb* **(a)** to enter data into a record in a file; **(b)** to submit a message to an online discussion group, newsgroup or mailing list; *he posted a new message to the newsgroup advertising his car for sale*

post- *prefix* action that occurs after another; **post-editing** = to edit and modify text after it has been compiled *or* translated by a machine; **post-formatted** = (text) arranged at printing rather than on screen; **post mortem** = examination of a computer program *or* piece of hardware after it has failed to try to find out why; **post production** = final editing process of a video or animation in which titles are added and sequences finalised

post office protocol *see* POP3

poster *noun* large printed sheet, used to advertise something

posterisation *noun* special effect in which an image is processed to reduce the number of colours or tones

postfix *noun* word *or* letter written after another; **postfix notation** = mathematical operations written in a logical way, so that the symbol appears after the numbers to be acted upon, this removes the need for brackets; *normal notation: (x-y) + z, but using postfix notation: xy - z* (NOTE: often referred to as **reverse Polish notation**)

postmaster *noun* person in charge of email within a company; *if you are having problems reaching a user at a site, try sending a message to the postmaster*

postprocessor *noun* **(a)** microprocessor that handles semi-processed data from another device **(b)** program that processes data from another program, which has already been processed; *see also* CPU

PostScript standard page description language developed by Adobe Systems; PostScript offers flexible font sizing and positioning; it is most often used in DTP systems, high-quality laser printers and phototypesetters; *if you do a lot of DTP work, you will benefit from a PostScript printer*; **Display PostScript** = graphics language system that allows a user to see on the screen exactly what would appear on the printer; **encapsulated PostScript (EPS)** = PostScript commands stored in a file that describe an image or page; *insert the EPS image in this box in the DTP software*

> COMMENT: an encapsulated PostScript file contains PostScript commands that describe an image or page, the commands are stored in a file and this can be placed on a page; an encapsulated PostScript file often contains a preview image in TIFF format

pot = POTENTIOMETER

potential *noun* ability of energy to carry out work (by transformation); **potential difference** = voltage difference between two points in a circuit

potentiometer *noun* mechanical variable resistance component consisting of a spindle which is turned to move a contact across a resistance track to vary the resistance of the potentiometer; *see also* VARIABLE RESISTOR

POTS = PLAIN OLD TELEPHONE SERVICE basic, standard telephone line without any special features (such as call waiting or forwarding) and without high-speed digital access; *compare with* ADSL, ISDN

power 1 *noun* **(a)** unit of energy in electronics equal to the product of voltage and current, measured in Watts; **automatic power off** = equipment that will switch itself off if it has not been used for a certain time; **PowerCD** = CD-ROM player produced by Apple that can connect to a television to display Photo CD images, or to a Macintosh as a standard CD-ROM drive, or to play back music CDs; **power loss** = amount of power lost (in transmission or connection equipment); **power off** = switching off *or* disconnecting an electrical device from its power supply; **power on** = indication that a voltage is being supplied to a piece of electrical equipment; **power on self test (POST)** = series of hardware tests that a computer carries out when it is first switched on; **power pack** = self-contained box that will provide a voltage and current supply for a circuit; **PowerPC** = RISC-based processor developed by Motorola and used in the PowerPC range of Apple Macintosh computers; **power supply** *or* **power supply unit (PSU)** = electrical circuit that provides certain direct current voltage and current levels from an alternating current source for use in other electrical circuits (a PSU will regulate, smooth and reduce the mains voltage level for use in low power electronic circuits); **power up** = to switch on *or* apply a voltage to a electrical device; **power user** = user who needs the latest, fastest model of computer because he runs complex or demanding applications; **power zoom** = motor that drives a zoom lens; **uninterruptable power supply (UPS)** = power supply that can continue to provide a regulated supply to equipment even after mains power failure **(b)** mathematical term describing the number of times a number is to be multiplied by itself; *5 to the power 2 is equal to 25* (NOTE: written as small figures in superscript: 10^5 say: 'ten to the power five')

powered *adjective* driven by a type of energy *or* motor; *a motor powered by electricity; a solar-powered calculator* **2** *verb* to provide electrical or mechanical energy to a device; *the monitor is powered from a supply in the main PC*; **power down** = to turn off the power to a device; *once you have shut down the software, you can power off the server*

ppm = PAGES PER MINUTE

PPM = PULSE POSITION MODULATION pulse modulation method that varies the time between pulses in relation to the magnitude of an input signal; *see also* PULSE MODULATION

PPP = POINT TO POINT PROTOCOL protocol that allows a computer to use the TCP/IP protocol over a telephone connection

PPQN = PARTS PER QUARTER NOTE most common time format used with standard MIDI sequences

PPS = PICTURES PER SECOND film or video frame speed

PPTP = POINT-TO-POINT TUNNELING PROTOCOL network protocol that allows one type of network protocol to be sent over a network that uses a different network protocol

COMMENT: used to send LAN protocols, such as Novell's IPX or Microsoft's NetBEUI over the Internet in a transparent manner; used by companies that want to use the Internet to connect servers in different offices

pre- *prefix* meaning before; **pre-agreed** = which has been agreed in advance

pre-amplifier *noun* low noise electronic circuit that increases the magnitude of very small signals, used before a power amplifier

precede *verb* to come before; *instruction which cancels the instruction which precedes it*

precedence *noun* computational rules defining the order in which mathematical operations are calculated (usually multiplications are done first, then divisions, additions and subtractions last); **operator precedence** = order in which a number of mathematical operations will be carried out

precise *adjective* very exact; *the atomic clock will give the precise time of starting the process*

precision *noun* being very accurate; **precision of a number** = number of digits in a number

precompiled code *noun* code that is output from a compiler, ready to be executed

predefined *adjective* which has been defined in advance

predesigned *adjective* (graphic material) provided to the customer already designed; *a wide selection of predesigned layouts help you automatically format typical business and technical documents*

predetermined *adjective* which has already been determined

pre-edit *verb* to change text before it is run through a machine to make sure it is compatible

pre-emphasise *verb* to boost certain frequencies of a signal before transmission *or* processing to minimize noise (signals are de-emphasised on reception)

preemptive multitasking *noun* form of multitasking in which the operating system executes a program for a period of time, then passes control to the next program so preventing any one program using all the processor time

pre-fade listen *noun (film)* sound desk device which permits channels to be heard before fading up

pre-fetch *noun* CPU instructions stored in a short temporary queue before being processed, increasing the speed of execution; often used to speed up processing of complex image files

prefix *noun* **(a)** code *or* instruction *or* character at the beginning of a message *or* instruction **(b)** word attached to the beginning of another word to give it a special meaning; *'kilo-' is the prefix meaning 'one thousand', so a kilogram is a thousand grams*

prefix notation method of writing mathematical formulae with the operator before the arguments; *in normal notation we write (x-y) + z, but using prefix notation we would write: - xy + z*

pre-flash *or* **pre-fog** *noun (film)* exposing film to light before filming so that it has a higher sensitivity to light and reduces contrast

preformatted *adjective* which has been formatted already; *a preformatted disk*

pre-imaging *noun* generating one frame of an animation or video in a memory buffer before it is transferred on-screen for display

premix *noun* combination of a number of signals before they have been processed in any way

preparation *noun* getting something ready; **data preparation** = conversion of data into a machine-readable form (usually by keyboarding) before data entry

preprinted *adjective* already printed *or* printed in advance; **preprinted form** = paper used for printing databases *or* applications programs that already contain some information printed; **preprinted stationery** = computer stationery (such as invoices) which has already been printed with the company's logo and address as well as the blank columns, etc.

preprocess *verb* to carry out initial organization and simple processing of data

preprocessor *noun* **(a)** software that partly processes *or* prepares data before it is compiled *or* translated **(b)** small computer that carries out some initial processing of raw data before passing it to the main computer

preproduction *noun* organization of the filming *or* recording of a video *or* compact disk, taking the form of diagrams and scene descriptions

preprogrammed *adjective* (chip) which has been programmed in the factory to perform one function

prerecord 1 *verb* to record something which will be played back later *or* to record sound effects that are added to a film at a later date; *the answerphone plays a prerecorded message* **2** *noun* section of text stored in a word-processor system which will be used as the basis for a form letter

pre-roll *noun (film)* time needed after having started a telecine, projector or video tape recorder in order to produce steady sound and picture

prescan *noun* feature of many flat-bed scanners and control software that carry out a quick, low-resolution scan to allow the operator to re-position the original or mark the area that is to be scanned at a higher resolution

presentation graphics *noun* graphics used to represent business information or data; *the sales for last month looked even better thanks to the use of presentation graphics*

presentation layer *noun* ISO/OSI standard network layer that agrees on formats, codes and requests for start and end of a connection; *see also* ISO/OSI MODEL, LAYER

presentation software *noun* software application that allows a user to create a business presentation with graphs, data, text and images

preset *verb* to set something in advance; *the printer was preset with new page parameters* (NOTE: presetting - preset)

press 1 *noun* **(a)** newspapers and magazines; **press conference** = meeting where reporters from newspapers are invited to hear news of a new product *or* of a takeover bid, etc.; **press coverage** = reports about something in the press; *we were very disappointed by the press coverage of the new car*; **press cutting** = piece cut out of a newspaper *or* magazine, which refers to an item which you find interesting; *we have kept a file of press cuttings about the new software package*; **press release** = advance publicity material about a new product given out to newspapers and other media; *the company sent out a press release about the launch of the new scanner*; **the local press** = newspapers which are sold in a small area of the country; **the national press** = newspapers which sell in all parts of the country; *the new car has been advertised in the national press; we plan to give the product a lot of press publicity; there was no mention of the new product in the press* (NOTE: no plural) **(b)** printing **press** = machine which prints; **the book is on the press** = the book is being printed **2** *verb* to push with the fingers; *to end the program press ESCAPE*

pressure pad *noun* transducer that converts pressure changes into an electrical signal; *the pressure pad under the carpet will set off the burglar alarm if anyone steps on it*

pressure plate *noun (film)* mechanical device which holds the film in place at the gate of a camera or projector

prestore *verb* to store data in memory before it is processed

presynchronization *noun (film)* the pre-recording of dialogue which is used in synchronization with lip movements in animation work

Pretty Good Privacy (PGP) *noun* software encryption technique developed to provide security against unauthorized people reading email and messages sent over the Internet; uses a form of public key encryption

prevent *verb* to stop something happening; *we must try to prevent the takeover bid; the police prevented anyone from leaving the building; we have changed the passwords to prevent hackers getting into the database*

prevention *noun* preventing something happening

preventive *or* **preventative** *adjective* which tries to stop something happening; **preventive maintenance** = regular checks on equipment to correct and repair any small faults before they cause a major problem; *we have a preventive maintenance contract for the system*

preview 1 *noun* special showing of a new film to a select audience before release to the general public **2** *verb* to display text *or* graphics on a screen as it will appear when it is printed out; in video, to view a picture *or* programme before transmission *or* recording

previewer *noun* feature that allows a user to see on screen what a page will look like when printed; *the built-in previewer allows the user to check for mistakes*

previous *adjective* which happens earlier; *copy data into the present workspace from the previous file*

previously *adverb* happening earlier; *the data is copied onto previously formatted disks*

primarily *adverb* mainly

primary *adjective* first *or* basic *or* most important; **primary channel** = channel that carries the data transmission between two devices; *compare with* SECONDARY CHANNEL; **primary colours** = colours (red, yellow and blue) from which all other colours can be derived; **primary group** = number of signals that are merged into one signal (which may be merged with others) prior to transmission; **primary key** = unique identifying word that selects one entry from a database; **primary station** = the single station in a data network that can select a path and transmit, the primary status is temporary and moves between stations; **primary memory** *or* **storage** *or* **main memory** = (i) small fast-access internal memory of a computer system (whose main memory is slower secondary storage) which stores the program currently being used; (ii) main internal memory of a computer system; *compare with* SECONDARY STORAGE

prime 1 *adjective* very important; **prime attribute** = most important feature *or* design of a system; **prime time** = (i) time when there are the greatest number of TV viewers; (ii) most expensive advertising time for TV commercials; *we are putting out a series of prime-time commercials* **2** *noun* number that can only be divided by itself and one; *the number seven is a prime*

prime lens *noun* (a) lens with a fixed focal length (b) the camera or projector objective, which is usually of a fixed focal length, to which is added an additional attachment range

primer *noun* manual *or* simple instruction book with instructions and examples to show how a new program *or* system operates

primitive *noun* (a) *(in programming)* basic routine that can be used to create more complex routines (b) *(in graphics)* simple shape (such as circle, square, line, curve) used to create more complex shapes in a graphics program

print 1 *noun* (a) image produced using an etched printing plate; *he collects 18th-century prints; the office is decorated with Japanese prints* (b) positive photographic image in which black is black and white is white; *compare with* NEGATIVE; **print contrast ratio** = difference between the brightest and darkest areas of an image; **print film** *or* **print film stock** = film which carries positive images and sound tracks which are to be projected onto a screen (c) characters made in ink on paper; *he was very pleased to see his book in print; the print from the daisy-wheel printer is clearer than that from the line printer*; **print control character** = special character sent to a printer that directs it to perform an action *or* function (such as change font), rather than print a character; **print hammer** = moving arm in a typewriter that presses the metal character form onto the printer ribbon leaving a mark on the paper; **printhead** = (i) row of needles in a dot-matrix printer that produce characters as a pattern of dots; (ii) metal form of a character that is pressed onto an inked ribbon to print the character on paper; **print job** = file in a print queue that contains all the characters and printer control codes needed to print one document *or* page; **print life** = number of characters a

component can print before needing to be replaced; *the printhead has a print life of over 400 million characters*; **print modifiers** = codes in a document that cause a printer to change mode, i.e. from bold to italic; **Print Manager** = software utility that is part of Microsoft Windows and is used to manage print queues; **printout** = final printed page; **print pause** = temporarily stopping a printer while printing (to change paper, etc.); **print preview** = function of a software product that lets the user see how a page will appear when printed; **print quality** = the quality of the text *or* graphics printed; normally measured in dots per inch; *a desktop printer with a resolution of 600dpi provides good print quality*; **print queue** = area of memory that stores print jobs ready to send to the printer when it has finished its current work; **print screen** = *see* PRTSC; **print server** = computer in a network that is dedicated to managing print queues and printers; **print spooling** = automatic printing of a number of different documents in a queue at the normal speed of the printer, while the computer is doing some other task; **print style** = typeface used on a certain printer *or* for a certain document **2** *verb* (a) to put letters *or* figures in ink on paper; *printed agreement; printed regulations; the printer prints at 60 characters per second;* **print out** = to print information from a computer through a printer (b) to put letters *or* illustrations onto sheets of paper so that they form a book; *the book was printed in Hong Kong; the book is printing at the moment, so we will have bound copies at the end of the month* (c) to write in capital letters; *please print your name and address on the top of the form* (d) take to be used in the finished film if it is not cut out during the editing process

printed circuit *or* **printed circuit board (PCB)** *noun* flat insulating material that has conducting tracks of metal printed *or* etched onto its surface which complete a circuit when components are mounted on it

printer *noun* (a) device that produces text or image on paper using ink or toner under the control of a computer; **computer printer** *or* **line printer** = machine which prints information from a computer, printing one line at a time; **barrel printer** = type of printer where characters are located around a rotating barrel; **bi-directional printer** = printer which is able to print characters from left to right *or* from right to left as the head moves backwards and forwards; **bubble-jet printer** = printer that produces characters by sending a stream of tiny drops of ink onto the paper; **chain printer** = printer whose characters are located on a continuous belt; **computer printer** = machine which prints information from a computer; **daisy-wheel printer** = printer with characters arranged on interchangeable wheels; **dot-matrix printer** = printer which forms characters from a series of tiny dots printed close together; **impact printer** = printer that prints text and symbols by striking an inked ribbon onto paper with a metal character; **ink-jet printer** = printer that produces characters by sending a stream of tiny drops of electrically charged ink onto the paper (the movement of the ink drops is controlled by an electric field); **laser printer** = high-resolution printer that uses a laser source to print high quality dot-matrix characters; **line printer** = printer which prints draft-quality information at high speed (typical output is 200 - 3000 lines per minute); **page printer** = printer which composes one page of text, then prints it rapidly; **printer buffer** = temporary store for character data waiting to be printed (used to free the computer before the printing is completed making the operation faster); **printer control characters** = command characters in a text which transmit printing commands to a printer; **printer control language (PCL)** = standard set of commands, defined by Hewlett Packard, that allow a computer to control a printer; **printer driver** = dedicated software that converts and formats the user's commands ready for a printer; **printer emulation** = printer that is able to interpret the standard set of commands used to control another brand of printer; *this printer emulation allows my NEC printer to emulate an Epsom*; **printer-plotter** = high resolution printer that is able to operate as a low resolution plotter; **printer ribbon** = roll of inked material which passes between a printhead and the paper; **printer quality** = standard of printed text from a particular printer (high resolution dot matrix printers produce near

letter quality, daisy wheel produce letter quality); **thermal printer** = printer where the character is formed on thermal paper with a printhead containing a heating element **(b)** company which prints books *or* newspapers; *the book will be sent to the printer next week; we are using Japanese printers for some of our magazines*

printhead *noun* **(a)** row of needles in a dot matrix printer that produce characters as a series of dots **(b)** metal form of a character that is pressed onto an inked ribbon to print the character on paper

printing *noun* **(a)** action of printing a book *or* a document; *the printing will take about two weeks* **(b)** number of copies printed at one time; *the first printing was 50,000 copies*

printing negative *noun (film)* a negative copy of an optical sound track on a positive picture print which is used to improve the quality of sound

prior *adjective* happening before; *he could not attend the meeting because he had a prior engagement*; **prior to** = before; *the password has to be keyed in prior to accessing the system*

priority *noun* importance of a device *or* software routine in a computer system; *the operating system has priority over the application when disk space is allocated; the disk drive is more important than the printer, so it has a higher priority*; **job priority** = importance of a job compared to others; **priority interrupt** = signal to a computer that takes precedence over any other task; *see also* INTERRUPT, NON-MASKABLE INTERRUPT; **priority scheduler** = system that organizes tasks into correct processing priority to improve performance

prism lens *noun (film)* a lens which creates multiple images in the camera

prism shutter *noun (film)* in editing machines, film viewers and a few high-speed cameras, a four- or more sided rotating prism through which the viewer light enters as the film moves through it

privacy *noun* the right of an individual to limit the extent of and control the access to the data that is stored about him; **privacy of data** = rule that data is secret and must not be accessed by users who have not been authorized; **privacy of information** = rule that unauthorized users cannot obtain data about private individuals from databases *or* that each individual has the right to know what information is being held about him on database; **privacy statement** = policy of a company (published on their website) that explains to visitors and customers what the company will (and preferably will not) do with a customer's personal details - such as their email address. Used to reassure customers that you're not about to resell their details as a mailing list.; **privacy transformation** = encryption of messages *or* data to ensure that it remains private

private *adjective* belonging to an individual *or* to a company, not to the public; **private address space** = memory address range that is reserved for a single user, not for public access; **private automatic branch exchange (PABX)** = small telephone exchange in a company that handles all internal and external calls to the main public network; **private automatic exchange (PAX)** = small telephone exchange in a company that only allows internal calls within the company to be made; **private branch exchange (PBX)** = small manual *or* automatic exchange in a company that can handle internal *or* external calls; **private dial port** = unlisted telephone number that connects one user to a packet network system; **private line** = special telephone line, rented from the telephone company and used only by the user; **private manual branch exchange (PMBX)** = small telephone exchange inside a company where all telephone calls coming in *or* going out have to be placed through a switchboard; **private mobile radio (PMR)** = *see* MOBILE; **private telephone system** = telephone system in a company that cannot be accessed from a public telephone system

privilege *noun* status of a user referring to the type of program he can run and the resources he can use; *the systems manager has a privileged status so he can access any file on the system*; **privileged account** = computer account that allows special programs *or* access to sensitive system data; *the system manager can access anyone else's account from his privileged account*

PRN = PRINTER acronym used in MS-DOS to represent the standard printer port

problem *noun* question to which it is difficult to find an answer; **to solve a problem** = to find an answer to a problem; **problem-orientated language (POL)** = high-level programming language that allows certain problems to be expressed easily

procedural *adjective* using a procedure (to solve a problem); **procedural language** = high-level programming language in which the programmer enters the actions required to achieve the result wanted

procedure *noun* **(a)** small section of computer instruction code that provides a frequently used function and can be called upon from a main program; *this procedure sorts all the files into alphabetic order, you can call it from the main program by the instruction SORT*; *see also* SUBROUTINE **(b)** method *or* route used when solving a problem; *you should use this procedure to retrieve lost files; the procedure is given in the manual*; **procedure-orientated language** = high-level programming language that allows procedures to be programmed easily

proceed *verb* to move forward; *after spellchecking the text, you can proceed to the printing stage*

process 1 *noun* a number of tasks that must be carried out to achieve a goal; *the process of setting up the computer takes a long time; there are five stages in the process*; **process camera** = a special effects camera, used for matte and bi-pack printing, as opposed to cameras which are used for recording live action; **process control** = automatic control of a process by a computer **2** *verb* to carry out a number of tasks to produce a result (such as sorting data *or* finding the solution to a problem); *we processed the new data; processing all the information will take a long time*

processing *noun* **(a)** sorting of information; using a computer to solve a problem *or* organize data; *page processing time depends on the complexity of a given page*; *see also* CPU; **batch processing** = computer system, where information is collected into batches before being loaded into the computer; **data processing** *or*

information processing = selecting and examining data in a computer to produce information in a special form; **word-processing** *or* **text processing** = working with words, using a computer to produce, check and change texts, reports, letters, etc. **(b)** the treatment of exposed film with chemicals in order to make the latent image everlastingly visible **(c) order processing** = dealing with orders; **the processing of a claim for insurance** = putting a claim for insurance through the usual office routine in the insurance company (NOTE: no plural)

> COMMENT: the central processing unit is a hardware device that allows a computer to manipulate and modify data; a compiler is a software language processor that translates data and instructions in one language into another form

processor *noun* hardware *or* software device that is able to manipulate *or* modify data according to instructions; **dual processor** = computer system with two processors for faster program execution; **image processor** = electronic *or* computer system used for image processing; **processor controlled keying** = data entry by an operator which is prompted and controlled by a computer; **word-processor** = small computer which is used for working with words, to produce texts, reports, letters, etc.

```
each chip will contain 128
processors and one million
transistors
                    Computer News
```

produce *verb* **(a)** to bring out; *he produced documents to prove his claim; the sales representative produced a set of figures; the customs officer asked him to produce the relevant documents* **(b)** to make *or* to manufacture; *to produce books or magazines or printers or disks*; **to mass produce** = to make large quantities of a product

producer *noun* **(a)** person *or* company *or* country which manufactures; *country which is a producer of high quality computer equipment; the company is a major magnetic tape producer* **(b)** person who is in charge of a film *or* TV show, who

has the idea for the show, and organizes the filming, the actors, etc.

producing *adjective* which produces; **producing capacity** = capacity to produce

product *noun* **(a)** item which is made *or* manufactured; **basic product** = main product made from a raw material; **end product** *or* **final product** *or* **finished product** = product made at the end of a production process **(b)** manufactured item for sale; **product advertising** = advertising a particular named product, not the company which makes it; **product analysis** = examining each separate product in a company's range to see why it sells *or* who buys it, etc.; **product design** = design of consumer products; **product development** = improving an existing product line to meet the needs of the market; **product engineer** = engineer in charge of the equipment for making a product; **product line** *or* **product range** = series of different products made by the same company which form a group (such as printers in different models *or* different colours, etc.); **product management** = directing the making and selling of a product as an independent item; **product mix** = group of quite different products made by the same company **(c)** result after multiplication

production *noun* **(a)** showing something; **on production of** = when something is shown; *the case will be released by the customs on production of the relevant documents; goods can be exchanged only on production of the sales slip* **(b)** making *or* manufacturing of goods for sale; *production will probably be held up by industrial action; we are hoping to speed up production by installing new machinery*; **batch production** = production in batches; **mass production** = manufacturing of large quantities of goods; *mass production of monitors or of calculators*; **production control** = control of the manufacturing of a product (using computers); **production cost** = cost of making a product; **production department** = section of a company which deals with the making of the company's products; **production line** = system of making a product, where each item (such as a TV set) moves slowly through the factory with new sections added to it as it goes along; *he* *works on the production line; she is a production line worker; a typical use of an image processor includes production line control*; **production manager** = person in charge of the production department; **production run** = manufacturing a product *or* running a program, as opposed to a test run; **production unit** = separate small group of workers producing a certain product; **rate of production** *or* **production rate** = speed at which items are made **(c)** the preparation for broadcast of a programme or advertisement **(d)** *(film)* the complete process of making a film; **production assistant** = the person who is assistant to the producer or director of a production and is in charge of scripts and continuity; **production camera** = camera used to record live action, as opposed to a process camera; **production level video** = *see* PLV (NOTE: no plural)

PROFS electronic mail system developed by IBM that runs on mainframe computers

program 1 *noun* **(a)** complete set of instructions which direct a computer to carry out a particular task; **program branch** = one or more paths that can be followed after a conditional statement; **program coding sheet** = specially preprinted form on which computer instructions can be written, simplifying program writing; **program counter (PC)** *or* **instruction address register (IAR)** = register in a CPU that contains the location of the next instruction to be processed; *see also* SEQUENCE CONTROL REGISTER; **program crash** = unexpected failure of a program due to a programming error *or* a hardware fault; *I forgot to insert an important instruction which caused my program to crash, erasing all the files on the disk!*; **program design language (PDL)** = programming language used to design the structure of a program; **program development** = all the operations involved in creating a computer program from first ideas to initial writing, debugging and the final product; **program development system** = all the hardware and software needed for program development on a system; **program documentation** = set of instruction notes, examples and tips on how to use a program; *see also* MANUAL; **program evaluation and review technique** = *see* PERT; **program execution** = instructing a processor to

execute in sequence the instructions in a program; **program flowchart** = diagram that graphically describes the various steps in a program; **program generator** = software that allows users to write complex programs using a few simple instructions; *(in a GUI)* **program icon** = icon that represents an executable program file; *to run the program, double-click on the program icon*; *(in Microsoft Windows)* **program information file (PIF)** = file that contains the environment settings for a particular program; **program instruction** = single word *or* expression that represents one operation (in a high level program each program instruction can consist of a number of low level machine code instructions); *(in a GUI)* **program item** = an icon that represents a program; **program library** = collection of useful procedures and programs which can be used for various purposes and included into new software; **program listing** = list of the set of instructions that make up a program (program listings are displayed in an ordered manner, BASIC listings by line number, assembly listings by memory location; they do not necessarily represent the order in which the program will be executed, since there could be jumps *or* subroutines); **program maintenance** = keeping a program free of errors and up to date; **Programs menu** = sub-menu that is accessed from the Start button in Microsoft Windows and displays the programs installed on the computer; **program relocation** = moving a stored program from one area of memory to another; **program report generator** = software that allows users to create reports from files and other stored data; **program specification** = document that contains details on all the functions and abilities of a computer program; **program stack** = section of memory reserved for storing temporary system *or* program data; **program statement** = high level program instruction that is made up of a number of machine code instructions; **program structure** = the way in which sections of program code are interlinked and operate; **program testing** = testing a new program with test data to ensure that it functions correctly; **program verification** = number of tests and checks performed to ensure that a program functions correctly **(b)** *(in MIDI)* data that defines a sound in a synthesizer; a program is also called a patch and can be altered by issuing a program-change message **2** *verb* to write *or* prepare a set of instructions which direct a computer to perform a certain task; **programmed learning** = using educational software which allows a learner to follow a course of instruction (NOTE: **programs - programming - programmed**)

programmable *adjective & noun* (device) that can accept and store instructions then execute them; **programmable calculator** = small calculator which can hold certain basic mathematical calculating programs; **programmable logic array (PLA)** = integrated circuit that can be permanently programmed to perform logic operations on data using a matrix of links between input and output pins; **programmable key** = special key on a computer terminal keyboard that can be programmed with various functions *or* characters; **programmable memory (PROM)** = electronic device in which data can be stored; *see also* EAROM, EEPROM, EPROM, ROM; **programmable read only memory (PROM)** = memory integrated circuit that can be programmed with data by a user (some PROMs provide permanent storage, others such as EPROMs are erasable); **hand-held programmable** = very small computer, which can be held in the hand, used for inputting information when a larger terminal is not available (as by a salesman on a call)

programme *or US* **program** *noun* TV *or* radio broadcast which is separate from other broadcasts, and has its own producer, director, etc.; *they were filming a wild life programme; children's programmes are scheduled for early evening viewing*

programmer *noun* **(a)** person who is capable of designing and writing a working program; *the programmer is still working on the new software*; **applications programmer** = programmer who writes applications software; **systems programmer** = programmer specializes in writing systems software **(b)** device that allows data to be written into a programmable read only memory;

programmer's hierarchical interactive graphics standard = *see* PHIGS

programming *noun* writing programs for computers; **programming in logic** = PROLOG; **programming language** = software that allows a user to write a series of instructions to define a particular task, which will then be translated to a form that is understood by the computer; **programming language for microprocessors** = *see* PL/M; **programming standards** = rules to which programs must conform to produce compatible code

COMMENT: programming languages are grouped into different levels: the high-level languages such as BASIC and PASCAL are easy to understand and use, but offer slow execution time since each instruction is made up of a number of machine code instructions; low-level languages such as assembler are more complex to read and program in but offer faster execution time

the other use for the socket is to program 2, 4, 8 or 16Kbyte eproms
Electronics & Wireless World

each of the 16 programmable function keys has two modes - normal and shift - giving 32 possible functions
Micro Decision

project 1 *noun* planned task; *his latest project is computerizing the sales team; the design project was entirely worked out on computer; CAD is essential for accurate project design* **2** *verb* to forecast future figures from a set of data; *the projected sales of the new PC*

projection *noun* **(a)** forecast of a situation from a set of data; *the projection indicates that sales will increase* **(b)** showing pictures on a screen; **projection room** = room in a cinema where the projectors which show the films are housed; **projection speed** = speed at which film is projected, generally 24 seconds per frame for sound film and 18 seconds for silent film

projector *noun* **projector leader** = short part of the beginning of a reel of film which allows projectionists to make fast changeovers from one reel to the next when projecting a film; **film projector** *or* **slide projector** = mechanical device that displays films *or* slides on a screen; *see also* OVERHEAD

PROLOG = PROGRAMMING IN LOGIC high-level programming language using logical operations for artificial intelligence and data retrieval applications

PROM (a) = PROGRAMMABLE READ ONLY MEMORY read-only memory which can be programmed by the user (as opposed to ROM, which is programmed by the manufacturer); **PROM burner** *or* **programmer** = electronic device used to program a PROM; *see also* EPROM **(b)** = PROGRAMMABLE MEMORY electronic memory in which data can be stored

prompt *noun* message *or* character displayed to remind the user that an input is expected; *the prompt READY indicates that the system is available to receive instructions*; **command prompt** = symbol displayed to show that a command is expected; *MS-DOS normally displays the command prompt C:\ to indicate that it is ready to process instructions typed in by a user*

prompter *noun (film)* person on a set who gives cues to performers during action filming; *see* CUE

proof 1 *noun* printed matter from a printer that has to be checked and corrected; **galley proofs** = proofs in the form of long pieces of text, not divided into pages, printed on long pieces of paper; **page proofs** = proofs which are divided into pages, but may not have page numbers or headings inserted **2** *verb* to produce proofs of a text

proofer *noun* printer which produces proofs, as opposed to finished printed pages; *output devices such as laser proofers and typesetters*

proofing *noun* producing proofs of text which have to be read and corrected

proofread *verb* to correct spelling and printing errors in a printed text; *has all the text been proofread yet?*

proofreader *noun* person who reads and corrects proofs

COMMENT: the stages of full proofing are galley proofs, page on galley (where the pages are indicated, but the proofs

are still printed on long pieces of paper), and page proofs. It is usual to miss out some of these stages, and many books are proofed in pages from the start

propagate *verb* to travel *or* spread; **propagated error** = one error in a process that affects later operations

propagation delay *noun* time taken for a signal to travel through a circuit; *propagation delay in the transmission path causes signal distortion*

properties *plural noun* attributes of an object that define its appearance and behaviour, such as its position, colour, shape, and name

proportion *noun* size of something as compared to others

proportional spacing *noun* printing system where each letter takes a space proportional to the character width ('i' taking less space than 'm'); *compare with* MONOSPACING

proprietary file format *noun* method of storing data devised by a company for its products and incompatible with other products; *you cannot read this spreadsheet file because my software saves it in a proprietary file format*

props *plural noun (film)* any objects used for scenery, such as guns or furniture, in a shot

protect *verb* to stop something being damaged; **copy protect** = switch used to prevent copies of a disk being made; *all the disks are copy protected*; **crash protected** = (disk) which uses a head protection *or* data corruption protection system; *if the disk is crash protected, you will never lose your work*; **protected location** = memory location that cannot be altered *or* cannot be accessed without authorization; **protected mode** = operating mode of some CPUs that supports multitasking, virtual memory, and data security; *compare with* REAL MODE; **protected storage** = section of memory that cannot be altered

protection *noun* action of protecting; **copy protection** = preventing copies being made; *a hard disk may crash because of faulty copy protection; the new product will come without copy protection*; **data protection** = making sure that data is not copied by an unauthorized user; **Data**

Protection Act = act which prevents confidential data about people being copied; **protection key** = signal checked to see if a program can access a section of memory; **protection master** = spare copy of a master film *or* tape

protective *adjective* which protects; *the disks are housed in hard protective cases*

protocol *noun* pre-agreed signals, codes and rules to be used for data exchange between systems; **protocol stack** = separate parts of a protocol, each with a different function, that work together to provide a complete set of network functions; **protocol standards** = standards laid down to allow data exchange between any computer system conforming to the standard

```
there is a very simple
protocol that would exclude
hackers from computer networks
using the telephone system
                    Practical Computing
```

prototype *noun* first working model of a device *or* program, which is then tested and adapted to improve it

prototyping *noun* making a prototype

provider *noun* **information provider** = company *or* user that provides an information source for use in a videotext system (such as the company providing weather information *or* stock exchange reports)

proxar *noun (film)* additional lens which is used in close-up shots to shorten the focal length

proxy server *noun* (i) computer connected to an intranet or Internet that stores copies of files and data held on slower servers and so allows users to access files and data quickly; (ii) a computer connected to a local area network and to the Internet that acts as a gateway, it retrieves web pages from remote Internet servers as required by a user but shields the user (for security) from direct access to the Internet

PrtSc = PRINT SCREEN *(on an IBM PC keyboard)* key that sends the contents of the current screen to the printer

pS = PICOSECOND

PSA *US* = PUBLIC SERVICE ANNOUNCEMENT advertisement for a public service *or* charity, which is shown on

TV, but for which the TV company is not paid

pseudo- *prefix* meaning similar to something, but not genuine

pseudo-code *noun* English sentence structures, used to describe program instructions which are translated at a later date into machine code

pseudo-digital *adjective* (modulated analog signals) produced by a modem and transmitted over telephone lines

pseudo-operation *noun* assembler command

pseudo-random *noun* generated sequence that appears random but is repeated over a long period; **pseudo-random number generator** = hardware *or* software that produces pseudo-random numbers

psophometer *noun* a meter which measures noise

PSS = PACKET SWITCHING SERVICE

PSTN = PUBLIC SWITCHED TELEPHONE NETWORK

PSU = POWER SUPPLY UNIT electrical circuit that provides certain direct current voltage and current levels from an alternating current source to other electrical circuits

COMMENT: a PSU will regulate, smooth and step down a higher voltage supply for use in small electronic equipment

PTR = PAPER TAPE READER

p-type semiconductor *noun* semiconductor material that has been doped with a chemical to provide extra holes (positive charge carriers), giving it an overall positive potential compared to intrinsic semiconductor

public *adjective* open to anyone to use; made for the use of everyone; **public address system (PA)** = microphone, amplifier and loudspeaker set up to allow one person to be heard by a group of people; **public data network** = data transmission service for the public; **public dial port** = port connecting a packet network to a public telephone system; **public domain (PD)** = documents *or* images *or* sound *or* text *or* program that has no copying fee or

publication *noun* **(a)** making something public; *the publication of the report on data protection; the publication date of the book is November 15th* **(b)** printed book *or* leaflet, etc. which is sold to the public *or* which is given away; *government publications can be bought at special shops; the company specializes in publications for the business reader*

publicity *noun* attracting the attention of the public to products *or* services by mentioning them in the media *or* by advertising them; **publicity bureau** = office which organizes publicity for companies; **publicity campaign** = period when planned publicity takes place; **publicity department** = department in a company which organizes the publicity for the company's products; **publicity matter** = leaflets *or* posters, etc., which publicize a product *or* service

publicize *verb* to attract people's attention to a product *or* service; *they are publicizing their low prices for computer stationery; the new PC has been publicized in the press*

publish *verb* **(a)** to design, edit and print a text (such as a book *or* newspaper *or* catalogue) and sell *or* give it to the public; *institute has published a list of sales figures for different home computers; the company specializes in publishing reference books* **(b)** to produce and sell software **(c)** to share a local resource with other users on a network (such as a file or folder)

publisher *noun* company which prints books *or* newspapers and sells *or* gives them to the public

publishing *noun* the business of printing books *or* newspapers and selling them *or* giving them to the public; **desktop publishing (DTP)** = design, layout and printing of documents using special software, a small computer and a printer; **electronic publishing** = (i) use of desktop publishing packages and laser printers to produce printed matter; (ii) using computers to write and display information (such as viewdata); **professional publishing** = publishing books on law, accountancy, and other professions

> desktop publishing or the ability to produce high-quality publications using a minicomputer, essentially boils down to combining words and images on pages
>
> *Byte*

pull-down *verb (film)* moving film frame to frame in a camera or projector by means of a claw

pull-down *or* **pull-up menu** *noun* set of options that are displayed below the relevant entry on a menu-bar; *the pull-down menu is viewed by clicking on the menu bar at the top of the screen*; *compare with* POP-UP MENU

pull up 1 *verb* to pull up a line = to connect *or* set a line to a voltage level; *pull up the input line to a logic one by connecting it to 5 volts* **2** *noun (film)* loop of film used to keep the film flowing steadily through the picture gate over the sound head

> the gated inputs lower the standby current and also eliminate the need for input pull-up or pull-down resistors
>
> *Electronics & Power*

pulse 1 *noun* short rush of electricity; short period of a voltage level; **pulse amplitude modulation (PAM)** = pulse modulation where the height of the pulse depends on the input signal; *(film)* **pulse and bar** = video test waveform; **pulse code modulation (PCM)** = pulse stream that carries data about a signal in binary form; **pulse cross** = device which permits the study of sync pulses on a television monitor; **pulse-dialling** = telephone dialling that

restrictions and can be used or copied by anyone; *compare with* SHAREWARE; **public key cipher system** = cipher that uses a public key to encrypt messages and a secret key to decrypt them (conventional cipher systems use one secret key to encrypt and decrypt messages); *see also* CIPHER, KEY; **public service announcement** = *see* PSA; **public switched telephone network (PSTN)** = national telephone system *or* country and world-wide exchanges, lines and telephone sets that are all interconnected and can be used by the public dials a telephone number by sending a series of pulses along the line; *pulse-dialling takes longer to dial than the newer tone-dialling system*; **pulse duration modulation (PDM)** = pulse modulation where the pulse width depends on the input signal; **pulse generator** = electronic test equipment used to produce different size pulses; **pulse modulation** = use of a series of short pulses which are modified by an input signal, to carry information; **pulse position modulation (PPM)** = pulse modulation where the time between pulses depends on the input signal; **pulse stream** = continuous series of similar pulses; **pulse width modulation (PWM)** = pulse modulation where the pulse width depends on the input signal **2** *verb* to apply a short-duration voltage level to a circuit; *we pulsed the input but it still would not work*

COMMENT: electric pulse can be used to transmit information, as the binary digits 0 and 1 correspond to 'no pulse' and 'pulse'

punch 1 *noun* **(a)** device for making holes in punched cards **(b)** mechanism which punches a cue mark in a film leader to show when printing or editorial synchronization should start **(c)** mechanism which eliminates the splicing noises in prints which are made from an optical sound negative **2** *verb* to make a hole; **punched card** = small piece of card which contains holes which represent various instructions *or* data; **punched card reader** = device that transforms data on a punched card to a form that can be recognized by a computer; **punched tag** = card attached to a product in a shop, with punched holes containing data about the product; **punched tape** = strip of paper tape that contains holes to represent data

punch-down block *noun* device used in a local area network to connect UTP cable

punctuation mark *noun* printing symbol, which cannot be spoken, but which helps to understand the text

COMMENT: the main punctuation marks are the question mark and exclamation mark; inverted commas (which show the type of text being written); the comma, full stop, colon and semicolon (which show how the words are broken up into sequences); the apostrophe (which shows that a letter or word is missing); the dash and hyphen and brackets (which separate or link words)

pup *noun (film)* tiny 500 watt spotlight

pure *adjective* clean *or* not mixed with other things; **pure code** = code that does not modify itself during execution; **pure semiconductor** = semiconductor material that has not had extra doping substances added; *see also* INTRINSIC; **pure tone** = single frequency containing no harmonics

purge *verb* to remove unnecessary *or* out of date data from a file or disk; *each month, I purge the disk of all the old email messages*

push *verb* to press something *or* to move something by pressing on it; **pushdown list** = temporary storage queue system where the last item added is at the top of the list; *see also* LIFO; **push instruction** = computer instruction that stores data on a LIFO list *or* stack; **push on** *or* **push off** = *see* CONCEAL, REVEAL; **push up list** = temporary storage queue system where the last item added is at the bottom of the list; *see also* FIFO

pushbutton 1 *noun* square shape displayed on a screen that will carry out a particular action if selected with a pointer or keyboard **2** *adjective* which works by pressing on a button; **pushbutton dialling** = using buttons rather than a dial on a telephone to dial a number; **pushbutton telephone** = telephone operated with buttons rather than a dial

COMMENT: a pushbutton is normally made up of two images: one displayed with shading to appear as if it is protruding from the screen and a second, displayed when the user selects the button, that is shaded differently to appear to sink into the screen

PWM = PULSE WIDTH MODULATION

Qq

Q Channel *noun (in a CD audio disc)* one of the eight information channels that holds data identifying the track and the absolute playing time; *see also* SQL

QAM = QUADRATURE AMPLITUDE MODULATION

QBE = QUERY BY EXAMPLE simple language used to retrieve information from a database management system by, normally, entering a query with known values, which is then matched with the database and used to retrieve the correct data; *in most QBE databases, the query form looks like the record format in the database - retrieving data is as easy as filling in a form*

QL = QUERY LANGUAGE

qty = QUANTITY

quad *noun* **(a)** sheet of paper four times as large as a basic sheet **(b)** meaning four times; **quadbit** = four bits that are used by modems to increase transmission rates when using QAM; **quad density** = four bits of data stored in the usual place of one; **em quad** = space printed that is equal in size to an em; **en quad** = space that is half the width of an em quad space

quad *or* **quadruplex** *noun* a four unit video tape recorder which produces video information in continuous almost vertical stripes

quadding *noun* insertion of spaces into text to fill out a line

> in this case, interfacing is done by a single quad-wide adapter
>
> *Minicomputer News*

quadlite *noun (film)* a lighting unit that contains four 500 watt floodlights

quadr- *prefix* meaning four

quadraphony *noun (film)* a four-channel system of sound

quadrature amplitude modulation (QAM) *noun* data encoding method used by high-speed modems (transmitting at rates above 2,400bps); QAM combines amplitude modulation and phase modulation to increase the data transmission rate

quadrature encoding *noun* system used to determine the direction in which a mouse is being moved; in a mechanical mouse, two sensors send signals that describe its horizontal and vertical movements - these signals are transmitted using quadrature encoding

quadrophonic *adjective* (audio music system) using four speakers

quadruplex *noun* four signals combined into a single one

quadruplicate *noun* in quadruplicate = with the original and three copies; *the statements are printed in quadruplicate* (NOTE: no plural)

quad-speed drive *noun* CD-ROM drive that spins the disc at four times the speed of a single-speed drive, providing higher data throughput of 600Kbps and shorter seek times

quality *noun* **(a)** what something is like *or* how good or bad something is; *there is a market for good quality secondhand computers*; high quality *or* top quality = very best quality; *the store specializes in high quality imported items* **(b)** quality control = checking that the quality of a product is good; quality controller = person who checks the quality of a product (NOTE: no plural)

> the computer operates at 120cps in draft quality mode

```
and    30cps    in    near
letter-quality mode
```
Minicomputer News

Quantel hardware graphics company that developed Paintbox and Harry production graphics systems

quantifiable *adjective* which can be quantified; *the effect of the change in the pricing structure is not quantifiable*

quantifier *noun* sign *or* symbol which indicates the quantity *or* range of a predicate

quantify *verb to quantify the effect of something* = to show the effect of something in figures; *it is impossible to quantify the effect of the new computer system on our production*

quantity *noun* **(a)** amount *or* number of items; *a small quantity of illegal copies of the book have been imported; he bought a large quantity of spare parts* **(b)** large amount; *the company offers a discount for quantity purchase*; **quantity discount** = discount given to a customer who buys large quantities of goods

quantization *noun* conversion of an analog signal to a numerical representation; **quantization error** = error in converting an analog signal into a numerical form due to limited accuracy *or* rapidly changing signal; *see also* A/D

quantize *verb* **(a)** to convert an analog signal into a numerical representation **(b)** to process a MIDI file and align all the notes to a regular beat, so removing any timing errors; *an analog to digital converter quantizes the input signal*; **quantizing noise** = noise on a signal due to inaccuracies in the quantizing process

quantizer *noun* device used to convert an analog input signal to a numerical form that can be processed by a computer

quantum *noun* smallest unit of energy of an electromagnetic radiation at a certain frequency

quarter-inch tape *noun (film)* standard diameter of magnetic tape which is used in tape cartridges and reel-to-reel recorders

quartile *noun* one of three figures below which 25%, 50% *or* 75% of a total falls

quarto *noun* paper size, made when a sheet is folded twice to make eight pages

quartz iodine lamp *noun* a tungsten-halogen lamp which holds iodine gas to lengthen the life of the filament and to help maintain its colour temperature

quartz lamp *noun* any lighting unit which uses tungsten-halogen lamps

quasi- *prefix* almost *or* which seems like; *a quasi-official body*

quaternary *adjective* referring to four bits *or* levels *or* objects

query 1 *noun* question; *the salesman had to answer a mass of queries from the public*; **query by example (QBE)** = simple language used to retrieve information from a database management system by, normally, entering a query with known values, which is then matched with the database and used to retrieve the correct data; **query language (QL)** = language in a database management system, that allows a database to be searched and queried easily; **query message** = message sent to an object to find out the value of one of the object's properties, such as its name, active state or position; **query processing** = processing of queries, either by extracting information from a database *or* by translating query commands from a query language; **query window** = (i) window that appears when an error has occurred, asking the user what action he would like to take; (ii) window that is displayed with fields a user can fill in to search a database **2** *verb* to ask a question about something *or* to suggest that something may be wrong; *he queried the last statement; you must query the conversion costs*

```
The Query By Example features
now found on some database
packages,    Foxpro    in
particular,  are easy to use
and very powerful
```
Computing

question 1 *noun* **(a)** words which need an answer; *the managing director refused to answer questions about faulty keyboards; the market research team prepared a series of questions to test the public's reactions to colour and price* **(b)** problem; *he raised the question of moving to less expensive offices; the main question is that of cost; the board discussed the question of launching a new business computer* **2** *verb* **(a)** to ask questions; *the police questioned* *the accounts staff for four hours; she questioned the chairman on the company's sales in the Far East* **(b)** to query *or* to suggest that something may be wrong; *we all question how accurate the computer printout is*

question mark *noun* the character (?) which is often used as a wildcard to indicate that any single character in the position will produce a match; *to find all the letters, use the command DIR LETTER?.DOC which will list LETTER1.DOC, LETTER2.DOC and LETTER3.DOC*; *see also* ASTERISK

questionnaire *noun* printed list of questions, especially used in market research; *to send out a questionnaire to test the opinions of users of the system; to answer or to fill in a questionnaire about holidays abroad*

queue 1 *noun* **(a)** line of people waiting one behind the other; *to form a queue or to join a queue; queues formed at the doors of the bank when the news spread about its possible collapse* **(b)** list of data *or* tasks that are waiting to be processed; series of documents (such as orders, application forms) which are dealt with in order; **file queue** = number of files temporarily stored in order before being processed; *output devices such as laser proofers and typesetters are connected on-line with automatic file queue*; **his order went to the end of the queue** = his order was dealt with last; **job queue** = number of tasks arranged in order waiting to be processed in a batch system; **queue management** *or* **queue manager** = software which orders tasks to be processed; *this is a new software spooler with a built-in queue management* **2** *verb* **(a)** to form a line one after the other for something; *when food was scarce, people had to queue for bread; we queued for hours to get tickets* **(b)** to add more data *or* tasks to the end of a queue; **queueing time** = amount of time messages have to wait before they can be processed *or* transmitted; **queued access method** = programming method which minimises input/output delays by ensuring that data transferred between software and an I/O device is synchronised with the I/O device

> It had two weeks of parallel running, which threw out some problems
>
> *Computing*

quick *adjective* fast *or* not taking any time; *the company made a quick recovery; he is looking for a quick return on his investment; we are hoping for a quick sale*; *(film)* **quick cuts** = fast cutting from one shot to the next without the use of dissolves

QuickDraw *(in an Apple Macintosh)* graphics routines built into the Macintosh's operating system that control displayed text and images

quickly *adverb* without taking much time; *the sale of the company went through quickly; the accountant quickly looked through the pile of invoices*

quicksort *noun* very rapid file sorting and ordering method

QuickTime *(in an Apple Macintosh)* graphics routines built into the Macintosh's operating system that allow windows, boxes and graphic objects (including animation and video files) to be displayed

> COMMENT: a QuickTime file can contain 32 tracks of audio, video, or MIDI data. QuickTime is also available as an add-on driver for Microsoft Windows PC environments; normally plays video at 15 frames per second

quiet *adjective* not making any noise; *laser printers are much quieter than dot-matrix*

quit *verb* **(a)** to leave a system *or* a program; *do not forget to save your text before you quit the system* **(b)** to resign *or* to leave (a job); *he quit after an argument with the managing director; several of the managers are quitting to set up their own company* (NOTE: **quitting - quit**)

quonking *noun (film)* undesired sounds which are picked up by a microphone

quotation marks *noun* inverted commas *or* signs printed at the beginning and end of text to show that it has been quoted from another source

quotation *noun* part of a text borrowed from another text

quote 1 *verb* **(a)** to repeat words used by someone else; to repeat a reference number; *he quoted figures from the newspaper report; in reply please quote this number;*

when making a complaint please quote the batch number printed on the computer case; he replied, quoting the number of the account **(b)** to estimate *or* to say what costs may be; *to quote a price for supplying stationery; their prices are always quoted in dollars; he quoted me a price of $1,026; can you quote for supplying 20,000 envelopes?* **2** *noun* **double quotes** = double inverted commas; *the name of the company should be put in double quotes*; **single quotes** = single inverted commas; **quotes** = quotation marks *or* inverted commas

quoting feature of many electronic mail applications that allows you to reply to a message and include the text of the original message; to distinguish the original text, each line normally starts with a '' symbol

QWERTY *noun* **QWERTY keyboard** = English language keyboard for a typewriter *or* computer, where the top line of letters are Q-W-E-R-T-Y; *the computer has a normal QWERTY keyboard*; *see also* AZERTY KEYBOARD

```
the keyboard does not have a
QWERTY layout but is easy to
use
```
Micro Decision

Rr

R & D = RESEARCH AND DEVELOPMENT **R & D department** = department in a company that investigates new products, discoveries and techniques

R/W cycle = READ/WRITE CYCLE sequence of events used to retrieve *or* store data

R/W head = READ/WRITE HEAD electromagnetic device that allows data to be read from *or* written to a storage medium

R/W *short for* read/write

race *verb* error condition in a digital circuit, in which the state *or* output of the circuit is very dependent on the exact timing between the input signals

rack *noun* **(a)** frame to hold items for display; *a display rack; a rack for holding mag tapes* **(b)** metal supporting frame for electronic circuit boards and peripheral devices such as disk drives; **rack mounted** = system consisting of removable circuit boards in a supporting frame

racking *see* FRAMING

rackover *verb* to move a camera's viewfinder in to line with its objective lens system

radar *noun* method of finding the position of objects such as aircraft, by transmitting radio waves which are reflected back if they hit an object and are displayed on a screen

radial transfer *noun* data transfer between two peripherals *or* programs that are on different layers of a structured system (such as an ISO/OSI system)

radiant *adjective* which radiates; **radiant energy** = amount of energy radiated by an aerial

radiate *verb* **(a)** to go out in all directions from a central point **(b)** to send out rays **(c)** to convert electrical signals into travelling electromagnetic waves; **radiating element**

= single basic unit of an antenna that radiates signals

radiation *noun* **(a)** sending out of waves of energy from certain substances **(b)** conversion of electrical signals in an antenna into travelling electromagnetic waves

radiator *noun* single basic unit of an antenna *or* any device that radiates signals

radio *noun* medium used for the transmission of speech, sound and data over long distances by radio frequency electromagnetic waves

radio button *noun* *(in a GUI)* circle displayed beside an option that, when selected, has a dark centre; radio buttons are a method of selecting one of a number of options; *see also* BUTTON, PUSHBUTTON

radio communications *noun* transmission and reception of sound and data by radio waves

radio frequency (RF) *noun* electromagnetic spectrum that lies between the frequency range 10KHz and 3000GHz; **radio frequency (RF)** = range of electromagnetic waves used for radiocommunications; *the radio frequency range extends from a few hertz to hundreds of gigahertz*; **radio microphone** = audio microphone with a small radio transmitter attached allowing the transmission of sound signals without wires; **radio pager** *or* **radio paging device** = small pocket receiver that responds to a certain unique transmitted code to alert the user; *you could contact your salesman if he had a radio pager*; **radio paging** = calling someone by transmitting a code to their radio pager; **radio phone** *or* **radio telephone** = mobile two-way radio communications system that can access the public telephone network; **radio receiver** = device that can receive signals broadcast on one radio frequency and convert them into their original audio form; **radio spectrum** = range of radio frequencies; **radio telegraphy** = telegraph codes transmitted via radio; **radio transmission of data** = sending data by radio; **radio waves** = electromagnetic radiation waves

radix *noun* the value of the base of the number system being used; *the hexadecimal number has a radix of 16*; **radix point** = dot which indicates the division between a whole unit and its fractional parts

ragged *adjective* not straight *or* with an uneven edge; **ragged left** = printed text with a flush right-hand margin and uneven left-hand margin; **ragged right** = printed text with a flush left-hand margin and uneven right- hand margin; **ragged text** = unjustified text *or* text with a ragged right margin

RAID = REDUNDANT ARRAY of INEXPENSIVE DISKS fast, fault-tolerant disk drive system that uses multiple drives which would, typically, each store one byte of a word of data, so allowing the data to be saved faster; one drive in the array also stores a check byte for error detection

```
A Japanese investor group led
by     system    distributor
Technography has pumped $4.2
million (£2.8 million) into US
disk   manufacturer   Storage
Computer  to  help  with  the
development  costs  of  RAID 7
hard disk technology
                     Computing
```

rails *plural noun (film)* transportable, light tracks laid on the ground on which a moveable camera support or dolly can be mounted

RAM = RANDOM ACCESS MEMORY memory that allows access to any location in any order, usually in the form of ICs; *compare with* SEQUENTIAL; **dynamic RAM** = most common RAM ICs, which use capacitative charge to retain data but which must be refreshed (read from and rewritten to) every few thousandths of a second; **RAM cache** = section of high-speed RAM that is used to buffer data transfers between the (faster) processor and a (slower) disk

drive; **RAM card** = expansion card which contains RAM chips; it is plugged into a computer *or* device to increase the main memory capacity; **RAM cartridge** = plug-in device that contains RAM chips and increases a computer *or* device's memory; *you can increase the printer's memory by plugging in another RAM cartridge*; **RAM chip** = chip which stores information, allowing random access; **RAM disk** = section of RAM that is made to look like and behave as a high-speed disk drive; **RAM refresh** = signals used to update the contents of dynamic RAM chips every few thousandths of a second, involving reading and rewriting the contents; **RAM resident program** *or* **TSR** = program that loads itself into main memory and carries out a function when activated; *when you hit Ctrl-F5, you will activate the RAM resident program and it will display your day's diary;* **static RAM** = RAM ICs that do not have to be refreshed but cannot store as much data per chip as dynamic RAM; *compare with* CHIP; ROM (NOTE: there is no plural for RAM, and it often has no article: **512K of RAM; the file is stored in RAM**)

COMMENT: dynamic RAM needs to have each location refreshed from time to time to retain the data, but is very fast and can contain more data per unit area than static RAM which has the advantage of not requiring to be refreshed to retain its data, and will keep data for as long as power is supplied

```
in addition the board features
512K of video RAM, expandable
up to a massive 1MB
                 PC Business World
```

```
fast memory is RAM that does
not  have  to  share  bus  access
with the chip that manages the
video display
                            Byte
```

```
The   HP   Enterprise   Desktops
have  hard-disk  capacities  of
between  20Gb  and  80Gb,  with
RAM  ranging  from  128Mb  up  to
256Mb
                     Computing
```

ramcorder *noun* digital video recorder which stores images as digital data in RAM rather than on film

random *adjective* (event) that cannot be anticipated; **random number** = number that cannot be predicted; **random number generator** = program which generates random numbers (used in lotteries, games, etc); **random process** *or* **direct access** = system whose output cannot be related to its input *or* internal structure; *see also* PSEUDO-RANDOM

random access *noun* ability to access immediately memory locations in any order; *disk drives are random access; magnetic tape is not, it is sequential access memory*; **random access memory (RAM)** = memory that allows access to any location in any order, usually in the form of ICs; **random access storage** = memory that allows access to any location in any order

range 1 *noun* **(a)** series of items from which the customer can choose; *a wide range of products; the catalogue lists a wide range of computer stationery* **(b)** set of allowed values between a maximum and minimum; *the telephone channel can accept signals in the frequency range 300 - 3400Hz; magnetic tape is stable within a temperature range of 0° to 40°C*; **frequency range** = range of allowable frequencies, between two limits; **number range** = set of allowable values **2** *verb* **(a)** to vary *or* to be different; *the company's products range from a cheap lapheld micro to a multistation mainframe* **(b)** to put text in order to one side; **range left** = move text to align it on the left margin

rank *verb* to sort data into an order usually according to size *or* importance

raster *noun* system of scanning the whole of a TV screen with a picture beam by sweeping across it horizontally, moving down one pixel *or* line at a time; **raster graphics** = graphics where the picture is built up in lines across the screen *or* page; **raster image processor** = raster which translates software instructions into an image *or* complete page which is then printed by a printer *or* typesetter; *an electronic page can be converted to a printer-readable video image by an on-board raster image processor*; **raster scan** = one sweep of the picture beam horizontally across the front of a television screen

rate 1 *noun* **(a)** quantity of data *or* tasks that can be processed in a set time; *the processor's instruction execution rate is better than the older version*; *(film)* **rate of development** = speed at which an image appears when photographic film is being developed **(b)** price charged per unit of time; *the engineer's rate is twenty pounds per hour* **2** *verb* to evaluate how good something is *or* how large something is

ratings *noun* calculation of how many people are watching a TV programme; **ratings battle** *or* **war** = fight between two TV companies to increase their share of the market

ratio *noun* proportion of one number to another; *the ratio of 10 to 5 is 2:1; the ratio of corrupt bits per transmitted message is falling with new technology*

rational number *noun* number that can be written as the ratio of two whole numbers; *24 over 7 is a rational number; 0.333 can be written as the rational number 1/3*

raw *adjective* in the original state *or* not processed; **raw data** = (i) pieces of information that have not yet been input into a computer system; (ii) data in a database which has to be processed to provide information to the user; *this small computer collects raw data from the sensors, converts it and transmits it to the mainframe*; *(in DOS and UNIX operating systems)* **raw mode** = method of accessing a file which, when data is read from the file, does not carry out any data translation or filtering; **raw stock** = undeveloped and unexposed photographic film

ray *noun* one line of light *or* radiation in a beam *or* from a source; *the rays of light pass down the optical fibre*

ray tracing *noun (in graphics)* method of creating life-like computer-generated graphics which correctly show shadows and highlights on an object as if coming from a light source; *to generate this picture with ray tracing will take several hours on this powerful PC*

COMMENT: ray tracing software calculates the direction of each ray of light, its reflection and how it looks on an object

RCA connector   *see*   PHONO CONNECTOR

RD *or* **RMDIR**   =   REMOVE DIRECTORY *(in DOS)* command to remove an empty subdirectory

RDBMS = RELATIONAL DATABASE MANAGEMENT SYSTEM

react *verb* **to react to something** = to act in response to something; **to react with something** = to change because a substance is present

reactance *noun* impedance associated with a component (capacitor *or* inductor)

reaction *noun* action which takes place because of something which has happened earlier

read *verb* **(a)** to look at printed words and understand them; *conditions of sale are printed in such small characters that they are difficult to read; can the OCR read typeset characters?* **(b)** to retrieve data from a storage medium; *we read in the data; this instruction reads the first record of a file; access time can be the time taken to read from a record*; **read error** = error that occurs during a read operation, often because the stored data has been corrupted; **read head** = transducer that reads signals stored on a (magnetic) medium and converts them back to their original (electrical) form; **read only** = device *or* circuit whose stored data cannot be changed; **read only attribute** = attribute bit of a file that, if set, prevents new data being written to the file or its contents edited; **read only memory (ROM)** = memory device that has had data written into it at the time of manufacture, and now its contents can only be read; *the manufacturer provided the monitor program in two ROM chips*; *(film)* **read-out lines** = lines on light meters and lenses which go from one scale to another; **read/write cycle** = sequence of events used to retrieve and store data; **read/write head** = transducer that can read *or* write data from the surface of a magnetic storage medium, such as a floppy disk

readable *adjective* that can be read *or* understood by someone *or* an electronic device; *the electronic page is converted to a printer-readable video image*

reader *noun* device that reads data stored on one medium and converts it into another form; **card reader** = device that transforms data on a punched card to a form that can be recognized by the computer; **reader level** = one of two modes in authoring software that allows a user to run and interact with a multimedia application, but not modify it in any way; the second mode is author level that is used by the developer to design the application; **tape reader** = machine that reads punched holes in paper tape *or* signals on magnetic tape; *see also* OPTICAL

reading *noun* note taken of figures *or* degrees, especially of degrees on a scale; = **readme file** = file that contains last-minute information about an application; the file is normally stored on the disk or CD-ROM together with the application files

readout *noun* display of data; *the readout displayed the time; the clock had a digital readout*

```
some  OCR  programs  can  be
taught  to  read  typefaces  that
are  not  in  their  library
                        Publish
```

```
the  machine  easily  reads  in
text  from  typewriters  and
daisy-wheel  printers
                PC Business World
```

ready *adjective* fit to be used *or* sold; (equipment) that is waiting and able to be used; *the green light indicates the system is ready for another program; the programming will not be ready until next week; the maintenance people hope that the system will be ready for use in 24 hours*; **ready state** = communications line *or* device that is waiting to accept data

Real proprietary system used to transmit sound and video over the Internet, normally used to transmit live sound, for example from a radio station; *to use Real Audio, your web browser needs a special plug-in that can be downloaded from www.real.com; see* PLUG-IN, STREAMING DATA

real address *noun* absolute address that directly accesses a memory location; *compare with* PAGED ADDRESS

real memory *noun* actual physical memory that can be addressed by a CPU; *compare with* VIRTUAL MEMORY

real mode *noun (in an IBM PC)* the default operating mode for an IBM PC and the only mode in which DOS operates; *compare with* PROTECTED MODE

COMMENT: real mode normally means a single-tasking operating system in which software can use any available memory *or* I/O device

real number *noun* *(in computing)* number that is represented with a fractional part (sometimes refers to numbers represented in a floating-point form)

real time *noun* actions *or* processing time that is of the same order of magnitude as the problem to be solved; *a navigation system needs to be able to process the position of a ship in real time and take suitable action before it hits a rock; US* **program shown in real time** = TV program which is broadcast live; **real-time animation** = animation in which objects appear to move at the same speed as they would in real life; *real-time animation requires display hardware capable of displaying a sequence with tens of different images every second*; **real-time authorization** *or* **authentication** = online system that can check the authenticity and validity of a customer's credit card within a few seconds, allowing an Internet shop to deliver goods or confirm an order immediately; *see also* E-WALLET, SHOPPING CART, SSL; **real-time clock** = clock in a computer that provides the correct time of day; *compare with* RELATIVE-TIME CLOCK; **real-time input** = data input to a system as it happens *or* is required; **real-time multi-tasking** = executing several tasks simultaneously; **real-time operating system** = operating system designed to control a real-time system *or* process-control system; **real-time processing** = processing operations that takes a time of the same order of magnitude as the problem to be solved; **real-time simulation** = computer model of a process where each process is executed in a similar time to the real process; **real-time system** = system whose processing time is within that of the problem, so that it can influence the source of the data; *in a real-time system, as you move the joystick left, the image on the screen moves left; if there is a pause for processing it is not a true real-time system;* **real-time video** = *see* RTV

define a real-time system as any system which is expected

to interact with its environment within certain timing constraints

Quotron provides real-time quotes, news and analysis on equity securities through a network of 40,000 terminals to US brokers and investors

realize *or* **realizing the palette** *verb* to select a particular set of colours for a 256-colour palette and use this palette when displaying an image, normally by mapping the colours in a logical palette into the system palette; (in Windows) an application asks Windows to carry out the mapping; *see also* LOGICAL PALETTE

RealNames system of assigning a trade name or descriptive name to a website address; for example, if you want to find the web page that covers Panasonic DVD players, you could type in 'Panasonic DVD' and RealNames will translate this to the correct website address; the service is supported by many of the major search engines, portals and web browser software programs; for more information, visit www.realnames.com.

rear projection *see* BACK PROJECTION

reboot *verb* to reload an operating system during a computing session; *we rebooted and the files reappeared*; *see also* BOOT

recall 1 *noun* bringing back text *or* files from store **2** *verb* to bring back text *or* files from store for editing

automatic recall provides the facility to recall the last twenty commands and to edit and re-use them

receive *verb* to accept data from a communications link; *the computer received data via the telephone line*; **receive only** = computer terminal that can only accept and display data (but not transmit)

receiver *noun* electronic device that can detect transmitted signals and present them in a suitable form; **radio receiver** = device that detects signals broadcast on one radio frequency and converts them into their original audio form; *the radio receiver picked up your signal very strongly*

reception *noun* quality of a radio *or* TV signal received; *signal reception is bad with that aerial*

re-chargeable *adjective* (battery) which can be charged again with electricity when it is flat

recode *verb* to code a program which has been coded for one system, so that it will work on another

recognition *noun* (a) being able to recognize something (b) process that allows something to be recognized, such as letters on a printed text *or* bars on bar codes, etc; **recognition logic** = logical software used in OCR, AI etc; **optical character recognition** = process that allows printed *or* written characters to be recognized optically (using an optical character reader), and converted into a form that can be input into a computer; **optical mark recognition** = process that allows certain marks *or* lines *or* patterns to be recognized optically (using an optical character reader), and converted into a form that can be input into a computer

recognizable *adjective* which can be recognized

recognize *verb* to see something and remember that it has been seen before; *the scanner will recognize most character fonts*

recompile *verb* to compile a source program again, usually after changes or debugging

reconfiguration *noun* altering the structure of data in a system; *I reconfigured the field structure in the file; this program allows us to reconfigure the system as we require; see also* CONFIGURE, SET UP

reconfigure *verb* to alter the structure of data in a system

reconnect *verb* to connect again; *the telephone engineers are trying to reconnect the telephone*

record 1 *noun* (a) set of items of related data; *your record contains several fields that have been grouped together under the one heading; this record contains all their personal details*; **logical record** = number of items of related data that are held in temporary memory ready to be processed; **physical record** = record and control data

combination stored on a backing device; **record format** *or* **layout** = organization and length of separate fields in a record; **record length** = quantity of data in a record; **record locking** = in a multiuser system, software method of preventing more than one user writing data to a record at the same time; **record structure** = list of the fields which make up a record, together with their length and data type; **records management** = program which maintains records and can access and process them to provide information (b) plastic disk on the surface of which music *or* other sounds are recorded **2** *verb* to store data *or* signals on tape *or* on disk *or* in a computer; *record the results in this column; this device records signals onto magnetic tape; digitally recorded data are used to generate images*; **recordable CD** = *see* CD-R; **record button** = key pressed on a recorder when ready to record signals onto a medium; **record head** *or* **write head** = transducer that converts an electrical signal into a magnetic field to write the data onto a magnetic medium

```
Micro Focus provides Fileshare
2,    which    it    claims
substantially reduces network
traffic, and provides features
such as full record locking,
update    logging    and
roll-forward recovery
```
Computing

recorder *noun* equipment able to transfer input signals onto a storage medium; **magnetic tape recorder** = device with a magnetic motor and circuitry to allow electrical signals to be recorded onto *or* played back from magnetic tape

COMMENT: the signal recorded is not always in the same form as the input signal since many recorders record a modulated carrier signal for better quality. A recorder is usually combined with a suitable playback circuit since the read/write head is often the same physical device

recording *noun* (a) action of storing signals *or* data on tape *or* in a computer; **recording density** = number of bits of data that can be stored in a unit area on a magnetic disk *or* tape; **recording indicator** = light or symbol that shows when a device is recording; **recording level** =

amplification of an input signal before it is recorded; *if a voice is very quiet, you can increase the recording level to ensure that it is not degraded by noise*; **recording trunk** = telephone line between a local and long distance exchange for operator use **(b)** signal (especially music) which has been recorded on tape *or* disk; *a new recording of Beethoven's quartets*

```
file and record-locking
procedures have to be
implemented to make sure that
files cannot be corrupted when
two users try to read or write
to the same record
simultaneously
```
Micro Decision

recordset *noun* group of records selected from a main database by a filter, search or query

recover *verb* to get back something which has been lost; *it is possible to recover the data but it can take a long time*

recoverable error *noun* error type that allows program execution to be continued after it has occurred

recovery *noun* **(a)** returning to normal operating after a fault; **recovery procedure** = processes required to return a system to normal operation after an error **(b)** getting back something which has been lost; *the recovery of lost files can be carried out using the recovery procedure*

rectangular waveguide *noun* microwave channel that is rectangular in cross section

rectifier *noun* electronic circuit that converts an alternating current supply into a direct current supply

rectify *verb* **(a)** to correct something *or* to make something right; *they had to rectify the error at the printout stage* **(b)** to remove the positive *or* negative sections of a signal so that it is unipolar

recto *noun* right hand page of a book (usually given an odd number)

recursion *or* **recursive routine** *noun* subroutine in a program that calls itself during execution

recursive filtering *noun* *(film)* technique which reduces video noise and defects

red book audio *see* CD-DA

red, green, blue (RGB) *noun* **(a)** high definition monitor system that uses three separate input signals controlling red, green and blue colour picture beams **(b)** three colour picture beams used in a colour TV **(c)** method of defining the colours in a colour image in which the colour of each pixel in the image is described by three bytes (24bits), one for red, green and blue; *compare with* CMYK

> COMMENT: in a colour TV there are three colour guns producing red, green and blue beams acting on groups of three phosphor dots at each pixel location

redefinable *adjective* which can be redefined

```
the idea of the packages is
that they enable you to
redefine the keyboard
```
Practical Computing

```
one especially useful command
lets you redefine the
printer's character-
translation table
```
Byte

redefine *verb* to change the function *or* value assigned to a variable *or* object; *we redefined the initial parameters*; **to redefine a key** = to change the function of a programmable key; *I have redefined this key to display the five when pressed*

redirect *verb* **(a)** to send a message to its destination by another route **(b)** *(in DOS and UNIX operating systems)* process of treating the output of one program as input for another program; *you can sort the results from a DIR command by redirecting to the SORT command*; **redirect** *or* **redirection operator** = character used by an operating system to indicate that the output of one program is to be sent as input to another

redirection *noun* sending a message to its destination by another route; *call forwarding is automatic redirection of calls*

redliner *noun* feature of workgroup *or* word-processor software that allows a user to highlight text in a different colour

redo *verb* to do something again; **redo from start** = start again from the beginning

redraw *verb* to draw again; *the artwork will have to be redrawn; can the computer redraw the graphics showing the product from the top view*

reduce *verb* to make (a photograph *or* a typesize) smaller

reduced instruction set
computer (RISC) *noun* CPU design whose instruction set contains a small number of simple fast-executing instructions, that can make program writing more complex, but increases speed of execution of each instruction

reduction *noun* **(a)** act of reducing; proportion by which something is made smaller; *we need a 25% reduction to fit the halftone in the space*; *(film)* **reduction print** = a positive 16mm print which is produced from a 35mm original positive print and generally results in a reduction of quality **(b)** method of combining signals from multitrack master tapes in order to create a master tape ready for production

redundancy *noun* providing extra components in a system in case there is a breakdown; **redundancy checking** = checking of received data for correct redundant codes to detect any errors

redundant *adjective* **(a)** (data) that can be removed without losing any information; *the parity bits on the received data are redundant and can be removed*; **redundant array of inexpensive disks (RAID)** = fast, fault-tolerant disk drive system that uses multiple drives which, typically, each store one byte of a word of data, so allowing the data to be saved faster; one drive in the array also stores a check byte for error detection; **redundant code** = data added for error detection purposes that carries no information **(b)** extra piece of equipment for a task in case of faults

reel *noun* circular holder around which a tape *or* film is rolled; *he dropped the reel on the floor and the tape unwound itself*; **pick-up reel** = empty reel used to store tape as it is played from a full reel

reel to reel *noun* copying one tape of data onto another magnetic tape; **reel to reel recorder** = magnetic tape recording machine that uses tape held on one reel and feeds to a pick-up reel

re-entrant program *or* **code** *or* **routine** *noun* one program *or* code shared by many users in a multi-user system and called again before it has finished its previous run

refer *verb* to mention *or* to deal with *or* to write about something; *the manual refers to the serial port, but I cannot find it*

reference 1 *noun* **(a)** value used as a starting point for other values, often zero; **reference level** = signal level to which all others are calibrated **(b)** mentioning *or* dealing with something; **reference file** = file of data which is kept so that it can be referred to; **reference mark** = printed symbol to indicate the presence of a note *or* reference not in the text; **reference retrieval system** = index which provides a reference to a document **2** *verb* to access a location in memory; *time taken to reference an item in memory is 'access time'*

reflect *verb* to send back (light *or* image) from a surface; *in a reflex camera, the image is reflected by an inbuilt mirror*

reflectance *noun* difference between the amount of light *or* signal incident and the amount that is reflected back from a surface (NOTE: the opposite is **absorptance**)

reflection *noun* light *or* image which is reflected; **signal reflection** = amount of transmitted signal that is reflected at the receiver due to an impedance mismatch *or* fault

reflective disk *noun* videodisc that uses a reflected laser beam to read the data etched into the surface

reflex (camera) *noun* camera with an optical mirror that allows a scene to be viewed through the camera lens so that the user sees exactly what will be photographed

reflex projection *(film)* *see* FRONT AXIAL PROJECTION

reflex shutter *noun* *(film)* shutter which is positioned at a 45 degree angle to the axis of the lens and reflects light into the viewfinder as it goes through the lens; the shutter moves up and out of the way when the exposure is made

reformat *verb* to format a disk that already contains data, and erasing the data by doing so; *do not reformat your hard disk unless you can't do anything else*

reformatting *noun* act of formatting a disk which already contains data; *reformatting destroys all the data on a disk*; *see also* FORMAT

refract *verb* to change the direction of light as it passes through a material (such as water *or* glass)

refraction *noun* change in direction of light rays as they pass through a material

refractive index *noun* measure of the angle that light is refracted by, as it passes through a material

refresh *verb* **(a)** to update regularly the contents of dynamic RAM by reading and rewriting stored data to ensure data is retained; *memory refresh signal* **(b)** **refresh cycle** = period of time during which a controller updates the contents of dynamic RAM chips; **refresh rate** = number of times every second that the image on a CRT is redrawn; **screen refresh** = to update regularly the images on a CRT screen by scanning each pixel with a picture beam to make sure the image is still visible

Philips autoscan colour monitor, the 4CM6099, has SVGA refresh rates of 72Hz (800 x 600) and 70Hz (1,024 x 768)

Computing

regenerate *verb* **(a)** to redraw an image on a screen many times a second so that it remains visible **(b)** to receive distorted signals, process and error check them, then retransmit the same codes; *the signals are regenerated every ten kilometres to provide clean signals at the receiver*

regeneration *noun* process of regenerating a signal

regenerator *noun* device used in communications that amplifies or regenerates a received signal and transmits it on; regenerators are often used to extend the range of a network

region *noun* a defined area (of an image or territory); **region fill** = to fill an area of a the screen or a graphics shape with a particular colour

register 1 *noun* **(a)** reserved memory location used for special storage purposes; **accumulator register** = most important internal storage register in a CPU, containing the data to be processed; **address register** = register in a computer that is able to store all the bits of an address which can then be processed as a single unit; **control register** = storage location used for control data; **index register** = computer address register that is added to a reference address to provide the location to be accessed; **instruction address register (IAR)** = register in a CPU that stores the location where instructions are found; **register file** = number of registers used for temporary storage; **register map** = display of the contents of all the registers; **sequence control register (SCR)** = CPU register that contains the address of the next instruction to be processed; *see also* INSTRUCTION ADDRESS REGISTER, NEXT INSTRUCTION REGISTER **(b)** superimposing two images correctly; **the two colours are out of register** = the colours are not correctly printed one on top of the other **2** *verb* **(a)** to react to a stimulus; *light-sensitive films register light intensity* **(b)** to correctly superimpose two images; **register marks** = marks at the corners of a film used to help in lining up two images; *(film)* **register pins** = small prongs which are shaped to fit into a film's perforation holes and provide the possibility of locating an exact part of a film by means of its perforations

regulate *verb* to control a process (usually using sensors and a feedback mechanism); **regulated power supply** = constant, controlled voltage *or* current source whose output will not vary with input supply variation

COMMENT: a regulated power supply is required for all computers where components cannot withstand voltage variations

regulation *noun* law *or* rule, which most people have to obey; *government regulations on the export of computer equipment*; **regulation line** = ability of a power supply to prevent input line changes affecting output supplies; **regulation load** = ability of a power supply to prevent output load changes affecting output supplies

rehyphenation *noun* changing the hyphenation of words in a text after it has been put into a new page format *or* line width

reject *verb* to refuse to accept something; *the computer rejects all incoming data from incompatible sources*

rejection *noun* refusing to accept something; **rejection error** = error by a scanner which cannot read a character and so leaves a blank

relational database *or* **relational database management system (RDBMS)** *noun* set of data where all the items are related; *if you search the relational database for the surname, you can pull out his salary from the related accounts database*; **relational operator** *or* **logical operator** symbol that compares two items

relationship *noun* way in which two similar things are connected

```
Data replication is the
process of duplicating data
on, or distributing it
between, databases, usually on
different servers. It is not
new, having been around for
many years: nor is it confined
to relational databases
                      Computing
```

relative *adjective* which is compared to something; **relative address** = location specified in relation to a reference *or* base address; **relative coordinates** = positional information given in relation to a reference point; **relative data** = data that gives new coordinate information relative to previous coordinates; **relative error** = difference between a number and its correct value; **relative pointing device** = input device (such as a mouse) in which the movement of a pointer on screen is relative to the movement of the input device; **relative-time clock** = regular pulses that allow software in a computer to calculate the real time

relay 1 *noun* electromagnetically controlled switch; *there is a relay in the circuit; it is relay-rated at 5 Amps*; **microwave relay** = radiocommunications equipment used to receive microwave signals, then boost and retransmit them **2** *verb* to receive data from one source and then retransmit it to another point; *all messages are relayed through this station*

release 1 *noun* **(a)** version of a product; *the latest software is release 5*; **release number** = number of the version of a product; *see also* VERSION **(b)** putting a new product on the market; **new releases** = new records put on the market; **on general release** = (i) available to the public; (ii) (film) shown at many cinemas **(c) press release** = sheet giving news about a news item which is sent to newspapers and TV and radio stations so that they can use the information in it; *(film)* **release negative** = negative copy from which release prints are created; **release print** = the completed motion picture composite print which is ready for showing in cinemas **2** *verb* **(a)** to put a new product on the market **(b)** *(of software)* to relinquish control of a block of memory *or* file

relevance *noun* **(a)** way in which something has a connection with something else **(b)** importance of something in a situation *or* process

relevant *adjective* which has an important connection

reliability *noun* the ability of a device to function as intended, efficiently and without failure; *it has an excellent reliability record; the product has passed its reliability tests*

reliable *adjective* which can be trusted to work properly; *the early version of the software were not completely reliable*

relief printing *noun* printing process in which the ink is held on a raised image

reload *verb* to load again

relocatable *adjective* which can be moved to another area of memory without affecting its operation; **relocatable program** = computer program that can be executed from any area of memory; *the operating system can load and run a relocatable program from any area of memory*

relocate *verb* to move data from one area of storage to another; *the data is relocated during execution*

relocation *noun* moving to another area in memory

REM = REMARK

remainder 1 *noun* number equal to the dividend minus the product of the quotient and divider; *7 divided by 3 is equal to 2 remainder 1* **2** *verb* to sell products below cost price; *this computer model is out of* *date so we have to remainder the rest of the stock*

remark (REM) *noun* statement in a BASIC program that is ignored by the interpreter, allowing the programmer to write explanatory notes

remedial maintenance *noun* maintenance to repair faults which have developed in a system

remote *adjective* (communications) with a computer at a distance from the systems centre; *users can print reports on remote printers*; **remote access** = link that allows a user to access a computer from a distance (normally using a modem); **remote control** = control of a process *or* machine from a distance; *the video recorder has a remote control facility*; **remote control software** = software that runs on a local computer and a remote computer allowing a user to control the remote computer; *this remote control software will work with Windows and lets me operate my office PC from home over a modem link*; **remote device** = input/output device located away from the computer (and send data to it by line *or* modem); **remote job entry (RJE)** = batch processing system where data is transmitted to the computer from a remote terminal; **remote procedure call** = *see* RPC; **remote station** = communications station that can be controlled by a central computer; **remote terminal** = computer terminal connected to a distant computer system

removable *adjective* which can be removed; *a removable hard disk*

removal *noun* taking away; *the removal of this instruction could solve the problem*

remove *verb* to take away *or* to move to another place; *the file entry was removed from the floppy disk directory*; **remove directory** = *see* RD

rename *verb* to give a new name to a file; *save the file and rename it CUSTOM*

rendering *noun* colouring and shading a (normally wire-frame or vector object) graphic object so that it looks solid and real

renumber *noun* feature of some computer languages that allows the programmer to allocate new values to all *or* some of a program's line numbers; *see also* LINE NUMBER

reorganize *verb* to organize again; *wait while the spelling checker database is being reorganized*

repaginate *verb* to change the lengths of pages of text before they are printed; *the text was repaginated with a new line width*

repagination *noun* action of changing pages lengths; *the DTP package allows simple repagination*

repeat *verb* to do an action again; **repeat key** = key on a keyboard which repeats the character pressed

repeater *noun* device that receives a signal, amplifies it, then retransmits it (sometimes regenerating the received signal); *this cheap repeater does not regenerate the signals*

repeating group *noun* pattern of data that is duplicated in a bit stream

reperforator *noun* machine that punches paper tape according to received signals; **reperforator transmitter** = a reperforator and a punched tape transmitter connected together

repertoire *noun* the range of functions of a device *or* software; *the manual describes the full repertoire*

repetitive letter *noun* form letter *or* standard letter into which the details of each addressee (such as name and address) are inserted

repetitive strain injury *or* **repetitive stress injury (RSI)** *noun* pain in the arm felt by someone who performs the same movement many times over a certain period, as when operating a computer terminal; *RSI can be avoided by adjusting your chair so that you do not excessively flex your wrists when typing*

replace *verb* **(a)** to put something back where it was before; to put something in the place of something else; *the printer ribbons need replacing after several thousand characters* **(b)** instruction to a computer to find a certain item of data and put another in its place; *see also* SEARCH AND REPLACE

replay 1 *noun* **(a)** playback *or* reading back data *or* a signal from a recording **(b)** repeating a short section of filmed action, usually in slow motion; *the replay clearly showed the winner; this video recorder has a replay feature*; **instant replay** = feature of video recording systems that allows an action that has just been recorded to be viewed immediately **2** *verb* to play back (something which has been recorded); *he replayed the tape; she recorded the TV programme on video tape and replayed it the next evening*

replenish *verb* to charge a battery with electricity again

replicate *verb* to copy; *the routine will replicate your results with very little effort*

report program generator (RPG) *noun* programming language used mainly on personal computers for the preparation of business reports

represent *verb* **(a)** to act as a symbol for something; *the hash sign is used to represent a number in a series* **(b)** to act as a salesman for a product

representation *noun* action of representing something

representative 1 *adjective* typical example of something **2** *noun* salesman who represents a company; *the representative called yesterday about the order*

reprint 1 *verb* **(a)** to print more copies of a document *or* book **(b)** to create a positive film print from a negative **2** *noun* printing of copies of a book after the first printing; *we ordered a 10,000 copy reprint*

reprise shots *plural noun (film)* shots that are to be repeated further on in a film

repro *noun informal* finished artwork *or* camera-ready copy, ready for filming and printing; **repro proof** = perfect proof ready to be reproduced

reproduce *verb* to copy data *or* text from one material *or* medium to another similar

reproduction *noun* action of copying

reprogram *verb* to alter a program so that it can be run on another type of computer

request 1 *noun* thing which someone asks for **2** *verb* to ask for something

require *verb* to need something *or* to demand something; *delicate computer systems require careful handling*

required hyphen *or* **hard hyphen** *noun* hyphen which is always in a word, even if the word is not split (as in co-administrator); *see also* SOFT HYPHEN

requirements *noun* things which are needed; *memory requirements depend on the application software in use*

re-route *verb* to send by a different route; *the call diverter re-routes a call*

rerun *verb* to run a program *or* a printing job again; **rerun point** = place in the program from where to start a running again after a crash *or* halt

res *see* RESOLUTION

resample *verb* to change the number of pixels used to make up an image; *if you scan an image at 400dpi and your printer is only capable of 300 dpi, you could resample the bitmap image to 300dpi, losing some detail but ensuring that what you edit is printed*

resave *verb* to save again; *it automatically resaves the text*

rescue dump *noun* data saved on disk automatically when a computer fault occurs (it describes the state of the system at that time, used to help in debugging)

research *noun* scientific investigation to learn new facts about a field of study; **research and development (R & D)** = investigation of new products, discoveries and techniques; *the company has spent millions of dollars on R & D*

reserved character *noun* special character which is used by the operating system *or* which has a particular function to control an operating system and cannot be used for other uses; *in DOS, the reserved character \ is used to represent a directory path*

reserved sector *noun* area of disk space that is used only for control data storage; **reserved word** = word *or* phrase used as an identifier in a programming language (it performs a particular operation *or* instruction and so cannot be used for other uses by the programmer *or* user)

reset *verb* **(a)** to return a system to its initial state, to allow a program *or* process to be started again; **hard reset** = electrical signal that usually returns the system to its initial state when it was switched on, requiring a reboot; **reset button** *or* **key** = switch that allows a program to be terminated and reset manually; **soft reset** = instruction that terminates any program execution and returns the user to the monitor *or* operating system **(b)** to set a register *or* counter to its initial state; *when it reaches 999 this counter resets to zero* **(c)** to set data equal to zero

reset-set flip-flop *see* RS-FLIP-FLOP

reshape handle *noun (in a GUI)* small square displayed on a frame around an object or image that a user can select and drag to change the shape of the frame or graphical object

resident *adjective* (person *or* data) that is always in a company *or* machine; **resident engineer** = engineer who works permanently for one company; **resident font** = font data which is always present in a printer *or* device and which does not have to be downloaded; **resident software** *or* **memory-resident software** = program that is held permanently in memory; **terminate and stay resident software (TSR)** = program that is started from the command line, then loads itself into memory, ready to be activated by an action, and passes control back to the command line

residual *adjective* which remains behind; **residual error rate** = ratio between incorrect and undetected received data and total data transmitted; **residual magnetism** = magnetic effects remaining in a material after the removal of an external magnetic field

resist 1 *verb* to fight against something *or* to refuse to do something **2** *noun* substance used to protect a pattern of tracks on a PCB, that is not affected by etching chemicals; *see also* PHOTORESIST

resistance *noun* measure of the voltage drop across a component with a current flowing through it; *see also* OHM'S LAW

resistor *noun* electronic component that provides a known resistance; **resistor transistor logic (RTL)** = circuit design method using transistors and resistors; **variable resistor** = component whose resistance can be changed by turning a knob

resolution *noun* **(a)** number of pixels that a screen *or* printer can display per unit area; *the resolution of most personal computer screens is not much more than 70 dpi (dots per inch)* **graphic display resolution** = number of pixels that a computer is able to display on the screen; **high resolution (hi-res)** = ability to display *or* detect a very

large number of pixels per unit area; **limiting resolution** = maximum number of lines that make up a television picture; **low resolution (low-res)** = ability of a display system to control a number of pixels at a time rather than individual pixels **(b)** difference between two levels that can be differentiated in a digitized signal **(c)** degree of accuracy with which something can be measured or timed

---

the resolution is 600 dots per inch and the throughput is up to eight pages per minute
Practical Computing

Group IV fax devices can send a grey or colour A4 page in about four seconds, at a maximum resolution of 15.7 lines per millimetre over an Integrated Services Digital Network circuit

---

Computing

resolver *noun* *(film)* system which regulates the speed of a magnetic film recorder or a tape playback machine

resolving power *noun* measurement of the ability of an optical system to detect between fine black lines on a white background (given as the number of lines per millimeter)

resonance *noun* situation where a frequency applied to a body being the same as its natural frequency, causes it to oscillate with a very large amplitude

resource *noun* device *or* memory *or* graphic object which can be used by an application *or* system software; **resource allocation** = dividing available resources in a system between jobs; *(in an Apple Macintosh)* **resource fork** = one of two forks of a file; the resource fork contains the resources that the file needs (fonts, code or icons); **resource interchange file format** = *see* RIFF; **resource sharing** = the use of one resource in a network *or* system by several users

respond *verb* to reply *or* to react because of something

response *noun* reaction caused by something; **response frame** = a page in a videotext system that allows a user to enter data; **response position** = area of a form that is to be used for optical mark reading data; **response time** = (i) time which passes between the user starting an action (by pressing a key) and the result appearing on the screen; (ii) speed with which a system responds to a stimulus; *the response time of this flight simulator is very good*

rest in proportion *see* RIP

restart *verb* to start again; *first try to restart your system*; **Restart** = software function of Windows that performs a soft reset of the operating system; click on the Start button and choose ShutDown then choose Restart to stop and restart the Windows software; *compare with* BOOT

restore *verb* to put back into an earlier state

first you have to restore the directory that contains the list of deleted files
Personal Computer World

restrict *verb* to keep something within a certain limit; to allow only certain people to access information; *the document is restricted, and cannot be placed on open access*

restriction *noun* something which restricts (data flow *or* access)

result code *noun* message sent from a modem to the local computer indicating the state of the modem

retain *verb* to keep

retention *noun* keeping; **image retention** = time taken for a TV image to disappear after it has been displayed, caused by long persistence phosphor

retention *noun* time taken for a TV image to disappear after it has been displayed, caused by long persistence phosphor

reticles *or* **reticle lines** *plural noun (film)* lines which are imprinted onto the viewfinder of a camera and show the centre of the film frame or the areas of safe-action in the projection of television

reticulation *noun* the distortion or wrinkling of film emulsion

retouch *verb* to change a print *or* photograph slightly by hand, to make it clearer *or* to remove any blemishes; *I retouched the scratch mark on the last print; the artwork for the line drawings needs retouching in places*

retrain *verb* to re-establish a better quality connection when the quality of a line if very bad

retransmission *noun* signal *or* data that has been retransmitted

retransmit *verb* to transmit again (a received signal)

retrieval *noun* the process of searching, locating and recovering information from a file *or* storage device; **information retrieval** = locating quantities of data stored in a database and producing information from the data; **information retrieval centre** = research system, providing specific information from a database for a user

retrieve *verb* to extract information from a file *or* storage device; *these are the records retrieved in that search; this command will retrieve all names beginning with S*

retro- *prefix* meaning going back; progress backwards; **retrofit** = device *or* accessory added to a system to upgrade it; **retrofocus lens** = a telephoto lens which has a long back-focus distance

retrospective parallel running *noun* running a new computer system with old data to check it is accurate

retrospective search *noun* search of documents on a certain subject since a certain date

return *noun* (a) instruction that causes program execution to return to the main program from a subroutine; *the program is not working because you missed out the return instruction at the end of the subroutine* (b) key on a keyboard used to indicate that all the required data has been entered; *you type in your name and code number then press return* (c) indication of an end of line (in printing)

return to zero signal recording reference mark taken as the level of unmagnetized tape (NOTE: opposite is **non return to zero**)

reveal 1 *verb* to display previously hidden information once a condition has been met **2** *noun* the pulling back of the camera from the area of action in order to create a wider view of the scene

reverb *or* **reverberation** *noun* sound effect caused by multiple delays to a signal; *this hall has a lot of reverb*; **reverberation time** = measure of the amount of reverberation of a room (given as the time taken for a signal to decay to one millionth of its initial amplitude)

reversal film *noun* photographic film that produces a positive image when developed (NOTE: often called slide or transparency film)

reverse 1 *adjective* going in the opposite direction; **reverse channel** = low speed control data channel between a receiver and transmitter; **reverse characters** = characters which are displayed in the opposite way to other characters for emphasis (as black on white *or* white on black, when other characters are the opposite); **reverse engineering** = method of product design in which the finished item is analysed to determine how it should be constructed; **reverse index** = movement of a printer head up half a line to print superscripts; **reverse interrupt** = signal sent by a receiver to request the termination of transmissions; **reverse polarity** = situation where the positive and negative terminals have been confused, resulting in the equipment not functioning; **reverse Polish notation (RPN)** = mathematical operations written in a logical way, so that the operator appears after the numbers to be acted upon, this removes the need for brackets; *three plus four, minus two is written in RPN as 3 4 + 2 - = 5; normal notation: (x-y) + z, but using RPN: xy - z*; *same as* POSTFIX NOTATION; *(film)* **reverse printing** = printing film and print stock which pass in opposite directions through an optical printer to give the illusion that the action is moving backwards during print projection; **reverse video** = screen display mode where white and black are reversed (colours are complemented) **2** *verb* to go in the opposite direction; **reverse L to R** = to print an image laterally reversed

revert *verb* to return to a normal state; *after the rush order, we reverted back to our normal speed*; **revert command** = command (in text) that returns a formatted page to its original state

review *verb* to see again *or* replay and check; *the program allows the user to review all wrongly spelled words*

revise *verb* to update *or* correct a version of a document *or* file; *the revised version has no mistakes*

rewind *verb* to return a tape *or* film *or* counter to its starting point; *the tape rewinds onto the spool automatically*

rewrite 1 *verb* to write something again **2** *noun* act of writing something again; *the program is in its second rewrite*

RF = RADIO FREQUENCY electromagnetic spectrum that lies between the frequency range 10KHz and 3000GHz; *(film)* **RF cues** = cues imprinted into the edge of a film negative in the form of small metal patches which are picked up by a radio-frequency detector in motion picture printing; **RF modulator** *or* **radio frequency modulator** = electronic circuit that modulates a high frequency carrier signal with a video signal to enable it to be displayed on a domestic TV; *(film)* **RF patter** = distortion of a picture which is caused by high-frequency interference; **RF shielding** = thin metal foil wrapped around a cable that prevents the transmission of radio frequency interference signals; *without RF shielding, the transmitted signal would be distorted by the interference*

RGB = RED, GREEN, BLUE **(a)** high-definition monitor system that uses three separate input signals controlling red, green and blue colour picture beams **(b)** the three colour picture beams used in a colour TV; in a colour CRT there are three colour guns producing red, green and blue beams acting on groups of three phosphor dots at each pixel location **(c)** method of defining colours in a colour image in which the colour of each pixel in the image is described by three bytes (24bits), one for red, green and blue; *compare with* CMYK

RGB display *or* **monitor** *noun* high-definition monitor system that uses three separate input signals controlling red, green and blue colour picture beams

rheostat *noun* resistance with a movable wiper that will provide a variable output voltage (NOTE: also called **variable potential divider**)

RI = RING INDICATOR

RIAA curve *noun* *(film)* standards for recording and equalization set by the RIAA (Recording Industries Association of America)

ribbon *noun* long thin flat piece of material; *printer ribbons or typewriter* *ribbon*; **ribbon cable** = number of insulated conductors arranged next to each other forming a flat cable; *see* TAPE CABLE; *(film)* **ribbon microphone** = a microphone which works through currents which are induced in a metal ribbon in a magnetic field

rich text format (RTF) *noun* text file format that includes text commands that describe the page, type, font and formatting; *the RTF format allows formatted pages to be exchanged between different word processing software*

ride focus *noun (film)* the act of adjusting the lens focus to keep a sharp picture by using the focus rings

RIFF = RESOURCE INTERCHANGE FILE FORMAT multimedia data format jointly introduced by IBM and Microsoft that uses tags to identify parts of a multimedia file structure and allow the file to be exchanged between platforms

RIFF chunk *noun* chunk with the ID RIFF

RIFF file *noun* file that contains tagged information that complies with the RIFF file format, such as the WAVE audio file format

rifle microphone *noun (film)* a long, highly directional microphone which can pick up sound over a great distance

rifle spot *or* **spotlight** *noun (film)* long ellipsoidal spotlight that provides a narrow beam of light

right *adjective* not left; **right-click menu** = pop-up menu that appears when you click on the right-hand button of a two-button mouse; often used to select formatting or the properties of an object

right-hand button *noun* button on the right-hand side of a two or three-button mouse; **right justify** = to align the right margin so that the text is straight; **right justification** = aligning the text and spacing characters so that the right margin is straight; **right shift** = to move a section of data one bit to the right; *see also* LOGICAL SHIFT, ARITHMETIC SHIFT

rightsizing *noun* process of moving a company's information technology structure to the most cost-effective hardware platform; often used to mean moving from a mainframe-based network to a PC-based network

rigid *adjective* hard *or* which cannot bend; **rigid disk** = rigid magnetic disk that is able to store many times more data than a floppy disk, and usually cannot be removed from the disk drive

ring 1 *noun* **(a)** a data list whose last entry points to the first entry **(b)** topology of a network in which the wiring sequentially connects one workstation to another; **ring (data) network** = type of network where each terminal is connected one after the other in a circle; *see also* NETWORK; **Token Ring network** = IEEE 802.5 standard that uses a token passed from one workstation to the next in a ring network; a workstation can only transmit data if it captures the token (Token Ring networks, although logically a ring, are often physically wired in a star topology); *Token Ring networks are very democratic and retain performance against increasing load*; *compare with* BUS NETWORK, ETHERNET **2** *verb* to telephone; **ring back system** = remote computer system in which a user attempting to access it phones once, allows it to ring a number of times, disconnects, waits a moment, then redials (usually in a bulletin board system); **ring down** = to call a number of users in a telephone network; **ring indicator (RI)** = signal from a line answering device that it has detected a call to the DTE and has answered by going into an off-hook state

ring counter *noun* electronic counter in which any overflow from the last digit is fed into the input

ringing *noun (film)* **(a)** interference in a television picture **(b)** noise caused by an alternating or pulsating current

RIP 1 = RASTER IMAGE PROCESSOR computer which translates software instructions into an image or complete page which is then printed by a printer or imagesetter (often used to speed up typesetting images) **2** = REST IN PROPORTION printing instruction to indicate that all the material is to be reduced *or* enlarged in the same proportion

ripple *noun* **(a)** small alternating current voltage apparent on a badly regulated direct current output supply **(b)** a visual effect which creates wavy images during film dissolves

ripple-through effect *noun (in a spreadsheet)* results *or* changes *or* errors appearing in a spreadsheet as a result of the value in one cell being changed

RISC = REDUCED INSTRUCTION SET COMPUTER CPU design whose instruction set contains a small number of simple fast-executing instructions, that makes program writing more complex, but increases speed

rise time *noun* time taken for a voltage to increase its amplitude (from 10 to 90 per cent or zero to RMS value of its final amplitude); **the circuit has a fast rise time** = electronic circuit that is able to handle rapidly changing signals such as very high frequency signals

Rivest, Shamir, Adleman *see* RSA

RJ11 connector *noun* popular standard of four-wire modular connector

RJ45 connector *noun* popular name for an eight-pin modular connector used in 10BaseT or 100BaseT networks to connect UTP cables

RJE = REMOTE JOB ENTRY

RLE = RUN-LENGTH ENCODING data compression technique that stores any sequence of bits of data with the same value to a single vlaue

RLL encoding = RUN-LENGTH LIMITED ENCODING fast and efficient method of storing data onto a disk in which the changes in a run of data bits are stored

rm *(in UNIX)* command to remove an empty subdirectory

RMDIR *or* **RD** = REMOVE DIRECTORY *(in DOS)* command to remove an empty subdirectory

RMS = ROOT MEAN SQUARE **RMS line current** = the root mean square of the electrical current on a line

RO = RECEIVE ONLY

roam *verb (in wireless communications)* to move around freely and still be in contact with a wireless communications transmitter

robot *noun* device which can be programmed to carry out certain manufacturing tasks which are similar to tasks carried out by people

robotics *noun* study of artificial intelligence and programming involved with robot construction

```
so far no robot sensor has been
devised which can operate
quickly enough to halt the
robot if a human being is in
its path of work
```

IEE News

robust *adjective* solid *or* (system) which can resume working after a fault

robustness *noun* **(a)** strength of a system's casing and its ability to be knocked *or* dropped; *this hard disk is not very robust* **(b)** system's ability to continue functioning even with errors *or* faults during a program execution

rock and roll *verb (of picture and film)* to move backwards and forwards in synchronization during editing

rogue indicator *noun* special code used only for control applications such as end of file marker

rogue value *or* **terminator** *noun* item in a list of data, which shows that the list is terminated

role indicator *noun* symbol used to show the role of a index entry in its particular context

roll scroll *verb* displayed text that moves up *or* down the computer screen one line at a time

roll 1 *noun* **(a)** length of film *or* tape wound around itself; *he put a new roll of film into the camera* **(b)** unwanted vertical movement in a picture **2** *verb* **(a)** to rotate a device about its axis **(b)** to start filming; **roll in/roll out** = the transfer of one process (in a multiprogramming system) from storage to processor then back once it has had its allocated processing time

rollback *noun* reloading software after the master software has been corrupted

rolling headers *noun* titles *or* headers of (teletext) pages displayed as they are received

rolling title *noun* titles which move vertically up a picture area; *see* CRAWLING TITLE

rollover *noun* keyboard that can still transmit correct data when several keys are pressed at once; **key rollover** = use of a buffer between the keyboard and computer to provide rapid keystroke storage for fast typists

ROM = READ ONLY MEMORY; **CD-ROM** or **compact disc-ROM** = small plastic disc that is used as a high capacity ROM device; data is stored in binary form as holes etched on the surface which are then read by a laser; **ROM BIOS** = code which makes up the BIOS routines stored in a ROM chip (normally executed automatically when the computer is switched on); **ROM cartridge** = software stored in a ROM mounted in a cartridge that can be easily plugged into a computer or printer (NOTE: there is no plural for ROM, and it is often used without the article: **the file is stored in ROM)**

roman *noun* ordinary typeface, neither italic nor bold; *the text is set in Times Roman*

Roman numerals *noun* figures written I, II, III, IV, etc. (as opposed to Arabic numerals such as 1, 2, 3, 4, etc.)

romware *noun* software which is stored in ROM

root *noun* **(a) root directory** = (i) starting node from which all paths branch in a data tree structure; (ii) *(in a disk filing system)* the topmost directory from which all other directories branch; *in DOS, the root directory on drive C: is called C:* **(b)** fractional power of a number; **root mean square (RMS)** measure of the amplitude of a signal (equal to the square root of the mean value of the signal); *the root mean square of the pure sinusoidal signal is 0.7071 of its amplitude;* **square root** = number raised to the power one half; *square root of 25 is 5*

roping *noun (film)* damage to film caused by the teeth of sprockets leaving indentations in the film; *see* RUN OFF

rostrum *noun (film)* **(a)** camera stand which can light and hold in position the subject to be filmed **(b)** platform which can elevate actors and scenery to the necessary height

rostrum camera *noun (film)* vertically mounted film and television camera which is used for filming graphics and animation artwork

rotary *adjective* which works by turning; **rotary camera** = camera able to photograph microfilm as it is moved in front of the lens by moving the film at the same time; *(film)* **rotary erase head** = a video tape recorder's erase head; **rotary movement** = the effect of spinning images on film created by an optical-spin device in an optical printer; **rotary press** = printing press whose printing plate is cylindrical; **rotary printer** = constant contact printing machine where the two films at the time of exposure are transported on a revolving sprocket; **rotary** or **rotating shutter** = rotating camera or projector shutter which intermittently blocks the passage of light as it moves through

rotate *verb* to turn an object about one of its axes; *to rotate the image move the joystick forward*

rotating helical aperture scanner *noun* type of scanner in which the original image is lit and the reflection sent, through a lens and mirror, through a rotating spiral slit and finally onto a photodetector cell; as the spiral slit turns, it has the effect of moving up the image

rotation *noun* amount by which an object has been rotated; **bit rotation** or **rotate operation** = to shift a pattern of bits in a word to the left or right, the old last bit moving to the first bit position; **matrix rotation** = swapping the rows with the columns in an array (equal to rotating by 90 degrees); *see also* SHIFT (CYCLIC)

rotoscope *noun* device which projects a film frame-by-frame on to the surface of an animation stand, either for the preparation of animated drawings or for the animation cels' background

rough cut *noun* the first edit of a film or a television programme

round 1 *adjective* which goes in a circle; **round robin** = way of organizing the use of a computer by several users, who each use it for a time and then pass it on the next in turn **2** *verb* **round off errors** = inaccuracies in numbers due to rounding off; **to round down** = to approximate a number to a slightly lower one of lower precision; *we can round down 2.6512 to 2.65;* **to round off** = to approximate a number to a slightly larger or smaller one of lower precision; *round off 23.456 to 23.46;* **to round up** = to approximate a number to a slightly larger one of lower precision; *we can round up 2.647 to 2.65*

rounding *noun* approximation of a number to a slightly larger or smaller one of lower precision; **rounding characters** making a displayed character more pleasant to look at (within the limits of pixel size) by making sharp corners and edges smooth

route *noun* path taken by a message between a transmitter and receiver in a network; *the route taken was not the most direct since a lot of nodes were busy*

router *noun* (a) communications device that receives data packets in a particular protocol and forwards them to their correct location via the most efficient route (b) *(in a LAN)* device that connect two or more LANs and allows data to be transmitted between each network

routine *noun* a number of instructions that perform a particular task, but are not a complete program; they are included as part of a program; *the routine copies the screen display onto a printer; the RETURN instruction at the end of the routine sends control back to the main program*; **closed routine** *or* **subroutine** = one section of code that is used by all calls to the routine; **open routine** *or* **subroutine** = the set of instructions in a routine, that are copied to whichever part of the program requires them; *see also* FUNCTION, SUBROUTINE, PROCEDURE

COMMENT: routines are usually called from a main program to perform a task, control is then returned to the part of the main program from which the routine was called once the task is complete

Hewlett Packard has announced software which aims to reduce PC-network downtime and cut support costs by automating housekeeping routines such as issuing alerts about potential problems

Computing

routing *noun* determining a suitable route for a message through a network; *there is a new way of routing data to the central computer*; **routing information protocol (RIP)** = protocol used on the Internet to calculate the best route by which to transfer information over the Internet, basing its selection on the distance that each route takes; **routing overheads** = actions that have to be taken when routing messages; *the information transfer rate is very much*

less once all routing overheads have been accommodated; **routing page** = videotext page describing the routes to other pages; **routing table** = list of preferred choices for a route for a message

row *noun* (a) line of printed *or* displayed characters (b) horizontal line on a punched card; *the figures are presented in rows, not in columns; each entry is separated by a row of dots* (c) horizontal set of data elements in an array *or* matrix

RPC = REMOTE PROCEDURE CALL method of communication between two programs running on two separate, but connected, computers

RPG = REPORT PROGRAM GENERATOR

RS-232C EIA approved standard used in serial data transmission, covering voltage and control signals

RS-422 EIA approved standard that extends the RS-232's 50ft limit

RS-423 EIA approved standard that extends the RS-232's 15m limit, introduced at the same time as the RS-422 standard, but less widely used; **RS-485** = standard that defines how serial devices are connected together for multipoint communications; this standard, approved by the EIA (Electronics Industries Association) supports higher rates of data transfer than the older RS-232C standard and allows more connections to one line than the RS-422 standard

RSA cipher system the Rivest, Shamir and Adleman public key cipher system

RS-flip-flop = RESET-SET FLIP-FLOP electronic bistable device whose output can be changed according to the Reset and Set inputs; *see also* FLIP-FLOP

RTF = RICH TEXT FORMAT text file format that includes text commands that describe the page, type, font and formatting; *the RTF format allows formatted pages to be exchanged between different word processing software*

RTL = RESISTOR TRANSISTOR LOGIC

RTV = REAL-TIME VIDEO real-time video compression used within DVI software to provide usable, but lower-quality, images that are compressed in real-time at 10 frames per second

rubber banding *see* ELASTIC BANDING

rubber numbers *plural noun (film)* identification numbers which are imprinted on developed rush prints and sound records during film editing

rubric *noun* printed headings of a book chapter *or* section

rule *noun* **(a)** set of conditions that describe a function; *the rule states that you wait for the clear signal before transmitting*; **rule based system** = software that applies the rules and knowledge defined by experts in a particular field to a user's data to solve a problem **(b)** thin line in printing; **em rule** = dash as long as an em, used to show that words are separated; **en rule** = dash as long as an en, used to show that words are joined

ruler *noun* bar displayed on screen that indicates a unit of measurement; often used in DTP or word-processor software to help with layout; **ruler line** = line displayed at the top of a document or page, showing the ruler currently in use (including tab stops)

run 1 *noun* **(a)** execution by a computer of a set of instructions *or* programs *or* procedures; *the next invoice run will be on Friday* **(b)** amount of time that a film is shown in a particular cinema **2** *verb* to make a device work; *the computer has been running ten hours a day; do not interrupt the spelling checker while it is running; the new package runs on our PC*; **run around** = to fit text around an image on a printed page; **Run command** = *(in Windows)* menu option (Start/Run) that lets a user type in the name of a program or command to execute; *type in 'telnet' at the Run command to start the telnet software*; **run in** = to operate a system at a lower capacity for a time in case of any faults

run off *noun (film)* error in positioning of film which causes it to move over a sprocket's teeth and be damaged

run on *verb* **(a)** to make text continue without a break; *the line can run on to the next without any space* **(b)** to print more copies to add to a print run; *we decided to run on 3,000 copies to the first printing*; **run-on price** = price of extra copies printed after a fixed print run

run out *noun (film)* section of blank film at the end of a reel to prevent damage occurring to the film

run up *noun (film)* section of tape or film which must be run through a projector, audio or video tape recorder before it reads the correct speed

rundown *noun (film)* broadcast order of programme events

run-length limited encoding (RLL) *noun* fast and efficient method of storing data onto a disk in which the changes in a run of data bits are stored

running head *noun* title line of each page in a document

run-time *or* **run-duration 1** *noun* **(a)** period of a time a program takes to run **(b)** time during which a computer is executing a program **2** *adjective* (operation) carried out only when a program is running; **run-time error** = fault only detected when a program is run *or* error made while a program is running; *see also* EXECUTION ERROR; **run-time library** = library of routines that are only accessed by an application when it is running; **run-time licence** = licence granted to a user to run an application; *the software is designed with all the graphics routines in this run-time library file*; **run-time system** = the software that is required in main storage while a program is running (to execute instructions to peripherals, etc.); **run-time version** = (i) program code that has been compiled and is in a form that can be directly executed by the computer; (ii) commercial interpreter program that is sold with an application developed in a high-level language that allows it to run

rushes *plural noun (film)* **(a)** the initial prints made from a picture or sound negative in order to check the quality; *see* DAILIES **(b)** unedited video tape

RX = RECEIVE, RECEIVER; *the RXed signal needs to be amplified*

Ss

S100 bus *or* **S-100 bus** *noun (old)* standard IEEE 696 bus, a popular 8 and 16 bit microcomputer bus using 100 lines and a 100-pin connector; *see also* BUS (NOTE: say 'S one hundred bus')

s/n ratio = SIGNAL TO NOISE RATIO ratio of the amplitude of the transmitted signal to the noise on the received signal

SAA = SYSTEMS APPLICATION ARCHITECTURE standard developed by IBM which defines the look and feel of an application regardless of the hardware platform

COMMENT: SAA defines which keystrokes carry out standard functions (such as F1 to display help), the application's display and how the application interacts with the operating system

safe area *noun* area of a TV image that will be seen on a standard television set

safe format *noun* format operation that does not destroy the existing data and allows the data to be recovered in case you formatted the wrong disk

safe mode *noun* special operating mode of Microsoft Windows that is automatically selected if Windows detects that there is a problem when it is starting

SAFE = SIGNATURE ANALYSIS USING FUNCTIONAL ANALYSIS signature validation technique

safebase *noun (film)* a plastic film material used as a base for film which is almost non-flammable (e.g. cellulose triacetate)

safelight *noun (film)* a coloured light which is used in a photographic darkroom to allow workers to see but which will not harm photographic emulsion or unprocessed film

safety net *noun* software *or* hardware device that protects the system *or* files from excessive damage in the event of a system crash; *if there is a power failure, we have a safety net in the form of a battery*

salami technique *noun* computer fraud involving many separate small transactions that are difficult to detect and trace

SAM = SERIAL-ACCESS MEMORY storage where a particular data item can only be accessed by reading all the previous items in the list (as opposed to random access)

COMMENT: magnetic tape is a form of SAM; you have to go through the whole tape to access one item, while disks, on the other hand, are random access

sample 1 *noun* measurement of a signal at a point in time; *the sample at three seconds showed an increase*; **sample and hold circuit** = circuit that freezes an analog input signal for long enough for an A/D converter to produce a stable output; *(film)* **sample print** = composite print which has not been approved for release; **sample rate** = number of measurements of a signal recorded every second; a PC sound card supports one of the following three standard rates: 11.025, 22.05 and 44.1KHz; *see also* ANALOG TO DIGITAL, MPC, QUANTIZE; **sample size** = size of the word used to measure the level of the signal when it is sampled: normally either 8-bit or 16-bit words are used; an 8-bit word means that each sample can have 256 separate levels, a 16-bit word can have 65,536 levels and so is more precise for capturing the finer detail in the signal **2** *verb* to obtain a number of measurements of a signal that can be used to provide information about the signal; **sampling interval** = time period between two consecutive samples; **sampling rate** =

number of measurements of a signal recorded every second

sampler *noun* **(a)** electronic circuit that takes many samples of a signal and stores them for future analysis **(b)** electronic circuit used to record audio signals in digital form and store them to allow future playback

COMMENT: if the sampling is on a music signal and the sampling frequency is great enough, digitally stored signals sound like the original analog signal. For analog signals, a sampling rate of at least two times the greatest frequency as required to provide adequate detail

sans serif *noun* typeface whose letters have no serifs

sapphire *noun* blue-coloured precious stone used as a substrate for certain chips

SAS = SINGLE ATTACHMENT STATION

satellite *noun* **(a)** device that orbits the earth receiving, processing and transmitting signals *or* generating images *or* data to be transmitted back to earth, such as weather pictures; **communications satellite** = satellite that relays radio *or* TV signals from one point on the earth's surface to another; **direct broadcast satellite (DBS)** = TV and radio signal broadcast over a wide area from an earth station via a satellite to homes (received with a dish aerial); **satellite broadcasting** *or* **satellite TV** = sending public radio and TV signals from one part of the earth to another, using a communications satellite; **satellite link** = use of a satellite to allow the transmission of data from one point on earth to another; **satellite master antenna television;** *see* SMATV; **satellite network** = series of satellites which provide wide coverage of an area; **weather satellite** = device that orbits the earth, transmitting images of the weather systems above the earth's surface **(b)** small system that is part of a larger system; **satellite computer** = computer doing various tasks under the control of another computer; **satellite terminal** = computer terminal that is outside the main network

saturation *noun* excessive signals present either on a magnetic medium *or* in a

displayed colour; **saturation testing** = testing to see if a communications network is operating correctly, by transmitting large quantities of data and messages over it

save *verb* to store data *or* a program on an auxiliary storage device; *this WP saves the text every 15 minutes in case of a fault; don't forget to save the file before switching off*; **save area** = temporary storage area of main memory, used for registers and control data; **save as** = option in an application that allows the user to save the current work in a file with a different name

sawtooth waveform *noun* waveform that regularly rises to a maximum and drops to a minimum in a linear way

SBC = SINGLE BOARD COMPUTER computer whose main components such as processor, input/output and memory are all contained on one PCB

SBM *see* SUPER BIT MAPPING

S-box *noun* matrix transformation process used in certain cipher systems

scalable font *noun* method of describing a font so that it can produce characters of different sizes; *see also* OUTLINE FONT

scalable software *noun* groupware application that can easily accommodate more users on a network without having to invest in new software

scalar *noun* variable that has a single value assigned to it; *a scalar has a single magnitude value, a vector has two or more positional values*; **scalar data** = data type containing single values which are predictable and follow a sequence; **scalar processor** = processor designed to operate at high-speed on scalar values; **Scalar Processor Architecture (SPARC)** = RISC processor designed by Sun Microsystems and used in its range of workstations; **scalar value** = single value rather than a matrix or record (scalar values are not normally floating-point numbers); **scalar variable** = variable which can contain a single value rather than a complex data type (such as an array or record)

scale 1 *noun* ratio of two values; **large scale** *or* **small scale** = working with large *or* small amounts of data *or* numbers of staff; **large scale integration (LSI)** = integrated circuit with 500 - 10,000 components;

medium scale integration (MSI) = integrated circuit with 10 - 500 components; **small scale integration (SSI)** = integrated circuit with 1 - 10 components; **very large scale integration (VLSI)** = integrated circuit with 10,000 - 100,000 components **2** *verb* **to scale down** *or* **scale up** = to lower *or* increase in proportion

scan 1 *noun* examination of an image *or* object to obtain data; *the heat scan of the computer quickly showed which component was overheating*; **scan code** = number transmitted from the keyboard to an IBM PC compatible computer to indicate that a key has been pressed and to identify the key; **scan conversion** = process of converting an interlaced video signal to a non-interlaced signal or a composite to a separated RGB signal; **scan head** = device used in scanners, photocopiers and fax machines, which uses photo-electric cells to turn an image into a pattern of pixels; *this model uses a scan head that can distinguish 256 different colours*; **scan length** = number of items in a file or list that are examined in a scan; **scan line** = one of the horizontal lines of phosphor (or phosphor dots) on the inside of a CRT or monitor; the monitor's picture beam sweeps along each scan line to create the image on the screen; **scan rate** = number of times every second that the image on a CRT is redrawn **2** *verb* **(a)** to examine and produce data from the shape *or* state of an object *or* drawing **(b)** *(optical)* to convert a printed image or photograph into a digital bitmap form **(c)** *(in a display)* to move a picture beam across a screen, one line at a time, to refresh the image on the CRT **(d)** to convert an optical image (from a video camera) into a digital form by examining each pixel on one line of a frame, then moving down one line; *he scanned the old photograph of Teddington; the facsimile machine scans the picture and converts this to digital form before transmission; the machine scans at up to 1200 dpi resolution*; **scan area** = section of an image read by a scanner

scanner *noun* **(a)** device that scans **(b)** a mobile video production vehicle; **flat-bed scanner** = device with a flat sheet of glass on which the image *or* photograph *or* document is placed; the scan head moves below the glass and converts the image into data which can be manipulated by a

computer; **hand-held scanner** = device that is held in your hand and contains a row of photo-electric cells which, when moved over an image, convert it into data which can be manipulated by a computer; **image scanner** = input device that converts documents *or* drawings *or* photographs into digitized machine-readable form; *a 1200 dpi image scanner*; **optical scanner** = equipment that converts an image into electrical signals which can be stored in and displayed on a computer **scanner memory** = memory area allocated to store images which have been scanned

COMMENT: a scanner can be a device using photoelectric cells as in an image digitizer, or a device that samples data from a process

scanning *noun* **(a)** action of examining and producing data from the shape of an object *or* drawing **(b)** method which examines an area line-by-line through the use of an electron beam, and is particularly used in television; **scanning device** = device that allows micrographic images to be selected rapidly from a reel of film; **scanning error** = error introduced while scanning an image; **scanning radio receiver** = radio receiver that can check a range of frequencies to find a strong signal *or* a particular station; **scanning line** = path traced on a TV screen by the picture beam; **scanning rate** = time taken to scan one line *or* image; **scanning resolution** = ability of a scanner to register small pixels (usual resolution is 1200 dpi); **scanning software** = dedicated program that controls a scanner and allows certain operations (rotate *or* edit *or* store, etc.) on a scanned image; **scanning speed** = how fast a line *or* image is scanned; *throughput is 1.3 inches per second scanning speed; its scanning speed is 9.9 seconds for an 8.5"x 11"document; (of modem)* **auto-baud scanning** *or* **auto-baud sensing** = circuit that can automatically sense and select the correct baud rate for a line

COMMENT: a modem with auto-baud scanning can automatically sense which baud rate to operate on and switches automatically to that baud rate

scanning spot *noun* **(a)** small area of an image that is being read by a facsimile machine that moves over the whole image **(b)** small area (i) covered by the picture beam on a TV screen that moves to follow a scanning line to write the whole of an image onto the screen; (ii) satellite transmission to a number of areas, as the satellite passes over them

SCART connector special connector normally used to carry video or audio signals between video equipment

scatter *noun* part of a beam that is deflected *or* refracted; **scatter graph** = individual points *or* values plotted on a two axis graph; **scatter proofs** = proofs not arranged in any order prior to PMT; *see also* BACKSCATTER

scavenging *see* BROWSE

scene sync *noun (film)* system which allows both movement of the foreground camera to be synchronised with the mask camera in chroma key, and colour separation overlay special effects

scene *noun (film)* **(a)** a group of interrelated shots combined into a continuous action **(b)** location for a specific shot or a group of shots

schedule 1 *noun* order in which tasks are to be done *or* order in which CPU time will be allocated to processes in a multi-user system **2** *verb* to organize the broadcasting of TV *or* radio programmes at certain times

scheduled circuits *noun* telephone lines for data communications only

scheduler *noun* program which organizes use of a CPU *or* of peripherals which are shared by several users

scheduling *noun* **(a)** method of working which allows several users to share the use of a CPU; **job scheduling** = arranging the order in which jobs are to be processed **(b)** **programme scheduling** = organizing the broadcasting of radio *or* TV programmes at certain times

schema *noun* graphical description of a process *or* database structure

schematic *adjective & noun* (diagram) showing system components and how they are connected

schlieren lens *noun* optical system which is used in video projection

scientific *adjective* referring to science; **scientific calculator** = specially adapted

calculator which has several scientific functions built into it

scissor *verb* to remove the areas of text *or* graphics that lie outside a page's limits

scissoring *noun* **(a)** defining an area of an image and then cutting out this part of the image so that it can then be pasted into another image **(b)** defining an area of an image and deleting any information that is outside this area

scoop *noun (film)* a lighting unit that has a matt white reflector and is used for fill lighting

scope *noun* **(a)** *(informal)* = OSCILLOSCOPE electronic test equipment that displays on a CRT the size and shape of an electrical signal; **scope leads** = wires that allow circuits under test to be connected to an oscilloscope **(b)** range of values that a variable can contain

score *noun* **(a)** list of actions that control how objects or cast members move with time within a presentation **(b)** description of a piece of music using musical notes

SCR = SEQUENCE CONTROL REGISTER

scramble *verb* to code speech *or* data which is transmitted in such a way that it cannot be understood unless it is decoded

scrambler *noun* **(a)** device that codes a data stream into a pseudorandom form before transmission to eliminate any series of one's or zero's *or* alternate one's and zero's that would cause synchronization problems at the receiver and produce unwanted harmonics **(b)** device that codes speech *or* other signals prior to transmission so that someone who is listening in without authorization cannot understand what is being transmitted (the scrambled signals are de-scrambled on reception to provide the original signals); *he called the President on the scrambler telephone*

scrapbook *noun* utility (on an Apple Macintosh) that stores frequently used graphic images; *we store our logo in the scrapbook*

scrape flutter *noun (film)* an error in magnetic recording which is caused by the recording tape sticking which produces flutter

scratch 1 *noun* **(a)** area of memory *or* file used for temporary storage of data **(b)** mark on the surface of a disk; *this scratch makes the disk unreadable* **2** *verb* to delete *or* move an area of memory to provide room for other data; **scratch file** *or* **work file** = work area which is being used for current work; **scratch tape** = magnetic tape used for a scratch file; *(film)* **scratch track** = sound track used only for editing purposes

scratchpad *noun* workspace *or* area of high speed memory that is used for temporary storage of data in current use; **scratchpad memory** = cache memory used to buffer data being transferred between a fast processor and a slow I/O device (such as a disk drive)

screen 1 *noun* **(a)** display device capable of showing a quantity of information, such as a CRT *or* VDU; the surface on to which a picture image is projected *or* shown; *compare with* READOUT; **on-screen** = information displayed on a screen; *on-screen font display; (in some operating systems, including DOS)* **screen attribute** = attribute bits which define how each character will be displayed on screen; they set background and foreground colour and bold, italic or underline; **screen border** = margin around text displayed on a screen; **screen buffer** = temporary storage area for characters *or* graphics before they are displayed; **screen burn** = problem caused if a stationary image is displayed for too long on a monitor, burning the phosphor; **screen capture** = to store the image currently displayed on screen in a file; it is useful when creating manuals about a software product (NOTE: in Windows, you can capture the current screen to the Clipboard by pressing the PrtScrn key; on a Macintosh you can capture the current screen by pressing Shift-Option-3); **screen dump** = outputting the text *or* graphics on a screen to a printer; **screen editor** *or* **text editor** = software that allows the user to edit text on-screen, with one complete screen of information being displayed at a time; **screen flicker** = image on a display that moves slightly or whose brightness alternates due to a low image refresh rate *or* signal corruption; *(in a GUI)* **screen font** = typeface and size designed to be used to display text on screen rather than be printed out; *the screen font is displayed at 72dpi on a monitor, rather than printed at 300dpi on this laser printer;* **screen format** = way in which a screen is laid out;

screen grab = (i) digitizing a single frame from a display *or* television; (ii) screen capture; **screen memory** = in a memory-mapped screen, the area of memory that represents the whole screen, usually with one byte representing one *or* a number of pixels; **screen saver** = software which, after a pre-determined period of user inactivity, replaces the existing image on screen and displays moving objects to protect against screen burn; **screen shot** = *see* SCREEN CAPTURE **(b)** grid of dots or lines placed between the camera and the artwork, which has the effect of dividing the picture up into small dots, creating an image which can be used for printing; **screen angle** = angle at which a screen is set before a photograph is taken (different angles are used for the four process colours so as to avoid a moire effect); the normal angles are black: 45; magenta: 75; yellow: 90; cyan: 105 **(c)** thing which protects; **magnetic screen** = metal screen to prevent stray magnetic fields affecting electronic components **2** *verb* **(a)** to display *or* show information; *the film is now being screened* **(b)** to protect something with a screen; *the PSU is screened against interference*

screenful *noun* complete frame of information displayed on a screen

scrim *noun (film)* gauze or netting which is used to diffuse light

script *noun* **(a)** text which will be spoken by actors in a film *or* TV programme **(b)** set of instructions which carry out a function, normally used with a macro language or batch language; *I log in automatically using this script with my communications software; (in Movie Player)* **script channel** = one channel in a score that contains commands; **script editor** = editor that lets a user edit a script or program in an authoring package; **scripting language** = simple programming language (normally proprietary to an application) that allows a user to automate the application's functions; *this communications software has a scripting language that lets me dial and log in automatically;* **script recorder** = function of an authoring package that records the functions and actions a user carries out and converts these into commands in a script

scriptwriter *noun* person who writes film *or* TV scripts

ScriptX authoring tool and utilities that allow a developer to write multimedia applications that can be played (unchanged) on a range of different platforms - such as Macintosh and PC; developed by Kaleida Labs, a joint venture between IBM and Apple

scroll 1 *verb* to move displayed text vertically up *or* down the screen, one line *or* pixel at a time; *(in a GUI)* **scroll arrows** = arrows that when clicked, move the contents of the window up or down or sideways; **scroll bar** = bar displayed along the side of a window with a marker which indicates how far you have scrolled; *the marker is in the middle of the scroll bar so I know I am in the middle of the document*; **Scroll Lock key** = key (on an IBM PC keyboard) that changes how the cursor control keys operate; their function is dependent on the application; **scroll mode** = terminal mode that transmits every key press and displays what is received; **smooth scroll** = text that is moved up a screen pixel by pixel rather than line by line, which gives a smoother movement **2** *noun* **(a)** video transition effect when one image pushes the existing image off the screen in a vertical direction **(b)** translucent roll of film which is used on an overhead projector

scrub *verb* to wipe information off a disk *or* remove data from store; *scrub all files referring to 2001 taxes*

SCSI = SMALL COMPUTER SYSTEMS INTERFACE standard high-speed parallel interface used to connect computers to peripheral devices (such as disk drives and scanners); **Fast-SCSI** = development that allows data to be transferred at a higher rate than with the original SCSI specification; **SCSI-2** = newer standard that provides a wider data bus and transfers data faster than the original SCSI specification; **Wide-SCSI** = development that provides a wider data bus than the original SCSI specification, so can transfer more data at a time

COMMENT: SCSI is the current standard used to interface high-capacity, high-performance disk drives to computers; smaller disk drives are connected with an IDE interface,

which is slower, but cheaper. SCSI replaced the older ESDI interface and allows several (normally eight) peripherals to be connected, in a daisy-chain, to one controller

The Tricord ES4000 is an entry-level superserver machine, with 60Gb of SCSI-2 fixed disk, 256Mb of ECC memory, and support for Raid levels 0, 1 and 10

Computing

SD = SINGLE DENSITY DISK

SDLC = SYNCHRONOUS DATA LINK CONTROL data transmission protocol most often used in IBM's Systems Network Architecture (SNA) and defines how synchronous data is transmitted

seal *verb* to close something tightly so that it cannot be opened; *the hard disk is in a sealed case*

seamless integration *noun* the process of including a new device or software into a system without any problems; *it took a lot of careful planning, but we succeeded in a seamless integration of the new application*

search 1 *noun* process of identifying a character *or* word *or* section of data in a document *or* file; **global search and replace** = word-processor search and replace function covering a complete file *or* document; **search and replace** = feature on some word processors that allows the user to find certain words *or* phrases, then replace them with another word *or* phrase; **search engine** = software that performs the search on a database or title; **search key** = (i) word *or* phrase that is to be found in a text; (ii) field and other data used to select various records in a database; **search memory** = method of data retrieval that uses part of the data rather than an address to locate the data; **sequential search** = search where each item in a list (starting at the beginning) is checked until the required one is found **2** *verb* **(a)** to look for an item of data **(b)** *(film)* to move quickly backwards and forwards to different parts of a programme without losing the synchronisation of the sound and picture

searching storage *noun* method of data retrieval that uses part of the data rather than an address to locate the data

> a linear search of 1,000 items takes 500 comparisons to find the target, and 1,000 to report that it isn't present. A binary search of the same set of items takes roughly ten divisions either to find or not to find the target
>
> *Personal Computer World*

SECAM = SYSTEME ELECTRONIQUE COULEUR AVEC MEMOIRE standard which defines television and video formats, used in France and Saudi Arabia

second *adjective* (thing) which comes after the first; *we have two computers, the second one being used if the first is being repaired*; **second generation computers** = computer which used transistors instead of valves; **second sourcing** = granting a licence to another manufacturer to produce an electronic item *or* component when production capacity is not great enough to meet demand; **second user** *or* **second hand** = (old equipment) that has already been used and is be sold again

secondary *adjective* second in importance *or* less important than the first; **secondary channel** = second channel containing control information transmitted at the same time as data; **secondary colour** = colour produced from two primary colours; = **secondary service provider** = organisation that provide Internet access for a particular region of a country; **secondary station** = temporary status of the station that is receiving data; **secondary storage** = any data storage medium (such as magnetic tape *or* floppy disk) that is not the main, high-speed computer storage (RAM)

> COMMENT: this type of storage is usually of a higher capacity, lower cost and slower access time than main memory

sector 1 *noun* smallest area on a magnetic disk that can be accessed by a computer; *the disk is divided into concentric tracks, and each track is divided into sectors which, typically, can store 512 bytes of data*; **bad sector** = sector which has been identified as faulty and cannot be used to reliably store data (bad sectors are stored in a sector map); **sector interleave** = ratio of sectors skipped between access operations on a hard disk; in a hard disk with an interleave of 3, the first sector is read, then three sectors are skipped and the next sector is read; this is used to slow down the transfer of data from a fast hard disk to a slower controller card; **sector map** = table which contains the addresses of unusable sectors on a hard disk **2** *verb* to divide a disk into a series of sectors; **hard-sectored** = disk with sector start locations described by holes *or* other physical marks on the disk, which are set when the disk is manufactured; **sectoring hole** = hole in the edge of a disk to indicate where the first sector is located; **soft-sectored** = disk where sectors are described by an address and start code data written onto it when the disk is formatted

> COMMENT: a disk is divided into many tracks, each of which is then divided into a number of sectors which can hold a certain number of bits

secure electronic transactions *see* SET

secure encryption payment protocol *see* SEPP

secure hypertext transfer protocol *see* S-HTTP

secure/multipurpose internet mail extension (S/MIME) method of providing secure electronic mail messages; the system encrypts the main message using a standard cipher such as DES then sends the key in encrypted form using a second, public-key encryption system; *see* DES, ELECTRONIC MAIL, MIME, PUBLIC-KEY

secure site *or* **website** *noun* website that includes features to ensure that any information transferred between the user and the site is encrypted and cannot be read by a hacker; normally used in a shopping site to allow a customer to type in their personal details (such as their credit-card number) without risk; *see* SSL

> COMMENT: Secure websites almost always use a system called SSL (secure sockets layer) that creates a secure

channel when you visit the site; a small padlock icon in the status bar at the bottom of the web browser indicates if a site is ecure: if the padlock icon is open, this is not a secure site and you should not type in sensitive information, such as a credit card number.

secure sockets layer *see* SSL

secure system *noun* system that cannot be accessed without authorization

secured *adjective* (file) that is protected against accidental writing *or* deletion *or* against unauthorized access

security *noun* being protected *or* being secret; *the system has been designed to assure the security of the stored data*; **security backup** = copy of a disk *or* tape *or* file kept in a safe place in case the working copy is lost *or* damaged; **security check** = identification of authorized users (by a password) before granting access

seed *noun* starting value used when generating random or pseudorandom numbers

seek *verb* to try to find; **seek area** = section of memory to be searched for a particular item of data *or* a word; **seek time** = time taken by a read/write head to find the right track on a disk

Sega *noun* videogame company that develops software and hardware for the console games market; developed the Mega-Drive console

segment 1 *noun* section of a main program that can be executed in its own right without the rest of the main program being required; **LAN segment** = part of a network separated from the rest by a bridge; *(in a bus network)* an electrically continuous piece of cable **2** *verb* to divide a long program into shorter sections which can then be called up when required; **segmented address space** = memory address space divided into areas called segments; to address a particular location, the segment and offset values must be specified; *see also* OVERLAY

select *verb* **(a)** to position a pointer over an object (such as a button or menu option) and click on the mouse-button **(b)** to find and retrieve specific information from a database; **chip select (CS)** = connection to a chip that will enable it to function when a

signal is present (often ICs do not function even when power is applied, until a CS signal is provided)

selectable *adjective* which can be selected; *see also* JUMPER-SELECTABLE

selection *noun* **(a)** action *or* process of selecting; *selection of information from a large database may take some time* **(b)** *(in a paint program)* defining an area of an image (often used to cut out an area of the image, or to limit a special effect to an area); *(in a GUI)* **selection handle** = small square displayed on a frame around a selected area that allows the user to change the shape of the area; **selection tool** = icon within a toolbar that allows a user to select an area of an image

selective *adjective* which chooses certain items; **selective calling** = calling a remote station from a main site; **selective dump** = display *or* printout of a selected area of memory; **selective focus** = the filming in clear focus of only a section of the action area; **selective sort** = to sort into order a section of data items

selectivity *noun* ability of a radio receiver to distinguish between two nearby carrier frequencies

selector *noun* mechanical device that allows a user to choose an option *or* function; *the selector knob for the amplification is located there; turn the selector control*; **selector channel** = communications link that operates with only one transmitter/receiver at a time

self- *prefix* referring to oneself; **self-adapting system** = system that can change adapt itself to various tasks; **self-blimped** = a film camera whose working noise level is so low that no sound-proofing is necessary; **self-checking code** = character coding system that can detect an error *or* bad character without correcting it; **self-checking system** = system that carries out diagnostic tests on itself usually at switch on; **self-correcting codes** = character coding system that can detect and correct an error *or* bad character; **self-documenting program** = computer program that provides the user with operating instructions as it runs; *(film)* **self-matting** = visual process where colour mattes are used to eliminate rotoscoping

semantics *noun* **(a)** part of language which deals with the meaning of words, parts of words *or* combinations of words **(b)** *(in computing)* meanings of words *or* symbols used in programs

semaphore *noun* **(a)** coordination of two jobs and appropriate handshaking to prevent lockouts *or* other problems when both require a peripheral *or* function **(b)** signalling system that uses two flags held in different positions by two mechanical *or* human arms

semi- *prefix* meaning half *or* partly; **semi-processed data** = raw data which has had some processing carried out, such as sorting, recoding, error detection, etc.

semicolon *noun* printing sign (;) which indicates a separation between parts of a sentence *or* marks the end of a program line *or* statement

semiconductor *noun* material that has conductive properties between those of a conductor (such as a metal) and an insulator; **semiconductor device** = electronic component that is constructed on a small piece of semiconductor (the components on the device are constructed using patterns of insulator *or* conductor *or* semiconductor material whose properties can be changed by doping); **semiconductor** *or* **solid-state laser** = piece of semiconductor bar that has a polished end, and a semi-silvered mirror, generating pulses of photons that reflect inside the bar until they have enough power to leave via the semi-silvered end

COMMENT: semiconductor material (such as silicon) is used as a base for manufacturing integrated circuits and other solid-state components, usually by deposition of various types of doping substances on *or* into its surface

sender *noun* person who sends a message; *the telex machine will check the message by verifying the sender*

senior *or* **senior spotlight** *noun (film)* 5,000 watt spotlight

sense *verb* to examine the state of a device *or* electronic component; *the condition of the switch was sensed by the program; this device senses the holes punched in a paper tape*; **sense switch** = switch on a computer front panel whose state can by examined by the computer; **auto-baud sensing**; *see* SCANNING

sensitive *adjective* which can sense even small changes; *the computer is sensitive even to very slight changes in current; light-sensitive film changes when exposed to light*

sensitivity *noun* **(a)** being sensitive to something **(b)** minimum power of a received signal that is necessary for a receiver to distinguish the signal; *the scanner's sensitivity to small objects* **(c)** *(film)* the degree to which a film emulsion responds to light

sensitize *verb* to make a substance sensitive to something

sensitometer *noun (film)* system which is used to expose film with precisely measured emulsion speed

sensor *noun* electronic device that produces an output dependent upon the condition *or* physical state of a process; *see also* TRANSDUCER; *the sensor's output varies with temperature; the process is monitored by a bank of sensors*; **image sensor** = photoelectric device that produces a signal related to the amount of light falling on it; **sensor glove** = glove that fits over a user's hand and has sensors that detect when the user moves his fingers *or* arm and so control an image on screen; for virtual reality separation

sentinel *noun* marker *or* pointer to a special section of data

separate 1 *adjective* not together; **separate channel signalling** = use of independent communications channel *or* bands in a multichannel system to send the control data and messages **2** *verb* to divide; **separated graphics** = displayed characters that do not take up the whole of a character matrix, resulting in spaces between them

separation *noun* act of separating; **colour separation** = process by which colours are separated into primary colours; **colour separations** = different artwork *or* film for the various colours to be used in multicolour printing

separator *noun* symbol used to distinguish parts of an instruction line in a program, i.e. command and argument; *see also* DELIMITER

sepmag *noun* *(film)* magnetic sound record which is separate from the picture with which it is connected

sequence *noun* **(a)** number of items *or* data arranged as a logical, ordered list; *the sequence of names is arranged alphabetically; the program instructions are arranged in sequence according to line numbers*; **sequence control register (SCR)** *or* **instruction address register** = CPU register that contains the address of the next instruction to be processed; **the logon sequence** = order in which user number, password and other authorization codes are to be entered when attempting to access a system **(b)** a series of musical notes that define a tune **(c)** a series of video frames

sequence shot *noun* *(film)* a long shot in which both cameras and actors move about; used to remove the necessity of shooting close-ups when the action is very intense

sequencer *noun* **(a)** software that allows a user to compose tunes for MIDI instruments, record scores from instruments and mix together multiple tracks **(b)** hardware device that can record or playback a sequence of MIDI notes; *see also* MIDI SEQUENCER

sequential *adjective* arranged in an ordered manner; **sequential batch processing** = completing one job in a batch before the next can be started; **sequential computer** = type of computer, for which each instruction must be completed before the next is started, and so cannot handle parallel processing; **sequential file** *or* **serial file** = stored file whose records are accessed sequentially; **sequential logic** = logical circuit whose output depends on the logic state of the previous inputs; *if the input sequence to the sequential logic circuit is 1101 the output will always be zero (0);* **compare with COMBINATIONAL CIRCUIT**; **sequential operation** = operations executed one after the other; **sequential processing** = data *or* instructions processed sequentially, in the same order as they are accessed; *see also* INDEXED SEQUENTIAL STORAGE

sequential access *noun* method of retrieving data from a storage device by starting at the beginning of the medium (such as tape) and reading each record until the required data is found; **sequential access storage** = storage medium whose data is accessed sequentially

> COMMENT: a tape storage system uses sequential access, since the tape has to be played through until the section required is found. The access time of sequential access storage is dependent on the position in the file of the data, compared with random access that has the same access time for any piece of data in a list

sequentially *adverb* (done) one after the other, in sequence

serial *adjective* (data *or* instructions) ordered sequentially (one after the other) and not in parallel; **serial access** = one item of the data accessed by reading through all data until the correct one is found (as on a tape); **serial-access memory (SAM)** = storage where a particular data item can only be accessed by reading all the previous items in the list (as opposed to random access); **serial adder** = addition circuit that acts on one digit at a time from larger numbers; **serial computer** = computer system that has a single ALU and carries out instructions one at a time; *see also* SEQUENTIAL COMPUTER; **serial data transmission** = transmission of the separate bits that make up data words, one at a time down a single line; **serial file** = stored file whose records are accessed sequentially; **serial input/output (SIO)** = *see* SERIAL TRANSMISSION; **serial input/parallel output (SIPO)** = device that can accept serial data and transmit parallel data; **serial interface** *or* **port** = circuit that converts parallel data in a computer to and from a serial form that allows serial data to be transmitted and received from other equipment; the most common form is the RS232C interface; *parallel connections are usually less trouble to set up and use than serial interfaces, but are usually limited to 20 feet in length*; **serial line Internet protocol** = *see* SLIP; **serial mouse** = mouse which connects to the serial port of a PC and transfers positional data via the serial port; **serial operation** = device that acts on data in a sequential manner; **serial port** = connector and circuit used to convert parallel data in a computer to and from a serial form in which each bit is transmitted one at a time over a single wire; **serial printer** = printer that prints characters one at a time; **serial processing** = data *or* instructions processed sequentially, in the same order as they are retrieved; **serial to parallel converter** = electronic device that converts data from a serial form to a parallel form; **serial transmission** *or* **serial input/output** = data transmitted one bit at a time (this is the normal method of transmission over long distances, since although slower it uses fewer lines and so is cheaper than parallel transmission)

serially *adverb* one after the other *or* in a series; *their transmission rate is 60,000 bits per second through a parallel connection or 20,000 serially*

series *noun* group of related items ordered sequentially; **series circuit** = circuit in which the components are connected serially

> COMMENT: in a series circuit the same current flows through each component; in a parallel circuit the current flow is dependent upon the component impedance

serif *noun* small decorative line attached to parts of characters in certain typefaces; **sans serif** = typeface without serifs

server *noun* dedicated computer *or* peripheral that provides a function to a network; **file server** = small microcomputer and large backing storage device that is used for the management and storage of users' files in a network; **LAN server** = dedicated computer and backing storage facility used by terminals and operators of a LAN; **LAN Server** = network operating system for the PC developed by IBM; **print server** = computer in a network which is dedicated to managing print queues and printers; **server-based application** = application program, stored on a server's hard disk, which can be accessed (and executed) by several users at one time; **server message block (SMB)** = system (developed by Microsoft) which allows a user to access another computer's files and peripherals over a network as if they were local resources

> COMMENT: in a network the hard disk machine is called the 'server' and the

> floppy disk units the 'satellites'. In a star network each satellite is linked individually to a central server

```
Sequent   Computer   Systems'
Platform  division  will  focus
on   hardware   and   software
manufacture,  procurement  and
marketing, with the Enterprise
division   concentrating   on
services      and      server
implementation
```
Computing

server access logs   *see*   ACCESS LOG

service *verb* to check *or* repair *or* maintain a system; *the disk drives were serviced yesterday and are working well*; **service bureau** = company which provides a specialist service, such as outputting DTP files to a typesetter, converting files or creating slides from graphics files; **service contract** = agreement that an engineer will service equipment if it goes wrong

service provider *noun* company that offers users a connection to the Internet; the service provider has a computer that acts as a domain name server and has a high-speed link to the Internet; it provides modem access to the Internet via point-of-presence telephone numbers

services *noun* **(a)** set of functions provided by a device **(b)** *(in an OSI network model)* set of functions provided by one OSI layer for use by a higher layer

servo *or* **servomechanism**   *noun* mechanical device whose position *or* state can be accurately controlled

session *noun* **(a)** period of work **(b)** time during which a program *or* process is running or active **(c)** *(in a PhotoCD)* separate occasion when image data is recorded onto a disc; **session key** = cipher key used for a particular session; **session layer** = layer in the ISO/OSI standard model that makes the connection/disconnection between transmitter and receiver

set 1 *noun* **(a)** number of related data items; **set theory** = mathematics related to numerical sets **(b)** width of a printed typeface; **set size** = measurement of horizontal dimensions in sets (one set equals one point); **set width** = width of the body of a printed character **(c)** radio *or* television receiver; **set-top converter** = device that converts TV signals from a network *or* satellite into a form that can be displayed **(d)** physical layout of a stage *or* filming studio including props and background **2** *verb* **(a)** to make one variable equal to a value **(b)** to define a parameter value; *we set the margin to 80 characters* **(c)** to give a bit the value of 1 **(d)** to compose a text into typeset characters; *the page is set in 12 point Times Roman*; *see also* TYPESET

set up 1 *verb* to initialize *or* define *or* start an application *or* system; *the new computer worked well as soon as the engineer had set it up*; **set-up option** = the choices available when setting up a system; **set-up time** = period of time between a signal to start an operation and the start **2** *noun* **(a)** *(in film production)* the finished arrangement of the scene which is to be shot **(b)** *(in a television system)* the difference between zero level or true black, and the real level of the picture reproduced

setting *noun* **(a)** action of fixing *or* arranging something; **brightness setting** = TV brightness control position; **contrast setting** = TV contrast control position; **tab settings** = preset points along a line, where the printing head *or* cursor will stop for each tabulation command **(b)** action of composing text into typeset characters; *the MS has been sent to the typesetter for setting; setting charges have increased since last year*; **computer setting** = typesetting using a computerized typesetting machine

sex changer *noun* device for changing a female connection to a male or vice versa

sf signalling = SINGLE FREQUENCY SIGNALLING

SGML = STANDARD GENERALIZED MARKUP LANGUAGE hardware-independent standard which defines how documents should be marked up to indicate bolds, italics, margins and so on; *see also* HTML

COMMENT: generally used to code data for database entry or to mark up a book before it is typeset

shade *noun* **(a)** variation in a printed colour due to added black **(b)** quantity of black added to a colour to make it darker

shading *noun* **(a)** showing darker sections of a line drawing by adding dark colour *or* by drawing criss-cross lines **(b)** the adjustment of contrast in a television picture

shadow *noun* area where broadcast signals cannot be received because of an obstacle that blocks the transmission medium; *the mountain casts a shadow over those houses, so they cannot receive any radio broadcasts*

shadow memory *noun* duplicate memory locations accessed by a special code

shadow ROM *noun* read-only shadow memory

shadowmask *noun* sheet with holes placed just behind the front of a colour TV screen to separate the three-colour picture beams

shallow depth *or* **shallow focus** *noun (film)* a small part of the action area which is in clear focus, with the rest of the action blurred

shannon *noun* measure of the information content of a transmission

Shannon's Law *noun* law defining the maximum information carrying capacity of a transmission line

COMMENT: Shannon's Law is defined as B lg(1 + S/N) where B = Bandwidth, lg is logarithm to the base two and S/N is Signal to Noise ratio

shaper *noun* video engineer who is responsible for the quality of a television picture

share *verb* to own *or* use something together with someone else; *the facility is shared by several independent companies;* **share-level access** = security system used to protect resources on a local area network that allows any other user to access a resource if they know the password; **share level security** = network operating system which assigns passwords to resources rather than setting up user accounts to limit access; **shared access** = computer *or* peripheral used by more than one person *or* system; *see also* TIME-SHARING, MULTI-USER; **shared directory** = directory (on a file server or workstation) which can be accessed by several users connected to a network; **shared file** = stored file that can be accessed by more than one user *or* system; **shared line** *or* **party line**= one telephone line shared by a number of subscribers; **shared logic system** = one computer and backing storage device used by a number of people in a network for an application; **shared logic text processor** = word-processing available to a number of users of a shared logic system; **shared network directory** = directory (on a file server or workstation) which can be accessed by several users connected to a network; **shared resources system** = system where one peripheral *or* backing storage device *or* other resource is used by a number of users

shareware *noun* software which is available free to sample, but if kept the user is expected to pay a fee to the writer (often confused with public domain software which is completely free)

```
Internet  users  know  the
dangers   of    'flaming'
(receiving  hostile  comments
following   a   naive   or
ridiculous assertion)
```
Computing

sheet *noun* large piece of paper; **(single) sheet feed** = paper feed system that puts single sheets of paper into a printer, one at a time; **sheet feed attachment** = device which can be attached to a printer to allow single sheets of paper to be fed in automatically

shelf life *noun* maximum storage time of a product before it is no longer guaranteed good to use; *the developer has a shelf life of one year* ·

shell *noun* software which operates between the user and the operating system, often to try and make the operating system more friendly or easier to use; *MS-DOS's COMMAND.COM is a basic shell that interprets commands typed in at the prompt; the Macintosh Finder is a sophisticated shell with a GUI front-end*; **shell out** = *(when running an application)* to exit to the operating system, whilst the original application is still in memory; the user then returns to the application; *I shelled out from the word-processor to check which files were on the floppy, then went back to the program*; **shell script** = scripting language (such as Perl) that runs on a server at the same time as other

software and is used to create programs that can enhance a website, for example to search a site

shell sort *noun* algorithm for sorting data items, in which items can be moved more than one position per sort action

SHF = SUPER HIGH FREQUENCY

shield 1 *noun* metal screen, connected to earth, that prevents harmful voltages *or* interference reaching sensitive electronic equipment **2** *verb* to protect a signal *or* device from external interference *or* harmful voltages; **shielded cable** = cable made up of a conductive core surrounded by an insulator, then a conductive layer to protect the transmitted signal against interference; **shielded twisted pair (STP) cable** = cable consisting of two insulated copper wires twisted around each other (to reduce induction and so interference); the pair of wires are then wrapped in an insulated shielding layer to further reduce interference; **unshielded twisted pair (UTP) cable** = cable made of two insulated copper wires twisted around each other (to reduce induction and so interference), unlike STP cable the pair of wires are not wrapped in any other layer

shift *verb* **(a)** to move a bit *or* word of data left or right by a certain amount (usually one bit); **arithmetic shift** = word *or* data moved one bit to the right *or* left inside a register, losing the bit shifted off the end; **cyclic shift** = rotation of bits in a word with the previous last bit inserted in the first bit position; **logical shift** = data movement to the left *or* right in a word, the bits falling outside the word boundary are discarded, the free positions are filled with zeros; **shift register** = temporary storage into which data can be shifted **(b)** to change from one character set to another, allowing other characters (such as capitals) to be used; **shift character** = transmitted character code that indicates that the following code is to be shifted; **shift code** = method of increasing total possible bit combinations by using a number of bits to indicate that the following code is to be shifted

shift key *noun* key on a keyboard that switches secondary functions for keys, such as another character set, by changing the output to upper case

shoot *verb* to take a picture or record a video sequence with a camera; *they shot hundreds of feet of film, but none of it was any good; the programme was shot on location in Spain*

shopping basket *or* **shopping cart** *noun* software that runs on a web server and provides an electronic version of a real shopping basket; the software allows a visitor to the web site to view items in the catalogue, add items to their shopping basket and then pay for the goods at an electronic checkout; some products (such a software) can then be downloaded from the web site and use immediately; *see also* REAL-TIME AUTHORIZATION, SECURE WEBSITE

short circuit **1** *noun* electrical connection of very low resistance between two points **2** *verb* to connect two points together with a (very low resistance) link; **short-circuited** = two points that are electrically connected, usually accidentally

COMMENT: short circuits can be accidental, due to bad circuit design or used as a protective measure

short end *noun* *(film)* a section of unexposed film or magnetic tape, which is too short to be used, at the end of a reel

short focal-length lens *or* **short-focus lens** *see* WIDE-ANGLE LENS

short message service (SMS) system that allows short text messages to be sent between and to mobile telephones; the service depends upon the telephone company

short-run *adjective* with a printrun of only a few hundred copies; *a printer specializing in short-run printing; the laser printer is good for short-run leaflets*

short wave (SW) *noun* radio communications frequency below 60 metres; **short-wave receiver** = radio receiver able to pick up broadcasts on the short wave bands

shortcut *noun* *(in Microsoft Windows)* feature that links an icon to a file or application; *place shortcut icons on the Windows Desktop so that you can start an application without using the menu commands; a shortcut has the same icon as the original file but has a tiny arrow in the bottom left-hand corner; the shortcut is not a duplicate of the original, rather it is a pointer to the original file*

shorten *verb* to make shorter; *we had to shorten the file to be able to save it on one floppy*

shot *noun* the continuous recording of action or images by a film camera in a small number of frames

shotgun microphone *noun* long, highly directional microphone; *see* RIFLE MICROPHONE

show copy *noun* selected copy of a finished film, video or programme which is to be shown to an audience

show-through *noun* text printed on one side of a piece of paper that can be seen from the other

shrink *verb* to become smaller; *the drawing was shrunk to fit the space* (NOTE: shrinks - shrank - has shrunk)

shut down *verb* to switch off and stop the functions of a machine *or* system

shut-off mechanism *noun* device which stops a process in case of fault

COMMENT: most hard disks have an automatic shut-off mechanism to pull the head back from the read position when the power is turned off

shutter *noun* **(a)** revolving device which protects a film from light at the aperture in a camera and diminishes the projection light in a projector while the film is moving at the aperture **(b)** device to control intensity of a spotlight

shutter control *noun* **(a)** device on a camera which diminishes exposure by partly closing the shutter **(b)** camera device which slowly opens and closes the shutter in order to attain fade-in and fade-out effects

shutter speed *noun* time span for which a shutter is open during the required frame exposure

shuttle search *noun* capacity to play back a film, video and audio tape in both directions and to duplicate the picture over a large range of speeds

SI units = SYSTÈME INTERNATIONAL UNITS international measurement units such as candela, lumen, and ampere; *see also* MKS

sibilance *noun* excess signal recorded when certain letters such as 's' are spoken

side lobe *noun* side sections of an aerial's response pattern

sideband *noun* frequency band of a modulated signal, a little above or below the carrier frequency; *upper sideband; lower sideband;* **double sideband** = modulation technique whose frequency spectrum contains two modulated signals above and below the unmodulated carrier frequency; **double sideband suppressed carrier (DSBSC)** = modulation technique that uses two modulated signal sidebands, but no carrier signal; **single sideband** = modulated signal filtered to leave just one sideband, usually the upper (this is very economical on bandwidth but requires more complex circuitry)

sideways ROM *noun* software which allows selection of a particular memory bank *or* ROM device

SIG = SPECIAL INTEREST GROUP

sign 1 *noun* polarity of a number *or* signal (i.e. whether it is positive *or* negative); **sign and magnitude** *or* **sign and modules** = way of representing numbers, where one bit shows if the number is positive *or* negative (usually 0 = positive, 1 = negative); **sign bit** = single bit that indicates if a binary number is positive *or* negative (usually 0 = positive, 1 = negative) **2** *verb* **(a)** to write your name in a special way, to show that you have written *or* approved a document; *the letter is signed by the managing director; all cheques have to be signed by two directors* **(b)** *(of a user)* to identify oneself to a computer using a personalized signature; **signed field** = storage field which can contain a number and a sign bit; **to sign off** = to logoff a system; **to sign on** = to logon to a system

signal 1 *noun* **(a)** generated analog *or* digital waveform used to carry information **(b)** short message used to carry control codes; *the signal received from the computer contained the answer*; **signal conditioning** = converting or translating a signal into a form that is accepted by a device; **signal converter** = device that converts signals from one format to another, usually from UHF to VHF for TV signals; **signal element** = smallest basic unit used when transmitting digital data; *the signal element in this system is a sort voltage pulse, indicating a binary one; the signal elements for the radio transmission system are 10mS of 40KHz and 10mS of 60KHz for binary 0 and 1 respectively*; **signal generator** = device that can produce various signals of varying amplitude, frequency and shape; **signal to noise ratio (S/N)** = ratio of the amplitude of the transmitted signal to the noise on the received signal; **signal processing** = processing of signals to extract the information contained; *the system is used by students doing research on signal processing techniques; the message was recovered by carrier signal processing* **2** *verb* to send a radio signal *or* a message to a computer; *signal to the network that we are busy*

signalling *noun* **(a)** method used by a transmitter to warn a receiver that a message is to be sent **(b)** communication to the transmitter about the state of the receiver; **in band signalling** = use of a normal voice grade channel for data transmission

signature *noun* **(a)** name written in a special way by someone; *do you recognize the signature on the cheque?* **(b)** series of printed and folded pages in a book (usually 8, 16 or 32 pages) **(c)** special authentication code which a user gives, prior to access to a system *or* prior to the execution of a task; **signature analysis using functional analysis** = *see* SAFE

> COMMENT: in some systems this can be written by the user or determined from the user in some way (such as fingerprint or eye scan: these are very advanced and secure systems)

significance *noun* special meaning

significant *adjective* which has a special meaning; **significant digit codes** *or* **faceted codes** = codes which indicate various details of an item, by assigning each one a value

signify *verb* to mean; *a carriage return code signifies the end of an input line*

silicon *noun* element with semiconductor properties, used in crystal form as a base for IC manufacture; **silicon chip** = small piece of silicon in and on the surface of which a complete circuit *or* logic function has been produced (by depositing other substances *or* by doping); **silicon disk** _or_ **RAM disk** = section of RAM that is made to look and behave like a high-speed disk drive; **silicon foundry** = works where pure silicon crystals are grown, sliced into wafers and cleaned ready for use; **silicon gate** = type of MOS transistor gate that uses doped silicon regions instead of a metal oxide to provide the function; _see also_ MOS, GATE; **silicon on sapphire (SOS)** = manufacturing technique that allows MOS devices to be constructed onto a sapphire substrate for high speed operation; **Silicon Glen** = area of Scotland where many Scottish IT companies are based; **silicon transistor** = microelectronic transistor manufactured on a silicon semiconductor base; **Silicon Valley** = (i) area in California where many US semiconductor manufacturers are based; (ii) part of the Thames Valley, west of London, where many British IT companies are based; **silicon wafer** = thin slice of a pure silicon crystal, usually around 4 inches in diameter on which integrated circuits are produced (these are then cut out of the wafer to produce individual chips)

COMMENT: silicon is used in the electronics industry as a base material for integrated circuits. It is grown as a long crystal which is then sliced into wafers before being etched or treated, producing several hundred chips per wafer. Other materials, such as germanium or gallium arsenide, are also used as a base for ICs

---

silk _noun_ fine white material used to diffuse light when photographing a subject

silver halide _noun_ light-sensitive formula used when making film emulsions

SIMD = SINGLE INSTRUCTION STREAM MULTIPLE DATA STREAM architecture of a parallel computer that has a number of ALUs and data buses with one control unit

SIMM = SINGLE IN-LINE MEMORY MODULE small, compact circuit board with an edge connector along one edge that carries densely-packed memory chips; _you can expand the main memory of your PC by plugging in two more SIMMs_

simple device _noun_ MCI device that does not require a data file for playback, such as a CD drive used to play audio CDs

simple mail transfer protocol (SMTP) standard protocol which allows electronic mail messages to be transferred from one system to another

simple network management protocol (SNMP) network management system which defines how status data is sent from monitored nodes back to a control station; SNMP is able to work with virtually any type of network hardware and software

simplex _noun_ data transmission in a single direction (NOTE: opposite is **duplex**)

simplify _verb_ to make something simpler

simulate _verb_ to copy the behaviour of a system _or_ device with another; _this software simulates the action of an aeroplane_

simulation _noun_ operation where a computer is made to imitate a real life situation _or_ a machine, and shows how something works _or_ will work in the future; _simulation techniques have reached a high degree of sophistication_

simulator _noun_ device that simulates another system; **flight simulator** = computer program which allows a user to pilot a plane, showing a realistic control panel and moving scenes (either as training programme _or_ computer game)

simulcast _noun_ to broadcast a programme at the same time on both television and radio

simultaneous _adjective_ which takes place at the same time as something else; **simultaneous processing** = two or more processes executed at the same time; **simultaneous transmission** = transmission of data _or_ control codes in two directions at the same time (NOTE: same as duplex)

simultaneously _adverb_ at the same time

COMMENT: true simultaneous processing requires two processors, but can be imitated by switching rapidly between two tasks with a single processor

---

sin _or_ **sine** _noun_ mathematical function defined as: the sine of an angle (in a right-angled triangle) is equal to the ratio of opposite to hypotenuse sides

sine wave _noun_ waveform that is the sine function with time (classic wave shape, changing between a maximum and minimum with a value of zero at zero time)

> COMMENT: sine waves are usually the basic carrier waveform shape in modulation systems

single *adjective* only one; **single address instruction** = machine code instruction that contains one operator and one address; **single address message** = message with a single destination; *(in an FDDI network)* **single attachment station (SAS)** = station with only one port through which to attach to the network; SAS stations are connected to the FDDI ring through a concentrator; **single board computer (SBC)** = micro *or* mini computer whose components are all contained on a single printed circuit board; **single density disk (SD)** = standard magnetic disk and drive able to store data; **single frame** = (i) a sole image in a strip of film or video tape; (ii) the slow exposure or projection of an individual picture; **single-frame shooting** *or* **single framing** = use of a camera release device for every frame of exposed film in order to accelerate action when the film is projected at standard speeds; **single frequency signalling** *or* **sf signalling** = use of various frequency signals to represent different control codes; **single function software** = applications program that can only be used for one kind of task; **single in-line memory module (SIMM)** = small, compact circuit board with an edge connector along one edge that carries densely-packed memory chips; **single in-line package (SIP)** = electronic component which has all its leads on one side of its package; **single instruction stream multiple data stream (SIMD)** = architecture of a parallel computer that has a number of ALUs and data buses with one control unit; **single instruction stream single data stream (SISD)** = architecture of a serial computer, that has one ALU and data bus, with one control unit; **single key response** = software that requires only one key to be pressed (no CR) to select an option; **single line display** = small screen which displays a single line of characters at a time; **single mode** *or* **monomode** = optic fibre which allows the light signal to travel along only one path; **single operand instruction** = *see* SINGLE ADDRESS INSTRUCTION; **single operation** = communications system that allows data to travel in only one direction at a time

(controlled by codes S/O = send only, R/O = receive only, S/R = send or receive); *see also* SIMPLEX; **single pole** = switch that connects two points; **single scan non segmented** = video tape system that allows freeze framing by recording one complete television picture field at a time; **single sheet feed** = device attached to a printer to allow single sheets of paper to be used instead of continuous stationery; **single shot** = the exposure of one frame of film at a time, as in animation work; **single sideband** = modulated signal filtered to leave just one sideband, usually the upper (this is very economical on bandwidth, but needs more circuitry); **single-sided disk (SSD)** = floppy disk that can only be used to store data on one side, because of the way it is manufactured *or* formatted; **single speed** = definition of the speed at which a CD-ROM is spun by a drive - normally 230rpm; **single standard** = a video tape recorder, television monitor or other system which has the ability to receive only video signals of one standard, such as NTSC, PAL, or SECAM; **single step** = to execute a program one instruction at a time; **single-strike ribbon** = printer ribbon which can only be used once; *compare with* MULTI-STRIKE PRINTER RIBBON; **single system** = method of recording both picture and sound at the same time on the same film strip; **single-system image** = operational view of multiple networks, distributed databases or multiple computer systems as if they were one system; **single time code** = *see* STC; **single-user system** = computer system which only a single user can use (as opposed to a multi-user system)

sink *noun* receiving end of a communications line; **heat sink** = metal device used to conduct heat away from an electronic component to prevent damage; **sink tree** = description in a routing table of all the paths in a network to a destination (NOTE: the opposite of sink is **source**)

sinusoidal *adjective* waveform *or* motion that is similar to a sine wave; *the carrier has a sinusoidal waveform*

SIO = SERIAL INPUT/OUTPUT

SIP = SINGLE IN-LINE PACKAGE

siphoning *noun* transmission of a direct broadcast TV programme over a cable network

SIPO = SERIAL INPUT/PARALLEL OUTPUT

SISD = SINGLE INSTRUCTION STREAM SINGLE DATA STREAM

SISO = SERIAL INPUT/SERIAL OUTPUT

site *noun* place where something is based

site licence *noun* licence between a software publisher and a user which allows any number of users in that site to use the software; *we have negotiated a good deal for the site licence for our 1200 employees in our HQ*

site poll *verb* to poll all the terminals *or* devices in a particular location *or* area; *see also* POLLING

sixteen-bit system *noun* (microcomputer system or CPU) which handles data in sixteen-bit words

sixteen mm film *or* **16 mm** *noun* film which is 16 mm wide, with 40 frames to the foot and 24 frames per second

sixteenmo *or* **16mo** *noun* size of a book page, where the sheet of paper has been folded four times to make a signature of 32 pages

size 1 *noun* physical dimensions of an image *or* object *or* page; *the size of the print has been increased to make it easier to read*; **page size** = physical dimensions of a printed page; *our page sizes vary from 220 x 110 to 360 x 220*; **screen size** = (i) number of characters a computer display can show horizontally and vertically; (ii) size of a display screen, normally measured diagonally across the screen; *a 15-inch screen* **2** *verb* to calculate the size of a picture and reduce *or* enlarge the artwork to fit

sizing *noun* reducing *or* enlarging a picture to fit; *photographs can be edited by cropping, sizing, etc*

sketch 1 *noun* rough drawing made rapidly **2** *verb* to make a rough rapid drawing

skew 1 *noun* (a) the amount by which something which is not correctly aligned (b) a television picture distortion in a zig zag shape which can be caused by a mechanical fault in the video tape motion or tension **2** *verb* to align something incorrectly; *this page is badly skewed*

skip *verb* (a) to transmit radio waves over an abnormally long distance due to the reflective properties of the atmosphere (b) to ignore an instruction in a sequence of instructions; *the printer skipped the next three lines of text*; **skip capability** = feature of certain word-processors to allow the user to jump backwards *or* forwards by a quantity of text in a document; **high-speed skip** = rapid movement of paper in a printer, ignoring the normal line advance; **skip frame** = in motion picture printing, when only particular frames are chosen and printed at systematic intervals in order to create the effect of speeded up action

sky filter *noun* lens filter which has colour only on its upper half and is used to diminish the impact of atmospheric haze

sky pan *noun* large lighting unit with a matte white reflector used for lighting backdrops

slash *or* **oblique stroke** *noun* printing sign (/) like stroke sloping to the right

slashed zero *noun* a printed *or* written sign (0 to distinguish O from 0)

slave *noun* (a) remote secondary computer *or* terminal controlled by a central computer; **slave processor** = dedicated processor that is controlled by a master processor (b) a recorder which dubs playbacks from a master tape; the video tape used for this dubbing process

sleep *noun* state of a system that is waiting for a signal (log-on) before doing anything

sleeve *noun* cover for a magnetic disk *or* for a record

slew *noun* rapid movement of paper in a printer, ignoring the normal line advance

slice architecture *noun* construction of a large word size CPU by joining a number of smaller word size blocks

slicing *noun* cutting thin round wafers from a bar of silicon crystal

slide 1 *noun* (a) transparent photograph which is projected into a camera in order to be broadcast on television (b) transparency which is to be projected by transmitted light; **slide film** = group of 35mm slides which are shown separately in a cartridge slide projector; **slide projector** = device that projects slide images onto a screen; **slide/sync recorder** = audio tape recorder that can control a slide projector in sync with music *or* commentary; **slide show** = feature of a presentation graphics software in which slides (static images) are displayed in a sequence under the control of the presenter **2** *verb* to move smoothly across a surface; *the disk cover slides on and off easily*

slip pages *or* **slip proofs** *noun* proofs, where each page of text is printed on a separate piece of paper

slit *noun (in photographic sound)* a thin aperture through which the film is exposed when recording, and scanned when duplicating

slot 1 *noun* **(a)** long thin hole; *the system disk should be inserted into the left-hand slot on the front of the computer*; **expansion slot** = expansion connector available on a computer's backplane *or* motherboard; *there are two free slots in the micro, you only need one for the add-on board* **(b)** **message slot** = number of bits that can hold a message which circulates round a ring network **2** *verb* to insert an object into a hole; *the disk slots into one of the floppy drive apertures*

slow lens *noun* camera lens with a highest aperture of f12.8

slow motion *noun* **(a)** playing back of a video tape *or* disk sequence slower than recorded; *the film switched to slow motion; play the film again in slow motion* **(b)** filming with a motion picture camera with the film moving at a more accelerated speed than normal so that when the film is projected at a normal rate, the action seems to be slowed down

slow scan *noun* television transmission and scanning at a slower frame rate than usual; **slow scan television** = television images transmitted line by line over a transmission link at a slow rate

SLSI = SUPER LARGE SCALE INTEGRATION

slug *noun* piece of metal type, with a character at the end

slur *noun* **(a)** printed image which is blurred because of movement during printing **(b)** distortion of voice during transmission

small *adjective* not large; **small caps** = printing style, with capital letters which are the same size as ordinary letters

small computer systems interface (SCSI) *noun* standard high-speed parallel interface used to connect computers to peripheral devices (such as disk drives and scanners)

COMMENT: Fast-SCSI allows data to be transferred at a higher rate than with the original SCSI specification; SCSI-2 is a newer standard that provides a wider data bus and transfers data faster than the original SCSI specification; Wide-SCSI is a development that provides a wider data bus than the original SCSI specification, so can transfer more data at a time; SCSI is the current standard used to interface high-capacity, high-performance disk drives to computers; smaller disk drives are connected with an IDE interface, which is slower, but cheaper. SCSI replaced the older ESDI interface and allows several (normally eight) peripherals to be connected, in a daisy-chain, to one controller

small scale integration (SSI) *noun* integrated circuit with 1 to 10 components

Smalltalk object-oriented programming language developed by Xerox; often used to develop GUI applications

smart *adjective* intelligent; **smart card** = plastic card with a memory and microprocessor embedded in it, so that it can be used for direct money transfer *or* for identification of the user; **smart terminal** *or* **intelligent terminal** = computer terminal that is able to process information; **smart wiring hub** = network hub *or* concentrator which can transmit status information back to a managing station and allows management software to configure each port remotely; *using this management software, I can shut down Tom's port on the remote smart wiring hub*

SMATV = SATELLITE MASTER ANTENNA TELEVISION distributor of cable or microwave satellite broadcasts to separate viewers from a central antenna

SMB = SERVER MESSAGE BLOCK system (developed by Microsoft) which allows a user to access another computer's files and peripherals over a network as if they were local resources

smog *see* ELECTRONIC SMOG

SMPTE division type *noun* timing format which specifies the number of frames per second used, and in which time is shown as hours, minutes, seconds, frames; standard SMPTE division types are 24, 25 and 30 frames per second

SMPTE offset *noun* MIDI event that defines when a MIDI file is to be played back

SMPTE time code *noun* method of assigning a unique identifying number to each frame in a video sequence

SMPTE = SOCIETY FOR MOTION PICTURE AND TELEVISION ENGINEERS organization that defines standards for television production systems; *the SMPTE time code standard is widely used to synchronize audio and video equipment using hours, minutes, seconds, frame data*

SMS *see* SHORT MESSAGE SERVICE

SMT = SURFACE-MOUNT TECHNOLOGY method of manufacturing circuit boards in which the electronic components are bonded directly onto the surface of the board rather than being inserted into holes and soldered into place; *surface-mount technology is faster and more space-efficient than soldering*

SMT *see* SURFACE-MOUNT TECHNOLOGY

SMTP = SIMPLE MAIL TRANSFER PROTOCOL standard protocol allowing electronic mail messages to be transferred from one system to another

SNA = SYSTEMS NETWORK ARCHITECTURE design methods developed by IBM which define how communications in a network should occur and allow different hardware to communicate

snapshot *noun* (a) recording of all the states of a computer at a particular instant (b) recording of a screen full of information at an instant (c) personal photograph taken quickly

snd = SOUND (a) *(in a PC)* filename extension used to indicate a file that contains digitized sound data (b) *(in a Macintosh)* the resource that contains sound information

SNMP = SIMPLE NETWORK MANAGEMENT PROTOCOL

SNOBOL = STRING ORIENTATED SYMBOLIC LANGUAGE high-level programming language that uses string processing methods

snoot *noun* spotlight attachment which is used to decrease the light beam's size and assist the placing of the beam

snow *noun* television image distortion in the form of random moving white dots due to a low quality signal

soak *verb* to run a program *or* device continuously for a period of time to make sure it functions correctly; *the device was soak-tested prior to delivery*

Society for Motion Picture and Television Engineers *see* SMPTE

socket *noun* device with a set of holes, into which a plug fits; **female socket** = hole into which a pin *or* plug can be inserted to make an electrical connection

socket driver *see* WINSOCK

SOCKS *(network)* protocol developed to support the transfer of TCP/IP traffic through a proxy server; commonly used to provide a way for users on a local area network to access the Internet via a single shared connection

sodium light *noun* lighting of a screen with sodium vapour which creates a yellow light, the sole colour which is unable to be photographed; used to provide a clear background for travelling matte shots

SOF = SOUND-ON-FILM indication of synchronised picture and sound on film

soft *adjective* (a) *(in graphics)* one shape that gradually changes to another; **soft edge** = a blurred edge to the image area of a picture, used in matte or wipe effects; **soft focus** = creating an image which is less sharply defined than normal; **soft goods** = software that is purchased and paid for at an online shop and is then downloaded directly onto your computer instead of receiving the product by post; **soft light** = lighting unit which creates a bright, diffused illumination (b) *(material)* that loses its magnetic effects when removed from a magnetic field (c) *(data)* that is not permanently stored in hardware (soft usually refers to data stored on magnetic medium); **soft copy** = text listed on screen (as opposed to hard copy on paper); **soft font** = fonts *or* typefaces stored on a disk, which can be downloaded *or* sent to a printer and stored in temporary memory *or* RAM; **soft hyphen** = hyphen which is inserted when a word is split at the end of a line, but is not present when the word is written normally; **soft keys** = keys which can be changed by means of a program; **soft keyboard** = keyboard where the functions of the keys can be changed by programs; **soft-sectored disk** = disk where the sectors are described by an address and start code data written onto it when the disk is formatted; **soft zone** = text area to the left of the right margin in a word-processed document, where if a word does not fit completely, a hyphen is automatically inserted

software *noun* **(a)** any program *or* group of programs which instructs the hardware on how it should perform, including operating systems, word processors and applications programs; **applications software** = programs which are used by the user to perform a certain task; **software compatible** = (computer) which will load and run programs written for another computer; **software development** = processes required to produce working programs from an initial idea; **software documentation** = information, notes and diagrams that describe the function, use and operation of a piece of software; **software engineer** = person who can write working software to fit an application; **software engineering** = field of study covering all software-related subjects; = **software flow control** = *see* XON/OFF; **software house** = company which develops and sells computer programs; **software interrupt** = high priority program generated signal, requesting the use of the central processor; **software library** = number of specially written routines, stored in a library file which can be inserted into a program, saving time and effort; **software licence** = agreement between a user and a software house, giving details of the rights of the user to use or copy software; **software life cycle** = period of time when a piece of software exists, from its initial design to the moment when it becomes out of date; **software maintenance** = updates and modifications to a software package to make sure the program is up to date; **software modem** = modem that uses the main computer's processor to carry out the functions of a

modem including all the signal processing required to modulate and demodulate data signals; external modems, in comparison, have their own processing components and transfer data to and from the computer, leaving the main computer's processor to carry on its other tasks; **software-only video playback** = full-motion video standard that can be played back on any multimedia computer, and does not need special hardware - the decompression and display is carried out by software drivers; any software-only standard does not normally provide as sharp an image as a hardware compression system (such as MPEG) or full-screen playback; **software package** = complete set of programs (and the manual) that allow a certain task to be performed; **software piracy** = illegal copying of software for sale; **software quality assurance (SQA)** = making sure that software will perform as intended; **software reliability** = ability of a piece of software to perform the task required correctly; **software specification** = detailed information about a piece of software's abilities, functions and methods; **software system** = all the programs required for one or more tasks; **software tool** = program used in the development of other programs; **systems software** = programs which direct the basic functions, input-output control, etc., of a computer **(b)** programmes for broadcast which are presented on electronic equipment **(c)** films, audio tapes and audio disks that are commercially accessible (NOTE: no plural for **software**; for the plural say · **pieces of software**)

solar *adjective* referring to the sun; **solar cell** = component that converts the light of the sun into electrical energy; **solar power** = (electrical) power derived from the sun; **solar-powered calculator** = calculator with a battery powered by light

solarization *or* **solarisation** *noun* **(a)** flare in a film image due to the film having been struck by light during processing **(b)** photographic effect where the picture image colours or tones are reversed, such as normally light areas becoming darker and vice versa; an almost identical effect can be created by video techniques

solder 1 *noun* soft lead which, when melted, forms a solid electrical connection to join wires, pins and metal components (NOTE: no plural) **2** *verb* to join two pieces of metal with molten solder

solderless *adjective* which does not use solder; (board, such as a breadboard) which does not need solder

solenoid *noun* mechanical device operated by an electromagnetic field

solid *adjective* (printed text) with no spaces between the lines; **solid colour** = colour that can be displayed or printed without dithering; **solid font printer** = printer which uses a whole character shape to print in one movement, such as a daisy wheel printer; **solid modelling** = function in graphics that creates three-dimensional solid-looking objects by shading

solid-state *adjective* referring to semiconductor devices; **solid-state device** = electronic device that operates by using the effects of electrical *or* magnetic signals in a solid semiconductor material; **solid-state memory device** = solid-state memory storage device (usually in the form of RAM or ROM chips)

solution *noun* (a) answer to a problem (b) liquid in which certain chemicals have been dissolved

solve *verb* to find the answer to a problem

son file *noun* latest working version of a file; *compare with* FATHER FILE, GRANDFATHER FILE

sonar *noun* device that uses sound waves to determine the state and depth of water

song *noun* complete musical tune

song key *noun* musical key used to play a MIDI song

sonic *adjective* referring to sound; (sound signals) within the human hearing range (20 - 20,000Hz); **ultrasonic** = (sound pressure waves) at a frequency above the audio band (above 20kHz)

Sony electronics company that has developed a wide range of products including the Betamax video system and camcorder

sophisticated *adjective* technically advanced; *a sophisticated desktop publishing program*

sophistication *noun* being technically advanced; *the sophistication of the new package is remarkable*

sort *verb* to put data into order, according to a system, on the instructions of the user; *to sort addresses into alphabetical order; to sort orders according to account numbers*; **bubble sort** = sorting method which repeatedly exchanges various pairs of data items until they are in order; **sort/merge** = program which allows new files to be sorted and then merged in correct order into existing files

sortkey *noun* field in a stored file that is used to sort the file; *the orders were sorted according to dates by assigning the date field as the sortkey*

SOS = SILICON ON SAPPHIRE

Sound Recorder utility included with Microsoft Windows that allows a user to play back digitized sound files (the .WAV standard) or record sound onto disk

sound *noun* noise *or* something which can be heard; **sound advance** = distance between a film frame and its sound track on a film due to the difference in position of the sound head and camera aperture; **sound bandwidth** = range of frequencies that a human ear can register, normally defined as the range from 20Hz to 20KHz; **sound capture** = conversion of an analog sound into a digital form that can be used by a computer; *see also* ANALOG TO DIGITAL; **sound card** = expansion card which produces analog sound signals under the control of a computer; *this software lets you create almost any sound - but you can only hear them if you have a sound card fitted*; **sound chip** = electronic device that can generate sound signals; **sound drum** = roller which holds the film steady as a scanning-beam slit scans, or a magnetic head reads, the sound track; **sound editor** = person in charge of the putting together, synchronising and editing of all sound tracks on a film; also gives the sound engineer the cue sheets to use in dubbing; **sound effects** = artificially produced sounds used when recording to give the impression of real sounds; *all the sound effects for the film were produced electronically*; **sound file** = file stored on disk that contains sound data; this can either be a digitized analog sound signal or notes for a MIDI instrument; **sound gate** = gate which can be used to replace the sound drum to hold the film in alignment with the scanning beam;

sound head = device that converts to or from a magnetic signal stored on tape; **sound hood** = cover which cuts down the noise from a noisy printer; **sound-on-film** = *see* SOF; **sound pressure level (SPL)** = measurement of the magnitude of the pressure wave conveying sound; **sound speed** = standard exposure rate of sound film which is 24 frames per second; **sound synthesizer** = device able to produce complex real sounds by the combination of various generated signals; **sound track** = track on a film on which the sound is recorded; **sound waves** = pressure waves produced by vibrations, which are transmitted through air (or a solid) and detected by the human ear or a microphone (in which they are converted to electrical signals)

SoundBlaster sound card for PC compatibles developed by Creative Labs that allows sounds to be recorded to disk and played back; also includes an FM synthesizer and a MIDI port

soundproof *adjective* which does not allow sound to pass through; *the telephone is installed in a soundproof booth*

source *noun* **(a)** point where a transmitted signal enters a network (NOTE: opposite is **sink**) **(b)** name of a terminal on an FET device **(c)** original *or* initial point; **source address filtering** = feature of some bridges which detects a particular address in the received packet and either rejects or forwards the data; **source book** = multimedia book from which elements or objects are copied and used in another book; **source code** = set of codes written by the programmer which cannot be directly executed by the computer, but has to be translated into an object code program by a compiler *or* interpreter; **source document** = form *or* document from which data is extracted prior to entering it into a database; **source file** = program written in source language, which is then converted to machine code by a compiler; **source listing** = (i) listing of a text in its original form; (ii) listing of a source program; *(in a drag and drop operation)* **source object** = the object that is first clicked on and dragged; *see also* DESTINATION OBJECT, DRAG IMAGE; **source program** = program, prior to translation, written in a programming

language by a programmer; **source routing** = method (originally developed by IBM for its Token Ring networks) of moving data between two networks which examines the data within the token and passes the data to the correct station; **source transparent routing (SRT)** = standard developed by IBM and the IEEE; it allows IBM networks and non-IBM Token Ring networks to be bridged and so exchange data

source language *noun* **(a)** language in which a program is originally written in **(b)** language of a program prior to translation (NOTE: opposite is **object** *or* **target language**)

space 1 *noun* **(a)** gap (printed *or* displayed in text); **space bar** = long bar at the bottom of a keyboard, which inserts a space into the text when pressed **(b)** transmitted signal representing a binary zero (NOTE: opposite is **mark**) **(c)** region extending out and around from the earth's atmosphere; **space craft** = vehicle that travels in space; **space station** = space craft which remains in orbit for a long time, and can be visited by other space vehicles **2** *verb* to spread out text; *the line of characters was evenly spaced out across the page*

spacer *noun* **intelligent spacer** = facility on a word-processing system used to prevent words from being hyphenated *or* separated at the wrong point

spacing *noun* way in which spaces are inserted in a printed text; *the spacing on some lines is very uneven*

spanning tree *noun* method of creating a logical topology for a widely-spread network that does not contain any loops

SPARC = SCALAR PROCESSOR ARCHITECTURE RISC processor designed by Sun Microsystems which is used in its range of workstations

spark printer *noun* thermal printer which produces characters on thermal paper by electric sparks

sparks *noun (film) (informal)* electrician

sparse array *noun* data matrix structure containing mainly zero *or* null entries

spatial measurement *noun* method of allowing a computer to determine the position of a pointer within three dimensions (often using a sensitive glove)

speaker *see* LOUDSPEAKER

spec *(informal)* = SPECIFICATIONS

special *adjective* which is different *or* not usual; **special character** = character which is not a normal one in a certain font (such as a certain accent *or* a symbol); **special effects** = (i) illusory effects required for a scene which are produced through the use of special equipment; (ii) a video mixer which enables parts of two or more pictures to be montaged and displayed on the screen; **special purpose** = system designed for a specific *or* limited range of applications; **special sort** = extra printing character not in the standard font range

special interest group (SIG) *noun* group (within a larger club) which is interested in a particular aspect of software or hardware; *our local computer club has a SIG for comms and networking*

specialist *noun* expert in a certain field of study; *you need a specialist programmer to help devise a new word-processing program*

specialize *verb* to study and be an expert in a subject; *he specializes in the design of CAD systems*

specific code *noun* binary code which directly operates the central processing unit, using only absolute addresses and values

specifications *noun* detailed information about what is to be supplied *or* about a job to be done; **high specification** *or* **high spec** = high degree of accuracy *or* large number of features; *high spec cabling needs to be very carefully handled*; **program specification** = detailed information about a program's abilities, features and methods; **the work is not up to specification** *or* **does not meet the customer's specifications** = the product was not manufactured in the way which was detailed in the specifications; **to work to standard specifications** = to work to specifications which are accepted anywhere in the same industry

specificity *noun* ratio of non-relevant entries not retrieved to the total number of non-relevant entries contained in a file, database or library

specify *verb* to state clearly what is needed

spectrum *noun* range of frequencies; range of colours; **spectrum analyzer** = electronic test equipment that displays the amplitudes of a number of frequencies in a signal

speech *noun* speaking *or* making words with the voice; **speech chip** = integrated circuit which generates sounds (usually phonemes) which when played together sound like human speech; **speech plus** = method of transmitting a bandlimited speech signal and a number of low speed data signals in a voice grade channel; **speech processor** = device that alters speech, such as a scrambler; **speech quality** = sound recorded at a low bandwidth with a small sample size; *in CD-i speech quality is Level C with 4-bit samples and a rate of 18.9KHz*; **speech recognition** = analysing spoken words in such a way that they can be processed in a computer to recognize spoken words and commands; **speech signal** = signal which transmits spoken words; **speech synthesis** = production of spoken words by a speech synthesizer; **speech synthesizer** = device which takes data from a computer and outputs it as spoken words, often by combining a series of phonemes; *see also* PHONEME

speech conveys information, and the primary task of computer speech processing is the transmission and reception of that information

Personal Computer World

speed *noun* **(a)** measure of the sensitivity of a photographic material (film *or* paper) to light; *high-speed film is very sensitive to light*; *see* ASA **(b)** time taken for a movement divided by the distance travelled; **playback speed** = rate at which tape *or* film travels past a playback head; **speed of loop** = method of benchmarking a computer by measuring the number of loops executed in a certain time

spellcheck *verb* to check the spelling in a text by comparing it with a dictionary held in the computer

spellchecker *or* **spelling checker** *noun* dictionary of correctly spelled words, held in a computer, and used to check the spelling of a text; *the program will be upgraded with a word-processor and a spelling checker*

spherical aberration *or* **distortion** *noun* optical distortion causing lines to appear curved

spherical optics *plural noun* camera or spotlight lenses which have surfaces with different curvatures which are used to create changes in the paths followed by light rays

spherization *noun* special effect provided by a computer graphics program that converts an image into a sphere, or 'wraps' the image over a spherical shape

spider *noun* program that searches through the millions of pages that make up the world wide web for new information, changes or pages that have been deleted; these changes are then added to a search engine index to ensure that it is always up to date

spike *noun* very short duration voltage

spill *or* **spill light** *noun* unwanted light created by a diffusion of light along the principal beam of a light source

spillage *noun* situation when too much data is being processed and cannot be contained in a buffer

spin *verb* to turn round fast; *the disk was spun by the drive; the disk drive motor spins at a constant velocity* (NOTE: spinning - span - spun)

spindle *noun* device which grips and spins a disc in its centre hole

spindling *noun* turning a disk by hand

spine *noun* back edge of the book which is covered by the binding; *the author's name and the title usually are shown on the spine as well as on the front cover*

spirit duplicator *noun* short-run printing method using spirit to transfer ink onto the paper

SPL = SOUND PRESSURE LEVEL

splash screen *noun* text or graphics displayed when an application or multimedia book is run; normally displays the product name, logo and copyright information and is only displayed for a few seconds before the main screen appears

splice 1 *verb* to join two lengths of magnetic tape *or* film by taping, cementing or butt-welding to form a continuous length; *you can use glue or splicing tape to splice the ends*; **splicing block** = device used to correctly position the ends of two lengths of tape *or* film that are to be spliced; **splicing tape** = non-magnetic, transparent tape which is applied to the back of the two ends

of tape *or* film to be joined **2** *noun* join between two film *or* magnetic tape sections

split edit *noun* (*in video editing*) when sound and picture cuts occur at separate times

split-field lens *or* **split-focus lens** *noun* camera lens which is able to achieve perfect focus at two different planes

split-focus shot *noun* shot where the focus of the camera is altered from one plane to another

split screen *noun* (**a**) software which can divide the display into two or more independent areas, to display two text files *or* a graph and a text file; *we use split screen mode to show the text being worked on and another text from memory for comparison* (**b**) shot where two or more images are visible in different areas of the same picture

splitter *noun* device which allows a number of other devices to be plugged into one supply *or* line; **beam splitter** = optical device to redirect part of a light beam

spool 1 *noun* reel on which a tape *or* printer ribbon is wound **2** *verb* to transfer data from a disk to a tape

spooler *or* **spooling device** *noun* device which holds a tape and which receives information from a disk for storage

spooling *noun* transferring data to a disk from which it can be printed at the normal speed of the printer, leaving the computer available to do something else

spot *noun* point on a CRT screen that is illuminated by the electron beam

spot beam *noun* narrow (satellite) antenna coverage of a select region (on earth)

spot wobble *noun* vertical fluctuation of a television display's scanning beam in order to make the raster spacing less obvious

spotting *noun* the retouching, with an opaque substance, of undesirable marks on film which appeared during the developing process

spray processing *noun* film developing method which moves the film through a chemical spray rather than putting it in a bath of developing fluid

spreadsheet *noun* program which allows calculations to be carried out on several columns of numbers

sprite *noun* graphic object which moves around in its own plane, independent of other graphic objects on screen

COMMENT: a sprite can normally be given attributes that determine whether it will pass through, over or under any other graphic object which it hits; sprites provide simpler image programming for games and multimedia applications

sprocket *or* **sprocket wheel** *noun* wheel with teeth round it which fit into holes in continuous stationery *or* punched tape

sprocket feed *noun* paper feed, where the printer pulls the paper by turning sprocket wheels which fit into a series of holes along each edge of the sheet; *see also* TRACTOR FEED

sprocket holes *noun* **(a)** series of small holes on each edge of continuous stationery, which allow the sheet to be pulled through the printer **(b)** perforations in the edges of a strip of film

spur *noun* connection point into a network

spurious data *noun* unexpected or unwanted data or an error in a signal, often due to noise; the part of the captured signal that is not useful

SPX = SIMPLEX

SQA = SOFTWARE QUALITY ASSURANCE

SQL = STRUCTURED QUERY LANGUAGE simple, commonly used standard, database programming language that is only used to create queries to retrieve data from the database

squawk *verb* to activate specific modes *or* functions on a transponder

square wave *noun* pulse that rises vertically, levels off, then drops vertically; the ideal shape for a digital signal

squeeze room *noun* system which alters the shape of a television image for an artistic effect

squeeze *noun* horizontal compression of film images by using an anamorphic lens

SRT = SOURCE TRANSPARENT ROUTING

SSD = SINGLE-SIDED DISK

SSI = SMALL SCALE INTEGRATION

ST connector *noun* connector used to terminate optical fibres

ST range of personal computers developed by Atari that use the Motorola 68000 series CPU

COMMENT: the ST includes the GEM graphical user interface, sound card, MIDI interface and colour graphics

ST506 standard *noun* (old) disk interface standard used in early IBM PCs, developed by Seagate; *the ST506 standard has now been replaced by IDE and SCSI*

stability *noun* being stable; **image stability** = ability of a display screen to provide a flicker-free picture

stabilizer *noun* a mount which holds the camera steady

stable *adjective* not moving *or* not changing; **stable state** = the state of a system when no external signals are applied

stack *noun* temporary storage for a list of data *or* tasks for a computer to process, where items are added *or* retrieved from the same end of the list; *see also* LIFO; **pushdown stack** *or* **pushdown list** = method of storing data, where the last item stored is always at the same location, the rest of the list being pushed down by one address; **stack pointer** = address register containing the location of the most recently stored item of data *or* the location of the next item of data to be retrieved; **stackware** = an application developed using the Apple Macintosh HyperCard system

stage *noun* one of several points in a process; *the text is ready for the printing stage; we are in the first stage of running in the new computer system*; **stage window** = window in which a video or animation sequence is viewed (normally refers to a window in which a Movie Player sequence is played)

staged *adjective* carried out in stages, one after the other; **staged changeover** = change between an old and a new system in a series of stages

stagehand *see* GRIP

stand-alone *or* **standalone** *adjective & noun* (device *or* system) which can operate without the need of any other devices; *the workstations have been* *networked together rather than used as standalone systems*; **stand-alone system** = system that can operate independently; **stand-alone terminal** = computer terminal with a processor and memory which can be directly connected to a modem, without being a member of a network *or* cluster

standard *adjective* normal *or* usual; **standard colours** = range of colours that are available on a particular system and can be shared by all applications; depends on hardware and type of display adapter installed; **standard document** *or* **standard form** *or* **standard paragraph** *or* **standard text** = normal printed document *or* form *or* paragraph which is used many times; **standard film** = 35mm film; **standard function** = special feature included as normal in a computer system; **Standard Generalized Markup Language** = *see* SGML; **standard interface** = interface between two or more systems that conforms to pre-defined rules; **standard letter** = letter which is sent without any change to the text, to several different people *or* addresses; *(in an IBM PC)* **standard mode** = mode of operation of Microsoft Windows which uses extended memory but does not allow multi-tasking of DOS applications

standardize *verb* to make a series of things conform to a standard; *the standardized control of transmission links*

standards *plural noun* normal quality *or* normal conditions which are used to judge other things; **modem standards** = rules defining transmitting frequencies, etc., which allow different modems to communicate; **production standards** = quality of production; **up to standard** = of an acceptable quality; *this batch of disks is not up to standard*; **standards converter** = device to convert received signals conforming to one standard into a different standard; *the standards converter allows us to watch US television broadcasts on our UK standards set*; **video standards** = *see* VIDEO

COMMENT: modem standards are set by the CCITT in the UK, the Commonwealth and most of Europe, while the USA and part of South America use modem standards set by Bell

standby *noun* (device *or* program) which is ready for use in case of failure; **cold standby** = backup system that will allow the equipment to continue running but with the loss of any volatile data; **hot standby** = backup equipment that is kept operational at all times in case of system failure; **standby equipment** = secondary system identical to the main system, to be used if the main system breaks down

```
before        fault-tolerant
systems, users had to rely on
the   cold   standby,   that   is
switching on a second machine
when   the   first   developed   a
fault; the alternative was the
hot   standby,   where   a   second
computer   was   kept   running
continuously
```
Computer News

staple 1 *noun* bent metal pin which attaches pages together **2** *verb* to attach papers together with a bent metal pin; *the booklet is stapled together; the collator gathers signatures together before stapling*

star filter *noun* filter with an engraved design which creates star effects on strong light sources

star network *noun* network of several machines where each terminal *or* floppy disk unit *or* satellite is linked individually to a central hard disk machine *or* server; *compare with* BUS NETWORK, RING NETWORK

start *adjective* beginning *or* first part; **start bit** *or* **element** = transmitted bit used in asynchronous communications to indicate the start of a character (NOTE: opposite is **stop bit**); **start of header** = transmitted code indicating the start of address *or* destination information for a following message; **start of text** = transmitted code indicating the end of control *or* address information and the start of the message; **warm start** = restarting a program which has stopped, without losing any data

Start button *noun* button that is normally in the bottom left-hand corner of a Microsoft Windows Desktop screen and provides access to software and settings on the computer

startup disk *noun* floppy disk which holds the operating system and system configuration files which can, in case of hard disk failure, be used to boot the computer

startup screen *noun* text or graphics displayed when an application or multimedia book is run; normally displays the product name, logo and copyright information and is only displayed for a few seconds before the main screen appears

stat *(informal)* = PHOTOSTAT

state-of-the-art *adjective* very modern *or* technically as advanced as possible

statement *noun* (a) expression used to convey an instruction *or* define a process (b) instruction in a source language which is translated into several machine code instructions; **input statement** = computer programming command that waits for data entry from a port *or* keyboard

static 1 *noun* (a) loud background noise *or* interference in a radio broadcast due to atmospheric conditions (b) background noise in a recorded signal (c) charge that does not flow (NOTE: no plural) **2** *adjective* (a) (data) which does not change with time (b) (system) that is not dynamic; **static colours** = *see* SYSTEM COLOURS; **static dump** = printout of the state of a system when it has finished a process; **static object** = object in an animation or video that does not move within the frame; **static RAM** = RAM which retains data even if the power supply is switched off, and where the data does not have to be refreshed (as opposed to dynamic RAM)

station *noun* (a) point in a network *or* communications system that contains devices to control the input and output of messages, allowing it to be used as a sink *or* source; **station management (SMT)** = software and hardware within the FDDI specification which provides control information; **workstation** = desk with computer, keyboard, monitor, printers, etc., where a person works (b) **earth station** = dish antenna and circuitry used to communicate with a satellite; **radio station** = broadcast signal booster *or* relay point consisting of a receiver and transmitter linked with ancillary equipment; *the signal from this radio station is very weak; we are trying to jam the signals from that station*

stationary *adjective* not moving; **geostationary orbit** = orbit of a satellite which keeps it above the same part of the earth

stationery *noun* office supplies for writing, especially paper, envelopes, labels, etc.; **computer stationery** = paper specially made for use in a computer printer; **continuous stationery** = printer stationery which takes the form of a single long sheet; **preprinted stationery** = computer stationery (such as invoices) which is preprinted with the company heading and form onto which the details will be printed by the computer (NOTE: no plural)

statistical *adjective* based on statistics; **statistical time division multiplexing (STDM)** = time division multiplexing system that allocates time slots when they are required, allowing greater flexibility and a greater number of devices to transmit; *see also* TIME DIVISION MULTIPLEXING

statistician *noun* person who analyses statistics

statistics *noun* (study of) facts in the form of figures

status *noun* importance *or* position; **status bar** *or* **status line** = line at the top or bottom of a screen which gives information about the task currently being worked on (position of cursor, number of lines, filename, time, etc.); **status bit** = single bit in a word used to provide information about the state *or* result of an operation; **status line** = line at the top *or* bottom of a screen which gives information about the task currently being worked on (number of lines, number of columns, filename, time, etc.); **status poll** = signal from a computer requesting information on the current status of a terminal; **status word** = word which contains a number of status bits, such as carry bit, zero bit, overflow bit, etc.

STD = SUBSCRIBER TRUNK DIALLING

STDM = STATISTICAL TIME DIVISION MULTIPLEXING

steadicam *noun* device which prevents camera shake and provides smooth action with a hand-held camera

stencil *noun* material with component shapes and symbols already cut out, allowing designers to draw components and other symbols rapidly; *the stencil has all the electronic components on it; the* *schematic looks much neater if you use a stencil*

step 1 *noun* a single unit; **single step** = executing a computer program one instruction at a time, used for debugging **2** *verb* to move forward *or* backwards by one unit; *we stepped forward the film one frame at a time*

step frame *verb* to capture a video sequence one frame at a time, used when the computer is not powerful or fast enough to capture real-time full-motion video

step printing *noun* printing process where the film is exposed one frame at a time

step through *noun* function of a debugger that allows a developer to execute a program one instruction at a time to see where the fault lies

stepper motor *or* **stepping motor** *noun* motor which turns in small steps as instructed by a computer (used in printers and robots)

steradion *noun* unit of solid angle

stereo *(informal)* = STEREOPHONIC

stereophonic *adjective* using two audio signals recorded from slightly different positions to provide a three-dimensional sound effect when replayed through two separate loudspeakers; **stereophonic microphone** = one device containing two microphones allowing stereo signals to be recorded; **stereophonic recorder** = tape recorder that records two audio signals onto magnetic tape

stereophony *noun* sound reproduction using two or more channels to produce a three dimensional effect of sound

stereoscopy *noun* photography system which provides a three dimensional effect

stick model *see* WIRE FRAME MODEL

still *noun* single image or frame within a video or film sequence

still frame *noun* an individual film or video tape frame which is continuously reproduced

stochastic model *noun* mathematical representation of a system that includes the effects of random actions

stock *noun* unexposed film, also called raw stock

stock control program *noun* software designed to help manage stock in a business

stock numbers *see* EDGE NUMBERS

stop 1 *verb* to cease doing something; **stop code** = instruction that temporarily stops a process to allow the user to enter data; **stop instruction** = computer programming instruction that stops program execution; **stop list** = list of words that are not to be used *or* are not significant for a file *or* library search **2** *noun* aperture opening of a lens which regulates the volume of light which enters the lens, sized from 1.5 to 22

stop-action photos *noun* images in which objects have been intermittently filmed one frame at a time so that when they are projected at a normal speed the changes that occur to these objects will be apparent

stop and wait protocol *noun* communications protocol in which the transmitter waits for a signal from the receiver that the message was correctly received before transmitting further data

stop bath *noun* chemical solution which stops the film developer working in a film bath; generally contains acetic acid

stop bit *or* **stop element** *noun* transmitted bit used in asynchronous communications to indicate the end of a character

stop down *verb* to decrease the width of a lens aperture by altering the diaphragm of the iris

stop frame *see* STILL FRAME

stop motion *noun* the filming, projecting or printing of one frame at a time

storage *noun* memory *or* part of the computer system in which data *or* programs are kept for further use; **archive storage** = storage of data for a long period of time; **storage capacity** = amount of space available for storage of data; **storage device** = any device that can store data and then allow it to retrieved when required; **storage disk** = disk used to store data; **storage dump** = printout of all the contents of an area of storage space; **storage media** = various materials which are able to store data; **storage tube** = special CRT used for computer graphics that retains an image on screen without the need for refresh actions; *see also* REFRESH

store 1 *noun* memory *or* part of the computer system in which data *or* programs are kept for further use; **store location** *or* **cell** = unit in a computer system which can store information **2** *verb* to save data, which can then be used again as necessary; *storing a page of high resolution graphics can require 3Mb*; **store and forward** = communications system that stores a number of messages before retransmitting them; **stored program signalling** = system of storing communications control signals on computer in the form of a program

COMMENT: storage devices include hard and floppy disk, RAM, punched paper tape and magnetic tape

story board *noun* visual plan of a proposed film, video or slide production made up of drawings which outline the draft contents

straight cut *noun* the cutting from one shot to another with no intervening visual effect

stray *adjective* lost *or* wandering; (something) which has avoided being stopped; *demagnetization involves removing stray magnetic fields from a disk or tape*

streaking *noun* **(a)** vertical stripes on a camera pick-up tube which can divide an image light into red-blue-green components without using dichroic mirrors **(b)** horizontal television picture distortion

stream *noun* long flow of serial data; **job stream** = number of tasks arranged in order waiting to be processed in a batch system

streamer *noun* **tape streamer** *or* **streaming tape drive** = (device containing a) continuous loop of tape, used for backing storage

streaming *noun* reading data from a storage device in one continuous operation, without processor intervention

the product has 160Mb of memory, 45Gb of Winchester disk storage and 95Gb streaming tape storage
Minicomputer News

streaming audio digital audio data that is continuously transmitted (normally over the Internet) using a streaming protocol to provide stereo sound; *see* STREAMING DATA, REALAUDIO

streaming data *or* **streaming protocol** method of sending a continuous stream of data over the Internet to provide live video or sound transmission

streaming video video image data that is continuously transmitted (normally over the Internet) using a streaming protocol to provide smooth moving images; *see* STREAMING DATA, ASF, VIVO, VXTREME

COMMENT: older methods of sending continuous live data used a standard web server (an HTTP server) to transmit the data - however, an HTTP server is designed to send data when it is ready rather than sending a regular stream of data that is required by multimedia. Video clips viewed over an Internet connection are prone to burst-transmission problems amd the quality of the video seen depends on the network traffic. To provide a good multimedia server, the data delivery must be regulated and ideally synchronised. There are many different standards used to deliver sound and video over the Internet including Progressive Network's RealAudio, Microsoft's NetShow server (that supports both audio and video) and Netscape's MediaServer. Each of these streaming data technologies allow the user or publisher to limit the delivery of data to a maximum data rate. There are several standard formats used including Microsoft's multimedia delivery format, ASF (active streaming format) and other standards developed by Macromedia, VDOnet, Vivo, and VXtreme.

string *noun* any series of consecutive alphanumeric characters *or* words that are manipulated as a unit by the computer; **string area** = section of memory in which strings of alphanumeric characters are stored; **string concatenation** = linking a series of strings together; **string function** = program operation which can act on strings; **string variable** = variables used in a computer language that can contain alphanumeric characters as well as numbers

string orientated symbolic language *see* SNOBOL

stringy floppy *or* **tape streamer** *noun* continuous loop of tape, used for backing storage

strip 1 *noun* long thin piece of material; **strip window** = display which shows a single line of text; **magnetic strip** = layer of magnetic material on the surface of a plastic card, used for recording data **2** *verb* to remove the control data from a received message, leaving only the relevant information

stripe *noun* (a) long thin line of colour (b) thin band of magnetic material which is applied to 35mm film for sound recording and reproduction; **balance stripe** = thin magnetic strip on a cine film on the opposite side to the sound track, so that the whole film will lie flat when played back

striping *noun* (a) applying of a magnetic stripe to film (b) adding longitudinal time-code to video rushes

strobe 1 *verb* to send a pulse (usually on the selection line) of an electronic circuit **2** *noun* pulse of an electric circuit

strobe lighting *noun* electronic flash lighting working at the same rate as a motion picture camera frame, creating sharp images of fast-moving objects

stroboscope *or* **strobe** *noun* light source which produces flashes of light

stroke *noun* (a) basic curved *or* straight line that makes up a character (b) the width (in pixels) of the pen or brush used to draw on-screen

strowger exchange *noun* telephone exchange worked by electromechanical switches

structure 1 *noun* way in which something is organized *or* formed **2** *verb* to organize *or* to arrange in a certain way; *you first structure a document to meet your requirements and then fill in the blanks*; **structured cabling** = (organisation which is cabled) using UTP cable feeding into hubs designed in such a way that it is easy to trace and repair cable faults and also to add new stations or more cable; **structured design** = problem solved by a number of interconnected modules; **structured programming** = well-ordered and logical technique of assembling programs; **structured query language (SQL)** = simple, commonly used, standard database

programming language which is only used to create queries to retrieve data from the database

stub *noun* short program routine which contains comments to describe the executable code that will, eventually, be inserted into the routine

stuck beacon *noun* (error condition in which) a station continuously transmits beacon frames

studio *noun* place where a designer draws; place where recordings take place; place where films are made

STX = START OF TEXT

style *noun* typeface, font, point size, colour, spacing and margins of text in a formatted document

style sheet *noun* (a) sheet giving the style which should be followed by an editor (b) template that can be preformatted to generate automatically the style *or* layout of a document such a manual, a book, a newsletter, etc.

stylus *noun* (a) (transducer) needle which converts signals on an audio record into electrical signals (b) pen-like device that is used in computer graphics systems to dictate cursor position on the screen; *use the stylus on the graphics tablet to draw* (c) (transducer) that detects data stored on a videodisc; **stylus printer** = *see* DOT-MATRIX PRINTER

sub- *prefix* meaning less (important) than *or* lower than; **subaudio frequencies** = frequencies below the audio range (below 20Hz); **subclass** = number of data items to do with one item in a master class; **subbing** *or* **sub-editing** = editing of a manuscript before it is sent for typesetting; **subrange** = below the normal range

subdirectory *noun* directory of disk *or* tape contents contained within the main directory

```
if you delete a file and then
delete the subdirectory where
it was located, you cannot
restore the file because the
directory does not exist
```
Personal Computer World

subjective camera *noun* scenes shot from the point of view of the camera in order to intensify audience reaction

submenu *noun* secondary menu displayed as a choice from a menu; used if there are too many choices to fit into one menu

submit button *noun* button displayed on a web page that sends information entered by a user on a web form to a program running on a web server for processing (for example, the submit button could be used to start a search query)

subnet *noun* self-contained part of a large network (normally refers to one, independently-managed part of the Internet); a subnet is located using part of the IP address called the subnet address; *see also* IP ADDRESS

subnet address *or* **subnet number** *noun* part of an IP address that identifies a subnet that is connected to a larger network; the first part of the IP address identifies the network, the next part of the IP address identifies the subnet and the last part of the IP address identifies a single host server; *see also* IP ADDRESS

subnet mask filter that is used to select the portion of an IP address that contains the subnet address

subnotebook *noun* very small portable computer that is smaller and lighter than a standard full-size notebook or laptop computer

COMMENT: a subnotebook often has a smaller keyboard and display and normally only has a hard disk drive with any floppy disk drive or CD-ROM drive in a separate, external unit that can be plugged in when needed

subprogram *noun* (a) subroutine in a program (b) program called up by a main program

subroutine *noun* section of a program which performs a required function and that can be called upon at any time from inside the main program; **closed subroutine** = number of computer instructions in a program that can be called at any time, with a control being returned on completion to the instruction after the call; **open subroutine** = code for a subroutine which is copied into memory whenever a call instruction is found; **subroutine call** = computer programming instruction that directs control to a subroutine

COMMENT: a subroutine is executed by calling its address and when finished it returns to the instruction after the call in the main program

subscriber *noun* (a) person who has a telephone; **subscriber trunk dialling (STD)** = system where a person can dial direct from one telephone to another, without referring to the operator (b) person who pays for access to a service

subscript *noun* small character which is printed below the line of other characters; *see also* SUPERSCRIPT (NOTE: used in chemical formulae: CO_2); **subscripted variable** = element in an array, which is identified by a subscript

subset *noun* small set of data items which forms part of a another larger set

substance *noun* any matter whose properties can be described

substitute *verb* to put something in the place of something else; **substitute character** = character that is displayed if a received character is not recognized (NOTE: you substitute one thing **for** another)

substitution *noun* replacing something by something else; **substitution error** = error made by a scanner which mistakes one character *or* letter for another; **substitution table** = list of characters *or* codes that are to be inserted instead of received codes

substrate *noun* base material on which an integrated circuit is constructed; *see also* INTEGRATED CIRCUIT

subsystem *noun* one smaller part of a large system

subtitle *noun* a caption which is inserted over the filmed action, generally at the bottom of the screen, to provide information, to give a direct translation of dialogue in a foreign language, or as an aid to the hard of hearing

subtotal *noun* total at the end of a column, which when added to others makes the grand total

subtractive primaries *plural noun* the colours cyan, magenta and yellow.

subtrahend *noun* (in a subtraction operation) the number to be subtracted from the minuend

subvoice grade channel *noun* communications channel using frequencies

(240 - 300Hz) below a voice channel, used for low speed data transmission

successive *adjective* which follow one after the other; *each successive operation adds further characters to the string*

suffix notation *noun* mathematical operations written in a logical way, so that the symbol appears after the numbers to be acted upon; *see also* POSTFIX NOTATION

suitcase *noun (in the Apple Macintosh environment)* way of grouping together all the screen and printer font files for a typeface within one object that can be easily installed onto the system

suite of programs *noun* (i) group of programs which run one after the other; (ii) number of programs used for a particular task; *the word-processing system uses a suite of three programs, editor, spelling checker and printing controller*

summation check *noun* error detection check performed by adding together the characters received and comparing with the required total

sun outage *noun* length of time during which a satellite does not operate due to the position of the moon *or* earth, causing a shadow over the satellite's solar cells

super- *prefix* meaning very good *or* very powerful; **supercomputer** = very powerful mainframe computer used for high-speed mathematical tasks; **supergroup** = a number (60) of voice channels collected together into five adjacent channels for simultaneous transmission

super 8mm film *noun* a larger form of standard 8mm film which has 72 frames per foot

super bit mapping (SBM) *noun* extension to the Red Book CD-Audio specification in which studio-quality 20-bit sound samples are stored in the CD-A 16-bit word

super high frequency (SHF) *noun* frequency range between 3 - 30GHz

super large scale integration (SLSI) *noun* integrated circuit with more than 100,000 components

super master group *noun* collection of 900 voice channels

super trouper *noun* a very large spotlight

super VGA (SVGA) *noun* (old) enhancement to the standard VGA graphics display system which allows resolutions of up to 800x600pixels with 16 million colours

super VHS *see* S-VHS

superheterodyne radio *noun* radio receiver that converts a received signal by means of a heterodyne process to an intermediate frequency for easier processing

superimpose *verb* **(a)** to lay one picture over another so that they both remain visible **(b)** to add a graphic or a caption over a picture

superior number *noun* superscript figure

superscript *noun* small character printed higher than the normal line of characters; *compare with* SUBSCRIPT (NOTE: used often in mathematics: 10^5 say: **ten to the power five**)

supersede *verb* to take the place of something which is older *or* less useful; *the new program supersedes the earlier one, and is much faster*

superstation *noun* US TV system, where a single TV station broadcasts many programmes simultaneously via satellite and cable

supervise *verb* to watch carefully to see if work is well done; *the manufacture of circuit boards is very carefully supervised*

supervision *noun* being supervised

supervisor *noun* **(a)** person who makes sure that equipment is always working correctly **(b)** section of a computer operating system that regulates the use of peripherals and the operations undertaken by the CPU

supervisory *adjective* as a supervisor; **supervisory sequence** = combination of control codes that perform a controlling function in a data communications network; **supervisory signal** = (i) signal that indicates if a circuit is busy; (ii) signal that provides an indication of the state of a device

supplier *noun* company which supplies; *a supplier of computer parts; a supplier of disk drives or a disk drive supplier; Japanese suppliers have set up warehouses in the country*

supply 1 *noun* providing goods *or* products *or* services; *the electricity supply has failed; they signed a contract for the supply of computer stationery* **2** *verb* to provide something which is needed (for which someone will pay); *the computer was supplied by a recognized dealer; they have signed a contract to supply on-line information*

supply spool *noun* spool in the camera on to which is wound the unexposed film

support *verb* to give help to *or* to help to run; *the main computer supports six workstations*

suppress *verb* to remove; *the filter is used to suppress the noise due to static interference*; **suppressed carrier modulation** = modulated waveform where the carrier signal has been suppressed prior to transmission, leaving only the modulated sidebands; **double sideband suppressed carrier (DSBSC)** = amplitude modulation that uses a suppressed carrier, leaving only two sidebands; **single sideband suppressed carrier (SSBSC)** = amplitude modulation that uses a suppressed carrier, and only one sideband for data transmission

suppression *noun* act of suppressing

suppressor *noun* device which suppresses interference; **echo suppressor** = device used on long-distance speech lines to prevent echoing effects

surface-mount technology (SMT) *noun* method of manufacturing circuit boards in which the electronic components are bonded directly onto the surface of the board rather than being inserted into holes and soldered into place; *surface-mount technology is faster and more space-efficient than soldering*

surge *noun* sudden increase in electrical power in a system, due to a fault *or* noise *or* component failure; **surge protector** = electronic device that cuts off the power supply to sensitive equipment if it detects a power surge that could cause damage

COMMENT: power surges can burn out circuits before you have time to pull the plug; a surge protector between your computer and the wall outlet will help prevent damage

sustain 1 *verb* to keep a voltage at a certain level for a period of time **2** *noun* body of a sound signal; *compare with* ATTACK, DECAY

SVGA = SUPER VGA enhancement to the standard VGA graphics display system which allows resolutions of up to 800x600 pixels with 16 million colours

SVHS *or* **S-VHS** = SUPER VHS high-resolution version of the standard VHS video cassette standard which can record 400 lines of a video signal rather than the usual 260 lines of VHS

SW = SHORT WAVE

swap 1 *noun* = SWAPPING **2** *verb* to stop using one program, put it into store temporarily, run another program, and when that is finished, return to the first one

swap file *noun* file stored on the hard disk used as a temporary storage area for data held in RAM, to provide virtual memory; *see also* VIRTUAL MEMORY

swapping *or* **swap** *noun* system where a program is moved to backing storage while another program is being used

sweep *noun* movement of the electron beam over the area of a television screen in regular horizontal and vertical steps, producing the image

sweetening *noun* **(a)** addition of new sound to a voice track **(b)** addition of sound effects to the visual images **(c)** *(in video)* the improvement of the quality of image, colour, etc., through electronic modification

swim *noun* computer graphics that move slightly due to a faulty display unit

swish pan *noun* a fast, horizontal pan shot which causes blurring of the filmed images

switch 1 *noun* **(a)** point in a computer program where control can be passed to one of a number of subroutines **(b)** *(in some command-line operating systems)* an additional character entered on the same line as the program command and which affects how the program runs; *add the switch '/W' to the DOS command DIR and the directory listing will be displayed across the screen* **(c)** mechanical *or* solid state device that can electrically connect *or* isolate two *or* more lines; **switch train** = series of switches between a caller and a receiver in a telephone network **2** *verb* to connect *or* disconnect two lines by activating a switch; **switched network**

backup = user's choice of a secondary route through a network if the first is busy; **switched star** = cable television distribution system; **switched virtual call** = connection between two devices in a network that is only made when required, after a request signal; **to switch off** = to disconnect the power supply to a device; **to switch on** = to start to provide power to a system by using a switch to connect the power supply lines to the circuit; **to switch over** = to start using an alternative device when the primary one becomes faulty

switchback *noun* camera shot which goes back to the original subject after a cut-away shot

switchboard *noun* central point in a telephone system, where the lines from various telephone handsets meet, where calls can be directed to any other telephone; **switchboard operator** = person who works a central telephone switchboard, by connecting incoming and outgoing calls to various lines

switching *noun* constant update of connections between changing sinks and sources in a network; **line switching** = communications line and circuit established on demand and held until no longer required; **switching centre** = point in a communications network where messages can be switched to and from the various lines and circuits that end there; **switching circuit** = electronic circuit that can direct messages from one line *or* circuit to another in a switching centre; **switching error** = video playback error due to the heads being wrongly aligned

symbol *noun* sign *or* picture which represents something; **symbol table** = list of labels *or* names in a compiler *or* assembler, which relate to their addresses in the machine code program

symbolic *adjective* which acts as a symbol *or* which uses a symbol; **symbolic address** = address represented by a symbol *or* name; **symbolic language** = any computer language where locations are represented by names

sync *noun* (*informal*) = SYNCHRONISATION *or* SYNCHRONIZATION (i) two events or timing signals which happen at the same time; (ii) the exact aligning of the sound and

picture components of a film so that they coincide; **in sync** = synchronized; **sync bit** = transmitted bit used to synchronize devices; **sync mark** *or* **punch** = a hole punched into a film sound track or leader as an indication of the synchronization points for other strips of film; **sync pulse** = (i) (*in film production*) the signal linked to the speed of the camera which is recorded on magnetic tape for later synchronization; (ii) section of a composite video signal which regulates the repetition rate of the scanning system; (iii) (*in communications*) transmitted pulse used to make sure that the receiver is synchronized with the transmitter; **the two devices are out of sync** = the two devices are not properly synchronized

synchronization *or* **synchronisation** *noun* action of synchronizing two or more devices; **synchronization pulses** = transmitted pulses used to make sure that the receiver is synchronized with the transmitter

synchronize *or* **synchronise** *verb* to make sure that two or more devices *or* processes are coordinated in time or actions

synchronizer *or* **synchroniser** *noun* (a) device that will perform a function when it receives a signal from another device; *the synchronizer ensures that the correct slide is displayed with the correct soundtrack* (b) machine used to edit the sound track and the film at the same time; **frame synchronizer** = device which holds a complete frame of video information which may be released at a separate rate to the input to produce a synchronous output

synchronous *adjective* which runs in sync with something else; **synchronous computer** = computer in which each action can only take place when a timing pulse arrives; **synchronous data link control (SDLC)** = data transmission protocol most often used in IBM's Systems Network Architecture (SNA) and defines how synchronous data is transmitted *or* received; **synchronous data network** = communications network in which all the actions throughout the network are controlled by a single timing signal; **synchronous detection** = method of obtaining the signal from an amplitude modulation carrier; **synchronous idle**

character = character transmitted by a DTE to ensure correct synchronization when no other character is being transmitted; **synchronous mode** = system mode in which operations and events are synchronized with a clock signal; **synchronous network** = network in which all the links are synchronized with a single timing signal; **synchronous transmission** = transmission of data from one device to another, where both devices are controlled by the same clock, and the transmitted data is synchronized with the clock signal

synonym *noun* word which means the same thing as another word

synonymous *adjective* meaning the same; *the words 'error' and 'mistake' are synonymous*

syntactic error *noun* programming error in which the program statement does not follow the syntax of the language

syntax *noun* grammatical rules that apply to a programming language; **syntax analysis** = stage in compilation where statements are checked to see if they obey the rules of syntax; **syntax error** = programming error in which the program statement does not follow the syntax of the language

synthesis *noun* producing something artificially (from a number of smaller elements)

synthesize *verb* to produce something artificially (from a number of smaller elements); **synthesized voice** = speech created by an electronic device that uses phonemes (the separate sounds that make up speech)

synthesizer *noun* device which generates something (signals *or* sound *or* speech); **speech synthesizer** = device which generates sounds which are similar to the human voice; **music synthesizer** = device which makes musical notes which are similar to those made by musical instruments

SyQuest manufacturer of storage devices, including a range of removable hard disk drives and backup units; *see also* ZIP DISK

System *noun* (Apple Macintosh) operating system that provides multitasking, virtual memory and peer-to-peer file sharing

system *noun* any group of hardware *or* software *or* peripherals, etc., which work together; **expert system** = software which applies the knowledge, advice and rules defined by experts in a particular field to a user's data to help solve a problem; **operating system** = basic software that controls the running of the hardware and the management of data files, without the user having to operate it; **system colours** = a palette of 20 colours that are used by Windows for colouring window elements such as borders, captions, buttons; **system console** = main terminal or control centre for a computer which includes status lights and control switches; **system crash** = situation where the operating system stops working and has to be restarted; **system design** = identifying and investigating possible solutions to a problem, and deciding upon the most appropriate system to solve the problem; **system diagnostics** = messages that help find hardware *or* software faults; **system disk** = disk which holds the system software that is used to boot up a computer and load the operating system ready for use; **system exclusive data** = MIDI messages that can only be understood by a MIDI device from a particular manufacturer; **system flowchart** = diagram that shows each step of the clerical *or* computer procedures needed in a system; *(in the Apple Macintosh environment)* **system folder** = folder that contains the program files for the operating system and Finder; **system generation** = process of produce an optimum system for a particular task; **system library** = stored files that hold the various parts of a computer's operating system; **system life cycle** = time when a system exists, between its initial design and its becoming out of date; **system palette** = range of colours that are available on a particular operating system and can be shared by all applications; depends on hardware and type of display adapter installed; **system prompt** = prompt which indicates the operating system is ready and waiting for the user to enter a system command; **system security** = measures, such as password, priority protection, authorization codes, etc., designed to stop browsing and hackers; **system software** = software which makes everything in a computer work correctly;

see also OPERATING SYSTEM; **system specifications** = details of hardware and software required to perform certain tasks; **system support** = group of people that maintain and operate a system; **system tray** = *(in Windows)* area of the taskbar in the bottom right-hand corner that displays tiny icons that show which system software programs were run automatically when Windows started and are now running in the background; *see also* TASKBAR; **system unit** = main terminal or control centre for a computer which includes status lights and control switches; **system variable** = variable that contains data generated by the system software that can be used by applications; **System X** = digital telephone switching system that allows data transmission and provides control for the integrated services digital network (ISDN) in the UK

System Monitor utility provided with Windows that allows you to view how the resources on your PC are performing and, if you have shared the device, who else on the network is using them.

Système Electronique Couleur Avec Mémoire *see* SECAM

Système International units *see* SI UNITS

systems analysis *noun* **(a)** analysing a process *or* system to see if it could be more efficiently carried out by a computer **(b)** examining an existing system with the aim of improving *or* replacing it; **systems analyst** = person who undertakes system analysis; **systems integration** = combining different products from different manufacturers to create a system; **systems program** = program which controls the way in which a computer system works; **systems programmer** = person who writes system software

Systems Application Architecture (SAA) *noun* standard developed by IBM which defines the look and feel of a software application; SAA defines which keystrokes carry out standard functions (such as F1 to display help), the application's display and how the application interacts with the operating system

Systems Network Architecture (SNA) *noun* design methods developed by IBM which define how communications in a network should occur and allow different hardware to communicate

Tt

T = TERA- *prefix meaning 10^{12}* one million million

T carrier *noun US* standard for digital data transmission lines, such as T1, T1C, and corresponding signal standards DS1, DS1C

T connector *noun* coaxial connector, shaped like the letter 'T', which connects two thin coaxial cables using BNC plugs and provides a third connection for another cable or network interface card

T junction *noun* a connection at right angles with a main signal *or* power carrying cable

T network *noun* simple circuit network with three electronic components connected in the shape of a letter T

T1 committee *noun* ANSI committee which sets digital communications standards for the US, particularly ISDN services

T1 link *noun* long distance data transmission link (not related to the T1 committee) that can carry data at 1.544Mbits per second

TAB = TABULATE

tab *verb* **(a)** to tabulate *or* to arrange text in columns with the cursor automatically running from one column to the next in keyboarding; **tab character** = ASCII character 09hex which is used to align text at a preset tab stop; **tab key** = key on a keyboard, normally positioned on the far left, beside the 'Q' key, with two arrows pointing opposite horizontal directions, used to insert a tab character into text and so align the text at a preset tab stop; **tab memory** = ability of a editing program (usually a word-processor) to store details about various tab settings; **tab rack** *or* **ruler line** = graduated scale, displayed on the screen, showing the position of tabulation columns; **tab settings** *or* **tab stops** = preset points along a line, where the printing head *or* cursor will stop for each tabulation command **(b)** in a GUI, method of moving from one button or field to another without using the mouse, but by pressing the tab key to move the focus

tabbing *noun* movement of the cursor in a word-processing program from one column to the next; **tabbing can be done from inside the program; decimal tabbing** = adjusting a column of numbers so that the decimal points are aligned vertically; *(in a GUI)* **tabbing order** = order in which the focus moves from one button or field to the next as the user presses the tab key

table of contents *noun* **(a)** list of the contents of a book, usually printed at the beginning **(b)** *(in a CD)* data at the start of the disc that describes how many tracks are on the CD, their position and length **(c)** *(in a multimedia title)* page with a list of the headings of all the other main pages in the title and links so that a user can move to them

table *noun* list of data in columns and rows on a printed page *or* on the screen; **lookup table** = collection of stored results that can be accessed very rapidly; *this is the value of the key pressed, use a lookup table to find its ASCII value*; **reference program table** = list produced by a compiler *or* system of the location, size and type of the variables, routines and macros within a program; **symbol table** = list of all the symbols which are accepted by a language or compiler and their object code translation; **table lookup** = using one known value to select one entry in a table, providing a secondary value

tablet *noun* **graphics tablet** = graphics pad *or* flat device that allows a user to input graphical information into a computer by drawing on its surface

tabular *adjective* **in tabular form** = arranged in a table

tabulate *verb* to arrange text in columns, with the cursor moving to each new column automatically as the text is keyboarded

tabulating *noun* processing punched cards, such as a sorting operation

tabulation *noun* **(a)** arrangement of a table of figures **(b)** the moving of a printing head *or* cursor to a preset distance along a line; **tabulation markers** = symbols displayed to indicate the position of tabulation stops; **tabulation stops** = preset points along a line at which a printing head *or* cursor will stop at for each tabulation command

tabulator *noun* part of a typewriter *or* computer which sets words *or* figures automatically in columns

tachometer *noun* device which specifies a camera's frame speed

TACS = TOTAL ACCESS COMMUNICATION SYSTEM *UK* standard for cellular radio systems

tactile *adjective* using the sense of touch; **tactile feedback** = information provided by using the sense of touch

tag image file format (TIFF) *noun* standard file format used to store bitmap graphic images

tag *noun* **(a)** one section of a computer instruction **(b)** identifying characters attached to a file *or* item (of data); *each file has a three-letter tag for rapid identification*

tail *noun* **(a)** data recognized as the end of a list of data **(b)** control code used to signal the end of a message

tail gate *noun* film projector on an optical printer

take *noun* a camera shot of an individual piece of action

take-up *noun* a device such as a reel on which film or tape is wound from a projector, camera gate or editing machine

take-up reel *noun* reel onto which magnetic tape is collected

Taligent operating system developed by IBM and Apple that can be used on both PC and Macintosh platforms

talk *verb* to speak *or* to communicate

talkback *noun* speech communications between a control room and a studio

a variety of technologies exist which allow computers to talk to one another
Which PC?

tallylight *noun* the cue light on a television camera

tandem *noun* **tandem processors** = two processors connected so that if one fails, the second takes over; **tandem switching** = one switch controlling another switch in the same exchange by means of a secondary switch; **working in tandem** = situation where two things are working together

tape *noun* a long, thin strip of storage or recording material which can take the form of a magnetic-coated plastic base or a paper strip with perforations; **(magnetic) tape** = narrow length of thin plastic coated with a magnetic material used to store signals magnetically; **(paper) tape** *or* **punched tape** = strip of paper on which information can be recorded in the form of punched holes; **(video cassette) tape** = magnetic tape used in a video recorder to store pictures and sound; **cassette tape** = tape stored on two small reels protected by a solid casing; **open reel tape** = tape on a reel which is not enclosed in a cassette *or* cartridge; **tape cable** *or* **ribbon cable** = number of insulated conductors arranged next to each other forming a flat cable; **tape cartridge** = cassette box containing magnetic tape (on a reel); **tape cassette** = small plastic, sealed box containing a reel of magnetic tape and a pickup reel; used in a cassette recorder; **tape counter** = indication (on a tape recorder) of the amount of tape that has been used; **tape deck** = device which plays back *or* records on magnetic tape; **tape drive** = mechanism which pulls magnetic tape over the tape heads; *our new product has a 96Gb streaming tape drive*; **tape format** = way in which blocks of data, control codes and location data is stored on tape; **tape guide** = method by which the tape is correctly positioned over the tape head; *the tape is out of alignment because one of the tape guides has broken*; **tape head** = transducer that can read and write signals onto the surface of magnetic tape; **tape header** = identification information at the beginning of a tape; **tape library** = (i) secure area for the storage of computer data tapes; (ii) series of computer tapes kept in store for reference; **tape punch** = machine that punches holes into paper tape; **tape reader** = machine that reads punched holes in paper tape *or* signals on magnetic tape; **tape recorder** = machine that records data and signals onto magnetic tape; **tape splicer** = device which cuts film so that it can be joined together without overlapping with the use of splicing tape; **tape streamer** = continuous loop of tape used for backing storage; **tape timer** = device that displays the total time left *or* amount of playing time used on a reel of magnetic tape; **tape to card converter** = device that reads data from magnetic tape and stores it on punched cards; **tape transmitter** = device that reads data from paper tape and transmits it to another point; **tape transport** = method (in a magnetic tape recorder) by which the tape is moved smoothly from reel to reel over the magnetic heads; **tape unit** = device with tape deck, amplifier, circuitry, etc., for recording and playing back tapes

COMMENT: cassettes *or* reels of tape are easy to use and cheaper than disks. They are less adaptable and only provide sequential access. The cassette casing usually conforms to a standard size and is most used in home audio cassette *or* video recorders

Targa graphics file format (which uses the .TGA extension on a PC) developed by Truevision to store raster graphic images in 16-, 24- and 32-bit colour; also used to refer to high-resolution colour graphics adapters made by Truevision

target *noun* **(a)** goal which you aim to achieve **(b)** part of a video camera tube where the visual image is produced and scanned

target computer *noun* computer on which software is to be run (but not necessarily written on, for example using a cross-assembler)

target disk *noun* disk onto which a file is to be copied

target language *noun* language into which a language will be translated from its source language; *the target language for this PASCAL program is machine code*

target program *noun* object program *or* computer program in object code form, produced by a compiler

target window *noun* window in which text or graphics will be displayed

the target board is connected to the machine through the in-circuit emulator cable
Electronics & Wireless World

tariff *noun* charge incurred by a user of a communications *or* computer system; *there is a set tariff for logging on, then a rate for every minute of computer time used*

TASI = TIME ASSIGNED SPEECH INTERPOLATION method of using a voice channel for other signals during the gaps and pauses in a normal conversation

task *noun* job which is to carried out by a computer; **multi-tasking** = ability of a computer system to run two or more programs at the same time; **task swapping** *or* **switching** = exchanging one program in memory for another which is temporarily stored on disk

TAT = TURNAROUND TIME

TBC = TIME-BASE CORRECTOR

TCIP = TIME CODE IN PICTURE discernable time-code numerals in video-tape editing

TCM = THERMAL CONTROL MODULE

TCP/IP = TRANSMISSION CONTROL PROTOCOL/INTERFACE PROGRAM data transfer protocol used in networks and communications systems (often used in Unix-based networks)

TCP = TRANSMISSION CONTROL PROTOCOL standard data transmission protocol that provides full duplex transmission, the protocol bundles data into packets and checks for errors

TDM = TIME DIVISION MULTIPLEXING method of combining several signals into one high-speed transmission carrier

COMMENT: each input signal is sampled in turn and the result transmitted. The receiver re-constructs the signals

TDR = TIME DOMAIN REFLECTOMETRY test that identifies where cable faults lie by sending a signal down the cable and measuring how long it takes for the reflection to come back

TDS = TRANSACTION-DRIVEN SYSTEM

tearing *noun* distortion of a television image due to bad sweep synchronization

technical *adjective* referring to a particular machine *or* process; *the document gives all the technical details on the new computer*; **technical director** = engineer in charge of the video control cable; **technical support** = (person who provides) technical advice to a user to explain how to use software *or* hardware or explain why it might not work

technically *adverb* in a technical way; *their system is technically far more advanced than ours*

technician *noun* person who is specialized in industrial work; *the computer technicians installed the new system*; **laboratory technician** = person who deals with practical work in a laboratory

technique *noun* skilled way of doing a job; *the company has developed a new technique for processing customers' disks; he has a special technique for answering complaints from users of the software*; **management techniques** = skill in managing a business; **marketing techniques** = skill in marketing a product

technological *adjective* referring to technology; **the technological revolution** = changing of industry by introducing new technology

technology *noun* applying scientific knowledge to industrial processes; **information technology** = technology involved in acquiring, storing, processing, and distributing information by electronic means (including radio, TV, telephone and computers); **the introduction of new technology** = putting new electronic equipment into a business *or* industry

tel = TELEPHONE

tele- *prefix* **(a)** meaning long distance **(b)** referring to television

telebanking *noun* system by which an account holder can carry out transactions with his bank via a terminal and communications network

telecine *noun* method of displaying a cine film on television

telecommunications *noun* technology of passing and receiving messages over a distance (as in radio, telephone, telegram, satellite broadcast, etc.)

telecommuting *noun* practice of working on a computer in one place (normally from home) that is linked by modem to the company's central office allowing messages and data to be transferred

teleconference *or* **teleconferencing** *noun* **(a)** linking video, audio and computer signals from different locations so that distant people can talk and see each other, as if in a conference room **(b)** part of video-conferencing where the image is renewed only at intervals in order to decrease the transmission bandwidth required

telecontrol *noun* control of a remote device by a telecommunications link

telegram *noun* message sent to another country by telegraph; *to send an international telegram*

telegraph 1 *noun* message transmitted using a telegraphy system; **telegraph office** = office from which telegrams can be sent **2** *verb* to send a telegram to another person; to send printed *or* written *or* drawn material by long-distance telegraphy; *they telegraphed their agreement; the photographs were telegraphed to New York*

telegraphic *adjective* referring to a telegraph system; **telegraphic address** = short address to which a telegram is sent

telegraphy *noun* system of sending messages along wires using direct current pulses; **carrier telegraphy** = system of transmitting telegraph signals via a carrier signal

teleinformatic services *noun* any data only service, such as telex, facsimile, which uses telecommunications

telematics *noun* interaction of all data processing and communications devices (computers, networks, etc.)

telemessage *noun* GB message sent by telephone, and delivered as a card

telemetry *noun* data from remote measuring devices transmitted over a telecommunications link

teleordering *noun* book ordering system, in which the bookseller's orders are entered into a computer which then puts the order through to the distributor at the end of the day

telephone 1 *noun* machine used for speaking to someone over a long distance; *we had a new telephone system installed last week; the managing director is on the telephone to Hong Kong; she has been on the telephone all day*; **by telephone** = using the telephone; *to place an order by telephone; to reserve a room by telephone*; **conference telephone** = telephone specially made to be used in a teleconference; **house telephone** *or* **internal telephone** = telephone for calling from one room to another in an office *or* hotel; **telephone answering machine** = device that answers a telephone, plays a prerecorded message and records any response; **telephone book** *or* **telephone directory** = book which lists people and businesses in alphabetical order with their telephone numbers; *he looked up the number of the company in the telephone book*; **telephone call** = speaking to someone on the telephone; **to make a telephone call** = to dial a number and speak to someone on the telephone; **to answer the telephone** *or* **to take a telephone call** = to speak in reply to a call on the telephone; **telephone (data carrier)** = using a modem to send binary data as sound signals over a telephone line; **telephone exchange** = central office where the telephones of a whole district are linked; **telephone number** = set of figures for a particular telephone subscriber; *can you give me your telephone number?*; **telephone operator** = person who operates a telephone switchboard; **telephone orders** = orders received by telephone; *since we mailed the catalogue we have received a large number of telephone orders*; **telephone repeater** = receiver, transmitter and associated circuits that boost a telephone signal; **telephone subscriber** = person who has a telephone connected to the main network; **telephone switchboard** = central point in a private telephone system where all internal and external lines meet; **to be on the telephone** = to be speaking to someone using the telephone **2** *verb* his secretary telephoned to say he would be late; **he telephoned the order through to the warehouse** = he telephoned the warehouse to place an order; **to telephone a place** *or* **a person** = to call a

place *or* a person by telephone; **to telephone about something** = to make a telephone call to speak about something; *he telephoned about the order for computer stationery*; **to telephone for something** = to make a telephone call to ask for something; *he telephoned for a taxi*

telephonist *noun* person who works a telephone switchboard

telephony *noun* data *or* signal transmission over a telephone using audio frequencies

telephoto distortion *noun* the compression result which occurs in shots filmed with a telephoto lens; objects far away from the camera seem to be closer, and a performer's movement towards or away from the camera seems to be slower

telephoto lens *noun* camera objective lens with long focal length and short back focus; this type of lens gives the impression that an object is closer than it really is

teleprinter *noun* device that is capable of sending and receiving data from a distant point by means of a telegraphic circuit, and printing out the message on a printer; **teleprinter interface** = terminal interface *or* hardware and software combination required to control the functions of a terminal; **teleprinter roll** = roll of paper onto which messages are printed

teleprocessing (TP) *noun* processing of data at a distance (as on a central computer from outside terminals)

telerecording *noun* the transferral of a television or video programme to motion picture film

telesales *noun* sales made by telephone

teleshopping *noun* use of a telephone-based data service such as viewdata to order products from a shop

telesoftware (TSW) *noun* software which is received from a viewdata *or* teletext service

teletext *noun* method of transmitting text and information with a normal TV signal, usually as a serial bit stream that can be displayed using a decoder and an ordinary TV set; **teletext decoder** = electronic device that allows a standard television to display teletext pages

COMMENT: teletext constantly

transmits pages of information which are repeated one after the other; the user can stop one to read it. This is different from viewdata, where the user calls up a page of text using a telephone line

COMMENT: in a colour TV there are three electron guns corresponding to red, green and blue signals. In the UK the TV screen has 625 lines to be scanned; this is normally done in two sweeps of alternate lines, providing a flicker-free image

teletype *noun* term used for teleprinter equipment

teletypesetting *noun* typesetter operated from a punched paper tape

teletypewriter *noun* keyboard and printer attached to a computer system which can input data either direct *or* by making punched paper tape

television (TV) *noun* **(a)** system for broadcasting pictures and sound using high-frequency radio waves, captured by a receiver and shown on a screen **(b)** device that can receive broadcast signals with an aerial and display images on a CRT screen with sound **(c)** the actual broadcasts themselves, or the set on which they are seen; **television camera** = optical lenses in front of an electronic device which can convert images into electronic signals in a form that can be transmitted *or* displayed on a TV; **television mask** = (i) a mask used in a viewfinder, or by an animation artist, to point out the limits of the safe-action area on a television set; (ii) a mask used when designing titles so that they will appear in the safe-action area; **television monitor** = device able to display signals from a TV camera *or* computer without sound, but not broadcast signals (this is usually because there is no demodulator device which is needed for broadcast signals); **television projector** = device that projects a TV image onto a large screen; **television receive only** = *see* TVRO; **television receiver** = device able to display with sound, broadcast signals *or* other modulated signals (such as signals from a video recorder); **television receiver/monitor** = device able to act as a TV receiver *or* monitor; **television scan** = horizontal movement of the picture beam over the screen, producing one line of an image; **television tube** = CRT with electronic devices that provide the line by line horizontal and vertical scanning movement of the picture beam; *see also* CRT, RGB

telex 1 *noun* **(a)** system for sending messages using telephone lines, which are printed out at the receiving end on a special printer; *to send information by telex; the order came by telex*; **telex line** = wire linking a telex machine to the telex system; *we cannot communicate with our Nigerian office because of the breakdown of the telex lines*; **telex operator** = person who operates a telex machine; **telex subscriber** = company which has a telex **(b) a telex** = (i) a machine for sending and receiving telex messages; (ii) a message sent by telex; *he sent a telex to his head office; we received his telex this morning* **2** *verb* to send a message using a teleprinter; *can you telex the Canadian office before they open? he telexed the details of the contract to New York*

telnet *noun* software that allows you to connect to and control a remote computer via the Internet as if you were there

template *noun* **(a)** plastic *or* metal sheet with cut-out symbols to help the drawing of flowcharts and circuit diagrams **(b)** *(in text processing)* standard text (such as a standard letter *or* invoice) into which specific details (company address *or* prices *or* quantities) can be added **(c)** an opaque sheet which is placed in a spotlight and which has been cut into a certain shape in order to produce a patterned shadow; **template command** = command that allows functions *or* other commands to be easily set; *a template paragraph command enables the user to specify the number of spaces each paragraph should be indented*

tempo *noun* **(a)** *(in MIDI or music)* the speed at which the notes are played, measured in beats per minute (a typical MIDI tempo is 120bpm) **(b)** *(in a multimedia title)* the speed at which frames are displayed

temporarily *adverb* for a certain time *or* not permanently

temporary storage *noun* storage which is not permanent

temporary swap file *noun* file on a hard disk which is used by software to store data temporarily or for software that implements virtual memory, such as Microsoft's Windows

10Base2 IEEE standard specification for running Ethernet over thin coaxial cable with a data transfer rate of 10Mbps; **100Base2** = IEEE standard specification for running Ethernet over thin coaxial cable with a data transfer rate of 100Mbps; *see also* ETHERNET, STRUCTURED CABLING, UTP

10Base5 IEEE standard specification for running Ethernet over thick coaxial cable with a data transfer rate of 10Mbps; **100Base5** = IEEE standard specification for running Ethernet over thick coaxial cable with a data transfer rate of 100Mbps

10BaseT IEEE standard specification for running Ethernet over unshielded twisted pair cable with a data transfer rate of 10Mbps; **100BaseT** = IEEE standard specification for running Ethernet over unshielded twisted pair cable with a data transfer rate of 100Mbps

tenner *noun* 10,000 watt-spotlight with a Fresnel lens

tera- *prefix* one million million (ten to the power 12); **terabyte** = one thousand gigabytes or one million megabytes of data; **terahertz** = frequency of one million million hertz

terminal 1 *noun* (a) device usually made up of a display unit and a keyboard which allows entry and display of information when on-line to a central computer system; **terminal adapter** = device that connects a computer to a digital communications line; for example, to link a PC to an ISDN line; a terminal adapter transfers digital signals from the computer to the line, wheras a modem is used to connect a computer to an analogue communications line, such as a telephone line, and needs to convert digital signals to and from an analogue form; **terminal emulation** = ability of a terminal to emulate the functions of another type of terminal so that display codes can be correctly decoded and displayed and keystrokes correctly coded and transmitted; **terminal identity** = unique code transmitted by a viewdata terminal to provide identification and so authorization of a user; **terminal interface** = hardware and software combination required to control the functions of a terminal from a computer; *(slang)* **terminal junky** = person (a hacker) who is obsessed by computers; **terminal session** = period of time when a terminal is on-line or in use; *see also* DUMB TERMINAL, INTELLIGENT TERMINAL, INTERACTIVE TERMINAL **(b)** an electrical connection point; **terminal block** = strip of insulated connection points for wires; **terminal strip** = row of electrical connectors that allow pairs of wires to be electrically connected using a screw-down metal plate **(c)** point in a network where a message can be transmitted *or* received; *see also* SOURCE, SINK **2** *adjective* fatal *or* which cannot be repaired; *the computer has a terminal fault*

COMMENT: computer terminals can be intelligent, smart or dumb according to the inbuilt processing capabilities

```
The London Borough of Hackney
has standardised on terminal
emulator software from
Omniplex to allow its
networked desktop users to
select Unix or DOS
applications from a single
menu
```
Computing

terminate *verb* to end

terminate and stay resident (TSR) program *noun* program which loads itself into main memory and carries out a function when activated

termination *noun* ending *or* stopping; **abnormal termination** = unexpected stoppage of a program which is being run, caused by a fault *or* power failure

terminator *or* **rogue value** *noun* **(a)** *(in a LAN)* resistor that fits onto the each end of a coaxial cable in a bus network to create an electrical circuit **(b)** *(in a SCSI installation)* resistor that fits onto the last SCSI device in the daisy-chain, creating an electrical circuit **(c)** item in a list of data, which shows that the list is terminated

ternary *adjective* (number system) with three possible states

test 1 *noun* **(a)** action carried out on a device *or* program to establish whether it is working correctly, and if not, which component *or* instruction is not working **(b)** an exposed and developed film strip which is used to gauge whether the film is suitable for further printing or not **2** *verb* to carry out an examination of a device *or* program to see if it is working correctly; **test data** = data with known results prepared to allow a new program to be tested; **test equipment** = special equipment which tests hardware *or* software; **test pattern** = graphical pattern displayed on a TV screen to test its colour, balance, horizontal and vertical linearity and contrast; *see also* BENCHMARK

text *noun* alphanumeric characters that convey information; **text compression** = reducing the space required by a section of text, by using one code to represent more than one character, by removing spaces and punctuation marks, etc.; **text-editing facilities** = word-processing system that allows the user to add, delete, move, insert and correct sections of text; **text-editing function** = option in a program that provides text-editing facilities; *the program includes a built-in text-editing function*; **text editor** = piece of software that provides the user with text-editing facilities; **text file** = stored file on a computer that contains text rather than digits *or* data; **text formatter** = program that arranges a text file according to preset rules, such as line width and page size; **text management** = facilities that allow text to be written, stored, retrieved, edited and printed; **text manipulation** = facilities that allow text editing, changing, inserting and deleting; **text processing** = word-processing *or* using a computer to keyboard, edit and output text, in the forms of letters, labels, etc.; **text register** = temporary computer storage register for text characters only; **text retrieval** = information retrieval system that allows the user to examine complete documents rather than just a reference to one; **text screen** = area of computer screen that has been set up to display text; **text to speech converter** = electronic device that uses a speech synthesizer to produce the spoken equivalent of a piece of text that has been entered

textual *adjective* referring to text; *the editors made several textual changes*

before the proofs were sent back for correction

texture mapping *noun* **(a)** special computer graphics effect using algorithms to produce an image that looks like the surface of something (such as marble, brick, stone or water) **(b)** covering one image with another to give the first a texture

TFT screen = THIN FILM TRANSISTOR SCREEN method of creating a high-quality LCD display often used in laptop computers; *see also* LCD

> COMMENT: TFT screens provide a sharper, clearer image with better colour display than a backlit LCD display - however, they are more complex to manufacture, more expensive and consume more power

TFTP = TRIVIAL FILE TRANSFER PROTOCOL simple form of the standard FTP (file transfer protocol) system; commonly used to load the operating system software onto a diskless workstation from a server when the workstation boots up when it is switched on; *see also* FTP

thaw *noun (film)* special effect in which action starts again after a freeze frame effect, especially in videowall presentation

thermal *adjective* referring to heat; **thermal control module (TCM)** = device that brings together over 100 ICs onto a water-cooled ceramic base providing over 1500 connection points (pins) per device; **thermal dye diffusion** = method of printing similar to thermal wax transfer, except that a dye is used instead of coloured wax; thermal dye diffusion can print continuous colour to produce a near-photographic output; **thermal imaging** = TV camera system that is sensitive to various temperatures rather than light; **thermal inkjet printer** = computer printer which produces characters by sending a stream of tiny drops (created by heating the ink) of electrically charged ink onto the paper (the movement of the ink drops is controlled by an electric field; this is a non-impact printer with few moving parts); **thermal magnetic duplication** = *see* TMP; **thermal noise** = random noise always present in any electronic component due to the effect of temperature on the materials (thermal noise power is proportional to the temperature of the component); **thermal paper** = special paper whose coating turns black when heated, allowing characters to be printed by using a matrix of small heating elements; **thermal printer** = type of printer where the character is formed on thermal paper with a printhead containing a matrix of small heating elements

> COMMENT: this type of printer is very quiet in operation since the printing head does not strike the paper

thermal printing *noun* **(a)** a printing system which has a print head with a number of quick-heating elements which work with heat-sensitive paper, or with ordinary paper when using a special ribbon **(b)** an imaging system which uses enclosed bubbles in an emulsion

thermal transfer *or* **thermal wax** *or* **thermal wax transfer printer** *noun* method of printing where the colours are produced by melting coloured wax onto the paper; *a thermal transfer printer; colour ink-jet technology and thermal transfer technology compete with each other*

thermistor *noun* electronic device whose resistance changes with temperature

thermo-sensitive *adjective* which is sensitive to heat

thesaurus *noun* file which contains synonyms that are displayed as alternatives to a misspelt word during a spell-check

thick *adjective* with a large distance between two surfaces; **thick film** = miniature electronic circuit design in which miniature components are mounted on an insulating base, then connected as required; often used to provide a package that is larger but cheaper on short runs than chips

thick-Ethernet *noun* network implemented using thick coaxial cable and transceivers to connect branch cables; can stretch long distances; *see also* ETHERNET, THIN-ETHERNET

thimble printer *noun* computer printer using a printing head similar to a daisy wheel but shaped like a thimble

thin *adjective* with only a small distance between two surfaces; **thin film** = method of constructing integrated circuits by depositing in a vacuum very thin patterns of various materials onto a substrate to form the required interconnected components; *see also* CHIP, SUBSTRATE; **thin film memory** = high speed access RAM device using a matrix of magnetic cells and a matrix of read/write heads to access them; **thin film transistor screen** = *see* TFT SCREEN; **thin window** = single line display window

thin-Ethernet *noun* network implemented using thin coaxial cable and BNC connectors; it is limited to distances of around 1000m

third *adjective* coming after second; **third generation (3G)** = latest specification for mobile communication systems (including mobile telephones); the third generation includes very fast data transfer rates of between 128Kbps and 2Mbps (depending on whether the person is walking, in a car or at their base station). This will allow high-speed Internet access, even live video links, to a portable telephone. Previous generations included: the first generation of mobile telephone were analogue cellular telephones, digital PCS were the second generation.; **third generation computers** = range of computers where integrated circuits were used instead of transistors; **third party** = company which supplies items *or* services for a system sold by one party (the seller) to another (the buyer)

> COMMENT: a third party might supply computer maintenance *or* might write programs, etc.

```
they expect third party
developers to enhance the
operating systems by adding
their own libraries
                  PC Business World
```

thirty-two bit system (32-bit) *noun* microcomputer system or CPU that handles data in thirty-two bit words; *see* INTEL, MOTOROLA, PROCESSOR

thrashing *noun* **(a)** excessive disk activity **(b)** configuration *or* program fault in a virtual memory system, that results in a CPU wasting time moving pages of data between main memory and disk or backing store

thread *noun* **(a)** program that consists of many independent smaller sections **(b)** the accurate positioning of film or tape in the path of a projector, or another film mechanism for take-up (NOTE: 'thread up' also used in the context of definition (b))

threaded language *noun* programming language that allows many small sections of code to be written then used by a main program

three input adder *see* FULL ADDER

three-colour process *noun* a process used to convert a colour image into three separate colours (red, blue and green)

three-dimensional *or* **3D** *adjective* (image) which has three dimensions (width, breadth and depth), and therefore gives the impression of being solid

the software can create 3D images using data from a scanner or photographs from an electronic microscope

PC Business World

three-pin plug *noun* standard plug with three connections, to connect an electric device to the mains electricity supply

COMMENT: the three pins are for the live, neutral and earth connections

threshold *noun* preset level which causes an action if a signal exceeds or drops below it; *if using a microphone in a noisy environment you might set the threshold high so that only loud noises are recorded*

threshold howl *noun* acoustic feedback which is created by sound from the loudspeakers re-entering the microphone

through-the-lens focus *noun* a camera viewfinder which can focus through the camera lens without parallax

throughput *noun* rate of production by a machine *or* system, measured as total useful information processed in a set period of time; *for this machine throughput is 1.3 inches per second (ips) scanning speed*

throw *noun* (a) distance from a film projector lens to the screen (b) distance from lighting units to the action area

thrystor *noun* semiconductor device that will allow the control of an AC voltage according to an input signal

thumbnail *noun* miniature graphical representation of an image; used as a quick and convenient method of viewing the contents of graphics or DTP files before they are retrieved

tie line *or* **tie trunk** *noun* communications link between switchboards *or* PBX systems

TIFF = TAG IMAGE FILE FORMAT standard file format used to store bitmap graphic images

COMMENT: developed by Aldus and Microsoft, TIFF can store monochrome, grey-scale, 8-bit or 32-bit colour images. There have been many different versions of TIFF that include several different compression algorithms

tight *adjective & noun (film)* (a) close camera shot where the subjects fill the whole frame (b) programme material that takes up all of the broadcast time allotted for it

tilde *noun* printed accent (~), commonly used over the letter 'n' in Spanish, vowels in Portuguese, etc.

tile *verb (in a GUI)* to arrange a group of windows so that they are displayed side by side without overlapping

tilt *verb* (a) to sweep a video camera up and down; *compare with* PAN (b) to alter the slope of the frequency response in a sound reproducer

tilt and swivel *adjective* (monitor) which is mounted on a pivot so that it can be moved to point in the most convenient direction for the operator

time 1 *noun* period expressed in hours, minutes, seconds, etc.; **time address code** = signal recorded on a video tape to display time elapsed when editing; **time assigned speech interpolation** = *see* TASI; **time base** = (i) signal used as a basis for timing purposes; (ii) regular sawtooth signal used in an oscilloscope to sweep the beam across the screen; **time-base corrector** = mechanism used to rectify timing faults in video signals, usually caused by speed deviations in video tape recorders; **time-base signal** = a signal which is recorded on the edge of a film in order to match up with a signal on a magnetic recording; assists the synchronisation of film and sound workprints; **time code** = a method of encoding video and audio tape, and sometimes film, for the later synchronisation and editing; shows hours, minutes and seconds and allows frames to be identified; *see also* SMPTE; **time code**

in picture = *see* TCIP; **time coded page** = teletext page that contains additional text which is displayed after a period of time; **time derived channel** = communications channel using time division multiplexing techniques; **time display** = digits *or* dial which show the current time; **time division multiple access** = time division multiplexing system that allocates time slots to various users according to demand; **time division multiplexing (TDM)** = multiplexing system that allows a number of signals to be transmitted down a single line by sending a sample of the first signal for a short period, then the second, and so on; **time division switching** = moving data from one time slot to another; **time domain analysis** = signal analysis as it varies with time; **time domain reflectometry (TDR)** = test which identifies where cable faults lie by sending a signal down the cable and measuring how long it takes for the reflection to come back; **time-lapse** = in film or video, the recording of a series of images with a controlled time delay between each image, and the subsequent projection at normal speed in order to show a process which is usually invisible to the human eye; **time-lapse motor** = motor which is attached to a camera to produce the intermittent single frame exposures for time-lapse cinematography; *(of an event or option)* **time out** = to become no longer valid after a period of time; **time shift viewing** = use of a video recorder to record programs which are then replayed at a more convenient time; **time slice** = amount of time allowed for a single task in a time-sharing system *or* in multiprogramming; **time slot** = period of time that contains an amount of data about one signal in a time division multiplexing system; *(within a MIDI sequence)* **time stamp** = a MIDI message that is tagged with a time so that a sequencer can play it at the correct moment **2** *verb* to measure the amount of time taken by an operation; **timed backup** = backup which occurs automatically after a period of time, or at a particular time each day; **timing loop** = computer program loop that repeats a number of times to produce a certain time delay

time-sharing *noun* computer system that allows several independent users to be on-line to it at the same time

COMMENT: in time-sharing, each user appears to be using the computer all the time, when in fact each is using the CPU for a short time slice only

timeout 1 *noun* **(a)** logoff procedure carried out if no data is entered on an on-line terminal **(b)** period of time reserved for an operation **2** *verb (of an event or option)* to become no longer valid after a period of time; *if you do not answer this question within one minute, the program times out and moves onto the next question*

timer *noun* device which records the time taken for an operation to be completed

tiny model *noun* memory model of the Intel 80x86 processor family that allows a combined total of 64Kb for data and code

title *noun* name given to a book *or* film *or* TV programme *or* multimedia software product, etc.; **title bar** = horizontal bar at the top of a window which displays the title of the window or application; **title of disk** = identification of a disk, referring to its contents; **title page** = first main page of a book, with the title, the name of the author and the name of the publisher; **titles** = words superimposed over a film or television programme which are not part of the scene

TK = TELECINE

TMP = THERMAL MAGNETIC DUPLICATION high-speed duplication of a videotape from a master tape

TMSF time format = TRACKS, MINUTES, SECONDS, FRAMES MCI time format used mainly by audio CD devices to measure time in frames and tracks

T-number *see* T-STOP

toggle *verb* to switch between the two states of a bistable device; **toggle switch** = electrical switch that has only two positions

the symbols can be toggled on or off the display
Micro Decision

token *noun* internal code which replaces a reserved word *or* program statement in a high-level language; **control token** = special sequence of bits transmitted over a

LAN to provide control actions; **token ring network** = network in which a device can transmit data by taking one free token which circulates and inserting the message after it

token bus network *noun* IEEE 802.4 standard for a local area network formed with a bus-topology cable; workstations transfer data by passing a token

token passing *noun* method of controlling access to a local area network by using a token packet: a workstation cannot transmit data until it receives the token

token ring network *noun* IEEE 802.5 standard that uses a token passed from one workstation to the next in a ring network, a workstation can only transmit data if it captures the token; *token ring networks are very democratic and retain performance against increasing load*

> COMMENT: token ring networks, although logically a ring, are often physically wired in a star topology

tomo- *prefix* meaning a cutting *or* section

tomogram *noun* picture of part of the body taken by tomography

tomography *noun* scanning of a particular part of the body using X-rays *or* ultrasound; **computerized axial tomography (CAT)** = X-ray examination where a computer creates a picture of a section of a patient's body

tone *noun* **(a)** sound at one single frequency; **dialling tone** = sound made by a telephone to show that it is ready for the number to be dialled; **engaged tone** = sound made by a telephone showing that the number dialled is busy; **tone dialling** = telephone dialling system that uses different frequency tones to represent the dialled number; **tone signalling** = tones used in a telephone network to convey control *or* address signals **(b)** shade of a colour; *the graphics package can give several tones of blue*

toner *noun* finely powdered ink (usually black) that is used in laser printers and photocopiers; the toner is transferred onto the paper by electrical charge, then fixed permanently to the paper by heating; **toner cartridge** = sealed cartridge containing toner; *change toner and toner cartridge according to the manual; the toner*

cartridge and the imaging drum can be replaced as one unit when the toner runs out

tool *noun* (*in a graphical front-end*) function accessed from an icon in a toolbar, such as a circle-draw option

toolbar *noun* window that contains a range of icons that access tools; *paint programs normally have a toolbar that includes icons for colour, brush, circle, text and eraser tools; a floating toolbar is a moveable window that can be positioned anywhere on screen*

Toolbox (*in an Apple Macintosh*) set of utility programs stored in ROM to provide graphic functions

toolbox *noun* **(a)** box containing instruments needed to repair *or* maintain *or* install equipment **(b)** set of predefined routines *or* functions that are used when writing a program

toolkit *noun* series of functions which help a programmer write *or* debug programs

tools *noun* set of utility programs (backup, format, etc.) in a computer system

top *noun* part which is the highest point of something; **top down programming** *or* **structured programming** = method of writing programs where a complete system is divided into simple units and each unit is written and tested before proceeding with the next one; **top hat** = small camera mount used for support when a low position is needed; **top of stack** = the latest data item added to a stack; **top space** = number of blank lines left at the top of a printed text

topology *noun* way in which the various elements in a network are interconnected; **bus topology** = network topology in which all devices are connected to a single cable which has terminators at each end; *Ethernet is a network that uses the bus topology; token ring uses a ring topology;* **network topology** = layout of machines in a network (a star network *or* a ring network *or* a bus network) which will determine what cabling and interfaces are needed and what possibilities the network can offer; **star topology** = network topology in which all devices are connected by individual cable to a single central hub; *if one workstation cable snaps in a star topology, the rest continue, unlike a bus topology*

TOPS software that allows IBM PCs and Apple Macintoshes to share files on a network

torn tape *noun* communications switching method, in which the received message is punched onto a paper tape which is fed by hand into the appropriate tape reader for transmission to the required destination

total access communication system *see* TACS

touch up *verb* to remove scratches *or* other marks from a photograph *or* image

touch *verb* to make contact with something with the fingers; **touch pad** = flat device that can sense when it is touched, used to control a cursor position *or* switch a device on or off; **touch screen** = computer display that has a grid of infrared transmitters and receivers, positioned on either side of the screen (when a user wants to make a selection *or* move the cursor, he points to the screen, breaking two of the beams, which gives the position of his finger)

TP = TELEPROCESSING, TRANSACTION PROCESSING

TPI = TRACKS PER INCH

trace *noun* (a) method of verifying that a program is functioning correctly, in which the current status and contents of the registers and variables used are displayed after each instruction step; **trace program** = diagnostic program which executes a program that is being debugged, one instruction at a time, displaying the states and registers; **trace trap** = selective breakpoint where a tracing program stops, allowing registers to be examined (b) *(in graphics program)* function that can take a bitmap image and process it to find the edges of the shapes and so convert these into a vector line image (c) cathode ray tube image which is produced by a flowing electronic stream

traceroute *noun* software utility that finds and displays the route taken for data travelling between your computer and a distant server on the Internet

tracing function *noun* function of a graphics program that takes a bitmap image and processes it to find the edges of the shapes and so convert these into a vector

line image that can be more easily manipulated

track 1 *noun* (a) one of a series of thin concentric rings on a disk *or* thin lines on a tape, which the read/write head accesses and on which the data is stored in separate sectors (b) the rails on which a dolly moves (c) *(in a music CD)* a song (d) *(in a MIDI file)* method of separating the notes within a tune either by channel or by part or instrument (e) *(in authoring software)* series of instructions that define how an object moves with time; **tracks per inch (TPI)** = number of concentric data tracks on a disk surface per inch **2** *verb* (a) to follow a path *or* track correctly; *the read head is not tracking the recorded track correctly* (b) to move a camera and its mount towards or away from the action, or to follow a moving subject

COMMENT: the first track on a tape is along the edge and the tape may have up to nine different tracks on it, while a disk has many concentric tracks around the central hub

trackball *noun* device used to move a cursor on-screen, which is controlled by turning a ball contained in a case with the palm of your hand

tracks, minutes, seconds, frames *see* TMSF

tractor feed *noun* method of feeding paper into a printer, where sprocket wheels on the printer connect with the sprocket holes on either edge of the paper to pull the paper through

the printer is fairly standard with both tractor and cut sheet feed system
Which PC?

traffic *noun* term covering all the messages and other signals processed by a system; *our Ethernet network begins to slow down if the traffic reaches 60 per cent of the bandwidth;* **incoming traffic** = data and messages received; **traffic analysis** = study of the times, types and quantities of messages and signals being processed by a system (NOTE: no plural)

trail *noun* line followed by something; **audit trail** = recording details of the use made of a system by noting transactions carried out (used for checking on illegal use *or* malfunction)

trailer *noun* (a) leader *or* piece of non magnetic tape to the start of a reel of magnetic tape to make loading easier (b) final byte of a file containing control *or* file characteristics (c) a brief film which advertises a motion picture that is about to be released

transaction *noun* one single action which affects a database (a sale, a change of address, a new customer, etc.); **transaction-driven system (TDS)** = computer system that will normally run batch processing tasks until interrupted by a new transaction, at which point it allocates resources to the transaction; **transaction file** *or* **change file** *or* **detail file** *or* **movement file** = file containing recent changes *or* transactions to records which is then used to update a master file; **transaction processing (TP)** = interactive processing in which a user enters commands and data on a terminal which is linked to a central computer, with results being displayed on-screen

COMMENT: similar to a multiprocessing system; compare with a batch processing system

At present, users implementing client-server strategies are focusing on decision support systems before implementing online transaction processing and other mission-critical applications

Computing

transborder data flow *noun* passing of data from one country to another using communications links such as satellites *or* land lines

transceiver *noun* transmitter and receiver *or* device which can both transmit and receive signals (such as a terminal *or* modem); **radio transceiver** = radio transmitter and receiver in a single housing

transcoder *noun* electronic device used to convert television signal standards; *use the transcoder to convert PAL to SECAM*

transcribe *verb* to transfer data from one system to another *or* from one medium to another

transcription *noun* action of transcribing data

transducer *noun* electronic device which converts signals in one form into signals in another; *the pressure transducer converts physical pressure signals into electrical signals*

transfer 1 *verb* (a) to change command *or* control; *all processing activities have been transferred to the mainframe* (b) to copy a section of memory to another location; **transfer rate** = speed at which data is transferred from backing store to main memory; *with a good telephone line, this pair of modems can achieve a transfer rate of 56Kbps* **2** *noun* changing command or control

transform *verb* to change something from one state to another

transformation *noun* action of changing

transformational rules *noun* set of rules that are applied to data that is to be transformed into coded form

transformer *noun* device which changes the voltage *or* current amplitude of an AC signal

COMMENT: a transformer consists of two electrically insulated coils of wire; the AC signal in one induces a similar signal in the other which can be a different amplitude according to the ratio of the turns in the coils of wire

transient 1 *adjective* state *or* signal which is present for a short period of time; **transient error** = temporary error which occurs for a short period of time **2** *noun* **line transient** *or* **voltage transient** = spike of voltage that is caused by a time delay in two devices switching *or* noise on the line

transistor *noun* electronic semiconductor device which can control the current flow in a circuit (there are two main types of transistors: bipolar and unipolar); **bipolar** *or* **junction transistor (BJT)** = transistor constructed of three layers of alternating types of doped semiconductor (p-n-p or n-p-n), each layer has a terminal labelled emitter, base and collector, usually the base controls the current flow between emitter and collector; **field effect transistor (FET)** = electronic device that can act as a variable current flow control; an external signal varies the resistance of the device and current flow by changing the width of a conducting channel by means of a field; it has three terminals: source, gate and drain; **transistor-resistor logic (TRL)** = early logic gate design method using bipolar transistors and resistors; **transistor-transistor logic (TTL)** = most common family of logic gates and high-speed transistor circuit design, in which the bipolar transistors are directly connected (usually collector to base) to provide the logic function; **unipolar transistor** = FIELD EFFECT TRANSISTOR

transition *noun* **(a)** (short) period of time between two events **(b)** period between two frames in a slide show or animation; the user can normally define how one frame changes to the next; *see also* DISSOLVE, FADE, WIPE

translate *verb* **(a)** to convert a program written in one language to a different programming language; *you can translate a HyperCard stack into a ToolBook script* **(b)** *(graphics)* to move an image on screen without rotating it

translation tables *or* **conversion tables** *noun* lookup tables *or* collection of stored results that can be accessed very rapidly by a process without the need to calculate each result when needed; *translation tables may be created and used in conjunction with a client's data to convert it to typesetting*

translator (program) *noun* program contained in the operating system that translates a high level language program into machine code

translucent *adjective* material which allows light to pass through

transmission *noun* sending of signals from one device to another; sending out radio *or* TV signals; **transmission channel** = physical connection between two points that allows data to be transmitted (such as a link between a CPU and a peripheral); **transmission control protocol** = *see* TCP; **transmission control protocol/interface program (TCP/IP)** = data transfer protocol used in networks and communications systems (often used in Unix-based networks); **transmission media** = means by which data can be transmitted, such as radio, light, etc.; **transmission rate** =

measure of the amount of data transmitted in a certain time; *their average transmission is 60,000 bits per second (bps) through a parallel connection or 20,000 bps through a serial connection*; **transmission window** = narrow range of wavelengths to which a fibre optic cable is most transparent

transmissive disk *noun* optical data storage disk in which the reading laser beam shines through the disk to a detector below; *compare with* REFLECTIVE DISK

transmit *verb* to send information from one device to another, using any medium, such as radio, cable, wire link, etc.

transmittance *noun* amount of light transmitted through a material in ratio to the total light incident on the surface of the material

transmitter *noun* device that will take an input signal, process it (modulate *or* convert to sound, etc.) then transmit it by some medium (radio, light, etc.)

> an X-ray picture can be digitized and transmitted to a specialist at another for diagnosis
> *Electronics & Business World*

> modern high-power transmitters are much reduced in size and a simple and uncluttered appearance
> *Electronics & Power*

transparency *noun* **(a)** transparent positive film, which can be projected onto a screen *or* to make film for printing **(b)** *(in graphics)* amount one image shows of another image beneath it; **transparent GIF** = graphic image stored in the GIF file format with one colour (from the palette) assigned as the transparent colour - when the image is displayed, any part of the image in this colour will be transparent to allow any image beneath to show through; *see also* GIF

transparent *noun* **(a)** computer program which is not obvious to the user *or* which cannot be seen by the user when it is running **(b)** device *or* network that allows signals to pass through it without being altered in any way

transphasor *noun* optical transistor, that is constructed from a crystal which is able to switch a main beam of light according to a smaller input signal

> COMMENT: this is used in the latest research for an optical computer which could run very fast - at the speed of light

transponder *noun* communications device that receives and retransmits signals

transport *verb* to carry from one place to another; **transport layer** = layer in the ISO/OSI standard that checks and controls the quality of the connection; *see also* LAYER

transportable *adjective* which can be carried; *a transportable computer is not as small as a laptop*

> WSL has potential as the repository's 'meta transport layer for program objects', claims Healey, but it would need to be significantly extended. 'It only handles a 10th of the translation problem,' says Healey
> *Computing*

transposition *noun* changing the order of a series of characters (as 'comupter' for 'computer' *or* '1898' for '1988'); *a series of transposition errors caused faulty results*

transputer *noun* single large very powerful chip containing a 32-bit microprocessor running at around 10 Mips

transverse mode noise *noun* interference which is apparent between power supply lines

transverse scan *noun* method of reading data from a video tape in which the playback head is at right angles to the tape

trap *noun* device, software or hardware that will detect something, such as a variable, fault or value; **trap handler** = software that accepts interrupt signals and acts on them (such as running a special routine *or* sending data to a peripheral)

trapezium distortion *noun* in a visual or video system, image distortion which produces a rectangular shape

trashcan *noun (in a GUI)* icon which looks like a dustbin or trash can; it deletes any file that is dragged onto it

travelling matte *noun* in the printing process, the combining of an action shot with another action shot or background shot

which has been filmed previously; used to create special effects

travelling matte printing *noun* printing of a film where a travelling matte is used

travelling peg bars *plural noun* peg bars encased in an animation table which are able to be moved in an easterly or westerly direction

tree *noun* **tree (structure)** = data structure system where each item of data is linked to several others by branches (as opposed to a line system where each item leads on to the next); **binary tree** = data system where each item of data *or* node has only two branches; **tree and branch network system** = system of networking where data is transmitted along a single output line, from which other lines branch out, forming a tree structure that feeds individual stations; **tree selection sort** = rapid form of selection where the information from the first sort pass is used in the second pass to speed up selection

trellis coding *noun* method of modulating a signal that uses both amplitude and phase modulation to give a greater throughput and lower error rates for data transmission speeds of over 9600bits per second

tremendously high frequency (THF) *noun* radio frequency between 300GHz and 3000GHz

triacetate base *noun* emulsion coating for film

triad *noun* triangular shaped grouping of the red, green and blue colour phosphor spots at each pixel location on the screen of a colour television

trial *noun* test for new equipment to see if it works; **trials engineer** = person who designs, runs and analyses trials of new equipment

triangle *noun (film)* a spreader with three sides for tripod legs

triax *noun (film)* coaxial cable with an additional screen which conveys power and coded commands to a television camera, and also receives the video signal from the camera; *triax is used when the camera is far away from the control unit*

tributary station *noun* any station on a multilink network other than the main control station

trim *verb* to cut off the edge of something; *the printed pages are trimmed to 198 x 129mm; you will need to trim the top part of the photograph to make it fit*

triniscope *noun* colour video display system which uses three different cathode ray tubes to produce the red, green and blue images

Trinitron *noun* colour television cathode ray tube which uses striped phosphors and aperture grille

tripack *noun* three emulsion layered colour film

triple standard *noun* a video tape recorder, television monitor or other apparatus which can receive NTSC, PAL or SECAM standard video signals

TRL = TRANSISTOR-RESISTOR LOGIC

Trojan Horse *noun* program inserted into a system by a hacker that will perform a harmless function while copying information in a classified file into a file with a low priority, which the hacker can then access without the authorized user knowing

trombone *noun* (*film*) a support clamp used to connect a lighting unit to a flat

troposphere *noun* region of space extending up to six miles above the earth's surface, causing radio wave scatter; *see also* IONOSPHERE

troubleshoot *verb* **(a)** to debug computer software **(b)** to locate and repair faults in hardware

troubleshooter *noun* person who troubleshoots hardware *or* software

trough *noun* lowest point in a waveform; *compare with* PEAK

trucking shot *noun* (*film*) shot filmed whilst the camera is moving with the action, supported on a truck or other such vehicle

TRUE *noun* logical condition (representing binary one); *compare with* FALSE

TrueType outline font technology introduced by Apple and Microsoft as a means of printing exactly what is displayed on screen

truncate *verb* **(a)** to cut short **(b)** to give an approximate value to a number by reducing it to a certain number of digits

truncation *noun* turning a real number into an integer by removing fractions (3.5678 truncated to 3.56); **truncation error** = error caused when a number is truncated

trunk *noun* bus *or* communication link consisting of wires *or* leads, which connect different parts of a hardware system

trunk call *noun* *GB* long-distance telephone call

trunk exchange *noun* *GB* telephone exchange that only handles trunk calls

truth table *noun* method of defining a logic function as the output state for all possible inputs; **truth value** = two values (true *or* false, T *or* F, 1 *or* 0) used in Boolean algebra

TSR = TERMINATE AND STAY RESIDENT (PROGRAM)

T-stop *noun* (*film*) a lens setting which shows the actual light transmission through the lens after being absorbed and reflected

> COMMENT: it differs from the f-stop which only loosely estimates the light transmission

TSW = TELESOFTWARE

TTL *noun* **(a)** = TRANSISTOR-TRANSISTOR LOGIC most common family of logic gates and high-speed transistor circuit design in which the bipolar transistors are directly connected (usually collector to base); **TTL compatible** = MOS or other electronic circuits *or* components that can directly connect to and drive TTL circuits; **TTL logic** = use of TTL design and components to implement logic circuits and gates; **TTL monitor** = design of monitor which can only accept digital signals, so can only display monochrome images or a limited range of colours **(b)** = THROUGH THE LENS; a camera viewfinder system

tune *verb* **(a)** to set a system at its optimum point by careful adjustment **(b)** (i) to adjust a radio receiver's frequency until the required station is received clearly; (ii) to adjust a transmitter to the correct frequency

tuner *noun* electronic circuit that detects a transmitted television carrier signal at a particular frequency and removes the audio or video information to display on a CRT

tungsten halogen lamp *noun* (*film*) small, competent lamp with tungsten filament enclosed in a quartz or hard glass envelope filled with halogen glass

tungsten rating *noun* a number which indicates the related sensitivity of a film to artificial light

Turing machine *noun* mathematical model of a device that could read and write data to a controllable tape storage while altering its internal states

Turing test *noun* test to decide if a computer is 'intelligent'

turn off *verb* to switch off *or* to disconnect the power supply to a machine; *turn off the power before unplugging the monitor*

turn on *verb* to switch on *or* to connect the power supply to a machine

turnaround document *noun* document which is printed out from a computer, sent to a user and returned by the user with new notes *or* information written on it, which can be read by a document reader

turnaround time (TAT) *noun* **(a)** length of time it takes to switch data flow direction in a half duplex system **(b)** time taken for a product to be constructed and delivered after an order has been received **(c)** *US* time taken to activate a program and produce the result which the user has asked for

turnkey system *noun* complete system which is designed to a customer's needs and is ready to use (to operate it, the user only has to switch it on or turn a key)

turret *noun* *(film)* rotary camera or projector attachment which permits any one of two or more lenses to be moved quickly into place on the optical axis to facilitate rapid shooting

turtle *noun* device whose movement and position are controllable, which is used to draw graphics (with instructions in computer language LOGO), either a device which works on a flat surface (floor turtle) *or* which draws on a VDU screen (screen turtle), used as a teaching aid; **turtle graphics** = graphic images created using a turtle and a series of commands; *the charts were prepared using turtle graphics*

TV = TELEVISION

TVRO = TELEVISION RECEIVE ONLY equipment for reception and display without transmission

TWAIN application programming interface standard developed by Hewlett-Packard, Logitech, Eastman Kodak, Aldus, and Caere that allows software to control image hardware

tweak *verb* to make small adjustments to a program *or* hardware to improve performance

tweening *noun* *(in computer graphics)* calculating the intermediate images that lead from a starting image to a different finished image; *using tweening, we can show how a frog turns into a princess in five steps*; *see also* MORPHING

tweeter *noun* *(informal)* small loudspeaker used for high frequency sounds only; *compare with* WOOFER

twisted pair cable *noun* cable which consists of two insulated copper wires twisted around each other (to reduce induction and so interference); **shielded twisted pair (STP) cable** = cable which consists of two insulated copper wires twisted around each other (to reduce induction and so interference) with the pair of wires then being wrapped in an insulated shielding layer to further reduce interference; **unshielded twisted pair (UTP) cable** = cable which consists of two insulated copper wires twisted around each other (to reduce induction and so interference), but unlike STP cable the pair of wires are not wrapped in any other layer

twitter *noun* video picture distortion which produces a flicker at the horizontal edges of objects

two's complement *noun* formed by adding one to the one's complement of a binary number, often used to represent negative binary numbers

two-bladed shutter *noun* a shutter with two blades and two apertures which decrease the flicker when each film frame is projected twice

two-dimensional *adjective* which has two dimensions (that is, flat, with no depth); **two-dimensional array** = array which locates items both vertically and horizontally

two-input adder *see* HALF ADDER

two-part *noun* paper (for computers *or* typewriters) with a top sheet for the original and a second sheet for a copy; *two-part invoices; two-part stationery*

two-shot *noun* a camera shot of two performers from the waist or shoulders up

two-way cable *noun US* system of cable TV, where the viewer can take which programmes he wants by selecting them *or* where the viewer can respond to broadcast questions by sending his response down the cable

two-way radio *noun* radio transmitted and receiver in a single housing, allowing duplex communication with another user

two-wire circuit *noun* two insulated wires used to carry transmitted and received messages independently

TX   =   TRANSMISSION, TRANSMITTER

tyler mount *noun (film)* a camera mount which prevents vibration

type 1 *noun* **(a)** metal bars with a raised character used for printing **(b)** characters used in printing *or* characters which appear in printed form; *they switched to italic type for the heading* **(c)** definition of the processes *or* sorts of data which a variable in a computer can contain (this can be numbers, text only, etc.); **string type** = variable that can contain alphanumeric characters only; **variable data type** = variable that can contain any sort of data, such as numerical, text, etc. **2** *verb* to write with a typewriter *or* to enter information via a keyboard; *he can type quite fast; all his reports are typed on his portable typewriter; I typed in the command again, but it still didn't work*

type style *noun* weight and angle of a font, such as bold or italic

typeface *or* **typestyle** *or* **font** *noun* set of characters designed in a certain style; *most of this book is set in the Times typeface*

typescript *noun* copy of a text written by an author on a typewriter; *compare with* MANUSCRIPT

typeset *verb* to set text in type for printing; *in desktop publishing, the finished work should look almost as if it had been typeset*

typesetter *noun* **(a)** company which typesets; *the text is ready to be sent to the typesetter* **(b)** machine which produces very

high-quality text output using a laser to create an image on photosensitive paper (normally at a resolution of 1275 or 2450dpi)

typesetting *noun* action of setting text in type; *typesetting costs can be reduced by supplying the typesetter with prekeyed disks*; *see also* PHOTOTYPESETTING

typesize *noun* size of type, calculated in 'points' which refer to the height of the character, but not its width

typewriter *noun* machine which prints letters *or* figures on a piece of paper when a key is pressed by striking an inked ribbon onto the paper with a character type; *she wrote the letter on her portable typewriter; he makes fewer mistakes now he is using an electronic typewriter*; **typewriter faces** = spacing, size and font of characters available on a typewriter

typewritten *adjective* written on a typewriter; *he sent in a typewritten job application*

typing *noun* writing letters with a typewriter; **typing error** = mistake made when using a typewriter; *the secretary must have made a typing error*; **copy typing** = typing documents from handwritten originals, not from dictation; **typing pool** = group of typists, working together in a company, offering a secretarial service to several departments (NOTE: no plural)

typist *noun* person whose job is to write letters using a typewriter; **copy typist** = person who types documents from handwritten originals not from dictation; **shorthand typist** = typist who takes dictation in shorthand and then types it

typo *noun informal* typographical error which is made while typesetting

typographer *noun* person who designs a section of art *or* text to be printed

typographic *or* **typographical** *adjective* referring to typography *or* to typesetting; *no typographical skills are required for this job; a typographical error made while typesetting is called a 'typo'*; **typographical error** = mistake made while typesetting

typography *noun* art and methods used in working with type

Uu

UART = UNIVERSAL ASYNCHRONOUS RECEIVER-TRANSMITTER chip which converts asynchronous serial bit streams to a parallel form *or* parallel data to serial bit streams; *see also* USART

U-format cassette *noun* standard size videocassette which uses a three-quarter inch tape for use with the U-matic system

UHF = ULTRA HIGH FREQUENCY range of frequencies normally used to transmit television signals

ULA = UNCOMMITTED LOGIC ARRAY

Ultra ATA version of the AT Attachment (ATA) hard disk drive interface standard that can support a data transfer rate of up to 33MBps; to manage this high-speed data transfer from the hard disk interface to the rest of your PC, it needs to have a high-speed version of DMA.

ultra- *prefix* meaning very large *or* further than; **ultra high frequency (UHF)** = very high frequency range between 300MHz and 3GHz; **ultrafiche** = microfiche with images that have been reduced by more than ninety times; **ultrasonic** = sound pressure waves at a frequency above the audio band, above 20KHz; **ultrasonic film cleaner** = a machine which uses ultrasonic frequencies to remove dust or dirt from film; **ultrasound** = sound emitted at a frequency above the audio band; **ultraviolet (light) (UV)** = electromagnetic radiation with wavelength just greater than the visible spectrum, from 200 to 4000 angstrom; **ultraviolet matte** = a matte which is created by filming the action in front of a translucent screen which is back-lighted with ultraviolet light

U-Matic *noun* video tape format, 3/4-inch wide, used for professional video recording;

U-Matic SP = an enhanced format of this tape standard that offers better quality

umbrella *noun (film)* a light-diffusing system made of white or silver coloured fabric

umlaut *noun* accent consisting of two dots over a German a, o or u

UMTS = UNIVERSAL MOBILE TELECOMMUNICATIONS SYSTEM third generation (3G) mobile communication system that supports voice, data, and video signals to the handset; *see also* THIRD GENERATION

un- *prefix* meaning not; **unauthorized** = which has not been authorized; *the use of a password is to prevent unauthorized access to the data*; **unbalanced** = a film emulsion which has been exposed to light and does not maintain proper colour temperature; **uncut** = (pages of a book) whose edges have not been cut

unallowable digit *noun* illegal combination of bits in a word, according to predefined rules

unary operation *noun* computing operation on only one operand

unattended operation *noun* system that can operate without the need for a person to supervise

unbundled software *noun* software which is not included in the price of the equipment

unclocked *adjective* electronic circuit *or* flip-flop that changes state as soon as an input changes, not with a clock signal

uncommitted logic array (ULA) *noun* chip containing a number of unconnected logic circuits and gates which can then be connected by a customer to provide a required function

unconditional *adjective* (jump) which does not depend on any condition being met

undelete *verb* to restore deleted information *or* a deleted file; *don't worry, this function will undelete your cuts to the letter*

under-cranking *noun* the running of a camera at slow frame speeds which creates abnormally fast motion when projected at normal speed

underdevelop *verb* to not leave film for a long enough time in the developer for an image to be sufficiently visible

underexposed *adjective* (photograph) that is too dark because it did not receive a long enough exposure

underflow *noun* result of a numerical operation that is too small to be represented with the given accuracy of a computer

underline *or* **underscore 1** *noun* line drawn *or* printed under a piece of text; *the chapter headings are given a double underline and the paragraphs a single underline* **2** *verb* to print *or* write a line under a piece of text; **underlining** = word-processing command which underlines text

undertake *verb* to agree to do something; *he has undertaken to reprogram the whole system* (NOTE: **undertaking - undertaken - undertook**)

undetected *adjective* which has not been detected; *the programming error was undetected for some time*

undo *verb* (option in a program) to reverse the previous action, normally an editing command; *you've just deleted the paragraph, but you can undo it from the option in the Edit menu*

unedited *adjective* which has not been edited; *the unedited text is with the publisher for editing*

unexposed *adjective* (film) which has not been exposed to light; which has not been used in a camera or printer

unformatted *adjective* (text file) which contains no formatting commands, margins or typographical commands; *it is impossible to copy to an unformatted disk; the cartridge drive provides 12.7Mbyte of unformatted storage*; **unformatted capacity** = capacity of a magnetic disk before it has been formatted; **unformatted disk** = magnetic disk which has not been formatted (disks must be formatted before use)

ungroup *verb* to convert a single complex object back into a series of separate objects; *compare with* GROUP

uni- *prefix* meaning one *or* single

unidirectional microphone *noun* microphone that is most sensitive in one direction only; *compare with* OMNIDIRECTIONAL

uniform resource locator (URL) *(Internet)* system used to standardize the way in which website addresses are written; *the URL of the Peter Collin Publishing home page is 'http://www.pcp.co.uk'*

uninterruptable power supply (UPS) *noun* power supply that can continue to provide a regulated supply to equipment even after a mains power failure (using a battery)

unipolar *adjective* **(a)** (transistor) that can act as a variable current flow control an external signal varies the resistance of the device; *see also* FET, TRANSISTOR **(b)** (transmission system) in which a positive voltage pulse *or* zero volts represents binary data; *compare with* POLAR; **unipolar signal** = signal that uses only positive voltage levels

unique *adjective* which is different from everything else; *each separate memory byte has its own unique address*

unique identifier *noun* set of characters used to distinguish between different resources in a multimedia book; *each button, image, sound and text is given a unique identifier that allows a programmer to identify and control the object from a program script*

unit *noun* **(a)** smallest element; **unit buffer** = buffer that is one character long (NOTE: usually used to mean that there are no buffering facilities); **unit record** = single record of information **(b)** single machine (possibly with many different parts); **desk top unit** = computer *or* machine that will fit onto a desk

universal *adjective* which applies everywhere *or* which can be used everywhere *or* used for a number of tasks; **universal asynchronous receiver-transmitter (UART)** = chip which converts an asynchronous serial bit stream to a parallel form *or* parallel data to a serial bit stream; **Universal Product Code (UPC)** = standard printed bar coding system used to identify products for sale; *see also* EAN; **universal serial bus** = *see* USB; **universal set** = complete set of elements that conform to a set of rules; *the universal set of prime numbers less than ten and greater than two is 3,5,7*; **universal synchronous asynchronous receiver-transmitter (USART)** = chip that can be instructed by a CPU to communicate with asynchronous or synchronous bit streams *or* data lines

UNIX *noun* popular multiuser, multi-tasking operating system developed by AT&T Bell Laboratories to run on almost any computer, from a PC, to minicomputers and large mainframes; *there are a number of graphical user interfaces, such as Open Look, that hide the Unix command-line*; **UNIX-to-UNIX copy (UUCP)** = software utilities that help make it easier for a user to copy data from one computer (running UNIX) via a serial link to another computer (running UNIX)

Hampshire fire brigade is investing 2 million in a command and control system based on the new SeriesFT fault-tolerant Unix machine from Motorola

Computing

unjustified *adjective* (text) which has not been justified; **unjustified tape** *or* **idiot tape** = tape containing unformatted text, which cannot be typeset until formatting data (such as justification, line width and page size) has been added by a computer

unlock *verb* action to allow other users to write to a file *or* access a system

unmodulated *adjective* (signal) which has not been modulated; **unmodulated track** = photographic sound track on which no sound has been recorded

unmount *verb* **(a)** to remove a disk from a disk drive **(b)** *(instruction)* to inform the operating system that a disk drive is no longer in active use

unpack *verb* to remove packed data from storage and expand it to its former state

unplug *verb* to take a plug out of a socket; *do not move the system without unplugging it*

unpopulated *adjective* printed circuit board which does not yet contain any components *or* whose sockets are empty; *you can buy an unpopulated RAM card and fit your own RAM chips*

unprotected *adjective* (data) that can be modified and is not protected by a security measure; **unprotected field** = section of a computer display that a user can modify

unrecoverable error *noun* computer hardware *or* software error that causes a program to crash

unshielded twisted-pair (UTP) cable *noun* cable consisting of two insulated copper wires twisted around each other (to reduce induction and so interference), unlike STP cable the pair of wires are not wrapped in any other layer

COMMENT: UTP is normally used for telephone cabling, but is also the cabling used in the IEEE 802.3 (10BaseT) standard that defines Ethernet running over UTP at rates of up to 10Mbits per second

unsigned *adjective* (number system) that does not represent negative numbers

unsolicited mail *noun* email message advertising something that has been received without being requested; often called 'spam' email; *don't send out unsolicited mail to unknown email addresses unless you want to annoy the recipients and damage your company's reputation; compare with* OPT-IN MAILING LIST

unsorted *adjective* (data) which has not been sorted

unsqueezed *adjective* (film print) where the compressed picture of an anamorphic negative has been altered for normal projection

unwanted *adjective* which is not needed; *use the global delete command to remove large areas of unwanted text*

up *adverb* (of computer *or* program) working *or* running; *they must have found the fault - the computer is finally up and running* (NOTE: opposite is **down**)

up and down propagation time *noun* total length of time that a transmission takes to travel from earth to a satellite and back to an earth station

up/down counter *noun* electronic counter that can increment *or* decrement a counter with each input pulse

UPC = UNIVERSAL PRODUCT CODE

update 1 *noun* (a) master file which has been made up-to-date by adding new material (b) printed information which is an up-to-date revision of earlier information (c) new version of a system which is sent to users of the existing system; **update file** *or* **transaction file** = file containing recent changes *or* transactions to records which is used to update the master file **2** *verb* to change *or* add to specific data in a master file so as to make the information up-to-date; *he has the original and updated documents on disks*

it means that any item of data stored in the system need be updated only once
Which PC?

upgrade *verb* to make (a system) more powerful *or* more up-to-date by adding new equipment; *they can upgrade the printer; the single processor with 64Mbytes of memory can be upgraded to 128Mbytes; all three models have an on-site upgrade facility*

the cost of upgrading a PC to support CAD clearly depends on the peripheral devices added
PC Business World

upkeep *noun* keeping data up-to-date; keeping in working order; *the upkeep of the files means reviewing them every six months*

uplink *noun* transmission link from an earth station to a satellite

upload *verb* to transfer data files *or* programs from a small computer to a main CPU; *the user can upload PC data to update mainframe applications* (NOTE: the opposite is **download**)

uploading *noun* action of transferring files to a main CPU; *the image can be manipulated before uploading to the host computer*

upper case *noun* series of capital letters and other symbols on a typewriter *or* keyboard, which are accessed by pressing the shift key

upper memory *noun (in an IBM PC)* 384Kb of memory located between the 640Kb and 1Mb limits

COMMENT: upper memory is after the 640Kb conventional memory but before the high memory areas above the 1Mb range

UPS = UNINTERRUPTABLE POWER SUPPLY

Magnum Power Systems has launched a new UPS for PCs. The BI-UPS prevents loss of data due to power dips or 'brown-outs' – voltage drops because of circuit overload
Computing

uptime *noun* time when a computer is functioning correctly (as opposed to downtime)

upwards compatible *or US* **upward compatible** *adjective* (hardware *or* software) designed to be compatible either with earlier models *or* with future models, not yet invented

URL = UNIFORM RESOURCE LOCATOR *(Internet)* system used to standardize the way in which website addresses are written; *the URL of the Peter Collin Publishing home page is 'http://www.pcp.co.uk'*

usability *noun* the ease with which hardware *or* software can be used; *we have studied usability tests and found that a GUI is easier for new users than a command line*

usable *adjective* which can be used *or* which is available for use; *the PC has 128Mb of usable memory*; **maximum usable frequency** = highest signal frequency which can be used in a circuit without distortion

USART = UNIVERSAL SYNCHRONOUS ASYNCHRONOUS RECEIVER-TRANSMITTER chip that can be instructed by a CPU to communicate with asynchronous *or* synchronous bit streams or data lines

USASCII *US* = USA STANDARD CODE FOR INFORMATION INTERCHANGE; *see* ASCII

USB = UNIVESAL SERIAL BUS standard that defines a high-speed serial interface that transfers data at up to 12Mbps and allows up to 127 compatible peripherals to be connected to a computer; *see also* FIREWIRE, SERIAL

use 1 *noun* **(a)** way in which something can be used; *the printer has been in use for the last two hours; the use of that file is restricted*; **to make use of something** = to use **(b)** value; being useful; *what use is an extra disk drive? it's no use, I cannot find the error*; **in use** = already in operation; *sorry, the printer is already in use* **2** *verb* **(a)** to operate something; *if you use the computer it will be much quicker; the computer is used to often by this sales staff* **(b)** to consume heat, light, etc.; *it's using too much electricity*

used *adjective* which is not new; *special offer on used terminals; our latest system is hardly used*

Usenet *noun* section of the Internet that provides forums (called newsgroups) in which any user can add a message or comment on other messages; often the busiest part of the Internet; *see also* NEWSGROUP

user *noun* **(a)** person who uses a computer *or* machine *or* software **(b)** especially, a keyboard operator; *(in a network or multiuser system)* **user account** = record which identifies a user, contains his password and holds his rights to use resources; *I have a new user account on this LAN but I cannot remember my password*; **user area** = part of the memory which is available for the user, and does not contain the operating system; **user-definable** = feature *or* section of a program that a user can customize as required; *the style sheet contains 125 user-definable tags*; **user-defined characters** = characters which are created by the user and added to the standard character set; **user documentation** = documentation provided with a program which helps the user run it; **user-friendly** = (language *or* system *or* program) that allows easy use and interaction; **user group** = association *or* club of users of a particular system *or* computer; **user ID** = unique identification code that allows a computer to recognize a user; **user interface** = hardware *or* software designed to make it easier for a user to communicate with the machine; *see also* GUI, SHELL; *(in authoring software)* **user level** = one of two modes that allows a user to run and interact with a multimedia application, but not modify it in any way; *compare with* AUTHOR LEVEL; *(in a network or multiuser system)* **user name** = name by which a user is known to the system and which opens the correct user account; **user-operated language** = high-level programming language that allows certain problems *or* procedures to be easily expressed; **user port** = socket which allows peripherals to be connected to a computer; **user's program** = computer software written by a user rather than a manufacturer; **user-selectable** = which can be chosen *or* selected by the user; *the video resolution of 300, 240 or 200 pixels is user-selectable*

> the first popular microcomputer to have a user-friendly interface built into its operating system
>
> *Micro Decision*

> ModelMaker saves researchers a great deal of time and effort, and provides a highly user-friendly environment using menus and 'buttons', instant output, and instant access to a wide variety of mathematical techniques built into the system
>
> *Computing*

utility program *noun* useful program that is concerned with such routine activities as file searching, copying files, file directories, sorting and debugging and various mathematical functions; *a lost file cannot be found without a file-recovery utility*

UTP cable = UNSHIELDED TWISTED-PAIR CABLE

UUCP = UNIX-TO-UNIX COPY

UV (light) = ULTRAVIOLET (LIGHT)

U-wrap *noun* in a helical scan video tape system, a tape path giving 180 degrees contact on the drum, therefore needing the use of two or more revolving heads

Vv

V = VOLT

V & V = VERIFICATION AND VALIDATION

V series series of CCITT recommendations for data communications

> COMMENT: **V.21** = 300 bits/second transmit and receive, full duplex **V.22** = 1200 bits/second transmit and receive, half duplex **V.22 BIS** = 1200 bits/second transmit and receive, full duplex **V.23** = 75 bits/second transmit, 1200 bits/second receive, half duplex **V.24** = interchange circuits between a DTE and a DCE **V.25 BIS** = automatic calling and answering equipment on a PSTN **V.26** = 2400 bits/second transmission over leased lines **V.26 BIS** = 2400 bits/second transmit, 1200 bits/second receive, half duplex for use on a PSTN **V.26 TER** = 2400 bits/second transmit, 1200 bits/second receive, full duplex for use on a PSTN **V.27** = 4800 bits/second modem for use on a leased line **V.27 BIS** = 4800 bits/second transmit, 2400 bits/second receive for use on a leased line **V.27 TER** = 4800 bits/second transmit, 2400 bits/second receive for use on a PSTN **V.29** = 9600 bits/second modem for use on a PSTN or leased line **V.42** = error control and correction protocol **V.42 BIS** = data compression used with V.42 error control **V.54** = standard for a modem loop-back test **V.80** = synchronous connection between PC and modem with a variable data rate, often used for video links **V.90** = modem standard for analogue data transfer at 56Kbps

vaccine *noun* software utility used to check a system to see if any viruses are present, and remove any that are found

vacuum *noun* state with no air; *there is a vacuum in the sealed CRT*; **vacuum tube** = electronic current flow control device consisting of a heated cathode and an anode in a sealed glass tube with a vacuum inside it

> COMMENT: used in the first generation of computers, now replaced by solid state current control devices such as the transistor

valid *adjective* correct, according to a set of rules

validate *verb* to check that an input *or* data is correct according to a set of rules

validation *noun* check performed to validate data

validity *noun* correctness of an instruction *or* password

value *noun* what something is worth (either in money *or* as a quantity); **absolute value** = value of a number regardless of its sign; *the absolute value of -62.34 is 62.34*; **initial value** = starting point (usually zero) set when initializing variables at the beginning of a program

value-added network (VAN) *noun* network where the transmission lines are leased from a public utility such as the telephone service, but where the user can add on private equipment

value-added reseller (VAR) *noun* retailer who sells equipment and systems which are specially tailored to certain types of operation

value-added *adjective* (something) with extra benefit for a user

value rollers *plural noun* couples of small rollers through which film passes in a projector and which assist in the prevention of the spreading of fire

valve *noun* electronic current flow control device consisting of a heated cathode and an anode in a sealed glass vacuum tube

COMMENT: used in the first generation of computers, now replaced by solid state current control devices such as a transistor

VAN = VALUE-ADDED NETWORK

vanishing point perspective *noun* graphics displayed in two-dimensions that have the appearance of depth as all lines converge at a vanishing point and objects appear smaller as they are further from the user

vapourware *noun informal* products which exist in name only

```
Rivals      dismissed     the
initiative as IBM vapourware,
designed   to  protect  its
installed  base  of  machines
running under widely differing
operating systems
```
Computing

VAR = VALUE-ADDED RESELLER

variable 1 *adjective* is able to change; **variable area track** = photographic sound track where the picture's diameter differs according to the sound modulation; **variable data** = data which can be modified, and is not write protected; **variable density** *or* **variable density sound track** = photographic sound track where the picture's density differs according to the sound modulation; **variable focus lens** = a camera lens which permits changes in focal length to be made during filming; **variable hue-sound recording** = an audio recording with a photographic sound track that has many different colours; **variable length record** = record which can be of any length; **variable-opening shutter** = a camera shutter with an additional leaf which can be set at various openings or can be completely closed; used in fade-ins and fade-outs; **variable word length computer** = computer in which the number of bits which make up a word is variable, and varies according to the type of data **2** *noun* computer program identifier for a storage location which can contain any number or characters and which may vary during the program; **global variable** = number that can be accessed by any routine or structure in a program; **local variable** = number which can only be accessed by certain routines in a certain section of a computer program

varifocal lens *see* ZOOM LENS

varispeed *noun* variable speed control on magnetic audio recorders which generally provide a large range; can also be a pitch control

vary *verb* to change; *the clarity of the signal can vary with the weather*

Vbox = VIDEO BOX device that allows several VCRs, videodiscs and camcorders to be attached and controlled by one unit, developed by Sony

VBX = VISUAL BASIC EXTENSION (in Microsoft Windows) special software module that adds functionality to another application

COMMENT: originally developed as a way of adding extra programming features to the Microsoft Visual Basic programming language, it is now a standard that can be used by many Windows programming tools; a VBX can be used in 16-bit or 32-bit Windows wheras an OCX control will only work with 32-bit Windows (version 95 and later)

VCPS *GB* = VIDEO COPYRIGHT PROTECTION SOCIETY

VCR = VIDEO CASSETTE RECORDER machine that can record analog video signals onto a magnetic cassette tape and play back the tape to display video on a monitor

COMMENT: the most popular formats are: one-inch tape used for studio-quality mastering; 3/4-inch tape was widely used but has now been mostly replaced by 1/2-inch tape; 1/2-inch VHS format tape was first used only in the home but has now mostly replaced 3/4-inch tape; and 1/2-inch Beta format tape was the first home VCR format but is no longer used. Some VCRs can be used to store digital data for data backup

VDT = VISUAL DISPLAY TERMINAL; *see* MONITOR

VDU = VISUAL DISPLAY UNIT

```
it  normally  consists  of  a
keyboard to input information
and either a printing terminal
or a VDU screen to display
messages and results
```
Practical Computing

```
a VDU is a device used with a
computer   that   displays
information in the form of
characters and drawings on a
screen
```
Electronics & Power

vector *noun* **(a)** address which directs a computer to a new memory location **(b)** coordinate that consists of a magnitude and direction; **vector graphics** *or* **vector image** *or* **vector scan** = computer drawing system that uses line length and direction from an origin to plot lines and so build up an image rather than a description of each pixel, as in a bitmap; *a vector image can be easily and accurately re-sized with no loss of detail*; *compare with* BIT MAP **(c)** a line which connect points on a cathode ray tube

vector font *noun* shape of characters within a font that are drawn using vector graphics, allowing the characters to be scaled to almost any size without changing the quality; *compare with* BIT-MAPPED FONT

vector processor *noun* coprocessor that operates on one row or column of an array at a time

vectored interrupt *noun* interrupt which interrupts and directs the processor to a routine at a particular address

vectorscope *noun* in television, an oscilloscope to show the form of the chroma signals in colour television systems

```
the great advantage of the
vector-scan display is that it
requires little memory to
store a picture
```
Electronics & Power

velocity *noun* speed; *the disk drive motor spins at a constant velocity*; **velocity compensator** = in video tape playback, a device which eliminates any distortion in the transmission of horizontal colour; **velocity of sound** = speed of sound which is equal to 331 metres per second through air; the speed of sound varies in different materials

vendor *noun* person who manufactures *or* sells or supplies hardware *or* software products; **vendor independent** = hardware *or* software that will work with hardware and software manufactured by other vendors; *compare with* PROPRIETARY FILE FORMAT; **vendor-independent messaging** = *see* VIM

Venn diagram *noun* graphical representation of the relationships between states

verification *noun* checking that data has been keyboarded correctly *or* that data transferred from one medium to another has been transferred correctly; **keystroke verification** = check made on each key pressed to make sure it is valid for a particular application; **verification and validation (V & V)** = testing a system to check that it is functioning correctly and that it is suitable for the tasks intended

verifier *noun* special device for verifying input data

verify *verb* to check that data recorded *or* entered is correct

version *noun* a copy *or* statement which is slightly different from others; *the latest version of the software includes a graphics routine*; **version control** = utility software that allows several programmers to work on a source file and monitors the changes that have been made by each programmer; **version number** = number of the version of a product

verso *noun* left hand page of a book (usually given an even number)

vertical *adjective* at right angles to the horizontal; **vertical application** = application software that has been designed for a specific use, rather than for general use; *your new software to manage a florist's is a good vertical application*; **vertical blanking interval** = interval between television frames in which the picture is blanked to enable the picture beam to return to the top left hand corner of the screen; *see* RASTER; **vertical format unit (VFU)** = part of the control system of a printer which governs the vertical format of the document to be printed (such as vertical spacing, page length); **vertical interval** = the field blanking time between pictures; cuts which occur in the vertical interval cannot be detected on the picture; **vertical interval time code** = *see* VITC; **vertical justification** = adjustment of the spacing between lines of text to fit a section of text into a page; **vertical portal (VORTAL)** = website which contains information for just one particular industry or interest group; *the* *vertical portal Buzzsaw (www.buzzsaw.com) provide news and resources for the construction industry;* **vertical resolution** = the number of horizontal lines in a televised picture; **vertical scan frequency** = number of times a picture beam in a monitor moves from the last line back up to the first; **vertical scrolling** = displayed text that moves up or down the computer screen one line at a time; **vertical sync signal** = in a video signal, a signal which indicates the end of the last trace at the bottom of the display; **vertical tab** = number of lines that should be skipped before printing starts again

vertically *adverb* from top to bottom *or* going up and down at right angles to the horizontal; *the page has been justified vertically*; **vertically polarized signal** = signal whose waveforms are all aligned in one vertical plane

very high density *see* VHD

very high frequency (VHF) *noun* range of radio frequencies between 30-300 MHz

very large scale integration (VLSI) *noun* integrated circuit with 10,000 to 100,000 components

very low frequency (VLF) *noun* range of radio frequencies between 3-30 KHz

VESA = VIDEO ELECTRONICS STANDARDS ASSOCIATION; *(in an IBM PC)* **VESA local bus** *or* **VL-bus** = standard defined by VESA which allows up to three special expansion slots that provide direct, bus-master control of the central processor and allow very high-speed data transfers between main memory and the expansion card without using the processor; *for a high-performance PC, choose one with a VESA bus*

vestigial sideband *noun* single sideband transmission with a small part of the other sideband kept to provide synchronization data, often used in TV transmissions

vf band = VOICE FREQUENCY BAND

VFU *see* VERTICAL FORMAT UNIT

VFW *see* VIDEO FOR WINDOWS

VGA = VIDEO GRAPHICS ARRAY *(in an IBM PC)* standard of video adapter developed by IBM that can support a display with a resolution up to 640x480

pixels in up to 256 colours, superseded by SVGA; **super VGA (SVGA)** = enhancement to the standard VGA graphics display system that allows resolutions of up to 800x600pixels with 16 million colours; **VGA feature connector** = 26-pin edge connector or port (normally at the top edge) of a VGA display adapter that allows another device to access its palette information and clock signals; *VGA feature connectors are often used to provide overlays*

VHD = VERY HIGH DENSITY capacitance type video disk able to store very large quantities of data

VHF = VERY HIGH FREQUENCY radio frequency between 30MHz and 300MHZ (used for broadcasting radio and TV programmes)

VHS = VIDEO HOME SYSTEM video cassette tape format, using 1/2-inch wide tape, developed by JVC and now the standard for home and consumer markets; *see also* S-VHS

VHS-C a video cassette system which uses the VHS format

via *preposition* going through something *or* using something to get to a destination; *the signals have reached us via satellite; you can download the data to the CPU via a modem*

VIBGYOR the colours in the visible spectrum: violet, indigo, blue, green, yellow, orange and red

COMMENT: ultra-violet and infra-red are not included in this range

video *noun* **(a)** an electronic system which records, stores and reproduces visual images **(b)** text *or* images *or* graphics viewed on television *or* a monitor; **analog video display system** = display board that creates the analog signals sent to the monitor; **digital video display adapter** = display board that generates digital signals for the monitor which then converts from digital to analog (NOTE: the monitor must be able to display the frequency range of the adapter or, in the case of multisync monitors, accept the range of frequencies used by the display adapter); **video adapter** *or* **board** *or* **controller** = add-in board which converts data into electrical signals to drive a monitor and display text and graphics; **video analyser** =

an electro-optical device which scans colour negatives to discover the correct printing exposures; **video bandwidth** = frequency range required to carry TV images; **video box** = *see* VBOX; **video buffer** = memory in a video adapter that is used to store the bit-map of the image being displayed; **video camera** = optical lenses in front of an electronic device that can convert images into electronic signals in a form that can be displayed on a TV; **video capture board** = high-speed digital sampling circuit which stores a TV picture in memory so that it can then be processed by a computer; **video cassette** = cassette with video tape in it (either blank for recording, or with a prerecorded film); **video cassette recorder (VCR)** = device attached to a TV set, which can be programmed to record TV programmes on videotape and play them back at another time; **video codec** = electronic device to convert a video signal to or from a digital form; **video compressor** = device that reduces the bandwidth of a TV signal allowing it to be transmitted over a (telephone), using a video expander at the receiving end; **video conferencing** = linking video, audio and computer signals from different locations so that distant people can talk and see each other, as if in a conference room; **video controller** = (i) device that allows a computer to control a video recorder or camera; (ii) a video display board; **video digitiser** = high-speed digital sampling circuit which stores a TV picture in memory so that it can then be processed by a computer; **videodisc** = read-only optical disc able to store TV pictures and sound in binary form, also capable of storing large amounts of computer data; **video display** = device which can display text or graphical information, such as a CRT; **video display adapter** *or* **board** *or* **card** = device which allows information in a computer to be displayed on a CRT (the adapter interfaces with both the computer and CRT); **video editing** = method of editing a video sequence in which the video is digitized and stored in a computer; **video editor** = computer that controls two videotape recorders to allow an operator to play back sequences from one and record these on the second machine; **Video Electronics Standards Association** = *see* VESA; **video**

expander = device that stores one frame of a video image as it is slowly received over a voice grade communications link, with a video compressor used at the transmitting end; **video frame** = single image on a video tape *or* TV; *with an image processor you can freeze a video frame*; **video game** = game played on a computer, with action shown on a video display; *(in an IBM PC)* **video graphics array (VGA)** = standard of video adapter developed by IBM that can support a display with a resolution up to 640x480 pixels in up to 256 colours, superseded by SVGA; **video graphics card** *or* **overlay card** = expansion card that allows a computer to display both generated text and graphics and moving video images from an external camera or VCR; **video home system** = *see* VHS; **video image** = single frame from a video tape *or* **TV**; *a printer-readable video image can be sent to a basic laser printer through a video port*; **video interface chip** = chip that controls a video display allowing computer information to be displayed; **video lookup table** = collection of pre-calculated values of the different colours that are stored in memory and can be examined very quickly to produce an answer without the need to recalculate; **video memory** *or* **video RAM (VRAM)** = high-speed RAM used for storing video image data; **video monitor** = device able to display, without sound, signals from a computer or TV camera (that are then recorded onto video tape); *(informal)* **video nasties** = horror films available on video cassette; **video phone** = two-way voice and image transmission; **video player** = device that can play back video recordings but cannot record; **video port** = connection on a video recorder allowing the data read from the tape to be used in other ways, such as being stored in a computer; **video RAM** = *see* VRAM; **video recorder** = device for recording TV images and sound onto video tape; **video scanner** = device which allows images of objects or pictures to be entered into a computer; *new video scanners are designed to scan three-dimensional objects*; **video server** = dedicated computer on a network used to store video sequences; requires special software or high-speed transmission hardware to ensure smooth playback; **video signal** = signal which provides line picture information and synchronization pulses with a frequency of between 1-6MHz; **video standards** = protocols defining video signal format (there are three main international video standards: NTSC, PAL and SECAM); **video system control architecture** = *see* VISCA; **videotape** = magnetic tape used in a video recorder, for storing TV pictures and sound information; **videotape recorder (VTR)** = device that can record and play back TV images and sound on video tape rather than on enclosed cassette used by a VCR; **video teleconferencing** = linking computers that can capture and display video, so that distant people can talk and see each other, as if in a conference room; **video terminal** = keyboard with a monitor; **video window** = window that displays a moving video image, independent of other displayed material; *see also* OVERLAY; **infrared video camera** = video camera sensitive to infrared light; *some instructors monitor their trainees with infrared video cameras*

video-CD *noun* CD-ROM that stores digital video data conforming to the Philips White Book standard and uses MPEG compression for the full-motion video data; *see also* WHITE BOOK

Video for Windows (VFW) software driver and utilities for Microsoft Windows 3.1, developed by Microsoft, that allows AVI-format video files to be played back in a window

videotext *or* **videotex** *noun* system for transmitting text and displaying it on a screen

COMMENT: this covers information transmitted either by TV signals (teletext) *or* by signals sent down telephone lines (viewdata)

Vision Dynamics has upgraded its video capture and display boards for PCs. Elvis II will now display TV pictures on a VGA screen at a resolution of 1,024 x 768 square pixels and 2 million colours to provide enhanced picture quality from PAL, NTSC and S-VHS sources
Computing

view *verb* to look at something, especially something displayed on a screen; *the user has to pay a charge for viewing pages on a bulletin board*

viewdata *noun* interactive system for transmitting text *or* graphics from a database to a user's terminal by telephone lines

COMMENT: the user calls up the page of information required, using the telephone and a modem, as opposed to teletext, where the pages of information are repeated one after the other automatically

Viewer multimedia authoring tool for Microsoft Windows and Sony DataDiscman platforms, developed by Microsoft, which uses RTF formatted files with embedded commands

viewer *noun* **(a)** person who watches television **(b)** device with an eyepiece through which a person can look at film *or* transparencies **(c)** utility that allows a user to see what is contained in an image or formatted document file, without having to start the program that created it

viewfinder *noun* eyepiece in a camera that allows a user to see what is being filmed; **electronic viewfinder** = miniature cathode ray tube in a television *or* video camera, that allows the camera operator to see the images being recorded; **viewfinder objective** *or* **objective lens** = the lens of a visual monitoring viewfinder, in which the picture is formed

vignetting *noun* (*film*) the shading of the borders of a picture

virgin *adjective* (tape) that has not been recorded on before

virtual *adjective* feature *or* device which does not actually exist but which is simulated by a computer and can be used by a user as if it did exist; **virtual address** = an address referring to virtual storage; **virtual circuit** = link established between a source and sink (in a packet switching network) for the duration of the call ; **virtual desktop** *or* **screen** = area that is bigger than the physical limits of the monitor, and which can contain text, images, windows, etc; the monitor acts as a window on the virtual screen and can be scrolled around to view a different part of the virtual screen; **virtual disk** = section of RAM used with a short controlling program as if it were a fast disk storage system; **virtual image** = complete image stored in memory rather than the part of it that is displayed; **virtual machine** = simulated machine and its operations; **virtual memory** *or* **virtual storage (VS)** = large imaginary main memory made available by loading smaller pages from a backing store into the main memory as they are required; **virtual reality** = simulation of a real-life scene or environment by computer; *this new virtual reality software can create a three-dimensional room that you can navigate around*; **virtual terminal** = ideal terminal specifications used as a model by a real terminal

---

anyone wishing to build Virtual Reality applications with the Cyberspace Developer's Kit should have solid knowledge of programming

Computing

---

virus *noun* program which adds itself to an executable file and copies (or spreads) itself to other executable files each time an infected file is run; a virus can corrupt data, display a message or do nothing; *if your PC is infected with a virus, your data is at risk*; **anti-virus software** = software which removes a virus from a file; **virus detector** = utility software which checks executable files to see if they contain (have been infected) with a known virus

---

COMMENT: viruses are spread by downloading unchecked files from a bulletin board system or via unregulated networks or by inserting an unchecked floppy disk into your PC - always use virus detector

---

ViSCA = VIDEO SYSTEM CONTROL ARCHITECTURE protocol used to synchronize multiple video devices, developed by Sony

viscous processing *noun* a method of film-developing where the film is submerged in chemical liquids

visible *adjective* which can be seen; **visible light** = range of light colours that can be seen with the human eye

visual 1 *adjective* which can be seen *or* which is used by sight; **visual effects** = motion picture special effects which are usually created during the printing process; **visual programming** = method of programming a computer by showing it or

taking it through the processes of what it has to do rather than writing a series of instructions **2** *noun* **visuals** = graphics *or* photographs *or* illustrations, used as part of a printed output

Visual Basic programming language and development tool produced by Microsoft that allows programmers to create Windows applications quickly and easily by dragging objects onto the design pad and defining how each object works

Visual C development product by Microsoft that allows Windows applications to be created by drawing the user interface and attaching C code

visual display terminal (VDT) *or* **visual display unit (VDU)** *noun* screen attached to a keyboard, on which text *or* graphics can be seen

visualization *noun* conversion of numbers or data into a graphical format that can be more easily understood

visualize *verb* to imagine how something will appear, even before it has been created

VITC = VERTICAL INTERVAL TIME CODE time code recorded onto tape between video frames

---

COMMENT: preferred to LTC because it does not use the audio track and can be read at slow playback speeds

---

VL-bus *or* **VL local bus** *noun* standard defined by VESA which allows up to three special expansion slots that provide direct, bus-master control of the central processor and allow very high-speed data transfers between main memory and the expansion card without using the processor

VLF = VERY LOW FREQUENCY radio frequency between 30Hz and 30KHz

VLSI = VERY LARGE SCALE INTEGRATION system with between 10,000 and 100,000 components on a single IC

VM *see* VIRTUAL MACHINE

VME bus = VERSAMODULE EUROCARD BUS expansion bus standard that supports 32-bit data transfer; this bus is mostly used in industrial and test equipment.

voice *noun* **(a)** *(in MIDI)* another name for a note or sound effect (such as a whistle); *instruments that are multi-voice can play* *several notes at the same time* **(b)** sound of human speech; **voice answer back** = computerized response service using a synthesized voice to answer enquiries; **voice band** = minimum bandwidth required for recognizable transmission of speech (usually 300 - 3400Hz); **voice coil** = (i) element in a dynamic microphone that vibrates when sound waves strike it and cause variations in an electrical signal; (ii) element in a loudspeaker that vibrates according to a signal and so produces sound waves; **voice data entry** *or* **input** = input of information into a computer using a speech recognition system and the user's voice; **voice frequency band** = *see* VF BAND; **voice grade channel** = communications channel (bandwidth usually equal to voice band), able to carry speech and some data (such as facsimile); **voice mail** = computer linked to a telephone exchange that answers a person's telephone when they are not there and allows messages to be recorded (in digital form); *I checked my voice mail to see if anyone had left me a message*; **voice messaging** = device for recording a caller's spoken message if the number he calls does not reply; **voice output** = production of sounds which sound like human speech, made as a result of voice synthesis; **voice print** = identification of a person by registering tones and signals in that person's speech; **voice recognition** = ability of a computer to recognize certain words in a human voice and provide a suitable response; **voice response** = replies by a computer to the user's commands by voice rather than by displayed text; **voice synthesis** = reproduction of sounds similar to those of the human voice; **voice synthesizer** = device which generates sounds which are similar to the human voice; **voice track** = a recording track for dialogue and narration

the technology of voice output is reasonably difficult, but the technology of voice recognition is much more complex

Personal Computer World

voice-over *noun* spoken commentary by an actor who does not appear on the screen (as the text of a TV commercial)

voice unit *noun* unit of signal measurement equal to a one millivolt signal across a 600 ohm resistance

volatile memory *or* **volatile store** *or* **volatile storage** *noun* memory *or* storage medium which loses data stored in it when the power supply is switched off (NOTE: opposite is **non-volatile memory**)

volatility *noun* number of records that are added *or* deleted from a computer system compared to the total number in store

volt *noun* SI unit of electrical potential; defined as voltage across a one ohm resistance when one amp is flowing

voltage *noun* electromotive force expressed in volts; **voltage dip** *or* **dip in voltage** = sudden fall in voltage which may last only a very short while, but which can affect the operation of a computer system; **voltage regulator** = device which provides a steady voltage output even if the input supply varies; **voltage transient** = spike of voltage that is caused by a time delay in two devices switching *or* noise on the line

COMMENT: electricity supply can have peaks and troughs of current, depending on the users in the area. Fluctuations in voltage can affect computers; a voltage regulator will provide a steady supply of electricity

volume *noun* **(a)** total space occupied by data in a storage system; **volume label** *or* **name** = name assigned to identify a particular disk *or* tape **(b)** intensity of sound; **volume control** = knob which turns to increase the volume from a radio, TV or amplifier

von Neumann architecture method of designing a computer, developed by mathematician John von Neumann

COMMENT: used for the design of most personal computers, this type of architecture is sequential (operates on one instruction at a time) and uses the concept of a stored program; parallel-processing is a different type of computer design and avoids the bottleneck with this design that can occur when the supply of instructions from memory is faster than the speed at which the processor can process the instructions

VORTAL *see* VERTICAL PORTAL

VR = VIRTUAL REALITY

VRAM = VIDEO RAM memory on a video adapter that is used to buffer image data sent from the computer's main memory or to store an image as it is built up

VS = VIRTUAL STORAGE

VSB = VESTIGIAL SIDE BAND method of transferring data over coaxial cable, used to modulate and transmit digital television signals

VT = VIDEOTAPE

VTR = VIDEO TAPE RECORDER system which records and replays television pictures and sound on magnetic tape

VT-terminal emulation *noun* standard set of codes developed by Digital Equipment Corporation to control how text and graphics are displayed on its range of terminals; **VT-52** = popular standard of a terminal that defines the codes used to display text and graphics

VU = VOICE UNIT

VxD = VIRTUAL DEVICE DRIVER device driver used to control one part of the Windows operating system or to link a peripheral to the Windows operating system

Ww

W = WATT

W3 = WORLD WIDE WEB *see* WWW

W3C = WORLD WIDE WEB CONSORTIUM group of international industry members that work together to develop common standards for the world wide web; visit the www.w3.org website for new standards and developments

wafer *noun* thin round slice of a large single crystal silicon onto which hundreds of individual integrated circuits are constructed, before being cut into individual chips

wafer scale integration *noun* one large chip, the size of a wafer, made up of smaller integrated circuits connected together (these are still in the research stage)

Rockwell International has signed a letter of intent to buy Western Digital's silicon wafer fabrication facility in Irvine, California for a proposed price of $115 million (77 million)

Computing

wait condition *noun* state where a processor is not active, but waiting for input from peripherals

wait loop *noun* processor that repeats one loop of program until some action occurs

wake up *verb* to switch on *or* start *or* initiate; **wake up a system** = code entered at a remote terminal to indicate to the central computer that someone is trying to log-on at that location

wake-on-LAN technology that allows a personal computer or workstation to be switched on automatically by sending it a signal over a local area network connection; the system is built into the network interface card fitted to the computer and allows a network manager or network server software to manage the computers linked to the network.

walk through *verb* to examine each step of a piece of software

wallpaper *noun* (*in a GUI*) image or pattern used as a background in a window

WAN = WIDE AREA NETWORK network in which the computers, peripherals and terminals are far apart and are linked by radio, telephone or microwave connections

wand *noun* bar code reader *or* optical device which is held in the hand to read bar codes on products in a store

WAP = WIRELESS APPLICATION PROTOCOL system that allows a user to access information on an Internet server using a wireless handheld device, such as a mobile telephone

COMMENT: WAP can be used over almost all of the current wireless networks, including the popular GSM mobile telephone standard, and can run on almost any operating system or hardware device. A device that supports WAP provides a very simple browser that can display basic graphics and text-based pages of information on a small, monochrome, 6-10 line display, similar to a tiny, simple web page. The user can navigate between pages using two or three buttons on the handheld device or mobile telephone. WAP allows users to access email and news-based websites from a mobile telephone, but users have been put off by the very slow speed (no more than 9600bps) at which data can be transferred over current wireless telephone systems. The new transmission standard GPRS provides faster access, making new WAP devices more usable.

WAP Browser *noun* simple web browser that works on a handheld WAP device

> COMMENT: a WAP browser supports the HTML and XML web page markup standards, but also supports its own markup system, WML (WAP markup language) that allows designers to create simple pages that can be transferred efficiently over the often slow wireless link (normally at a maximum of 9600bps) and navigated using two or three buttons on the handheld device or mobile telephone.

WAP markup language (WML)

simple web page formatting language that is similar to a very simple version of the standard HTML web page coding system, but does not include many of the extra features that cannot be displayed on the small screen of a WAP handheld device or navigated with two or three buttons; *see also* HTML

WAP markup language script

(WMLScript) simple scripting language similar to a very simple version of JavaScript that allows WML web pages to include scripting functions

warm boot *noun* system restart which normally reloads the operating system but does not reset or check the hardware; *compare with* HARD RESET

warm standby *noun* secondary backup device that can be switched into action a short time after the main system fails; *compare with* COLD STANDBY, HOT STANDBY

warm start *noun* restarting a programme which has stopped, but without losing any data; *compare with* COLD START

warm up *verb* to allow a machine to stand idle for a time after switching on, to reach the optimum operating conditions

> warm-up time measures how long each printer takes to get ready to begin printing
>
> *Byte*

warn *verb* to say that something dangerous is about to happen; to say that there is a possible danger; *he warned the keyboarders that the system might become overloaded* (NOTE: you warn someone **of** something, or **that** something may happen)

warning *noun* notice of possible danger; *to issue a warning; warning notices were put up around the construction site*; **warning light** = small light which lights up to show that something dangerous may happen; *when the warning light comes on, switch off the system*

warrant *verb* to guarantee; *all the spare parts are warranted*

warrantee *noun* person who is given a warranty

warrantor *noun* person who gives a warranty

warranty *noun* **(a)** guarantee *or* legal document which promises that a machine will work properly *or* that an item is of good quality; *the printer is sold with a twelve-month warranty; the warranty covers spare parts but not labour costs* **(b)** promise in a contract; **breach of warranty** = failing to do something which is a part of a contract

wash (a PROM) *verb* to erase the data from a PROM

Watt *noun* SI unit of measurement of electrical power, defined as power produced when one amp of current flows through a load that has one volt of voltage across it

WAV file *see* WAVE

wave *noun* signal motion that rises and falls periodically as it travels through a medium; **microwave** = high frequency, short wavelength signals used for communication links, such as an earth station to satellite link; **sound wave** = pressure wave that carries sound; **WAVE** *or* **WAV file** = standard method of storing an analog signal in digital form under Microsoft Windows (files have the .WAV extension)

waveform *noun* display of the changing amplitude of a signal in relation to time; **waveform audio** = method of storing analog audio signals as digital data; **waveform digitization** = conversion and storing a waveform in numerical form using an A/D converter; **waveform editor** = software program that displays a graphical representation of a sound wave and allows a user to edit, adjust levels, frequencies or add special effects; **waveform monitor** = an oscilloscope for showing and measuring the waveform of electrical signals; **waveform**

synthesizer = musical device that creates sounds of an instrument by using recorded samples of the original waveform produced by the instrument; *compare with* FM SYNTHESIZER; **waveform table** = data that describes a sound clip

waveguide *noun* physical system used to direct waves in a particular direction (usually metal tubes for microwave signals *or* optical fibres for light signals)

wavelength *noun* distance between two corresponding points of adjacent waves in a periodic waveform; defined as the speed of the wave divided by the frequency

WBFM = WIDEBAND FREQUENCY MODULATION

weave *noun* unwanted sideways movement of film through a projector gate

web *or* **www** *or* **world wide web**
noun collection of all the websites on the Internet

> COMMENT: the web is the collection of the millions of websites and web pages that together form the part of the Internet that is most often seen by users (although the Internet also includes electronic mail, Usenet and newsgroups); each website is a collection of web pages and each web page contains text, graphics and links to other web pages and websites. Each page is normally created using the HTML language and is viewed by a user with a web browser. To navigate between web pages and web sites is called surfing; this requires a computer with a link to the Internet (often using a modem) and a web browser to view the web pages stored on the remote web servers.

web application *noun* software program that runs on a web server to provide special functions or to display information via a website to a user; *the new web application lets visitors to our website search our product database; the web application displays the latest stock price for our company*

web browser *see* BROWSER

web cam *noun* video camera linked to a web server that allows visitors to see live video images of a scene displayed on a website; *we have a web cam pointing at the street to show visitors to our website how bad the traffic is around the office*

web crawler *noun* software that automatically finds and reads every new web page on the Internet and produces an index based on the content of the web pages, normally used by search engines to ensure that they are up to date

web page design software *noun* software that provides features to help a user or designer create web pages for a website; *this web page design software is very similar to our desktop publishing software and allows you to drag text and images onto a page, create tables and change the style of text from menu options, without having to edit complex HTML commands*

web page *noun* single file stored on a web server that contains HTML instructions that describe formatted text, graphics and hypertext links to other pages on the Internet; *see* BROWSER, HTML

web portal *noun* website that provides a wide range of information and resources for the needs and interests of all users; *the biggest web portals include AOL, MSN, ad Yahoo! that offer a wide range of general services including news, sports, email, weather, shopping and a search engine*; *see also* VERTICAL PORTAL

web server *noun* computer that stores the collection of web pages that make up a website

> COMMENT: Web servers often store hundreds of separate websites, but some websites are so big and complex that they have their own dedicated web server, for example BBC (www.bbc.co.uk) or CNN (www.cnn.com)

webBot *noun* software utility program used in some Microsoft Internet applications that carry out a particular special function in a website, for example, adding a search function to a website; *see also* BOT

weber *noun (film)* a unit of magnetic flux

webmaster *noun* person in charge of a website; *if you have a problem or complaint about our website you could send an email message to 'webmaster@pcp.co.uk'*

website *noun* collection of web pages that have been produced by one company or individual and are linked together by hyperlinks; *see also* HTML, INTERNET, WWW

> COMMENT: Although the individual web pages within a website can be accessed separately, the initial, opening page of a website is viewed if you enter the domain name of the website - for example, the Peter Collin Publishing website contains pages that describe each of our specialist dictionaries; you can see the opening web page by typing our domain name 'www.petercollin.com' in your web browser

WebTV *noun* television that also lets you view web pages; some TVs include a computer and modem, other systems use an external box that links to the TV and a telephone socket; some interactive television and cable television installations do not use a telephone socket but instead download and display web pages via the television cable.

weigh *verb* (a) to measure how heavy something is; *he weighed the packet at the post office* (b) to have a certain weight; *the packet weighs twenty-five grams*

weighing machine *noun* machine which measures how heavy a thing *or* a person is

weight *noun* measurement of how heavy something is; **gross weight** = weight of both the container and its contents; **net weight** = weight of goods after deducting the packing material and container; **paper weight** = amount which a certain quantity of paper weighs; *our paper weight is 70 - 90 gsm*

weighted *adjective* sorted according to importance *or* priority; **weighted average** = average calculated taking several factors into account, giving some more value than others

weighting *noun* (a) sorting of users, programs or data by their importance or priority (b) additional salary *or* wages paid to compensate for living in an expensive part of the country; *salary plus a London weighting*

wetware *noun* US *informal* the human brain *or* intelligence which writes software to be used on hardware

What You See Is All You Get (WYSIAYG) *noun* program where the output on screen cannot be printed out in any other form (that is, it cannot contain hidden print *or* formatting commands)

What You See Is What You Get (WYSIWYG) *noun* program where the output on the screen is exactly the same as the output on printout; including graphics and special fonts

whip pan *noun* (*film*) when the pan shot is done at such a high speed that the image being filmed becomes blurred beyond recognition

white *adjective & noun* the colour of snow; **white flag** = signal indicating a new frame on a video disk; **white level** = maximum TV signal strength corresponding to maximum brightness on the screen; **white noise** = random noise that is of equal power at all frequencies; = **white pages** = database of users and their email address stored on the Internet to help other users find an email address; normally you have to add your own email address to the database; **white writer** = laser printer which directs its laser beam on the points that are not printed (NOTE: the opposite is **black writer**)

> COMMENT: with a white writer, the black areas are printed evenly but edges and borders are not so sharp

White Book formal video-CD standard published by Philips and JVC that defines how digital video can be stored on a CD-ROM; the specification provides 72 minutes of full motion video compressed with the MPEG algorithm

whois (Internet) utility that displays information about the owner of a particular domain name

wholesale *noun & adverb* buying goods from manufacturers and selling in large quantities to traders who then sell in smaller quantities to the general public; **he buys wholesale and sells retail** = he buys goods in bulk at a wholesale discount and then sells in small quantities to the public; **wholesale dealer** = person who buys in bulk from manufacturers and sells to retailers (NOTE: no plural)

wholesaler *noun* person who buys goods in bulk from manufacturers and sells them to retailers

wide area network (WAN) *noun*
network where the various terminals are far
apart and linked by radio, satellite and
cable; *compare with* LAN

> COMMENT: WANs use modems, radio
> and other long distance transmission
> methods; LANs use cables *or* optical
> fibre links

wide-angle lens *noun* lens which has a
large acceptance angle; **wide-angle shot** =
shot which is taken by a camera with a
wide-angle lens in order to show more of
the action area than would be revealed by a
camera with a normal lens from the same
distance

wideband *noun* transmission with a
bandwidth greater than that of a voice
channel; *compare with* BASEBAND;
**wideband frequency modulation
(WBFM)** = frequency modulation that uses
a large frequency bandwidth and has more
than one pair of sidebands

wide-open *adjective* a lens setting at its
lowest f-stop rating in order to ensure that
the iris is opened to its greatest width

widescreen *adjective* pictures presented
with a larger aspect ratio than 1.4:1

widow *noun* first line of a paragraph which
is printed by itself at the bottom of a
column; *compare with* ORPHAN

width *noun* size of something from edge to
edge; **page width** *or* **line width** = number of
characters across a page *or* line

wild card *noun* symbol used when
searching for files *or* data that represents all
files; *a wild card can be used to find all
files names beginning DIC*

> COMMENT: in DOS, UNIX and PC
> operating systems, the wild card
> character '?' will match any single
> character in this position; the wild card
> character '*' means match any number
> of any characters

wild track *noun* sound recorded without a
synchronised picture

WIMP = WINDOW, ICON, MOUSE,
POINTER description of an integrated
software system that is entirely operated
using windows, icons and a
mouse-controlled pointer; *see also*
ENVIRONMENT, GUI; *compare with*
COMMAND LINE INTERFACE

> COMMENT: WIMPs normally use a
> combination of windows, icons and a
> mouse to control the operating system.
> In many GUIs, such as Microsoft
> Windows and Apple Macintosh System,
> you can control all the functions of the
> operating system just using the mouse.
> Icons represent programs and files;
> instead of entering the file name, you
> select it by moving a pointer with a
> mouse

Winchester disk *or* **drive** *noun*
compact high-capacity hard disk which is
usually built into a computer system and
cannot be removed; **removable
Winchester** = small hard disk in a sealed
unit, which can be detached from a
computer when full *or* when not required

wind *verb* **(a)** to roll film on to a reel, spool
or core **(b)** to tighten the spring device on a
camera by rotating a crank or a key

window 1 *noun* **(a)** reserved section of
screen used to display special information,
that can be selected and looked at at any
time and which overwrites information
already on the screen **(b)** part of a document
currently displayed on a screen **(c)** area of
memory *or* access to a storage device; *you
can connect several remote stations (to the
network) and each will have its own
window onto the hard disk; the operating
system will allow other programs to be
displayed at the same time in different
windows*; **active window** = area of the
display screen where the operator is
currently working; **command window** =
area of the screen that always displays the
range of commands available; *the
command window is a single line at the
bottom of the screen*; **edit window** = area of
the screen in which the user can display and
edit text *or* graphics; **text window** = window
in a graphics system, where the text is held
in a small space on the screen before being
allocated to a final area; **window, icon,
mouse, pointer (WIMP)** = program display
which uses graphics *or* icons to control the
software and make it easier to use; system
commands do not have to be typed in **2** *verb*
to set up a section of screen by defining the
coordinates of its corners, that allows
information to be temporarily displayed,
overwriting previous information but

without altering information in the workspace

windowing *noun* (i) action of setting up a window to show information on the screen; (ii) displaying *or* accessing information via a window; *the network system uses the latest windowing techniques*

Windows multi-tasking graphical user interface for the IBM PC developed by Microsoft Corp. that is designed to be easy to use; **Windows API** = set of standard functions and commands, defined by Microsoft, that allow a programmer to control the Windows operating system from a programming language; **Windows for Workgroups** = version of Windows that includes basic peer-to-peer file-sharing functions and email, fax and scheduler utilities; **Windows GDI** = set of standard functions, defined by Microsoft, that allow a programmer to draw images in windows within the Windows operating system; **Windows ME** = operating system that is designed for home use and provides easy access to software and integration with the Internet; **Windows NT** = high-performance operating system that is designed for use in multiuser network environments; **Windows SDK** = set of software tools, including definitions of the Windows API, libraries that make it easier for a programmer to write applications that will work under the Windows operating system; **Windows XP** = latest version of Microsoft Windows operating system that improves on the speed and features of Windows 98, adds closer integration with the Internet, information sources and networks and better support for plug-and-play and error-detection and prevention

COMMENT: Windows uses icons to represent files and devices and can be controlled using a mouse, unlike MS-DOS which requires commands to be typed in

you can connect more satellites to the network, each having its own window onto the hard disk

PC Plus

the network system uses the latest windowing techniques

Desktop Publishing

the functions are integrated via a windowing system with pull-down menus used to select different operations

Byte

For instance, if you define a screen window using PowerBuilder, you can build a whole family of windows, which automatically inherit the characteristics of the first

Computing

windshield *noun (film)* device which is attached to a microphone in order to reduce wind noise

WINS = WINDOWS INTERNET NAMING SERVICE *(in Microsoft Windows)* database of the IP addresses of each computer on a local area network; *see also* = DNS, IP ADDRESS, NAME RESOLUTION

wipe 1 *noun (in a film sequence)* optical transition where one image is replaced by another at a boundary edge which is moving across the picture **2** *verb* to clean data from a disk; *by reformatting you will wipe the disk clean*

wiper *noun* movable arm in a potentiometer, a variable resistor *or* selector switch that can be turned to select a new resistance *or* function

wire frame model *noun (in graphics and CAD)* objects displayed using lines and arcs rather than filled areas or having the appearance of being solid

wire tap *noun* unauthorized connection to a private communications line in order to listen to conversations *or* obtain private data

wire 1 *noun* (a) thin metal conductor; **wire wrap** = simple method of electrically connecting terminals of components together using thin insulated wire wrapped around each terminal then soldered into place, usually used for prototype systems (b) telegram; *he sent a wire to say he was coming* **2** *verb* (a) to install wiring; *the studio is wired for sound*; **wired program computer** = computer with a program built into the hardware which cannot be changed; *see also* HARDWIRED CONNECTION (b) to send a telegram to (someone); *he wired the head office to say that the deal had been signed*

Wireless Application Protocol

(WAP) system that allows a user to access information on an Internet server using a wireless handheld device, such as a mobile telephone; *see also* WAP BROWSER, WML

COMMENT: WAP can be used over almost all of the current wireless networks, including the popular GSM mobile telephone standard, and can run on almost any operating system or hardware device. A device that supports WAP provides a very simple browser that can display basic graphics and text-based pages of information on a small, monochrome, 6-10 line display, similar to a tiny, simple web page. The user can navigate between pages using two or three buttons on the handheld device or mobile telephone. The arrival of WAP allows users to access email and news-based websites from a mobile telephone, but users have been put off by the very slow speed (no more than 9600bps) at which data can be transferred over current wireless telephone systems but the new telephone standard GPRS improves this speed

wireless 1 *noun (old use)* device that can receive radio broadcasts **2** *adjective* communication system that does not require wires to carry signals; **wireless microphone** = audio microphone with a small transmitter attached allowing the transmission of signals without interconnecting wires

wireless modem *noun* modem that can be used with a wireless mobile telephone system (a wireless modem normally includes the telephone hardware and an aerial, so does not need to be plugged into a separate mobile telephone)

wiring *noun* series of wires; *the wiring in the system had to be replaced*; **wiring closet** = box in which the cabling for a network or part of network is terminated and interconnected; **wiring frame** = metal structure used to support incoming cables and provide connectors to allow cables to be interconnected

WML WAP MARKUP LANGUAGE = web page formatting language similar to a very simple version of the standard HTML web page coding system, but does not include many of the extra features that cannot be displayed on the small screen of a WAP handheld device or navigated with two or three buttons; *see also* HTML, SGML, WAP, XML

WMLScript WAP MARKUP LANGUAGE SCRIPT = scripting language similar to a very simple version of JavaScript that allows WML web pages to include scripting functions; *see also* JAVASCRIPT, WAP

woofer *noun (informal)* large loudspeaker used to produce low frequency sounds

word *noun* **(a)** separate item of language, which is used with others to form speech *or* writing which can be understood; **word break** = division of a word at the end of a line, where part of the word is left on one line with a hyphen, and the rest of the word is taken over to begin the next line; **word count** = number of words in a file *or* text; **WordPad** = software utility included with Windows that provides the basic functions of Microsoft Word 6. It can read and save Word 6 files and lets you format text and write complex documents; **words per minute (wpm)** = method of measuring the speed of a printer *or* shorthand typist; **word wrap** *or* **wraparound** = system in word processing where the operator does not have to indicate the line endings, but can keyboard continuously, leaving the program to continue the text on the next line **(b)** separate item of data on a computer, formed of a group of bits, stored in a single location in a memory; **word length** = length of a computer word, counted as the number of bits; **word serial** = data words transmitted along a parallel bus one after the othe.

WordPerfect popular word-processing application developed by WordPerfect Corp. to run on a wide range of hardware platforms and operating systems

word-process *verb* to edit, store and manipulate text using a computer; *it is quite easy to read word-processed files*

word-processing (WP) *noun* using a computer to keyboard, edit, and output text, in the form of letters, labels, address lists, etc.; *load the word-processing program before you start keyboarding*; **word-processing bureau** = office which specializes in word-processing for other companies (NOTE: no plural)

word-processor *noun* **(a)** small computer *or* typewriter with a computer in it, used for word-processing text and documents **(b)** word-processing package *or* program for a computer which allows the editing and manipulation and output of text, such as letters, labels, address lists, etc.

WordStar popular word-processing application developed by MicroPro International for CP/M and IBM PC computers

work 1 *noun* **(a)** things done using the hands *or* brain; **casual work** = work where the workers are hired for a short period; **clerical work** = work done in an office; **work area** = memory space which is being used by an operator; **work disk** = disk on which current work is stored; **work file** *or* **scratch file** temporary work area which is being used for current work; **working store** *or* **scratch pad** = area of high-speed memory used for temporary storage of data in current use **(b)** job *or* something done to earn money; *he goes to work by bus; she never gets home from work before 8 p.m.; his work involves a lot of travelling; he is still looking for work; she has been out of work for six months* (NOTE: no plural) **2** *verb* **(a)** to do things with your hands *or* brain, for money; *the factory is working hard to complete the order; she works better now that she has been promoted;* **to work a machine** = to make a machine function **(b)** to function; *the computer system has never worked properly since it was installed*

workflow *noun* network software designed to improve the flow of electronic documents around an office network, from user to user

workgroup *noun* small group of users who are working on a project *or* connected with a local area network; **workgroup enabled** = feature added to standard software package to give it more appeal to a group of networked users; *this word-processor is workgroup enabled which adds an email gateway from the standard menus;* **workgroup software** = application designed to be used by many users in a group to improve productivity - such as a diary or scheduler

working *adjective* **(a)** (person) who works; *the working population of a country* **(b)** referring to work; **working conditions** = general state of the place where people work (if it is hot, noisy, dark, dangerous, etc.)

workload *noun* amount of work which a person *or* computer has to do; *he has difficulty in dealing with his heavy workload*

workplace *noun* place where you work

work print *noun film* positive print of a film scene which has been selected by the editor

work-sharing *noun* system where two part-timers share one job

worksheet *noun* (*in a spreadsheet program*) a two-dimensional matrix of rows and columns that contains cells which can, themselves, contain equations

workspace *noun* space on memory, which is available for use *or* is being used currently by an operator

workstation *noun* place where a computer user works, with a terminal, VDU, printer, modem, etc.; *the system includes five workstations linked together in a ring network; the archive storage has a total capacity of 1200 Mb between seven workstations*

```
an      image    processing
workstation must provide three
basic facilities: the means to
digitize,    display    and
manipulate the image data
                         Byte
```

World Wide Web *see* WWW

worlds *noun* three-dimensional scene that is displayed on a website and allows a user to move around the scene exploring the objects visible; the entire scene is often called a 'world' and is created using a special plug-in extension to the web browser; *see* VRML

WORM = WRITE ONCE READ MANY times memory optical disc storage system that allows the user to write data to the disc once, but the user can then read the data from the disc many times

wow *noun* fluctuation of the frequency of a recorded signal at playback (usually caused by uneven tape movement)

WP = WORD-PROCESSING
WPM = WORDS PER MINUTE

wrap 1 *noun* **omega wrap** = system of threading video tape round a video head (the tape passes over most of the circular head and is held in place by two small rollers **2** *verb* **to wrap (up)** = to cover something all over (in paper); *he wrapped (up) the parcel in green paper* (NOTE: wrapping - wrapped)

wraparound *or* **word wrap** *noun* system in word processing where the operator does not have to indicate the line endings, but can keyboard continuously, leaving the program to continue the text on the next line; **horizontal wraparound** = movement of a cursor on a computer display from the end of one line to the beginning of the next; **wrapper** = special software that is used to combine multiple files to provide a single, convenient file that can be distributed over the Internet

COMMENT: wrapper software often includes security features, to prevent unauthorised copying, and compression to reduce the size of the files. A user double-clicks the file and it automatically installs the software enclosed in the wrapper on their computer

writable instruction set computer (WISC) *noun* CPU design that allows a programmer to add extra machine code instructions using microcode, to customize the instruction set

write *verb* **(a)** to put words *or* figures on to paper; *she wrote a letter of complaint to the manager; the telephone number is written at the bottom of the notepaper* **(b)** to put text *or* data onto a disk *or* tape; *access time is the time taken to read from or write to a location in memory*; **write** *or* **write-back** *or* **write-behind cache** = temporary storage used to hold data intended for a storage device until the device is ready; *write-back cacheing improves performance, but can be dangerous; see also* CACHE; **write error** = error reported when trying to save data onto a magnetic storage medium; **write head** = transducer that can write data onto a magnetic medium; **write once, read many times memory (WORM)** = optical disk storage system that allows one writing

action but many reading actions in its life; **writing pad** = special device which allows a computer to read in handwritten characters which have been written onto a special pad; *see* OCR (NOTE: you write data **to** a file. Note also: writing - wrote - has written)

write black printer *noun* printer where toner sticks to the points hit by the laser beam when the image drum is scanned; *compare with* WHITE WRITER

COMMENT: a write black printer produces sharp edges and graphics, but large areas of black are muddy

write-on slides *plural noun* during a film's production, slides with a matte covering are used, on which information is hand drawn to show the final image

write-permit ring *noun* ring on a reel of magnetic tape which allows the tape to be overwritten *or* erased

write protect *verb* to make it impossible to write to a floppy disk *or* tape by moving a special tab; **write-protect tab** = tab on a floppy disk which if moved, prevents any writing to *or* erasing from the disk

writer *see* BLACK WRITER, WHITE WRITER

writing *noun* something which has been written; *to put the agreement in writing; he has difficulty in reading my writing* (NOTE: no plural); **writing speed** = *(in a cathode ray tube)* the speed at which the electron beam crosses the phosphor while writing; *(in video tapes)* the rate at which the moving recording *or* replay head crosses the magnetic tape surface, which is much faster than the transport speed of the tape itself

WWW = WORLD WIDE WEB *(within the Internet)* thousands of pages of formatted text and graphics (stored in HTML) that allow a user to have a graphical user interface to the Internet rather than a less user-friendly command-line interface; *see also* HTML, INTERNET

WYSIAYG = WHAT YOU SEE IS ALL YOU GET

WYSIWYG = WHAT YOU SEE IS WHAT YOU GET

Xx

X = EXTENSION

X2 communications standard developed by US Robotics for its range of high-speed modems that can transfer data at 56,000 bits per second; *see also* V SERIES

X.25 CCITT standard that defines the connection between a terminal and a packet-switching network

X.400 CCITT standard that defines an electronic mail transfer method

X.500 CCITT standard that defines a method of global naming that allows every individual user to have a unique identity and allows any user to address an electronic mail message to any other user

XA *see* CD-ROM/XA

X-axis *noun* horizontal axis of a graph

X-coordinate *noun* horizontal axis position coordinate

X direction *noun* horizontally

X distance *noun* distance along an X-axis from an origin

xenon lamp *noun* a DC quartz-glass projection lamp which uses xenon gas to produce lasting and efficient light

> COMMENT: xenon lamps are widely used in motion picture film projectors

xerographic *adjective* referring to xerography; **xerographic printer** = printer (such as a photocopier) where charged ink is attracted to areas of a charged picture

xerography *noun* copying method that relies on ink being attracted to dark regions of a charged picture

Xerox 1 *noun* **(a)** trademark for a type of photocopier; *to make a xerox copy of a letter; we must order some more xerox paper for the copier; we are having a new xerox machine installed tomorrow* **(b)** photocopy made with a xerox machine; *to send the other party a xerox of the contract; we have sent xeroxes to each of the agents*; **Xerox networking system** = *see* XNS **2** *verb* to make a photocopy with a xerox machine; *to xerox a document; she xeroxed all the file*

Xerox PARC *noun* Xerox development centre that has developed a wide range of important products including the mouse and GUI

XGA EXTENDED GRAPHICS ARRAY standard for colour video graphics adapter for PCs, developed by IBM, which has a resolution of 1,024x768 pixels with 256 colours on an interlaced display; **XGA-2** = provides a resolution of 1,024x768 pixels with 64,000 colours

XHTML = EXTENSIBLE HYPERTEXT MARKUP LANGUAGE combination of the HTML and XML web page markup languages; XHTML is created from the XML language and provides a simpler way of creating web pages that will be displayed in the same way over a wide range of web browser platforms

XML = EXTENSIBLE MARKUP LANGUAGE web page markup language that is a simplifed version of the SGML system and allows a designer to create their own customised markup tags to improve flexibility

XMODEM standard file transfer and error-detecting protocol used in asynchronous (modem) data transmissions; **XMODEM 1K** = version of XMODEM that transfers 1024-byte blocks of data; **XMODEM CRC** = enhanced version of XMODEM that includes error checking

XMS = EXTENDED MEMORY SPECIFICATION rules that define how a program should access extended memory fitted in a PC

XNS = XEROX NETWORKING SYSTEM proprietary protocol developed by Xerox and used in many local area networks

XON/XOFF *noun* asynchronous transmission protocol in which each end can regulate the data flow by transmitting special codes

X/OPEN *noun* group of vendors that are responsible for promoting open systems

X-ray *noun* **(a)** ray with a very short length, which is invisible, but can go through soft tissue and register as a photograph on a film; **X-ray imaging** = showing images of the inside of a body using X-rays **(b)** photograph taken using X-rays; *the medical text is illustrated with X-ray photographs* **(c)** *(film)* a lighting unit that hangs above the set

X-series *noun* recommendations for data communications over public data networks

X-sheet *noun* written orders for the exposure of animation film

XT *noun* version of the original IBM PC, developed by IBM, that used an 8088 processor and included a hard disk; **XT keyboard** = keyboard used with the IBM PC which had ten function keys running in two columns along the left-hand side of the keyboard

X-Window System *or* **X-Windows**
noun standard set of API commands and display handling routines, that provides a hardware-independent programming interface for applications

COMMENT: originally developed for UNIX workstations, the X-Window System can also run on a PC or minicomputer terminals

```
X is the underlying technology
which allows Unix applications
to run under a multi-user,
multitasking GUI. It has been
adopted as the standard for
the Common Open Software
Environment, proposed
recently by top Unix vendors
including Digital, IBM and Sun
```
Computing

X-Y *noun* coordinates for drawing a graph, where X is the vertical and Y the horizontal value; **X-Y plotter** = device for drawing lines on paper between given coordinates

Yy

Y *noun* luminance element of a colour television signal

Y/C *noun* refers to the two signal (luminance, Y, and chroma, C) that make up a video signal

yaw *noun* rotation of satellite about a vertical axis with the earth

Y-axis *noun* vertical axis of a graph

Y-coordinate *noun* vertical axis position coordinate

Y-direction *noun* vertically

Y-distance *noun* distance along a Y-axis from an origin

year 2000 *or* **Y2K** problem that, it was predicted, would affect millions of computers and businesses around the world on the 1st of January 2000; *see also* MILLENNIUM COMPLIANCE

COMMENT: original PCs and other types of computer system were often designed with the assumption that the year would start 19xx and so only supported the last two numbers for each year (no one thought of this problem in 1983 when PCs were first developed). In the event, there was little disruption - the banks, telephone companies, and air-traffic systems were modified before the end of the last millenium and few businesses suffered the catostrophic chaos that was predicted.

Yellow Book *noun* formal specification for CD-ROM published by Philips, includes data storage formats and has an extension to cover the CD-ROM XA standard

yellow-magenta-cyan-black *see* YMCK

YIQ *noun (in the NTSC colour television system)* whole set of component signals, consisting of luminance Y and the two colour difference signals, I and Q

YMCK = YELLOW-MAGENTA-CYAN-BLACK colour definition based on these four colours used in graphics and DTP software when creating separate colour film to use for printing (NOTE: normally written as CMYK)

YMODEM *noun* variation of the XMODEM file transfer protocol that uses 1024-byte blocks and can send multiple files

yoke *noun* **deflection yoke** = magnetic coils around a TV tube used to control the position of the picture beam

YUV *noun (in the PAL colour television system)* the whole set of component signals, consisting of luminance Y and the two colour difference signals, U (= B-Y) and V (= R-Y)

YUV encoding *noun* video encoding system in which the video luminance (Y) signal is recorded at full bandwidth but the chrominance signals (U&V) are recorded at half their bandwidth

Zz

Z = IMPEDANCE

Z80 8-bit processor developed by Zilog, used in many early popular computers

zap *verb* to wipe off all data currently in the workspace; *he pressed CONTROL Z and zapped all the text*

z-axis *noun* axis for depth in a three-dimensional graph or plot

zeppelin (windscreen) *noun* a long, pierced tube connected to a shotgun microphone used to decrease wind noise

zero 1 *noun* **(a)** the digit 0; *the code for international calls is zero zero (00)* **(b)** equivalent of logical off or false state; **jump on zero** = conditional jump executed if a flag *or* register is zero; **zero compression** *or* **zero suppression** = shortening of a file by the removal of unnecessary zeros **2** *verb* to erase *or* clear a file; **to zero a device** = to erase the contents of a programmable device; **to zero fill** = to fill a section of memory with zero values

zero insertion force (ZIF) *noun* chip socket that has movable connection terminals, allowing the chip to be inserted with no force then a small lever turned to grip the legs of the chip

zero slot LAN *noun* local area network that does not use internal expansion adapters, instead it uses the serial port (or sometimes an external pocket network adapter connected to the printer port)

zero wait state *noun* state of a device (normally processor *or* memory chips) that is fast enough to run at the same speed as the other components in a computer, so does not have to be artificially slowed down by inserting wait states

ZIF = ZERO INSERTION FORCE

zip code *noun* US letters and numbers used to indicate a town *or* street in an address on an envelope (NOTE: the GB English for this is **postcode**); **Zip disk** = proprietary type of removable storage device, similar to a removable hard disk drive, manufactured by Iomega Corp. to provide a convenient backup and storage medium with 100Mb, 250Mb or 1Gb disk capacity; *see also* IOMEGA

ZMODEM *noun* enhanced version of the XMODEM file transfer protocol that includes error detection and the ability to re-start a transfer where it left off if the connection is cut

zone 1 *noun* **(a)** region *or* part of a screen defined for specialized printing; **hot zone** = text area to the left of the right margin in a word-processed document, if a word does not fit completely into the line, a hyphen is automatically inserted **(b)** area of a town *or* country (for administrative purposes); **development zone** *or* **enterprise zone** = area which has been given special help from the government to encourage businesses and factories to set up there **(c)** division of the area of a television picture raste; usually, zone 1 is the part held within a circle of 0.8 of picture height, zone 2 is the circle equal to picture width, and zone 3 is the rest of the area outside zone 2 **2** *verb* to divide (a town) into different areas for planning purposes

zoom lens *noun* lens whose focal length can be varied to make an object larger in the viewfinder

zoom microphone *noun* a microphone which can give a zoom effect by moving towards or away from sound

```
there  are  many  options  to
allow you to zoom into an area
for precision work
```
Electronics & Wireless World

> any window can be zoomed to
> full-screen size by pressing
> the F5 function key
>
> *Byte*

zoom *verb* **(a)** to change the focal length of a lens to enlarge the object in the viewfinder **(b)** to enlarge an area of text (to make it easier to work on)

zooming *noun* enlarging an area; *variable zooming from 25% to 400% of actual size*

ZV Port = ZOOMED VIDEO PORT *noun* interface port that allows data to be transferred from a PC Card directly to the computer's video controller without passing through the computer's central processor; used to allow a laptop computer to display live images from a video camera plugged into the computer's PC Card socket

SUPPLEMENT

TML codes

ie following is a list of the basic HTML codes (or tags) used to format web pages.

﹥a﹥ .. </a>

eates a hyperlink target or source. For example,

```
<a href="www.pcp.co.uk">link to PCP</a>
```

ill create a hyperlink to the PCP web page.

address﹥ .. </address>

closed text is formatted in smaller typeface as an address

applet﹥ .. </applet>

fines an applet within the document

area>

fines the area of a graphic image that will respond to a mouse click using a client-side
iage map

﹥ .. </b>

rmats enclosed text in a bold typeface

base>

fines the URL address that is added in front of all relative URLs used within the
cument

asefont>

fines the point size of the font used to format for the following text

gsound>

fines the audio file that is played as a background sound to the document (used in
S-IE 2 and later)

ig> .. </big>

rmats enclosed text in a bigger typeface

lockquote> .. </blockquote>

rmats the enclosed text as a quotation

ody> .. </body>

fines the start and finish of this document is body text; also used to define a graphic
iage used as a background, and to set the default colour of the text, hyperlinks and
argins for the document

r>

serts a line break in the text, the <p> code also inserts a carriage return

aption> .. </caption>

fines the caption for a table

enter> .. </center>

rmats enclosed text to be centered across the line

ite> .. </cite>

rmats enclosed text as a citation

ode> .. </code>

rmats enclosed text as program code, normally using the Courier typeface

\<col\>
defines the properties for a column that has been defined using \<colgroup\>; available in MS-IE 2 and above

\<colgroup\>
defines a column; available in MS-IE 2 and above

\<comment\> .. \</comment\>
defines the enclosed text to be a comment; only works in MS IE 2, with any other browser you should use the \<!\> comment \<\> tag format

\<dd\> .. \</dd\>
defines one element of a definition list

\<dfn\> .. \</dfn\>
formats enclosed text as a definition

\<dir\> .. \</dir\>
creates a directory list using the \<li\> to create entries

\<div\> .. \</div\>
divides the text within a document and formats each division

\<dl\> .. \</dl\>
creates a definition list using the \<dd\> and \<dt\> tags to create entries

\<dt\> .. \</dt\>
defines the definition part of an entry within a definition list

\<em\> .. \</em\>
formats enclosed text with emphasis (often the same as a bold typeface)

\<embed\> .. \</embed\>
points to an object to embed in a document

\<font\> .. \</font\>
defines the size, colour and typeface of the font to use for the enclosed text

\<form\> .. \</form\>
defines the following tags to be treated as one form; also defines how to process the form and where to send the encoded information

\<frame\> .. \</frame\>
defines a frame, including its border, colour, name and text

\<frameset\> .. \</frameset\>
defines a collection of frames

\<h\> .. \</h\>
defines a pre-set font size, such as \<h1\> for a large headings, \<h4\> for small headings

\<hr\>
breaks the current line of text and inserts a horizontal rule across the page

\<html\> .. \</html\>
defines the start and end of the entire html document

\<i\>.. \</i\>
formats enclosed text using an italic typeface

<iframe> .. </iframe>
defines a floating frame, used only in MS-IE 3

<img>
includes an image within a document, also defines a border for the image, size, alternative caption text and whether the image is a video clip

<input type=checkbox>
defines a checkbox button within a form

<input type=file>
defines a file-selection list within a form

<input type=image>
defines an image input element within a form

<input type=password>
defines a text input that displays an asterisk when text is entered

<input type=radio>
defines a radio button within a form

<input type=reset>
defines a button to reset the formis contents

<input type=submit>
defines a button to submit the formis contents to the named process

<input type=text>
defines a text input element to allow users to enter a line of text

<isindex>
defines the html document to be searchable by a defined search engine

<kbd> .. </kbd>
formats enclosed text as a keyboard input

<li> .. </li>
defines an item in a list; the list can be ordered using <ol> or unordered using <ul>

<link>
defines a link within a document header

<listing> .. </listing>
old tag that is the same as a the <pre> tag

<map> .. </map>
defines an image map that contains hotspots

<marquee> .. </marquee>
creates an animated scrolling text line, used in MS-IE 2 and after

<menu> .. </menu>
defines a menu that has items created using the <li> tag

<meta>
allows the programmer to include extra information about the document

<multicol> .. </multicol>
defines multiple columns within the document, used in Netscape Navigator 3 only

\<nextid\>
used by automated html document generators as a reference point within a file

\<nobr\> .. \</nobr\>
prevents the browser adding breaks within the enclosed text

\<noframes\> .. \</noframes\>
defines content that should be displayed if the browser does not support frames

\<noscript\> .. \</noscript\>
defines content that should be used if the browser does not support Java; only for Netscape Navigator 3 and after

\<object\> .. \</object\>
defines an object, applet or OLE object to be inserted into the document; used for MS-IE and after

\<ol\> .. \</ol\>
defines the start and end of a numbered list; items are inserted using the \<li\> tag

\<option\> .. \</option\>
defines one option within a \<select\> tag

\<p\> .. \</p\>
defines the start and end of a paragraph

\<param\> .. \</param\>
defines the paramaters to be passed to an enclosed applet or object

\<plaintext\>
formats the rest of the document as plain text with spaces and breaks

\<pre\> .. \</pre\>
formats the enclosed text as plain text with spaces and breaks

\<s\> .. \</s\>
formats enclosed text with a strikethrough, horizontal line

\<samp\> .. \</samp\>
defines enclosed text as a sample

\<script\> .. \</script\>
defines the start and end of a script written in a language, such as JavaScript or VBScript

\<select\> .. \</select\>
defines a list of options within a form, each created using the \<option\> tag

\<small\> .. \</small\>
formats enclosed text in a small typesize

\<spacer\>
inserts a character space within a line of text; only used in Netscape Navigator 3

\<span\> .. \</span\>
define a style sheet that formats text over several tags; only used in MS-IE 3

\<strike\> .. \</strike\>
formats enclosed text with a strikethrough line

\<strong\> .. \</strong\>
formats enclosed text with emphasis, similar to bold

style> .. </style>
fines a collection of text formatting commands that can be referred to with this style
mmand; used for MS-IE 3 only

sub> .. </sub>
rmats enclosed text as subscript

sup> .. </sup>
rmats enclosed text as superscript

able> .. </table>
fines a table including border, colour, size and width; columns are added with <td> and
ws with <tr>

body>
oup of rows within a table; used in MS-IE 2

d> .. </td>
fines a cell within a table, effectively adds a column to the table

extarea> .. </textarea>
fines a multiple line text input element for a form

foot>
fines rows within a table that are formatted as a footer to the table; used in MS-IE 2

h> .. </th>
fines the header to each column in a table

head>
fines rows within a table that are formatted as a header to the table; used in
icrosoft-IE 2

itle> .. </title>
fines the title to this html document

r> .. </tr>
fines a row of cells within a table

t> .. </tt>
rmats enclosed text in a monospaced typewrite-style font

l> .. </ul>
fines the start and end of a bulleted list of elements, each element is add using <li>

ar> .. </var>
closed text is the name of a variable

vbr>
fines a possible point for a word break within a <nobr> line

mp> .. </xmp>
l tag that formats enclosed text, similar to <pre>

Modulation

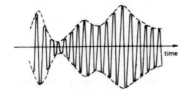

Amplitude Modulation

Original Signal

Frequency Modulation

Pulse Amplitude Modulation

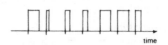

Pulse Width Modulation

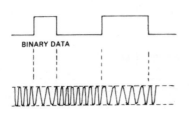

FSK of binary data

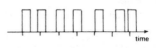

Pulse Position Modulation

ogic Function Tables

Written as	Drawn as	logic table		

A	A
0	0
1	1

A

A	B	A·B
0	0	0
0	1	0
1	0	0
1	1	1

A AND B

A	B	A+B
0	0	0
0	1	1
1	0	1
1	1	1

A OR B

A	B	A exor B
0	0	0
0	1	1
1	0	1
1	1	0

A EXOR B

A	$\overline{A}$
0	1
1	0

NOT A

A	B	$\overline{A.B}$
0	0	1
0	1	1
1	0	1
1	1	0

A NAND B

A	B	$\overline{A+B}$
0	0	1
0	1	0
1	0	0
1	1	0

A NOR B

A	B	A exnor B
0	0	1
0	1	0
1	0	0
1	1	1

A EXNOR B

Numbers

You write	You say
0	zero or nought or oh
0.4	point four or nought point four
¼	one quarter or (informal) a quarter
1	one
2	two
3	three
4	four
5	five
6	six
7	seven
8	eight
9	nine
10	ten
12	twelve or (informal) one dozen or a dozen
15	fifteen or one-five
50	fifty or five-oh
67	sixty-seven
100	one hundred or (informal) a hundred
106	one hundred and six or (US) one hundred six
556	five hundred and fifty-six
1000	one thousand or (informal) a thousand or one K
10,000	ten thousand
1,000,000	one million or (informal) a million

Decimals

0.5	zero point five
0.23	zero point two three
2.5	two point five

Roman Numerals

I or I	1
II or ii	2
III or iii	3
IV or iv	4
V or v	5
VI or vi	6
VII or vii	7
VIII or viii	8
IX or ix	9
X or x	10
XX or xx	20
L	50
C	100
D	500
M	1000

ymbols

	per cent
	degrees
	equals
	is approximately equal to
	is not equal to
	is less than
	is more than
	plus
	minus
	divided by
	multiplied by
	therefore
	and
	infinity
	root

ecimal Conversion Table

	Decimal	BCD	Binary	Octal	Hexadecimal
se	10	2	2	8	16
	00	0000 0000	0000	00	0
	01	0000 0001	0001	01	1
	02	0000 0010	0010	02	2
	03	0000 0011	0011	03	3
	04	0000 0100	0100	04	4
	05	0000 0101	0101	05	5
	06	0000 0110	0110	06	6
	07	0000 0111	0111	07	7
	08	0000 1000	1000	10	8
	09	0000 1001	1001	11	9
	10	0001 0000	1010	12	A
	11	0001 0001	1011	13	B
	12	0001 0010	1100	14	C
	13	0001 0011	1101	15	D
	14	0001 0100	1110	16	E
	15	0001 0101	1111	17	F

ternational Standard Paper Sizes

	1189 x 841mm	A5	210 x 148mm
	841 x 594mm	A6	148 x 105mm
	594 x 420mm	A7	105 x 74mm
	420 x 297mm	A8	74 x 52mm
	297 x 210mm	A9	52 x 37mm
		A10	37 x 26mm

SI Units and Abbreviations

A	ampere	electrical current
C	coulomb	electrical charge (As)
cd	candela	light intensity
F	farad	capacitance (C/V)
H	henry	inducatance (Vs/A)
Hz	hertz	frequency (cycles per second)
J	joule	energy (Kg m/s)
K	kelvin	temperature
kg	kilogram	mass
lm	lux	illumination (cd/sr)
lx	lumen	illumination density (lm/m)
m	metre	distance
N	newton	force (J/m)
Pa	pascal	pressure
rad	radian	plane angle
s	second	time
sr	steradian	solid angle
S	siemens	electrical conducance (1/ohm)
T	tesla	magnetic flux density (WB/m)
V	volt	electrical potential (W/A)
W	watt	power (J/s)
Wb	weber	magnetic flux (Vs)
Ω	ohm	electrical resistance (V/A)
C	degree Celsius	temperature (K+273)

Prefixes

T	tera-	10^{12}
G	giga-	10^{9}
M	mega-	10^{6}
k	kilo-	10^{3}
d	deci-	10^{-1}
c	centi-	10^{-2}
m	milli-	10^{-3}
μ	micro-	10^{-6}
n	nano-	10^{-9}
p	pico-	10^{-12}
f	femto-	10^{-15}
a	atto-	10^{-18}

ASCII in Decimal, Hexadecimal

dec	hex	char	dec	hex	char	dec	hex	char	dec	hex	char
0	00	NUL	32	20	SP	64	40	@	96	60	
1	01	SOH	33	21	!	65	41	A	97	61	a
2	02	STX	34	22	"	66	42	B	98	62	b
3	03	ETX	35	23	#	67	43	C	99	63	c
4	04	EOT	36	24	$	68	44	D	100	64	d
5	05	ENQ	37	25	%	69	45	E	101	65	e
6	06	ACK	38	26	&	70	46	F	102	66	f
7	07	BEL	39	27	'	71	47	G	103	67	g
8	08	BS	40	28	(	72	48	H	104	68	h
9	09	HT	41	29	)	73	49	I	105	69	i
10	0A	LF	42	2A	*	74	4A	J	106	6A	j
11	0B	VT	43	2B	+	75	4B	K	107	6B	k
12	0C	FF	44	2C	,	76	4C	L	108	6C	l
13	0D	CR	45	2D	-	77	4D	M	109	6D	m
14	0E	SO	46	2E	.	78	4E	N	110	6E	n
15	0F	SI	47	2F	/	79	4F	O	111	6F	o
16	10	DLE	48	30	0	80	50	P	112	70	p
17	11	DC1	49	31	1	81	51	Q	113	71	q
18	12	DC2	50	32	2	82	52	R	114	72	r
19	13	DC3	51	33	3	83	53	S	115	73	s
20	14	DC4	52	34	4	84	54	T	116	74	t
21	15	NAK	53	35	5	85	55	U	117	75	u
22	16	SYN	54	36	6	86	56	V	118	76	v
23	17	ETB	55	37	7	87	57	W	119	77	w
24	18	CAN	56	38	8	88	58	X	120	78	x
25	19	EM	57	39	9	89	59	Y	121	79	y
26	1A	SUB	58	3A	:	90	5A	Z	122	7A	z
27	1B	ESC	59	3B	;	91	5B	[	123	7B	{
28	1C	FS	60	3C	<	92	5C	\	124	7C		
29	1D	GS	61	3D	=	93	5D	]	125	7D	}
30	1E	RS	62	3E	>	94	5E	^	126	7E	~
31	1F	US	63	3F	?	95	5F	_	127	7F	DEL

ASCII Symbols

NUL	null	FF	form feed	ESC	esape
SOH	start of heading	CR	carriage return	FS	file separator
SOT	start of text	SO	shift out	GS	group separator
STX	end of text	SI	shift in	RS	record separator
EOT	end of transmission	DLE	data link escape	US	unit separator
ENQ	enquiry	DC	device control	SP	space
ACK	acknowledge	NAK	negative ack.		
BEL	bell	SYN	synchronous idle		
BS	backspace	ETB	end of transmission block		
HT	horizontal tab	CAN	cancel		
LF	line feed	EM	end of medium		
VT	vertical tab	SUB	substitute		

Request for further information

Use this form to request information about our range of dictionaries. Send t
Peter Collin Publishing   fax: +44 20 7222 1551   email: info@petercollin.com
Visit our website: **www.petercollin.com** for more information and resources.

Title	ISBN	Send Detail
English Dictionaries		
English Dictionary for Students	1-901659-06-2	☐
English Study Dictionary	1-901659-63-1	☐
Basic English Dictionary	1-901659-96-8	☐
Accounting, 2nd ed	1-901659-85-2	☐
Aeronautical Terms	1-901659-10-0	☐
Agriculture, 2nd ed	0-948549-78-5	☐
American Business, 2nd ed	1-901659-22-4	☐
Automobile Engineering	0-948549-66-1	☐
Banking & Finance, 2nd ed	1-901659-30-5	☐
Business, 3rd ed	1-901659-50-X	☐
Computing, 4th ed	1-901659-46-1	☐
Ecology & Environment, 4th ed	1-901659-61-5	☐
Government & Politics, 2nd ed	0-948549-89-0	☐
Hotels, Tourism, Catering Management	0-948549-40-8	☐
Human Resources & Personnel, 2nd ed	0-948549-79-3	☐
Information Technology, 3rd ed	1-901659-55-0	☐
Law, 3rd ed	1-901659-43-7	☐
Library and Information Management	0-948549-68-8	☐
Marketing, 2nd ed	0-948549-73-4	☐
Medicine, 3rd ed	1-901659-45-3	☐
Military Terms	1-901659-24-0	☐
Multimedia	1-901659-51-8	☐
PC and the Internet	1-901659-52-6	☐
Printing and Publishing, 2nd ed	0-948549-99-8	☐
Vocabulary Workbooks		
Banking and Finance	0-948549-96-3	☐
Business, 2nd ed	0-948549-72-6	☐
Computing, 2nd ed	1-901659-28-3	☐
Colloquial English	0-948549-97-1	☐
English for FCE	1-901659-11-9	☐
English for IELTS	1-901659-60-7	☐
English for PET	1-903856-23-X	☐
English for TOEFL	1-901659-86-2	☐
Hotels, Tourism, Catering	0-948549-75-0	☐
Law, 2nd ed	1-901659-21-6	☐
Marketing	1-901659-48-8	☐
Medicine, 2nd ed	1-901659-47-X	☐
Bilingual Dictionaries		
Chinese-English		☐
French-English		☐
German-English		☐
Spanish-English		☐
Portuguese-English		☐

Name: ....
Dept: ....
Address:..
....
....Postcode: ....Country: ....